Figure E.3 Education Expenditures per Student in 15 Industrial Countries

Country	Expenditure
Sweden	$4,279
Canada	$4,054
Denmark	$3,997
Switzerland	$3,733
Norway	$3,636
United States	$3,398
Austria	$2,972
Netherlands	$2,495
Belgium	$2,492
France	$2,486
United Kingdom	$2,474
West Germany	$2,450
Japan	$2,379
Italy	$2,320
Australia	$2,060

Figure E.4 Gross Domestic Product per Capita in 15 Industrial Countries

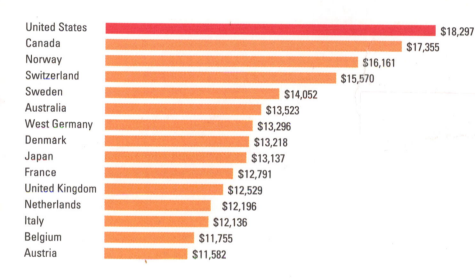

United States	$18,297
Canada	$17,355
Norway	$16,161
Switzerland	$15,570
Sweden	$14,052
Australia	$13,523
West Germany	$13,296
Denmark	$13,218
Japan	$13,137
France	$12,791
United Kingdom	$12,529
Netherlands	$12,196
Italy	$12,136
Belgium	$11,755
Austria	$11,582

Figure E.5 Ratio of Pupils to Teachers in 15 Industrial Countries

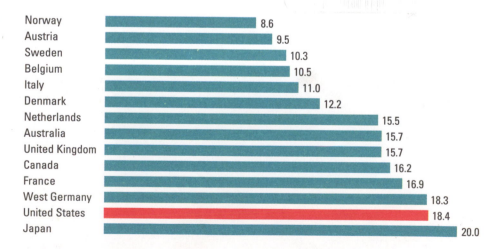

Norway	8.6
Austria	9.5
Sweden	10.3
Belgium	10.5
Italy	11.0
Denmark	12.2
Netherlands	15.5
Australia	15.7
United Kingdom	15.7
Canada	16.2
France	16.9
West Germany	18.3
United States	18.4
Japan	20.0

For more information about education around the world, see Chapter 15, "International Education."

FOUNDATIONS
OF
EDUCATION

Allan C. Ornstein
*Loyola University
of Chicago*

Daniel U. Levine
*University of Nebraska
at Omaha*

FOUNDATIONS
OF
EDUCATION

Fifth Edition

Houghton Mifflin Company   Boston   Toronto   Dallas   Geneva, Illinois   Palo Alto   Princeton, New Jersey

To the children of Hubbard Woods School,
whose innocence and ideal of childhood were stripped away
by an adult with a gun.

Another dawn, another day.
The children are bright and fresh,
brimming with life.
And they want the world to know
that they still expect to make it
a better place.

Senior Sponsoring Editor: Loretta Wolozin
Senior Development Editor: Susan Granoff
Senior Project Editor: Rosemary Winfield
Design/Production Coordinator: Martha Drury
Manufacturing Coordinator: Sharon Pearson
Marketing Manager: Rebecca Dudley

Cover design by Lisa De George.
Cover photograph copyright © 1987 by Steve Rosenthal.

Part-opening credits: Part 1, p. 1, Kindra Clineff/The Picture
Cube; Part 2, p. 76, Snark/Art Resource, New York; Part 3,
p. 196, Paul Conklin; Part 4, p. 314, Harvey Finkle; Part 5,
p. 446, Elizabeth Crews/The Image Works; Part 6, p. 568,
Jerry Howard/Positive Images.

Acknowledgments for the color insert and endpapers appear
on p. 657.

Printed in the U.S.A.
Library of Congress Catalog Card Number: 92-72390
ISBN: 0-395-63782-1

123456789-CS-96 95 94 93 92

Contents

7

8

PART IV   SOCIAL ◄●► FOUNDATIONS   315

9

Preface

Foundations of Education, Fifth Edition, is a comprehensive overview of the foundations of education in the United States. We have written it for students who are preparing for a teaching career as well as those who simply wish to learn more about the key educational issues and policies affecting American education.

AUDIENCE AND PURPOSE

The text is designed for use both in introductory courses in the foundations of education and in a variety of upper-level foundations courses. For beginning students in education, it provides a clear understanding of the teaching profession and the issues and controversies confronting American education today. The book is appropriate also for upper-level foundations courses because of its solid research base drawn extensively from primary sources and its systematic attention to providing up-to-date research references and documentation.

Our purpose in writing this book remains the same as in the previous four editions: to provide a comprehensive body of information on the various foundations of education and significant contemporary educational issues from a broad, substantive, and interdisciplinary viewpoint. We have sought to summarize and synthesize the important concepts and research findings in a practical way and to provide balanced treatment of many controversial issues without making the text overly complicated for students.

FEATURES OF THE REVISION

One of the major changes in this edition is a *new chapter on international education.* Chapter 15, "International Education," offers readers a comparative look at education and schools throughout the world. Especially noteworthy is its coverage of exemplary programs such as school choice and school-based management in England and Wales, vocational education in Germany, and mathematics and science education in Japan. In addition to familiarizing readers with important global educational issues and developments, we hope this new international perspective will help readers gain a better understanding of what is truly unique about the U.S. educational system.

Another key change is a *new feature, "Getting to the Source,"* which appears in every chapter. Consisting of a one-page excerpt from a high-interest, significant, and relevant primary source along with author commentary and questions relating the document to chapter content, this feature exposes students to a wide variety of primary sources. Sources range from Erasmus's description of the conditions of schools during the Renaissance to selections from the writings of DuBois, Counts, Bronfenbrenner, and Coleman; from a page in a nineteenth-century teaching manual to a landmark school finance court decision to a first-hand account of a Japanese math class today. Our goals in introducing this new feature are to help students feel more comfortable using and referring to primary sources and to make chapter coverage more meaningful and real to students. A complete index of this feature appears at the front of this book.

Among the most significant changes in this edition is the *increased coverage of multiculturalism and student diversity.* The new content coverage, which reflects the rapidly changing demographics of American society and American classrooms, includes:

- An expanded section on the critical shortage of minority teachers (Chapter 1)
- An expanded discussion of the education of minorities throughout American history (Chapter 5)
- New sections on legal issues related to religion and public schools, including coverage of the 1992 Supreme Court decision (Chapter 8)
- Updated statistics for school performance by various minority groups (Chapter 10)
- New figures and tables reflecting 1990 Census data on racial and ethnic groups (Chapter 11)
- A new section on multicultural curriculum and instruction (Chapter 11)
- New recommendations for implementing and evaluating multicultural programs (Chapter 11)
- A new section on "Multicultural Education in Europe and the United States" that assesses U.S. success in providing educational opportunities for a diverse population (Chapter 15)
- A new six-page, full-color insert on "The Changing Face of American Education" with numerous full-color graphs illustrating various aspects of America's multicultural and diverse classrooms and society

This expanded coverage of multiculturalism will help students better understand the educational implications of an increasingly diverse student population and, at the same time, prepare them to respond effectively to these changes.

In addition, because education is such a dynamic and rapidly changing field, *every chapter has been updated and changed,* most quite substantially, to provide students with the most current information and scholarship available. We have added coverage of such significant trends and topics as fifth-year and five-year programs, alternative certification, reflective teaching, school-based management, disputes about political correctness, drug testing of teachers, sexual harassment, school choice, year-round schools, national curriculum, teleconferencing and distance education, current multicultural controversies, privatization of educational services, promising instructional innovations, and much more. Throughout, the text provides the latest statistical data (including 1990 Census findings) on such topics as teacher employment trends, demographics, school enrollments, poverty, adolescent drug and alcohol use, school finance, and student performance. Over 50 percent of the citations in this edition are from 1990 or later.

Finally, the resource package accompanying this textbook has been expanded to include a *test bank data disk* and an *improved Instructor's Resource Manual* with many new multiple-choice items that test for higher-order thinking skills.

CONTENT AND ORGANIZATION

The text consists of sixteen chapters divided into six parts. All the foundations of education are covered. *Part I* ("Understanding the Teaching Profession") considers the climate in which teachers work today and its impact on teaching. Changes in the job market and in the status of the profession and issues such as teacher empowerment and alternative certification are treated in detail.

The three chapters in *Part II* ("Historical Foundations") provide an historical context for understanding current educational practices and trends by examining the events and ideas that have influenced the development of American education.

Part III ("Political, Economic, and Legal Foundations") presents an overview of the organization, governance, and administration of elementary and secondary education; the financing of public education; and the legal aspects of education.

Part IV ("Social Foundations") examines the relationship between society and the schools that society has established to serve its needs. The three chapters in this part discuss culture and socialization, the complex relationship of social class and race to school achievement, and the various programs aimed at providing equal educational opportunity for all students.

Part V ("Philosophical and Curricular Foundations") examines the philosophical ideas that have shaped education and the ways in which changes in social priorities have led to changes in educational aims, curriculum, and instructional methods. Throughout these three chapters, we explicitly point out how particular philosophical ideas are linked to aims, curriculum, and other facets of contemporary education. This section concludes with a look at emerging curriculum trends.

Part VI ("Effective Education: International and American Perspectives") provides a comparative look at effective schools and school reform throughout the world and an in-depth analysis of current efforts to improve school effectiveness in the United States.

SPECIAL PEDAGOGIC FEATURES

The Fifth Edition of *Foundations of Education* includes many special features designed to help students easily understand and master the material in the text.

Three unique pedagogical features are particularly noteworthy:

■ *"Getting to the Source"*—a new feature—offers students the opportunity to become familiar with a wide variety of primary source materials. Appearing in every chapter, this feature consists of one-page excerpts from a variety of high-interest, significant and relevant primary source materials, along with author commentary and questions.

■ *Charts entitled "Taking Issue"* present controversial issues in the field of education, offering arguments on both sides of a question so that students can understand why the topic is important and how it affects contemporary schools. One of these charts appears in each chapter, covering issues such as alternative certification, merit pay, magnet schools, and establishing a national curriculum. Instructors may wish to use these charts as the basis for class discussion or essay assignments.

■ *Topic overview charts,* set off in screened boxes throughout the text, summarize and compare key developments and topics. The overview charts from the previous edition have been updated and several new ones have been added.

To help you easily locate these three features, special indexes for each of them appear at the front of this book.

In addition, all the other pedagogic features of the preceding edition have been retained, including the following important elements:

■ *Focusing questions* at the beginning of each chapter highlight the major topics to be discussed.

■ *Marginal notations* reinforce central points throughout the text.

■ *Annotated lists of selected readings* that may be of special interest to readers appear at the end of each chapter.

■ *A list of key terms,* with cross-references to text pages, appears near the end of each chapter as a convenient recapitulation and guide for the student.

■ *End-of-chapter features* also include *summary lists* that facilitate understanding and analysis of content and *discussion questions* to stimulate class discussion of text material.

■ *An extensive glossary* at the end of the book defines important terms and concepts.

ANCILLARIES

Accompanying the text is an *Instructor's Resource Manual with Test Items.* It contains over eight hundred test items, developed according to sound principles and standards of test construction. The multiple-choice items have been extensively revised and now include many items that test for higher order thinking skills. In addition, the instructional resource material of the manual has been thoroughly updated and revised to reflect new text content; it offers for each chapter of the text a chapter outline, a chapter overview, student objectives, lecture and discussion topics, student projects, and selected references.

The test items contained in the *Instructor's Resource Manual* are also available in computerized form in a *Test Bank Data Disk,* new to this edition.

Finally, a *set of forty transparencies,* both two- and-one-color, is available to each instructor upon adoption of the text. The transparencies include figures from the text and new material as well.

ACKNOWLEDGMENTS

The fifth edition represents an ambitious undertaking that would not have been possible without the help of many individuals. We especially wish to acknowledge Gerald Gutek, Professor of Education and History at Loyola University of Chicago, who wrote chapters 3, 4, 5, and 12 and brought them up to date for this new edition. We would also like to thank Rayna Levine for her collaboration on Chapter 8, "Legal Aspects of Education."

A number of reviewers made useful suggestions and provided thoughtful reactions at various stages in the development of the manuscript. We wish to thank the following individuals for their conscientiousness and for their contributions to the content of this edition:

Louis Alfonso, *Rhode Island College*

Terryl J. Anderson, *The University of Texas of the Permian Basin*

Mario L.M. Baca, *California State University, Fresno*

James F. Cummings, *Newberry College, South Carolina*

Arnold Danzig, *Northern Arizona University*

Judith A. Green, *Kansas State University*

Ralph R. Karst, *Northeast Louisiana University*

June Kreutzkampf, *University of Minnesota, Duluth*

Colleen A. Moore, *Central Michigan University*

John P. Strouse, *Ball State University*

Margaret D. Tannenbaum, *Glassboro State College*

Cheryl Valdez, *Chapman University, California*

J.W. Weatherford, *University of Central Oklahoma*

Jody Messinger Wolfe, *West Virginia University*

We also wish to note out gratitude to our mentors, Virgil Clift of New York University and the late Robert Havighurst, who appreciated good friends, vintage wine, and new ideas. Then there are Stanley Elam of *Phi Delta Kappan,* Tom Koerner of *NASSP Bulletin,* and Gerald Unks of *High School Journal*—all of whom, as editors of these journals, have been receptive for many years to our ideas about schools and society. Thanks must also be given to our editors, who provided varied and continuous assistance at every step from planning to completion and whose Yankee wit and style seem to blend well with our view, from the heartland, of what is important in education.

In particular, Susan Granoff and Loretta Wolozin continued to provide vigorous and perceptive leadership and support as they have for previous editions, Rosemary Winfield and Karen Donovan made sure that the multitude of details involved in moving from manuscript to book received appropriate attention, and Doug Gordon worked tirelessly and with great skill to improve the substantive and stylistic quality, integrity, and coherence of this edition. Finally, the patience and understanding of our wives, Valerie and Rayna, are greatly appreciated—and a special thanks is owed to Joel, Stacey, and Jason for everything they've taught their Dad.

Allan C. Ornstein   *Daniel U. Levine*

UNDERSTANDING THE TEACHING PROFESSION

*T*hose who intend to teach should be aware of the trends that affect the work of classroom teachers, the issues that involve their status as professionals, and the changes that occur in these trends and issues over time. In Part 1, we look at the climate in which teachers operate, observe how this climate affects both the act of teaching and the status of the teaching profession, and examine what teachers are doing to shape their future.

The first part of Chapter 1 examines why people choose to become teachers and discusses the economic position and prestige and the demand for teachers. We consider the basic decision to teach, we analyze salary trends, and we review the current and prospective job market for teachers.

The focus shifts in the second part of the chapter to teacher preparation. Several questions arise: What is the appropriate mix of general or liberal education, specialization, and professional education courses for preparing effective teachers? How are teachers certified? What are the trends in teacher preparation programs? The chapter then describes recent concern with the quality of the teacher workforce and the need for increasing the number of minority teachers. We conclude by describing several current efforts to improve the situation of teachers.

Chapter 2 inquires into the question of whether teaching is a full profession. After explaining the debate regarding the professional status of teachers, we look at recent trends toward greater professionalism. Chapter 2 also describes a variety of teacher organizations and associations.

Our portrayal of the teaching profession may be viewed as generally encouraging. On the one hand, teachers' salaries and prestige are not as high as those of some other professions, and problems and pressures in the schools can make teaching a stressful job. On the other hand, teachers' salaries have been improving, and there no longer is a large surplus of teachers. As in previous eras, teachers enter the field because it provides an opportunity to help children learn and grow. Teaching should continue to be a rewarding field for persons interested in making this important contribution to schools and society.

1

Motivation, Status, and Preparation of the Teacher

FOCUSING QUESTIONS

What are the reasons for becoming a teacher?

What is satisfying and dissatisfying about teaching?

How does the prestige teachers possess compare to that of other occupations?

What do teachers earn? How does this compare with other occupations?

What are the employment trends for teachers?

How are teachers prepared? How are they certified?

What are the trends in teacher education?

What developments are taking place regarding the quality of the teacher workforce and the conditions of teaching?

Anyone who is thinking about becoming a teacher should understand something about the situation of the teacher. Why do people become teachers? To what degree do teachers enjoy the respect of the public? What level and range of salaries do they earn? Are teachers still underpaid? What are the supply-demand trends for the profession? How are teachers prepared for elementary and secondary education? These are some of the important concerns that will be explored in this chapter.

CHOOSING A CAREER IN TEACHING

Reasons for entering the profession

There are many motives, both idealistic and practical, for choosing a career in teaching. People who are thinking of entering the teaching profession — and even those who are already teaching — should ask themselves why they are making this choice. Their motives may include (1) a love of children, (2) a desire to impart knowledge, (3) an interest in and excitement about teaching, and (4) a desire to perform a valuable service to society. Other reasons may include job security, pension benefits, and the relative ease of preparing for teaching compared with the training required by some other professions.[1]

It is especially essential for prospective teachers to understand the importance of this career decision. Your reasons for choosing teaching as a career will undoubtedly affect your attitude and behavior with your students when you eventually become a teacher. Whatever your reasons for wanting to teach, it might be helpful for you to consider the thoughts and feelings that have motivated others to become teachers.

Motives for teaching

A 1987 study of future teachers from a nationally representative sample of seventy-six schools and colleges of teacher education examined respondents' reasons for selecting the teaching profession. Ninety percent of the respondents cited "Helping children grow and learn" as one of their reasons. Next highest was the statement "Seems to be a challenging field" (63 percent), followed closely by "Like work conditions" (54 percent), "Inspired by favorite teachers" (53 percent), and "Sense of vocation and honor of teaching" (52 percent). These reasons were basically similar to those cited in several other studies conducted in the 1980s.[2]

Satisfaction with Teaching

Once people become teachers, are they generally satisfied with their work? An answer to this question was sought from a nationally representative sample of elementary and secondary teachers in a poll conducted for the Metropolitan

---

[1]Pamela B. Joseph and Nancy Green, "Perspectives on Reasons for Becoming Teachers," *Journal of Teacher Education* (November–December 1986), pp. 28–33; Frances O. Rust, "A Comparative Analysis of Beliefs About Teaching Among Preservice Teachers" (Paper presented at the Annual Meeting of the American Educational Research Association, Chicago, April 1991).

[2]*Teaching Teachers: Facts and Figures* (Washington, D.C.: American Association of Colleges for Teacher Education, 1987); Donald R. Cruickshank, *Research That Informs Teachers and Teacher Educators* (Bloomington, Ind.: Phi Delta Kappa, 1990).

There are many motives for becoming a teacher, but perhaps the most powerful is the desire to work with young people. (© Eric Neurath/ Lightwave)

Life Insurance Company. Respondents were asked the question, "All in all, how satisfied would you say you are with teaching as a career?" Eighty-six percent responded that they were either "very satisfied" or "somewhat satisfied"; only 3 percent said they were "very dissatisfied."[3] Similarly, a poll conducted in 1990 found that 85 percent of teachers were generally satisfied, and nearly half reported that they were more enthusiastic about teaching than when they began their careers.[4]

National surveys

Job aspects that teachers find most satisfying and most dissatisfying can be inferred from Figure 1.1, which shows the responses of public-school teachers in a Metropolitan Life Survey. Large majorities rated their schools "excellent" or "good" with respect to their colleagues' competence and caring for students; the overall quality of the education offered; and relations between parents and teachers. Teachers were somewhat less satisfied with physical facilities, support shown by parents, and student motivation. Nevertheless, more teachers rated their schools either "excellent" or "good" than "poor" or "fair" on these latter characteristics.

Satisfaction generally high

The generally high ratings that teachers assign to the schools in which they work help explain their relatively high level of satisfaction. Research indicates that two of the most important determinants of teachers' satisfaction are the extent to which they feel successful in advancing students' learning and growth,

Main sources of satisfaction

---

[3]Humphrey Taylor and Robert Leitman, *The American Teacher 1989* (New York: Metropolitan Life, 1990).

[4]*The Condition of Teaching: A State-by-State Analysis 1990* (Lawrenceville, N.J.: Princeton University Press, 1990).

Percentage of Teachers Choosing "Excellent" or "Good" in Rating Selected Aspects of Their Schools

Figure 1.1

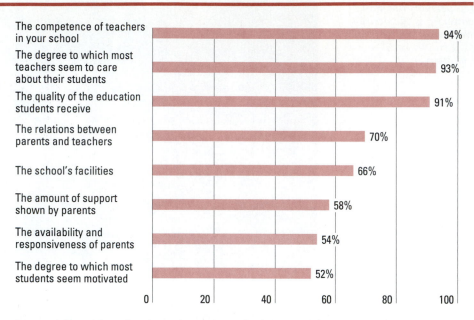

Source: Adapted from data in Louis Harris, Michael Kagay, and Jane Ross, *The American Teacher 1987* (New York: Metropolitan Life, 1987), p. 20. Used with permission.

and the quality of the teachers' interpersonal relationships with students and parents.[5] Since teachers appear to be mostly positive about these two aspects, it is not surprising that they tend to be satisfied with their jobs.

Aspects of dissatisfaction

Conversely, however, many teachers report dissatisfaction with those aspects of their work that they think interfere with their ability to help students learn and to establish positive relationships with students. Nationwide surveys have indicated that many teachers believe they have insufficient time for counseling students, planning lessons, and other instructional functions.[6] Other aspects of work that substantial proportions of respondents find problematic include ambiguity in the expectations of supervisors; lack of supplies and equipment; extensive paperwork and record keeping; and insufficient opportunity to participate in organizational decisions.[7] In addition, many teachers are dissatisfied with what they perceive as unduly low salaries. Recent improvements in

[5]Douglas E. Mitchell, Flora Ida Ortiz, and Tedi K. Mitchell, *Work Orientation and Job Performance: The Cultural Basis of Teaching Awards and Incentives* (New York: State University of New York Press, 1987); Betty J. Young, "Teacher Empowerment and Job Satisfaction" (Paper presented at the Annual Meeting of the American Educational Research Association, Boston, April 1990).

[6]*Characteristics of Stayers, Movers, and Leavers* (Washington, D.C.: U.S. Department of Education, 1991).

[7]Ann Bradley, "Poll Finds Drop in Teacher Satisfaction with Degree of Control Over Their Jobs," *Education Week*, September 5, 1990, p. 9; "Teachers Take Charge," *Instructor* (May 1990), pp. 23–25.

teacher salaries and efforts underway to improve teaching conditions (described later in this chapter) may reduce these aspects of dissatisfaction in the future.

Stress and Burnout

Teaching can be stressful

Like other occupations, teaching has its difficult and stressful moments. This is particularly true in the "caregiving" professions, in which 20 percent or more of persons may suffer from "burnout" during some stage of their professional careers. Evidence that accumulated in the 1970s and 1980s indicates that elementary and secondary teaching has become more stressful than it was in earlier periods and that greater stress is causing burnout among some teachers.[8]

Burnout

Definitions of burnout generally characterize it in terms of emotional and, in many cases, physical exhaustion. Recent research indicates that much of the stress and burnout among teachers stems from their perceptions that many students have serious problems that impede learning, and that time pressures and administrative regulations are interfering with the effectiveness of instruction.[9]

Counteracting burnout

The emphasis in recent years has been to encourage professionals who experience stress to develop a variety of coping techniques. Counselors point out that exercise, rest, hobbies, good nutrition, meditation or other relaxation techniques, efficient scheduling of personal affairs, and vacations can help individuals cope with high-stress jobs. Recommendations for avoiding burnout also advise teachers to participate in professional renewal activities, to separate their jobs from their home life, and to try to maintain flexibility and an open-minded attitude toward change. Activities or projects undertaken by professional organizations and school districts to help teachers avoid burnout include a variety of courses and workshops emphasizing coping techniques and other stress-reduction activities.[10] Specialists on this topic also point out that some educators view stressful conditions as a challenge and in doing so apparently are better able to cope with the stress they experience.[11]

Attrition

Low recent attrition

Research on attrition (that is, on people leaving the teaching profession) indicates that a significant proportion of teachers resign from their positions in any given year. Data also show, however, that attrition currently is less than it has been in the last twenty-five or thirty years: rates of attrition in recent years

---

[8]Barry A. Farber, *Crisis in Education* (San Francisco: Jossey-Bass, 1991).

[9]Joseph J. Blase, "A Qualitative Analysis of Sources of Teacher Stress: Consequences for Performance," *American Educational Research Journal* (Spring 1986), pp. 13–40; Farber, *Crisis in Education;* and Daniel P. Liston and Kenneth M. Zeichner, "Teacher Education and the Social Context of Schooling," *American Educational Research Journal* (Winter 1990), pp. 610–636.

[10]Jim Sweeney, "Responsibility and Fulfillment of Needs: Burnout Remedies?" *Phi Delta Kappan* (May 1981), p. 676; Edward F. Pajak, Deborah Williams, and Carl D. Glickman, "Teacher Stress: Implications for Supervision," *Educational Leadership* (December 1987–January 1988), p. 95; and Marc Cecil and Susan Forman, "Effect of Stress Inoculation Training," *Journal of School Psychology* (Summer 1990), pp. 105–118.

[11]James C. Sarros, "The Stress Stories of School Teachers and Administrators" (Paper presented at the Annual Meeting of the American Educational Research Association, San Francisco, April 1986); Madeleine Fuchs Holzer, "Teaching Is Still a Noble Profession," *Education Week*, October 16, 1991, p. 25.

have been between 4 and 9 percent, down from twice that level in the 1960s and 1970s. Much of this decline probably is due to the fact that relatively few young teachers were hired during the teacher surplus of the 1970s and early 1980s; consequently, an unusually high proportion of the teaching force currently consists of experienced teachers with tenure who are least likely to leave the field. However, this situation is likely to change in the near future as many teachers reach retirement age.[12]

Likelihood of attrition

Data on the likelihood that teachers may leave teaching have been collected as part of recent annual surveys conducted for the Metropolitan Life Insurance Company. When asked the question "Within the next five years how likely is it that you will leave the teaching profession to go into some different occupation?" about one-quarter of teachers have responded "very likely" or "fairly likely." Female teachers in elementary schools and teachers working in rural areas were least inclined to answer "very likely" or "fairly likely."[13]

The preceding analysis indicates that most teachers have been motivated by a desire to work with young people and to enter a challenging and honorable field. A large majority of teachers are satisfied with most aspects of their jobs, but there is some dissatisfaction with salary and other "nonteaching" considerations, and a significant percentage leave teaching for other fields. As we shall see later in this chapter, nationwide efforts are underway to improve salaries and other conditions in teaching.

STATUS AND SUPPLY OF TEACHERS

Occupational prestige and salary level are two of the major determinants of the social status of persons in a given occupation. Prestige and salary in turn are affected by **supply and demand.** When the supply of persons in an occupation exceeds demand, the prestige and salaries of such workers tend to decline, which leads to a decrease in social status. Conversely, high demand and low supply tend to increase salaries, prestige, and social status. (See color insert.)

Occupational Prestige

Occupations with high prestige

Occupational prestige refers to the esteem in which an occupation is held by individuals or groups in a particular society. Some occupations are highly esteemed in the sense that people generally perceive them as socially important and desirable, whereas other occupations are viewed as less important. Occupations with high prestige tend to include those that are perceived as making a particularly valuable contribution to society and that require a high level of education or skill and little manual or physical labor. The job of elementary or secondary teacher historically has ranked relatively high on this aspect of social status.

---

[12]David W. Grissmer and Sheila N. Kirby, *Teacher Attrition: The Uphill Climb to Staff the Nation's Schools* (Santa Monica, Calif.: Rand, 1987); "Fewer Teachers Leave the Ranks," *Teacher Magazine* (August 1990), p. 14.

[13]Taylor and Leitman, *The American Teacher 1989.*

Prestige of teachers

Perhaps the best-known studies of occupational prestige are those conducted by the National Opinion Research Center (NORC), affiliated with the University of Chicago. In 1947, NORC asked 2,290 persons throughout the country to rank eighty-eight occupations.[14] The study showed that school teachers ranked thirty-seventh in prestige, and college professors outranked others in the teaching profession. The NORC conducted a related study of ninety occupations in 1964.[15] Teachers ranked 29.5, moving up 7.5 places. Later surveys conducted in the 1970s and 1980s provided prestige ratings of more than five hundred overlapping occupational titles. The highest average score was 82 for physicians and surgeons, and the lowest was 9 for shoe shiners.[16] Elementary school teachers were rated at 60, and secondary school teachers were rated at 63 — both above the 90th percentile.[17] In addition, the percentage of teachers who say they "feel respected in today's society" has increased from 39 percent in 1984 to 49 percent in 1989.[18]

Causes of higher teacher status

One reason why the occupational prestige of teachers seems to have remained high or even increased is that their average level of education has risen greatly in the twentieth century. Since requirements for entering teaching have been increasing recently (as detailed later in this chapter) and larger proportions of teachers earn graduate degrees, the occupational prestige and status of teachers should improve still more. Traditionally, teachers had relatively high occupational prestige but relatively low salaries; recent and prospective improvements in teachers' salaries also are likely to generate improvements in their status. Among other interrelated trends that may raise the status of teaching are a growing national concern for the quality and effectiveness of education, and movement toward greater specialization in the teaching force (for example, master teachers and counselors).[19]

Pay Scales and Trends

Increase in salaries

In 1930 the average teacher salary in 1991 dollars was $26,085. By 1991 this figure had risen to $32,880. Today it is not uncommon for some experienced teachers in wealthy school districts to earn $60,000 to $70,000. Moreover, teachers have opportunities to supplement their income by supervising after-school programs, athletics, and other extracurricular activities, and some can advance to administrative positions with annual salaries well over $80,000. In addition, one should keep in mind that public-school teachers usually have

---

[14]C. C. North and Paul K. Hatt, "Jobs and Occupation: A Popular Evaluation," *Opinion News*, September 1, 1947, pp. 3–13; Richard Centers, "Social Class, Occupation, and Imputed Values," *American Journal of Sociology* (May 1953), pp. 543–555.

[15]Robert W. Hodge, Paul M. Siegel, and Peter H. Rossi, "Occupational Prestige in the United States, 1925–63," *American Journal of Sociology* (November 1964), pp. 286–302.

[16]Paul M. Siegel, "Prestige in the American Occupational Structure" (Ph.D. diss., Department of Sociology, University of Chicago, 1971).

[17]Donald J. Treiman, *Occupational Prestige in Comparative Perspective* (New York: Academic Press, 1977); Daniel W. Rossides, *Social Stratification* (Englewood Cliffs, N.J.: Prentice-Hall, 1990).

[18]Taylor and Leitman, *The American Teacher 1989*.

[19]Allan C. Ornstein, "Teacher Salaries Look Good for the 1990s," *Education Digest* (December 1990), pp. 21–23.

Getting to the Source ◆

Teachers and Teaching / Jacques Barzun

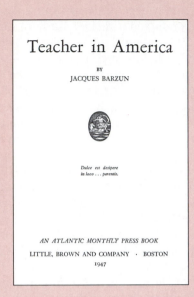

Teacher in America

BY
JACQUES BARZUN

*Dulce est desipere
in loco . . . parentis.*

AN ATLANTIC MONTHLY PRESS BOOK

LITTLE, BROWN AND COMPANY · BOSTON
1947

Jacques Barzun, who emigrated from France to the United States, was admitted to Columbia University at age sixteen in 1923 and later served as a professor of history at that institution for more than 30 years. Many of his publications provide thoughtful analysis of teaching and learning at all levels of education. In the following excerpt, from a book published in 1944,

he discusses the status and power of teachers and the "American state of mind about Education."

There is an age-old prejudice against teaching. Teachers must share with doctors the world's most celebrated sneers, and with them also the world's unbounded hero-worship. Always and everywhere, "He is a schoolteacher" has meant "He is an underpaid pitiable drudge." Even a politician stands higher, because power in the street seems less of a mockery than power in the classroom. But when we speak of Socrates, Jesus, Buddha, and "other great teachers of humanity," the atmosphere somehow changes and the politician's power begins to look shrunken and mean. August examples show that no limit can be set to the power of a teacher. . . .

The odd thing is that almost everybody is a teacher at some time or other during his life. Besides Socrates and Jesus, the great teachers of mankind are mankind itself — your parents and mine. First and last, parents do a good deal more teaching than doctoring, yet so natural and necessary is this duty that they never seem aware of performing it. It is only when they are beyond it, when they have thoroughly ground irremediable habits of speech, thought, and behavior into their offspring that they discover the teacher as an institution and hire him to carry on the work.

excellent benefits (such as pensions and health insurance) compared to other workers.[20]

Teaching pay varies considerably among and within states. Table 1.1 shows a state-by-state breakdown of average teacher salaries in 1991. Beginning teacher salaries that year ranged from $15,685 in Idaho to $29,950 in Alaska. Average overall salaries in the three highest-paying states (Alaska, New York,

Differences among states

---

[20]Myron Lieberman, "Are Teachers Underpaid?" *Public Interest* (Summer 1986), pp. 12–28; Gary Sykes, "Present Views of Teachers Past," *Educational Researcher* (January–February 1991), pp. 31–32.

. . . [N]ot long ago, I joined a club which described its membership as made up of Authors, Artists, and Amateurs — an excellent reason for joining. Conceive my disappointment when I found that the classifications had broken down and I was now entered as an Educator. Doubtless we shall have to keep the old pugilistic title of Professor, [but] we can and must get rid of "Educator." Imagine the daily predicament: someone asks, "What do you do?" — "I profess and I educate." It is unspeakable and absurd.

Don't think this frivolous, but regard it as a symbol. Consider the American state of mind about Education at the present time. An unknown correspondent writes to me: "Everybody seems to be dissatisfied with education except those in charge of it." This is a little less than fair, for a great deal of criticism has come from the profession. But let it stand. Dissatisfaction is the keynote. Why dissatisfaction? Because Americans believe in Education, because they pay large sums for Education, and because Education does not seem to yield results. At this point one is bound to ask: "What results do you expect?"

The replies are staggering. Apparently Education is to do everything that the rest of the world leaves undone. . . . An influential critic, head of a large university, wants education to generate a classless society; another asks that education root out racial intolerance (in the third or the ninth grade, I wonder?); still another requires that college courses be designed to improve labor relations. One man, otherwise sane, thinks the solution of the housing problem has bogged down — in the schools; and another proposes to make the future householders happy married couples — through the schools. . . .

Well, this is precisely where the use of the right word comes in. . . . The advantage of [the word] "teaching" is that in using it you must recognize — if you are in your sober senses — that practical limits exist. You know by instinct that it is impossible to "teach" democracy, or citizenship or a happy married life. I do not say that these virtues and benefits are not somehow connected with good teaching. They are, but they occur as by-products. They come, not from a course, but from a teacher; not from a curriculum, but from a human soul.

Questions

1. When you become a teacher, do you want to be known as an "educator"? What are the positives and negatives attached to this designation?

2. What noninstructional problems and tasks have been thrust at least in part on the schools in recent years?

Source: Jacques Barzun, *The Teacher in America* (Boston: Little, Brown, 1944), cover pp. 4–5, 6, 7, 9. Copyright © renewed by Jacques Barzun. By permission of Little, Brown and Company.

and Connecticut) were nearly twice as high as those in the three lowest-paying states (Idaho, North Dakota, and South Dakota). Of course, comparative living costs must be taken into account. It is much more expensive to live in Alaska, for example, than to live in the Southeast or the North Central states.

Variations based on experience and education

Salary differences within states are wide, especially in states where average state pay scales are high. For example, in Niles, Illinois, the average teacher salary in 1990 was approximately $20,000 more than the average for Illinois teachers statewide. In southern states where average salaries are low, the range is narrower, but there are still considerable differences. If you settled in Cobb County, Georgia, for example, your maximum salary in the early 1990s was about $10,000 lower than the maximum salary for Atlanta teachers.

Teachers often supplement their salaries by taking on additional responsibilities, such as supervising extracurricular activities. (© Frederick D. Bodin/ Stock Boston)

Table 1.1

Average Beginning and Overall Salaries of Public School Teachers, 1991

State	Beginning Salary	Average Salary
50 states and D.C.	$21,542	$32,880
Alaska	29,950	43,406
New York	26,375	42,080
Connecticut	25,312	43,398
California	24,570	39,118
New Jersey	24,500	38,411
Nevada	24,358	35,269
Hawaii	23,792	33,548
Maryland	23,548	38,312
D.C.	23,327	39,362
Pennsylvania	23,250	36,057
Michigan	22,400	37,800
Virginia	22,206	32,692
Alabama	22,114	26,846
Illinois	21,954	34,642
Massachusetts	21,800	36,090
Arizona	21,375	30,773
Florida	21,368	30,555
Delaware	21,112	35,246
Minnesota	21,029	33,128
Rhode Island	20,887	38,220

(Cont.)

Wisconsin	20,689	33,077
New Hampshire	20,635	31,273
Washington	20,612	32,975
Georgia	20,471	28,950
Oregon	20,357	32,295
Missouri	20,293	27,636
Indiana	20,247	32,931
Tennessee	20,150	28,248
Texas	20,150	28,100
North Carolina	19,810	29,165
Colorado	19,786	31,819
South Carolina	19,757	28,174
Iowa	19,404	27,949
Kentucky	19,311	29,115
Wyoming	19,238	28,996
New Mexico	19,124	25,800
Kansas	18,954	28,188
Mississippi	18,950	24,609
Maine	18,878	28,531
West Virginia	18,728	25,966
Oklahoma	18,575	24,378
Vermont	18,509	29,714
Ohio	18,452	31,964
Montana	18,400	26,696
Nebraska	18,344	26,592
Louisiana	17,486	26,170
Arkansas	17,458	23,735
Utah	17,234	25,415
South Dakota	16,676	22,363
North Dakota	16,274	23,574
Idaho	15,685	25,510

Note: Some data are derived from preliminary figures or estimates.

Source: F. Howard Nelson, *Survey and Analysis of Salary Trends 1991* (Washington, D.C.: American Federation of Teachers, 1991), Table III-1, p. 43. Used by permission.

Variations based on experience and education

The greatest variation in salaries is accounted for by years of experience and education. Teachers with more years of experience and more education earn more than those with less of either. Table 1.2 shows the range based on years of experience and additional education in a typical salary schedule — that of the Kansas City, Missouri, public schools. The salary schedule negotiated for 1992 provided $22,215 for a first-year teacher with a B.A. degree and $44,430 for a teacher at the highest level of experience and education. Salary schedules in wealthy suburban districts generally are substantially higher than those in most other school districts. In the Glenbrooke suburb of Chicago, for example, first-year teachers with a B.A. earned $27,100 in 1991, fifth-year teachers with an M.A. earned $36,043, and teachers with at least 20 years of experience and 45 graduate hours past the M.A. were paid $65,040.

Table 1.2

Selected Steps in the Salary Schedule for the Kansas City, Missouri, Public Schools, 1992

	Bachelor's Degree	Master's Degree or Bachelor's Degree + 36 Graduate Hours	Master's Degree + 32 Graduate Hours	Doctorate or Master's Degree + 60 Graduate Hours
First year (Step 1)	$22,215	$24,548	$27,213	$29,813
Fifth year (Step 5)	25,436	28,102	30,768	33,989
Tenth year (Step 10)	29,213	32,545	35,211	39,209
Maximum (Step 15)	—	37,654	39,654	44,430

Note: Teachers with a bachelor's degree must earn at least thirty-six graduate hours by their thirteenth year of teaching.

Source: Reference sheet distributed by Kansas City, Missouri, Public Schools, 1992.

Beginning salaries

Although a teacher at the top of the salary schedule can earn an attractive salary considering that the academic year is less than ten months long, starting salaries still tend to be low relative to some other professions. Recognizing this problem, many political and educational leaders are working to increase salaries for both first-year and experienced teachers in order to attract and retain high-quality staff. Some states provide additional funds so that all school districts can raise beginning salaries to a specified minimum, and most states have increased funding to the extent that school districts can raise general salary levels substantially. Figure 1.2 shows the results of recent efforts to improve teacher salaries. During the inflationary period of the 1970s, teachers' salaries declined relative to inflation and to the average salary of all workers, but large and steady gains in both these measures of teacher compensation have been registered since 1981.

Supply and Demand

From 1950 until the mid-1960s, the schools were bursting at the seams with record enrollments that originated in the post–World War II baby boom. These high-birthrate groups had to rely on teachers born during the low-birthrate years of the Great Depression — a trickle of teachers for a flood of students. Thus, a widespread shortage of teachers developed in the 1950s and early 1960s.

Excess of teachers in 1970s

The pattern was reversed in the late 1960s, and a general oversupply of teachers was available in the 1970s and early 1980s. This surplus of teachers reflected two major interrelated factors. First, the U.S. birthrate fell steadily from 1955 to 1973 and then remained low, thereby leading to a decline in school enrollment in the elementary and then the secondary schools. Second, the college-age population increased as the baby boom generation grew up, and many of this generation entered teaching.[21] However, it should be noted that a teacher shortage in certain subject areas has persisted through much of the past twenty

---

[21]"Trends in Teacher Supply and Demand in Public Schools, 1973–76," *NEA Research Memo* (June

Average Annual Earnings of Teachers, Government Workers, and All Workers in the United States, in Constant 1991 Dollars

Figure 1.2

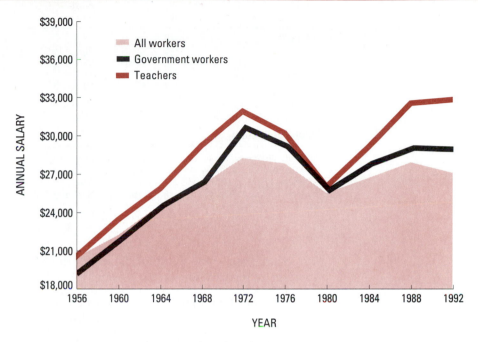

Source: F. Howard Nelson, *Survey and Analysis of Salary Trends 1991* (Washington, D.C.: American Federation of Teachers, 1991), Table II-2, p. 31. Used with permission.

years. These fields include special education, bilingual education, and early childhood education, which have been expanding rapidly despite general enrollment decline; and science, mathematics, and industrial arts, in which financial rewards are far better in business and industry than in teaching.[22]

Changing enrollment in teacher education

As college students, teacher educators, and state government officials realized that there was a substantial oversupply of teachers, enrollment in teacher-education programs decreased, and the percentage of college freshmen interested in becoming teachers declined from 23 percent in 1968 to 5 percent in 1982. In part because the resulting decline in the production of new teachers helped to reduce the surplus, the percentage of college students interested in teaching then began to increase, rising to 9 percent in 1990. Enrollment in teacher-education institutions rose by more than 60 percent during the latter part of the 1980s.[23]

1973), pp. 2–3; Stanley M. Elam, "A Somber Economic Picture for Teachers," *Phi Delta Kappan* (November 1974), p. 170; Linda Darling-Hammond, "Achieving Our Goals," *Phi Delta Kappan* (December 1990), pp. 286–294.

[22]Robert Rothman, "Freshmen Need Math Help, Survey Finds," *Education Week*, January 31, 1990, p. 7; "Teacher-Education Update," *The Chronicle of Higher Education*, January 8, 1992, p. A17.

[23]Beverly T. Watkins, "Teacher-Education Update," *The Chronicle of Higher Education*, April 25, 1990, p. A18.

Table 1.3
Public- and Private-School Enrollments, 1965–2000 (in millions)

	Total K–12	Public K–12	Private K–12	Private as Percentage of Total
1965	49.4	43.1	6.3	12.9%
1970	51.3	45.9	5.4	10.6
1980	45.9	41.0	4.9	10.7
1985	44.5	39.5	5.0	11.1
1990	46.2	40.8	5.4	11.7
1995 (projected)	49.4	43.6	5.7	11.5
2000 (projected)	49.9	44.1	5.8	11.6

Source: *The Condition of Education 1991* 1 (Washington, D.C.: U.S. Government Printing Office, 1991), Table 1.17, p. 64; *Projections of Education Statistics to 2001* (Washington, D.C.: U.S. Government Printing Office, 1991), Table 1, p. 4. Also see *United States Catholic Elementary and Secondary Schools 1990–1991* (Washington, D.C.: National Catholic Education Association, 1991), Table 5, p. 7.

What, then, is the trend for the rest of the 1990s? Some educators predict a shortage of teachers for several reasons:[24]

1. Now that the original baby boom generation has grown up and begun to produce its own children, a "mini" baby boom has developed. As a result, school enrollment will increase in the next decade (see Table 1.3).

2. A significant proportion of the current teaching force will reach retirement age within the next ten years.

Reasons to expect a future teacher shortage

3. Educational reformers are attempting to reduce class size, expand preschool education, place greater emphasis on science and mathematics, and introduce other changes that require more teachers.

4. Higher standards for teachers are serving to limit the supply of new teachers.

5. Because general opportunities for women have increased, the number of women in teacher education will probably not increase substantially.

Other educators, however, argue that there will not be a major shortage of teachers in the mid- and late 1990s.[25] Widespread layoffs attributed to economic recession in the early 1990s indicate a temporary reduction in demand. On the supply side, the attrition rate among teachers appears to have declined, and recent improvements in teacher salaries may reduce attrition still further. The improved salaries may also bring ex-teachers back to the schools and attract people who trained as teachers but did not originally enter the profession. More-

Reasons to expect no shortage

[24]Ann Bradley, "Even as Gaps in Data Are Filled, Teacher-Supply Debate Lingers," *Education Week,* September 19, 1990, pp. 1, 14–15; Robert K. Dornan, "New Careers in Education," *Congressional Record,* June 12, 1991, p. E2170; and Frank V. Auriemma, "Retiring and Hiring Teachers," *National Forum of Applied Educational Research Journal* 5 (no. 1, 1991–1992), pp. 49–54.

[25]*The Supply Side of the Teacher Labor Market in the Southeast* (Research Triangle Park, N.C.: Southeastern Educational Improvement Laboratory, 1990); Daniel Gursky, "Continued Gains in Number of School Employees Seen," *Education Week,* January 29, 1992, p. 5.

over, many states are making it easier to become a teacher through the process of alternative certification (see later section in this chapter).[26]

Given the arguments on each side of the issue, it is difficult to determine whether teacher shortages will be widespread in the next decade.[27] However, shortages should continue to exist in such "special needs" fields as education of students with handicaps, remedial education, bilingual education, science and mathematics, and foreign languages. In addition, teachers will remain in short supply in many rural areas and in some city and suburban communities that register significant population growth, particularly in the South and Southwest.[28]

Shortages in "special needs" fields

Opportunities in Nonpublic Schools. Certain trends suggest that numerous job opportunities may be available for prospective teachers in nonpublic schools during the mid- and late 1990s. As Table 1.3 shows, private-school enrollments have risen since 1980, and these schools now enroll more than 11 percent of the nation's elementary and secondary students. Moreover, many Catholic schools have been increasing the percentage of lay teachers on their faculties, and this trend is likely to continue in the future.

Increase in lay teachers

Years ago a large majority of students attending nonpublic schools were in Catholic schools, but this situation has now changed; in the past three decades Catholic enrollment has declined and many other nonpublic schools have been established. Enrollment has increased most in the independent (nonreligious) sector and in schools sponsored by evangelical and fundamentalist church groups.[29] In the future, many nonpublic schools may emulate the public schools in trying to upgrade their instructional programs by hiring more teachers specializing in such areas as science, math, computers, education of children with disabilities, and bilingual education.

Upgrading in nonpublic schools

Enhancing Employment Opportunities. Regardless of whether a large teacher shortage does or does not develop in the 1990s, there are some steps that prospective teachers can and should take to enhance their opportunities for rewarding employment.[30]

Pursuing a teaching job

Begin applying for teaching jobs as soon as possible.

Maintain an up-to-date placement file.

Apply for several vacancies.

[26]*The Supply Side of the Teacher Labor Market;* Jeff Neade, "Back to School," *Teacher Magazine* (March 1991), pp. 58–59; and Ann Bradley, "Where Have All the Jobs Gone?" *Teacher Magazine* (January 1992), pp. 12–13.

[27]Debra Viadero, "Survey Offers Glimpse of Interviews for Teaching Jobs," *Education Week,* March 7, 1990, p. 12.

[28]Ann Bradley, "Sweet Forgiveness," *Teacher Magazine* (May 1990), pp. 14–18; *Patterns of Attrition Among Indiana Teachers, 1965–1987* (Santa Monica, Calif.: Rand, 1992).

[29]*Characteristics of Private Schools: 1987–88* (Washington, D.C.: U.S. Department of Education, 1990); "Catholic Educators Come Out Fighting," *Teacher Magazine* (January 1992), p. 9.

[30]Charles B. Myers and Ann M. Neely, "Finding the First Teaching Job in Today's 'Unsettled Market,'" *Education Week,* March 13, 1987, p. 6; Maria Mihalik, "Thirty Minutes to Sell Yourself," *Teacher Magazine* (April 1990), pp. 78–80.

Prepare a neat, accurate, clear résumé.

Collect information on school districts that have vacant positions.

Prepare a "professional portfolio" including lesson plans, descriptions of relevant experience, and, if possible, a videotape of your teaching.

Be prepared for interview questions. In particular, anticipate questions that deal with classroom management, lesson design, teaching philosophy, and your employment history.

Make sure you follow certification requirements correctly.

Acquire adjunct skills to assist in activities such as journalism and coaching.

PREPARATION OF TEACHERS

Evolution of teacher training

During the colonial period and well into the early nineteenth century, an individual who wanted to become a teacher usually obtained approval from a local minister or a board of trustees associated with a religious institution. A high-school or college diploma was not considered a necessary prerequisite. If you could read, write, and spell and were of good moral character, you could teach school. By the 1820s, future teachers had begun attending normal schools (discussed in Chapter 5), although formal certification procedures still were not required. These teaching institutions did not grant a degree; rather, they offered a number of courses that prepared the candidate for teaching. Eventually, the normal schools became teacher colleges, and most of the latter have now become diversified colleges and universities. Today, except for alternative certification or temporary certification, all states require a bachelor's degree or five years of college work for entrance into teaching.

Preservice Teacher Education

Major components of preservice preparation

The preparation of teachers usually consists of three major components: (1) liberal (or general) education, (2) specialized subject-field education, and (3) professional education. In general, the purpose of a *liberal education* is to liberate the mind, to provide knowledge of self and culture worthy of a citizen in a free society. A liberal program combines the arts and sciences and seeks to give the student a broad cultural background. The *specialized subject field* comprises a cluster of courses in a specific subject area and provides the prospective teacher with in-depth preparation for his or her chosen teaching field. In most colleges and universities this subject field is called the student's "major" or "minor." Whereas secondary teachers are typically certified in one subject field, and for this reason usually complete a greater amount of coursework in one or two areas, most elementary teachers are responsible for many subject fields. Elementary teachers may also specialize, however, in areas such as music, art, physical education, and foreign language. *Professional education* consists of courses designed to provide knowledge and skills regarding the art and science of teaching.[31]

---

[31]Debra Viadero, "How Best to Train Teachers?" *Teacher Magazine* (January 1990), pp. 16–17; Gary R. Galluzo and Roger S. Pankratz, "Five Attributes of a Teacher Education Program–Knowledge Base," *Journal of Teacher Education* (September–October, 1991), pp. 7–14.

Almost all educators agree that the preparation of good teachers rests on these three components. What provokes strong argument are differing ideas about the relative emphasis that each component should receive. How much time, for example, should the education student devote to courses in liberal education, versus courses in a specialized subject field and professional education? Viewpoints also differ concerning the extent to which clinical experience, which emphasizes practice in actual school settings, should be incorporated in professional education courses.

Credit requirements

The typical school of education requires about 25 semester hours of professional studies for elementary teacher candidates and 20 hours for secondary teacher candidates. For both groups, an average of 16 of these hours is devoted to student teaching. For future elementary teachers, curriculum and methods courses account for about 25 percent of the professional studies curriculum, but such courses comprise only about 15 percent of professional studies for secondary school candidates. Of course, some colleges of education encourage or require more than this number of credits or specify courses beyond state certification requirements. Most colleges and universities distribute education courses throughout the four-year program, but some cluster them during the last year. Others either have implemented a fifth-year component consisting of subject-field and professional courses or have initiated a five-year program providing for fieldwork in schools beginning the second or third year and culminating in a graduate-credit internship in schools during the fifth year.[32]

Certification

In order to teach in a public school in the United States, prospective teachers are required to be certificated by the state in the subject areas or grade levels they wish to teach. Until recently, most states granted **certification** based on documentation that the candidate possessed sufficient appropriate professional preparation and good moral character. However, increasing public dissatisfac-

Competency requirements

tion with the quality of education has led to the introduction of competency tests for future teachers. Nearly every state has passed some type of competency requirement for teachers seeking initial certification.[33]

In past decades teaching certificates usually were issued for life. Some states have revised these laws and now issue certificates valid for only three to five

Renewing certificates

years. Teachers currently holding life certificates are not affected, but those possessing renewable certificates usually have to furnish proof of positive evaluations or university coursework.

Variation in Certification Requirements. One of the things that makes the preparation of teachers such a bedeviling problem is that certification requirements vary so widely from state to state. The situation can be summarized as follows: The power to determine requirements for teacher certification is divided among legislatures, state departments of education, schools and colleges of ed-

---

[32]Cruickshank, *Research That Informs Teachers;* Mary M. Kennedy, "Some Surprising Findings on How Teachers Learn to Teach," *Educational Leadership* (November 1991), pp. 14–17.

[33]Lynn Olson, "Teaching Our Teachers," *Education Week,* December 12, 1990, pp. 11–15, 20–21, 24–26.

Sources of variations

ucation, superintendents of public instruction, and boards of education. The range of semester hours in general education (that is, arts and sciences) required for a secondary certificate varies nationwide from about 30 hours at the low end to about 75 at the high end. The minimum hours required in professional education courses and the number of semester or quarter hours needed to teach an academic subject also vary in accordance with differing state requirements. But throughout the country, it is usually the responsibility of the teacher-preparation institution, not the state, to decide what courses in the subject field will be used to meet the semester requirements. Add to this the fact that even when education course titles at differing institutions are similar, there are often wide differences in content, intellectual level, and mandated competencies. The result is that state and institutional requirements, even when taken together, do not guarantee that teachers have studied a uniform set of skills and concepts.

NASDTEC requirements

How do we end this confusion? Perhaps teachers will soon exercise a greater role in shaping programs for their own training and certification. Or, perhaps more likely, state departments of education may agree on a common set of requirements for training and testing teachers. This already has happened to a significant degree; more than half the states follow broad requirements endorsed by the National Association of State Directors of Teacher Education Certification (NASDTEC).

Reciprocity of Teacher Certificates.   Differences in the certification requirements of the individual states traditionally have inhibited the free movement of teachers throughout the country. A teacher certified to teach in New York, for example, might not meet the requirements for teaching in Illinois. Organizations concerned with the quality of education generally view such lack of reciprocity as undesirable because interstate movement of teachers can be helpful in (1) nationally balancing teacher supply and demand, (2) improving opportunities for teachers, (3) reducing inbreeding and provincialism in local school systems, and (4) increasing morale among teachers.

Advantages of interstate movement of teachers

With varying degrees of success, reciprocity compacts were established between some states as early as 1900. In recent years, some states have taken action to establish two regional teaching certificates that provide reciprocity among Iowa, Kansas, Missouri, and Nebraska, and among the New England states, respectively. In addition, the NASDTEC and the Educational Testing Service are cooperating to develop a nationwide data base to facilitate teachers' geographic mobility by providing certification information on all fifty states.[34]

Reciprocity agreements

Where formal reciprocity agreements exist, persons graduating from approved programs leading to certification in one state are supposed to be automatically eligible for similar certification in other participating states. However, certified teachers who expect to move from one state to another should always be sure to obtain information on requirements and interpretations that may affect their status and employability, even when reciprocal agreements are in place.[35]

---

[34]"One Small Step for Teachers, One Giant Leap for Bureaucrats," *Teacher Magazine* (April 1990), p. 54.

[35]Mary Koepke, "How to Avoid Getting Trapped in License Hell," *Teacher Magazine* (April 1990), pp. 51–53, 55–56.

Alternative Certification. Partly in order to increase opportunities for attracting talented candidates into teaching and partly in reaction to current or anticipated shortages in teaching fields such as science and math, most states have introduced **alternative certification** programs. These provide ways for prospective teachers to obtain certification without following the traditional preparation path at schools and colleges of education. New Jersey, for example, has initiated a program to attract "talented persons who did not study education in college." More than 12,000 teachers were certified through alternative certification programs in the late 1980s.[36]

Nontraditional preparation

Alternative certification programs try to provide for intense supervision and compressed formal coursework during the first few years of assignment to a teaching position. Many educators in the public schools as well as in colleges and universities are troubled by alternative certification, however. Short-term preparation may not prove as adequate as traditional training programs, and pressures to respond rapidly to shortages of personnel in key teaching areas may lead schools to tolerate superficial preparation and supervision. In addition, alternative certification tends to undercut efforts to improve the quality of the teacher force through reform of teacher-education programs and preservice testing of future teachers' competencies.[37]

Compressed preparation

One of the first systematic examinations of alternative certification programs provided some encouraging indications that "well educated individuals with a sincere interest in teaching" are being attracted and that "intense supervision" generally is being provided. However, some recent assessments have raised questions about the quality and adequacy of alternative preparation. For example, data on several of these programs indicate that many participants received little or none of the training or supervision that school districts are supposed to provide, and many others who could not obtain jobs acquired large debts while preparing to participate.[38]

Assessment of alternative programs

Probably the best known alternative certification program established in recent years is a national effort called Teach For America. Designed to attract recent graduates from colleges at which students have high achievement scores, Teach For America spent more than $2.5 million in 1990 to recruit, train intensively for eight weeks, and place in school districts with severe urban problems nearly 500 participants. The program spent more than $5 million during the 1991–1992 school year to prepare and support over 1,000 participants. Some of the initial data were promising. For example, more than one-quarter of the teacher participants were minority individuals, and more than one-half of the secondary-school students were math or science majors. But the data also indicated that many of these potential new teachers were frustrated by conditions

Teach For America

---

[36]"More Alternative Paths Lead to Teaching Jobs," *The New York Times,* June 6, 1990, p. B9; "Professional Resources," *AACTE Briefs,* September 16, 1991, p. 3; and Patricia Hines, "From the Armed Forces to the Teaching Force," *The Wall Street Journal,* January 10, 1992, p. A8.

[37]Susan W. Masland and Robert T. Williams, "Teacher Surplus and Shortage: Getting Ready to Accept Responsibilities," *Journal of Teacher Education* (July–August 1983), p. 6; James P. Steffersens, "The Privatization of Teacher Education," *Education Week,* January 30, 1991, p. 40.

[38]Nancy E. Adelman, *An Exploratory Study of Teacher Alternative Certification and Retraining Programs* (Washington, D.C.: Policy Studies Associates, 1986), pp. 55–61; Joe M. Smith, "The Alternate Route: Flaws in the New Jersey Plan," *Educational Leadership* (November 1991), pp. 32–36.

Taking Issue

Alternative Certification

Alternative certification programs that bypass traditional teacher education requirements have been introduced in many states. In general, these programs provide orientation experiences for college graduates and then place them in full-time teaching positions where they receive training leading to certification at the same time they are learning about teaching and education.

Question: Should alternative certification programs that bypass traditional teacher education requirements be encouraged?

Arguments PRO

1   Learning to teach on the job is potentially more effective because it provides better opportunities to determine what does and doesn't work in the real world and to talk with, observe, and emulate successful teachers.

2   Professional studies are likely to be more meaningful and practical when they are integrated with full-time teaching than when they are presented in largely theoretical college courses.

3   Alternative programs, which do not require years of study for certification, can help attract teacher candidates to shortage areas such as mathematics, science, and bilingual education.

4   Alternative programs help attract minority teachers, retired persons with special skills in technical subjects, and other candidates who can make important contributions in improving the education system.

5   The existence of competing alternative programs will stimulate colleges and universities to improve their teacher-training programs.

Arguments CON

1   Learning to teach on the job generally will prove unsuccessful because many or most participants will be overwhelmed by the immediate demands placed on a new teacher and will be unable to develop and hone their skills adequately.

2   In practice, school districts either lack sufficient resources to provide professional studies for participants or have other priorities. Initial data on several alternative certification programs support this point.

3   These programs offer short-term relief only. Many participants will withdraw during or soon after the first year of teaching, once they realize they are not suited for or interested in the work.

4   Alternative certification reinforces inequity in education because it often places inexperienced persons at inner-city schools, which have high turnover and the most need for well-trained and experienced faculty.

5   Competing alternative programs may distract colleges and universities from offering training that develops the understanding and skills of reflective teachers over several years of study.

in difficult schools and/or withdrew before completing their initial assignments. Critics also raised questions about the adequacy of the eight-week training, the possible "arrogance" inherent in a program that recruits high-ability but thinly trained teachers from elite colleges for placement in low-income schools, the failure of participating schools and districts to provide recruits with promised support, and other aspects of the program design and implementation.[39]

---

[39]Michel Marriott, "For Fledgling Teacher Corps Hard Lessons," *New York Times*, December 5, 1990, pp. A1, B9; Michel Marriott, "Program to Recruit Top Graduates to Be Teachers Is

Trends in Preservice Education

Over the past two decades, many teacher-education programs have placed significant emphasis on competency-based preparation, on school-based field centers, and on earlier field experience. In recent years major developments also have included movements toward fifth-year and five-year programs, increased emphasis on producing "reflective" teachers, and the growing use of computers and other technology.

Competency-Based Teacher Education. A program using **competency-based teacher education (CBTE)** requires prospective teachers to demonstrate minimum levels of performance on specified teaching tasks. For example, rather than identifying an appropriate teaching strategy by writing a brief essay or selecting from among multiple-choice alternatives, a candidate may be required to teach a simulated class and then discuss the reasons for his or her teaching behaviors. The skills and understandings tested are based on research findings about the characteristics of effective teachers.

Testing of teaching performance

Data collected in the 1970s indicated that as many as half the teacher-training institutions in the United States utilized some degree of CBTE in their preservice programs, but this figure declined as colleges and universities experienced financial problems (CBTE is expensive if done well) and as questions were raised about CBTE's utility and feasibility.[40] Criticisms directed at CBTE have included the following:[41]

Decline of CBTE

1. CBTE fragments teaching and teacher education by introducing and attempting to assess too many skills. For example, some implementations included hundreds of skill modules.

Criticisms of CBTE

2. The reliability and validity of competency tests are not well established.

3. It is difficult to translate CBTE information about prospective teachers into certification units and licensing requirements.

School-Based Field Centers. One innovation designed to make teacher preparation more realistic and practical involves field centers at cooperating elementary or secondary schools. Much of the training previously provided at the college or university campus is now conducted at these **school-based field centers,** which frequently have office space for college faculty, special equip-

From college classrooms to school centers

Given a Boost," *The New York Times*, January 12, 1992, p. 12. Wendy Kopp, "Teach For America: No Private-Sector 'Quick Fix,'" *Education Week*, March 6, 1991, pp. 29, 31; Julie L. Nicklin, "Alternative Teacher-Education Project Draws Mixed Review," *Chronicle of Higher Education*, June 19, 1991, pp. A21–A22.

[40]Kenneth Howey, Sam Yarger, and Bruce Joyce, "Reflections on Preservice Preparation: Impressions from the National Survey, Part III: Institutions and Programs," *Journal of Teacher Education* (January–February 1978), pp. 38–40; Kenneth M. Zeichner and Daniel P. Liston, *Traditions of Reform in U.S. Teacher Education* (East Lansing, Mich.: National Center for Research on Teacher Education, 1990).

[41]Sam J. Yarger and Bruce R. Joyce, "Going Beyond the Data: Reconstructing Teacher Education," *Journal of Teacher Education* (November–December 1977), pp. 21–25; Zeichner and Liston, *Traditions of Reform;* and Nancy Green, "The Role of Foundations of Education in Teacher Preparation" (Paper presented at the Annual Meeting of the American Educational Studies Association, Kansas City, October 1991).

ment for use in teacher training, and outstanding teachers who serve as supervisors and models.

Whereas in 1968 less than 20 percent of higher education teacher-training institutions had established school-based centers, 36 percent had done so by 1975. The trend toward establishing these centers was particularly evident among public colleges and universities: 64 percent of the public higher education institutions had established a school-based center of some kind. The number of centers seems to have declined in the 1980s as federal support for them decreased and many colleges experienced financial distress, but this decline may reverse as educators explore possibilities for establishing "professional development schools" (see p. 33) as part of a national movement to reform U.S. schools.[42]

Reduction in federal support

Early Field Experience.   Many teacher-education programs have become more practical by requiring or encouraging future teachers to spend a significant amount of time in elementary or secondary schools early on in their preparation. Professional courses dealing with subjects such as introduction to education, educational psychology, or pedagogical methods are closely coordinated with classroom observation, assignments as a teacher aide, or other field experiences in local schools. Institutions that require early and continual field experience have constructed a sequence of assignments by which students move from observation to service as a teacher's aide to relatively full-scale teaching responsibility similar to the traditional "practice teaching" semester.[43]

Early assignments in schools

Fifth-Year and Five-Year Programs.   During the 1980s several states and numerous schools and colleges of education either introduced fifth-year programs or expanded teacher education across five years of preparation. We define fifth-year programs as those which include few or no professional studies components during the four years in which the future teacher earns a bachelor's degree; professional preparation is concentrated in the fifth year. In contrast, five-year programs spread professional preparation across the undergraduate years and focus increasingly on clinical experience and training. Some institutions modify these programs by shifting some professional studies components to a fifth year while retaining substantial undergraduate teacher-education requirements.

Professional preparation postponed

Fifth-year programs sometimes arise as a response to state government mandates to greatly reduce or eliminate undergraduate teacher-education courses. This would ensure that future teachers spend more time acquiring a comprehensive general education and more adequate knowledge of subjects they eventually will teach. In Virginia, for example, the state has placed a maximum of eighteen hours on teacher-education courses taken as part of a four-year preparation program; additional education courses are taken during the fifth year of

State mandates

---

[42]Marilyn Cochran-Smith, "Student Teaching and Teacher Research" (Paper presented at the Annual Meeting of the American Educational Research Association, Boston, April 1990); Edward J. Meade, Jr., "Reshaping the Clinical Phase of Teacher Preparation," *Phi Delta Kappan* (May 1991), pp. 666–669.

[43]Lynn Cornett, "Teacher Education: Action by SREB States" (Atlanta: Southern Regional Education Board, 1987); David G. Armstrong, "Early Field Experiences: Some Key Questions," *Teacher Educator* (Winter 1989–1990), pp. 2–7.

study. More commonly, though, teacher-education institutions create five-year programs in which the professional studies begin with orientation in the freshman or sophomore year and conclude with concentrated field experience (sometimes as an intern) in the fifth year. Some institutions have further complicated training by extending traditional requirements in a program that requires more than five years.[44]

Reflective Teaching. In accordance with the recent stress on improving students' thinking and comprehension skills, many institutions have begun to emphasize **reflective teaching** as a central theme in teacher education. Reflective

"Thoughtful" practitioners

teachers are "thoughtful and wise practitioners" who frequently reflect on the results of their teaching and adjust their methods accordingly.[45] Closely related terms such as "inquiry-oriented teacher education," "expert decisionmaking," "higher-order self-reflection," and "action research" also have been widely used to describe this concept. Hundreds of schools of education have reorganized their programs to try to prepare reflective teachers, but the programs and activ-

Many definitions of reflective teaching

ities being developed are very diverse, and there is little agreement on what reflective teaching should mean in theory or in practice or on how it should be advanced as part of teacher-education programs.[46]

Computer and Technology Use. The introduction of computer and technology requirements into teacher education has occurred very rapidly. Data collected as part of a national survey of teacher-education programs indicate that approximately 90 percent established computer laboratories during the 1980s, and a more intensive study of all teacher-certification programs in Michigan found that 95 percent offer computer-related experiences for preservice teachers.

Multiple objectives in learning about computers

Computers and computer/technology laboratories encompass a wide variety of activities and objectives, such as orienting future teachers in computer use, introducing hardware and software developed for elementary and secondary schools, and strengthening interest and capability in technology for lesson design or delivery.[47]

EFFORTS TO IMPROVE THE TEACHING FORCE

In recent years, there has been much discussion about possibilities for improving the quality of the teaching workforce. Many political and educational leaders have expressed alarm about a perceived decline in the average scholastic ability

---

[44]"Herbst's Recommendations," *The Holmes Group Forum* (Winter 1992), p. 7; Olson, "Teaching Our Teachers"; Debra Viadero, "Massachusetts Abolishes Undergraduate Teacher Education Major," *Education Week*, January 31, 1990, p. 5.

[45]Cruickshank, *Research That Informs Teachers*, p. 119.

[46]Zeichner and Liston, *Traditions of Reform;* Mary Catherine Ellwein, M. Elizabeth Grave, and Ronald E. Comfort, "Talking About Instruction," *Journal of Teacher Education* (November–December 1990), pp. 3–14; and Joseph J. Onosko, "Exploring the Thinking of Thoughtful Teachers," *Educational Leadership* (April 1992), pp. 40–43.

[47]Richard J. Arends and Gary Galluzzo, "Institutional Structures and Practices" (Paper presented at the Annual Meeting of the American Educational Research Association, Boston, April 1990);

of teachers and about school conditions that make effective teaching difficult. Much of the effort to improve the quality of teachers and teaching has centered on testing of teachers, on the shortage of minority teachers, and on a variety of recommendations publicized in influential national reports on the problems of the U.S. educational system.

Ability of Teachers

Discussions and data on the "quality" of the teaching workforce generally are misleading because they almost always focus on "ability" scores derived from standardized tests such as the Scholastic Aptitude Test (SAT) and the American College Test (ACT). In most cases, there is either an explicit assertion or an implied assumption that the aptitudes and performance measured by such tests are synonymous with the "quality" of the workforce.

Standardized tests imperfect

Many other variables are at least as important as academic performance and ability. In many instances, stress on academic performance, as measured by standardized tests, may lead to the selection of teachers who are intellectually superior but have relatively little understanding of or commitment to teaching and to students. Nevertheless, it is important that teachers possess sufficient intellectual ability to master the subject matter they teach and to function successfully in a difficult job. Although one should be careful about equating such terms as "quality," "academic ability," and "effective teachers," the intellectual performance level of teachers is a legitimate concern.

Changes in SAT scores

Data on the academic performance of potential teachers indicate that a decline occurred in the 1970s, as it did for students majoring in business and numerous other subjects. For example, between 1973 and 1982, the average SAT verbal score of college students intending to teach fell from 418 to 394, and the average math score fell from 449 to 419. These scores were far below the average for all college students. Since 1982, however, the average SAT scores of college students who say they intend to become teachers have appreciably increased. By 1990 the average SAT score of future teachers was slightly above the national average and the typical future teacher was maintaining a B+ grade point average in college classes.[48]

High ratings of teacher-education students

Other encouraging data on the capabilities of students preparing to be teachers have been provided by the American Association of Colleges for Teacher Education (AACTE). It reported that a national sample of school administrators rated recent teacher-education graduates significantly higher than earlier graduates on eight characteristics such as "ability to organize the classroom" and "motivating all students to reach their maximum potential."[49] In addition, approximately two-thirds of education faculty now rate their undergraduate stu-

---

Dianne I. Novak and Carl F. Berger, "Integrating Technology into Teacher-Education," *T.H.E. Journal* (April 1991), pp. 83–86; and Karen Diegmueller, "Embracing Technology as Tool in Teacher Training," *Education Week,* January 8, 1992, special report p. 11.

[48]Daniel Koretz, *Educational Achievement: Explanations and Implications of Recent Trends* (Washington, D.C.: Congressional Budget Office, 1987); Susan Chira, "In the Drive to Revive Schools, Better Teachers But Too Few," *New York Times,* August 2, 1990, pp. A1, A12.

[49]"School Administrators Report New Teachers Are Better Prepared Than Predecessors," *AACTE Briefs,* May 13, 1991, pp. 1, 8.

dents as "above average" or "outstanding," and almost 70 percent report that their students are well prepared in instructional methods and approaches.[50]

In considering students' readiness to teach, it should be noted that clinical preparation for many future teachers consists of less than a semester of poorly supervised "practice" or "student" teaching, and that the average annual per-student expenditure for training teachers typically is much less than the average annual per-student expenditure in elementary and secondary schools. Some observers trace this problem at least in part to the tendency of schools and colleges of education frequently to serve as a "cash cow" that generates revenue used to fund other campus units.[51] Resulting inadequacies in teacher-preparation programs became a matter of widespread national concern when a number of well-publicized reports on problems in education were released in the 1980s.[52] We will review these reports' implications for teachers and teaching later in this chapter and in subsequent chapters.

Schools of education subsidize other activities

Testing of Teachers

Some of the efforts being made to improve the quality of the teaching force in elementary and secondary education focus on **basic skills testing** of pre-service teachers, new teachers, and — sometimes — experienced teachers. Drawing on the argument that teachers who have very low reading, mathematics, communications, and/or professional knowledge probably are ineffective in their teaching, some educators and many laypersons have advocated that qualifying examinations be introduced to test teachers' basic skills and knowledge. These efforts have led to developments such as the following:[53]

Testing basic skills

■   Since 1980 many states have introduced requirements that prospective teachers pass some form of minimum skills test in reading and language, math, subject-area specialty, and/or professional knowledge, and other states are planning to introduce such tests. In particular, more than thirty states now use the National Teacher Examination (NTE) for this purpose. All but a few states require applicants to pass tests before entering or exiting teacher-education programs or obtaining certification.

[50]Kenneth R. Howey, "The American Association of Colleges for Teacher Education Research About Teacher Education Study" (Paper presented at the Annual Meeting of the American Educational Research Association, San Francisco, March 1989); Cruickshank, *Research That Informs Teachers.*

[51]Robert N. Bush, "Teacher Education Reform: Lessons from the Past Half Century," *Journal of Teacher Education* (May–June 1987), pp. 13–19; Howard Ebmeier, Susan Twombley, and Deborah J. Teeter, "The Comparability and Adequacy of Financial Support for Schools of Education" (Paper presented at the Annual Meeting of the American Educational Research Association, Chicago, April 1991); and "New Respect for Teacher Education?" *Teacher Magazine* (January 1992), pp. 8–9.

[52]Mary M. Kennedy, "Policy Issues in Teacher Education," *Phi Delta Kappan* (May 1991), pp. 659–665.

[53]Robert A. Roth, *Teaching and Teacher Education: Implementing Reform* (Bloomington, Ind.: Phi Delta Kappa, 1986); Linda Darling-Hammond, *The Evolution of Teacher Policy* (Santa Monica, Calif.: Rand, 1988); Olson, "Teaching Our Teachers"; and Ann Maria Villegas, "Equity Issues in the Assessment of Teacher Performance" (Paper presented at the Annual Meeting of the American Educational Research Association, Chicago, April 1991).

■ A 1987 study conducted for the U.S. Department of Education reported that passing rates on tests for admission to teacher education varied from 55 percent to 95 percent in the eleven states that provided data for analysis.

■ In 1982 the state of California began to administer a test in reading, writing, and math to new candidates for teaching positions. Slightly more than 6,000 applicants took the first test, and 27 percent failed, even though state government officials described the test as "relatively easy." In 1985–1986 the Florida Department of Education decertified thirty-two teacher-training programs because less than 80 percent of their graduates passed the state-wide teacher certification exam.

■ The Arkansas legislature enacted a law in 1983 specifying that all teachers in the state must pass an academic skills test. This law made Arkansas the first state to require experienced teachers to pass a basic skills test. Texas followed in 1985, and Georgia in 1987.

■ Dallas and several other school districts now require that all teachers pass a basic skills test.

Criticisms of testing

Testing of prospective and current teachers has become a controversial topic that is not likely to be resolved soon. Many political leaders see testing as one of the few feasible steps they can take to quickly improve public confidence in the teacher workforce. Opponents argue that the tests unjustifiably exclude persons who do poorly on paper-and-pencil instruments of the kind typically used for basic skills testing of teachers. Most opponents also believe that we do not have sufficient knowledge about effective teaching to allow for construction of valid tests — particularly of the paper-and-pencil variety — and that existing tests are biased against minority candidates whose background and experience do not provide equal or adequate preparation.[54] Many opponents also cite data indicating that scores on standardized tests such as the NTE do not correlate well with subsequent on-the-job measures of teaching effectiveness and that existing tests of professional knowledge have "failed miserably in their attempts both to

Deficiencies in tests

define this elusive domain of knowledge and to write items that measure it."[55] Given these perceived deficiencies in existing tests, opponents worry that the tests are "driving" both teacher education and subsequent teaching in the classroom toward unproductive overemphasis on the kinds of factual subject matter and knowledge that are most easily tested.[56]

---

[54]John G. Weiss, "Testing Teachers: Strategies for Damage Control," in *What Is the Appropriate Role of Testing in the Teaching Profession* (Washington, D.C.: National Education Association, 1987), pp. 34–48; Edith Guyton and Elizabeth Farokhi, "Relationships Among Academic Performance, Basic Skills, Subject Matter Knowledge, and Teaching Skills of Teacher Education Graduates," *Journal of Teacher Education* (September–October 1987), pp. 37–42; and Ed Wiley III, "Teacher Exams Still Wreaking Havoc on Minority Teachers," *Black Issues in Higher Education,* May 23, 1991, pp. 1, 12–14.

[55]George F. Madaus and Diana Pullin, "Teacher Certification Tests: Do They Really Measure What We Need to Know?" *Phi Delta Kappan* (September 1987), p. 34. Also see "Teacher Test Flunks New York Study: Movement to Overhaul Exam Grows," *Fair Test Examiner* (Winter 1988), pp. 1, 7; and S. E. Phillips, "Extending Teacher Licensure Testing" (Paper presented at the Annual Meeting of the American Educational Research Association, Chicago, April 1991).

[56]Susan L. Melnick and Diana Pullin, "Testing Teachers' Professional Knowledge: Legal and Educational Policy Implications," *Educational Policy* (no. 2, 1987), pp. 215–228; Martha M. McCarthy, "Teacher-Testing Programs," in Joseph Murphy, ed., *The Educational Reform Movement of the 1980s* (Berkeley, Calif.: McCutchan, 1990), pp. 189–214.

Proponents of basic skills testing generally counter that all or nearly all teachers must be able to demonstrate that they can function at least at the seventh- or eighth-grade level in reading, writing, and math — the minimum level currently specified on some of the tests — if they are to perform effectively in their jobs. Many proponents also argue that recent research has provided information sufficient to justify minimum standards and to allow for creation of more valid exams.[57]

Diversity of the Teaching Force and the Critical Shortage of Minority Teachers

Widespread testing of teachers has led to a growing concern about the performance of minority candidates for teaching, many of whom do not perform well on paper-and-pencil tests. In Alabama, for example, only about one-third of African-American students completing teacher-education programs passed the state teacher candidacy exams during the 1980s, compared to approximately three-fourths of nonminority candidates. Low passing rates for African-American and/or Hispanic candidates also have been reported in Arizona, California, Georgia, Mississippi, New Mexico, Oklahoma, Texas, and other states. Some observers believe that testing of prospective teachers has eliminated as many as 40,000 African-American and Hispanic candidates during the past decade.[58]

Among current elementary and secondary teachers, the percentage who are African-American or Hispanic is generally estimated at 10 percent or less. In contrast, African-Americans and Hispanics make up about 28 percent of the public school student population in public schools. (See color insert.) This underrepresentation of minority groups in the teaching force is expected to grow even more severe in future years. Currently, only 6 to 7 percent of teacher-education majors are African-American or Hispanic; yet members of these minority groups are predicted to constitute nearly 30 percent of elementary and secondary students in the year 2000.[59]

Possible contributions of minority teachers

Increasing the diversity of the teaching force to reflect growing minority enrollment in the student population is widely viewed as an important goal for the U.S. educational system. For one thing, minority teachers generally are in a better position than nonminority teachers to serve as positive role models for minority students. They also may have more inherent credibility in working to guide and instruct minority students. Minority teachers may have a better understanding of how to plan and carry out lessons that are appropriate in terms of minority students' expectations and learning styles (see Chapters 10 and 11). For example, Lisa Delpit, Jacqueline Irvine, and other analysts have pointed out that African-American teachers should be less prone than middle-class nonminority teachers to mistakenly assume that low-income black students will re-

[57]W. James Popham and W. N. Kirby, "Recertification Tests for Teachers: A Defensible Safeguard for Society," *Phi Delta Kappan* (September 1987), pp. 45–49; Richard J. Murmane, "The Case for Performance-Based Licensing," *Phi Delta Kappan* (October 1991), pp. 137–142.

[58]"Tests Keep Thousands of Minorities out of Teaching," *Fair Test Examiner* (Winter 1989), pp. 8–9; Susan Chira, "Efforts to Reshape Teaching Focus on Finding New Talent," *New York Times*, August 28, 1990, pp. A1, A14; and "States," *Education Week*, October 23, 1991, p. 2.

[59]Olson, "Teaching Our Teachers"; "Educators Advocate Steps to Lure Minority Teachers," *New York Times*, May 30, 1990, p. B7.

The shortage of minority teachers has been characterized as a "crisis-like situation," and efforts are being made to increase the number of minority teacher-education candidates. (© Paul Conklin)

spond well to a teacher who is informal and overly friendly rather than "authoritative" and demanding.[60]

After reviewing data on the low proportion of minority teachers and the low passing rates of prospective minority teachers, AACTE officials have stated that these figures reflect a "devastating" crisis and that "teacher education programs and staff . . . must change to reflect current demographic reality."[61] In conjunction with other organizations, the AACTE has proposed and helped initiate legislation for a variety of new programs to increase the number of minority teachers. Proposals that have received the most attention specify increasing fi-

---

[60]Lisa D. Delpit, "The Silenced Dialogue: Power and Pedagogy in Educating Other People's Children," *Harvard Educational Review* (August 1988), pp. 280–298; Jacqueline Jordan Irvine, "Beyond Role Models: An Examination of Cultural Influences on the Pedagogical Perspectives of Black Teachers," *Peabody Journal of Education* (Summer 1989), pp. 51–63.

[61]Steven Teske, "AACTE to Seek Funds for Minority Teacher Education Initiatives," *Education Daily,* December 15, 1987, pp. 1–2; Blake Rodman, "AACTE Outlines Plan to Recruit Minorities into Teaching," *Education Week,* January 13, 1988, p. 6; Chris Pipho, "A Closer Look at the Shortage of Minority Teachers," *Education Week,* May 17, 1989, p. 29; and *Minority Teacher Supply and Demand* (Washington, D.C.: American Association of Colleges of Teacher Education, 1990), p. 3.

nancial aid for prospective minority teachers, enhancing recruitment of minority candidates, and providing coursework to improve admissions test scores of minority students interested in teaching.[62]

Recommendations of National Reports

Since the mid-1980s a large number of reports — prepared by various national commissions as well as individuals supported by philanthropic and government grants — have focused on problems of education in the United States. Frequently referred to collectively as the **national reports,** they are discussed in detail in Chapter 13.

National Commission on Excellence

A Nation at Risk, the best known and most influential of the national reports, was prepared by the National Commission on Excellence in Education sponsored by the U.S. Department of Education. Arguing that the United States is "at risk" in the sense that its "once unchallenged preeminence in commerce, industry, service, and technological innovation is being overtaken by competitors throughout the world," the commission concluded that one major aspect of decline has been a "rising tide of mediocrity" in the schools.[63] The commission pointed to a variety of risk indicators, such as a twenty-year fall in SAT scores of students graduating from high school, a high functional illiteracy rate among minority youth, and declines in science and math achievement — particularly among high achievers. The commission's recommendations centered on the following themes:

Content of education. Increase high-school graduation requirements in "five new basics": English, mathematics, science, social studies, and computer science.

Time. Devote more time to the new basics. Make more effective use of the existing school day, extend the school day, and/or lengthen the school year.

Recommendations in **A Nation at Risk**

Teaching. Make teaching a more rewarding and respected profession. Set higher standards for entry into the profession. Increase salaries so they are "professionally competitive, market-sensitive, and performance-based," thus making them part of a system that gives greater rewards to superior teachers (in other words, institute merit pay). Add an additional month of employment with pay for teachers. Institute a "career ladder" that distinguishes among beginning, experienced, and master teachers. Use incentives such as grants and loans to attract outstanding candidates into teaching, particularly into shortage areas such as science and mathematics. Involve master teachers in preparing and supervising probationary teachers.

[62]*Minority Teacher Recruitment and Retention: A Call for Action* (Washington, D.C.: American Association of Colleges for Teacher Education, 1987); Sheryl Stein, "Minority Teacher Recruitment," *AACTE BRIEFS* (October 1990), p. 7; *Teach America* (Washington, D.C.: American Association of State Colleges and Universities, 1991); and "SEF Study Finds More Programs Needed to Address Minority Teacher Shortage," *SEF News* (February 1992), p. 3.
[63]National Commission on Excellence in Education, *A Nation At Risk: The Imperative for Education Reform* (Washington, D.C.: U.S. Department of Education, 1983), p. 5.

Carnegie recommendations

In 1986, three years after the publication of *A Nation at Risk,* the Carnegie Task Force on Teaching as a Profession released *A Nation Prepared: Teachers in the 21st Century.*[64] This report stressed the urgent need to improve education for the nation's growing proportion of low-income and minority students and the importance of teaching "complex, non-routine intellectual" skills. Like *A Nation at Risk,* the Carnegie report recommended increasing teachers' salaries and establishing a career hierarchy so that "lead teachers" exercise leadership responsibilities in the schools. The report also called for incentives to increase the pool of minority teachers. Undergraduate education majors should be replaced with a new "professional" curriculum at the graduate level. Teachers should be given more control over their work environment and in turn should be held accountable for student performance. Finally, the report proposed the establishment of a national board, as in medicine and law, to set high standards for teachers and certify those who met them.

National Board for Professional Teaching Standards

In 1987, in accordance with this last recommendation, the Carnegie Corporation helped establish the **National Board for Professional Teaching Standards (NBPTS),** a nonprofit organization whose purpose is to issue certificates to teachers who meet the board's standards for professional ability and knowledge. Two-thirds of the board's members are teaching professionals; the remaining one-third represents the larger educational community and the public.[65] By 1991 the board had begun work on standards for teaching certificates and licenses. The standards, which will focus on both content knowledge and effective teaching methods, will be considerably more rigorous than those for state government certification tests, but the assessment methods will include interviews, portfolios, computer and video simulations, and other innovative approaches. To be eligible for board certification, teachers will need a bachelor's degree and at least three years of successful teaching. In several states school officials have proposed large salary increases for teachers who pass the NBPTS certification exams.[66]

NBPTS certification

Holmes reports and recommendations

Holmes and Renaissance Groups.   Reform of the teaching profession has been a primary concern of the Holmes Group, a consortium of deans of education at major research universities. Since 1986 the group has commissioned a series of reports, including *Tomorrow's Teachers* and *Tomorrow's Schools.* In addition to the reforms stressed in other reports, the Holmes Group has emphasized the need for teacher-education students to have early experience in schools, beginning in the sophomore year and culminating in a fifth-year internship supervised by a mentor teacher and university faculty. Consequently, the group

---

[64]Carnegie Task Force on Teaching as a Profession, *A Nation Prepared: Teachers in the 21st Century* (New York: Carnegie Corporation, 1986).

[65]Stephen Teske, "Teacher Certification Board Awaits Nod from Carnegie to Begin Work This Summer," *Education Daily,* May 15, 1987, pp. 1–3.

[66]*Towards High and Rigorous Standards* (Detroit: National Board for Professional Teaching Standards, 1990); Ann Bradley, "Request for Developing Teaching Assessment Prepared," *Education Week,* March 7, 1990, p. 11; and Beverly T. Watkins, "Teaching-Standards Board Foresees a Battle for Recognition, Acceptance," *Chronicle of Higher Education,* July 11, 1990, p. A14. Also see Arthur Wise, "Teacher Accountability," in Atelia Melaville, Daphne Moore, and Tasha Harris, eds., *Voices from the Field* (Washington, D.C.: William T. Grant Foundation Commission on Work, Family and Citizenship, 1991), pp. 23–24.

Professional Development Schools

has focused on the creation of **professional development schools (PDSs).** Like a traditional "laboratory" school, the PDS is designed to link a local school district with a college or school of education, but in a more comprehensive and systematic fashion. Classroom teachers function as college faculty while serving as mentors for new teachers. According to the Holmes Group, PDSs will encourage thoughtful, long-term inquiry into teaching and learning; experienced teachers, beginning teachers, teacher educators, and administrators will work together to create a community of learning.[67]

Widespread support for PDSs

Other groups, including the American Federation of Teachers, the American Association of Colleges of Teacher Education, and the National Education Association, have been working on plans for schools similar to PDSs. The efforts are in the early stages, but an AACTE survey indicates that a large majority of schools and colleges of education have enhanced their relationships with elementary and secondary schools.[68]

Renaissance Group recommendations

Additional support for reform of the teaching profession has come from the Renaissance Group, a consortium of higher education institutions composed primarily of former teacher-training colleges that historically focused on undergraduate teaching education. The Renaissance Group contends that teacher training should be integrated throughout a student's university experience rather than reserved for the student's final year. Further, the training should incorporate extensive, sequenced field and clinical experience.[69]

Mixed reactions and criticisms

Reactions to the National Reports.   Reaction to the plethora of national reports has been mixed. There is no doubt that the reports have helped focus attention on the problems of education, and the specific proposals have generated a great deal of support. However, many educators believe that the reports have been too simplistic in their diagnoses and solutions,[70] and some of the proposals have met with substantial resistance and criticism. For example, some educators have criticized the emphasis on "lead teacher" and "career ladder" approaches that give some teachers greater authority and remuneration than their colleagues.[71] The NBPTS has drawn fire from the president of the American

---

[67]Holmes Group, *Tomorrow's Teachers* (East Lansing, Mich.: Holmes Group, 1986); Holmes Group, *Tomorrow's Schools* (East Lansing, Mich.: Holmes Group, 1990); Holmes Group, *Tomorrow's Schools of Education* [tentative title] (East Lansing, Mich.: Holmes Group, in preparation). Also see Lynn Olson, "Holmes Group Reflects on How to Sustain Its Momentum," *Education Week,* December 9, 1987, p. 6; *Work in Progress* (East Lansing, Mich.: Holmes Group, 1989); Kathleen Devaney, "3rd 'Vision Statement' to Be Shaped by Conferences and Case Studies," *The Holmes Group Forum* (Fall 1991), pp. 1–3; and "How PDS Can Facilitate Research," *The Holmes Group Forum* (Winter 1992), p. 15.

[68]Ann Lieberman and Lynne Miller, "Teacher Development in Professional Practice Schools," *Teachers College Record* (Fall 1990), pp. 105–122; Karen Diegmueller, "N.E.A. Launches Teacher-Training Initiative in Three States," *Education Week,* March 6, 1991, p. 5.

[69]J. T. Sandefur, *Analysis of Teacher Education Reform Initiatives* (Bowling Green, Ky.: Western Kentucky University, 1991).

[70]For examples, see Lawrence C. Stedman and Marshall S. Smith, "Recent Reform Proposals for American Education," *Contemporary Education Review* (Fall 1983), pp. 85–104; Thomas B. Timar and David L. Kirp, *Managing Educational Excellence* (New York: Falmer, 1988); John E. Chubb, "Why the Current Wave of School Reform Will Fail," *Public Interest* (Winter 1988), pp. 28–49; and Joseph Murphy, ed., *The Educational Reform Movement of the 1980s* (Berkeley, Calif.: McCutchan, 1990).

[71]William R. Johnson, "Empowering Practitioners: Holmes, Carnegie, and the Lessons of His-

Association of School Administrators, who described the national board as "an attempted takeover of American schools by teacher unions."[72] Others have pointed out the enormous expense involved in implementing NBPTS practices and the difficulties the board will face in constructing valid tests of teachers' skills and knowledge.[73] Similarly, critics of professional development schools have focused on the high costs of PDSs and the lack of available funds, as well as the divergent interests that hamper collaboration between school districts and higher education institutions. There is concern, as well, that teachers appointed to PDSs will carry too heavy a burden of duties.[74]

Widespread actions

Despite the lack of consensus on certain specific reforms, nearly all state governments have taken actions consistent with one or another of the national reports. In particular, they have increased high-school graduation requirements, established or expanded minimum competency testing of students, raised teacher salaries, stiffened entrance and exit requirements for teacher education, and expanded testing of new teachers.[75]

EDUCATIONAL REFORM AND TEACHER EMPOWERMENT

In conjunction with reform efforts, many states and local school districts have prescribed particular methods to be used in planning and delivering instruction. Teachers are evaluated, in large part, by their ability to follow these standard methods. In Arkansas, Missouri, and Texas, to take three examples, guidelines for teacher assessment specify the general instructional sequence — for instance, introduce the topic, present material, check for understanding, provide guided and independent practice, and discuss homework — that teachers should follow in executing a "model" lesson.

Prescriptions to improve education

To some extent, this type of reform appears to have reinforced and magnified rather than alleviated the problems in education. As noted earlier, teachers frequently express dissatisfaction with their limited opportunities to participate in decision making. Reforms that dictate particular instructional methods will reduce teachers' autonomy even further. As Linda McNeil's study in Texas concluded, legislative requirements for extensive testing of students, combined with administrative prescriptions of appropriate teaching methods, have contributed to "deprofessionalization" and "deskilling" of the teaching force. **Deprofes-**

Effects of legislative prescriptions

tory," *History of Education Quarterly* (Summer 1987), pp. 221–240; Ann Weaver Hart, "Impacts of the School Social Unit on Teacher Authority During Work Redesign," *American Educational Research Journal* (Fall 1990), pp. 503–532.

[72]Lynn Olson, "Certification Panel Gets Cool Reception from Some Administrators," *Education Week,* May 27, 1987, pp. 1–16, 17; Ann Bradley, "Wait a Minute . . . ," *Teacher Magazine* (March 1990), pp. 16, 18.

[73]Karen Diegmueller, "Teachers at Board's Forum Uncertain About Certification," *Education Week,* July 31, 1991, p. 19.

[74]Debra Viadero, "Holmes Group Outlines 'Clinical' Schools Network," *Education Week,* February 7, 1990, p. 5; Beverly T. Watkins, "Education-School Reform Group Set to Endorse Plan That Would Alter Teacher Training, Public Schools," *Chronicle of Higher Education,* February 7, 1990, pp. A15, A20.

[75]Richard F. Elmore and Susan H. Fuhrman, "The National Interest and the Federal Role in Education," *Journal of Federalism* (Summer 1990), pp. 149–162.

"Defensive teaching"

sionalization refers to the results of administrative control policies and practices that encourage or require teachers to simplify curriculum and instruction in order to ensure that students demonstrate mastery on easy-to-grade tests. McNeil reported that many teachers responded with "defensive teaching" in which they fragmented the curriculum to fit tests, "mystified" topics by emphasizing factual regurgitation over understanding, and simplified material to gain the compliance of students.[76]

Passive learning

The consequences of specifying instructional methods seem to have had a similarly negative effect in teacher evaluation. As described by one observer in the Southwest, this evaluative approach frequently rewards teachers who "lecture and question a relatively passive class but not teachers who help students struggle through difficult tasks — such as science experiments, English composition, or computer programming — on their own."[77] Researchers elsewhere also have described cases in which prescription of specific teaching methods has encouraged or required teachers to emphasize passive learning and memorization of low-level material and skills.[78]

Fundamental change difficult

Part of the reason why the educational reform movement has had some negative consequences is that it has tended to concentrate on changes (such as increased credit requirements for graduation, improved teacher salaries, and prescribed lesson sequences) that are relatively easy to mandate.[79] Comparatively little has been accomplished in terms of actually changing the way in which schools are organized and function, because fundamental change at the operating level is much more expensive and difficult (see Chapter 16). This limitation has been recognized and criticized by many educators, as is clear in the following statements. From the former president of the National Education Association:

Reform is complex

> Policymakers, by and large, do not want to hear that reform efforts, to be effective, must target a complex constellation of problems. . . . Above all, policymakers do not want to hear that educational reform is hard work. . . . Our schools today are structurally decrepit, still shaped by an organizational model appropriate to 19th century industry. That model does little to enliven the imagination. It does little to encourage collegial cooperation. . . . [Unless educators are released] from the structural straightjackets in which they are now strapped . . . all the reform documents that have been written will become no more than faded reminders of what might have been. . . . We cannot continue to assume that a system which has allowed 25–30% of the children to fall through the cracks will be the system that will take us into the 21st century.[80]

---

[76]Linda M. McNeil, *Contradictions of Control* (New York: Routledge & Kegan Paul, 1986). Also see Susan Moore Johnson, *Teachers At Work* (New York: Basic Books, 1990), and *Raising Standards for American Education* (Washington, D.C.: U.S. Government Printing Office, 1992).

[77]Harriett Tyson-Bernstein, "The Texas Teacher Appraisal System," *American Educator* (Spring 1987), pp. 26–31. Also see Arthur E. Wise, "Legislative Learning Revisited," *Phi Delta Kappan* (January 1988), pp. 328–333, and Bruce L. Wilson and H. Dickson Corbett, "Statewide Testing and Local Improvement: An Oxymoron?" in Murphy, ed., *The Educational Reform Movement of the 1980s*, pp. 243–264.

[78]Joseph O. Milner, "Suppositional Style and Teacher Evaluation," *Phi Delta Kappan* (February 1991), pp. 464–467.

[79]Murphy, *The Educational Reform Movement*; Daniel U. Levine and Robert J. Havighurst, *Society and Education*, 8th ed. (Needham Heights, Mass.: Allyn and Bacon, 1992).

[80]Mary Hatwood Futrell, "Restructuring Teaching: A Call for Research," *Educational Researcher* (December 1986), p. 6.

From the president of the American Federation of Teachers:

> So why won't most of the current education reforms do the job? Because they merely ask schools to do more of what they've always been doing. . . . [The typical reform approach] assumes that education is something teachers deliver to students and pour into their heads. If the student doesn't score well, it's because the teacher didn't pour the knowledge, didn't pour the right stuff, didn't pour enough, or didn't have the right pouring knack. . . . It's time to ask how schools can be restructured so that youngsters will be turned from passive into active students.[81]

Restructuring needed

Although many reform efforts have not moved very far, progress is being made in some locations. Changes associated with the effective schools movement, increasing concern for thinking skills, and other important developments will be discussed in the last chapter of this book. In addition, some of the reform efforts deal specifically with **teacher empowerment** — increasing the power of teachers and their role in decision making. For example, a contractual agreement reached between the United Federation of Teachers and the New York City Board of Education not only provided for a large increase in teacher salaries but also allowed teachers a large role in determining school policies and practices. One such provision gave teachers greater opportunities to challenge supervisors' decisions regarding grading of students, textbook selection, curriculum mandates, and other such matters.[82]

Teacher policy role

Recent experiments to improve education through enhanced teacher participation in decision making are even more ambitious and comprehensive in Dade County (Florida), Chicago, Denver, Memphis, Rochester (New York), and numerous other school districts. In Dade County, nearly 150 of the district's 263 schools are participating in a self-governance experiment in which teachers and administrators work together to redesign the educational programs and opportunities in their schools. To a significant extent, faculties can determine the number of staff to be employed, how staff will function, and how funds will be spent. As part of this project, the board of education has suspended requirements in such areas as maximum class size, length of the school day, and number of minutes per subject. The Dade County Federation of Teachers has agreed to waive contractual provisions so that teachers can work longer hours without more pay and can assist in evaluating other teachers.[83]

Movement toward self-governing schools

From some points of view, Rochester's approach is even more comprehensive. The 1987 contract between the board of education and the Rochester Teachers Association included the following key provisions:

1. Based on the Carnegie model for "lead" teachers, a career in teaching program was established. In this program, teachers move through four stages:

[81]Albert Shanker, "Education Now Being Served . . . But How Many Takers?" *New York Times,* December 13, 1987, p. E9. Also see Albert Shanker, "Reflections on Forty Years in the Profession," in Derek L. Burleson, ed., *Reflections* (Bloomington, Ind.: Phi Delta Kappa, 1991), pp. 324–339.

[82]Blake Rodman, "Two Unions Gain Sharp Pay Hikes, Role in Decisions," *Education Week,* September 9, 1987, pp. 1, 25; Dale Mann, "It's Time to Trade Red Tape for Accountability in Education," *Executive Educator* (January 1990), pp. 26, 28.

[83]Gene I. Maeroff, *The Empowerment of Teachers* (New York: Teachers College Press, 1988); Brian Peterson, "How School-Based Management Is Faring in Miami," *Education Week,* June 12, 1991, p. 26; and David Moberg, "Can Democracy Save Chicago's Schools?" *American Prospect* (Winter 1992), pp. 98–108.

Rochester career ladder

(a) *intern* (new) teachers working under the supervision of experienced colleagues; (b) *resident* teachers with a completed internship but only provisional certification; (c) *professional* teachers with a permanent certificate; and (d) *lead* teachers with at least ten years of experience who work 10 percent longer hours and devote as much as half their time to serving as mentors, to planning instructional improvements, or to other leadership roles. Promotion from one level to another depends on meeting various criteria at each stage. Lead teachers, who are selected by panels consisting of four teachers and three administrators, earn nearly $75,000 per year.[84]

Faculty governance

2. Instead of following traditional seniority practices in determining teachers' assignments and transfers, a faculty committee in each school interviews teachers who wish to transfer, examines their records, and makes decisions based on the problems and programs in the school. At the same time, professional teachers and lead teachers accept assignments on the basis of need rather than seniority or other criteria and thus more frequently teach the lowest-achieving students and classes. Rochester Teachers Association President Adam Urbanski views this aspect of the agreement as particularly important:

   Under the current structure, the most difficult students often fall, by default, to the least experienced and most vulnerable teachers. . . . It makes sense to match the most challenging students with the most experienced, expert practitioners. Certainly success with these students shouldn't be expected of first-year teachers, who have enough to do just to learn the job. Rookie teachers' taking on the toughest assignments would be tantamount in the medical profession to interns performing open-heart surgery while master surgeons treat skin abrasions.[85]

3. In return for large increases in salary and much more participation in decision making, teachers are to be held more accountable for students' achievement, attendance, and other outcomes. However, the board of education and the teachers' association have experienced severe difficulties and conflict in trying to implement this provision.[86]

Rochester magnet choices

4. Building on Rochester's already sizable magnet-school program, all schools become "schools of choice" that offer specialized learning opportunities and compete with each other to attract students. Teachers play a large role in selecting and implementing the unique combination of curricular themes and instructional arrangements in each school.[87]

It would be premature to reach conclusions about the success or failure of such experiments or to speculate as to whether they will be emulated on a

---

[84]Jerry Buckley, "A Blueprint for Better Schools," *U.S. News and World Report*, January 18, 1988, pp. 60–65; Ann Bradley, "'This Is Damn Hard'", *Teacher Magazine* (December 1989), pp. 12–14; and Jerry Buckley, "Blackboard Jungle," *U.S. News and World Report*, December 24, 1990, pp. 52–56.

[85]Adam Urbanski, "Restructuring the Teaching Profession," *Education Week*, October 28, 1987, p. 32.

[86]Susan Chira, "Rochester: An Uneasy Symbol of School Reform," *The New York Times*, April 10, 1991, p. B8; Adam Urbanski, "'Real Change Is Real Hard': Lessons Learned in Rochester," *Education Week*, October 23, 1991, p. 29.

[87]Magnet schools offer special curriculum or instruction for students who enroll voluntarily and may not live nearby.

Success uncertain

widespread basis. These reform efforts will encounter some obstacles, and educators involved in them will have to learn how to translate greater teacher decision making into improved school functioning and how to avoid potentially negative consequences associated with career ladders, new approaches to curriculum and instruction, and other related innovations.[88] As we point out in later sections of this book, it probably will be at least five or six years until adequate assessments can be made concerning the potential utility and eventual national implications of these fledgling efforts to empower teachers.

OUTLOOK FOR TEACHING

Bright prospects for teachers

In the 1970s and early 1980s, college students majoring in education were confronted with a buyer's market for teachers, and many wondered whether it was wise to enter a field that seemed to be declining in salary, status, and general attractiveness. Now national attention has focused on education, and there is good news regarding teachers' prospects for the future. The pattern of teacher oversupply has been reversed, and governments at all levels are initiating action to improve salary and other teaching conditions as well as teacher recruitment and preparation. Individuals dedicated to the task of helping children and young people learn and grow in the schools probably face much brighter professional opportunity now than has been true in the past two decades.

Summing Up

1. Although there are many reasons for entering the teaching profession, research indicates that most teachers do so to help young children and to provide a service to society.
2. Most teachers are satisfied with most aspects of their jobs, but there is significant dissatisfaction with salaries and some other aspects of the profession.
3. Teacher salaries have improved rapidly in recent years.
4. There was a sharp drop in demand relative to supply of teachers in the 1970s. This situation has been reversed, and there may be a serious shortage of teachers in the future.
5. The preservice preparation of teachers rests upon a threefold set of components: general education, specialized subject-field education, and professional studies. Each of these interrelated areas is important in preparing successful teachers.
6. Requirements for teacher certification vary from state to state and among institutions of higher learning.
7. In general, teacher education is becoming more practical and reality ori-

---

[88]Daniel U. Levine and Eugene E. Eubanks, "Site-Based Management: Engine for Reform or Pipedream?" in John J. Lane and Edgar Epps, eds., *Restructuring the Schools* (Berkeley, Calif.: McCutchan, 1992).

ented. Trends in this direction include the establishment of school-based centers for preparing future teachers and the provision of early field experience in elementary and secondary classrooms. Other important trends are the introduction of five-year and fifth-year programs and the interest in developing reflective teachers.

8. There is widespread national concern with the quality and diversity of the teaching workforce. Some efforts to address this concern emphasize testing of new and future teachers. The major national reports on education have proposed introducing performance-based remuneration, setting higher national standards for licensing, and establishing the highly paid position of "lead" or "master" teacher. Other proposals call for increasing the recruitment of prospective minority teachers in order to create a more diverse workforce.

9. Many school districts are attempting to work out approaches for empowering teachers in order to make schools more effective.

10. Increasing public concern for education, changes occurring in the schools, and improvements in the outlook for teachers are bringing new excitement and importance to the role of the teacher.

Key Terms

The number in parentheses indicate the pages where explanations of the key terms can be found.

supply and demand *(8)*

occupational prestige *(8)*

certification *(19)*

alternative certification *(21)*

competency-based teacher
   education *(23)*

school-based field centers *(23)*

reflective teaching *(25)*

basic skills testing *(27)*

national reports *(31)*

A Nation at Risk (31)

National Board for Professional
   Teaching Standards *(32)*

professional development schools
   (33)

deprofessionalization *(34)*

teacher empowerment *(36)*

Discussion Questions

1. Why are you thinking of becoming a teacher? Give some of your reasons. How do your reasons compare with those given in the chapter?

2. What jobs other than teaching in elementary or secondary schools may be open to persons with a teaching certificate? What additional preparation would be needed to obtain such jobs?

3. What kinds of education courses should be required for teacher preparation?

4. Do you believe that the trends in teacher education identified in this chapter are desirable? Why or why not?

5. What steps can be taken to improve teacher salaries?

6. What is the level of funding for teacher education at your campus? Is there any reason to believe that your school or college of education serves as a "cash cow" that provides substantial funding for other campus units?

Suggested Readings

Boyer, Ernest L. *High School.* New York: Harper & Row, 1983.
   Much of the discussion involves the situation of teachers and the steps that could be taken to improve the quality and conditions of teaching.

Clift, Renee T., W. Robert Houston, and Marleen C. Pugach, eds. *Encouraging Reflective Practice in Education.* New York: Teachers College Press, 1990.
   Discusses and analyzes a wide range of topics involving the nature of reflective teaching.

Freedman, Samuel G. *Small Victories.* New York: Harper, 1990.
   Describes the highs and lows in the work of dedicated teachers at a big-city high school.

Herndon, Joseph. *The Way It Spozed to Be.* New York: Bantam, 1968.
   This classic describes the satisfactions and difficulties of teaching in the inner city.

Journal of Teacher Education.
   Regularly provides information and analysis regarding important issues in preservice and in-service education.

Lane, John J., and Edgar Epps, eds. *Restructuring Schools.* Berkeley, Calif.: McCutchan, 1992.
   Includes national and international case studies and analysis of problems and issues involving school-based management and other restructuring approaches.

McNeil, Linda M. *Contradictions of Control.* New York: Routledge and Kegan Paul, 1986.
   Analyzes teachers' reactions to legislative and administrative mandates that sometimes distort instruction toward low-level concentration on facts.

2

The Teaching Profession

FOCUSING QUESTIONS

In what ways is teaching not fully a profession?

What trends show that teaching is becoming a full-fledged profession?

How does merit pay help (hinder) the teaching profession?

What are the essential differences between the NEA and the AFT? Can these differences be reconciled?

What are some other important professional organizations for teachers?

What professional organizations might education students and beginning teachers join?

Until the twentieth century, teachers had relatively little preparation for their jobs and relatively little voice in determining the conditions of their employment. Teacher training consisted of one or two years and sometimes less at a normal school or teachers college, and teachers had to follow strict rules and regulations concerning their behavior outside the school. Unorganized and isolated from one another in small schools and school districts, teachers could be summarily dismissed by a board of education. Many were told they could not teach any material that someone in the community might find objectionable.

Times have changed. Today, teachers aspire to be professionals with expert knowledge concerning the content and methods of instruction in their particular fields. In addition, teachers are well organized as a group and have gained greater rights to be judged mainly on the basis of their performance rather than on the basis of their behavior outside the school and to participate in making decisions about the conditions in which they work. In many cases, they are forging stronger links with school administrators, university researchers, and government officials. The first part of this chapter describes the ways in which teachers are striving for full professional status; the second discusses how teacher organizations have grown in power and prominence.

IS TEACHING A PROFESSION?

Whether teaching can be considered a profession in the fullest sense has been an issue of great concern to educators for many decades. A number of educators have tried to identify the ideal characteristics of professions and, by rating teachers on these, to determine whether teaching is a profession. Here is a list of the characteristics of a full **profession,** based on the works of noted authorities in the field over a twenty-five-year period.[1]

1. A sense of public service; a lifetime commitment to career

2. A defined body of knowledge and skills beyond that grasped by laypersons

3. Application of research and theory to practice (to human problems)

4. A lengthy period of specialized training

5. Control over licensing standards and/or entry requirements

6. Autonomy in making decisions about selected spheres of work

7. An acceptance of responsibility for judgments made and acts performed related to services rendered; a set of standards of performance

Characteristics of a profession

8. A commitment to work and client; an emphasis on service to be rendered

9. Common goals, common purpose — a shared sense among members of what they are trying to accomplish

10. Use of administrators to facilitate work of professionals; relative freedom from detailed on-the-job supervision

---

[1]Ronald G. Corwin, *Sociology of Education* (New York: Appleton-Century-Crofts, 1965); Robert B. Howsam et al., *Educating a Profession* (Washington D.C.: American Association of Colleges for Teacher Education, 1976); and Susan J. Rosenholtz, *Teachers' Workplace: The Social Organization of Schools* (New York: Longman, 1989).

11. A self-governing organization composed of members of the profession

12. Professional associations and/or elite groups to provide recognition for individual achievements

13. A code of ethics to help clarify ambiguous matters or doubtful points related to services rendered

14. A high level of public trust and confidence in individual practitioners

15. High prestige and economic standing

Viewed as a semiprofession

The general consensus is that teaching is not a profession in the fullest sense: it does not possess some of the above characteristics. In some ways, it may be viewed as a "semiprofession" or an "emerging profession" in the process of achieving these characteristics. Teaching is a semiprofession, according to Amitai Etzioni, because "the training [of teachers] is shorter, their status less legitimated [low or moderate], their right to privileged communication less established; theirs is less of a specialized knowledge, and they have less autonomy from supervision or societal control than 'the professions.'"[2] (Several sociologists contend that nursing and social work are also semiprofessions.)

Knowledge, control, autonomy, and prestige

Of the fifteen characteristics of a profession listed, perhaps the four most important are (1) a defined body of knowledge and skills beyond that grasped by laypersons, (2) control over licensing standards and/or entry requirements, (3) autonomy in making decisions about selected spheres of work, and (4) high prestige and economic standing. Although no profession has achieved the ideal, teaching seems to lag behind some others, such as law and medicine, in these four important areas.

A Defined Body of Knowledge

No agreed-upon knowledge

All professions have a monopoly on certain knowledge that separates their members from the general public and allows them to exercise control over the vocation. Members of a profession have mastered a body of knowledge that establishes their expertise and protects the public from quacks, untrained amateurs, and special-interest groups. There is, however, no agreed-upon specialized body of knowledge that is "education" or "teaching."[3] Whereas the behavioral sciences, physical sciences, and health fields are guided by extensive rules of procedure and established methodologies, education has no such agreed-upon set of procedures to guide teachers in the classroom.[4]

As a result, too many people, especially the lay public, talk about education as if they were experts — resulting in a great deal of conflicting and sometimes negative conversation. Another result of this ill-defined body of knowledge is that the content of teacher-education courses varies from state to state and among teacher-training institutions within states.

---

[2]Amitai Etzioni, *The Semiprofessions and Their Organizations: Teachers, Nurses, and Social Workers* (New York: Free Press, 1969), p. v.

[3]David Dill, *What Teachers Need to Know* (San Francisco: Jossey-Bass, 1990); John I. Goodlad, *Teachers for Our Nation's Schools* (San Francisco: Jossey-Bass, 1990).

[4]Frances S. Bolin and Judith M. Falk, *Teacher Renewal: Professional Issues, Personal Choices* (New York: Teachers College Press, Columbia University, 1987); Hendrik D. Gideonse, *Relating Knowledge to Teacher Education* (Washington, D.C.: American Association of Colleges for Teacher Education, 1989).

At the very least, there should be some agreement nationally on the mix of teacher-training courses devoted to liberal education, subject-matter specialization, and professional knowledge. However, agreement on this topic has eluded the profession for the last forty years. In the 1960s James Conant pointed out that professors of arts and science and professors of education were at war with each other over several important questions: the proper mix of teacher-training courses, who should teach those courses, and even whether methods courses were worthwhile at all.[5] James Koerner described the problem further in his highly critical book, *The Miseducation of American Teachers.* Koerner argued that by requiring too many education courses — as many as 60 hours at state teacher colleges — and by making these courses too ''soft,'' colleges of education were producing teachers versed in pedagogy at the expense of academic content.[6]

Although the influence of Conant and Koerner has helped reduce the number of required education courses, the controversy continues.[7] This has made it especially difficult to establish clear national standards for teacher preparation. The **National Council for Accreditation of Teacher Education (NCATE)** has set standards that specify courses to be taken and the qualifications of the faculty who teach those courses. However, a huge number of teacher-education institutions do not meet NCATE's standards; in the late 1980s and early 1990s as many as 55 percent of the 1,200 colleges involved in training teachers were not accredited by NCATE.[8] More recently, most institutions have worked diligently to meet NCATE requirements, and the approval rate increased to more than 70 percent in 1990 and 1991.[9]

Although twenty-four states have collaborative agreements with NCATE, teacher-training institutions can usually receive state accreditation even if they are not approved by NCATE. Moreover, the graduates of non-NCATE-accredited institutions find jobs just as readily as graduates of accredited schools. The new director of NCATE, Arthur Wise, hopes to remedy this confusing situation by making all teacher-education institutions measure up to rigorous national standards set by a single accrediting organization.[10] Many major education organizations support this policy. But the confusion will persist until educators reach greater agreement on the basic body of knowledge that teachers need to share.

---

[5]James B. Conant, *The Education of American Teachers* (New York: McGraw-Hill, 1964).

[6]James D. Koerner, *The Miseducation of American Teachers* (Boston: Houghton Mifflin, 1963).

[7]See, for example, Rita Kramer, *Ed School Follies: The Miseducation of America's Teachers* (New York: Free Press, 1991).

[8]*34th Annual List of Accredited Programs, 1987–1988* (Washington, D.C.: National Council for Accreditation of Teacher Education, 1988); telephone conversation with Richard C. Kunkel, Director, National Council for Accreditation of Teacher Education, May 12, 1988; and Arthur E. Wise, ''We Need More Than a Redesign,'' *Educational Leadership* (November 1991), p. 7.

[9]Karen Diegmueller, ''Higher Percentage of Schools Pass Latest Round of NCATE Review,'' *Education Week*, June 19, 1991, p. 15; *38th Annual List of Accredited Programs, 1991–1992* (Washington, D.C.: National Council for Accreditation of Teacher Education, 1992); and *Restructuring the Education of Teachers*, Report of the Commission on the Education of Teachers into the 21st Century (Washington, D.C.: Association of Teacher Educators, 1992).

[10]''Meet Teaching's Toughest Critic,'' *NEA Today* (April 1991), pp. 8–9; telephone conversation with Arthur E. Wise, Director, National Council for Accreditation of Teacher Education, July 22, 1991.

Control over Requirements for Entry and Licensing

Whereas most professions have uniform requirements for entry and licensing, historically this has not been the case in teaching. As indicated in Chapter 1, recent reforms have required prospective teachers in most states to pass minimum competency tests, and bodies such as the National Board for Professional Teaching Standards are trying to establish reliable methods for measuring a person's ability to teach. However, certification requirements still vary greatly from state to state, and the trend toward testing of teachers has generated widespread controversy.

Teaching out of license

It is estimated, moreover, that many teachers working in the secondary schools are teaching out of license — in other words, outside their recognized areas of expertise. For example, many teachers of English did not major in English in college, nor are they certified to teach English. This problem is especially acute in the areas of science and mathematics.

The outlook is further clouded by the trend toward alternative certification. As discussed in Chapter 1, this is a process by which teachers are recruited from the ranks of college-educated retirees, part-time industrial personnel, and experienced people seeking second careers. Intended to eliminate teacher shortages in certain subject areas (such as mathematics, science, and computer instruction) or to upgrade the quality of new teachers, alternative certification is often praised as practical and innovative by laypeople and school board members. Most teacher organizations, on the other hand, see alternative certification as a threat to the profession; critics have labeled such practices *irresponsible credentialism* and *pseudocredentialism*.[11] One critic wrote, "The assumption that those who know something can automatically teach . . . [will] not solve the problem of teacher quality."[12] The American Association of Colleges for Teacher Education (AACTE) has taken a middle position, supporting alternative licensing procedures only at the master's degree level and in conjunction with supervised field training.[13]

Debate about alternative certification

Involvement of teacher organizations

Whatever they may think about differing requirements for certification, teachers traditionally have had little to say on these matters. Teacher organizations now, however, are beginning to cooperate with state legislatures and departments of education to modify certification standards and establish professional practice boards (discussed later in this chapter). The more input teachers have — the more control they exercise over their own licensing procedures — the more teaching will become a full profession.

---

[11]Mary Hatwood Futrell, "The Holmes Group: A Teacher's Perspective," *Teachers College Record* (Spring 1987), pp. 378–383; Albert Shanker, "Tomorrow's Teachers," *Teachers College Record* (Spring 1987), pp. 423–429; and Shanker, "Restructuring Our Schools," *Peabody Journal of Education* (Summer 1989), pp. 88–100.

[12]Lee S. Shulman, "Knowledge and Teaching: Foundations and the New Reform," *Harvard Educational Review* (February 1987), p. 324.

[13]*Alternative Preparation for Licensure: A Policy Statement* (Washington, D.C.: American Association of Colleges for Teacher Education, 1989).

Autonomy in Deciding About
Spheres of Work

*Lay control vs.
professional control*

In a profession, every member of the group, but not outsiders, is assumed to be qualified to make professional judgments on the nature of the work involved. Professionals usually establish laws of exclusive jurisdiction in a given area of competence; custom and tradition are relied on to maintain effective control over matters relating to work and to dealing with clients. Indeed, lay control is considered the natural enemy of professions; it limits the power of the professional and opens the door to outside interference.

Teachers accept the assumption that local and state officials have the right to decide on the subjects, instructional materials, and books to be used — although they sometimes doubt the wisdom of the community in exercising such rights. Traditionally, teachers have been allowed little input in curriculum decisions, and they are vulnerable when they seek to introduce textbooks or discuss topics considered controversial by pressure groups. Today, in fact, school officials often hire outside "experts" with little teaching experience to help them select books, write grant proposals, or resolve local school-community issues.[14] Even in school reform, the initiative often comes from government officials, business leaders, and civic groups rather than from teachers. Taxpayers and their representatives are said to "reasonably" claim a large share in decision making because they foot the bill and provide the clients. Only recently have some public groups and reform groups alike begun to realize that teachers have important knowledge and expertise to contribute to the school enterprise — knowledge about the students they teach, the goals and objectives they implement, and the overall learning environment.

*Guarding against client
interference*

The physician and lawyer also provide services that their clients pay for, yet no one expects the client or the public to prescribe drugs or write the clauses in a contract. When the client interferes with the decisions of the practicing physician or lawyer, the professional-client relationship ends. This protects clients from being victimized by their own lack of knowledge, while it safeguards the professional from the unreasonable judgments of the lay public. Peter Blau and W. Richard Scott observe that "professional service . . . requires that the [professional] maintain independence of judgment and not permit the clients' *wishes* as distinguished from their *interests* to influence his decisions." The professional has the knowledge and expertise to make judgments, "and the client is not qualified to evaluate the services he needs." Professionals who permit their clients to tell them what to do "fail to provide optimum service."[15]

Teacher accountability

Teachers, on the other hand, can be told what to do by parents and other citizens, principals, superintendents, and school board members, even in opposition to the teachers' professional judgments. Although collective bargaining has resulted in new arrangements between teachers and administrators, most people still believe that teachers are public servants and are therefore account-

---

[14]Michael W. Apple, "Is There a Curriculum Voice to Reclaim?" *Phi Delta Kappan* (March 1990); Milbrey W. McLaughlin, "Test-Based Accountability as a Reform Strategy," *Phi Delta Kappan* (November 1991), pp. 248–251.

[15]Peter Blau and W. Richard Scott, *Formal Organizations* (San Francisco: Chandler, 1965), pp. 51–52.

able to the people and to the school officials who are hired, elected, or appointed by the people. Even though it is true that teachers must not lose sight of the welfare of their clients or ignore those who are in the position to make decisions for the public, they should not completely surrender the power to determine the nature of the service they render.

Teacher empowerment

Some school districts have taken steps toward teacher empowerment — that is, granting teachers a wider role in policy decisions. This movement can be enhanced by initiating collective negotiations that define areas in which teachers can make use of their experiences and competencies, by increasing teacher representation on school boards at the local level and teaching licensing and governing boards at the state level, and by helping to elect political candidates who are pro-teacher and pro-education. The idea of a strong teacher organization working to improve teaching conditions and to assume accountability, as well as decision-making authority, is supported by most education policy making organizations.[16]

High Prestige and Economic Standing

As pointed out in Chapter 1, teachers have registered major gains in salary and status during the past sixty years. Although teachers' salaries since 1930 have increased more than those of the average worker in industry, teacher pay remains lower than that of the average college graduate.[17] In addition, teachers still earn far less than lawyers, business executives, and some other professionals with similar levels of formal education.

In terms of occupational prestige, teachers have fared somewhat better. Still, the prestige of teachers has risen more slowly than that of some other professionals. For example, Figure 2.1 compares the prestige rankings of teachers, physicians, department heads in state government, and bankers, using data from the National Opinion Research Center surveys. As the graph demonstrates, between 1964 and 1989 teachers surpassed bankers in the survey rankings but fell behind doctors and state executives.

What are the implications of these gaps in salary and status? It may seem unrealistic to compare the salaries of teachers with master's degrees or doctorates with the salaries of physicians, lawyers, dentists, or top business executives. Members of the latter group, for example, despite a level of formal education similar to that of a teacher, might earn $150,000 per year, and some might earn $500,000 or more. Nevertheless, the *status-consistency hypothesis* holds that a group does tend to compare its achievements (both prestige and salary) with other groups, striving to match the rewards of people with similar jobs and similar years of education.[18] If this is true, we can expect teachers to make compar-

---

[16]Mary Hatwood Futrell, "Mission Not Accomplished: Education Reform in Retrospect," *Phi Delta Kappan* (September 1989), pp. 8–14; Marilee Rist, "Teacher Empowerment and Teacher Unions," *Education Digest* (February 1990); and Albert Shanker, "The End of the Traditional Models of Schooling," *Phi Delta Kappan* (January 1990), pp. 344–357.

[17]Victor R. Lindquist and Frank S. Endicott, *The Northwestern Lindquist-Endicott Report: Employment Trends for College Graduates*, Forty-sixth Annual Survey (Evanston, Ill.: Northwestern University, 1992); "Starting Salaries," *NEA Today* (March 1991), p. 12.

[18]Ronald G. Corwin, *Militant Professionalism: A Study of Militant Conflict in High Schools* (New York: Appleton-Century-Crofts, 1970).

Changes in Occupational Prestige Ratings Between 1964 and 1989 (Based on Ratio of Profession's Rating to Average Rating in Survey)

Figure 2.1

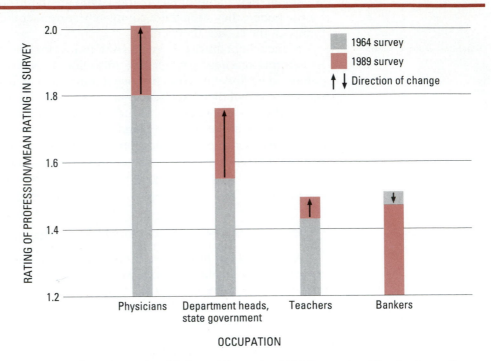

Source: Keiko Nakao and Judith Treas, "Computing 1989 Occupational Prestige Scores," Report No. 70 (Washington, D.C.: National Science Foundation and National Opinion Research Center, 1990); Paul M. Siegal, "Prestige in the American Occupational Structure" (Ph.D. diss., Department of Sociology, University of Chicago, 1971).

isons with other groups and to feel somewhat dissatisfied. In the past this dissatisfaction has been one of the major reasons for teacher militancy.

To its credit, educational reform has put teachers in the limelight and has brought pressure on school districts to increase salaries. By the early 1990s teacher salary raises had outpaced inflation in eight of the last ten years. Some experienced teachers today earn $70,000 per year, and by 1995 the average salary is expected to be over $48,000.[19] Perhaps the earnings gap between teachers and other highly educated groups will now begin to close. With help from their own professional organizations, coupled with pressure to upgrade educational standards, teachers should continue to experience increased status.

TRENDS TOWARD PROFESSIONALISM

Although teaching probably should not be considered a fully professionalized occupation, some trends have helped it move in that direction. Collective bar-

---

[19]Allan C. Ornstein, "Teacher Salaries in Social Context," *High School Journal* (December–January 1990), pp. 129–132; Ornstein, "Teacher Salaries Look Good for the 1990s," *Education Digest* (December 1990), pp. 21–23.

gaining, for example, can enhance teachers' capacity to make decisions about their work in the classroom. Several other major aspects of a long-range trend toward the professionalization of teaching are also apparent, as discussed below.

The Scope of Collective Bargaining

By 1980 teachers had won the right to have their representatives formally bargain with their employers in most of the United States. The extent and nature of **collective bargaining** varied from negotiations conducted in the absence of a law allowing or forbidding it to full-scale contract bargaining backed by the right to strike.

In some ways, collective bargaining may be considered a nonprofessional or even an antiprofessional activity. In the law, medicine, or the ministry, for example, few professionals work in organizations in which terms of employment are determined by collective bargaining. From another point of view, however, collective bargaining can significantly enhance professionalization of teaching by giving teachers greater authority to determine their work conditions and their effectiveness as teachers.

Changing focus of collective bargaining

The trend in collective bargaining has been to include a growing number of concerns other than the fundamental salary issue. Collective bargaining in the late 1980s was often concerned with educational problems and issues, such as class size, grouping of students in classes, instructional materials, testing, classroom discipline and management, teacher-supervisor relations, and community relations. Today, the focus is often on peer review, career ladders, merit pay, standards setting, school-based management, and school reform.[20] As the 1990s unfold, the movements toward school reform, school restructuring, and teacher empowerment will give teachers more professional autonomy, union strength, and higher salaries, in exchange for greater accountability and reduced adversarial bargaining.

Sharing of power

Collective bargaining now seems to be an integral part of the teaching profession. In the early days of militancy by teachers' unions, school boards and school administrators often saw the unions as obsessed with wages and working conditions; many believed the needs of schools and students had become secondary union concerns.[21] Today, educators on both sides of the negotiating table have gained maturity and experience; both unions and management have become more comfortable with collective bargaining. School board members, superintendents, principals, and teachers are learning to share power and to work as partners to improve the schools. Continuing in this vein, collective bargaining can not only resolve conflicts between school boards and teachers but also raise the overall status of the profession.[22]

---

[20]Grant Hendrickson, "After You Get to Yes," *Executive Educator* (November 1990), pp. 16–17; Marilee C. Rist, "Politics and Professionalism Top the Two Teacher Unions' Agenda," *American School Board Journal* (October 1990), pp. 6–12.

[21]Charles T. Kerchner and Douglas Mitchell, *The Changing Idea of a Teacher's Union* (New York: Falmer Press, 1988); Myron Lieberman, *Beyond Public Education* (New York: Praeger, 1986); and Richard Wynn, *Collective Bargaining* (Bloomington, Ind.: Phi Delta Kappa, 1983).

[22]Jerry J. Herman, "Coping with Conflict," *American School Board Journal* (August 1991), pp. 39–41; Del Stover, "Report from the Picket Line," *American School Board Journal* (December 1991), pp. 46–47.

Professional Practice Boards

Setting professional standards

It is not likely that educators will be allowed complete autonomy in setting standards for professional practice, but they have gained a greater role recently. As of 1990 all the states except two (Maine and South Dakota) had established state **professional practice boards,** or similar bodies, which set standards for certification of teachers.[23] These boards upgrade the profession by defining standards for minimum competency, reprimanding teachers for unprofessional or unproductive behavior, and in extreme cases suspending teachers' certificates.

Boards controlled by teachers

According to a 1990 survey, however, only six of the state boards possessed a majority of teachers, and some states did not even require teacher participation on the board.[24] The National Education Association (NEA) has endorsed the idea of state boards but believes they should be controlled by teachers — with other groups, such as school administrators and higher education officials, given minority representation. The NEA argues that teachers are just as capable of governing their own profession as are attorneys, doctors, and accountants.[25]

A national board

Other educators favor a single national board, rather than independent state boards. This has always been the position of the American Federation of Teachers (AFT), and the idea has been welcomed by many of the national task force groups. As mentioned in Chapter 1, the Carnegie Corporation has helped to found the **National Board for Professional Teaching Standards (NBPTS).** The NEA now supports this organization, since two-thirds of the directors of the NBPTS are "teaching professionals" — that is, representatives of teacher unions, subject-area associations, and teachers noted for classroom excellence. The NBPTS is expected to provide leadership in certifying teachers, clarifying the role of teachers in schools, guiding the creation of teacher assessment systems, rewarding excellence in teaching, and allowing greater professional responsibility to teachers.[26]

Advocates believe the NBPTS improves the image of teachers and raises the status and authority of teaching to a level enjoyed by that of other professions represented by national boards, such as accounting, architecture, and medicine. Critics argue that teacher-controlled boards give teachers too much authority; given that teaching is a public responsibility, they claim, boards should be governed by elected officials who represent the people. Nevertheless, the growth of professional practice boards at the state level, and now at the national level, helps strengthen the profession by clarifying and upgrading professional standards. It may also help establish a professional knowledge base that educators can agree upon, thus reducing disagreement about the structure of teacher-education programs.

---

[23]*Teacher Education Policy in the States, A 50 State Survey of Legislative and Administrative Actions* (Washington, D.C.: American Association of Colleges for Teacher Education, 1990).

[24]Ibid.

[25]Keith Geiger, "Holding America Accountable," *Washington Post,* May 6, 1991, p. 34; Blake Rodman, "NEA Pursues Its Plan to Establish State Boards Controlled by Teachers," *Education Week,* April 29, 1987, pp. 1, 20.

[26]John W. Porter, "A Call for National Certification of Teachers," *NASSP Bulletin* (October 1990), pp. 64–70; Joan Baratz-Snowden, "The NBPTS Begins Its Research and Development Program," *Educational Researcher* (August–September 1990), pp. 19–24; and *Toward High and Rigorous Standards for the Teaching Profession* (Washington, D.C.: National Board for Professional Teaching Standards, 1990).

Mediated Entry

Supervised stages of assistance

Mediated entry refers to the practice of inducting persons into a profession through carefully supervised stages that help them learn how to apply professional knowledge successfully in a concrete situation. For example, in the medical profession, aspiring physicians serve one or more years as interns and then as residents before being considered full-fledged professionals.

Dan Lortie has studied the teacher's job from a sociological perspective and concluded that in terms of sequenced professional entry, teaching ranks in between occupations characterized by "casual" entry and those that place protracted and difficult demands on would-be members.[27] The lack of more carefully mediated entry has profound consequences because it means that new teachers have relatively little opportunity to benefit from empirically derived and rigorously grounded principles and practices of pedagogy. Teachers too frequently report that their main teacher has been experience and that they learned to teach through trial and error in the classroom. They also report that the beginning years of teaching can be a period of anxiety and fear, even of trauma.[28] But, then, the beginning period of almost any occupation or profession has its problems and anxieties.

Trial and error in the classroom

Lack of effective induction

Although efforts have been made to provide for more effective induction of new teachers into the profession, they have not been sufficiently widespread or systematic. Most school districts, for example, now require a probationary period for new teachers, but in too many cases relatively little concrete assistance is provided to help those teachers develop and refine the skills needed for effective performance. Many school districts and a few states require a fifth year of preparation beyond the traditional bachelor's degree and initial certificate, but too often this requirement is implemented in a way that allows new teachers to take a few more courses that may or may not help them improve professionally.[29] As a rule, most new teachers are still largely on their own in their first professional position.

Probationary teachers

The teaching profession now recognizes the need to develop a period of induction and transition into teaching. The concept of mediated entry is supported by many school district officials, who no longer feel they must immediately accept and put new teachers to work as was done during the teacher shortage of the 1960s and early 1970s. Some school districts, such as Toledo, Ohio, provide the probationary or intern teacher with feedback and assistance from experienced teachers. In Greenwich, Connecticut, and Salt Lake City, Utah, as well as in all the schools of Colorado and North Carolina, all teachers are evaluated, but there are different expectations and training sessions for probationary teachers and experienced teachers.[30]

---

[27]Dan C. Lortie, *Schoolteacher: A Sociological Study* (Chicago: University of Chicago Press, 1975).

[28]Barry A. Farber, *Crisis in Education: Stress and Burnout in the American Teacher* (San Francisco: Jossey-Bass, 1991); Pamela L. Grossman, *The Making of a Teacher* (New York: Teachers College Press, Columbia University, 1990); and Susan Moore Johnson, *Teachers at Work* (New York: Harper & Row, 1990).

[29]William C. McGaghie, "Professional Competence Evaluation," *Educational Researcher* (January–February 1991), pp. 3–9; Lee S. Shulman, "Assessment for Teaching: An Initiative for the Profession," *Phi Delta Kappan* (September 1987), pp. 38–44.

[30]*Teacher Performance Appraisal System Training* (Raleigh: North Carolina Department of Public

Mediated entry linked to career ladders

The trend toward more carefully mediated entry will probably continue because it is supported by the NEA and AFT and several education reform groups; it will probably become linked with various career ladder and teacher appraisal plans. Most important, the notion of mediated entry should focus on the school as the workplace as well as the training place for beginning teachers. Mediated entry should address the practical nature of teaching, involve experienced teachers in training beginning teachers, establish closer ties between teacher educators and school people, and ensure greater control by the profession over teacher training.

Staff Development

Staff development is the further education and training of a school district's teaching staff — whether this additional education focuses on subject matter, teaching skills, or any other area that increases a teacher's effectiveness. To stay up to date in their preparation and to acquire new classroom skills, teachers have traditionally participated in various kinds of in-service training. Most of this training has been provided as a one- or two-day workshop on the school site or as a special off-campus university course. Besides the training they offer, these courses help teachers acquire additional college credits for continuing certification.

Keeping up to date

Increasing emphasis on staff development

Many observers have viewed this kind of in-service program as a "cafeteria of courses and workshops" with no relationship to job roles and student needs.[31] In the past few years, however, staff development has increasingly come to be seen as an important aspect of teacher education and career enhancement. The National Staff Development Council, an organization of educators interested in the problems of staff development, has grown from 246 members in 1978 to 6,500 in mid-1991.[32] Some commentators have argued that educators should follow the examples of management and government, which have long recognized the value of continued training and career development programs.[33] Most important, both the NEA and the AFT support the concept of staff development as an integral part of a teacher's professional growth. The National Council for Accreditation of Teacher Education (NCATE) also has begun to place greater emphasis on professional training throughout the teacher's career. Given the fact that U.S. teachers are an aging group (the average teacher is about fifty years old and has twenty years of experience), many states now require teachers to participate in staff development programs in order to retain their teaching certificates.

Instruction, 1986); Arthur E. Wise, Linda Darling-Hammond, and Barnett Berry, *Effective Teacher Selection: From Recruitment to Retention* (Santa Monica, Calif.: Rand Corporation, 1987). Also see David Holdzkom, "Teacher Performance Appraisal in North Carolina: Preferences and Practices," *Phi Delta Kappan* (June 1991), pp. 782–784; Joseph Kretovics, Kathleen Farber, and William Armaline, "Reform from the Bottom Up," *Phi Delta Kappan* (December 1991), pp. 295–299.

[31]Linda Lambert, "Staff Development Redesigned," *Phi Delta Kappan* (May 1988), pp. 665–668; and Thomas J. Sergiovanni, "Will We Ever Have a True Profession?" *Educational Leadership* (May 1987), pp. 44–49.

[32]Telephone conversation with Paul R. Burden, Editor, *Journal of Staff Development*, July 3, 1991.

[33]Bruce J. Joyce, "The Doors of School Improvement," *Educational Leadership* (May 1991), pp. 59–62; and Robert Garmston, "Staff Developers as Social Architects," *Educational Leadership* (November 1991), pp. 64–65.

Staff development programs, such as the in-service workshop these teachers are participating in, keep teachers up to date and help them acquire additional classroom skills. (© Robert Kalman/The Image Works)

Cooperation between school districts and colleges

Instead of allowing universities to dictate the courses offered and the requirements for advanced degrees and certificates, many recent staff development programs have stressed cooperation between the school district and a local college or university, so that courses are designed specifically for the district's needs.[34] Such programs not only introduce teachers to the latest instructional approaches; they also can provide feedback on the teacher's performance, help counter the isolation that long-term teachers may begin to feel, and encourage experimentation, such as the use of mini-sabbaticals (six to eight weeks with pay).[35] The professional development schools described in Chapter 1 are one example of such a trend.

Role of teacher centers

In-service training opportunities have also been provided in the past by *teacher centers*, where teachers can exchange ideas with colleagues about new instructional practices and talk about how to apply appropriate methods in the classroom. Largely as a result of cutbacks in federal funds, though, the number of teacher centers has dwindled from more than two hundred in 1980 to ap-

---

[34]Pamela B. Clarridge, "Multiple Perspectives on the Classroom Performance of Certified and Uncertified Teachers," *Journal of Teacher Education* (September–October 1990), pp. 15–26; Allan G. Glatthorn, "A New Concept of Supervision," *Educational Horizons* (Winter 1987), pp. 78–81; and Michael G. Fullan, "Staff Development, Innovation, and Institutional Development," in B. Joyce, ed., *Changing School Culture through Staff Development,* 1990 Yearbook (Alexandria, Va.: Association for Supervision and Curriculum Development, 1990), pp. 3–25.

[35]Lorin W. Anderson, "Staff Development and Instructional Improvement," *Educational Leadership* (February 1987), pp. 64–66; Patricia M. Dumser, "Mini-Sabbaticals Widen a Teacher's World," *Educational Leadership* (November 1991), pp. 77–78; and Thomas R. Guskey and Dennis Sparks, "Complexities in Evaluating the Effects of Staff Development Programs" (Paper presented at the annual meeting of the American Educational Research Association, Chicago, April 1991).

proximately twenty-five in 1991.[36] In many locations their functions have been taken over by regional service centers funded by state education agencies; these centers provide school districts with teacher workshops, in-service training, and instructional materials.

ER&D Program

The AFT has also recently developed an Educational Research and Dissemination (ER&D) Program to expose teachers to the growing body of important research findings in education. Through a series of collegial workshops, participants learn about the latest research and explore practical classroom applications. Some 1,000 teachers have already been trained by universities to act as workshop leaders.[37]

Taken as a whole, the new varieties of staff development programs give teachers a major voice in decisions that affect their professional careers. These programs also help to establish the concept that teaching requires lengthy and ongoing periods of training, like other full-fledged professions.

Collaboration Between Researchers and Teachers

In addition to working with universities in staff development programs, teachers have begun to collaborate with university researchers to study a wide range of educational questions. On the basis of the old "action research" and "field research" models of the 1950s and 1960s, Gary Griffin and Ann Lieberman developed three kinds of **collaborative research centers** in the 1980s, involving (a) a single school district, (b) a state intermediate or regional agency, and (c) a teacher center.[38] These centers tend to focus less on theory and more

Focus on practical benefits

on steps to improve teaching and benefit teachers. The research takes place in the classroom without disturbing the instruction received by the students. Through this type of collaboration, researchers learn to respect teachers and teachers learn to appreciate and "do" research.

Decisions regarding research questions, data collection, and reporting are made jointly by the university and the school. In the past, the teachers involved in such a project would have received little or no credit when the research findings were published; the emphasis was on protecting the rights and anonymity

More research credit for teachers

of the "informants" or "respondents." Now, however, teachers often seek full partnership in the research, so that they share in the recognition when it is published.[39] This is another step in teacher empowerment. Overall, increased

---

[36]Telephone conversations with Paul R. Burden, Editor, *Journal of Staff Development*, August 19, 1991, and Judy White, Staff Specialist, Department of Instruction and Professional Development, National Education Association, July 3, 1991; Sam J. Yarger, "The Legacy of the Teacher Center," in B. Joyce, ed., *Changing School Culture Through Staff Development*, pp. 104–116.

[37]*AFT Educational Research and Dissemination Program* (Washington, D.C.: AFT, 1990); telephone conversation with Karen L. Smith, Assistant Director of the Educational Research and Dissemination Program, American Federation of Teachers, July 24, 1991.

[38]Gary A. Griffin, Ann Lieberman, and Joann Jacullo-Noto, *Interactive Research and Development in Schooling* (Austin: University of Texas at Austin, Research and Development Center for Teacher Education, 1983); Griffin, ed., *Staff Development*, Eighty-second Yearbook of the National Society for the Study of Education (Chicago: University of Chicago Press, 1983). Also see Ann Lieberman and Lynne Miller, *Staff Development for Education in the 90s*, 2nd ed. (New York: Teachers College Press, Columbia University, 1991).

[39]Judith H. Shulman, "Now You See Them, Now You Don't," *Educational Researcher* (August–September, 1990), pp. 11–15.

collaboration between teachers and researchers will contribute to the professionalism of teaching.

Merit Pay

Salaries tied to performance

Critiques of merit pay

Real changes in teacher remuneration are under way. A growing number of school boards have taken the position that **merit pay** (a supplement to a teacher's base salary to reward superior performance) is a cost-effective method of motivating teachers and encouraging excellence in teaching. The NEA, the AFT, and other critics have expressed reservations about merit pay plans, however. Some argue that because what teachers do is very complicated and difficult to measure, assessments of merit are too often subjective.[40] Where merit plans have been implemented, both the NEA and the AFT claim, teachers have often felt that the wrong people were selected for preferential pay. Some observers fear that rewards given to a relatively small number of teachers will be at the expense of many others, thereby threatening the unity and collegiality among educators. The need, such critics say, is to increase all teachers' salaries, not just a few, and not to pit teachers against one another.[41]

AFT's position

Despite these criticisms, the AFT accepts merit pay as part of the national movement to improve the educational system — as long as there are sufficient safeguards in the evaluation procedures and as long as monetary awards do not compete with pay hikes for all teachers. According to AFT president Albert Shanker, the traditional system of rewarding teachers is outdated. To encourage teacher productivity, he contends, the federal government should provide bonuses of up to $15,000 per teacher in the 10 percent of the nation's schools that show the most improvement.[42]

Merit plans spread

Even as the arguments continue, the concept of merit pay has spread to many school districts and to entire states. Today, merit pay plans are sometimes linked with career ladders, which establish clear-cut stages through which a teacher may advance. In Rochester, New York, for example, the four ranks of teacher culminate in the position of lead teacher, which can pay nearly $75,000 per year; promotion to lead teacher is based on administrative and peer recommendations. On a statewide level, North Carolina in 1991 implemented a merit plan called "differential pay," whereby local school districts receive up to 3 percent above their normal salary totals to allocate to teachers on the basis of merit or additional responsibilities.[43] Denver's four-year contract for 1991–1994 calls for annual raises based in part on performance. The merit program for Granite School Districts (Salt Lake City) is a voluntary one developed by the

---

[40]Ron Brandt, "On Research on Teaching," *Educational Leadership* (April 1992), pp. 14–19; McGaghie, "Professional Competence Evaluation."

[41]Gene I. Maeroff, "A Blueprint for Empowering Teachers," *Phi Delta Kappan* (March 1988), pp. 472–477; telephone conversation with William Martin, Director of Public Relations, National Education Association, July 11, 1991. Also see "Salaries and Benefits," *NEA Handbook 1990–91* (Washington, D.C.: National Education Association, 1991), pp. 257–258.

[42]"A Call for 'Real' Incentives," *Teacher K-8* (September–October 1989), p. 26; Albert Shanker, "A Proposal for Using Incentives to Restructure Our Public Schools," *Phi Delta Kappan* (January 1990), pp. 344–357.

[43]Telephone conversations with Thomas Gillette, Chief Negotiator, Rochester Teachers Association, July 10, 1991, and David Holdzkom, chief consultant for the North Carolina Department of Public Instruction, July 8, 1991.

Taking Issue ◆

Merit Pay

Traditionally, teachers have earned salaries based on their number of years in teaching and their highest degree obtained. Some recent plans, however, offer extra pay to teachers judged to be above average in teaching skills, work habits, leadership, or student achievement.

Question: Should individual teachers be chosen to receive special increases in pay on the basis of merit?

Arguments PRO

1 Teachers whose students consistently score high on achievement tests or have healthy social attitudes must be outstanding teachers or models for citizenship. Such teachers merit extra compensation for their work.

2 Teachers who provide their students with creative and interesting educational experiences, work hard in preparation, and give many hours of their own time to their students also deserve special compensation.

3 Merit pay reduces teaching conformity by encouraging teachers to develop different teaching approaches, become more independent in thought, and exceed what is presented in texts or asked for in teaching guides.

4 Some merit pay plans allow teachers to earn $75,000 or more. Without such opportunities, as in business, to earn above the base salary, capable and ambitious people will not go into teaching.

5 Merit pay promotes excellence in teaching by acting as an incentive for teachers to improve their performance. Each teacher is encouraged to develop better teaching behaviors and a deeper concern for student welfare. Such incentives are found in business and most other professions: why not in teaching?

Arguments CON

1 Factors related to achievement and social attitudes are so diverse that is impossible to identify the teacher's contribution. Influences from the home, social class, and peer groups cannot readily be separated from the effects of teaching.

2 Hard work can perhaps be measured. But many "creative" activities do not necessarily correlate with good teaching. If creativity is a criterion, merit pay may be awarded more for the teacher's apparent inventiveness than for students' learning.

3 Those who evaluate teachers' merit may unconsciously favor people who do not challenge district policy or seem to threaten the stability of the school with innovative approaches. Thus, merit pay may encourage conformity.

4 The taxpayers will never be able or willing to support extensive merit pay rewards. Business can offset such rewards by raising prices. But merit pay in schools requires higher taxes, which are often not feasible.

5 Incentive pay, by definition, can be given to only a few. Such a plan penalizes equally qualified teachers who are not chosen simply because there are not enough positions. Moreover, competition for merit pay pits one teacher against another, encourages political games, and destroys the collegial cooperation essential to good education.

teachers themselves; in 1991, 60 percent of the 3,500 teachers signed up. In this plan each participating teacher is evaluated annually by the school principal and by two peer teachers from another school; the teachers also prepare self-evaluations.[44]

$100,000 teacher salaries

If traditional pay scales, based on experience and education, give way to some form of merit plan, highly rated teachers might soon have the opportunity to earn up to $100,000. Granted there are risks in merit pay plans, as the critics point out, but the possible benefits may outweigh the risks. Raising the ceiling on teaching salaries, and making distinctions based on merit, will improve the teaching profession; subsequently, this will raise the prestige of teachers, attract brighter students into the profession, and keep good teachers from leaving class-rooms for more competitive salaries in other fields.

School-Based Management

Many educational reforms, as we have seen, involve a movement toward teacher empowerment — increasing teachers' participation in decisions that affect their own work and careers. One such reform is frequently called **school-based management,** a system in which many decisions about curriculum, instruction, staff development, allocation of funds, and teaching assignments are made at the level of the individual school rather than by the superintendent or the board of education. Working together, the school's teachers and administrators develop their own plan for the school's future.

Teachers and administrators work together

The assumption underlying school-based management is the idea that people who share in responsibilities and decisions will believe in what they are doing and will work more effectively toward common goals. This concept of reform also recognizes that teachers are experts whose talents should be put to use in planning. The reform plans in Dade County, Florida, and Rochester, New York (described in Chapter 1), include a generous dose of school-based management; other districts with similar plans include Louisville, Chicago, Denver, Los Angeles, and Philadelphia.

The fate of school-based management — also known as "site-based management" or "collaborative decision making" — rests especially on the relationship between principals and their teachers, on the willingness of teachers to take responsibility for directing their own behavior, and on the amount of extra time teachers are willing to devote to working out problems and reaching consensus.[45] Advocates of school-based management claim that most teachers welcome the increased involvement and eventually reach greater personal and professional maturity. In addition, where such reforms are successful, teacher morale and the overall climate of the school are dramatically enhanced.[46]

---

[44]Anne Bradley, "Gov. Romer Unveils Teachers' Contract for Denver Schools," *Education Week*, April 3, 1991, pp. 1, 19; Briant Farnsworth, Jerry Debenham, and Gerald Smith, "Designing and Implementing a Successful Merit Pay Program for Teachers," *Phi Delta Kappan* (December 1991), pp. 320–325.

[45]Ron Brandt, "On Teacher Empowerment," *Educational Leadership* (May 1989), pp. 23–26; Gordon Cawelti, "Key Elements of Site-Based Management," *Educational Leadership* (May 1989), pp. 46–54; and Neal J. Powell, "School-Based Management in Small Secondary Schools," *NASSP Bulletin* (March 1991), pp. 11–15.

[46]Lew Allen and Carl D. Glickman, "School Improvement: The Elusive Faces of Shared Gover-

Critiques of school-based management

Critics contend that the result of collaboration is often not useful; considerable time devoted to discussing daily teaching problems such as classroom management, equipment needs, clerical routines, and working conditions means that little time remains for the larger issue of school effectiveness. In addition, some administrators argue that many teachers are ill-equipped for shared leadership because they are not trained for it; instead of cooperating, teachers may revert to a hostile collective bargaining stance.[47] The teachers surveyed for one report admitted that many of the issues they discussed with administrators reopened old wounds and resurrected old disagreements.[48]

The implementation of school-based management will require patience and a willingness to work out differences in expectations. Once it is put into practice, however, shared decision making will help empower teachers and further enhance their professional roles and status.

TEACHER ORGANIZATIONS

Restrictions on teachers

A critical factor in the development of teaching as a profession has been the growth of professional organizations for teachers. Although today's working conditions still need improvement, they sharply contrast with the restrictions teachers once endured. Here are the details of what is reputed to be a Wisconsin teacher's contract for 1922, calling for a salary of $75 a month.

Miss _____ agrees:

1. Not to get married. This contract becomes null and void immediately if the teacher marries.
2. Not to keep company with men.
3. To be home between the hours of 8 P.M. to 6 A.M. unless in attendance at a school function.
4. Not to loiter downtown in ice-cream parlors.
5. Not to leave town at any time without the permission of the chairman of the Trustees.
6. Not to smoke cigarettes.
7. Not to drink beer, wine, or whiskey.
8. Not to ride in a carriage or automobile with any man except her brother or father.
9. Not to dress in bright colors.
10. Not to dye her hair.
11. Not to wear less than two petticoats.
12. Not to wear dresses shorter than two inches above the ankles.

nance," *NASSP Bulletin* (March 1992), pp. 80–87; Bruce Joyce et al., "School Renewal as Cultural Change," *Educational Leadership* (September 1989), pp. 70–77; and Marilyn Rauth, "Exploring Heresy in Collective Bargaining and School Restructuring," *Phi Delta Kappan* (June 1990), pp. 781–784.

[47]Ted Elsberg, "Dade County, Florida — Three Years Later," *Education Week,* April 3, 1991, p. 19.
[48]Karen Diegmueller, "Report Raps Shared-Decisionmaking Effort in Los Angeles," *Education Week,* November 21, 1990, p. 5.

13. To keep the schoolroom clean:
    a. To sweep the classroom floor at least once daily.
    b. To scrub the classroom floor at least once weekly.
    c. To clean the blackboard at least once daily.
    d. To start the fire at 7 A.M. so that the room will be warm at 8 A.M. when the children arrive.
14. Not to wear face powder, mascara, or to paint the lips.[49]

Consider these requirements in the context of the times: the status of women, the image of teachers, and what Small Town, U.S.A., was like. Those were the days of the Model T Ford, the organizing struggles of labor, the "muck-rakers," and Sinclair Lewis's *Main Street* and *Babbitt.* According to David Tyack, this was the end of an era when male principals and superintendents, enamored by bureaucracy, designed tightly organized school districts and selected and supervised teachers, most of whom were female and expected innumerable restrictions on their private lives.[50] Most of the schools then were still rural, and provincial and puritanical values prevailed. Although teaching was a serious calling in the 1920s, it was hardly a "profession" or "semiprofession."

Obviously, the foregoing conditions no longer exist, and to a large extent the growth of teacher organizations and teacher militancy have played a role in changing them. The **National Education Association** and the **American Federation of Teachers** are the two most important organizations. They usually are considered rivals, competing for members, recognition, and power. Although some educators believe that perpetuation of this division is a healthy form of professional competition, others view it as detrimental to the teaching profession — a splitting of power and a waste of resources.

NEA and AFT are rivals

Regardless of which teacher organization you prefer or are inclined to join, the important step is to make a commitment and be an active member. Organizational membership will not only increase your own professionalism and gain you collegial relationships; your support also helps to improve working conditions and benefits. In addition, reading the journals, magazines, or newsletters that most professional organizations publish will keep you abreast of the latest developments in the field.

Becoming an active member

National Education Association (NEA)

The National Education Association, founded in 1857 by forty-three educators, is a complex, multifaceted organization involved in many areas of education on local, state, and national levels. The NEA, unlike the AFT, includes both teachers and administrators at the national level. As shown in Table 2.1, membership grew tenfold from 1900 to 1920 and another ninefold by 1940. Membership totaled 450,000 in 1950 and 2.1 million by 1991.[51]

2.1 million members

---

[49]*Chicago Tribune*, September 28, 1975, sect. 1, p. 3.
[50]David Tyack, "An American Tradition: The Changing Role of Schooling and Teaching," *Harvard Educational Review* (May 1987), pp. 171–174.
[51]*NEA Handbook, 1990–91*, Table 2, p. 151; "NEA Membership Nears 2.1 Million," *NEA Press Release*, July 5, 1991, p. 1.

Table 2.1
Membership of the NEA and AFT by Decades

Year	NEA Membership	AFT Membership
1857[a]	43	
1870	170	
1880	354	
1890	5,474	
1900	2,322	
1910	6,909	
1916[a]		1,500
1920	22,850	10,000
1930	216,188	7,000
1940	203,429	30,000
1950	453,797	41,000
1960	713,994	59,000
1970	1,100,000	205,000
1980	1,650,000	550,000
1985	1,700,000	600,000
1990	2,050,000	750,000
1995[b]	2,300,000	900,000

[a]Year organization was founded.
[b]Estimated membership.
Source: "The AFT Soars," *The 1988–90 Report of the Officers of the American Federation of Teachers* (Washington, D.C.: AFT, 1990), p. 15; *NEA Handbook, 1986–87* (Washington, D.C.: NEA, 1986), Table 4, p. 142; *NEA Handbook, 1990–91* (Washington, D.C.: NEA, 1991), Table 2, p. 151.

Among NEA members in 1991, approximately 55,000 were students, 90,000 were retired members, 175,000 were auxiliary staff (school secretaries, teacher aides, cafeteria workers, bus drivers, and custodians), 80,000 were college professors, 100,000 were professional support staff (guidance counselors, librarians, and administrators), and more than 1.6 million were classroom teachers.[52] This figure comprises two-thirds of the nation's 2.4 million teachers.

Suburban and rural members

Disproportionately suburban and rural, the membership is served by a large network of affiliates in every state, Puerto Rico, and the District of Columbia and by an Overseas Educational Association. There are more than 13,000 local affiliate groups. In sheer numbers, the NEA represents the second largest lobbying force in the country, outnumbering all other public employee organizations. Among unions it trails only the Teamsters. Its combined annual budget is over $145 million, and it averages about 4,000 members per congressional district.[53] The state affiliates are usually among the most influential education lobbies at the state level.

4,000 members per congressional district

The NEA offers a wide range of professional services. The Research Division, organized in 1922, conducts annual studies on the status of the profession; it also publishes several research memos and opinion surveys on an annual basis.

[52]*NEA Handbook, 1990–91*, Table 1, p. 150.
[53]"NEA Budget 1990–91," *NEA Handbook, 1990–91*, p. 335.

Today's Education

The NEA's major publication is *Today's Education,* now an annual publication, with a supplementary monthly newspaper called *NEA Today.* In addition, the national councils for the various subjects — mathematics, science, social studies, modern language, speech, home economics, business education, art, and so on — also publish professional journals. (These councils are loosely affiliated with the NEA.) Most of the fifty state affiliates publish a monthly magazine as well.

American Federation of Teachers (AFT)

The AFT was formed in 1916. It is affiliated with the AFL-CIO and was open only to classroom teachers until 1976, when it started to target professional employees, such as nurses, in order to increase membership. Membership in 1991 was 780,000, organized in some 2,200 locals in large and medium-sized cities. As shown in Table 2.1, membership limped along in the 1920s and 1930s. This was a result of antilabor sentiments and a feeling in some quarters that labor organizations were led by radicals.

Membership increase

Most of the AFT membership increase has taken place since 1960. Among its current membership are some 150,000 school personnel who work in cafeteria, custodial, maintenance, and transportation services, including some 25,000 paraprofessionals; 100,000 state and local municipal workers; 35,000 nurses, therapists, and social workers (all of whom are not teachers), 95,000 college professors, and 400,000 teachers.[54] The 1995 AFT membership is projected to be 900,000, with most of the increase coming from the ranks of classroom teachers, college professors, and school-related personnel.

American Teacher

In the past, the AFT has not been involved with research and publication to the extent the NEA has, but the union does publish a professional magazine, *Changing Education, a Consortium Yearbook,* and a monthly newspaper, *American Teacher.* In addition, the local affiliates each put out a monthly newsletter. Unlike the NEA, the AFT has always required its members to join the local, state (twenty-two in all), and national organizations simultaneously. Only in the last ten years has the NEA encouraged unitary membership. The NEA dues policy emphasizes local support, whereas the AFT channels a large portion of local funds to the national level. Most contracts negotiated with schools by an AFT

Automatic dues deduction

local affiliate require an automatic dues deduction and agency fee (whether or not the teachers belong to the union). Only a small number of local NEA contracts insist on this provision, although one might expect a move in this direction because of the obvious advantages to the organization.

The AFT remained quite small until criticism of the schools mounted at the end of the 1950s. The membership breakthrough came when AFT leaders decided to concentrate on the New York City school system. In 1961 the union group defeated the organization supporting the NEA, and the United Federation of Teachers (UFT), an affiliate of the AFT, was chosen to represent New York City teachers. The UFT engaged in a number of strikes in New York City during the next decade — for improved working conditions, salary increases, health benefits, pensions, and teacher rights. Success in New York City led to a series

[54]Telephone conversation with Robert Ripperjer, Secretary-Treasury Department, American Federation of Teachers, July 10, 1991; telephone conversation with Scott Trebitz, Assistant Director of Public Relations, American Federation of Teachers, July 14, 1991.

of victories over the NEA in several other large cities for the right to represent teachers. The AFT became the dominant teacher organization in many large urban centers where unions have traditionally flourished, where militant tactics such as collective bargaining and strikes have been common, and where teachers in general perceived a need for a powerful organization to represent them. In rural and suburban areas, where union tactics have typically received less support, the NEA remains dominant.

Strength in urban areas

Rivalry Between the NEA and AFT

Without question, there has been intense organizational rivalry between the NEA and the AFT for years. These two organizations have competed for members and for exclusive local rights to represent teachers. The NEA has historically viewed itself as a professional association, not a union. For many years it shunned collective bargaining, strikes, and other militant tactics. It vehemently criticized the AFT for its labor affiliation and maintained that this relationship was detrimental to the professional image of teachers. For its part, the AFT criticized the NEA's more conciliatory tactics as unrealistic and argued that union affiliation provided teachers with political and economic clout; it also criticized the NEA for permitting administrators to join the organization.

Professionalism vs. unionism

The differences between the two organizations were most pronounced in the 1960s, when the AFT spearheaded a dramatic increase in teacher strikes. The NEA at first condemned such strikes as illegal and unprofessional. By 1968, however, the NEA — facing pressure from its own members — joined the AFT in accepting the strike as a legitimate option. The total number of teacher strikes rose from thirty in 1966 to over a hundred per year in the 1970s, surpassing two hundred in 1975 and 1980.[55]

NEA adopts the strike tactic

Since then, both organizations have toned down their militancy; with the exception of 1984, there were fewer than one hundred strikes a year between 1981 and 1991. Both the NEA and the AFT have developed other strategies, such as coalitions with business and civic groups, binding arbitration, and attempts to increase their political clout. The decline in strikes also relates to several other factors: budget cutbacks in various government sectors; layoffs of striking employees in many industries in the 1980s; and the national recession in the early 1990s. Contract periods have generally been lengthened to three or four years, rather than one or two, which reduces the frequency of strikes. It's also significant that the strike era left many teachers emotionally and financially drained.[56]

Decline in strikes

Although the NEA and AFT no longer disagree about the use of strikes, a number of important differences still exist between the two organizations. The NEA continues to oppose any affiliation with labor organizations, a stance that

Continuing differences

---

[55]*Work Stoppages in Government, 1958–68* (Washington, D.C.: U.S. Department of Labor, 1970), Table 9, p. 13; annual reports from the U.S. Department of Labor, *Work Stoppages in Government,* from 1971 to 1980; and Stover, "Report from the Picket Line."

[56]Telephone conversations with Tom Gillette, Chief Negotiator, Rochester Teacher Association, July 10, 1991, and William Martin, Director of Public Relations, National Education Association, July 10, 1991.

Although the number of teacher strikes has declined in recent years, teacher organizations still consider the strike — or the threat to strike — to be an important tactic for improving teachers' salaries and working conditions. (© UPI/ Bettmann Newsphotos)

reflects its predominantly conservative and suburban-rural membership.[57] The AFT, on the other hand, values its affiliation with the AFL-CIO for collective bargaining power and political clout. Moreover, the AFT has mounted a major campaign to attract state and county white-collar government workers, social workers, library workers, health care workers, and nurses.[58] The NEA contends that enrolling such workers dilutes the AFT's educational focus, although the NEA itself compromised in 1990 by recruiting school maintenance workers, school nurses, school bus drivers, and other school-related personnel.[59]

Views on affirmative action

The NEA and AFT also differ in their attitudes toward affirmative action. Both organizations promote affirmative action but in distinct ways. The NEA has implemented affirmative action timetables and quotas to staff its own administrative positions; the AFT has not. The NEA strongly opposes the widespread use of standardized tests to evaluate student achievement and teacher competency, arguing that the tests are oversimplified in their measurements, culturally biased, and discriminatory against minorities. The AFT, in contrast, insists that standardized tests yield valid indicators of performance; to overcome

---

[57]Chester Finn, "Teacher Unions and School Quality: Potential Allies or Inevitable Foes?" *Phi Delta Kappan* (January 1985), pp. 331–338; Thomas W. Payzant, "Changing How the Bureaucracy Works," *Education Digest* (February 1990), pp. 10–11.

[58]"Membership: The Heart of the Union," *The 1988–90 Report of the Officers of the American Federation of Teachers* (Washington, D.C.: AFT, 1990), pp. 8–19.

[59]Telephone conversation with William Martin, Director of Public Relations, National Education Association, July 10, 1991.

any racial or ethnic differences the tests may reveal, the AFT advocates remedial, tutorial, and compensatory programs.

Different atmosphere and style

Perhaps most of all, the two organizations differ in their overall atmosphere and style of leadership. The differences in atmosphere can be seen at the various local offices and also at the AFT and NEA national offices in Washington, D.C. AFT offices are professionally staffed by a handful of informally dressed people (fifty in Washington), and the workplace is usually buzzing with noise and activity. The NEA office staff (five hundred in Washington) tend to be formally dressed and more deliberative and quiet.

Shanker's visibility

Then there is Albert Shanker, president of the AFT, who has a distinctive leadership philosophy and style. The AFT tends to be dominated by Shanker's visibility and, in some cases, his controversial ideas. Representing the AFT for nearly twenty years, he has traveled extensively both nationally and internationally for the purposes of organizing and strengthening AFT ties with political, labor, and education groups. He is frequently the main speaker at conventions, and he gives testimony or advice to government agencies, Congress, and the president. Until recently Shanker wrote a regular and outspoken column for the *New York Times* and now appears periodically in *Education Week*.

Low-profile NEA president

In contrast, the NEA leadership is diffuse, and until recently it has lacked well-known heads who could deliver votes on controversial issues. The president is elected for two years and is eligible for only two additional terms, a policy that makes it somewhat difficult for a strong leader to build a reputation. Few people in education, much less the public, have known the NEA presidents by name. This situation changed to some extent with Mary Hatwood Futrell, president from 1983 to 1989, who chose to publicize the NEA's view in paid advertisements in the *Washington Post, Education Week,* and professional journals; she also spoke frequently at professional conferences. Her successor, Keith Geiger, has continued this increased visibility. He has a vibrant public image and is seen, according to some observers, as a "savvy player" in the national educational arena and with the media.[60]

Competition for members

The upshot of the many contrasts and disagreements between the NEA and AFT has been a continuing competition for membership. Both organizations are courting college and university professors, and the rivalry to enroll these potential new members may grow more intense. Even more contentious is the battle over current members. Because about 85 percent of public-school teachers now belong to either the NEA or the AFT, the competition frequently involves existing turf. In Memphis, in Seattle, and in Prince George County, Maryland, the NEA and AFT have tried to take members from each other. Because it is becoming more difficult to win large contract concessions from school districts, teachers are more willing to switch to whichever side seems to be winning most. The raiding of one organization's membership by the other is so counterproductive

"No raid" agreements

that a few state affiliates have discussed "no raid" agreements — with some limited success.[61]

---

[60]Ann Bradley and Karen Diegmueller, "Geiger Is Seen as Savvy Player in Education's Political Arena," *Education Week,* June 19, 1991, pp. 1, 18–19.

[61]American Association of Colleges for Teacher Education, *Washington Highlights,* December 7, 1987, p. 1; telephone conversation with John Dunlop, Collective Bargaining Department, National Education Association, January 4, 1992.

Areas of Agreement Between the
NEA and AFT

Agreement on many issues

Despite these continuing differences, the NEA and AFT agree on most big issues concerning teachers and schools, including improved salaries and working conditions, smaller classrooms, reduced teacher patrol and clerical duties, free time for preparation, and released time with pay for attending professional conferences. Both organizations promote full academic freedom for teachers, including the right to participate in textbook selection committees, as well as due process and grievance procedures to protect teachers. They seek a credentialed position for all educators as a means of enhancing the image of the profession. Both organizations wish to increase financial support of all public schools and to extend free public education to all children and youth from prekindergarten to grade fourteen (or junior college).

Codes of ethics

The two organizations share a concern for professional ethics. Their respective codes of ethics clarify the roles and responsibilities of teachers and stress the special commitment that teachers must make to students and the profession. The AFT code also emphasizes a commitment to the public and the school districts. Both codes of ethics highlight the dignity of the individual, fulfillment of the student's human potential, the importance of truth, and respect for democratic principles.

Both the NEA and AFT wish to increase teacher involvement and influence in teacher-education programs, and they condemn recent assaults on teachers' tenure and security.[62] The two organizations have played an important role in the current effort to upgrade the teaching profession and academic standards in schools. They are active in promoting special education, compensatory education (especially Head Start), drug education, sex and AIDS education, environmental education, and global education.[63]

Upgrading the profession

Political activities

In the political arena, the NEA and AFT recognize the need to elect proteacher and pro-education political representatives. Through their national and state political action committees (PACs), they now spend millions of dollars annually on political campaigns and lobby efforts,[64] and they encourage their teachers to volunteer time in election contests and to run for political office.[65] They have been so successful in this approach that in many states they are considered the strongest lobby force; they usually support the same political candidates, and most of these individuals emerge victorious. Moreover, the AFT and

---

[62]Sam Ellis, "Laying Siege to Seniority," *Time,* December 23, 1991, p. 64.

[63]These issues are continuously discussed in *Education Week* in news items or paid advertisements. For example, see Albert Shanker, "Where We Stand," *Education Week,* January 9, 1991, p. 12; Keith Geiger, "A Message from the President of the National Education Association," *Education Week,* June 5, 1991, p. 4. Also, the annual NEA handbook and AFT report regularly discuss the organizations' agendas and issues.

[64]For example, the NEA's Political Action Committee for Education (NEA-PAC), some twenty years old, raised $4.2 million for federal candidates in 1990, up from $36,000 in 1972, placing fifth in contributions among all PACs. The AFT's PAC, called the Committee on Political Action (COPE), raised $1.5 million for use in federal campaigns and was ranked within the top ten contributors. These monies do not include funds raised by local and state affiliates for local and state campaigns.

[65]The most controversial example of this direct electoral participation was provided by Edward Doherty, president of the Boston Teacher Union, who ran against two-term incumbent mayor Raymond Flynn in 1992.

Getting to the Source —•◆•

The NEA Code of Ethics

all. The educator accepts the responsibility to adhere to the highest ethical standards.

The educator recognizes the magnitude of the responsibility inherent in the teaching process. The desire for the respect and confidence of one's colleagues, of students, of parents, and of the members of the community provides the incentive to attain and maintain the highest possible degree of ethical conduct. The Code of Ethics of the Education Profession indicates the aspiration of all educators and provides standards by which to judge conduct.

The remedies specified by the NEA and/or its affiliates for the violation of any provision of this Code shall be exclusive and no such provision shall be enforceable in any form other than one specifically designated by the NEA or its affiliates.

Nearly everyone agrees that a profession should have a code of ethics. Accordingly, both the NEA and the AFT have developed such codes, attempting to clarify the relationship between teachers and students as well as the behavior expected of teachers. Although the laws applying to teachers vary from state to state, courts are often influenced by the NEA and AFT codes. The NEA code printed below, established originally in 1929, has been revised six times, most recently in 1975.

PREAMBLE

The educator, believing in the worth and dignity of each human being, recognizes the supreme importance of the pursuit of truth, devotion to excellence, and the nurture of democratic principles. Essential to these goals is the protection of freedom to learn and to teach and the guarantee of equal educational opportunity for

PRINCIPLE I — COMMITMENT TO THE STUDENT

The educator strives to help each student realize his or her potential as a worthy and effective member of society. The educator therefore works to stimulate the spirit of inquiry, the acquisition of knowledge and understanding, and the thoughtful formulation of worthy goals.

In fulfillment of the obligation to the student, the educator —

1. Shall not unreasonably restrain the student from independent action in the pursuit of learning.

2. Shall not unreasonably deny the student access to varying points of view.

3. Shall not deliberately suppress or distort subject matter relevant to the student's progress.

4. Shall make reasonable effort to protect the student from conditions harmful to learning or to health and safety.

5. Shall not intentionally expose the student to embarrassment or disparagement.

6. Shall not on the basis of race, color, creed, sex, national origin, marital status, political or religious beliefs, family, social or cultural background, or sexual orientation, unfairly:
   a. Exclude any student from participation in any program;
   b. Deny benefits to any student;
   c. Grant any advantage to any student.

7. Shall not use professional relationships with students for private advantage.

8. Shall not disclose information about students obtained in the course of professional service, unless disclosure serves a compelling professional purpose or is required by law.

PRINCIPLE II — COMMITMENT TO THE PROFESSION

The education profession is vested by the public with a trust and responsibility requiring the highest ideals of professional service.

In the belief that the quality of the services of the education profession directly influences the nation and its citizens, the educator shall exert every effort to raise professional standards, to promote a climate that encourages the exercise of professional judgment, to achieve conditions which attract persons worthy of the trust to careers in education, and to assist in preventing the practice of the profession by unqualified persons.

In fulfillment of the obligation to the profession, the educator —

1. Shall not in an application for a professional position deliberately make a false statement or fail to disclose a material fact related to competency and qualifications.

2. Shall not misrepresent his/her professional qualifications.

3. Shall not assist entry into the profession of a person known to be unqualified in respect to character, education, or other relevant attribute.

4. Shall not knowingly make a false statement concerning the qualifications of a candidate for a professional position.

5. Shall not assist a noneducator in the unauthorized practice of teaching.

6. Shall not disclose information about colleagues obtained in the course of professional service unless disclosure serves a compelling professional purpose or is required by law.

7. Shall not knowingly make false or malicious statements about a colleague.

8. Shall not accept any gratuity, gift, or favor that might impair or appear to influence professional decisions or actions.

Questions

1. How does a code of ethics strengthen a profession? Are there any ways in which it could weaken a profession?

2. What is the best procedure for dealing with individuals who violate a code of ethics: closed hearings, arbitration, adjustments during contract negotiation, litigation? Why?

3. If you had the opportunity to add one clause and omit another one, what changes would you make in the NEA code?

Source: National Education Association, *Code of Ethics of the Education Profession*, adopted by the NEA Representative Assembly, 1975. Cover and excerpt reprinted by permission of the Association.

NEA have been very successful in increasing the number of teachers on school boards across the country: by 1991 teachers represented 14 percent of elected school board members nationwide.[66]

Mergers between affiliates

A Possible Merger.   If the two organizations are compatible enough to back the same political candidates, why shouldn't they end their rivalry? Many educators, faced with important questions about working conditions, tenure, teacher accountability, and teacher evaluation, have concluded that the best way to promote the interests of the teaching profession is for the two organizations to move toward greater unity — and ultimately toward merger. In the last several years, in fact, mergers have been successful between AFT and NEA affiliates in certain districts of California and Minnesota and throughout the entire state of Wisconsin. More than fifteen other states have been targeted for potential mergers. Presently, both organizations are trying to establish a uniform merger policy for their respective state and local affiliates.[67]

Benefits of merger

In 1990 AFT president Albert Shanker declared that an "AFT/NEA merger would best serve the profession"; the next year, NEA president Keith Geiger suggested that "the NEA, the AFT, and the American Association of University Professors combine into one powerful organization" that would represent more than three million educators.[68] Many of the nearly one million teachers and professors who presently belong to neither the NEA nor the AFT would probably join such a united "super" organization, which would provide enormous political power unavailable to the two separate organizations.

GENERAL PROFESSIONAL ORGANIZATIONS FOR TEACHERS

In addition to the NEA and AFT, there are more than 325 other national teacher organizations.[69]

Specialized Professional Organizations

At the working level of the classroom, the professional organization of greatest benefit to a teacher (and education student) is usually one that focuses on his or her major field. Each such subject-centered professional association provides a meeting ground for teachers of similar interests. The activities of these professional organizations customarily consist of regional and national meetings and publication of a professional journal, usually monthly or quarterly, that provides current teaching tips and describes accepted curriculum practices.

---

[66]Allan C. Ornstein, "School Superintendents and School Board Members: Who They Are," *Contemporary Education* (Winter 1992).

[67]Telephone conversation with William Martin, Director of Public Relations, National Education Association, July 10, 1991.

[68]Karen Diegmueller, "NEA to Discuss Policy on Teacher Union Mergers," *Education Week,* January 9, 1991, p. 15; "Teacher Unions Mull the Usual," *Executive Educator* (October 1990), pp. 28–29.

[69]See *Directory of Education Associations, 1991–92* (Washington, D.C.: U.S. Department of Education, 1991).

The following list names fifteen major organizations that focus on specific subject matter.

Subject-related teacher organizations

1. American Alliance for Health, Physical Education, Recreation and Dance
2. American Council on the Teaching of Foreign Languages
3. American Industrial Arts Association
4. American School Health Association
5. American Vocational Association
6. Association for Education in Journalism
7. International Reading Association
8. Modern Language Association
9. Music Teachers National Association
10. National Art Education Association
11. National Business Education Association
12. National Council for the Social Studies
13. National Council of Teachers of English
14. National Council of Teachers of Mathematics
15. National Science Teachers Association

For those readers who identify with a particular type of student — say by age or grade level, or by cognitive, physical, or ethnic characteristic — the teaching organizations that follow should be of interest. These professional organizations, also national in scope, focus on the needs and rights of special students and are organized to ensure that these children and youth are served by well-prepared school personnel. These associations hold regional and national meetings and publish monthly or quarterly journals.

Student-related teacher organizations

1. American Association for Gifted Children
2. American Association of Workers for the Blind
3. American Association for Asian Studies
4. American Montessori Society
5. American Speech-Language-Hearing Association
6. Association for Childhood Education International
7. Association for Children with Learning Disabilities
8. Council for Exceptional Children
9. Middle School Association
10. National Association for Bilingual Children
11. National Association for the Education of Young Children
12. National Association for Multicultural Education
13. National Rehabilitation Association
14. National Scholarship Service and Fund for Negro Students
15. Rural Education Association

Still another type of organization that merits comment is the professional organization whose members cut across various subjects and student types, such as the Association for Supervision and Curriculum Development and Phi Delta Kappa. These organizations tend to highlight innovative teaching practices in general, describe new trends and policies affecting the entire field of education, comprise a wide range of membership, and work for the advancement of the teaching profession in general.

Religious Education Organizations

As of 1991, there were approximately 340,000 nonpublic school teachers in grades K–12, of which 125,000 belonged to one of eighty religious education associations. One of the largest religious teacher organizations is the National Association of Catholic School Teachers (NACST), founded in 1978 and comprising in 1992 over 5,000 teachers, mainly from large cities. The organization is expected to grow in membership because the great majority of Catholic teachers are not organized on a national or local level.[70] Of the 91,000 Catholic school teachers K–12, no more than one thousand belong to either the NEA or AFT.[71]

Catholic teacher organizations

The largest and oldest Catholic education organization is the National Catholic Education Association, founded in 1904 and comprising 15,000 institutions and 200,000 Catholic educators. Most administrators, as supervisors, principals, or superintendents of their respective schools, join the organization. Few teachers are members.

Parent-Teacher Groups

A forum for parents and teachers to work together in resolving educational problems on the local, state, and national levels is provided by **parent-teacher groups.** Teachers usually take an active part in these associations and work with parents on curriculum and instructional programs, student policy, and school-community relations.

7.1 million members

Founded in 1897, the **Parent-Teacher Association (PTA)** — the most prominent of the groups — is a loose confederation of fifty-three branches and 27,000 local units, with over 7.1 million members (mostly mothers) in 1992. Its branches cover all fifty states, the District of Columbia, and both European and Pacific Congresses of American Parents, Teachers, and Students. No local unit is exactly like any other, although all local PTA members belong to the national PTA. Every PTA unit devises its own pattern of organization and service to fit its school and neighborhood. Membership in the PTA is open to anyone interested in promoting the welfare of children and youth, working with teachers and schools, and supporting the goals of the PTA.[72]

[70]"Summary Report of Basic School Statistics, Sorted by Region, State, and Diocese" (Washington, D.C.: National Catholic Education Association, 1991); telephone conversation with Rita Schwartz, Secretary-Treasurer, National Association of Catholic School Teachers, January 7, 1992.

[71]*United States Catholic Elementary and Secondary Schools, 1991–92* (Washington, D.C.: National Catholic Education Association, 1991).

[72]*Partners in Education: Teachers in the PTA* (Chicago: The National PTA, 1987); telephone conversation with Tari Marshal, Director of Public Relations, Parent-Teacher Association, July 9, 1991.

PTA Today and *What's Happening in Washington* are the official monthly magazines of the association. Many teacher and administrative associations, including the NEA and AFT, maintain a working relationship with the PTA on important issues; in fact, the NEA is loosely affiliated with the PTA.

In some school districts, however, parents and teachers have preferred not to affiliate with the state or national PTA organization because of political differences and because they want to keep local monies in the community. The Parent-Teacher Organization (PTO) and Parent-Teacher-Student Organization (PTSO) have replaced the PTA in some communities.[73]

Local school influence

Although the PTA claims to wield considerable power in shaping local school-community relations and local school policy, its actual local influence is often determined by the philosophy and attitudes of the superintendent, principal, and teachers. Overall, the PTA tends to have more influence nationally.

National impact

As the nation's largest child-advocacy organization, the national PTA is constantly assessing children's welfare so that it can respond to changes in society and in the needs of children. For a number of years, the national PTA has lobbied to reduce violence on television and to improve the quality of children's television programming. The national PTA is also very active in programs related to reading, urban education, sex education and AIDS education, child nutrition and safety education, and drug abuse prevention as well as in improving school discipline and combating censorship of school and library materials. The national PTA has developed programs and tips for parents to deal with alcohol abuse, child abuse, latchkey children, health education, and parental involvement in learning at home.

Organizations for Prospective Teachers

Students who are thinking of or are committed to a career as a teacher may join a number of professional organizations. These organizations help answer many questions; develop an understanding of the profession; stimulate ideals of professional ethics, standards, and training; provide an opportunity to meet other education students and educators at local and national meetings; and publish materials that help members keep up with current trends in the profession. The following list, summarized in Overview 2.1, describes several such organizations.

1. *Student National Education Association.* Founded in 1937, the Student NEA was originally called Future Teachers of America and admitted high-school and college students. Currently, there are about 53,000 Student NEA members (an increase of 25,000 since 1988) in about forty-five college chapters. Members receive *Today's Education* and the annual *NEA Handbook* and are entitled to request free research reports. They also obtain automatically free liability protection when they student teach.

Free insurance for students

The Student NEA strives to develop an understanding of the education profession; its major purpose is to encourage young men and women to enter teaching and join the NEA. Each state is allocated at least one student vote at the Representative Assembly, which makes the bylaws. The AFT has not established student organizations for prospective teachers, although local chapters are

---

[73] *The National PTA Handbook* (Chicago: The National PTA, 1991).

Overview 2.1 ◄●►

Professional Organizations for Students to Join

Name and Location	Membership Profile	Focus	Major Journal(s)
Student National Education Association, Washington, D.C.	Undergraduate college students (53,000)	Future teachers	*Today's Education* (annually); *NEA Handbook* (annually)
Pi Lambda Theta, Bloomington, Ind.	Undergraduate and graduate college students; teachers and administrators (12,000)	Honorary association; teaching	*Educational Horizons* (quarterly)
Phi Delta Kappa, Bloomington, Ind.	Graduate college students, teachers, administrators, and professors (175,000)	Honorary association; research and teaching	*Phi Delta Kappan* (monthly); fastbacks at reduced rates
Kappa Delta Pi, Lafayette, Ind.	Graduate college students, teachers, administrators, and professors (48,000)	Honorary association; teaching	*Educational Forum* (quarterly); *Kappa Delta Pi Record* (quarterly)
American Educational Research Association, Washington, D.C.	Graduate college students, professors (18,000)	Research, scholarship	*Educational Researcher* (bimonthly); *American Educational Research Journal* (quarterly); *Review of Educational Research* (quarterly); *Educational Evaluation and Policy Analysis* (quarterly)

exerting pressures to do so. The AFT takes the position that there is no pressing need to move in this direction.

2. *Honorary Educational Associations.* Professional and honorary groups in education include Pi Lambda Theta, Phi Delta Kappa, and Kappa Delta Pi. Pi Lambda Theta has initiated more than 100,000 individuals since its inception in 1910 and has grown from seven chapters to more than one hundred chapters (mostly campus based) in thirty-one states. Originally open to undergraduate and graduate female students and faculty members who met the necessary qualifications, it began to admit men in 1974. Membership in 1992 was 12,000. General qualifications include superior scholastic achievement (B+ or higher), evidence of high professional standards, and leadership potential. Pi Lambda Theta publishes a quarterly entitled *Educational Horizons,* as well as a newsletter.

Educational Horizons

Phi Delta Kappa, founded in 1906, now includes 670 local and 8 regional chapters in the United States and Canada as well as 10 international chapters. About half are campus based. As of 1992, there were approximately 175,000 members, with no distinctions made among graduate students, teachers, and administrators. Originally open only to men, it began admitting women in 1974. Membership requirements include high scholastic achievement, completion of a minimum of fifteen semester hours of graduate work in education, and commitment to a life career of educational services. The purpose of the organization is to promote quality education, with particular emphasis on publicly supported education. Members receive *Phi Delta Kappan*, a highly respected professional journal published ten times a year, and the fraternity newsletter. Other publications (such as short "fastback" books) are available at reduced rates.

Phi Delta Kappan

Kappa Delta Pi, founded in 1911, has always been open to men and women. Total membership (including retirees) is 430,000, of which 48,000 are considered active. Approximately 17,000 members are students. The purpose of the association is to recognize outstanding contributions to education. To this end, it invites to membership persons who exhibit worthy educational ideals, sound scholarship, and commendable personal qualities. The association is international in scope and comprises several hundred alumni and active chapters. Kappa Delta Pi publishes two well-known quarterly journals, *Educational Forum* and *Kappa Delta Pi Record*, as well as a limited number of books on education as part of the Kappa Delta Pi Research Publications series.

Educational Forum

3. *American Educational Research Association.* The American Educational Research Association (AERA), founded in 1915, is a national organization of educators and social scientists who have a vital interest in research in education and the application of research to education practice. It is considered by many to be the most prestigious research organization in education. AERA is constituted in eleven divisions and more than ninety special-interest groups. Membership in 1992 totaled 18,000, of which 3,200 were students. All members receive the *Educational Researcher*, a bimonthly news and feature magazine. In addition, members are entitled to choose two other periodicals from a list of four published by the AERA; the choices include *American Educational Research Journal, Review of Educational Research*, and *Educational Evaluation and Policy Analysis*, all quarterlies. Members also receive discounts for AERA-sponsored publications and research training sessions at the annual meeting. The annual meeting is held in a different city each year and attracts a wide array of researchers and educators from across the country; more than one thousand original papers on a broad spectrum of topics are presented at these meetings.

Review of Educational Research

Students interested in joining any of these organizations can ask their professors for appropriate information. If you visit your college library, you can track down the respective journals for each organization. The first or second page of each issue will list the membership address and membership dues; some journals will also indicate lower membership rates for students.

Summing Up

1. It is generally agreed that teaching is not yet a full profession, although it is moving toward becoming one.
2. Many trends in education are raising the level of teacher professionalism. State professional practice boards and the National Board for Professional

Teaching Standards, for example, enable teachers to participate in setting criteria for entering the profession. Mediated entry and staff development programs help to establish the idea that teaching is a full-fledged profession requiring lengthy and continued training. University-school colaboration in research projects gives teachers a chance to expand their professional horizons. Merit pay and school-based management provide opportunities for increased salaries and responsibilities.

3. The NEA and AFT now represent the large majority of classroom teachers; these organizations have improved teachers' salaries and working conditions and have gained them a greater voice in decisions that affect teaching and learning in the schools.

4. Although several differences in philosophy and practice separate the NEA and AFT, the possibility of merger may become a reality in the near future.

5. There are other professional organizations that work to improve education. Some of these, such as Phi Delta Kappa and the American Educational Research Association, are open to students of education.

Key Terms

profession *(42)*

National Council for Accreditation of Teacher Education (NCATE) *(44)*

collective bargaining *(49)*

professional practice boards *(50)*

National Board for Professional Teaching Standards (NBPTS) *(50)*

mediated entry *(51)*

staff development *(52)*

collaborative research centers *(54)*

merit pay *(55)*

school-based management *(57)*

National Education Association (NEA) *(59)*

American Federation of Teachers (AFT) *(59)*

parent-teacher groups *(70)*

Parent-Teacher Association (PTA) *(70)*

Discussion Questions

1. Is teaching a profession? Defend your answer.

2. Would a teacher surplus tend to make teaching more or less of a full-fledged profession? Why or why not?

3. What trends are giving teaching more status as a full-fledged profession than it has had in the past?

4. What are some similarities and differences between the NEA and the AFT? Is a merger desirable? Defend your answer.

5. What professional organizations other than the NEA or AFT might you join? Why?

Suggested Readings

Conant, James B. *The Education of American Teachers.* New York: McGraw-Hill, 1964.
   A classic text on improving teacher education and teacher professionalism.

Jackson, Philip W. *The Practice of Teaching.* New York: Teachers College Press, Columbia University, 1986.
   The author discusses the practice of teaching; emphasis is on the importance of teaching and how to define "teaching."

Johnson, Susan Moore. *Teachers at Work.* New York: Harper & Row, 1990.
   The rules and responsibilities teachers adapt in classrooms and schools.

Lieberman, Myron. *Beyond Public Education.* New York: Praeger, 1986.
   A critical view of teachers and schools — drawing on conservative, big-business ideas of efficiency and cost effectiveness.

Lortie, Dan C. *Schoolteacher: A Sociological Study.* Chicago: University of Chicago Press, 1975.
   An interesting book with observations on and interpretations of the nature of teaching and the social dynamics of the classroom and the school.

Ornstein, Allan C. *Strategies for Effective Teaching.* New York: Harper & Row, 1990.
   Current research on effective teaching and how students learn.

Rosenholtz, Susan J. *Teachers' Workplace: The Social Organization of Schools.* New York: Longman, 1989.
   A discussion of the profession of teaching and how teachers interact in school settings.

PART
II

HISTORICAL FOUNDATIONS

*I*nsight into the present and future rests on the ability to understand the past and raise intelligent questions about it. An appreciation of historical trends reveals the folly of attempting simple answers to complex problems. Schools do not exist in a vacuum; they are influenced by a changing society rooted in historical foundations. The three chapters in Part II examine the history of education in this context.

In each chapter we learn that certain lines of thought seem to have had a marked influence in shaping the character of American education. In Chapter 3, we see that our system of education originated in European movements and that it has been shaped by certain important periods — the ancient Greek and Roman eras, the medieval period, the Renaissance, and the Reformation.

Next, in Chapter 4, we examine some of the ideas advanced by philosophers and other scholars concerned with education. We discuss twelve major pioneers in education: Comenius, Locke, Rousseau, Pestalozzi, Herbart, Froebel, Spencer, Dewey, Montessori, Counts, Piaget, and Hutchins. Emphasis is placed on these scholars' ideas about learning and schooling and their influence on educational practice.

In Chapter 5, we look at the development of education in America, from the colonial period to contemporary events. We see the complex interaction of schools and society as we learn how changing institutions and national ideas influenced the development of American education. A particular focus is the development of universal education through the establishment of the common school and the extension of educational opportunity to the secondary level.

3

Roots of
American Education

FOCUSING QUESTIONS

Why should teachers study the history of education?

How did the leading educators of the past define knowledge, education, schooling, teaching, and learning?

What concepts of the educated person were dominant during each period of history discussed in this chapter?

Who received a formal education during each period of history treated in this chapter? Why?

How have educational ideas changed during the course of time?

How have the theories of leading educators contributed to modern education?

Prospective teachers need to possess, as a cultural and professional knowledge base, an understanding of how education and schooling originated, developed, and reached its present condition. Even the most contemporary and urgent of social and educational issues remains unclear unless its roots in the past are understood. Studying the history of education provides teachers with a sense of professional place and time. The Bradley Commission on History in Schools made some general recommendations about Americans' perspective on the past that are relevant to the history of education:

A perspective on the past

> Our students . . . need to confront the diverse cultural heritages of the world's many peoples, and they need to know the origins and evolution of the political, religious, and social ideas that have shaped our institutions and those of others. Without studying the history of the West and the history of the world, students remain out of touch with these realities. They will not understand the origins and major tenets of the world's religions, they will not be familiar with the ancient and worldwide struggles for freedom and justice, and they will not know the many roads that nations have taken to conquest and survival.[1]

Our study of history illustrates how the educational ideas of the past and present arose out of the human struggle for survival and enlightenment. In this chapter we focus on the educational heritage specifically of Western Civilization, since it has most directly influenced the shape of American education. It should be noted that Meso-American, African, and Asian civilizations also made significant contributions to world educational history. African traditions came to North America with the slaves who were forcibly transported to the New World. Also, the Mayans in Mexico's Yucatán peninsula and in Guatemala had a highly developed system of architecture and astronomy. They developed a type of writing based on logographs, or word signs, that Mayan priests taught to their apprentices in religious schools.[2] Chinese civilization developed an extensive educational system based on Confucian philosophy and used formal exams to prepare civil servants who administered the vast Chinese empire.[3]

Why study history?

As you read this chapter, keep in mind these important reasons for studying the history of education:

1. Educational issues and problems are often rooted in the past; the study of educational history can help us to understand and solve today's problems.
2. Realistic efforts to reform education begin with present conditions, which are a product of our past; by using our past, we can shape the future.
3. The study of education's past provides a perspective that explains and illuminates teachers' present activities.

In approaching the study of educational history from the perspective of your present concerns, it is helpful to look to the experience of past educators for

---

[1]The Bradley Commission on History in Schools, *Building a History Curriculum: Guidelines for Teaching History in Schools* (Washington, D.C.: Educational Excellence Network, 1988), pp. 3–4.
[2]Linda Schele and David Freidel, *A Forest of Kings: The Untold Story of the Ancient Maya* (New York: William Morrow, 1990), pp. 52–53.
[3]Conrad Schirokauer, *A Brief History of Chinese Civilization* (New York: Harcourt Brace Jovanovich, 1991), pp. 40–43.

answers to questions that you will face as a teacher. The questions put to these educators will be broad ones, dealing with the very nature of teaching and learning. For example: What is knowledge? What is education? What is the purpose of the school? Who should attend school? How should teaching and learning be carried on?

In addition to exploring these significant educational questions, we also shall examine the degree to which various groups had the opportunity to receive a formal education during major historic periods. For whom was formal education, or schooling, intended? To what extent was formal education based on gender and social class?

EDUCATION IN PRELITERATE SOCIETIES

In its long march to the present, humankind developed skills for creating, sustaining, and transmitting culture. Preliterate persons faced the problem of survival in an environment that pitted them against natural forces, animals, and other hostile human beings. In order to transform a frequently hostile environment into a life-sustaining one, humankind developed life skills that eventually became cultural patterns.[4]

Cultural transmission

For the culture of a particular group to continue, that culture had to be transmitted from the group's adults to its children. As the children learned the language, skills, knowledge, and values of their society, they inherited the culture. The earliest patterns of education involved (1) gathering food and providing shelter, (2) making tools or instruments, (3) inculcating the mores of group life, and (4) learning language.

Informal education

Through informal education rather than schooling, adult members of the group, such as parents, elders, and priests, instructed children in the specialized tasks and roles that they would perform as adults. Boys learned to make spears and other tools and to hunt and fish; girls learned to gather and prepare food. Over time, essential patterns of group life evolved into moral codes of behavior that were ritualized ways of dealing with the environment. Preliterate societies

Oral tradition

particularly relied on oral tradition as a means of passing on the cultural heritage. Elders of the group, often gifted storytellers, sang or recited stories or long narratives of the group's past. In this way, the oral tradition informed the young about the group's history, its victories and defeats, and its heroic figures and values.

Abstract thinking

Participating in the songs and stories of the oral tradition helped young people learn spoken language, and with it to develop the ability to function as abstract thinkers. As toolmakers, human beings could fashion and manipulate instruments; as language users, they could create, use, and manipulate symbols. When these symbols began to be expressed in signs, pictographs, and letters, human beings created a written language and made the great leap to literacy.[5]

---

[4]John P. McKay, Bennett D. Hill, and John Buckler, *A History of Western Society* (Boston: Houghton Mifflin, 1984), pp. 5–8.

[5]John B. Harrison, Richard E. Sullivan, and Dennis Sherman, *A Short History of Western Civilization* (New York: Knopf, 1985), pp. 12–13.

Overview 3.1 ━━◆━━━━━━━━━━━━━━━━━━━━━━━━━━━━━━━━━━━

Key Periods in Educational History, to A.D. 1600

Historical Group or Period	Educational Goals	Students	Instructional Methods	Curriculum	Agents	Influences on Western Education
Preliterate societies 7000 B.C.– 5000 B.C.	To teach group survival skills; to cultivate group cohesiveness	Children in the group	Informal means of education; children imitating adult skills and values	Practical skills of hunting, fishing, food gathering; stories, myths, songs, poems, dances	Parents, tribal elders, and priests	Emphasis on informal education in transmission of skills and values
Greek 1600 B.C.– 300 B.C.	To cultivate civic responsibility and identification with city-state Athenian: to develop well-rounded persons Spartan: to develop soldiers and military leaders	Male children of citizens; ages 7–20	Drill, memorization, recitation in primary schools; lecture, discussion, and dialogue in higher schools	Athenian: reading, writing, arithmetic, drama, music, physical education, literature, poetry Spartan: drill, military songs and tactics	Athens: private teachers and schools, Sophists, philosophers Sparta: military teachers, drill sergeants	Athens: the concept of the well-rounded, liberally educated person Sparta: the concept of the military state
Roman 750 B.C.– A.D. 450	To develop sense of civic responsibility for republic and then empire; to develop administrative and military skills	Male children of citizens; ages 7–20	Drill, memorization, and recitation in *ludus;* declamation in rhetorical schools	Reading, writing, arithmetic, Laws of Twelve Tables, law, philosophy	Private schools and teachers; schools of rhetoric	Emphasis on education for practical administrative skills; relating education to civic responsibility
Arabic A.D. 700– A.D. 1350	To cultivate religious commitment to Islamic beliefs; to develop expertise in mathematics, medicine, and science	Male children of upper classes; ages 7–20	Drill, memorization, and recitation in lower schools; imitation and discussion in higher schools	Reading, writing, mathematics, religious literature, scientific studies	Mosques; court schools	Arabic numerals and computation; reentry of classical materials on science and medicine

EDUCATION IN ANCIENT GREECE

Historians of education often look to ancient Greece as an originating source of Western culture. The study of classical Greek culture illuminates many problems that today's educators face. What are worthy models for children to imitate? How does education help to shape good citizens? How does education reflect

Historical Group or Period	Educational Goals	Students	Instructional Methods	Curriculum	Agents	Influences on Western Education
Medieval A.D. 500– A.D. 1400	To develop religious commitment, knowledge, and ritual; to reestablish social order; to prepare persons for appropriate roles	Male children of upper classes or those entering religious life; girls and young women entering religious communities; ages 7–20	Drill, memorization, recitation, chanting in lower schools; textual analysis and disputation in universities and in higher schools	Reading, writing, arithmetic, liberal arts; philosophy, theology; crafts; military tactics and chivalry	Parish, chantry, and cathedral schools; universities; apprenticeship; knighthood	Establishing the structure, content, and organization of the university as a major institution of higher education; the institutionalization and preservation of knowledge
Renaissance A.D. 1350– A.D. 1500	To cultivate a humanist who was expert in the classics (Greek and Latin); to prepare courtiers for service to dynastic leaders	Male children of aristocracy and upper classes; ages 7–20	Memorization, translation, and analysis of Greek and Roman classics	Latin, Greek, classical literature, poetry, art	Classical humanist educators and schools such as lycée, gymnasium, Latin grammar school	An emphasis on literary knowledge, excellence, and style as expressed in classical literature; a two-track system of schools
Reformation A.D. 1500– A.D. 1600	To cultivate a sense of commitment to a particular religious denomination; to cultivate general literacy	Boys and girls, ages 7–12, in vernacular schools; young men, ages 7–12, of upper-class background in humanist schools	Memorization, drill, indoctrination, catechetical instruction in vernacular schools; translation and analysis of classical literature in humanist schools	Reading, writing, arithmetic, catechism, religious concepts and ritual; Latin and Greek; theology	Vernacular elementary schools for the masses; classical schools for the upper classes	A commitment to universal education to provide literacy to the masses; the origins of school systems with supervision to ensure doctrinal conformity; the dual-track school system based on socioeconomic class and career goals

changing social, economic, and political conditions? How does education serve humankind's search for truth?

Generations of readers have thrilled to the tension and suspense of Homer's epic poems, the *Iliad* and *Odyssey*. Appearing about 1200 B.C., Homer's poems provided Greeks with a means of defining themselves and their culture. The poems offered an explanation of the Greeks' origins, a dramatic portrayal of their struggles, and a model of their common future.[6] In this way, Homer's epics served important educational purposes. Agamemnon, Ulysses, Achilles, and other characters in the epics vividly personified the heroic dimension of life. By studying the behavior of these heroes, the young Greek learned (1) the characteristics and qualities that made life worth living, (2) the behaviors expected of warrior-knights, and (3) the flaws or weaknesses in human character that brought harm to oneself and one's friends.[7]

Homeric education

The study of ancient Greek civilization provides valuable lessons on citizenship and civic education that illuminate the role of education in shaping good citizens. A number of small and often competing city-states, such as Athens, Sparta, and Thebes, were noteworthy for their well-defined conception of civic duties, responsibilities, and rights. Athens, in particular, emphasized the humane, rational, and democratic form of social and political organization. Sparta, the chief adversary of Athens, was a military dictatorship. As each city-state developed its own form of political organization, it also evolved an appropriate kind of education.

Education and the citizen

For the Greeks, **acculturation** — immersion and participation in the total culture — was more important than formal schooling. Through acculturation the Greek youth became a citizen of his society. Especially in Athens, formal education was generally reserved for the male children of citizens of the city-state, or *polis*. Although there were exceptions, resident aliens, women, and slaves had either no or very little opportunity to attend schools. Thus, about two-thirds of the population were excluded from formal education.[8]

Acculturation

The Athenians believed that a free man needed a liberal education in order to perform his duties to the state as well as for his own personal development. This was not thought to be true of the large populations of slaves, who were held as property by the free citizens. According to the Athenians, slaves should be trained in the skills required in various trades but did not need and should not have a liberal education.[9]

Education of women

The education and status of women depended upon the customs of the particular Greek city-state. In Athens, women had no legal or economic rights, and the vast majority of women did not receive a formal education. Some of the more fortunate, however, were educated at home by tutors. Certain others, such as priestesses of the religious cults, were educated in religious ritual at special schools associated with the cults. In contrast to Athens, girls in Sparta received more schooling, but it was almost exclusively athletic training to prepare them to be healthy mothers of future Spartan soldiers.

---

[6]Louis Goldman, "Homer, Literacy, and Education," *Educational Theory* (Fall 1989), pp. 391–400.

[7]Robert H. Beck, "The Iliad: Principles and Lessons," *Educational Theory* (Spring 1986), pp. 179–194.

[8]Donald Kagan, *Pericles of Athens and the Birth of Democracy* (New York: Free Press, Macmillan, 1990); Cynthia Farrar, *The Origins of Democratic Thinking: The Invention of Politics in Classical Athens* (New York: Cambridge University Press, 1988).

[9]Ellen Meiksins Wood, *Peasant-Citizen and Slave: The Foundations of Athenian Democracy* (New York: Verso, 1988).

More structured education began with the appearance of the Sophists. Following these teachers came Socrates and Plato, the moral philosophers; Aristotle, who attempted to formulate rational and systematic explanations of natural phenomena; and Isocrates, the educator and rhetorician.

The Sophists

In the middle of the fifth century B.C., altered economic conditions generated social and educational change in Greece, especially in Athens. The older landed aristocracy was slowly being displaced by commercial classes, which had profited from Athenian expansion and colonization. This social change created the conditions for the Sophists, who became the first professional educators.

Wandering teachers

The **Sophists** were a group of wandering teachers who developed a variety of methods for instructing the rising commercial class of Athens and other Greek city-states in needed intellectual and rhetorical skills. The Sophists claimed that they could teach any subject or skill to anyone who wished to learn it.[10] Although their pedagogical expertise was often exaggerated, they brought educational opportunities to more people than had previously enjoyed them and contributed to socioeconomic mobility.

Grammar, logic, and rhetoric

The Sophists specialized in teaching grammar, logic, and rhetoric; these subjects later developed into the liberal arts. Logic — the rules of argument — aided students in clarifying their own thinking; grammar helped them express ideas clearly; **rhetoric** — the power of persuading others through speech — was considered most important. Essentially, the Sophists were concerned with developing the communication skills of their students so that they might become successful advocates and legislators. Skill in communication was the means to power.

> In the middle of the fifth century B.C. there was a verbal explosion of unprecedented magnitude. . . . Men argued, debated, soliloquized, declaimed, contradicted, orated. In trade, in politics, in litigation, in estate management, in war, in courtship, in international relations, he who had the gift of words was victor.[11]

Protagoras' method

Some of the Sophists were excellent teachers who were well prepared to teach their subjects and skills. Unfortunately, others were fakes who offered instant success through tricks and gimmicks. Protagoras (485–415 B.C.) was one of the most effective teachers among the Sophists.[12] His method involved (1) the presentation of a simple lecture or declamation to his students to provide them with an excellent model of speech; (2) an examination of great orations that could be used as models of speech; (3) the study of rhetoric, grammar, and logic; (4) practice orations by the young orator which were criticized by the teacher; and finally (5) a public oration delivered by the student. Protagoras believed it

---

[10]Gerald L. Gutek, *Cultural Foundations of Education: A Biographical Introduction* (New York: Macmillan, 1991), pp. 14–15.

[11]James J. Jarrett, *The Educational Theories of the Sophists* (New York: Teachers College Press, Columbia University, 1969), p. 5.

[12]L. Glenn Smith, *Lives in Education: People and Ideas in the Development of Teaching* (Ames, Iowa: Education Studies Press, 1984), pp. 7–9.

was possible for one to argue for or against any proposition and to win any kind of argument.

The Sophists were not particularly concerned with knowledge as a search for truth. Rather, they promised to provide their students with techniques needed to acquire wealth, political power, and social prestige. In ancient Athens, the key to power in the assembly and courts was the ability to attract people and to persuade them to follow you. For the Sophists, knowledge was not speculation about abstract concepts of truth, beauty, and goodness. It was the ability to use information in such a way as to motivate and persuade people to accept your point of view. It was not what you said but how you expressed yourself that won the argument or the case of law.

Information for persuasion

As traveling teachers the Sophists did not establish schools in an institutional sense. They instructed anyone who could afford to pay them, trying to give their students the image of confidence, skill, and talent. In this sense, the Sophists were democratic educators who did not restrict their teaching to an upper class or a hereditary aristocracy. In another sense, they contributed to an opportunistic attitude that stressed appearance and technique rather than truth and honesty. In some respects, the Sophists resembled modern image-makers, who try to "package" political candidates as if they are products to be sold to voters. In fact, the word *sophistry,* which means misleading but clever and subtle argument, is derived from the methods used by the ancient Greek Sophists.

Opportunistic attitude

Socrates: Education by Self-Examination

Unlike the Sophists, the Athenian philosopher Socrates (469–399 B.C.) sought to discover the universal principles of truth, beauty, and goodness, which he believed should govern human conduct. Socrates is important in Western educational history because he firmly defended the freedom to think, to question, and to teach. He was also significant as the teacher of Plato, who later systematized many of Socrates' ideas. Because what we know about Socrates is from the writings of Plato, there is room for debate about the precise nature of Socrates' philosophy.[13] Most scholars, however, agree on the basic tenets.

Principles of truth, beauty, and goodness

Socrates' philosophy was a simple ethic; it stated that a person ought to seek to live a life of moral excellence. Such an individual would live wisely and act rationally. A true education was one that cultivated morally excellent people. Socrates held moral excellence to be superior to technical or vocational training. Unlike the Sophists, Socrates did not believe that knowledge or wisdom could be transmitted from a teacher to a learner. He asserted that true knowledge existed within everyone and needed to be brought to consciousness. A liberating education would stimulate learners to discover ideas by bringing to consciousness the truth that was latent in their minds.

Socrates' educational aim was for individuals to define themselves through self-examination and self-analysis. Through self-examination each person could seek the truth that is universally present in all people. As a teacher, Socrates used the method of asking probing questions that stimulated his students to investigate the perennial human concerns about the meaning of life, truth, and

Probing questions

---

[13]Alven Neiman, "Ironic Schooling: Socrates, Pragmatism and the Higher Learning," *Educational Theory* (Fall 1991), pp. 371–384.

The Roman educational ideal was exemplified by the broadly and liberally educated man of public life — the senator, lawyer, teacher, civil servant, and politician. (© Alinari/Art Resource, New York)

justice. As a result of the Socratic dialogue with the teacher, the student constructed, criticized, and reconstructed his basic conceptions. This technique is still known as the **Socratic method**.

Socrates frequented the Athenian marketplace, raising political, aesthetic, moral, and philosophical issues. As a social critic, he made powerful enemies. In 399 B.C., he was brought to trial on the charge of impiety to the gods and corruption of Athenian youth and was condemned to death by his fellow Athenians.

Plato: Eternal Truths and Values

Socrates' educational efforts were continued by his pupil Plato (427–346 B.C.).[14] A speculative philosopher, Plato founded the Academy in 387 B.C. He wrote *Protagoras,* a discourse on virtue, and the *Republic* and the *Laws,* treatises on political, legal, and educational theory. In general, Plato was a conservative social and educational philosopher who disliked the changes encouraged by the Sophists and held that reality consisted of an unchanging world of perfect ideas — universal concepts such as truth, goodness, justice, and beauty. According to Plato, individual examples of these concepts, as they appear to our senses, are imperfect representations of the universal and eternal ideas.

Reminiscence

Plato's theory of knowledge is based on the **theory of reminiscence,** by which individuals recall the truths or ideas that are present in latent form in their minds. Reminiscence implies that the human soul, before birth, has lived in a spiritual world of ideas, which is the source of all truth and knowledge. At

---

[14]Gutek, *Cultural Foundations of Education,* pp. 15–31.

birth, this knowledge of truth is represented within one's subconscious mind. For Plato, learning was the rediscovery or recollection of this latent knowledge of perfect forms.[15] Because sense impressions, according to Plato, are distortions of reality, genuine knowledge is intellectual, not sensory. True knowledge, as contrasted with sensation, is changeless and eternal. There is but one idea of perfection that is common to all human beings regardless of their time and circumstances. Given that truth is universal, education should also be universal and unchanging. Since reality can be apprehended only intellectually, education also should be intellectual.

Universal and unchanging education

Plato's Ideal Society.   In the *Republic*, his most famous work, Plato fashioned a plan for a perfect state ruled by an intellectual elite of philosopher-kings. Although **Plato's Republic** was never implemented in historical reality, Plato's ideas are useful as an idealized version of a certain kind of education. The Republic, existing to cultivate truth and virtue in its inhabitants, rested on the assumptions that only knowledgeable men should rule and that all inhabitants should contribute to the general welfare according to their particular aptitude. Inhabitants were divided into three major classes; the intellectual rulers, or philosopher-kings; the auxiliaries and military defenders; and the workers, who produced goods and services. A person's intellectual capacity, defined primarily in cognitive terms, determined the class to which he or she belonged.

Intellectual elite

The educational system rated individual intellectual competencies and sorted people into categories. Once assigned to a class, individuals received the education appropriate to their assigned social role. Plato gave the philosopher-kings the task of selecting those who were intellectually able. Because of their intellectual expertise, the philosopher-kings were judged to be virtuous and intelligent men who possessed the capacity for leadership. The second class, the auxiliaries (warriors) were subordinate to the philosopher-kings. Strong of will, rather than intellect, they were to defend the Republic. The lowest class, the workers, provided the needed economic products. For each class, there was an appropriate educational track to prepare its members for their functions. Plato believed that each class would fulfill a necessary socioeconomic function as it contributed to the community. Such a society, he believed, would be harmonious.

Contrary to the prevailing Athenian opinion that held women to be inferior, Plato believed that women should enjoy many of the intellectual and educational privileges and responsibilities accorded men.[16] Like their male counterparts, women, too, fell within the three basic categories to which Plato assigned human beings. Some women, possessing a high degree of intellectual powers, could become members of the ruling philosophical elite; others of lesser cognitive abilities were assigned to the ranks of defenders or workers. Like men, women would receive the education appropriate to their abilities and their destined occupation in the Republic.

Plato on women's education

Plato's Educational Curriculum.   Plato designed a curriculum to meet the educational needs of his ideal society. Although never put into practice, this

---

[15]Gerald L. Gutek, *Philosophical and Ideological Perspectives on Education* (Englewood Cliffs, N.J.: Prentice-Hall, 1988, pp. 17–18.

[16]Robert S. Brumbaugh, "Plato's Ideal Curriculum and Contemporary Philosophy of Education," *Educational Theory* (Spring 1987), pp. 169–177.

curriculum represents the kind of schooling Plato deemed appropriate to a hierarchical society.

State-run schools

Since Plato believed that parents often passed on their prejudices and ignorance to their children, children were separated from their parents and reared in state nurseries in the Republic. The nurseries constituted a prepared environment from which ideas and practices regarded as injurious to the child's proper development had been excised. From ages six to eighteen, children studied music and gymnastics. Music included letters, reading, writing, choral singing, and dancing. After mastering reading and writing, students read the classics, which had been carefully censored. Plato, who regarded literature as a powerful force in character formation, believed that children should read only poems and stories that epitomized truthfulness, obedience to authorities, courage, and control of emotions. After mastering basic arithmetic, students applied themselves to geometry and astronomy. Gymnastics, which consisted of functional exercises useful for military training, such as fencing, archery, javelin throwing, and horseback riding, was considered essential for character building and for physical development. Plato also included the rules of diet and hygiene in his curriculum.

Athletics for building character

Higher education

From ages eighteen to twenty, students pursued intensive physical and military training. At twenty, the future philosopher-kings were selected for ten years of additional higher education in mathematics, geometry, astronomy, music, and science. At age thirty, the less intellectually capable became civil servants; the most intellectually capable continued the higher study of metaphysics. When their studies were completed, the philosopher-kings began to direct the military and political affairs of the Republic. At age fifty, the philosopher-kings became the Republic's elder statesmen.

Metaphysics and dialectic studies

To Plato, intellectual capacity was related to a person's ability to reason in metaphysical terms. Since **metaphysics** dealt with questions of the nature of ultimate reality, the philosopher-kings had to penetrate beyond the effects of immediate sense perception and grasp intellectually the ultimate cause of existence. The search for this ultimate cause involved the process of **dialectic** — a term derived from the Greek word *dialektike,* which means "to converse." Corresponding to the Socratic dialogue, dialectic was an attempt to clarify ideas and arrive at truth through a rigorous give-and-take asking of questions and examination of answers. For Plato, the pursuit of dialectic would lead the truth-seeker to the Form of the Good, the single universal principle from which all truth is derived.

Focus on intellectual learning

Plato opposed the Sophists' relativistic stress on technique and method. For Plato, truth, learning, and education were intellectual, not technical. Hence, those who showed a propensity toward abstract thought were to be selected by teachers for studies that developed their reasoning powers. Individuals who were not suited to philosophical inquiry were given vocational training. Students admitted to a Platonic school were a carefully selected intellectual elite.

Aristotle: Cultivation of Rationality

Plato's student Aristotle (384–322 B.C.) was the tutor of Alexander the Great. Aristotle founded the Lyceum, an Athenian philosophical school, and wrote extensively on such subjects as physics, astronomy, zoology, botany, logic, ethics, and metaphysics. Aristotle's *Nichomachean Ethics* and *Politics* examine education in relation to society and government.[17]

In contrast to Plato, who believed that reality existed only in the realm of ideas, Aristotle held that reality exists objectively. In other words, objects, composed of form and matter, exist independently of our knowledge of them. Human beings are rational; therefore, they have the ability to know and observe the natural laws that govern them. Aristotle also saw a basic duality in human nature. Human beings possess both minds and material bodies. Like animals, people have appetites or physical needs that must be satisfied for them to survive. Unlike lower animals, men and women have intellect, which gives them the power to think. The good person has activated and fully uses this rational power. The truly educated person exercises reason in judging ethical and political behavior. Humankind's goal is happiness, and the good life is one of moderation — an avoidance of extremes.

Moderation

For Aristotle, thinking and knowing begin with one's sensation of objects in the environment. From this sensory experience, one forms concepts about objects. The Aristotelian emphasis on sensory experience as the beginning of knowing and of instruction later was stressed by eighteenth- and nineteenth-century educators, such as Locke and Pestalozzi. Aristotle's philosophical position was the historical predecessor of realism, which is discussed in Chapter 12.

Cultivation of rationality

Aristotle on Education.   In *Politics,* Aristotle set forth an educational theory that states that the good community is based on the cultivation of rationality. If education is neglected, then the community suffers.[18] Like most Greek theorists, Aristotle made a distinction between liberal education and vocational training. Aristotle saw the liberal arts as a liberating factor, enlarging and expanding one's choices. Occupational or vocational training in trade, commerce, or farming was a servile pursuit that interfered with intellectual pursuits. (Contemporary debates between liberal educators and career educators often reflect the same basic issues that Aristotle and other Greek theorists examined.)

Compulsory schooling

Aristotle, who saw that education cultivated both the rational person and the rational society, recommended compulsory public schools. Infant schooling was to consist of play, physical activity, and appropriate stories. Children from ages seven to fourteen were to develop proper habits by moral and physical education. They should have gymnastic training or physical education. Music cultivated proper emotional dispositions. The basic skills needed for liberal education — reading and writing — were to be taught. From age fifteen through twenty-one, youths would study mathematics, geometry, astronomy, grammar, literature, poetry, rhetoric, ethics, and politics. At age twenty-one, students would follow more theoretical subjects, such as physics, cosmology, biology, psychology, logic, and metaphysics. Like many other Greek theorists, Aristotle was concerned exclusively with the education of boys. Following the conventional mores of Athens, he believed women to be intellectually inferior to men. Girls were to be trained only to perform household and child-rearing duties necessary for their roles as future wives and mothers.

---

[17]J.J. Chambliss, *Educational Theory as Theory of Conduct: From Aristotle to Dewey* (Albany: State University of New York Press, 1987), pp. 23–25.

[18]Larry Arnhart, *Aristotle on Political Reasoning: A Commentary on the ''Rhetoric''* (DeKalb: Northern Illinois University Press, 1985).

Taking Issue ━●▶ ─────────────────────────────────────

Separate Vocational Education

Since the classical period in ancient Greece, philosophers such as Plato and Aristotle have argued that different kinds of education are appropriate for different classes of society. According to this view, a liberal, academic education is important for the intellectual classes, such as civic leaders, teachers, and clergy; but for the working classes, education should concentrate on vocational training. A similar distinction can be seen in many American secondary schools that separate academic programs for college-bound students from vocational or business programs for students who will probably not attend college. This dual-track system in secondary education has been opposed by many prominent American educators, including John Dewey and Robert Hutchins.

Question: Should secondary education in the United States be divided into separate programs for academic and vocational education?

Arguments PRO

1 Students have varying interests and aptitudes. Not all are interested in or motivated by academic programs. By offering specialized vocational programs, schools can challenge the interests of many different types of students.

2 Because socioeconomic life has grown increasingly specialized and technological, it is important that students be prepared for specialized careers as early as possible. For many students, this early training can best be obtained in a vocational program.

3 The United States faces severe economic competition from other industrialized nations. Specialized vocational programs improve economic productivity by providing well-trained technical personnel.

4 Specialized vocational schools can be organized to meet the economic needs of specific geographical areas. The graduates of such schools possess salable skills needed in the communities in which they live.

5 Vocational programs have been a useful, practical feature of American secondary schools for many years. Why change a system that is working?

Arguments CON

1 Although people may have varying aptitudes and interests, all of us share a common human nature and inhabit a common planet. A liberal education for all, regardless of future occupation, enhances a sense of community and helps students realize their full human potential.

2 Separate vocational programs cause premature specialization. Such early training locks young people into careers and limits their opportunities for future choice. Moreover, highly specialized training is likely to become obsolete as technology changes.

3 To improve its competitive position, the United States needs well-trained thinkers more than it needs technicians. As Aristotle understood, a liberal, academic education is the best way to train the human mind.

4 The nation's population is increasingly mobile. To prepare persons for specific job markets limits their ability to find work in other locations and thereby reduces their long-term employment opportunities.

5 Despite its supposed practicality, the system of separating vocational from academic programs is undemocratic. It reinforces class divisions and decreases the upward mobility of the working classes.

Knowledge, objects, and concepts

Aristotle's Theory of Knowledge.   For Aristotle, knowledge is always about an object. Whereas cognition begins with sensory data about an object, knowledge is conceptual — it is based on the form of the object. Concepts are generalized classes of objects. For example, if you walk through a forest, you might see such trees as pines, oaks, elms, and maples. Although these trees vary in some aspects of their appearance, they are all similar in that they are members of a class. As trees, they share or participate in the form of "treeness." If a teacher of botany uses the Aristotelian method, he or she can teach about trees as a class or as a general category in botanical reality and can also teach about the particular trees that are members of the class. Since knowledge is always about an object, education and teaching are always about an object and should have a content. In the Aristotelian teaching act, the teacher instructs a learner about some object, some body of knowledge, or some discipline. Teaching and learning never represent merely an interpersonal relationship or the expression of feelings.

Focus on scholarship and science

Since Aristotle defined human beings as rational, the Aristotelian school attempted to cultivate and develop each student's rationality. A school, in Aristotle's view, should be a highly academic institution. It should offer a prescribed subject-matter curriculum based on scholarly and scientific discipline. Within such a school, teachers would have expert knowledge of their subject and would be skilled in transmitting that knowledge to students who are motivated to learn it. Aristotle's philosophy became the foundation of medieval Scholastic education and is the basis of the educational philosophies of such modern educators as Robert Hutchins and Mortimer Adler.[19]

Isocrates: Oratory and Rhetoric

The Greek rhetorician Isocrates (436–388 B.C.) is significant in educational history because he developed a well-constructed educational theory based on rhetorical skills and knowledge. Isocrates wrote *Against the Sophists* as a prospectus for his own school and method of instruction.[20] He denounced the Sophists for their superficiality, their stress on tricks and gimmicks, and their often exaggerated promises. Isocrates considered education the means to prepare rational men who would be speakers of the truth. Civic reform, he believed, could be secured only by educating virtuous leaders who could capably administer the state. Of the liberal studies, Isocrates held that rhetoric, the rational expression of thought, was most important in cultivating morality and political leadership.

Rhetorical education as humanistic

Isocrates opposed those Sophists who taught rhetoric as a set of isolated persuasive routines or public relations techniques. Rather, he believed that rhetorical education should be humanistic and cultural, including the tools and techniques of speech. The worthy orator should serve honorable causes that advance the public good. As a man above reproach, the orator would persuade men to follow good programs. Isocrates' students, who enrolled in his school for three to four years, studied rhetoric, examined model orations, and practiced public speaking. To develop humanely educated men, Isocrates also taught pol-

[19]Mortimer J. Adler, *Paideia Problems and Possibilities* (New York: Macmillan, 1983).
[20]Gerald L. Gutek, *A History of the Western Educational Experience* (Prospect Heights, Ill.: Waveland Press, 1987), pp. 43–45.

itics, ethics, and history. The teacher was important in Isocrates' method of rhetorical education because he had to be capable of influencing his students through his own demonstration of knowledge, skill, and ethical conduct.

Although Isocrates opposed the Sophists' crass opportunism, he also rejected the Platonic perspective that education was purely speculative and abstract. For Isocrates, education had objectives that led to public service because informed action was based on and guided by knowledge.

Influence on Roman education

An effective and methodological educator, Isocrates contributed to the rhetorical tradition in education. He had a direct influence on the Roman theorists Cicero and Quintilian. By recognizing the humanistic dimension of rhetorical study, Isocrates contributed to the ideal of the liberally educated man.

The Greek Contribution to Western Education

Western culture and education inherited a rich legacy from ancient Greece. It included the following:

1. A profound conviction of the possibility of achieving human excellence
2. The idea that education had civic purposes related to the political well-being of the community
3. A distinction between liberal education and vocational training, which has led to curricular controversies throughout Western educational history
4. The legacy of the Socratic method, by which skilled teachers might use dialectical processes to ask universal questions relating to truth, goodness, and beauty

EDUCATION IN ANCIENT ROME

While the Greeks were developing their concepts of culture and education in the eastern Mediterranean, the Romans were consolidating their political position on the Italian peninsula and throughout the western Mediterranean. In their growth from small republic to great empire, the Romans first were preoccupied with war and politics. After they had created their empire, they concentrated on the administration, law, and diplomacy needed to maintain it. The Greeks were concerned with speculative philosophy; the Romans were most interested in educating the practical politician and able administrator.

War and politics

Access to education

As was true in ancient Greece, only a minority of the citizens of Rome received a formal education. Attendance at school was not a possibility for most children. Schooling was reserved for those who had both the money to pay the tuition and the time to attend school. As was true of Western history until the late nineteenth century, children of the Roman lower socioeconomic classes were used as workers. Although there were exceptions, the children of Rome's large slave population were trained to perform certain tasks rather than given an education that contributed to literacy.[21]

---

[21]Peter A. Brunt, "Work and Slavery in Rome," in Allan Mitchell and Istvan Deak, eds., *Everyman*

While girls might learn to read and write at home, boys from upper-class families attended a primary school, called a *ludus,* and secondary schools taught by teachers of Latin and Greek grammar. Boys were escorted to these schools by educated Greek slaves, called *pedagogues,* from which the term *pedagogy,* or art of instruction, is derived.

The Roman educational ideal was exemplified by a concept of oratory similar to that held by Isocrates. The Roman orator was the broadly and liberally educated man of public life — the senator, lawyer, teacher, civil servant, and politician. Cicero and Quintilian are important examples.

Cicero: Master Orator

Practical and liberal education

The distinguished Roman senator Cicero (106–43 B.C.) had himself studied both Greek and Latin grammar and literature, history, and rhetoric. He appreciated both the established Roman stress on practicality and utility and the Greek emphasis on humanistic and liberal culture. His work *de Oratore* combined the Roman and Greek conceptions of the educated man.[22] In the Roman context, the practical results of oratory were winning debates and arguments in the Forum. Cicero added the Greek perspective of rhetorical education, which stressed broad and liberal culture, or **humanitas**. Cicero recommended that the orator, as a rational man, should be educated in the liberal arts and should use his education in the public interest. Commenting on the education that was preparatory to rhetoric, Cicero also prescribed the role of the *grammaticus,* the secondary school teacher. The *grammaticus* was to comment on the poets, teach history, correct diction and delivery, and explain the meaning of language. Although Greek was the medium of instruction, the young Roman boy was also to be adept in using his own language, Latin.

Importance of history

After the prospective orator had been prepared adequately in grammar, he went on to the higher studies. Like Isocrates, Cicero believed that the humanistically educated orator should be prepared thoroughly in the liberal arts — ethics, psychology, military science, medicine, natural science, geography, astronomy, history, law, and philosophy. In particular, Cicero believed that the great orator needed a knowledge of history to provide a perspective on his own past and tradition. Students were to study the speeches of great statesmen and the ancient Roman Laws of the Twelve Tables. Cicero's emphasis on the Laws of the Twelve Tables revealed his desire to preserve the ethical principles of republican Rome as the basis of moral education. These laws covered one's duties to honor parents, to respect property, and to serve the state. Effective speakers also needed to be versed in philosophy, which then included psychology, ethics, politics, and logic.

Emphasis on rhetoric

Upon the broad framework of the liberal arts, the orator then studied rhetoric. As a public speaker, the orator had to select his words with care so that he could structure his arguments persuasively. He needed to use psychology to excite the emotions of his audience and to influence public affairs. The orator needed to be quick intellectually; he needed to be versatile in using various

---

in Europe: Essays in Social History, vol. 1 (Englewood Cliffs, N.J.: Prentice-Hall, 1981), pp. 25–29.

[22]Neal Wood, *Cicero's Social and Political Thought* (Berkeley: University of California Press, 1988).

speaking styles and types of argument. Cicero also believed that oratory was a functional study that could actively influence public opinion and shape state policy. The word *humanitas,* which signifies all that is worthy in an individual as a humane and intelligent being, best expresses his ideal of the educated man.[23]

Quintilian: Teacher of Rhetoric

Marcus Fabius Quintilianus, or Quintilian (A.D. 35–95), worked in Rome as a legal assistant. It was as a teacher of rhetoric, however, that he gained the fame that led to his appointment as holder of the first chair of Latin rhetoric. As the foremost Roman rhetorician, Quintilian served emperors. Cicero had written when Rome was a republic; Quintilian's program of oratorical education reflected the political realities of imperial Rome, which was ruled by decree rather than by group decisions shaped by oratorical argument.[24] Unlike Cicero, who served in Rome's Senate, Quintilian was primarily a teacher whose chief involvement was with education. Nevertheless, both Quintilian and Cicero believed that the orator should be a man of *humanitas,* of liberal disposition and culture.

Quintilian's *Institutio Oratoria,* appearing in A.D. 96, was a systematic educational work that dealt with education preparatory to the study of rhetoric, rhetorical theories and studies, and the practice of public speaking or declamation. Quintilian recognized that instruction should be based on the stages of human growth and development. In the first stage, from birth until age seven, the child was impulsive and concerned with immediately satisfying needs and desires. Since the early childhood years established later attitudes and values, parents were to select well-trained nurses, pedagogues, and companions for their children. It was very important that the future orator should have a Greek nurse and pedagogue who used correct speech and pronunciation so that good language usage became habitual to the student.

Stages of growth

In Quintilian's second stage of education, from seven to fourteen, the child learned from sense experiences, formed clear ideas, and exercised his memory. Now he wrote the languages that he already spoke. The reading and writing instructor, the *litterator,* was to be of good character *and* a competent teacher. Instruction in reading and writing was to be slow but thorough. The school should include games and recreation. A set of ivory letters was to aid in learning the alphabet. By tracing the outline of the letters, the child learned writing.

Reading and writing

In the third stage of education, from fourteen to seventeen, Quintilian stressed the study of the liberal arts with the *grammaticus* in the secondary school. Both Greek and Latin grammars were to be studied concurrently. Grammar involved Greek and Roman literature, history, and mythology. Students also studied music, geometry, astronomy, and gymnastics. After grammar and the liberal arts, the prospective orator began rhetorical studies, which constituted the fourth stage of education, covering ages seventeen to twenty-one.

Study of liberal arts

---

[23]*Cicero on the Good Life,* trans. Michael Grant (New York: Penguin, 1979).

[24]Edward J. Power, *A Legacy of Learning: A History of Western Education* (Albany: State University of New York Press, 1991), pp. 86–92.

Overview 3.2 ◀━▶

Major Educational Theorists, to A.D. 1600

Theorist	Philosophical Orientation	View of Human Nature	Views on Education and Curriculum	Contribution and Influence
Socrates 469–399 B.C. (Greek)	Social and educational iconoclast; tended toward philosophical idealism and political conservatism	Human beings can define themselves by rational self-examination	Use of a probing intellectual dialogue to answer basic human concerns; education should cultivate moral excellence	The Socratic dialogue as a teaching method; teacher as a role model
Plato 427–346 B.C. (Greek)	Philosophical idealist; sociopolitical conservative	Human beings can be classified on the basis of their intellectual capabilities	Music, gymnastics, geometry, astronomy, basic literary skills; philosophy for ruling elite of philosopher-kings	Use of schools for sorting students according to intellectual abilities; education tied to civic (political) purposes; basis of "Great Books" curriculum
Aristotle 384–322 B.C. (Greek)	Philosophical realist; view of society, politics, and education based on classical realism	Human beings have the power of rationality, which should guide their conduct	Objective and scientific emphasis; basic literary skills, mathematics, natural and physical sciences, philosophy	Emphasis on liberally educated, well-rounded person; importance of reason; basis of "Great Books" curriculum
Isocrates 436–388 B.C. (Greek)	Rhetorician; oratorical education in service of self and society	Men have the power of using their speech (discourse) for social and political improvement	Rhetorical studies; basic literary skills; politics, history, rhetoric, declamation, public speaking	Use of knowledge in public affairs and in political leadership; teacher education having both a content and a practice dimension
Cicero 106–43 B.C. (Roman)	Rhetorician; oratory as an instrument of humane culture and civic competency	Certain persons, namely orators, have the capacity to be liberally educated, humane, and skilled speakers	Arts and sciences, especially history; rhetoric	Emphasis on civic education or public service

Quintilian identified rhetorical studies as drama, poetry, history, law, philosophy, and rhetoric itself.[25]

Declamations — systematic speaking exercises — were of great importance for the orator. The themes of the declamations were factual rather than fictitious. If students proved incapable of oratory they were dismissed, so as not to waste the teacher's time and energy. As soon as possible, the novice orator spoke in the Forum before an audience and then returned to the master rhetorician for expert criticism. The teacher was to correct the student's mistakes with a sense of authority but also with patience, tact, and consideration.

For Quintilian, oratorical perfection depended on the speaker's own moral excellence.[26] To persuade, the orator had to be trustworthy. Quintilian's signifi-

---

[25]William M. Smail, *Quintilian on Education,* rev. ed. (New York: Teachers College Press, Columbia University, 1966).

[26]Alan Brinton, "Quintilian, Plato, and the Vir Bonus," *Philosophy and Rhetoric* (Winter 1983), pp. 167–184.

Theorist	Philosophical Orientation	View of Human Nature	Views on Education and Curriculum	Contribution and Influence
Quintilian A.D. 35–95 (Roman)	Rhetorician; oratory for personal gain and public service	Certain individuals have capacity for leadership, based on humane disposition, liberal knowledge, and oratorical skill	Basic literary skills; grammar, history, literature, drama, philosophy, public speaking, law	Role of motivation in learning; recognition of individual differences
Aquinas A.D. 1225–1274 (Italian medieval theologian)	Christian theology and Aristotelian (realist) philosophy	Human beings possess both a spiritual nature (soul) and physical nature (body)	Education should be based on human nature, with appropriate studies for both spiritual and physical dimensions	Teacher as moral agent; education related to universal theological goals; synthesis of the theological and philosophical; basis of philosophy used in Roman Catholic schools
Erasmus A.D. 1465–1536 (Dutch Renaissance humanist)	Christian orientation; the educator as social and intellectual critic	Human beings are capable of great achievements but also of profound stupidity	Education for a literary elite that stressed criticism and analysis	Role of secondary and higher education in literary and social criticism; emphasis on critical thinking
Luther A.D. 1483–1546 (German Protestant)	Reformed theology stressing salvation by faith and individual conscience	Human beings are saved by faith; individual conscience shaped by Scripture and Reformed theology	Elementary schools to teach reading, writing, arithmetic, religion; secondary schools to prepare leaders by offering classics, Latin, Greek, and religion; vocational training	Emphasis on universal literacy; schools to stress religious values, vocational skills, knowledge; close relationship of religion, schooling, and the state

Instruction appropriate to the learner's abilities

cance in Western educational history lies in his attention to the theory and practice of teaching and learning. In anticipating the modern teacher's concern for the learner's individual differences, he advised that instruction be made appropriate to the learner's abilities and readiness. He also recommended that the teacher motivate students by making learning interesting and attractive.

The Roman Contribution to Western Education

Many of the cultural and educational structures that shaped Western civilization developed in the Roman republic and empire. Among them were the following:

1. An emphasis on training administrators and civil servants who could maintain the political infrastructure of a vast and diverse empire
2. A pragmatic propensity to translate theories into practices

3. An institutionalization of informal educational practices into more formal school arrangements

4. The practice of cultural and educational borrowing and readaptation, which reached a high point in Rome's selective use of Greek philosophy and education

INFLUENCE OF ARABIC LEARNING ON WESTERN EDUCATION

Arabic learning

In the tenth and eleventh centuries, Arabic learning had a pronounced influence on Western educational development, particularly on the evolution of medieval scholasticism (the philosophy underlying medieval thought and higher learning). From contact with Arab scholars (the Moors) in North Africa and Spain, Western educators learned new ways of thinking about mathematics, natural science, medicine, and philosophy. For example, important Arabic advances in medical theory and practice were introduced to the medieval university of Salerno in Italy. The Arabic number system had a particularly dramatic influence: it became the basis of Western arithmetic. Arab scholars also preserved and translated into Arabic the works of such important Greek thinkers as Aristotle, Euclid, Galen, and Ptolemy. Because many of these works had disappeared from Europe by the Middle Ages, they might have been lost to European culture forever if the Arabs had not kept them alive.

Preservation of Greek works

Arabic scholarship and science stemmed from the earlier religious movement led by Mohammed (569–632), who developed the Islamic theological framework. United by a missionary zeal to spread the Islamic religion, Arabic scholars carried their culture and their ideas about education throughout North Africa, as far east as India, and as far west as Spain.[27] Because of their extensive conquests, the Arabs came into contact with a wide variety of peoples and cultures—Hindus, Egyptians, Syrians, and others. Although religious purists, they incorporated elements from these cultures into their own civilization. Along with the Islamic faith and the Arabic language, Arab culture also embraced literature, science, philosophy, and architecture. Under the influence of religious leaders, Arabic higher schools were established at Baghdad, Cairo, Córdoba, Grenada, Toledo, and Seville.

Arab scholars—Avicenna and Averroës

In time, a division developed among the Arabs. Whereas some were fundamentalist believers, others were more inclined to philosophy. The more philosophical of them, scholars such as Avicenna (980–1037) and Averroës (1126–1198), had an impact on Western European education. Avicenna, who believed that philosophy could illuminate and enrich religious experience, encountered Aristotle's texts and translated them into Arabic. Although Western European educators were familiar with Aristotle's logic, his philosophical texts were presumed to be lost. When European Scholastic educators encountered Avicenna's translations of Aristotle, they in turn translated them into Latin. Averroës, a physician in Córdoba, was also a translator of and a commentator on Aristotle.

---

[27]See Henry Munson, *Islam and Revolution in the Middle East* (New Haven: Yale University Press, 1988).

An original thinker, Averroës wrote treatises on medicine, astronomy, and philosophy. Keenly interested in education, Averroës believed that teachers should seek to find the truth and transmit it to their students.

Arab contributions to education

The influence of Arabic scholarship on Western thought is a prime example of the frequent cross-cultural transference of educational ideas. Through their advances in mathematics and science and their preservation of classical Greek texts, the Arabs not only contributed to their own educational system but also partially determined the future course of European and American education.[28]

MEDIEVAL CULTURE AND EDUCATION

The years between the fall of Rome and the Renaissance (c. 500–1400) have been labeled the Middle Ages, or the medieval period. This era of Western culture and education began at the end of the ancient classical period of Greece and Rome and ended at the beginning of the modern era. The medieval period was characterized first by a decline in learning and then by a revival by the Scholastic educators.[29] In the absence of centralized political authorities, the medieval order of life, society, and education was brought to a synthesis and unified by the Roman Catholic church, headed by the pope in Rome.

Decline, then revival in learning

Places of learning

During this period, European education took place at elementary parish, chantry, and monastic schools conducted under church auspices. At the secondary level, both monastic and cathedral schools offered a curriculum of general studies. Schools that provided basic education as well as training for a trade were also maintained by the merchant and craft guilds. Knights received their training in military tactics and the chivalric code in the palaces.[30] The rise of the medieval university merits attention because together with the flowering of Scholastic education, it was the major contribution to education during this period.

Formal education

As was true of the earlier Greek and Roman eras, only a small minority of the population attended school and received a formal education in the medieval period. Schools were attended primarily by persons planning to enter religious life as priests, monks, or other orders of clerics. The vast majority of people were serfs who were required to serve as agricultural workers on the estates of feudal lords. The large class of serfs was uneducated in the formal sense and was generally illiterate.

Education of medieval women

The condition of women in medieval society was mixed in terms of their status and educational opportunities. Although medieval Christianity stressed the spiritual equality of women and the sacramental nature of marriage, women were consigned to prescribed roles. For the vast serf and peasant classes of agricultural poor, women's roles were the traditional ones of household chores and child-rearing. Girls of the peasant classes learned their future roles by imitating their mothers. Women of the noble classes also followed the prescriptions

---

[28]Daniel G. Bates and Amal Rassam, *Peoples and Cultures of the Middle East* (Englewood Cliffs, N.J.: Prentice-Hall, 1982), pp. 29–57.

[29]John Van Engen, "The Christian Middle Ages as an Historiographical Problem," *American Historical Review* (June 1986), pp. 532–537.

[30]Nicholas Orme, *From Childhood to Chivalry: The Education of the English Kings and Aristocracy, 1066–1530* (New York: Methuen, 1984).

of their class and learned the roles accorded them by the code of chivalry, which often meant managing the domestic life of the castle or manor.[31]

As was true for men, the medieval church provided an institutional opportunity for the education of women through religious communities or convents. Convents, like monasteries, had libraries and schools to prepare nuns to follow the religious rules of their communities.

Aquinas: Scholastic Education

A method of inquiry and teaching

By the eleventh century, medieval educators had developed **scholasticism** — a method of inquiry, scholarship, and teaching.[32] The Scholastics, as the teaching clerics were called, relied on faith and reason as complementary sources of truth. They accepted the sacred Scriptures and the writings of the church fathers as sources of God's revealed word and also trusted in human reason. The Scholastics believed that the human mind could deduce first principles that, when illuminated by scriptural authority, were a source of truth.[33] When the Scholastics encountered the works of Aristotle and other Greek philosophers that came to them from Arabic scholars, they faced the problem of reconciling philosophical and theological principles.

Scholastic philosophy and education reached its zenith in the *Summa Theologica* of Saint Thomas Aquinas (1225–1274), a Dominican theologian who taught at the University of Paris.[34] Aquinas was primarily concerned with reconciling the authority of faith as represented by the Scriptures with the authority of Greek rationalism as represented by Aristotle. Aquinas used both faith and reason to answer basic questions dealing with the Christian concept of God, the nature of humankind and the universe, and the relationship between God and human beings. In Aquinas's view, human beings possess a physical body and a spiritual soul. Although they live temporarily on earth, their ultimate purpose is to experience eternity with God. Like Aristotle, Aquinas asserted that human knowledge of the world originates in sensation and is completed by abstraction or concept formation.

Relationship between God and human beings

In *De Magistro (Concerning the Teacher)*, Aquinas discussed the teacher's vocation as one that combines faith, love, and learning. The teacher needs to be a contemplative scholar, an active agent of learning, a master of his discipline, and a lover of humanity. The teacher needs to know subject matter thoroughly and also to be expert in the method of teaching it. Aquinas and the other Scholastic educators saw no conflict between research and teaching. The good teacher needs to do both and do them well so that teaching and scholarship are carefully blended.

The teachers in Scholastic schools were clerics, and the schools were governed and protected by the church. Teaching was organized by formal subject-

[31]See Joel T. Rosenthal, ed., *Medieval Women and the Sources of Medieval History* (Athens, Ga.: University of Georgia Press, 1990), and Mary Erler and Maryanne Kowsaleski, *Women and Power in the Middle Ages* (Athens, Ga.: University of Georgia Press, 1988).
[32]Frederick B. Artz, *The Mind of the Middle Ages, A.D. 200–1500* (Chicago: University of Chicago Press, 1980).
[33]Anders Pilitz, *The World of Medieval Learning* (Totowa, N.J.: Barnes & Noble, 1981).
[34]John W. Donohue, *St. Thomas Aquinas and Education* (New York: Random House, 1968).

Subject-matter disciplines

matter disciplines, following the liberal arts tradition; for example, in higher education the subject disciplines were logic, mathematics, natural and moral philosophy, metaphysics, and theology. Within such disciplines, Scholastic teachers used the syllogism — a form of deductive reasoning — to accumulate an ordered body of demonstrated knowledge. The teacher aided the student in recognizing basic principles and their implications. In addition to this formal schooling, Aquinas recognized the role of informal education in a student's life. Informal education involved *all* the agencies, such as family, friends, and environment, that developed a person's virtue or excellence.[35]

Medieval Universities

The work of Aquinas and other Scholastic educators centered about the medieval university, which established the basic patterns of higher education. The famous medieval universities of Paris, Salerno, Bologna, Oxford, Cambridge, and Padua grew out of the intellectual revival of the twelfth and thirteenth centuries.[36] It is believed that the major universities evolved from the expanding enrollments of the cathedral schools, which by the twelfth century were unable to accommodate the growing number of students. The universities evolved from associations, called *universitas,* which the students and teachers organized for their own security. Enrollment had increased because of the improved economic conditions stimulated by the Crusades. Crusaders had come into contact with Byzantine Greek and Arabic scholarship, which was then brought back to western Europe. As mentioned earlier, the medieval educators discovered the works of Aristotle, Euclid, Ptolemy, Galen, and Hippocrates through the Byzantine and Arab scholars.[37] Theological interpretation and investigation of these newly discovered works were of major interest to the Scholastics, especially at the University of Paris, where Thomas Aquinas attempted to reconcile Aristotle's rationalism with the Scriptures and doctrines of Christianity.

Intellectual revival

Because the authority of Scriptures and church teaching was considered a primary component of knowledge, the most important subjects in the medieval university were theological. But a high level of scholarship also developed in secular disciplines. The medieval universities established specialized professional schools of law, medicine, and theology in addition to the liberal arts curriculum. The University of Bologna in Italy and the University of Paris in France represented two distinctive patterns of institutional organization in higher education — the former was shaped by students; the latter, by faculty.

Professional schools

Other universities were established throughout Europe between the twelfth and fifteenth centuries: in Italy, the University of Padua and the University of Naples; in France, the universities of Montpellier, Orleans, and Toulouse; in England, Oxford University, and Cambridge University a hundred years later. By the fourteenth century, Europe had the Scottish universities of St. Andrew and

---

[35]Ibid., pp. 76–89.

[36]See Hastings Rashdall, *The Universities of Europe in the Middle Ages,* 3 vols., ed. R. M. Powicke and A. B. Emden (Oxford: Oxford University Press, 1936). Also see Stephen C. Ferruolo, *The Origins of the University: The Schools of Paris and Their Critics, 1100–1215* (Stanford, Calif.: Stanford University Press, 1985).

[37]A. P. Kazhdan and Ann Wharton Epstein, *Change in Byzantine Culture in the Eleventh and Twelfth Centuries* (Berkeley: University of California Press, 1985).

Forerunners of our modern institutions of higher learning, the medieval universities established specialized professional schools, such as the school of medicine shown in this rather humorous illustration. (© Bildarchiv Preussischer Kulturbesitz)

Aberdeen, the Spanish university of Salamanca, and the German universities of Erfurt, Heidelberg, and Cologne. There were also universities in Vienna and Prague.

The Medieval Contribution to Western Education

The medieval contribution to Western education primarily resulted from the institutionalization and preservation of knowledge. Parish, monastic, and cathedral schools were places of learning in which knowledge was transmitted in an organized, formal, and institutionalized framework. The epitome of such institutionalization was the medieval university, which served as the model for the modern university. In addition to institutionalizing knowledge, medieval centers of learning preserved it by recording and codifying it.

RENAISSANCE CLASSICAL HUMANISM

Revival in humanism and classics

The Renaissance, beginning in the fourteenth century and reaching its height in the fifteenth century, witnessed a marked revival of interest in the humanistic aspects of the Greek and Latin classics. It is considered a period of transition between the medieval and modern ages. The Renaissance scholar of **classical humanism,** like the medieval Scholastic, found his authorities in the past and stressed classical manuscripts. Unlike the Scholastics, the humanist educators were interested more in the earthly experience of human beings than in a God-centered world view.[38]

The effects of the Renaissance were particularly noticeable in Italy, where the revival of commerce had produced a financial surplus that fostered art, literature, and architecture. Wealth, flowing into the prosperous Italian cities, supported humanist educators and schools. The Italian classical humanists, considering themselves an aristocratic literary elite, were self-proclaimed "custodians of knowledge." In keeping with the spirit of the age, rulers in the Italian city-states established court schools to prepare their children in the new learning.

Classical humanists

The literary birth of the Italian Renaissance came with the works of Dante, Petrarch, and Boccaccio. Rejecting Scholastic techniques, the classical humanist writers and educators rediscovered Cicero and Quintilian. In the ancient classics of Greek and Rome, the humanist educators found models of literary excellence and style, the ideal of the educated person, and a view of life based on the wisdom of antiquity.

Challenge to scholasticism

Classical humanist education challenged the older Scholastic model. The cleric, trained in Scholastic logic, was no longer the preferred model of the educated man. In the Renaissance, the courtier became the model. The courtier was a man of style and elegance; he was liberally educated in classical literature; he was a capable diplomat and could serve his ruler well in the affairs of state. Baldesar Castiglione (1478–1529) described the courtier and his education in a famous work, *The Book of the Courtier.*[39]

Educated courtier

In northern Europe as well, classical humanist scholars began to critically examine the Scriptures and theological writing. They considered Scholastic education to be in a state of decay. Educators now sought to develop teaching methods and materials designed to produce the well-rounded, liberally educated courtier. The most suitable curriculum was classical Greek and Latin literature. The imitation of Cicero's style of writing would cultivate the elegance of style and expression needed by the cultured gentleman. An examination of the teaching style of Erasmus of Rotterdam provides an example of the northern Renaissance humanist educator.

Erasmus: Critic and Reformer

Desiderius Erasmus (1465–1536), who was born in the city of Rotterdam in the Netherlands, was educated in the schools of the Brethren of the Common Life and studied scholastic philosophy at the University of Paris. *The Praise of Folly* is his best-known book of a general nature.[40] Erasmus's writings reveal his interest in literary criticism and social reform. His contribution to Western education was that of a critic of contemporary institutions, a humanist educator, and an advocate of cosmopolitan humanism.

---

[38]De Lamar Jensen, *Renaissance Europe: Age of Recovery and Reconciliation* (Lexington, Mass.: D. C. Heath, 1981), pp. 103–113.

[39]Baldesar Castiglione, *The Book of the Courtier,* trans. C. S. Singleton (New York: Doubleday, 1959).

[40]William H. Woodward, *Desiderius Erasmus Concerning the Aim and Method of Education,* rev. ed. (New York: Teachers College Press, Columbia University, 1964).

Getting to the Source

A Renaissance Humanist's View /
Desiderius Erasmus

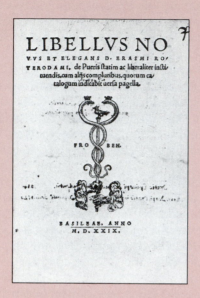

Desiderius Erasmus (1465–1536) was one of the leading humanist educators of the Renaissance. During an era that saw both the revival of classical

learning and rising sectarian conflicts, Erasmus, seeking a middle course, argued for cosmopolitan humanism. In the following selections, from his De Pueris Instituendis, *he describes the evil conditions of schooling in some schools during the Renaissance and comments on the character of the teacher.*

THE EVIL CONDITION OF THE SCHOOLS, ESPECIALLY THE PRIVATE SCHOOLS, IN THE PRESENT DAY

What shall we say then of the type of school too common at the present time? A boy scarce four years old is sent to school to a master about whose qualifications for the work no one knows anything. Often he is a man of uncouth manners, not always sober; maybe he is an invalid, or crippled, or even mentally deficient. Anyone is good enough to put over the grammar school in popular opinion. Such a man, finding himself clothed with an unlooked for and unaccustomed authority, treats his charges as we should expect. The school is, in effect, a torture chamber; blows and shouts, sobs and howls, fill the air. Then it is wondered that the growing boy hates learning; and that in riper years he hates it still. . . .

The Praise of Folly shows Erasmus to be a satirical critic of the professions and institutions of his day. He criticized the teachers of grammar for stressing obscure facts and for ignoring the important aspects of learning while emphasizing trivialities that only confused students. Philosophers, Erasmus charged, were concerned only with the most abstract speculations. Theologians, too, felt the jab of Erasmus's pen. Instead of examining the basic relationship of human beings with God, the doctors of theology were busily spinning subtle corollaries to demonstrate their own erudition. Erasmus, like Socrates, delighted in deflating the puffed-up egos of those who considered themselves to be exalted men of wisdom.

Erasmus was the leading classical scholar of the late Renaissance. Concerning the teaching of classical languages, he advised that the teacher should be well acquainted with archeology, astronomy, etymology, history, and Scripture because these areas were related to the study of classical literature. Recognizing the importance of early childhood, Erasmus recommended that the child's education begin as early as possible. Parents were to take their educational responsibilities seriously. Children should receive gentle instruction in good

Early childhood education

THE DISPOSITION OF THE TEACHER

Seeing, then, that children in the earliest stage must be beguiled and not driven to learning, the first requisite in the Master is a gentle sympathetic manner, the second a knowledge of wise and attractive methods. Possessing these two important qualifications he will be able to win the pupil to find pleasure in his task. It is a hindrance to a boy's progress, which nothing will ever nullify, when the master succeeds in making his pupil hate learning before he is old enough to like it for its own sake. For a boy is often drawn to a subject first for his master's sake, and afterwards for its own. Learning, like many other things, wins our liking for the reason that it is offered to us by one we love. But, on the other hand, there is a type of man of manners so uncouth, of expression so forbidding, of speech so surly, that he repels even when he by no means intends it. Now men of that stamp are wholly unfit to be teachers of children; a man who loves his horse would hardly put such a man to have charge of his stable. Yet there are parents who think such a temper as I have described well adapted to breaking in the young child, thinking, perhaps, that seriousness of that sort betokens a proper gravity. Therein may lie a great error, inasmuch as that demeanour may cloak a depraved nature, which, delighting in tyranny, cows and breaks the spirit of the pupil. *Fear is of no real avail in education:* not even parents can train their children by this motive. Love must be the first influence; followed and completed by a trustful and affectionate respect, which compels obedience far more surely than dread can ever do.

Questions

1. According to Erasmus, what are some of the evil conditions that were found in schools in the early sixteenth century?

2. Although he is arguing for improved conditions in schooling, how was Erasmus insensitive to issues of handicapping condition?

3. What does Erasmus identify as desirable characteristics of the teacher?

Source: William Harrison Woodward, *Desiderius Erasmus Concerning the Aim and Method of Education* (New York: Teachers College, Columbia University, 1964), pp. 203–204. Copyright © 1964 by Teachers College, Columbia University. Reprinted by permission of the publisher. All rights reserved.

manners and hear stories that had a beneficial effect on the development their characters.

Erasmus believed that understanding content was more important t mastering style and grammar. Students should understand the content t oughly; conversation in the language would make learning interesting. Gan. and contests were also to be encouraged. Erasmus's concern for content and not just for style is clearly seen in his discussion of teaching methods. The teacher *Teaching methods* of language, he recommended, should (1) present the author's biography, (2) examine the type of work under study, (3) discuss the basic plot, (4) analyze the author's style, (5) consider the moral implications of the work, and (6) explain the broader philosophical issues raised by the work.

The Renaissance's Contribution to Western Education

Study of Latin Most significantly, Renaissance humanists emphasized the study of Latin as the hallmark of the educated person. To be educated meant to have learned

Overview 3.3

Significant Events in the History of Western Education, to A.D. 1600

Period	Political and Social Events		Significant Educational Events	
Greek	1200 B.C.	Trojan War	c. 1200 B.C.	Homer's *Iliad* and *Odyssey*
	594 B.C.	Athenian constitutional reforms		
	479–338 B.C.	Golden Age of Greek (Athenian) culture		
	445–431 B.C.	Age of Pericles		
	431–404 B.C.	Peloponnesian War between Athens and Sparta		
			399 B.C.	Trial of Socrates
			395 B.C.	Plato's *Republic*
			392 B.C.	School established by Isocrates in Athens
			387 B.C.	Academy founded by Plato
	336–323 B.C.	Alexander the Great	330 B.C.	Aristotle's *Politics*
	146 B.C.	Rome conquers Greece		
Roman	753 B.C.	Traditional date of Rome's founding		
	510 B.C.	Roman republic established	449 B.C.	References appear to the existence of Latin schools, or *ludi*
	272 B.C.	Rome dominates Italian peninsula		
	146 B.C.	Greece becomes Roman province	167 B.C.	Greek grammar school opened in Rome
	49–44 B.C.	Dictatorship of Julius Caesar	55 B.C.	Cicero's *de Oratore*
	31 B.C.	Roman empire begins	A.D. 96	Quintilian's *Institutio Oratoria*
	A.D. 476	Fall of Rome in the West		
Medieval	713	Arab conquest of Spain		
	800	Charlemagne crowned Holy Roman Emperor		
	1096–1291	Crusades to the Holy Land	1079–1142	Abelard, author of *Sic et Non*
	1182–1226	St. Francis of Assisi	1180	University of Paris granted papal charter and recognition

classical languages and studied classical literature. For centuries, these classical humanist preferences would both shape and confine secondary and higher education. In Europe and in the United States, knowledge of Latin was required for admission to many colleges and universities until the end of the nineteenth century.

Erasmus and other Renaissance educators were moving slowly to a humanistic, or human-centered, conception of knowledge.[41] Rather than approaching their human subject as an object of scientific inquiry, the humanist educators preferred to deal with it indirectly through literature. The educated person was defined as one who acquired classical knowledge through books. The later pedagogical reforms of Rousseau, Comenius, Pestalozzi, and Dewey (discussed in Chapter 4) were directed against schools that gave exclusive emphasis to the study of literature, while neglecting experience.

Absence of scientific inquiry

---

[41]Gutek, *A History of the Western Educational Experience,* pp. 99–103.

Period	Political and Social Events		Significant Educational Events	
			1209	University of Cambridge founded
			1225–1274	Thomas Aquinas, author of *Summa Theologica*
	1295	Explorations of Marco Polo		
Renaissance	1304–1374	Petrarch, author of odes and sonnets		
	1313–1375	Boccaccio, founder of Italian vernacular literature		
	1384	Founding of Brethren of the Common Life		
	1393–1464	Cosimo de' Medici encourages revival of art and learning in Florence	1428	Da Feltre, classical humanist educator, established court school at Mantua
	1423	Invention of printing	1507–1589	Sturm, creator of gymnasiums in Germany
	1456	First book printed		
	1492	Columbus arrives in America	1509	Erasmus's *The Praise of Folly*
Reformation	1517	Luther posts Ninety-five Theses calling for church reform		
	1509–1564	John Calvin, Protestant reformer, founder of Calvinism	1524	Luther's "Letter . . . in Behalf of Christian Schools"
	1509–1547	King Henry VIII of England, founder of the Church of England	1524	Melanchthon, an associate of Luther, organizes Lutheran schools in German states
	1540	Jesuit order founded by Loyola		
	1545	Council of Trent launches Roman Catholic Counter Reformation	1630–1650	Calvinist schools organized in Scotland by John Knox

The Renaissance humanist educators were literary figures — writers, poets, and translators — as well as teachers. In many respects, they were artist-teachers, critics of taste and society as well as literature. Such persons brought a witty and penetrating mind to their work. In broad terms, the education advocated by the humanist produced a critical person who challenged existing customs and mediocrity in literature and in life.

But as artist-teachers the Renaissance humanists viewed their human subject with a sense of detachment. They kept a safe distance between themselves and humanity. Their conception of human nature was distilled from a carefully aged literature. As a vintage wine is used to grace a carefully prepared dinner, the humanist education was reserved for the connoisseur. Humanist education was not given to everyone but was reserved for an elite that could appreciate and savor it.

Elitist education

The invention of the printing press in 1423 made books and other printed materials more widely available and fostered the spread of literacy. But there was no large increase during the Renaissance in the numbers who attended

Printing press

school. Humanist secondary schools were primarily intended for children of the nobility and upper classes. Elementary schools served the needs of the commercial middle classes, and members of the lower classes received little, if any, formal schooling.

Women's education

The educational opportunities for women did improve slightly during the Renaissance, especially for the daughters of the upper classes. Girls of wealthy families might attend the humanist court school or receive private lessons. The curriculum pursued by young ladies of the upper classes still reflected the notion that certain studies were appropriate for their gender, such as art, music, needlework, dancing, and poetry. Convents and convent schools continued to educate a small minority of young women as they had in the medieval period. For the daughters of the working classes, especially the rural peasantry, education still consisted almost entirely of training in household duties.[42]

RELIGIOUS REFORMATION AND EDUCATION

The religious reformations of the sixteenth and seventeenth centuries were related to the northern European humanist criticism of institutional life and to the search for new authorities. In particular, as the new humanism began to replace the declining medieval scholasticism, there was a slow weakening of the central authority of the Catholic church and of its power to enforce authoritative religious doctrines. This situation paved the way for the expression of diverse religious opinions, which ultimately led to diverse claims about the legitimacy of teaching authority.[43]

Freedom from papal authority

The rise of the commercial middle classes and the concurrent rise of national states were important factors in the reformation movements. Primarily, however, the various Protestant religious reformers — such as John Calvin, Martin Luther, Philip Melanchthon, and Ulrich Zwingli — sought to free themselves and their followers from papal authority and to reconstruct religious doctrine and forms. These reformers, who were conversant with classical humanism, sought to develop educational philosophies and institutions that would support their religious reformations.[44]

Extension of mass literacy

The Protestant reformers reshaped educational philosophies and institutions. They developed their own educational theories, established their own schools, structured their own curricula, and convinced their children of the truth of the reformed creeds. The Protestant Reformation also extended literacy among the masses. Since most of the reformers insisted that the faithful should read the Bible in their own native tongue, the members of the various churches had to become literate. For Catholics, the Mass and other religious worship was still conducted in Latin rather than the vernacular languages; to compete with

[42]For a commentary on the emergence of women from educational restrictions during the Renaissance, see Katharina M. Wilson, ed., *Women Writers of the Renaissance and Reformation* (Athens, Ga.: University of Georgia Press, 1987).

[43]Alister McGrath, *The Intellectual Origins of the European Reformation* (New York: Basil Blackwell, 1987).

[44]Kenneth O. Gangel and Warren S. Benson, *Christian Education: Its History and Philosophy* (Chicago: Moody Press, 1983), pp. 135–151.

During the Renaissance, the curriculum pursued by young women of the upper classes reflected the notion that certain studies — such as art, music, needlework, dancing, and poetry — were appropriate for their gender. (© Giraudon/Art Resource, New York)

Protestants, however, Catholics also began to emphasize the vernacular language as well as Latin in schools.

Catechetical instruction

The Protestant reformers' commitment to defend the faith led to the use of the catechetical method of religious instruction. The catechism was an elementary book that summarized the principles of the Christian religion, as interpreted by the various denominations, into systematic questions and answers. It was believed that by memorizing the lessons in the catechism, students would internalize the principles of their religious faith. **Vernacular schools** (primary or elementary institutions that offered a basic curriculum of reading, writing, arithmetic, and religion) brought literacy to the lower classes by providing instruction in the community's own language. Vernacular schools in England, for example, used English as the language of instruction.

Attempt to increase school attendance

Unlike the historical periods that preceded it, the Protestant Reformation, with its emphasis on literacy, stimulated an increase in school attendance. Reformers encouraged both girls and boys to attend the primary vernacular schools. Accurate statistics are not available for school attendance or for the change in literacy rates. In fact, literacy is difficult to define in historical terms; in many instances, those who could merely sign their names were considered literate by their contemporaries. Nevertheless, estimates suggest that the Reformation era had a significant impact. According to one estimate, only 10 percent of the men and 2 percent of the women in England were literate (in the current meaning of the term) in the year 1500; by 1600 the percentages had risen to 28 for men and 9 for women; and by 1700 nearly 40 percent of English men and about 32 percent of English women were literate. Literacy rates were higher in

Literacy rates

Secondary schools

northern than in southern Europe, in urban as opposed to rural areas, and among the upper classes as compared to the lower classes.[45]

Despite the religious reformers' interest in widespread literacy, the prestigious preparatory and secondary schools remained the province of upper-class males. A variety of secondary schools were maintained to educate the sons of the upper classes in Latin and Greek. The gymnasium in Germany, the Latin grammar school in England, and the lycée in France were college preparatory schools that trained the leadership elite, particularly those who were to be clergymen, in the classical languages.

Although there were many strong personalities active during the Protestant Reformation and Roman Catholic Counter Reformation, special attention to the educational ideas of Martin Luther will exemplify the work of a major leader.

Luther: Advocate of Reform

Of the religious leaders of the era, Martin Luther (1483–1546) stands out as perhaps the most influential in shaping the history of Western civilization. Born and educated in Germany, Luther was awarded the Master of Arts in 1505 and then became an Augustinian monk. His intellectual brilliance brought him to the attention of the head of his religious order, and Luther was sent to Wittenberg to lecture on theology. In 1517 Luther nailed his famous Ninety-five Theses to the door of the castle church at Wittenberg. From this time on, Luther mounted a series of challenges to the Roman Catholic Church and the pope on matters dealing with indulgences, the sacraments, papal authority, and freedom of individual conscience. Luther's challenges stimulated great religious ferment and caused others to preach religious reform. The culmination of this ferment was the Protestant Reformation, which spread through western and northern Europe.

Educational and religious reformation

Luther, who had been a university professor, recognized that educational reform was a potent ally of religious reformation.[46] The church, state, family, and school were to be agents of reformation. The family, in particular, was an important agency in forming the character of children and in shaping values compatible with reformed Christian life. He admonished parents to teach their children reading and religion. Each family should pray together, read the Bible, study the catechism, and practice a useful trade. Once children had acquired the right values, they were ready to benefit from formal schooling. Luther believed that public officials needed to be made conscious of their educational responsibilities. His "Letter to the Mayors and Aldermen of All Cities of Germany in Behalf of Christian Schools" stressed the spiritual, material, and political benefits of schooling. Schools were to produce literate citizens and members of the church. They would prepare trained ministers to lead their flocks in the Reformed religion.

Luther on women's education

Luther's views of the social, religious, and educational status of women did not differ substantially from the medieval perspective. He believed that the husband, as the head of the household, had authority over his wife. Domestic duties

[45]Mary Jo Maynes, *Schooling in Western Europe: A Social History* (Albany: State University of New York Press, 1985).

[46]Marilyn J. Harran, ed., *Luther and Learning: The Wittenberg University Luther Symposium* (Cranbury, N.J.: Associated University Presses, 1985).

and child-rearing remained, in his view, the appropriate role for women. However, because of his emphasis on reading the Bible in one's own language, women, too, were afforded opportunities for elementary schooling. In turn, they had a shared, but subordinate, role in educating their children.

Vernacular schools

In implementing his educational reforms, Luther was assisted by Philip Melanchthon (1497–1560). Both wanted to end the monopoly of the Roman Catholic Church over formal schools. They looked to the state to supervise schools and to license teachers. In 1559 Melanchthon drafted the School Code of Würtemberg, which became a model for other German states. Vernacular schools were to be founded in every village to teach religion, reading, writing, arithmetic, and music. The classical secondary school, the gymnasium, was to provide instruction in the higher studies and the classical languages.

Even though Luther and Melanchthon argued for the establishment of elementary vernacular schools to teach reading, writing, and religion to the common people, they strongly believed that the Latin and Greek language curriculum patterned in the Renaissance was most appropriate to prepare the leaders of the church and state. Thus, the German gymnasium followed the basic pattern of humanist education, with the addition of Lutheran theology. It is especially important to note that the general effect of the Protestant Reformation on educational institutions was to fix firmly the **dual-track system of schools:** there was one set of schools for the common people and a second set of schools for the upper classes.

Reformation Views on Knowledge

Authority of the Bible

Luther, Melanchthon, Calvin, and the other Protestant reformers concerned themselves with questions of knowledge, education, and schooling because they wanted to use these powerful tools to advance the cause of Reformed theology. Although they differed in particular theological perspectives, they shared a number of educational ideas. On the question of the nature of knowledge, they emphasized the authority of the Christian Bible. Because they regarded Bible reading as necessary to gain salvation, the religious reformers emphasized literacy in the European vernacular languages. They favored universal schooling, to enable people to read the Bible and to make them useful citizens of the nation-state.

Since the reformers were deeply religious men, they emphasized religious education and values. Schooling was a means of indoctrinating the masses with religious tenets and values. The sixteenth and seventeenth centuries were times of fierce religious rivalries as the various Christian churches competed for adherents to their particular creeds. To achieve doctrinal conformity through schooling, teachers used the official catechisms prepared for that purpose. Through a question-and-answer approach, the teachers hoped to fix religious principles in the student's mind.

The Reformation's Contribution to Western Education

The educational consequences of the Protestant Reformation reconfirmed many institutional developments from the Renaissance, especially the dual-track system of schools. Vernacular schools, which provided primary instruction, were designed for the lower socioeconomic classes; the various classical humanist and

Latin grammar schools were preparatory for higher education. The colonists who settled in North America were transplanted Europeans who brought the dual structure of schools to the New World.

In addition to their adherence to the dual-track system of schools, the Protestant reformers bequeathed to Western education an emphasis on literacy. Luther, Calvin, and others related literacy to salvation. For many Protestants, Bible reading was a necessary feature of reformed Christianity. It was this emphasis on literacy that contributed ultimately to universal schooling.

INFLUENCE OF THE ENLIGHTENMENT ON WESTERN EDUCATION

As we examine the eighteenth-century Age of Enlightenment (also called the Age of Reason), we should keep in mind that our own governmental institutions are products of that era. The ideas of the Enlightenment influenced such major educational reformers as Rousseau, Pestalozzi, and Froebel. Although most of these reformers were European, their ideas were transplanted to the New World.

Reason and the scientific method

Foremost among the ideas of the Enlightenment was the supremacy of reason. The philosophers, scientists, and scholars of the Enlightenment clearly believed that it was possible for human beings to improve their lives and institutions by using their rational minds to solve problems. Using the scientific method, scientists of the day formulated "natural laws," which construed the universe as operating according to orderly processes. Philosophers and social reformers developed social theories as hypotheses for the investigation of society.[47] The ideas underlying the American and French revolutions were designed to reconstruct the political order according to the dictates of reason. These ideas implied that schools should cultivate the reasoning powers of their students.

Belief in progress

The learned men of the Enlightenment, such as Diderot, Rousseau, Franklin, and Jefferson, were committed to the view that humankind was progressing toward a new and a better world. No longer was it necessary to look backward to the "golden age" of Greece or Rome. If humankind followed reason and used the scientific method, it would be possible to have continual progress on this planet. Once again, the work of the schools would be to cultivate a questioning attitude, which meant a willingness to use scientific and empirical methods. Further, these methods were to be applied to the problems of human society.

Reforming society

As they sought to reform society, the Enlightenment theorists tried to create a new kind of education and a new pattern of schooling based on equality, individualism, civic responsibility, and intellectual reasoning. Enlightenment concepts were to have a significant influence on American education because the open environment of the New World permitted them to flourish. While the European nobility still rigidly defined human possibilities according to the ascriptions of birth, the American frontier acted to equalize these possibilities.

The ideas of the Enlightenment had their greatest impact on American education in the period after the American Revolution. In particular, Benjamin

[47]Margaret C. Jacob, *The Cultural Meaning of the Scientific Revolution* (New York: Alfred A. Knopf, 1988).

Franklin's emphasis on utilitarian and scientific education and Thomas Jefferson's stress on civic education were influenced by Enlightenment theories. In the twentieth century, the concept of "progress" that originated in the Enlightenment contributed to the progressive educational philosophy, which saw schooling as an instrument of social reform and improvement.

In the next chapter we examine the educational contributions of the major pioneers of education — beginning with those from the Enlightenment era.

Summing Up

1. We have examined in historical context questions about the nature of teaching and learning that were raised at the beginning of this chapter. What is knowledge? What is education? What is schooling? Who should attend school? How should teaching and learning be carried on? Often, the historical responses to these questions were incomplete, and the answers varied from time to time and place to place. Contemporary educators continue to examine and to answer these highly significant questions. Some seek to answer in universal terms, as did Plato; others to shape their answers to their changing perceptions of knowledge and the role of education.

2. Many elements of American education originated in European educational history. Although the relationship between education in preliterate societies and American society is remote, schooling throughout human history has involved the transmission of the cultural heritage from one generation to the next. This feature is common to both preliterate and modern education. In ancient Greece, the concepts of the educated person, of rational inquiry, and of freedom of thought were enunciated by Socrates, Plato, and Aristotle. The idea of rhetorical education was developed by the Sophists, refined by Isocrates, and further elaborated by the Roman rhetoricians Cicero and Quintilian.

3. During the medieval period, the foundations of the modern university were established at Bologna and Paris. Medieval education was influenced by mathematical and scientific contributions that entered the Western world by way of the Arabs. The classical humanist educators of the Renaissance developed the concept of the well-rounded, liberally educated person. With its emphasis on literacy and vernacular education, the Protestant Reformation had a direct impact on the schools established in colonial America. The ideas of the Enlightenment were especially influential in America after the Revolutionary War, but they continue to influence American education even today.

4. From the classical period of ancient Greece and Rome to the Protestant Reformation in the fifteenth century, only a minority of children received a formal education in schools. The majority of people were educated nonformally. Beginning with the Protestant Reformation, school attendance began to increase.

Key Terms

acculturation *(84)*	dialectic *(89)*
Sophists *(85)*	*humanitas (94)*
rhetoric *(85)*	scholasticism *(100)*
Socratic method *(87)*	classical humanism *(102)*
theory of reminiscence *(87)*	vernacular schools *(109)*
Plato's Republic *(88)*	dual-track system of schools *(111)*
metaphysics *(89)*	

Discussion Questions

1. What were the basic patterns of education in preliterate societies?

2. Explain the origin, development, and change of educational institutions and ideas in terms of the major historical periods highlighted in this chapter.

3. Reflect on the educational controversies that occurred in ancient Greece. Restate these issues in terms of their meaning for contemporary education.

4. How did Roman education borrow certain educational ideas from the Greek world and introduce them to the larger European context?

5. How did the bases of educational authority change from the medieval to the Reformation periods?

6. What were the differences between Renaissance and Enlightenment concepts of knowledge and education?

7. Who attended schools in the periods of history treated in this chapter? What conditions limited educational opportunities? In what ways do these limits exist today?

8. The Romans adapted Greek concepts, methodologies, and language to their educational system. In what ways is adaptation of "foreign" concepts positive or negative? How has this phenomenon occurred in education in the United States in recent years?

Suggested Readings

Chambliss, Joseph J. *Educational Theory as Theory of Conduct: From Aristotle to Dewey.* Albany: State University of New York Press, 1987.

> *The author analyzes the contributions of Aristotle, Cicero, Locke, Rousseau, Condillac, and others to educational theory.*

Gutek, Gerald L. *A History of the Western Educational Experience.* Prospect Heights, Ill.: Waveland Press, 1987.

> *The book describes and analyzes the historical development of educational ideas, institutions, and processes in Western civilization.*

Houston, R. A. *Literacy in Early Modern Europe: Culture and Education 1500–1800.* New York: Longman, 1988.

> *Houston examines the interrelationships between European education, literacy, and popular culture from 1500 to 1800, centering on the nature of education and schooling and the extent and uses of literacy (reading and writing) among the general population.*

Maynes, Mary Jo. *Schooling in Western Europe: A Social History.* Albany: State University of New York Press, 1985.

>   *The author examines the development of schools and school attendance as part of the new social history.*

Power, Edward J. *A Legacy of Learning: A History of Western Education.* Albany: State University of New York Press, 1991.

>   *Power examines the cultural and intellectual contexts of European and American educational history from the classical Greco-Roman eras to the twentieth century.*

Smith, L. Glenn. *Lives in Education: People and Ideas in the Development of Teaching.* Ames, Iowa: Educational Studies Press, 1984.

>   *Using the focusing themes of educational biography, Smith and other leading scholars in the history of education have produced a well-written and highly readable treatment of significant educational theorists.*

4

Pioneers in Educational Theory

FOCUSING QUESTIONS

Who qualifies as an educational pioneer?

How did the pioneers modify the traditional concepts of the child and the curriculum? What major innovations in teaching and learning did they bring about?

How have the pioneers expanded the definitions of knowledge, education, schooling, instruction, and learning?

What aspects of the pioneers' ideas or practices can be found in current educational practices or in modern thought about schools and the educational process?

Many distinguished individuals have contributed to educational theory and practice, but it is not possible to treat them all here. Therefore, judgment about whom to include must be made on the basis of two criteria: Was the person a genuine pioneer in education? Is the educator's work significant for you as a future teacher? Educational biography—the study of the lives and thoughts of educators—provides the means for identifying those pioneers who were the first to work in a particular field of educational theory and practice and who succeeded in opening that area to further development by others. Biography can also help us understand how certain pioneering ideas, transcending the historical context in which they emerged, have a significant impact on contemporary education.[1]

This chapter complements Chapter 3, which examined the historical evolution of educational ideas, institutions, and processes in Western culture. Chapter 3 concluded by considering the impact of the Protestant Reformation and the Enlightenment on education. Chapter 4 begins with a discussion of Comenius, who was a transitional figure between the Reformation and the Enlightenment. It then identifies and examines major educational theorists who helped to shape the course of education in the eighteenth, nineteenth, and twentieth centuries.

European influence on our schools

Before turning directly to the study of these educational pioneers, it is important to recognize that education in the United States has been influenced by pedagogical developments that took place in other nations. Although certain aspects of the American common school and high-school movements are unique to this country, other aspects of American education reveal a transatlantic influence. The study of the educational pioneers of other countries is part of a field called comparative education. By examining the educational contributions of such pedagogical pioneers as Comenius, Locke, Rousseau, Pestalozzi, Herbart, Froebel, Spencer, Montessori, and Piaget, we can appreciate the significance of the international diffusion of their educational theories and practices.

Child depravity theory

Despite differences in the educational methods proposed by these major theorists, certain patterns can be identified. Comenius developed an educational theory that incorporated a spiritual love of human beings along with an emphasis on the general goodness of nature. He, as well as such naturalistic educators as Rousseau, Pestalozzi, and Spencer, challenged the older view of child depravity and passive learning that had long dominated schooling. The **child depravity theory** held the child to be evil at birth, and it stressed that corruptive weakness could be corrected by a strong teacher who used authoritarian teaching methods.[2]

Innate goodness

In contrast, **naturalistic educators** believed that the child was innately good. Concerned with examining the child's nature, they believed that the stages of human growth and development provided clues for the development of educational method. These pioneering educators came to be called *naturalistic* because they believed that children learn by working with and by examining the

[1]Gerald L. Gutek, *Cultural Foundations of Education: A Biographical Introduction* (New York: Macmillan Co., 1991), pp. 4–7. Also see Edward Beauchamp, "Education and Biography in the Contemporary United States: An Introduction," *Biography* (Winter 1990), pp. 1–5.
[2]C. John Sommerville, *The Discovery of Childhood in Puritan England* (Athens, Ga.: University of Georgia Press, 1992).

objects in their immediate natural environment. The educative impact of the environment was a theme carried forward by such later American progressive educators as Dewey and Counts. Froebel's kindergarten and Montessori's prepared environment represent deliberate attempts to create learning situations that respect and utilize the child's own rate and pace of development.

COMENIUS: THE SEARCH FOR A NEW METHOD

Jan Komensky (1592–1670), known as Comenius, was born in the Moravian town of Nivnitz. His family were members of the Moravian Brethren, a small, frequently persecuted sect of Protestants. Young Comenius attended the Brethren's vernacular school, where he studied the conventional elementary curriculum of reading, writing, singing, arithmetic, and catechism. He attended a Latin preparatory school and then went on to the University of Heidelberg in Germany. Upon completing his education, Comenius returned to his native province to pursue a career as a teacher and administrator first in the Moravian schools and later in Poland and in the Netherlands. Religious persecution helped to keep him on the move; he settled in places where he was provided refuge. Out of these experiences, he developed a pioneering educational theory that stressed the establishment of a permissive school environment based on the natural principles of child growth and development.

Permissive school environment

As an educational reformer, Comenius occupied a middle position between the humanist educators of the Renaissance and later naturalistic reformers such as Rousseau, Pestalozzi, and Spencer. Although continuing to emphasize the centrality of Latin in the school curriculum, he thought it should be taught by methods that incorporated the active use of the senses rather than passive memorization. Since language, especially Latin, was necessary in order to acquire universal knowledge, Comenius wanted to make language instruction both interesting and efficient. In his book *Gates of Tongues Unlocked,* he approached the study of Latin through the learner's own vernacular.[3] Beginning with short, simple phrases, the student gradually progressed to more complicated sentences. Comenius also prepared a picture book for the teaching of Latin, *The Visible World in Pictures,* consisting of pictures that designated objects in both their Latin and vernacular names. The picture of the object combined language learning with sense perception, for Comenius believed that the formation of ideas began with the human being's immediate sensory response to external stimuli.[4] This tendency toward sensory learning would receive further emphasis in the work of Locke, Rousseau, and Pestalozzi.

Learning language by natural means

Principles of Learning and Instruction.   Comenius believed that nature revealed certain patterns of development, and he sought an efficient method of

---

[3]Jean Piaget, ed., *John Amos Comenius on Education* (New York: Teachers College Press, Columbia University, 1967).

[4]Edward A. Power, *A Legacy of Learning: A History of Western Education* (Albany: State University of New York Press, 1991), pp. 195–197.

instruction based on the principles of child growth.[5] Teachers, he argued, should recognize that children have stages of readiness for specific kinds of learning, and materials and instruction should be based on these developmental stages. Since nature was orderly and gradual, instruction should be organized carefully into easily assimilated steps so that learning might be gradual, cumulative, and pleasant.[6] Comenius did not believe that children should be hurried, coerced, or pressured to learn before they were ready.

Stages of growth and development

According to Comenius, instruction should be arranged according to four six-year periods: (1) infancy, when education is informal and primarily in the home; (2) childhood, when learning takes place in the formal school; (3) adolescence, when the student is to learn Latin; and (4) youth, when the student attends the university.

To implement his ideas about child development and his belief in the importance of sensory experience, Comenius developed nine principles of teaching: (1) teaching should involve presentation of the object or idea in a concrete and direct way, not merely through symbols or concepts; (2) instruction should involve practical application to life; (3) material taught should be presented in a direct, uncomplicated way; (4) material taught should be related to its true nature and origin; (5) general principles should be taught before details; (6) all things should be learned with reference to the whole and to how the parts are connected; (7) teachers should present material in succession, one thing at a time; (8) the teacher should not leave a specific subject until students understand it completely; and (9) differences among things should be taught so that the knowledge acquired is clear.[7]

Principles of teaching

Rejection of corporal punishment

Although many people believed children were inherently bad and that schools should use strict corporal punishment to discipline them, Comenius sought to enlist gentle and loving persons as teachers. He also argued that schools should be joyful and pleasant places.

Universal knowledge

Education and School. Comenius believed in making education available to all people, regardless of sex or socioeconomic status, because the road to peace was through universally shared knowledge. Comenius's educational philosophy of pan-Sophism, or universal wisdom, was a form of international education. Universal knowledge, Comenius reasoned, would stimulate a love of wisdom that would transcend nationalism and religious sectarianism, reduce the sort of persecution that he himself had experienced, and help humankind create a peaceful world order.[8]

Influence on Educational Practices Today. Comenius, a well-known and respected educator in his own lifetime, developed many ideas associated with

[5]M. W. Keatinge, ed. and trans., *Comenius* (New York: McGraw-Hill, 1931); M. W. Keatinge, *The Great Didactic of John Amos Comenius* (London: Adam Black, 1896).

[6]Josef Smolik, ''Comenius: A Man of Hope in a Time of Turmoil,'' *Christian History* (vol. 6, 1987), pp. 15–18.

[7]Edward J. Power, *Evolution of Educational Doctrine: Major Educational Theorists of the Western World* (New York: Appleton-Century-Crofts, 1969), pp. 238–241.

[8]Gerald Gutek, ''Knowledge: The Road to Peace,'' *Christian History* (vol. 6, 1987), pp. 29–30.

Child's interests and senses

modern and especially progressive education. To make universal education a reality, Comenius developed plans for organizing and administering effective schools. He believed that teaching methods should build on the child's interests and actively involve the senses. The teacher should be a patient and permissive person who gently leads children to use and to understand the world in which they live. Such later educational theorists as Rousseau and Pestalozzi would follow Comenius's pioneering work in naturalistic education.

LOCKE: EMPIRICIST EDUCATOR

John Locke (1632–1704) was an English scholar, physician, scientist, and philosopher. As a member of the Whig political party, Locke opposed the efforts of King James II to impose an absolute monarchy in England. After the Glorious Revolution of 1688, which exiled King James II, Locke gained prominence as the foremost philosophical champion of religious toleration and political liberalism.[9]

Locke's outstanding work on political philosophy was *Two Treatises of Government*, which appeared in 1689.[10] In it, he opposed the "divine right of kings" theory, which held that the monarch had the right to be an unquestioned and absolute ruler over his subjects. Locke argued that political order should be based on a contract between the people and the government, which ruled by the consent of those who had established it. He asserted that all human beings possessed inalienable rights of life, liberty, and property. Locke's political philosophy contributed to the concept of representative government and to the system of checks and balances among the legislative, executive, and judicial branches of government that would later characterize the American political system. His theories inspired Thomas Jefferson and the other founders of the American republic.[11]

Inalienable rights

Locke's political theory implied that the people were to establish their own government and select their own political leaders. No longer were aristocrats destined by birth to be rulers — the people were to elect their own leaders from among themselves. Locke's concept meant that the people should be educated to govern themselves intelligently and responsibly. This idea became a major theme of the nineteenth-century American common school movement and remains a major responsibility of American public schools.

Principles of Learning and Instruction.   Locke's major philosophical contribution, *An Essay Concerning Human Understanding*, published in 1690, examined the question of how we acquire ideas.[12] Locke held that at birth the human mind is a blank slate, a *tabula rasa*, empty of ideas. We acquire knowledge, he

Blank slate

---

[9]John Dunn, *Locke* (New York: Oxford University Press, 1984).

[10]John Locke, *Two Treatises of Government*, ed. Peter Laslett (New York: New American Library, 1965).

[11]Silvio A. Bedini, *Thomas Jefferson: Statesman of Science* (New York: Macmillan, 1990).

[12]John Locke, *An Essay Concerning Human Understanding*, ed. Alexander Fraser (New York: Dover, 1959).

argued, from the information about the world that our senses bring to us. Through sensation, we learn about the objects in the environment. Simple ideas become more complex through comparison, reflection, and generalization.

Empiricism and the scientific method

Although Comenius and others had stressed the role of sensation in forming ideas, Locke, because of his systematic writing on the subject, is often acclaimed as a pioneer of empiricism. According to **empiricism,** human knowledge is acquired only by means of the senses. Because it relies on sensation, empiricism is closely related to **induction,** which is the process of developing explanations or hypotheses from observed phenomena. In presenting his theory about how humans come to know, Locke attacked Plato's belief that knowledge or ideas are present latently in the mind. Locke also questioned the long-standing Renaissance view that knowledge came exclusively from literary sources, particularly the Greek and Latin classics. He argued that learning was an active process that used the senses to investigate and acquire data about the world. Locke's stress on studying objects present in the environment was shared and developed further by Rousseau, Pestalozzi, and Dewey. Later educators would use Locke's pioneering ideas as they came to advocate the **scientific method** — the testing of hypotheses by experimentation — as the best approach for teaching and learning.

Practical learning

Education and School.   In *Some Thoughts Concerning Education,* written in 1697, Locke recommended practical learning. Since it was a powerful force in shaping a person's life, a good education, he reasoned, should cultivate the ability to manage social, economic, and political affairs in a practical manner.[13]

Specifically, Locke believed that a sound education began very early in a child's life. Stressing the maxim of a sound mind in a strong and healthy body, Locke directed attention to a child's physical environment, diet, and activities. Children should breathe fresh air, have plenty of sleep, eat light and plain food, bathe frequently, exercise regularly, and have time for play and recreation.

Slow and cumulative learning

Learning, Locke insisted, should be a gradual process. The child's instruction in reading, writing, and arithmetic should be slow and cumulative. Beyond the basics, Locke's curricular recommendations included conversational learning of foreign languages, especially French; mathematics; and the study of civil government through history. Physical education, games, and athletics should be continual. Locke's educational goal was to cultivate the person who was ethical, who would manage economic affairs prudently, and who would participate in government effectively.

Influence on Educational Practices Today.   John Locke has exerted a significant influence on present-day educational practices. His emphasis on learning by sensory experience and on civic education helped to shape the practical and vocational aspects of Benjamin Franklin's plan for an English grammar school in Philadelphia in 1741. Franklin's proposal, in turn, was a forerunner of the modern high school. Locke's stress on empirical learning also influenced the more pragmatic and experimental views of modern education, which emphasizes "learning by doing" and interaction with the environment. Like Co-

---

[13]Henry J. Perkinson, *Since Socrates: Studies in the History of Western Educational Thought* (New York: Longman, 1980), pp. 111–127.

menius, Locke challenged inherited educational traditions and moved educators to a more modern conception of learning.

Because of his influence on Jefferson and other political thinkers of the American revolutionary generation, Locke has had a particularly enduring impact on civic education. His political theories of the separation of powers of government and individual freedom have shaped the way in which Americans are educated to think about citizenship and civic participation.[14]

Civic education

ROUSSEAU: THE NATURAL PERSON

Jean Jacques Rousseau (1712–1778), a Swiss-born French theorist, studied for a variety of careers but achieved fame as a social and educational philosopher. His works *On the Origin of the Inequality of Mankind* and *The Social Contract* state that the distinctions based on wealth, property, and prestige that give rise to social inequalities are artificial.[15] In the original state of nature, people were "noble savages," free and uncorrupted; it was the artificialities of society that corrupted people. Property produced inequalities, and government and other institutions legitimized these artificial distinctions.

Rousseau's most famous educational treatise, *Emile,* a novel he wrote in 1762, tells the story of a boy's education from infancy to adulthood.[16] Rousseau's novel attacks child depravity theory and an exclusively verbal and literary education. Such doctrines and practices, he felt, ignored the child's natural interests and inclinations. He also believed that the child needs to be freed from society's imprisoning institutions, of which the school was one of the most coercive.

The child's natural interests

Although many of the concepts developed in *Emile* could be applied to the education of both boys and girls, Rousseau was writing about the education of the upper-class French male. Many of his comments are clearly sexist in that Sophy, who eventually becomes Emile's wife, is educated to become a pleasing companion for her husband. Despite the book's orientation to the education of the male, later educators, including many who were progressive or child centered, found much in Rousseau's writing that contributed to the liberation of both boys and girls.[17]

Principles of Learning and Instruction. Like Comenius, Rousseau recognized stages of human growth and development. For Rousseau, there are five stages of growth: infancy, childhood, boyhood, adolescence, and youth. Each stage requires an appropriate education to stimulate further development and

Stages of growth

[14]Charles F. Bahmueller, ed., *CIVITAS: A Framework for Civic Education* (Calabasas, Calif.: Center for Civic Education, 1991), p. 384.

[15]James Miller, *Rousseau: Dreamer of Democracy* (New Haven: Yale University Press, 1984).

[16]William Boyd, *The Emile of Jean Jacques Rousseau* (New York: Teachers College Press, Columbia University, 1962); Allan Bloom, *Emile or On Education* (New York: Basic Books, 1979).

[17]Jane Roland Martin, *Reclaiming a Conversation: The Ideal of the Educated Woman* (New Haven: Yale University Press, 1985), pp. 381–369. Also see Helen E. Misenheimer, *Rousseau on the Education of Women* (Lanham: University Press of America, 1981).

growth. Most important, the early, formative stages of growth are to be free from the corruption of society. Emile, the subject of Rousseau's novel, was to be educated by a tutor on a country estate away from the blandishments and temptations of a ruinous society.[18]

Rousseau's first stage, infancy (from birth to five), sees the human being as essentially helpless and dependent on others. The infant needs freedom to move and to exercise his body. He needs to make his first contacts with the objects of the environment. The infant's diet should be simple but nourishing.

Pain and pleasure

During childhood (from five to twelve), the child is growing physically stronger. He is beginning to develop his own personality as he becomes aware that his actions have either painful or pleasurable consequences. During this stage, the child is egotistical but also curious. He explores the environment and learns about the world through his senses. Rousseau calls the child's eyes, ears, hands, and feet the first teachers. These natural teachers are far better and more efficient than the schoolmaster who teaches words that the learner does not comprehend; they are better than the schoolroom's silence and the master's rod. Emile's tutor did not attempt to introduce books at this stage. Reading was not substituted for the child's own direct experience with nature.

Nature as the best teacher

During boyhood (form twelve to fifteen), the boy's bodily strength is still increasing. Nature, still the best teacher, gives instruction in science and geography. By watching the cycles of growth and development of plants and animals, Emile learned natural science. By exploring his surroundings, he learned geography far more realistically than he could have from the study of maps. Emile now read *Robinson Crusoe*, the story of a man marooned on an island who had to meet nature on its own terms. Emile also learned a manual trade so that he could understand the relationship between mental and physical work.[19]

Next, in Rousseau's developmental schema, come the years of adolescence (from fifteen to eighteen). During these years, Emile returned to society. Becoming aware of and interested in sex, he asked his tutor questions about human sexuality, and the tutor was to answer his questions honestly, directly, and sincerely. Now that Emile had experienced a natural education, he was ready to cope with the outside world. He needed to be aware of society, government, economics, and business. His aesthetic tastes had to be cultivated by visits to museums, art galleries, libraries, and the theater. During the last stage of education (from eighteen to twenty), Emile traveled to Paris and to foreign countries to see different peoples and societies.

Interacting with society

Education and School. For Rousseau, knowledge was based on sensations and feelings. Preferring the natural to the social, Rousseau stressed human instincts as the means to knowledge.[20] He definitely opposed reliance on books as the pathway to truth. It was far better, he believed, to rely on direct and immediate experience with nature than to seek wisdom through the indirect source of the printed page. Rousseau, a true pioneer, challenged existing conventions

---

[18]David B. Owen, "History and the Curriculum in Rousseau's *Emile*," *Educational Theory* (vol. 32, 1982), pp. 117–130.

[19]Gutek, *Cultural Foundations of Education*, pp. 109–112.

[20]J. J. Chambliss, *Educational Theory as Theory of Conduct: From Aristotle to Dewey* (Albany: State University of New York Press, 1987), pp. 101–115.

and sought to destroy those that he felt impeded human freedom and progress. Rousseau was decidedly romantic and preferred the spontaneous, primitive, and emotional person to the rational and scientific individual. Rousseau's personal bent was to demolish restrictive and coercive social institutions and customs.

Schools impede learning

Unlike the classical humanists, who equated education and schooling, Rousseau carefully separated the two. Like advocates of de-schooling, Rousseau believed that the school often interferes with learning. As a social institution, the school puts children into a straightjacket that confines them to socially accepted customs, manners, and ideas. Rousseau wanted to liberate the child and adult from artificial social restrictions. Emile was a child of nature who followed his impulses and acted on them. If pleasure was the result, then Emile earned his own reward. If his actions caused pain, then Emile brought these consequences upon himself.

Influence on Educational Practices Today.   Rousseau influenced such innovative educators as Pestalozzi and contributed to broad movements in education, such as the child-study movement and child-centered progressive education. One of Rousseau's major contributions was the idea that educators should base the curriculum on the child's interests and needs rather than forcing the child to conform to a prescribed program of learning. In some respects, Rousseau anticipated the "romantic" view of child development, according to which children create their own reality rather than learn information given to them in a final form by adults.

Influential, progressive educators

Rousseau's *Emile* exerted a strong influence on Western education. Johann Pestalozzi put Rousseau's ideas into a more methodological and group-centered context. In the United States, such child-centered progressive educators as Francis Parker and Marietta Johnson elaborated a pedagogy based on the child's interests, needs, and inclinations.

PESTALOZZI: THEORETICIAN AND EXPERIMENTER

The Swiss educator Johann Heinrich Pestalozzi (1746–1827) was an attentive reader of Rousseau's *Emile.* He agreed with Rousseau's contentions that human beings are naturally good but are spoiled by the contagion of a corrupt society; that traditional schooling was a dull mess of deadening memorization and recitation; and that a pedagogical reform could lead to social reform. A natural society could arise based on the foundation created by a natural education.[21]

Natural education

Pestalozzi established an educational institute at Burgdorf to educate children and prepare teachers. Here he worked to devise a more efficient method of group instruction. He taught spelling by having the children begin with the shortest words and then proceed to longer ones by gradual and cumulative steps. Concrete objects, such as pebbles and beans, were used to teach counting. After becoming familiar with basic mathematical processes, children were introduced

[21]Robert B. Downs, *Heinrich Pestalozzi: Father of Modern Pedagogy* (Boston: Twayne, 1975); Gerald L. Gutek, *Pestalozzi and Education* (New York: Random House, 1968).

Johann Pestalozzi believed that teachers should encourage the development of the whole child in a secure, loving, and homelike school environment. (© Historical Pictures Service, Inc.)

to the numbers that represented the quantities of the objects they had counted earlier. The first writing exercises consisted of drawing lessons in which the children made a series of rising and falling strokes and open and closed curves. These exercises were intended to exercise the hand muscles and thus prepare the child for writing. The school's atmosphere was generally permissive, and there were physical exercises, play activities, and nature study walks.[22]

Permissive school atmosphere

Principles of Learning and Instruction. Pestalozzi's methods of instruction can be divided into the "general" and the "special." The general method is of great importance because it was used prior to the special method. In working with orphans and with the victims of poverty and ignorance, Pestalozzi felt that — to be effective — schools needed to be like secure and loving homes. The general method called for teachers who were loving persons, who were emotionally secure, and who could contribute to the emotional health of students by winning their trust and affection.

Warm and emotionally secure teachers

Once the general method had brought about the right emotional predispositions, then Pestalozzi used the special method. Since he believed that all learning comes through the senses, all teaching should likewise be sensory. To this end, Pestalozzi devised the **object lesson.** Children would study the common objects found in their environment — the plants, rocks, artifacts, and objects

Sensory learning

[22]Johann Pestalozzi, *How Gertrude Teaches Her Children,* trans. L. E. Holland and F. C. Turner (Syracuse, N.Y.: Bardeen, 1900).

Getting to the Source

A Pestalozzian Object Lesson / Elizabeth Mayo

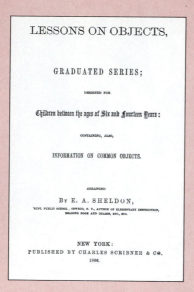

LESSONS ON OBJECTS,

GRADUATED SERIES;

DESIGNED FOR

Children between the ages of Six and Fourteen Years:

CONTAINING, ALSO,

INFORMATION ON COMMON OBJECTS.

ARRANGED

By E. A. SHELDON,

SUPT. PUBLIC SCHOOL, OSWEGO, N. Y.; AUTHOR OF ELEMENTARY INSTRUCTION,
READING BOOK AND CHARTS, ETC, ETC.

NEW YORK:
PUBLISHED BY CHARLES SCRIBNER & CO.
1866.

Johann Heinrich Pestalozzi (1746–1827) was a Swiss educational reformer who emphasized the use of the senses and object teaching in education. His ideas attracted disciples in many countries. In Eng-

land, Charles and Elizabeth Mayo founded a school that taught future teachers how to use the Pestalozzian method. The following excerpt from Elizabeth Mayo's 1835 text presents a model of the object lesson for a class of children aged six to eight. It should be noted that texts of this sort tended to formalize Pestalozzi's method, making it more rigid than Pestalozzi himself might have desired.

Glass has been selected as the first substance to be presented to the children, because the qualities which characterize it are quite obvious to the senses. The pupils should be arranged before a black board or slate, upon which the result of their observations should be written. The utility of having the lesson presented to the eyes of each child, with the power of thus recalling attention to what has occurred, will very soon be appreciated by the instructor.

The glass should be passed round the party to be examined by each individual.

TEACHER. What is this which I hold in my hand?

CHILDREN. A piece of glass.

TEACHER. Can you spell the word *glass*? (The teacher then writes the word "glass" upon the slate, which is thus presented to the whole class as the subject

that they saw and lived with in their daily experience. The object lesson focused on learning form, number, and sound. The children would determine the form of the object and would draw and trace the form or shape. They would count the objects and then name them.

From lessons in form, number, and sound came exercises in drawing, writing, counting, adding, subtracting, multiplying, dividing, and reading. Pestalozzi's methodological innovation was an insistence that learning begin with the senses rather than with words. Actually, he was following Rousseau's rule that mere verbal learning or abstract lessons are futile. Like Rousseau, Pestalozzi urged that lessons be based on sense experience originating in the learner's home and family life. This basic innovation became an important part of progressive school reform in the twentieth century.

From concrete to abstract

To ensure that instruction followed the ways of nature, Pestalozzi developed a set of instructional strategies that sum up his approach. Instruction, he urged, should (1) begin with the concrete object before introducing abstract concepts; (2) begin with the learner's immediate environment before dealing with what

of the lesson.) You have all examined this glass; what do you observe? What can you say that it is?

CHILDREN. It is bright.

TEACHER. (Teacher having written the word "qualities," writes under it — It is bright.) Take it in your hand and *feel* it.

CHILDREN. It is cold. (Written on the board under the former quality.)

TEACHER. Feel it again, and compare it with the piece of sponge that is tied to your slate, and then tell me what you perceive in the glass.

CHILDREN. It is smooth — it is hard.

TEACHER. What other glass is there in the room?

CHILDREN. The windows.

TEACHER. Look out at the window and tell me what you see.

CHILDREN. We see the garden.

TEACHER. (Closes the shutter.) Look out again, and tell what you observe.

CHILDREN. We cannot see anything.

TEACHER. Why cannot you see anything?

CHILDREN. We cannot see through the shutters.

TEACHER. What difference do you observe between the shutters and the glass?

CHILDREN. We cannot see through the shutters, but we can through the glass.

TEACHER. Can you tell me any word that will express this quality which you observe in the glass?

CHILDREN. No.

TEACHER. I will tell you then; pay attention, that you may recollect it. It is transparent. What shall you now understand when I tell you that a substance is transparent?

CHILDREN. That you can see through it.

TEACHER. You are right. Try and recollect something that is transparent.

CHILDREN. Water.

Questions

1. How was the Pestalozzian object lesson an improvement over the conventional teaching practices of the early nineteenth century?

2. How did Elizabeth Mayo's object lesson anticipate modern "hands-on" methods of teaching?

3. What are the strengths and weaknesses of object teaching?

Source: Elizabeth Mayo, *Lessons on Objects, as Given to Children Between the Ages of Six and Eight, in a Pestalozzian School, at Cheam, Surrey,* 5th ed. (London, 1835), pp. 5–8. Cover from E. A. Sheldon, *Lessons on Objects, Graduated Series; Designed for Children Between the Ages of Six and Fourteen Years: Containing, Also, Information on Common Objects* (New York: Charles Scribner, 1866).

is distant and remote; (3) begin with easy exercises before introducing complex ones; and (4) always proceed gradually, cumulatively, and slowly.[23]

Education and School.   As an educational pioneer, Rousseau had attacked schools as social institutions that chained humankind to conventional thinking. Like Rousseau, Pestalozzi wanted to base learning on natural principles and stressed the importance of human emotions. Unlike Rousseau, however, Pestalozzi did not abandon the school; he tried to reform it.

Rousseau and Pestalozzi were both naturalistic educators who believed that nature was the source of knowledge. To know, for Pestalozzi, meant to be involved with and to understand nature, its patterns, and its laws. Pestalozzi also had much in common with John Locke. Both stressed empirical learning,

Empirical learning

---

[23]Dieter Jedan, *Johann Heinrich Pestalozzi and the Pestalozzian Method of Language Teaching* (Bern, Switzerland: Peter Lang, 1981), pp. 45–67.

through which human beings come to know their environment by carefully observing natural phenomena.

Pestalozzi is significant to teachers because he stressed methodology. Learning could be efficient and enjoyable, he thought, if it were based on nature's own method. Like Comenius, Pestalozzi felt that children should learn in a slow and precise manner, understanding thoroughly whatever they were studying. Pestalozzi was especially dedicated to children who were poor, hungry, and socially or psychologically maladjusted. If children were hungry, Pestalozzi fed them before he attempted to teach them. If they were frightened, Pestalozzi comforted them. For him, a teacher was not only a person skilled in instructional methodology but also someone capable of loving all children. In fact, Pestalozzi believed that love of humankind was necessary for successful teaching.

Devotion to at-risk learners

Pestalozzi's principles of education were applicable to both boys and girls. However, because the customs of the day limited the use of boarding school facilities to one sex or the other, most of the children in Pestalozzi's schools were boys.

Influence on Educational Practices Today.   Pestalozzi's ideas and methods had a great impact on the course of western European and American education. William Maclure and Joseph Neef, in the early nineteenth century, were the first to import his practices to the United States. Through the work of Maclure, a pioneering early-nineteenth-century geologist and natural scientist, Pestalozzi's educational method became linked with scientific discovery and exploration. Basic scientific knowledge was transmitted through practical education based on the object lesson.[24]

Henry Barnard, U.S. commissioner of education in the late nineteenth century, also worked to introduce Pestalozzian ideas into the United States. Barnard's *Pestalozzi and Pestalozzianism* introduced American educators to the basic principles of the new method of instruction.[25] Edward Sheldon was important in introducing Pestalozzi's object lessons.[26] Horace Mann and William Woodward, leaders of the American common school movement, were familiar with Pestalozzianism and sought to incorporate its tenets into school practice. Many reforms associated with progressive education show the Pestalozzian imprint: the emphasis on the environment, for use of concrete objects, and the cultivation of sensory experience. When American educators came to focus on the education of at-risk children, Pestalozzi's ideas took on a special relevance. His claim that emotional security was a precondition of skill learning bore a strong resemblance to the emphasis many modern educators place on close school-home partnerships.

Impact on American progressive education

---

[24]Charlotte M. Porter, *The Eagle's Nest: Natural History and American Ideas, 1812–1842* (Tuscaloosa, Ala.: University of Alabama Press, 1986), pp. 93–95. Also see George E. DeBoer, *A History of Ideas in Science Education: Implications for Practice* (New York: Teachers College Press, Columbia University, 1991), pp. 21–24.

[25]Thomas A. Barlow, *Pestalozzi and American Education* (Boulder, Colo.: Este Es Press, University of Colorado Libraries, 1977), pp. 35–48, 74–88.

[26]Ned H. Dearborn, *The Oswego Movement in American Education* (New York: Teachers College Press, Columbia University, 1925).

HERBART: MORAL AND INTELLECTUAL DEVELOPMENT

Johann Herbart (1776–1841) was a German philosopher known for his contributions to moral development in education and for his creation of a methodology of instruction designed to establish a highly structured mode of teaching. Herbart attended the conventional German schools and then went on to study philosophy at the University of Jena, where he worked with the famous professor Gottlieb Fichte. Early in Herbart's career, while he was a tutor in Switzerland, he became interested in the educational theory of Pestalozzi. In 1809 Herbart was appointed to the chair of philosophy at the University of Königsberg. He now turned to serious scholarship and conducted a seminar in the psychological and philosophical aspects of education.[27]

Moral development

Principles of Learning and Instruction. For Herbart, the chief aim of education was moral development; it was basic and necessary to all other educational purposes. Herbart argued that virtue is founded on knowledge and that human beings do not deliberately choose evil. Misconduct is the product of inadequate knowledge or of inferior education. Thus, he gave education a vital role in shaping moral character. For Herbart, moral education involved the presentation of ethical ideas to the child's mind. In elaborating his work on moral education, Herbart specified five major ideas as the foundations of moral character: (1) the idea of inner freedom, which refers to action based on one's personal convictions; (2) the idea of perfection, which refers to the harmony and integration of behavior; (3) the idea of benevolence, by which a person is concerned with the social welfare of others; (4) the idea of justice, by which a person reconciles his or her individual behavior with that of the social group; and (5) the idea of retribution, which indicates that reward or punishment accrues to certain kinds of behavior.

Foundations of moral character

Knowledge and ethics

Drawing from his ideas on moral education, Herbart also specified two major bodies of interests that should be included in education: knowledge interests and ethical interests.[28] Knowledge interests involved empirical data, factual information, and speculative ideas. Knowledge interests were broadly conceived to include logic, mathematics, literature, music, and art. Ethical interests included sympathy for others, social relationships, and religious sentiments. Herbart wanted to produce an educated individual of good character and high morals. He believed that if people's cognitive powers are properly exercised and if their minds are stocked with ideas, then knowledge will guide their behavior. The person who lives and acts according to knowledge will be a moral person.

Integrating ideas

Education and School. In terms of organizing instruction, Herbart developed the concept of **curriculum correlation.** This was to have a decided impact on education in the United States. According to the doctrine of correlation, each subject should be taught in such a way that it refers to and relates to other subjects. Knowledge would then appear to the learner as an integrated system

---

[27]Harold B. Dunkel, *Herbart and Education* (New York: Random House, 1969).
[28]Johann F. Herbart, *Textbook of Psychology* (New York: Appleton, 1894).

This American kindergarten, circa 1910, drew on Froebel's theories that the child's first formal learning should be based on self-activity — in games, play, songs, and crafts — in a prepared, emotionally secure environment. (© Brown Brothers)

of ideas that forms an apperceptive mass—the whole of a person's previous experience—to which new ideas could be related. Herbart believed that history, geography, and literature were ideally suited as core subjects.

In the United States, Herbartian pedagogical principles were accepted enthusiastically.[29] The American Herbartians were especially interested in Herbart's **Formal steps of instruction** formal steps of instruction: (1) clearness; or the careful analysis and comprehension of each element of the lesson; (2) association, the relating of the facts with each other and with previously acquired information; (3) system, the ordering of ideas into a coherent system; and (4) method, the development of projects by the student to apply the learning acquired in the earlier steps.

Herbart's followers revised the four original steps and developed the well-**Herbartian method** known five phases of the Herbartian method that came to be popular in the United States. These five steps are (1) preparation, by which the teacher stimulates the readiness of the learner for the new lesson by referring to materials learned earlier; (2) presentation, in which the teacher presents the new lesson to the students; (3) association, in which the new lesson is deliberately related to ideas or materials studied earlier; (4) systematization, in which the teacher uses examples to illustrate the principles or generalizations to be mastered by the student; and (5) application, in which students test new ideas or materials of the new lesson to demonstrate their mastery of them.

Influence on Educational Practices Today. In the early twentieth century, Herbart's theories had a definite impact on American elementary and secondary schools and teacher education. His injunction that instruction follow a carefully **Lesson planning** designed sequence encouraged lesson planning, the organization of instruction

---

[29]Herbert M. Kliebard, *The Struggle for the American Curriculum, 1893–1958* (Boston: Routledge & Kegan Paul, 1986), pp. 44–45, 56–57.

into courses, units, and lessons—each with its own objectives, plan of presentation, and application. Although John Dewey and other progressive educators rebelled against the Herbartian approach because of its excessive reliance on prearranged lessons, its influence remains. For example, Herbart and his American followers were successful advocates of the inclusion of history and literature in the curriculum. According to Herbart, history and literature provided knowledge and contributed to moral and ethical sensitivity.

Science teaching

Herbart's emphasis on direct experience and social interaction also had an important impact on the teaching of science. Herbartian science teaching encouraged the observation of natural phenomena, the interpretation of such observations, and the correlation of scientific concepts with a broader network of knowledge.[30] Herbartianism, like Pestalozzianism, was an international movement that changed educational methods in other countries as well as in the United States. Japan, which modernized its educational system in the 1870s as a result of the Meiji restoration, imported and used the Herbartian method.

FROEBEL: THE KINDERGARTEN MOVEMENT

Friedrich Froebel (1782–1852), a German educator, is known for developing a school for early childhood education — the kindergarten, or child's garden. Froebel, the son of a Lutheran minister, was born in the German state of Thuringia. His mother died when he was only nine months old. As a mature person, Froebel frequently reflected on his childhood and youth. He believed that those who were to be teachers should continually think back to the days of their own childhood to find insights that could be applied to their teaching. Like Pestalozzi, *Student of Pestalozzi* with whom he studied, Froebel was very shy as a child and highly introspective as an adult.[31]

He worked as a forester, a chemist's assistant, and a museum curator before turning to education. His attraction to teaching led him to Pestalozzi's institute at Yverdon, where he interned from 1808 to 1810. He accepted certain aspects of Pestalozzi's method: the reliance on nature as the chief educator, the permissive school atmosphere, and the object lesson. Froebel believed, however, that Pestalozzi had not established an adequate philosophical underpinning for his theory. Froebel gave the object lesson a more symbolic meaning in that the concrete object was to stimulate recall of a corresponding idea in the child's mind.

Principles of Learning and Instruction. Like Pestalozzi, Froebel was determined to improve methods of teaching. Both protested vigorously against teaching children ideas that they did not understand. They believed that the *Active teachers* teacher must became an active instructor instead of a taskmaster and hearer of individual recitations.

The kindergarten

In 1837 Froebel founded the kindergarten in the city of Blankenburg. It emphasized games, play, songs, and crafts and subsequently attracted a number

---

[30]DeBoer, *A History of Ideas in Science Education*, pp. 24–30.
[31]Gutek, *Cultural Foundations of Education*, pp. 221–241.

Overview 4.1

Educational Pioneers

Pioneer	Purpose of Education	Curriculum	Methods of Instruction	Role of the Teacher	Significance	Influence on Today's Schools
Comenius 1592–1670 (Czech)	To relate instruction to children's natural growth and development; to contribute to peace and human understanding	Vernacular language, reading, writing, mathematics, religion, history, Latin; universal knowledge	Based on readiness and stages of human growth; gradual, cumulative, orderly; use of concrete objects	To be a permissive facilitator of learning, to base instruction on child's stages of development	Helped to develop a more humane view of the child; devised an educational method	Schools organized according to children's stages of development
Locke 1632–1704 (English)	To develop ideas in the mind based on sense perception; to educate individuals capable of self-government	Reading, writing, arithmetic, foreign language, mathematics, history, civil government, physical education	Sensation; slow, gradual, cumulative learning	To encourage sense experience; to base instruction on empirical method	Developed a theory of knowledge based on sensation	Schooling that emphasizes sensory observation
Rousseau 1712–1778 (Swiss-French)	To create a learning environment that allows the child's innate, natural goodness to flourish	Nature; the environment	Sensation; experience with nature	To assist nature; not to impose social conventions on the child	Led a romantic revolt against the doctrine of child depravity; a forerunner of child-centered progressivism	Permissive schooling based on child freedom
Pestalozzi 1746–1827 (Swiss)	To develop the human being's moral, mental, and physical powers harmoniously; use of sense perception in forming clear ideas	Object lessons; form, number, sound	Sensation; object lessons; simple to complex; near to far; concrete to abstract	To act as a loving facilitator of learning by creating a homelike school environment; skilled in using the special method	Devised an educational method that changed elementary education	Schooling based on emotional security and object learning
Herbart 1776–1841 (German)	To contribute to the human being's moral development through knowledge and ethics	Curriculum correlation, interests, morals; logic, mathematics, literature, history, music, art	Preparation, presentation, association, systematization, application	To stimulate the learner's intellectual and moral development by formal stages of instruction	Devised a formal method of instruction based on the planned and sequenced lesson	Schooling that stresses literary and historical materials designed to enlarge the learner's interest

Pioneer	Purpose of Education	Curriculum	Methods of Instruction	Role of the Teacher	Significance	Influence on Today's Schools
Froebel 1782–1852 (German)	To develop the latent spiritual essence of the child in a prepared environment	Songs, stories, games, gifts, occupations	Self-activity; play; imitation	To facilitate children's growth	Created the kindergarten, a special early childhood learning environment	Preschools designed to liberate the child's creativity
Spencer 1820–1903 (English)	To enable human beings to live effectively, economically, and scientifically	Practical, utilitarian, and scientific subjects	Sensation and the scientific method; activities	To organize instruction in basic life activities	A leading curriculum theorist who stressed scientific knowledge	Schooling that stresses scientific knowledge and competitive values
Dewey 1859–1952 (American)	To contribute to the individual's personal, social, and intellectual growth	Making and doing; history and geography; science; problems	Problem solving according to the scientific method	To create a learning environment based on the shared experience of the community of learners	Developed the pragmatic experimentalist philosophy of education	Schooling that emphasizes problem solving and activities in a context of community
Montessori 1870–1952 (Italian)	To assist children's sensory, muscular, and intellectual development in a prepared environment	Motor and sensory skills; preplanned materials	Spontaneous learning; activities; practical, sensory, and formal skills; exercises	To act as a facilitator or director of learning by using didactic materials in a prepared environment	Developed a widely used method and philosophy of early childhood education	Early childhood schooling that is intellectually and developmentally stimulating
Counts 1889–1974 (American)	To create a new society that encompasses science, technology, and democracy	Social issues, history, science, technology, and the social sciences	Problem solving according to social methodologies	To become an educational statesperson who serves as a leader in reconstructing society	Originated the social reconstructionist view of the school	Schools designed to stimulate social planning and reconstruction
Piaget 1896–1980 (Swiss)	To organize education in terms of children's patterns of growth and development	Concrete and formal operations	Individualized programs; exploration and experimentation with concrete materials	To organize instruction according to stages of cognitive development	Formulated a theory of cognitive development	Schooling organized around cognitive developmental stages
Hutchins 1899–1977 (American)	To educate human beings to search for truth, which is found in the wisdom of the human race	Liberal arts and sciences; great books	Identifying, analyzing, and reflecting on intellectual concerns	To ask leading and challenging questions that stimulate students to pursue truth	A leading spokesman for the perennialist perspective in education	Schooling that emphasizes the liberal arts curriculum

Prepared environment

of visitors.[32] Froebel intended his kindergarten to be a prepared environment in which the child's first formal learning would be based on self-activity. The kindergarten teacher was to be a moral and cultural model who was worthy of the child's love and trust. Froebel readily accepted the Pestalozzian general method of emotional security for the child but raised it to a spiritual and highly symbolic level. As a philosophical idealist, Froebel believed that every child's inner self contained a spiritual essence, which was the force that caused self-active learning. Therefore, he conceived the prepared environment of the kindergarten as a means to draw out or externalize this interior spirituality.

Gifts and occupations

The kindergarten curriculum included songs, stories, games, "gifts," and "occupations." The songs, stories, and games, generally a part of early childhood education, stimulated the child's imagination and introduced the child to the customs, heroes, and ideas of the cultural heritage. Games provided the cooperative activities that socialized children and developed their physical and motor skills. As the boys and girls played with other children, they became part of the group and were prepared for further group learning activities. Froebel's "gifts" consisted of objects with fixed form, such as spheres, cubes, and cylinders. The gifts stimulated children to bring to full consciousness the underlying concept the object implied. The kindergarten "occupations" consisted of materials the children could shape and use in designs and construction activity. For example, clay, sand, cardboard, and mud could be manipulated and shaped into castles, cities, and mountains.[33] Together these activities served as the learning environment; they were the garden in which children could grow naturally and correctly.

Dignity of the child

Education and School. Most of us acquired our first impressions of schools and of teachers in kindergarten. According to Froebel, the personality of the kindergarten teacher is paramount. The teacher should be a person who respects the dignity of human personality and who embodies the highest cultural values, so that children can imitate these values. Above all, the kindergarten teacher should be an approachable and open person.[34]

Influence on American educators

Influence on Educational Practices Today. Immigrants who fled from Germany after the Revolution of 1848 brought the concept of the kindergarten with them, and the kindergarten is now an established part of American education. Margarethe Meyer Schurz, wife of the German-American patriot Carl Schurz, established a kindergarten in Watertown, Wisconsin, in 1855. Elizabeth Peabody founded the first English-language kindergarten and a training school for kindergarten teachers in Boston in 1860. The kindergarten was greatly encouraged by William Harris, superintendent of schools in St. Louis, Missouri, and later U.S. commissioner of education. Harris believed that the kindergarten was an important first stage of the school system because it prepared the child for

[32]Robert B. Downs, *Friedrich Froebel* (Boston: Twayne, 1978), p. 43.
[33]Friedrich Froebel, *The Education of Man*, trans. W. Hailmann (New York: Appleton, 1889).
[34]Bernard Spodek, ed., *Today's Kindergarten: Exploring the Knowledge Base, Expanding the Curriculum* (New York: Teachers College Press, Columbia University, 1986).

the order and routine of the elementary school.[35] Froebelianism became an international education movement as Froebel's disciples established kindergartens in countries throughout the world.

SPENCER: UTILITARIAN EDUCATION

Herbert Spencer (1820–1903) was an English social theorist who sought to fit Charles Darwin's theory of biological evolution into a comprehensive sociological and educational theory. According to Darwin's theory, species evolved naturally and gradually over long periods of time. Members of certain species survived and reproduced themselves by means of selective adaptation to changes in the environment. As their offspring inherited these characteristics, they survived and reproduced themselves and thus continued the life of the species. Those who were unable to adapt perished.[36]

Evolutionary stages of human development

Spencer and other Social Darwinists translated the concept of selective adaptation into the arena of social relationships. Spencer believed that human development had gone through an evolutionary series of stages from the simple to the complex. Social development has also taken place according to an evolutionary process by which simple, homogeneous societies had evolved to more complex societal systems characterized by an increasing variety of specialized tasks. Spencer's theory of **Social Darwinism** was developed in the last half of the nineteenth century when industrialization was indeed transforming American and western European societies into more complicated social systems characterized by specialized professions and occupations.

Survival of the fittest

Spencer believed that in a modern industrialized society, as in earlier and simpler societies, the "fittest" individuals of each generation would survive because of their skill, intelligence, and propensity to adapt to environmental requirements. Winning the competition with other individuals, the fittest would inherit the earth and populate it with their intelligent and productive offspring. Those individuals who were lazy, stupid, or weak would slowly disappear. Thus, according to the doctrine of Social Darwinism, individual competition would gradually bring about socioeconomic progress.

Value of competition

Principles of Learning and Instruction. According to Spencer, human life exhibits a series of basic activities that foster the survival of the species. Education should be based on these activities; it should emphasize the practical subjects that allow humankind to perpetuate itself and to master the environment. In particular, he believed, industrialized society requires **utilitarian education** based on scientific and practical objectives rather than on the very general educational goals associated with humanistic and classical education.[37]

[35]Michael S. Shapiro, *Child's Garden: The Kindergarten Movement from Froebel to Dewey* (University Park, Pa.: Pennsylvania State University Press, 1983). Also see Barbara Beatty, "Child Gardening: The Teaching of Young Children in American Schools," in Donald Warren, ed., *American Teachers: Histories of a Profession at Work* (New York: Macmillan, 1989).

[36]Jonathan Howard, *Darwin* (New York: Oxford University Press, 1982).

[37]Gerald L. Gutek, *A History of the Western Educational Experience* (Prospect Heights, Ill.: Waveland Press, 1987), pp. 253–267.

In many respects, Spencer resembled Pestalozzi, since he argued that learning should be based on sensory experience that involved the learner with the environment. Like Pestalozzi, Spencer favored instruction that was gradual, cumulative, and unhurried. Disinclined to memorization and rote learning, he related schooling to the activities needed to earn a living. Spencer believed that education should be vocational and professional, readily applicable to industry, commerce, government, and society.

Education and School.   Like such naturalistic educational theorists as Rousseau and Pestalozzi, Spencer opposed the excessively verbal, literary, and classical education associated with traditional schooling. He believed that the traditional schools of England were impractical and ornamental; they failed to meet the needs of a modern industrial society.[38] The most valuable education, in Spencer's view, was based on the physical, biological, and social sciences.

Stress on the sciences

Spencer influenced curriculum construction by classifying human activities according to their capacities for advancing human survival and progress. According to Spencer's curriculum rationale, (1) educational priorities should be based on those human activities that sustain life; (2) education that is valuable should prepare men and women to perform these activities efficiently; and (3) science should have curricular priority because it aids in the effective performance of life activities.[39]

Self-preservation as a priority

In Spencer's view, the activities that contribute to self-preservation are basic to all other activities. Because physical health is the most obvious necessity for self-preservation, Spencer believed education should include the study of human physiology and health. Indirectly, activities connected to a person's economic occupation or profession also support self-preservation. For this reason, the basic skills of reading, writing, and arithmetic are necessary. Moreover, in an industrial society the populace requires an education that contributes to technological efficiency; hence the physical and biological sciences, the social sciences, and the applied and technological sciences are also important.

To prepare students for social and political participation, Spencer recommended the study of sociology and was a pioneer in developing the sociological foundations of educational theory and practice. According to Spencer, the educated members of modern societies need knowledge of the science of society, of how social progress occurs, and of sociopolitical structures. They need to be able to formulate scientific generalizations from masses of sociological data. Spencer relegated aesthetic and literary cultivation to the least important area of the curriculum. Such activities, he felt, are for leisure and do not directly relate to sustaining life or to earning a living. The defenders of the classical and literary curriculum attacked Spencer for neglecting the knowledge that develops one's artistic and literary nature.

Influence on Educational Practices Today.   Spencer's theories of society and education continue to influence contemporary thought and practice. The Social Darwinist concept of survival of the fittest often underlies situations in which individuals compete for grades, honors, distinctions, rank, and eventually

---

[38]Andreas Kazamias, *Herbert Spencer on Education* (New York: Teachers College Press, Columbia University, 1966).

[39]Herbert Spencer, *Education: Intellectual, Moral and Physical* (New York: Appleton, 1881).

social, economic, and political power. For the Spencerian educator, this individual competition leads to social progress. Spencer's greatest impact was on curriculum formulation and implementation. His educational ideas, which were readily accepted in the United States, influenced the National Education Association committee that published the *Cardinal Principles of Secondary Education* in 1918—a document that stressed education for practical and civic purposes. Modern curriculum designers continue to show Spencer's influence when they base curriculum on an analysis of necessary human activities.

DEWEY: LEARNING THROUGH EXPERIENCE

An examination of leading educational pioneers would be incomplete without some comments on John Dewey (1859–1952), the American philosopher and educator.[40] Dewey's synthesis of Darwinian evolutionary theory, the philosophy of pragmatism, and the scientific method formed the basis for his work as an educational reformer. Viewing education as a process of social activity, Dewey recognized that the school was intimately related to the society that it served.

Dewey was born in Vermont. After receiving his doctoral degree in philosophy from Johns Hopkins University in 1884, he taught philosophy at several universities. Dewey's years at the University of Chicago, where he headed the combined departments of philosophy, psychology, and pedagogy, were important for the development of his educational theory. As the director of the University of Chicago's Laboratory School from 1896 until 1904, he tested his pragmatic educational philosophy by using it as the basis of learning activities.[41]

Laboratory school

Principles of Learning and Instruction. Dewey's well-known work *The Child and the Curriculum* provides a guide to the ideas used at the laboratory school.[42] Viewing children as socially active human beings, Dewey believed that learners want to explore their environment and gain control over it. In exploring their world, learners encounter both personal and social problems. It is the problematic encounter that leads children to use their intelligence to solve the difficulty — to use the collected knowledge of the human race in an active and instrumental manner.

Scientific method

In Dewey's view, the scientific method is the means of solving problems. Through the scientific method, the learner comes to direct and control his or her experience. This is the process by which human beings think reflectively and publicly. It is also the method of intelligent teaching and learning. The contemporary movement toward reflective teaching, discussed in Chapter 1, bears some resemblance to Dewey's ideas. The following steps are extremely important in Dewey's educational theory:

1. The learner has a "genuine situation of experience" — involvement in an activity that interests him or her.

[40]Robert B. Westbrook, *John Dewey and American Democracy* (Ithaca: Cornell University Press, 1991).
[41]Gerald L. Gutek, *Education in the United States: An Historical Perspective* (Englewood Cliffs, N.J.: Prentice-Hall, 1986), pp. 218–220.
[42]John Dewey, *The Child and the Curriculum* (Chicago: University of Chicago Press, 1902).

2. Within this experience, the learner has a "genuine problem" that stimulates thinking.

3. The learner possesses the information or does research to acquire the information needed to solve the problem.

4. The learner develops possible and tentative solutions that may solve the problem.

5. The learner tests the solutions by applying them to the problem. In this way, the learner discovers their validity for him- or herself.[43]

For Dewey, knowledge was not an inert body of information. It was, rather, an instrument to solve problems. The fund of knowledge of the human race — past ideas, discoveries, and inventions — was to be used as the material for dealing with problems. People should test and reconstruct this accumulated wisdom of the cultural heritage as necessary in light of present needs. Since human beings and the environment were constantly changing, knowledge too would continually be repatterned.

Knowledge reconstructed

Education and School.   Dewey conceived of education as the social process by which the immature members of the group, especially children, are brought to participate in group life. Through education, immature human beings are introduced to the cultural heritage and learn to use that heritage to deal with their problems. Education's sole purpose is to contribute to the personal and social growth of individuals. According to Dewey, education "is that reconstruction or reorganization of experience which adds to the meaning of experience, and which increases ability to direct the course of subsequent experience."[44]

Personal and social growth

Dewey's concept of the school was social and scientific. The school introduced children to society and their heritage based on each child's own interests, needs, and problems. The school as a miniature society was the means of bringing children into social participation. The school was scientific in the sense that it was a social laboratory in which children and youth could test their ideas and values. It was also scientific in a methodological sense; the learner was to acquire the disposition and procedures associated with scientific, or reflective, thinking and acting.[45]

School as a miniature society

Dewey outlined three levels of activity that would be used at the school. The first level, for preschool children, involved exercise of the sensory organs and development of physical coordination. The second level involved use of the materials and instruments found in the environment. The school was to be rich in the raw materials that excited children's interests and caused them to build, to experiment, and to create. Children in the third stage discovered new ideas, examined them, and used them. Now learning moved from simple impulse to careful observation, planning, and thinking about the consequences of action.

Learning through activity

Dewey advocated democratic education and schooling, which meant that the learner must be free to test all ideas, beliefs, and values.[46] Cultural heritage,

---

[43]John Dewey, *Democracy and Education* (New York: Macmillan, 1916), p. 192.
[44]Ibid., pp. 89–90.
[45]Kliebard, *The Struggle for the American Curriculum*, pp. 58–88.
[46]Brian Hendley, *Dewey, Russell, Whitehead: Philosophers as Educators* (Carbondale: Southern Illinois University Press, 1986).

Taking Issue ◄•►

Dewey's Learning by Experience

Since John Dewey developed his experimentalist or pragmatic philosophy and applied it to education, his approach has been vigorously debated. Proponents of Dewey's method, many of whom are professors of education, emphasize learning by experience through the use of the scientific method. Opponents of Dewey's method claim that it lowers academic standards and achievement by weakening systematic subject-matter learning and encouraging relativistic values.

Question: Should Dewey's experimentalist method of inquiry be used as the basis of teaching and learning in American schools?

Arguments PRO

1 Dewey's method provides continuity between children's world of direct experience and a school curriculum that arises from and develops that experience. Because of this continuity, students readily become interested and motivated, eager to pursue their interests into areas of broader educational importance.

2 Free from absolutes based on previous concepts of reality, Dewey's method encourages students to question inherited traditions and values. It fosters an experimental attitude that leads to invention, discovery, and innovation and equips people to use knowledge as an instrument to solve the problems of a changing world.

3 Since Dewey's method of inquiry requires the freedom to think and to question, it encourages a democratic orientation to life and society. Dewey's method is therefore well suited to the American culture's stress on representative institutions and open discussion of issues.

4 Dewey's educational goal — human growth for the sake of further growth — promotes an instructional flexibility in which teachers and students are free to respond to personal and social issues. This type of education encourages the capacity for flexible responses to the environment, a capacity sorely needed in today's technological and interdependent world.

Arguments CON

1 By stressing the interests and needs of children and adolescents, Dewey's method fails to emphasize the important role of adults in transmitting the cultural heritage. It also minimizes the fact that learning often requires the child to apply effort *before* developing interests.

2 Dewey's method falsely assumes that the scientific method can be applied to any problem without a deep knowledge of the problem's context. On the contrary, it is important that students learn subjects systematically, not experimentally. The failure to master subject matter leads to many of the deficiencies of American students, especially in mathematics and science.

3 Dewey's method is highly relativistic and situational, denying the existence of universal truths and values. In order to survive and prosper, American democracy needs to reaffirm certain basic and traditional values, not call all values into question.

4 Dewey's argument that the only goal of education is growth for further growth neglects the need for standards that encourage intellectual achievement and economic productivity. Schools, teachers, and learners need substantive goals to guide the educational process; vague notions about human growth are not sufficient.

customs, and institutions are all subject to critical inquiry, investigation, and reconstruction. As a democratic institution, the school should be open to and used by all. He opposed barriers of custom or prejudice that segregate people from each other and believed that people ought to live, share, and work together to solve common problems. He opposed the authoritarian or coercive style of administration and teaching that blocked genuine inquiry; his ideal school was a place where children and teachers together planned the curriculum and activities that they would pursue and where there was enjoyment in teaching and learning.

Children and teachers plan together

Influence on Educational Practices Today.   John Dewey exercised an enormous influence on American education. He developed and applied the open-ended philosophy of pragmatism to education and helped to open the process of schooling to change and innovation. For him, education was a social activity and the school was a social agency that helped shape human character and behavior. Today, educators who relate schooling to social purposes are following Dewey's pioneering educational concepts.

Progressive education

Dewey's ideas became closely associated with the progressive education movement, which emphasized the child's interests, needs, and personal growth. Dewey has often been misunderstood, however. Although he advocated freedom to learn through inquiry, he did not encourage aimless educational anarchy. Similarly, although he emphasized the testing of ideas by their consequences in the present, he did not reject past knowledge or past experience. Dewey favored relative values, but his educational philosophy was not value free. For him, sharing, cooperation, community, and democracy were significant human values that schools should encourage.

Dewey's influence can still be seen in American schools that focus on experimentation and on learning from the reflective reconstruction of experience. His concept of learning through problem solving has also been particularly influential in American teacher education. Moreover, Dewey had a strong international influence; he visited and lectured in Japan, China, and the Soviet Union, all of which instituted various educational reforms stimulated by his ideas.[47]

International influence

MONTESSORI: PREPLANNED EXPERIENCES

Early childhood education

Maria Montessori (1870–1952), an Italian educator, devised a method of early childhood education that enjoys international popularity. Montessori schools can be found in Europe, the United States, and India. In her own education, Montessori left the conventional schooling that was considered appropriate for girls of the Italian upper-middle class to attend a technical school. She then became the first woman in Italy to earn the degree of doctor of medicine.[48]

As a physician, Montessori's work brought her into contact with children who were regarded as mentally handicapped and brain damaged. Her work was

---

[47]William A. Paringer, *John Dewey and the Paradox of Liberal Reform* (Albany: State University of New York Press, 1990).
[48]Gutek, *Cultural Foundations of Education,* pp. 305–324.

Maria Montessori developed an educational method that emphasized a structured and orderly prepared environment. (© Culver Pictures)

so effective with these children that Montessori concluded that it had merits for the education of all children.

Principles of Learning and Instruction.   In 1908 Maria Montessori established a children's school, the Casa dei Bambini, whose students came from the slums of Rome. The school as a "specially prepared environment" emphasized teaching methods and materials as well as learning exercises derived from Montessori's observations of children. Children, she found, are capable of sustained concentration and work. They enjoy order and prefer work to play. They also enjoy repeating actions until they have mastered a given activity. Montessori found that children have an inner need to work at what interests them without the prodding of teachers and without the use of external rewards and punishments. In fact, children's capacity for spontaneous learning leads them to begin pursuing reading and writing.[49]

Teaching and learning methods

---

[49]Maria Montessori, *The Discovery of the Child* (New York: Ballantine Books, 1972).

Education and School.   Montessori's curriculum included three major types of activity and experience: practical, sensory, and formal skills and studies. It was designed to introduce the child to such practical activities as setting the table, serving a meal, washing dishes, tying and buttoning clothing, and practicing basic manners and social etiquette. Repetitive exercises developed sensory and muscular coordination. Formal skills and subjects included reading, writing, and arithmetic. Children were introduced to the alphabet through the use of unmounted, movable sandpaper letters. Reading was taught after writing. Colored rods of various sizes were used to teach measuring and counting.

Sensory and muscular coordination

The preplanned materials designed to develop the practical, sensory, and formal skills included lacing and buttoning frames, weights, and packets to be identified by their sound or smell. The use of these materials was to follow a prescribed method so that the child would obtain the desired skill mastery, sensory experience, or intellectual outcome. The Montessori teacher served as a director of activities, rather than as a teacher in the conventional sense. He or she was to be a trained observer of children. Since the child in the Montessori school is primarily involved in individualized activity, the activities of the director are geared to each child rather than to group-centered teaching and learning.

Didactic materials

Influence on Educational Practices Today.   Montessori education has experienced two periods of popularity in the United States. The first round of enthusiasm occurred just before World War I. Montessori visited the United States in 1913 and lectured on her method. However, the criticisms of William Kilpatrick and other progressive educators weakened the movement, and it declined after an initial burst of popularity. The progressive critics charged that the Montessori method was overly structured and provided insufficiently for children's socialization. Kilpatrick, a progressive disciple of Dewey's experimentalist philosophy, believed that children learned and developed social skills as they worked together on group projects. According to Kilpatrick, the Montessori method concentrated too much on doing things correctly and in isolation and thereby restricted the opportunities for creative and experimental problem solving.[50]

Decline after burst of popularity

Kilpatrick's critique

Revival of interest

Since the 1950s, there has been a marked revival of Montessorian pedagogy and Montessori schools in the United States, coinciding with the rise of preprimary and early childhood education. In addition, interest in Head Start stimulated a renewed interest in the methods of the Italian educator. The Montessori revival that began in the 1950s has gained momentum. Today, private **Montessori schools** enroll preschool children throughout the country. Many parents send their children to Montessori schools to enhance their children's intellectual development and to give them an academic boost. It is difficult to assess the long-range significance of Montessorianism in American education. Although it has stimulated the rise of numerous private schools and early childhood programs, the Montessori method has not made a pervasive impact on teacher education here.

---

[50]William H. Kilpatrick, *The Montessori System Examined* (New York: Arno Press and New York Times, 1971).

Maria Montessori was an early childhood educator who concentrated her efforts on improving learning opportunities for children. Like Pestalozzi, she was concerned initially with educating the disadvantaged child, and when her methods proved so successful she applied them to all children. Like Froebel, she created a special setting for the child's first learning experiences. Her method of instruction was carefully organized and based on her conclusions about the patterns of human growth and the laws of learning.

COUNTS: BUILDING A NEW SOCIAL ORDER

George Counts (1889–1974) believed that education was not based on eternal truths but was relative to a particular society at a given time and place. Counts asked the profound but still unanswered question, Dare the school build a new social order?[51] A professor of education at Columbia University Teachers College, Counts asked this in 1932, when the United States was gripped by a severe economic depression. He believed that the American schools needed to identify with such progressive forces as labor unions, farmers' organizations, and minority groups. By allying themselves with groups that wanted to change or reconstruct society, the schools would become an instrument for social improvement rather than an agency for preserving the status quo.

Reconstructing society

Principles of Learning and Instruction. Counts, who was associated with experimentalist philosophy and the socially oriented wing of progressive education, believed that learning and instruction should incorporate content of a socially useful nature and a problem-solving methodology.[52] The subject matter most appropriate for social reform was based on history and the various social sciences. Historical knowledge, in Counts's view, should derive from the "new history," based on the interpretations of Charles A. Beard, the noted American historian.[53] The new history did not pretend to be completely neutral regarding the great social conflicts of the day. It was written from a point of view that saw America becoming a more cooperative and technological society. Although Counts did not neglect the sciences and mathematics, he favored sociology and economics. The new history and the emergent social sciences were expressly emphasized, as was a commitment to democratic ethics and values. Students would be encouraged to work on problems that had social importance.

Education for social reform

Education and School. Counts was a cultural relativist who believed that education is always conditioned by the particular culture of a given society. American education, as a whole, reflected the American historical experience. But American culture had been transformed radically by the Industrial Revolu-

[51]George S. Counts, *Dare the School Build a New Social Order?* (New York: John Day, 1932); a recent edition is Counts, *Dare the School Build a New Social Order?* (Carbondale: Southern Illinois University Press, 1978).

[52]Gerald L. Gutek, *The Educational Theory of George S. Counts* (Columbus: Ohio State University Press, 1970).

[53]Lawrence J. Dennis, *George S. Counts and Charles A. Beard: Collaborators for Change* (Albany: State University of New York Press, 1989).

Democracy and equalitarian ideas

tion, which, by uniting science and industry, had created a technological society.[54] Counts concluded that the democratic and equalitarian ethic of the American heritage needed to be reconstructed so that it had meaning in this modern technological society. The schools, Counts said, should emphasize the dynamic forces of democracy and technology in their curriculum and methods of instruction.

Lag between materialism and ethics

Counts was concerned that a cultural lag had developed between our material progress and our social institutions and ethical values. Material inventions and discoveries had pronounced effects on many areas of life. Unfortunately, organized education had not developed a method for understanding these effects. Counts wanted the schools to stress an attitude of planning and an engineering mentality so that students could begin to understand and cope with the problems of social change that arose from technology.[55]

Teachers as agents of change

Counts urged teachers to lead society rather than follow it. As leaders, they were to be policy makers who would choose between conflicting aims and values. In the broadest sense of the term, educational statesmanship not only would be concerned with school matters but also would come to bear on the controversial matters of economics, politics, and morality. For Counts, the school was

Schools involved in society

an agency involved in society's politics, economics, art, religion, and ethics. Involvement meant that the school could either reflect the knowledge, beliefs, and values of the society, or it could seek to change them. When schools reflected society, they were simply acting as mirrors. If schools were to be socially reconstructive, their involvement would have to express itself as an active attempt to solve problems. If schoolteachers were to act as statespersons, then the solving of major social issues would result in a new social order.

Equal opportunity

Counts saw the democratic ethic as an enduring value of the American heritage. For him, everyone had the right to attend school. Further, schools ought to provide an education that afforded equal learning opportunities to all students.[56]

Influence on Educational Practices Today. Counts has influenced American education in several ways. For him, the educator was an educational statesperson who was responsible for shaping humankind's future as well as transmitting its past. He urged educators to exercise their role in determining the

A new social order

future. Counts's argument that the school should build a new social order has inspired subsequent generations of activist teachers, who identify important social problems — environmental pollution, economic inequality, gender discrimination, and racial injustice — and enlist students in solving them. Such problem solving requires an investigation into the knowledge bases of the natural and social sciences for necessary information. Most importantly, it often requires deliberate action. Through engagement with social, political, and economic issues,

[54]George S. Counts, *Secondary Education and Industrialism* (Cambridge, Mass.: Harvard University Press, 1929).
[55]Gerald L. Gutek, *George S. Counts and American Civilization* (Macon, Ga.: Mercer University Press, 1984).
[56]Lawrence J. Dennis and William E. Eaton, eds., *George S. Counts: Educator for a New Age* (Carbondale: Southern Illinois University Press, 1980).

Counts's followers claim, the schools and their teachers and students contribute to forging a new and better society.

PIAGET: DEVELOPMENTAL GROWTH

Jean Piaget (1896–1980), a Swiss psychologist and early childhood educator, made a significant contribution to research in educational psychology and early childhood education. From 1921 on, Piaget was a member of the Rousseau Institute in Geneva, Switzerland, becoming codirector in 1932. He also founded the International Center of Genetic Epistemology in Geneva.

Piaget's contributions to early childhood education and developmental psychology, especially in the areas of the development of children's thought, cognition, and language, are notable. His research and writing examine children's conceptions of moral judgment, number, space, logic, geometry, and physical reality.

Child as primary agent

Principles of Learning and Instruction.   Piaget believed that children are the primary agents of their own cognitive development in that they shape their conceptions of reality by complex and continuous interactions with the environment.[57] Human cognitive development results from the child's adaptation to the environment: the child builds a sense of reality by assimilating stimuli from the environment and adjusting to their requirements. Through their own exploratory interactive processes, children develop the ability to generalize, differentiate, and coordinate their concepts of reality. They form mental constructs that correspond to their experience of the external world and continually reconceptualize these constructions by means of new experiences.

Developmental stages

Piaget theorized that human intelligence develops sequentially. Children proceed on their own from one developmental stage to the next through maturation and exploratory activity. Each stage depends on the preceding one and leads to the next. Piaget's four developmental stages are

1. Sensorimotor, from eighteen months to two years
2. Preoperational, from two to seven years
3. Concrete operations, from seven to eleven years
4. Formal operations, from eleven to fifteen years

Programs of instruction that follow Piagetian cognitive psychology generally are guided by these four stages of human cognitive development, although not mechanistically. The key, for Piaget, is that children think differently than adults do because they perceive reality differently. Each stage is not so much a passage through time as it is a qualitative exploratory experience of understanding the world in a new and more complex way.

---

[57]Jean Piaget, *The Origins of Intelligence in Children*, trans. Margaret Cook (New York: Norton, 1952), pp. 23–42.

Children's exploration

Education and School.   Although complete curricula and schools based on Piaget's psychology of learning are rare, it is possible to extrapolate certain guidelines for education and schooling by examining Piaget's stages.[58] In the **sensorimotor stage,** Piaget found that infants first carry out isolated explorations of their environment by using their mouths, eyes, and hands. Later, they coordinate their senses for more environmental exploration. Through this exploratory activity, children construct an organized view of the world.

The **preoperational stage** occurs between ages two and seven as children continue to organize their perception of the environment. They classify objects into related groups and name them. The child's organization and classification approximate those of adults. Although their thinking still differs from that of adults in many respects, children are now beginning to develop logical relationships.

Stages of cognitive development

The third stage, **concrete operations** occurs between ages seven and eleven as children isolate the general characteristics of objects — size, duration, length, and so on — and use them in more complex mental operations. Although the child's cognitive operations are still based on concrete objects, they are becoming more and more abstract. Children can comprehend number signs, processes, and relationships. Although outwardly appearing to accept adult authority, they question it in their own minds.

The stage of **formal operations,** which begins sometime between ages eleven and fifteen, is characterized by the individual's ability to formulate abstract conclusions. Since individuals at this stage understand causal relationships, they can use the scientific method to explain reality. They are capable of learning complex mathematical, linguistic, mechanical, and scientific processes.

For Piaget, the teacher's function is to assist children in their learning processes. Learning cannot be forced before the individual child is ready. Teaching should create situations where children can actually develop mental structures, or ways of organizing their concepts of reality. In the Piagetian school environment, the following things should occur:

1. Teachers should encourage children to explore and experiment.

2. Instruction should be individualized so that children can learn in accordance with their own readiness.

3. Children should be provided with concrete materials to touch, manipulate, and use.

Influence on Educational Practices Today.   Piaget's cognitive psychology has had its greatest impact on early childhood education, but it also has implications for elementary and secondary education. Schools should be places where teachers provide a setting for appropriate interactions between children and their environment. It is crucial that these interactions be occasions of exploration for children so that they can successfully progress through the stages of development.

---

[58]William O. Penrose, *A Primer on Piaget* (Bloomington, Ind.: Phi Delta Kappa Educational Foundation, 1979).

HUTCHINS: LIBERAL EDUCATOR

Robert Maynard Hutchins (1899–1977) was a leading voice for educational reform in the United States.[59] Although many of his criticisms were directed at higher education, his educational ideas were relevant to elementary and secondary schools as well. A graduate of Yale University and its law school, Hutchins became dean of the Yale Law School in 1928. He became a leader in legal education by advocating that law schools prepare lawyers as generally educated persons who knew the philosophical roots of jurisprudence and the social responsibilities of law. He did not believe that lawyers should know merely the rules and how to manipulate them.

Hutchins as a reformer

Hutchins's success as a reformer of legal education brought him national recognition. In 1929, at age thirty, he became president of the University of Chicago. As a university president, Hutchins was committed to major curricular changes and not solely to administration. Hutchins earned a national reputation as a storm center of educational criticism, change, and reform. Though he was often called a radical reformer, Hutchins's pioneering role in education was, nevertheless, very different from that of the other educators treated in this chapter. Whereas Pestalozzi and Herbart sought to devise new educational methods, Hutchins — like Aristotle and Aquinas — was more concerned with cultivating the learner's rational powers. Throughout his educational career, Hutchins was also concerned with the central issues of personal and national ethics and the relationship of education to ethical standards.

Emphasis on rationality

Principles of Learning and Instruction. Hutchins believed that principles of learning flowed from the rational nature of human beings. Genuine learning had to do with identifying, examining, and reflecting on intellectual issues. In Hutchins's search for intellectual excellence, learning was related to general education — the general cultivation of mind — rather than to vocational training. Learning was an intellectual effort to know the truth about reality.

Instruction, from Hutchins's perspective, occurred when teachers challenged students to think and to question — when teachers introduced the great ideas that were developed in the history of civilization, not as ends in themselves but as means to future ideas. Instructors were well advised to follow the Socratic method of searching for truth by asking significant and challenging questions.

Cultivating intellect

Education and School. Hutchins argued that the role of education was to cultivate human intellect by examining and reflecting on the great ideas of humankind. Eager to restore some of the educational premises of ancient Athens, he advanced an educational philosophy of perennialism, which included the following beliefs:

1. Education is based on humankind's perennial and constant search for truth; since what is true is always true and is everywhere true, the truth is universal and timeless. Therefore, education should also be universal and timeless.

---

[59]Harry S. Ashmore, *Unseasonable Truths: The Life of Robert Maynard Hutchins* (Boston: Little, Brown, 1989).

2. Since the life of the mind is intellectual and consists of ideas, education should also be about ideas; education's primary function is to cultivate human rationality.

3. The true purpose of education is to encourage students to think carefully about important ideas. Correct and critical thinking is the only defensible method for educators to use.[60]

Hutchins knew what he stood for in education; he also knew what he opposed. He rejected the tendency of American education to devote its resources to materialistic ends, to premature specialization and vocationalism, and to gimmicks and panaceas. Hutchins believed that the search for financial profit often distorted true educational purposes. The lure of moneymaking caused students to search for careers that promised wealth rather than careers that cultivated the mind. Instead of providing a liberal education based on the sciences, arts, and humanities, many colleges and secondary schools had introduced specialized vocational and career programs. These specialized programs, Hutchins felt, often came too early in the individual's life and quickly became obsolete. Hutchins also opposed the tendency of some educators to reduce learning to the mastery of techniques rather than of thinking and ideas.

Influence on Educational Practices Today. Through his leadership role in the *Encyclopaedia Britannica,* the Great Books of the Western World Foundation, and the Center for the Study of Democratic Institutions, Hutchins kept his educational philosophy before the American people. His influence continues to affect contemporary American education. It is expressed in secondary schools and colleges that are committed to intellectual disciplines and to the liberal arts and sciences, rather than specific career preparation, as the basic curriculum.

Hutchins's recommendation for an intellectually based curriculum was the foundation for Mortimer Adler's *Paideia Proposal,* which is discussed in Chapter 12. Essentially, Hutchins, as well as Adler, advocated an intellectually based curriculum for all students.

Summing Up

1. The pioneers discussed in this chapter made distinctive contributions to the development of education in their own countries and throughout the world.

2. In challenging the dogma of child depravity, Comenius, Locke, and Rousseau developed a method of education based on the learner's natural growth and on the child's natural goodness.

3. Pestalozzi's work led to instructional methods based on using the immediate environment and the objects in it. Throughout the nineteenth and early twentieth centuries, the Pestalozzian method was the basic strategy used in teacher-education institutions and schools throughout the United States. Froebel's theory was the basis of the kindergarten movement in the United

---

[60]Robert M. Hutchins, *A Conversation on Education* (Santa Barbara, Calif.: The Fund for the Republic, 1963).

States. Both Pestalozzi's and Froebel's methods liberalized the American conception of early childhood education by making teachers more sensitive to the interests and needs of children. Herbart's principles of instruction and moral development have also strongly influenced classroom teachers.

4. The concept of the sociological foundations of education developed by Spencer was a pioneering effort to relate the school to society. His theory of identifying social activities contributed to curriculum development based on social use and efficiency.

5. John Dewey's pioneering work at the University of Chicago Laboratory School pointed the way to progressive educational reform. The impact of Maria Montessori is currently felt in early childhood education.

6. George Counts was a progressive thinker who saw education as a means of creating a new social order. He challenged educators to become statespersons.

7. Jean Piaget's developmental psychology illuminated our thinking on children's cognitive operations.

8. Robert Hutchins, a perennialist thinker, used old truths to point the way to new educational reforms.

Key Terms

child depravity theory *(117)*

naturalistic educators *(117)*

empiricism *(121)*

induction *(121)*

scientific method *(121)*

object lesson *(125)*

curriculum correlation *(129)*

Social Darwinism *(135)*

utilitarian education *(135)*

Montessori schools *(142)*

sensorimotor stage *(146)*

preoperational stage *(146)*

concrete operations stage *(146)*

formal operations stage *(146)*

Discussion Questions

1. What are your conceptions of knowledge, education, and schooling? How do your conceptions agree or differ with those of the educators introduced in this chapter?

2. How did these pioneers of education function as innovators?

3. Identify the various educational methods devised by the pioneers discussed in this chapter. What are the strengths and weaknesses of each method?

4. Of the educators discussed in this chapter, whose ideas are most relevant to you as a prospective teacher? Whose are least relevant?

5. Can you find any evidence of the influence of these pioneering educators on your own education?

6. Identify a current educational controversy. How might the educators discussed in this chapter react to it?

Suggested Readings

Ashmore, Harry S. *Unseasonable Truths: The Life of Robert Maynard Hutchins.* Boston: Little, Brown, 1989.

> *Ashmore's well-reviewed biography examines Hutchins's educational ideas and his career as an educational administrator.*

Bloom, Allan. *Emile or On Education.* New York: Basic Books, 1979.

> *Bloom's annotated edition of Rousseau's* Emile *is well translated and includes an introductory essay.*

Dennis, Lawrence J. *George S. Counts and Charles A. Beard: Collaborators for Change.* Albany: State University of New York Press, 1989.

> *Based upon a skillful marshaling of primary sources, Dennis re-creates the intellectual relationship between Charles A. Beard, a leading American historian, and George S. Counts, a reformist educator.*

Froebel, Frederick. *The Education of Man.* Translated by W. N. Hailman. New York: Appleton, 1896.

> *Hailman's translation of Froebel's classic work remains the most useful version of the kindergarten founder's philosophy.*

Gutek, Gerald L. *Cultural Foundations of Education: A Biographical Introduction.* New York: Macmillan, 1991.

> *Considering each theorist's cultural context, Gutek examines the educational ideas of Plato, Quintilian, Aquinas, Calvin, Rousseau, Pestalozzi, Froebel, Spencer, Montessori, Addams, Dewey, Du Bois, Lenin, and Gandhi.*

Lillard, Paula. *Montessori: A Modern Approach.* New York: Schocken Books, 1973.

> *Lillard presents a contemporary appraisal of Montessori and her educational method.*

Stabler, Ernest. *Founders: Innovators in Education, 1830–1980.* Edmonton, Canada: University of Alberta Press, 1986.

> *Stabler examines the impact of selected innovators who stimulated significant change in education.*

Westbrook, Robert B. *John Dewey and American Democracy.* Ithaca: Cornell University Press, 1991.

> *Westbrook presents an exhaustive and definitive examination of the intellectual origins of John Dewey's thought.*

5

Historical Development of American Education

FOCUSING QUESTIONS

How were European educational ideas and institutions modified in the American environment?

How did American democratic ideas contribute to the rise of public schooling in the United States?

How does the American educational ladder differ from the European dual system?

What are the contributions of racial, ethnic, and language minority groups to American education?

What uniquely American problems of education have persisted over the course of time?

How has American education become more inclusive over time?

What are the recent trends in the history of American education?

C hapter 5 provides a historical overview of the origins and development of American education. It traces the evolution of educational institutions and identifies the contributions of individuals and groups whose decisions shaped American education. The chapter examines (1) the colonial period, when European educational ideas and institutions were transported to America; (2) the creation of a uniquely American educational system during the revolutionary and early national eras; (3) the spread of universal education; (4) the development of secondary education from the Latin grammar school, through the academy, to today's comprehensive high school; (5) the development of institutions of higher learning; (6) the education of minorities throughout American history; and (7) trends in the recent history of American education.

THE COLONIAL PERIOD

European colonists

The European colonists who settled in North America in the seventeenth and eighteenth centuries represented a variety of ethnic and language backgrounds. The major settlements were established by the French in Canada and the Mississippi Valley; the Spanish in Mexico and the southwest; the Dutch in New Netherlands, now New York State; and the English in the original thirteen colonies that would form the United States after the War for Independence. Other groups of colonists were Scotch-Irish, German, Scottish, Irish, Swedish, and Jewish.

As a result of the slave trade, a large African population grew in the southern colonies. The slaves were seized by force and brutally transported to North America. Over time, the African heritage developed into the foundations of African American culture. The European colonization of North America resulted in complex and often violent cultural encounters between the various groups of colonists and the many tribes of indigenous people. Among the consequences of the European and Native American encounter were the forced resettlement and decimation of large numbers of Native Americans.

Among all these groups, it was the English who would have the greatest impact on the political and educational institutions of the colonial period, institutions that profoundly influenced the later development of American education.

Influence of European schools

The English and other European colonists generally sought to re-create the European **dual-track system of schools,** in which the lower socioeconomic classes attended primary schools and the upper classes attended separate preparatory schools and colleges. In the colonies, as in Europe, the primary-school curriculum included reading, writing, arithmetic, and religious indoctrination. The language of instruction was the local vernacular — for example, English in English-speaking areas, Dutch in New Amsterdam.

For the upper classes, the chief preparatory school was the Latin grammar school, which stressed the Latin and Greek classics as the means to higher education. Education of the colonial upper classes was still heavily influenced by the Renaissance humanists, who believed that the classics contained the wisdom needed by an educated man. The two kinds of school, the primary school and the Latin grammar school (precollege), were separate systems. Neither the inherited European system nor the social ideas of the British colonists in North

America questioned the idea of class distinctions in education. The colonists also imported their Old World conceptions about the kind of education appropriate to males and females. Formal education, especially at the secondary and higher levels, was reserved for males. Although girls attended the primary schools and the dame schools (private schools taught by women in their homes), they rarely attended Latin grammar schools and colleges during the colonial period.

Different education for boys and girls

The modern idea of public education — a local system of schools supported by taxes and administered by public officials, which compels attendance of all children up to a certain age (usually sixteen years) — did not exist in the colonies. Granted, a colony sometimes organized the schools, but its role (outside of New England) was limited. Instead, other agencies assumed the major responsibility of education — the family, the apprenticeship system, and private schools of various sorts. Of these agencies, the family carried the greatest burden; frequently, children had no formal learning or picked up only a little vocational training.

Limited role of government

Limited role of government

The various colonies handled education matters differently. In New England, the governing bodies exerted general authority over education and directly supported their schools. In the Middle Atlantic colonies, a tolerant policy toward religion fostered several different sects, each group with its own religious schools and school policies. The southern colonies did not pass laws requiring communities to establish schools. Individual parents educated their own children by making arrangements with private tutors or by sending them to private schools.[1]

Regional differences on educational matters

New England Colonies

The New England colonies of Massachusetts Bay, Connecticut, and New Hampshire were very important in the development of American educational ideas and institutions. Massachusetts, in particular, enacted the first laws that governed formal education in the British colonies of North America. Much of the history of education in early America can be generalized from the educational experiences of colonial Massachusetts.

First education laws in Massachusetts

Massachusetts Bay Colony was settled mainly by the Puritans, a Protestant group that followed the theology of the Swiss religious reformer John Calvin. Unlike today, when a strict separation between church and public school exists in the United States, the first schools established in New England were closely related to the Puritan church. As practiced by the Puritans, Calvinist theology had several significant implications for education. First, the doctrine of predestination held that those souls who were elected (predestined) by God for salvation (others were damned to hell) were to exhibit outward signs of correct behavior. Second, the good person respected the sanctity of property and would prosper; he would use his income wisely and for the enlightenment of his fellows. Third, educated persons who knew God's commandments, as revealed by Calvin and preached by the Puritan ministers, were likely to resist the temptations of the world, especially the flesh and the devil. The school was seen as handmaiden of the church. Schooling was intended to cultivate a respect for the laws of the theocratic state and for the sanctity of property. In Puritan New England, education encouraged social conformity and religious commitment.

Calvinist theology and education

---

[1]Gerald L. Gutek, *Education in the United States: An Historical Perspective* (Englewood Cliffs, N.J.: Prentice-Hall, 1986), pp. 6–21.

The Puritans of New England were a literate people whose political ideas and Congregational form of church governance made it necessary for them to train an educated leadership and a literate and disciplined followership. (© Brown Brothers)

Schooling for economic and social usefulness

There was also an economic rationale for schooling in New England, which was reinforced by the Puritan outlook. The good citizen of the Puritan commonwealth was to be an economically productive individual who would produce wealth by hard work in farming, manufacturing, and trade. It was further assumed that schooling would contribute to a person's economic and social usefulness by cultivating literacy, resourcefulness, enterprise, punctuality, and thrift.

Child Depravity. The Puritan concept of the child was another important element in New England colonial education. The child was regarded as being naturally depraved — conceived in sin and born in corruption. Childish play was regarded as idleness, and child's talk was considered gibberish. In order to

Harsh discipline

civilize the child, the Puritan teacher applied constant discipline. Over time,

---

[2]Ross W. Beales, Jr., "In Search of the Historical Child: Miniature Adulthood and Youth in Colonial New England," in N. Ray Hiner and Joseph M. Hawes, eds., *Growing Up in America: Children in Historical Perspective* (Urbana: University of Illinois Press, 1985), pp. 7–24.

childish ways would yield to the disciplined behavior regarded as the outward sign of the elect. The good child appeared to be a miniature adult.[2] The Puritan children of New England had always before them the vision of their own evil and the punishment that they would receive in the hellfires of eternity. The stories they heard and the books they read were designed to impress on them the constant need for prayer and repentance. In their schools, New England children began to learn the alphabet with the rhyme "In Adam's fall/we sinned all."[3]

Religious rhymes

"Old Deluder Satan."   The Puritans of New England were a literate people. Their political ideas and the Congregational form of church governance made it necessary for them to train an educated leadership and a literate and disciplined followership. Even in the first years of their settlement of Massachusetts, the Puritans sought to establish schools. In 1642, legislation of the Massachusetts General Court required parents and guardians of children to make certain that their charges could read and understand the principles of religion and the laws of the commonwealth. In 1647 the General Court enacted the "Old Deluder Satan" Act, which required every town of fifty or more families to appoint a reading and writing teacher. Towns of one hundred or more families were required to employ a teacher of Latin so that students could be prepared for entry to Harvard College.[4] The Act of 1647 was designed to outwit Satan, who, the Puritans believed, led people into sin because of their ignorance.

A teacher for every town

The other New England colonies, except for Rhode Island, followed Massachusetts' example. These early laws indicated how important education was to the Puritan colonists of Massachusetts. Some historians have regarded these laws as the beginnings of American school law. It is clear that the Puritans did not want to see the growth of an illiterate class in North America. Such a class might be the beginning of a group of dependent poor, as had existed in England. They also wanted to ensure that the children of the commonwealth would grow up to be adults committed to Puritan theology.

A literate and committed citizenry

The Town School.   The New England **town school** was a locally controlled institution attended by both boys and girls. They might range in age from six to thirteen or fourteen. Attendance was not always regular; it depended on weather conditions and the family's need for children to work on the farm. The school's curriculum included reading, writing, arithmetic, catechism, and the singing of religious hymns. The child learned the alphabet, syllables, words, and sentences by memorizing the **hornbook,** a single sheet of parchment covered by a transparent material made by flattening the horns of cattle. The older children read the *New England Primer,* which included more detailed materials of a religious nature, such as the Westminster catechism.[5] Religion and reading were carefully integrated. Memorization of the Ten Commandments, the Lord's Prayer, and the Creed was combined with instruction in reading. Arithmetic was primarily a matter of counting, adding, and subtracting.

The three Rs

---

[3]Stanford Fleming, *Children and Puritanism: The Place of Children in the Life and Thought of New England Churches* (New Haven, Conn.: Yale University Press, 1933).

[4]Nathaniel Shurtleff, ed., *Records of the Governor and Company of the Massachusetts Bay in New England,* vol. 2 (Boston: Order of the Legislature, 1853).

[5]H. Warren Button and Eugene F. Provenzo, Jr., *History of Education and Culture in America* (Englewood Cliffs, N.J.: Prentice-Hall, 1983), pp. 12–14.

The New England town school was often a crude structure dominated by the teacher's pulpit located at the front of the single room. The students sat on benches. They studied their assignments until called before the schoolmaster to recite. The teachers were males. Some earned their living as teachers while preparing for the ministry. Others took the job to repay the passage money that had brought them to North America. Many, unfortunately, were incompetents who controlled their charges by the use of the rod. Although there were some variations, the New England town school was characterized by rote learning, memorized responses, and corporal punishment. It should be remembered that the children who attended town schools were often of the lower socioeconomic class.

Rote learning and corporal punishment

The Latin Grammar School.   The sons of the upper classes attended the **Latin grammar school,** which prepared them for entry to college. These children generally had learned to read and write English from private tutors. A boy would enter the Latin grammar school at the age of eight and remain there for eight years.[6] His lessons were based on such Latin authors as Cicero, Terence, Caesar, Livy, Vergil, and Horace. The Greek authors, such as Isocrates, Hesiod, and Homer, were read by advanced students who had already mastered Latin grammar and composition. Little or no attention was given to mathematics, science, history, or modern languages. Indeed, the regimen of study in the Latin grammar school was exhausting and unexciting. Nevertheless, the masters who taught in these schools possessed college degrees and were generally held in high esteem. As historian Samuel Morison points out, the Latin grammar school was one of colonial America's closest links to the European educational experience, resembling the classical humanist schools of the Renaissance.[7]

Classics

Harvard College

After completing the Latin grammar school, the early New England student applied for admission to Harvard College, established in 1636. Harvard was based on the Puritan conception that those called to the ministry and other positions of leadership needed to be soundly educated in the classics and the Scriptures. The student had to demonstrate his competency in Latin and Greek to be admitted to Harvard, where the curriculum consisted of grammar, logic, rhetoric, arithmetic, geometry, astronomy, ethics, metaphysics, and natural sciences. In addition, Hebrew, Greek, and ancient history were offered for their usefulness in scriptural study.

Middle Atlantic Colonies

The Middle Atlantic colonies — New York, New Jersey, Delaware, and Pennsylvania — differed from those in New England. Whereas New England had a common language, religion, and value structure, the Middle Atlantic colonies were characterized by linguistic, religious, and cultural pluralism. Although English-speaking people were in the majority, there were Dutch in New York, Swedes in Delaware, and Germans in Pennsylvania. In addition to lin-

Linguistic, religious, and cultural pluralism

---

[6]Robert Middlekauff, *Ancients and Axioms: Secondary Education in Eighteenth-Century New England* (New Haven, Conn.: Yale University Press, 1963).

[7]Samuel E. Morison, *The Intellectual Life of Colonial New England* (New York: New York University Press, 1956).

guistic pluralism, there was religious diversity. The Dutch were members of the Dutch Reformed Church, the Society of Friends dominated Pennsylvania, and the Germans might be Lutherans or members of small pietistic denominations. There were also Baptists, Roman Catholics, and a small Jewish population.

In such a situation of divergent ideas and values, no single system of schools could be established. Whereas New England created the town school, the Middle Atlantic colonies used parochial and independent schools that were closely related to the different churches.

New York. In New York, which had first been under Dutch control, the schools of the Dutch Reformed Church continued to operate when the colony came under English domination. The Dutch parochial schools taught reading, writing, and religion.[8] After the coming of English rule, a number of charity schools were established by a missionary society of the Church of England.

Since New York was a commercial colony, a number of private schools were established there to teach specific trades or skills. These private schools taught such subjects and skills as navigation, surveying, bookkeeping, Spanish, French, and geography. Some of them came to be known as "academies." These schools

Schools for middle-class children

made education available to middle-class children whose parents could afford tuition. The idea soon spread to other colonies. One of the most famous of these private schools was the Philadelphia Academy, founded in 1751 by Benjamin Franklin. Others were the Newark Academy in Delaware and the Washington Academy in New Jersey.

Pennsylvania. The colony of Pennsylvania became a haven for the Society of Friends under the leadership of William Penn. The Society of Friends, whose members are often called Quakers, was a religious sect that rejected violence. The Friends refused to support war efforts or to serve in the military forces. Their

Schools for all children

schools in Pennsylvania were open to all children, including blacks and Native Americans.[9] Although a very small minority, Pennsylvania, especially in Philadelphia, had a community of free African Americans. The Native Americans were the children of tribes that remained in the colony. Their teachers rejected corporal punishment. They respected the individual dignity of the child and opposed the commonly held view of child depravity. Like the other primary schools of the colonial period, the Quaker schools taught reading, writing, arithmetic, and religion. In addition to these basic skills, some vocational training was given in the form of handicrafts, domestic science, and agriculture.[10]

Southern Colonies

The southern colonies — Maryland, Virginia, the Carolinas, and Georgia — represented still another pattern of colonial education. Unlike in New England and

---

[8]William H. Kilpatrick, *The Dutch Schools of New Netherlands and Colonial New York* (Washington, D.C.: U.S. Government Printing Office, 1912).

[9]James D. Hendricks, "Be Still and Know!: Quaker Silence and Dissenting Educational Ideals, 1740–1812," *Journal of the Midwest History of Education Society* (Annual Proceedings, 1975), pp. 14–40.

[10]Thomas Woody, *Early Quaker Education in Pennsylvania* (New York: Teachers College Press, Columbia University, 1920).

the Middle Atlantic colonies, where concentrations of population had developed in cities and towns, the population of the southern colonies was dispersed over a large land area. This made it difficult to bring groups of children together in school classes. Those who could afford to do so resorted to tutorial education. Wealthy families engaged private teachers to educate their children; a few families sent their children to private schools.

Tutorial and private education

   The slave system of labor and the plantation system of landholding also deeply influenced the development of education in the South. The plantations often produced a single, staple crop, such as tobacco, cotton, or rice. This type of agriculture became the mainstay of the Southern economy and was supported by the use of a large unpaid labor force provided by the African slave trade. The children of the privileged class of white plantation owners had the benefit of private tutors, who often lived in the plantation manor.[11] Occasionally, the Anglican missionary society established a school for these children. In the late colonial period, boarding schools were established, usually in towns such as Williamsburg or Charleston. Slaves were trained to be agricultural workers, field hands, craftspeople, or domestic servants, but they generally were forbidden to learn reading or writing. For the poor whites, who tilled the infertile soils of the back country or the mountainous areas, formal education was nonexistent. Poor white children usually grew up to be subsistence farmers like their parents. Thus, the situation in the southern colonies delayed the development of large and uniform school systems. The lag in developing educational institutions remained until the Reconstruction period following the Civil War.

Effects of the plantation system

No schooling for blacks and poor whites

Colonial Education: A Summary View

   Despite regional variations, certain parallels existed among the schools of New England, the Middle Atlantic colonies, and the South. All three were dominated by British political rule and, despite linguistic and religious differences, were heir to the Western European educational tradition. Similar basic ideas and values governed individuals and groups.[12] Religion held a high priority in the value structure, and the family played a strong formative role in shaping ideas, values, and skills.[13]

Similarities among regions

   In all three regions, educational opportunities were limited by sex and by socioeconomic class. Both girls and boys attended the primary schools; Latin grammar schools and colleges were restricted to males. There were several reasons for such discriminatory practices.

Gender discrimination in the colonial era

1. The role of women was specifically defined as that of wife and mother. Since women in the colonial period did not have career choices, their schooling was limited to the basics (reading and writing) needed to carry out family and religious responsibilities.

2. There was a general prejudice, mainly held by males who controlled educational institutions, that women were incapable of higher studies.

---

[11]Jane Turner Censer, *North Carolina Planters and Their Children, 1800–1860* (Baton Rouge: Louisiana State University Press, 1984).

[12]Lawrence A. Cremin, *American Education: The Colonial Experience, 1607–1783* (New York: Harper & Row, 1970).

[13]Bernard Bailyn, *Education in the Forming of American Society* (New York: Random House, 1960).

3. The curriculum of the Latin grammar school and college stressed Latin and Greek classics, theology, and philosophy. These studies were designed to prepare future ministers and lawyers. During the eighteenth and nineteenth centuries, these professions were closed to women.

Class bias in schooling

Colonial schools also followed European social and economic class biases, according to which schooling was divided into two tracks. The primary or district schools, designed for the lower classes, provided basic literacy but did not encourage upward social mobility. There were some exceptions, but most pupils who completed their schooling in primary town and district schools did not pursue further study in the Latin grammar schools and colonial colleges. The sons of the upper classes, in contrast, attended the preparatory Latin grammar schools and, if successful, entered college. Throughout the nineteenth century, the forces of frontier egalitarianism, political democratization, and economic change worked to erode these European-based educational structures, creating the American system of universal, public education.

THE EARLY PERIOD OF NATIONHOOD

The American Revolution of 1776 ended British rule in the thirteen colonies. A new government based on a system of checks and balances distributed political power among the executive, legislative, and judicial branches. Although the inherited vernacular and denominational elementary schools and Latin grammar schools continued for some time, the leaders of the new republic sought to create new patterns of education that would be suited to the self-governing citizens of the United States.

Northwest Ordinance

The first national educational legislation was included in the Northwest Ordinance of 1785, which called for the surveying and division of the Northwest Territory into townships of 36 square miles. Each township was further divided into thirty-six sections, the sixteenth section of which was to be used for education. The provisions of the Northwest Ordinance established the pattern of financing education through land grants — a pattern often followed in the early nineteenth century.

Education reserved to the states

The U.S. Constitution made no mention of education, but the "reserved powers" clause of the Tenth Amendment (which reserved to the states all powers not specifically delegated to the federal government or prohibited to the states by the Constitution) served as the basis for leaving responsibility for education with the individual states. The colonial tradition of local school control and the opposition to centralized political power contributed to a state rather than a national school system in the United States.

Rejection of European ideas

In the years before and after the Revolution, many political and intellectual leaders put forth educational plans designed to suit the emerging nation. These plans shared certain aims: (1) education should meet the needs of a self-governing polity; (2) education should reflect the needs of a developing nation with vast expanses of frontier land and abundant natural resources; (3) education should be useful rather than classical or ornamental; and (4) education should be American rather than European. The nature of these early educational plans is evident in the proposals of Benjamin Franklin, Thomas Jefferson, and Noah Webster.

Franklin: The Academy

Benjamin Franklin (1706–1790) represented the rising American business class. His own formal education was brief, consisting of one year at the Boston grammar school, some writing and arithmetic lessons by private teachers, and experience as a printer's apprentice. He was a self-educated man who studied the major political and social tracts of his day. Franklin inaugurated several major scientific and educational organizations in Philadelphia, such as the Library Subscription Society, the Junto, and the American Philosophical Society. The proverbial folk wisdom of his *Poor Richard's Almanack* was very popular among the American middle classes, which readily accepted his emphasis on the virtues of frugality, diligence, thrift, hard work, and inventiveness.[14]

Virtues of thrift and hard work

In 1749 Franklin wrote "Proposals Relating to the Education of Youth in Pennsylvania." This treatise served as a basis for the academy that he founded. The **academy,** as Franklin conceived of it, was a private secondary school that offered a practical curriculum. Although others had suggested a replacement for the classically dominated Latin grammar school, Franklin's proposal for an English school clearly outlined an alternative institution and curriculum. English grammar, classics, composition, rhetoric, and public speaking were to be the chief language studies, rather than Latin and Greek. Students could also choose a second language based on their vocational interests. For example, prospective clergy might study Latin and Greek; physicians could choose Latin, Greek, and French; businessmen might elect French, German, and Spanish. Mathematics was to be taught for its practical application to bookkeeping rather than as an abstract intellectual exercise. History would be the chief ethical study. By studying biographies of great men, students were to learn moral and ethical principles. Franklin's curricular proposal was especially noteworthy because it brought many practical skills into the formal school that hitherto had been ignored. These included carpentry, shipbuilding, engraving, printing, painting, cabinetmaking, farming, and carving. With prophetic insight into the course of civilization and education, Franklin suggested that special attention be given to science, invention, and technology.[15]

Franklin's academy

Practical curriculum

By the mid-nineteenth century, many academies functioned throughout the nation, especially at the secondary level. They offered a wide variety of curricula and courses. The late nineteenth and twentieth centuries saw the emergence of high schools and the junior high or middle school, which incorporated utilitarianism, vocationalism, and commercialism, much as Franklin had recommended in his proposals of the mid-eighteenth century.[16]

Jefferson: Education for Citizenship

Thomas Jefferson (1743–1826), a leading statesman of the revolutionary and early republican periods, attended the local English vernacular school and

---

[14]Esmond Wright, ed., *Benjamin Franklin: His Life As He Wrote It* (Cambridge, Mass.: Harvard University Press, 1990).

[15]Bernard Cohen, *Benjamin Franklin's Science* (Cambridge, Mass.: Harvard University Press, 1990).

[16]W. J. Rorabaugh, *The Craft Apprentice: From Franklin to the Machine Age in America* (New York: Oxford University Press, 1986).

Latin grammar school near his home in Virginia. He also attended the College of William and Mary. Jefferson was a man of wide-ranging interests, which embraced politics, philosophy, architecture, agriculture, and science. His political career was distinguished by his service as a member of the Virginia Legislature and the Continental Congress, governor of Virginia, secretary of state, vice-president, and president of the United States. As the principal author of the Declaration of Independence, Jefferson stated his political belief that all persons are endowed with inalienable rights of "life, liberty, and the pursuit of happiness." Deeply involved in intellectual and educational affairs, he was a member of the American Academy of Sciences and was president of the American Philosophical Society.[17]

State responsibility for education

Jefferson's educational beliefs were embodied in his Bill for the More General Diffusion of Knowledge, introduced in the Virginia legislature in 1779. The major purpose of education, as the bill defined it, was to serve the welfare of a democratic society by cultivating an educated and literate citizenry. It was the responsibility of the state, not of religious denominations, to provide educational opportunities for both the common people and the leaders of society. This education would be offered "at the common expense of all" — funded, in other words, through public taxes.[18]

Jefferson's plan

Jefferson's plan would have subdivided the counties of Virginia into wards. All white children in Virginia, both girls and boys, were to attend a ward elementary school to study reading, writing, arithmetic, and history. Tuition would be free for the first three years. The proposal also would have established twenty grammar schools for education of males at the secondary level; here the young men would learn Latin, Greek, English, geography, and higher mathematics. In each ward school, the most gifted male student who could not afford tuition would be given a scholarship to continue his education in a grammar school. After grammar school, half of the scholarship students would be assigned positions as ward schoolteachers. The ten scholarship students of highest achievement would attend the College of William and Mary. By this means, Jefferson's plan sought to provide the most competent male students with continuing education.

Scholarships based on merit

Although Jefferson's proposal was not enacted by the Virginia legislature, the bill revealed the tenor of educational theorizing in the early republic. It demonstrated that a primary purpose of education was to promote good citizenship. It also showed that the earlier influence of religious denominations was beginning to decline. Ideas like those of Jefferson and Franklin would contribute to the nineteenth-century movement that created the American common school.

Education to promote citizenship

Webster: Schoolmaster of the Republic

Noah Webster (1758–1843) was one of the leading cultural nationalists of the early republic. A native of Connecticut and a Yale graduate, Webster was a

---

[17]Robert D. Heslep, *Thomas Jefferson and Education* (New York: Random House, 1969).

[18]Thomas Jefferson, "A Bill for the More General Diffusion of Knowledge," in P. L. Ford, ed., *The Writings of Thomas Jefferson* (New York: Putnam, 1893), vol. 2, p. 221.

Taking Issue ◆●▶

Schools and American Culture

A long-standing issue in American education is the degree to which public schools should transmit a distinctively American culture. Some educators believe there are key cultural concepts and values that all public schools should convey. Others contend that schools have no business deciding what constitutes Americanism or instilling such notions in students.

Question: Should American public schools transmit a distinctively American culture; that is, should there be a specific cultural core that schools deliberately convey?

Arguments PRO

1   As American leaders since Thomas Jefferson have recognized, a primary purpose of schooling is to educate responsible citizens. Without a basic knowledge of the ideas and values central to our national life, we could not function as citizens. Democratic institutions would founder.

2   Because the United States has always been a nation of immigrants, it is important that the schools transmit a core culture to bind these diverse groups together. Noah Webster looked to schools to forge a national identity from a cluster of former colonies, and the same need to integrate the many into one is evident today.

3   The cultural core includes tried and true values, ones imbedded in the nation's development from the Revolutionary era to the present. We know that these values are useful and worthy — over two hundred years of history bear witness to that fact.

4   Given the intense economic competition that the United States now faces from other countries, it is vital that American citizens share certain common purposes. Schools can encourage the growth of shared goals by transmitting the values and concepts unique to American culture.

Arguments CON

1   From the earliest days of American history, the nation has been characterized by cultural pluralism. There is no one set of ideas or values that makes a person American. In fact, the strength of U.S. institutions depends on the creativity and diversity of the people, not on whether all Americans think alike.

2   Those who advocate a core of common ideas and values have neglected ethnic and minority cultures. Inevitably, a single "American" culture means the culture of the white, English-speaking middle classes. Schools have no right to impose a uniform culture on their students, given the diverse backgrounds of the American population.

3   American life is an open and dynamic process. As the world changes, as new groups enter our society, American culture constantly evolves. Instead of perpetuating the status quo, schools should help students deal with the emerging values of contemporary society.

4   To make the United States more competitive with other countries, schools should teach multiculturalism and the need to appreciate foreign cultures. An increased international awareness — not a more rigidly defined Americanism — will bring the United States greater success on the world scene.

lawyer, schoolmaster, politician, and writer.[19] His prominence in American intellectual and educational history rests on his authorship of the *American Spelling Book* and the *American Dictionary*. Webster articulated a concept of cultural nationalism according to which nationality was based on and reflected the unique identity of a nation's citizens. For Webster, the major challenge was to create a sense of American cultural identity and unity.

Cultural independence from England

In 1789, when the Constitution went into effect, Webster argued that the United States should have its own system of "language as well as government." The language of Great Britain, he reasoned, "should no longer be our standard; for the taste of her writers is already completed, and her language on the decline."[20] By revolution, the American people had declared their political independence of England; now they needed to declare their cultural independence as well. Realizing that a sense of national identity was conveyed through a distinctive national language and literature, Webster set out to reshape the English language used in the United States.

Specific American language

Webster directly related the learning of language to organized education. As they learned the American language, children also would learn to think and act as Americans. The American language that Webster proposed would have to be taught deliberately and systematically to the young in the nation's schools. Since the curriculum of these Americanized schools would be shaped by the books that the students read, Webster spent much of his life writing spelling and reading books. His *Grammatical Institute of the English Language* was published in 1783. The first part of the *Institute* was later printed as the *American Spelling Book*, which was widely used throughout the United States in the first half of the nineteenth century.[21] Webster's *American Spelling Book* went through many editions; it is estimated that 15 million copies had been sold by 1837. Webster's great work was the *American Dictionary*, which was completed in 1825 after twenty-five years of laborious research.[22] Often called the "schoolmaster of the republic," Noah Webster was an educational statesman whose work helped to create a sense of American language, identity, and nationality.

Spelling books and dictionaries

THE RISE OF UNIVERSAL EDUCATION

In the first two decades of the nineteenth century, individuals and groups were seeking a new education suited to the republican needs of a frontier society. Although they rejected the highly class-centered European model, proponents of a new form of American education borrowed selectively from European educators. For example, Robert Owen's infant school, developed in the factory

Education designed for frontier society

---

[19]Harry R. Warfel, *Noah Webster: Schoolmaster to America* (New York: Octagon, 1936); Ervin C. Shoemaker, *Noah Webster: Pioneer of Learning* (New York: Columbia University Press, 1936).

[20]Noah Webster, *Dissertations on the English Language* (Boston: Isaiah Thomas, 1789).

[21]Henry Steele Commager, ed., *Noah Webster's American Spelling Book* (New York: Teachers College Press, Columbia University, 1962).

[22]Richard M. Rollins, "Words as Social Control: Noah Webster and the Creation of *The American Dictionary*," *American Quarterly* (Fall 1976), pp. 415–430.

community of New Lanark, Scotland, gained some support.[23] In the infant school, young children from three to six were given both play activity and intellectual experiences. Although some infant schools were established, they were not widely instituted in the United States.

Sunday schools

Like western Europe, early nineteenth-century America was undergoing the first phase of industrialization. Women and children worked in the factories of the industrial Northeast. To give the child factory workers some minimal learning, Sunday schools were opened in some of the larger cities, such as New York and Philadelphia. The Sunday school concept was developed by Robert Raikes, an English religious leader and publicist, who wanted to take children off the streets on the Lord's Day and give them basic literary and religious instruction. In the United States, classes were conducted on the one day of the week when the factories were closed. Writing, reading, arithmetic, and religion were taught to those who attended.

Monitorial method utilized student teachers

The European method of instruction that received the most attention in the early nineteenth century was the monitorial method, promoted by two rival English educators, Andrew Bell, an Anglican churchman, and Joseph Lancaster, a Quaker teacher. The **monitorial method,** as its name implies, relied heavily on the use of monitors, pupils who were trained by a master teacher to assist in conducting classes, taking attendance, and maintaining order.[24] First, the master teacher would train a number of monitors in a particular skill, such as adding single-digit numbers. These monitors were then assigned to teach that particular skill to subgroups of students. In this way, large numbers of students could learn basic literacy and numeracy skills. The monitorial method attracted those who believed it possible to have a large system of education at very little cost.

At first, monitorial schools were very popular in the United States, and they helped to make education more widely available. In New York, Philadelphia, and elsewhere, they were supported by private funds and by some state and city appropriations. When the New York Free School Society turned its property over to the public school system in 1853, more than 600,000 children had attended monitorial schools.[25] By the early 1840s, however, interest faded when people realized that the monitorial method provided only the barest minimum of learning.

Early industrialism

As the frontier moved west, the northern states continued to experience industrialization. The cities, growing into large urban centers with increasing populations of immigrants, needed schools that would provide systematic elementary education in reading, writing, arithmetic, and citizenship. Both industrialization and the frontier movement produced a spirit of practicality that encouraged schools to cultivate basic skills as opposed to the traditional and classical subjects.

The need for basic skill learning was one of the early nineteenth-century arguments for mass education. There was also a strong conviction that the char-

---

[23]Gerald L. Gutek, "Reconstructive Themes in Robert Owen's and William Maclure's Plans for New Harmony, Indiana, 1824–1830," *Journal of the Midwest History of Education Society* (vol. 15, 1987), pp. 226–233.

[24]David Salmon, *Joseph Lancaster* (London: Longman, Green, 1904).

[25]John Reigart, *The Lancasterian System of Instruction in the Schools of New York City* (New York: Teachers College Press, Columbia University, 1916).

acter and destiny of the United States required the participation of all citizens in the institutions of government. The advocates of popular education in both the West and North argued that in a democratic, self-governing society, citizens needed to be able to intelligently elect competent officials to conduct the affairs of state. Thus, a mixture of political, social, and economic motivations characterized the demand for universal schooling that culminated in the common school movement.

The Common School

Although the major thrust of the American common school movement of the first half of the nineteenth century was to win popular support for publicly financed elementary education, it also had broad social, political, intellectual, and economic ramifications. The **common school** may be defined as an institution devoted to elementary education in the basic tools of reading, writing, and arithmetic. It was common in that it was open to the children of all social and economic classes. Through a common program of civic education, it was to cultivate a sense of American identity and loyalty. Its major social purpose was to integrate children of various social, economic, and ethnic backgrounds into the broad American community. The political objective of common schooling, enunciated earlier by such leaders as Jefferson, was to educate the future citizens of a country founded on self-government.

Children of all social classes

Intellectually, the common school curriculum was to cultivate literacy that could be used in everyday life and for ongoing practical education. It was not intended to teach the traditional classical curriculum. Economically, the common school was a place to learn the skills and the attitudes that made one into a competent shopkeeper, merchant, artisan, and worker. It was an agency to develop the practical economic competencies that facilitated upward mobility and occupational choice.

Practical education

Because the Tenth Amendment reserved powers over education to each state, the patterns of common school establishment varied considerably across the nation. As noted earlier, the American educational system truly was a decentralized system. Even within a given state, especially in the frontier areas where a number of small school districts emerged, there might be significant variations in school support and organization from one local district to another.

State and local variations among school districts

The roots of the common school movement were established between 1820 and 1850. Common schools were first established mainly in the New England states, where Massachusetts and then Connecticut provided the leading examples.[26] The other northern states generally followed New England's common school model. As the frontier expanded and new states entered the Union, they too adopted the model and enacted the necessary provisions for setting up a

---

[26]In 1826, Massachusetts passed a law that required every town to choose a school committee responsible for all the schools in the local area. Thus began the policy of organizing public schools into a school system under a single authority. Eleven years later, the Massachusetts legislature established the first state board of education. Connecticut followed the example of its neighbor. See Lawrence A. Cremin, *The American Common School, A Historical Conception* (New York: Teachers College Press, Columbia University, 1951).

common or public elementary school system. In the South, the establishment of common schools was generally delayed until after the Civil War.

Three stages of legislation

Although the pattern varied from state to state, a common school usually was established in one of three legislative stages: *permissive, encouraging,* and *compulsory.* In the permissive stage, the state legislature gave permission for the organization of each local school district subject to the approval of the majority of voters in the district. In the second stage, the state legislature deliberately encouraged but did not compel the establishment of school districts, the election of school boards, and the raising of tax revenues for school support. In the third stage, the state did compel the establishment of school districts, the election of school boards, and the tax support of common schools. In the common school code the state also might specify a minimum curriculum and standards for school construction, lighting, and maintenance. Since the amount of taxation varied considerably from school district to school district, the quantity and quality of education were uneven. For a considerable period of time, many districts also charged a tuition payment per child, called a rate bill.

Tax support of common schools

Foundation of the American public school

The coming of the common school laid the foundation of the American public school system. Later in the nineteenth century, the public high school would be fashioned to complete the educational ladder that led to the state college and university. Perhaps the most prominent American educator who worked in establishing the common school system was Horace Mann.

Mann: The Fight for Free Schools

Horace Mann (1796–1859) was born in Massachusetts, attended Brown University, and prepared for a legal career. Elected to the Massachusetts legislature in 1827, he became a proponent of common schools. When the legislature created a state board of education in 1837, Mann was appointed secretary. His *Annual Reports* contained his philosophy of education and his surveys of the condition of common schooling in Massachusetts. As editor of the *Common School Journal,* Mann gained a nationwide audience for his arguments in support of popular elementary education. When he retired from the Massachusetts Board of Education in 1849, Mann was elected to Congress. Later, he served as president of Antioch College.[27]

Enlisting support for the common schools

Horace Mann skillfully executed a consensus style of leadership and administration to gain support for the common school cause. He had to convince several major segments of the Massachusetts population. First, taxpayers had to be shown that it was in their interest to support public schools. To enlist the support of the business community, Mann developed the stewardship theory. He argued that wealthy people had a special responsibility in providing public education. Those who had prospered, Mann asserted, were the guardians or stewards of wealth. Their support of public education actually would create an industrious class of men and women who would obey the law, be diligent in their work, and add to the state's economic well-being. Tax support of education was actually an investment that would yield high dividends in the form of public safety, progress, and prosperity. To the workers and farmers of Massachusetts, Mann argued that the common school would be a great social equalizer. It would be

A social equalizer

[27]Jonathan Messerli, *Horace Mann: A Biography* (New York: Knopf, 1972).

the means by which the children of a lower socioeconomic class could gain the necessary skills and knowledge to achieve a higher status. Common schooling would be the instrument of social and economic mobility; it would open the doors to greater opportunities.

As an administrator, Mann realized that he had to have the support of the common school teachers. He sought to improve teacher preparation by encouraging normal schools to professionalize teaching and to secure higher salaries for teachers. His efforts generally were supported, although some teachers opposed his liberal views on discipline and classroom management.

A unifying bond of common culture

In addition to being an effective administrator, Mann recognized the relationship between the common school and a democratic society. Citizens needed to be prepared to study the issues of the day and to vote intelligently. The United States differed from the more homogeneous nations of western Europe; it was composed of people of different religious beliefs and of varying ethnic origins and languages, crosscut by special and often conflicting interests. If the United States was to develop the unifying bond of a common culture, there needed to be a common basic education that developed a sense of national identity and purpose.[28]

According to Mann, the school would be part of the birthright of every child, financed by the state and local community. It would be for rich and poor alike; it would be not only free but also as good in quality as any private school; it would be nonsectarian, receiving children of all religions and classes. Through state legislatures and local boards, popularly elected officials rather than professional educators would exercise ultimate control and authority. Mann reasoned that the public, which must support the schools, should govern them. Thus, he set in motion the built-in dynamism that characterizes today's public schools and the underlying ideals of universal education.[29]

In addition to providing publicly supported elementary education for the majority of American children, the common school movement had two important complementary consequences: (1) it established the normal school as a teacher-preparation institution, and (2) it established elementary school teaching as an important career choice for women.

Normal schools

By the mid-nineteenth century, the normal school had become widely accepted as an institution for preparing teachers. It was modeled after the French *école normale*, from which its name was derived. **Normal schools,** first established in New England in 1823, were two-year institutions providing courses in history and philosophy of education, instructional principles, methodology, and practice or demonstration teaching for prospective teachers. At first, normal schools were somewhat like academies. By the end of the nineteenth century, however, many normal schools had been converted into four-year teacher-education colleges.[30]

The development of common schools created a demand for trained teachers, and many women were attracted to teaching careers in the expanding system of

---

[28]Lawrence A. Cremin, ed., *The Republic and the School: Horace Mann on the Education of Free Man* (New York: Teachers College Press, Columbia University, 1957).

[29]Horace Mann, *Lectures and Annual Reports on Education* (Cambridge, Mass.: Cornhill Press, 1867).

[30]For the development of American Teacher Education, see Jurgen Herbst, *And Sadly Teach: Teacher Education and Professionalization in American Culture* (Madison: University of Wisconsin Press, 1989).

Overview 5.1

Significant Events in the History of American Education

Major Political Events		Significant Educational Events	
1620	Arrival of Pilgrims in America	1635	Boston Latin grammar school established; one of oldest preparatory schools in United States
1630	Settlement of Massachusetts Bay Colony	1636	Harvard College founded, first English-speaking college in Western Hemisphere
		1642	First education law enacted in Massachusetts
		1647	Old Deluder Satan Act enacted in Massachusetts, requiring establishment of schools
		1751	Benjamin Franklin's Academy established in Philadelphia
1775–1783	American Revolution	1783	Noah Webster's *American Spelling Book* published
1788	U.S. Constitution ratified	1785	Northwest Ordinance, first national education law, enacted
		1821	First public high school in the United States opened in Boston
			Emma Willard's Female Seminary, first school of higher education for women, established in Troy, New York
		1823	First private normal school in the United States opened in Concord, Vermont
1824	Bureau of Indian Affairs established	1825	Webster's *American Dictionary* completed
		1827	Massachusetts law requiring public high schools passed
1830	Indian Removal Act	1837	Horace Mann appointed Massachusetts state board of education
1846–1848	Mexican-American War; U.S. acquisition of southwestern territories	1839	First public normal school opened in Lexington, Massachusetts
1849	Gold Rush to California	1855	First German-language kindergarten in the United States established
		1860	First English-language kindergarten in the United States established
1861–1865	Civil War	1862	Morrill Land Grant College Act passed, establishing in each state a college for agricultural and mechanical instruction
		1865	Freedmen's Bureau established
		1872	*Kalamazoo* decision upheld public taxation for high schools
		1877	Captain Richard Henry Pratt establishes Carlisle Indian Boarding School in Pennsylvania
1887	Dawes Act divides tribal lands into individual plots	1881	Tuskegee Institute established by Booker T. Washington

Major Political Events		Significant Educational Events	
1898	Spanish-American War; U.S. acquisition of Puerto Rico and the Philippines	1892	Committee of Ten established
		1896	*Plessy* v. *Ferguson* decision used to uphold constitutionality of "separate but equal" schools for white and black students
		1909	First junior high school established in Berkeley, California
		1910	First junior college established in Fresno, California
1914–1918	World War I	1917	Smith-Hughes Act passed, providing money grants for vocational education, home economics, and agricultural subjects
		1918	*Cardinal Principles of Secondary Education* published
		1919	Progressive Education Association organized
		1928	Meriam Report criticizes Indian education policies
1929	Start of the Great Depression	1930s	New Deal programs during the Great Depression provided federal funds for education of the unemployed and for school construction
		1933	John Collier, Commissioner of Indian Affairs, reaffirms indigenous Indian cultures
1939–1945	World War II	1944	G.I. Bill passed, providing federal funds for continued education of veterans
1950–1953	Korean War	1954	*Brown* v. *Board of Education of Topeka* decision required eventual racial integration of public schools
		1957	Soviet Union launched *Sputnik*, leading to criticism and reevaluation of American public education
		1958	National Defense Education Act passed, providing federal funds to improve science, math, and modern foreign language instruction and guidance services
		1964	Civil Rights Act authorizes federal lawsuits for school desegregation
1965–1973	Vietnam War	1965	Elementary and Secondary Education Act passed, providing federal funds to public schools, especially for compensatory education
		1968	Bilingual Education Act
		1972	Title IX Education Amendment passed, outlawing sex discrimination in schools receiving federal financial assistance
		1975	Education for All Handicapped Children (Public Law 94-142) passed
		1980	Department of Education established in federal government with cabinet status
		1983	Publication and dissemination of *A Nation at Risk* stimulated national movement to reform education
1990	End of Cold War	1988	Federal proposals for national testing and choice in education
1991	Gulf War		

In its approach to school government, the one-room school represented a form of direct democracy: the elected school board set the tax rate and hired and supervised the teacher. The small rural school also served as a cultural center for the community. (© Snark/Art Resource, New York)

elementary schools. The normal schools provided women with opportunities for higher education. Although it is true that salaries were low, teaching careers gave women a chance to begin developing other career opportunities.

Catharine Beecher: Training Women Teachers

Reform and feminism

The common school movement and the entry of women into teaching coincided with the rise of the movement for women's rights. The women's movement grew out of the general impetus for social, educational, and political reform that had stimulated the demands for the abolition of slavery and the enactment of common school legislation. Feminist leaders such as Elizabeth Cady Stanton, Emma Willard, Susan B. Anthony, and Catharine Beecher spoke out for the educational and political equality of women.

Women in teaching

Catharine Beecher (1800–1878), founder of the Hartford Female Seminary in 1828, was a pioneering educator who integrated women's education with their entry into teaching careers. Beecher, the sister of the famous author of *Uncle Tom's Cabin,* Harriet Beecher Stowe, combined her interest in women's education and common schooling with a semireligious zeal for social reform. To advance her educational cause, she founded and led the American Women's Educational Association.

Catharine Beecher believed that her generation lived on the verge of a new and progressive era that would be shaped by education. By assuming careers as teachers, educated women, she argued, were eminently suited to educate chil-

Teacher seminaries

Service on the frontier

dren both intellectually and morally. To prepare women as teachers for the common schools, Beecher urged that seminaries, or normal schools, be established.[31] Each seminary would have a model school where prospective teachers would do their practice teaching under the supervision of master teachers. Beecher was especially aware of the need for prepared teachers to staff the many one-room schools in America's western states and territories.[32] Among her educational goals was to prepare women, many of whom were from the eastern states, for this frontier service.

The One-Room School

A homely building

An especially distinctive type of common school was the one-room school, often called the district school. In rural areas it was usually small and plain, and it housed children of many different ages. Typically it would have a cast iron stove, a coat closet, several long seats and writing benches, and a raised desk for the teacher.[33] The simplicity of the "little red schoolhouse," which was established in almost every rural community, especially in the West, formed one of the nation's most lasting and sentimental pictures.[34] In this classroom students learned the basic skills of reading, writing, arithmetic, spelling, geography, and history and the virtues of punctuality, honesty, and hard work.

The "little red schoolhouse"

In its approach to school government, the one-room school represented a form of direct democracy. The elected school board set the tax rate; it also hired and supervised the teacher. Teacher certification was a simple but chaotic process. Each school board issued its own certificates to the teachers it employed, and in many cases these were not recognized in other districts.

School as cultural center

In addition to expressing the local commitment to schooling, the small rural school served as a cultural center for the community. Spelling bees, patriotic celebrations, and graduation exercises often drew community members to its steps.[35] Simple as it was, the one-room school helped to shape American society and culture.

The McGuffey Readers

120 million copies sold

The ideals of literacy, hard work, diligence, and virtuous living that characterized nineteenth-century American public schools were epitomized by **McGuffey readers.** William Holmes McGuffey (1800–1873), clergyman, professor, and college president, is best known for the series of readers that bears his name. It is estimated that more than 120 million copies of McGuffey's readers were sold between 1836 and 1920. McGuffey himself was nurtured in the the-

---

[31]Barbara M. Cross, ed., *The Educated Woman in America: Selected Writings of Catharine Beecher, Margaret Fuller, and M. Carey Thomas* (New York: Teachers College Press, Columbia University, 1965), ppl. 73–75.

[32]Polly Welts Kaufman, *Women Teachers on the Frontier* (New Haven, Conn.: Yale University Press, 1984).

[33]Warren Burton, *The District School as It Was* (Boston: Lee & Shepard, 1897), p. 4.

[34]Andrew Gulliford, *America's Country Schools* (Washington, D.C.: Preservation Press, 1984).

[35]Wayne E. Fuller, *The Old Country School: The Story of Rural Education in the Middle West* (Chicago: University of Chicago Press, 1982).

ology and values of Scotch Presbyterianism, and his readers emphasized the importance of individual virtue and goodness.[36]

Morality, patriotism, and heroism

Stressing the basic moral outlook of white Anglo-Saxon Protestant rural America, the McGuffey readers also emphasized patriotism and heroism. Among the selections included as representative of American literature were the orations of Patrick Henry, Daniel Webster, and George Washington. Through his readers, McGuffey was a teacher to several generations of Americans. McGuffey also provided the first graded readers for our school systems and paved the way for a totally graded system, which had its beginnings in the 1840s.

THE SECONDARY SCHOOL MOVEMENT

The establishment of the common school created the framework for a tax-supported and locally controlled public elementary school education in the United States. Upon this base was created the public high school — the institution that linked the elementary school with the state colleges and universities. Public secondary schooling forged the institutional rungs of the American **educational ladder.** As opposed to the dual-track system, which limited the education of students from lower socioeconomic classes, the single educational ladder gave all students the chance to progress to higher education.

The Academy: Forerunner of the High School

Decline of Latin grammar school

The Latin grammar school of the colonial period was replaced by the academy, which was the dominant institution of secondary education during the first half of the nineteenth century. Serving the educational needs of the middle classes, it offered a wide range of curricula and subject matter.[37] By 1855 there were more than 6,000 academies in the United States, with an enrollment of 263,000 students.

Unlike the Latin grammar schools, which were restricted to college preparatory male students, the academies enrolled both young men and women, including those preparing for college and those who would end their formal education at the secondary level. The curriculum of the academies also extended beyond the Latin and Greek offered by the grammar schools. The programs

Academy curricula

varied considerably in quality and quantity from academy to academy but usually followed three curriculum patterns: (1) the traditional college preparatory curriculum; (2) the English language course, which was the general curriculum for those who were completing their formal education; and (3) the normal course, which was intended for prospective common school teachers. There were, in addition, some specialized military academies.

The academies were generally under the control of private boards of trustees or governing bodies. Occasionally, they might be semipublic and receive some

---

[36]John H. Westerhoff, *McGuffey and His Readers: Piety, Morality, and Education in Nineteenth-Century America* (Nashville: Abingdon, 1978). Also see James M. Lower, "William Holmes McGuffey: A Book or a Man? Or More?" *Vitae Scholasticae* (Fall 1984), pp. 311–320.

[37]Theodore R. Sizer, *The Age of Academies* (New York: Teachers College Press, Columbia University, 1964).

support from cities or states. The era of the academies extended to the 1870s, when they declined in numbers and in popularity and were replaced by the public high school. Private academies still exist in the United States and continue to provide secondary education for a small percentage of the population.

Academies for women

The academies and the normal schools of the nineteenth century extended the opportunities for a formal education to young women. Some academies were founded expressly for young women, and others were coeducational. Among the academies founded for women was the Troy Female Seminary, established in 1821 in New York, by Emma Willard, a leader in the women's rights movement of the nineteenth century. Mary Lyon founded Mount Holyoke Female Seminary in Massachusetts in 1837. Along with the conventional domestic science program, female seminaries and academies offered classical and modern languages, science, mathematics, art, and music. The teacher-preparation, or normal, curriculum was also a popular course of study.

The High School

Although a small number of high schools had existed in the United States since the founding of the English Classical School of Boston in 1821, the **high school** did not become the major institution of American secondary education until the second half of the nineteenth century, when it gradually replaced the academy. In the 1870s the courts ruled in a series of cases (especially the *Kalamazoo*, Michigan, case in 1874) that the people of the states could establish and support public high schools with tax funds if they desired. After that, the public-high-school movement spread rapidly. By 1890 the 2,526 public high schools in the United States were enrolling more than 200,000 students. In contrast, the 1,600 private secondary schools and academies at that time enrolled fewer than 95,000 students.[38]

Taxes for public high school

Eventually the states passed compulsory school attendance laws. Provision of public secondary schools thereafter became a state obligation, rather than a voluntary matter. Children were permitted to attend approved nonpublic schools, but the states had the right to set minimum standards for *all* schools.

Urbanization and the High School.   The rise of the high school as the dominant institution of secondary education in the United States was the result of a variety of socioeconomic forces. The United States in the mid-nineteenth century experienced a great transition from an agricultural and rural society to an industrial and urban nation. For example, New York City's population grew from 1,174,779 in 1860 to 4,766,833 in 1910. By 1930, more than 25 percent of all Americans lived in seven great urban areas: New York, Chicago, Philadelphia, Boston, Detroit, Los Angeles, and Cleveland. Rapid urbanization also caused a growing need for specialization of occupations, professions, and services, and the high school was seen as the major institution for meeting this need.[39]

---

[38]Edward A. Krug, *The Shaping of the American High School, 1880–1920* (New York: Harper & Row, 1964).

[39]Edward A. Krug, *The Shaping of the American High School, 1920–1941* (Madison: University of Wisconsin Press, 1972).

As an educational agency of an urban and industrialized society, the high school provided a more intensive and specialized education for more and more people who were continuing their formal education beyond the eight years of elementary schooling. It served the needs of the so-called terminal students who would complete their formal schooling in the high school, and it continued to provide college preparatory schooling for those bound for institutions of higher education. In the late nineteenth and early twentieth centuries, it began to include career or vocational courses such as home economics, manual training, industrial and shop training, and clerical-commercial preparation.

Academic and vocational courses

A Democratic and Comprehensive Institution. As a school for students from varying social, economic, racial, religious, and ethnic backgrounds, the high school represented a new kind of secondary institution. In contrast to the European track system of secondary education, which separated academic from terminal students, the American high school evolved into a democratic and comprehensive institution that aimed at social integration while providing curricular differentiation. As a school for adolescents, the American high school was a product of a society that was becoming increasingly affluent. It was a society that could afford the financial costs of educating large numbers of fourteen- to eighteen-year-olds.

Social integration

When the high school became the dominant institution of American secondary education, it was possible for a student to attend an articulated sequence of publicly supported and controlled institutions that began with the kindergarten, extended to the elementary school, continued through high school, and reached the college and university.

Link between elementary and higher education

The Committee of Ten. The early years of the American high school witnessed some of the same confusion that had beset its institutional predecessor, the academy. Educators of the more traditional view defined the school as a college preparatory institution. Those who took a broader perspective saw the high school as a "people's school," which would offer a wide range of practical courses. In order to standardize the curricula of the high school, the National Education Association in 1892 established the **Committee of Ten.** This committee was chaired by Charles Eliot, president of Harvard University and a major leader in higher education who had extended his interests to both elementary and secondary education. Eliot, a forceful chairman, guided the committee to two major recommendations: earlier entry of several subjects and uniform treatment in the teaching of subjects for both college and terminal students.[40]

Efforts to standardize curricula

The committee recommended eight years of elementary and four years of secondary education. It advised four separate curricula as appropriate for the high school: classical, Latin-scientific, modern language, and English. Each curriculum included foreign languages, mathematics, sciences, English, and history — what we now call the basic academic courses. The first two curricula were more traditional in nature, and the latter two were considered more contemporary.

---

[40]National Education Association, *Report of the Committee on Secondary School Studies* (Washington, D.C.: U.S. Government Printing Office, 1893).

Although the Committee of Ten helped to liberalize the school program by identifying alternatives to the prevalent Latin and Greek classical curriculum, its recommendations nevertheless followed the traditional college preparatory program. Influenced by the popular educational psychology of the time, which stressed mental discipline, the committee concluded that the same subjects would be equally useful to both terminal and college preparatory students because these subjects trained the mind. This view was soon challenged by a number of educators who believed that a truly comprehensive secondary institution had to provide a broader program and a larger number of educational alternatives. From 1910 through 1930, several educators argued that the principle of social efficiency should be applied to high-school education.[41] *Social efficiency* meant that each person should be prepared to contribute to his or her own personal well-being and to the society's good; education should cultivate an individual's capacities as a producer, a citizen, and a parent. Although advocates of social efficiency sought to broaden high-school education, they sometimes narrowly defined their idea of efficiency, challenging the humanistic and aesthetic aspects of secondary education.

Emphasis on mental discipline

Social efficiency

The Commission on the Reorganization of Secondary Education. In the early twentieth century, the number of high-school students continued to rise. These students were no longer only the children of the professional and business classes; the population of the high school came from the adolescent population at large. The high school was indeed becoming comprehensive. By 1918, in fact, thirty states had laws requiring full-time school attendance until age sixteen.[42]

This fundamental change in the high school was revealed in *Cardinal Principles of Secondary Education,* set forth in 1918 by the National Education Association's **Commission on the Reorganization of Secondary Education.** Aware of the pervasive social changes in the United States, the commission stated that the high school should be a truly comprehensive institution serving the various social groups in the population. The curriculum could be differentiated to meet agricultural, business, commercial, industrial, and domestic as well as college preparatory needs without losing its integrative and comprehensive social character. All of the institutions in American education, the commission noted, should function together rather than in isolation.[43]

Comprehensive orientation

Secondary School Organization

As the high school assumed its institutional form, four curricular patterns emerged: (1) the college preparatory program, which included courses in English language and literature, foreign languages, mathematics, natural and physical sciences, and history and social sciences; (2) the commercial or business program, which offered courses in bookkeeping, shorthand, and typing; (3) industrial, vocational, home economics, and agricultural programs; and (4) a

Different programs for various students

---

[41]Walter H. Drost, *David Snedden and Education for Social Efficiency* (Madison: University of Wisconsin Press, 1967).

[42]Krug, *The Shaping of the American High School, 1920–1941,* p. 7.

[43]Commission on the Reorganization of Secondary Education, *Cardinal Principles of Secondary Education,* Bulletin no. 35 (Washington, D.C.: U.S. Government Printing Office, 1918).

modified academic program for terminal students whose formal education would end upon high-school graduation.

Despite some regional variations, the usual high-school pattern followed a four-year sequence that encompassed grades nine, ten, eleven, and twelve and generally included the age group from fourteen to eighteen.[44] There were exceptions, however, in that some reorganized six-year institutions could be found in which students attended a combined junior-senior high school after completing a six-year elementary school. Three-year junior high schools, which comprised seventh, eighth, and ninth grades, combined with three-year senior high schools, which encompassed tenth, eleventh, and twelfth grades, also began to appear in some large school districts in the 1920s.

The rise of junior high schools

The junior high school concept grew out of the Committee of Ten's suggestion that secondary education begin two years earlier in order to reduce the elementary school from eight to six years.[45] In many instances, the junior high school was initially the first three years of a six-year school. As it developed in the 1920s and 1930s, the **junior high school** often became a separate facility housing grades seven, eight, and nine. Today, the junior high school has become part of the pattern of school organization for many districts.

Emergence of middle schools

During the 1960s, the middle school appeared. The **middle school** generally includes grades six, seven, and eight. The middle school was designed to meet the needs of preadolescents, usually ages eleven through thirteen, in a transitional institution between elementary and high school. The middle school is intended to permit a gradual transition from childhood to adolescence by emphasizing special programs uniquely designed for preadolescents. Some educators classify the school as part of the elementary grade sequence.[46]

The American high school is a multipurpose institution. It provides a general education for all students; college preparation for those who wish to continue their formal schooling; and vocational and career preparation in agriculture, industry, and trade. It is comprehensive in the social sense, bringing together students of varying religions, social and economic classes, and ethnic and racial groups. Any institution that performs such varied social and educational services will necessarily by the scene of controversy and conflict. Despite disagreements about goals and programs, the high school serves as the main institution for achieving "equalization of opportunity" for most youth in our country.

THE AMERICAN COLLEGE AND UNIVERSITY

The British model

The colleges of the colonial period followed the British pattern of Oxford and Cambridge. In addition to preparing the scholar and theologian, the colleges in England sought to educate the well-rounded gentleman of the upper socio-

---

[44]Robert L. Hampel, *The Last Little Citadel: American High Schools Since 1940* (Boston: Houghton Mifflin, 1986).

[45]Nelson Bossing and Roscoe Cramer, *The Junior High School* (Boston: Houghton Mifflin, 1965).

[46]Judith L. Irvin, ed., *Transforming Middle Level Education: Perspectives and Possibilities* (Needham Heights, Mass.: Allyn and Bacon, 1992).

economic classes. The essential curriculum comprised grammar, rhetoric, logic, music, astronomy, geometry, and mathematics.

Religious roots of colonial colleges

The early colonial colleges were established under religious auspices. Believing that an educated ministry was needed to establish Christianity in the New World, the Massachusetts General Court created Harvard College in 1636. Yale was founded in 1701 as an alternative to Harvard, which some regarded as too liberal in theological matters. In 1693, Virginia's College of William and Mary, a Church of England institution, was granted a royal charter. Princeton, in New Jersey, was chartered in 1746 as a Presbyterian college, and King's College (later Columbia University) was chartered in 1754 to serve New York's Anglicans. Other colonial colleges were the University of Pennsylvania, Dartmouth in New Hampshire, Brown in Rhode Island, and Rutgers in New Jersey. Although there were curricular variations among these institutions, the general colonial college curriculum included (1) Latin, Greek, Hebrew, rhetoric, and logic during the first year; (2) Greek, Hebrew, logic, and natural philosophy during the second year; (3) natural philosophy, metaphysics, and ethics during the third year; and (4) mathematics and a review in Greek, Latin, logic, and natural philosophy during the fourth year.[47]

Land-Grant Colleges

During the first half of the nineteenth century, a liberal federal land-grant policy encouraged the establishment of many state colleges and universities. Many religious denominations also founded their own private colleges as a wave of religious revivalism swept the country. These colleges offered liberal arts and frequently included seminaries for training ministers.

Agricultural and technical colleges

By the early 1850s, critics of traditional liberal arts education were arguing that colleges for agriculture and mechanical science should be established with support from federal land grants.[48] Such institutions were deemed essential to further agricultural and industrial progress. Justin Morrill, a U.S. representative from Vermont, sponsored a bill to use federal land grants for the support of agricultural and industrial education. The Morrill Act of 1862 granted each state 30,000 acres of public land for each senator and representative in Congress, based on the apportionment of 1860. The income from this grant was to be used to support at least one state college for agriculture and mechanical instruction.[49]

Higher education for more individuals

The effect of the Morrill Act was to bring higher education within reach of the masses. The general impact of **land-grant colleges** was to further agricultural education, engineering, and other applied sciences, as well as the more traditional liberal arts and professional education. Many of today's leading state universities originated as land-grant colleges. Among these are the University of Illinois, Iowa State University, Michigan State University, Pennsylvania State University, and the University of Wisconsin.

---

[47]Frederick Rudolph, *The American College and University: A History* (Athens: University of Georgia Press, 1990).

[48]Allan Nevins, *The State Universities and Democracy* (Urbana: University of Illinois Press, 1962).

[49]Benjamin F. Andrews, *The Land Grant of 1862 and the Land-Grant College* (Washington, D.C.: U.S. Government Printing Office, 1918).

German University Model

American higher education was influenced in the late nineteenth century by the importation of the German research model of scholarship to the United States. Many American professors went to Germany in the late nineteenth century to complete their doctoral studies. While in residence, they engaged in research seminars with learned professors who investigated limited topics in the sciences and the humanities. When they returned to the United States, they brought with them the German concepts of the seminar and the scholarly dissertation.

Growth of Higher Education

Rising student enrollments

After World War II, American higher education experienced its greatest growth. From 1950 to 1965 college enrollments doubled from 2.4 million to 4.9 million students. By 1975 the number had almost doubled again to 9 million. By 1980, 12 million students were enrolled in institutions of higher education,[50] and in the early 1990s the figure reached 13.4 million.[51] Millions more were attending adult education classes offered by business, labor, the armed services, and social agencies. Educational television and adult continuing education programs enrolled thousands of others. The concept of "equality of educational opportunity" had reached the institutions of higher learning.

THE EDUCATION OF MINORITIES

A major historical tendency in American education has been to bring increasing numbers of children and youth into the educational mainstream. Unfortunately, some groups in the American population have not shared fully in the opportunities presented by public education until relatively recent times. African Americans, Native Americans, Hispanic Americans, and Asian Americans, for example, have had to struggle to gain admittance to the institutions that make up the American educational ladder. For them, it has been a slow and painful struggle.

African Americans

The Civil War, Reconstruction, and the Thirteenth Amendment ended slavery in the United States. Although free blacks had attended school in some northern states long before the Civil War, southern states had prohibited the teaching of African American children, whether slave or free. Emancipation brought with it the challenge of providing educational opportunities for the freedmen and women and their children, particularly in the former Confederate states.

---

[50]*Digest of Education Statistics, 1980*, Table 94, p. 102; *Projections of Educational Statistics, 1986–87* (Washington, D.C.: U.S. Government Printing Office, 1978), Table 2, p. 14; Table 5, p. 20.

[51]*Digest of Education Statistics, 1990* (Washington, D.C.: U.S. Government Printing Office, 1990), p. 5.

Freedmen's Bureau

In 1865, Congress created the Freedmen's Bureau to help former slaves adjust to freedom. The bureau continued to function until 1872 and, under the leadership of General O. O. Howard, established schools throughout the South. At their peak in 1869, these schools enrolled some 114,000 students. The schools followed a New England common school curriculum of reading, writing, grammar, geography, arithmetic, and music, especially singing. As their northern counterparts did, the Freedmen's Bureau schools relied on the standard textbooks — including Webster's spellers and McGuffey's readers.

A small number of black teachers were trained in these schools, but the schools were usually staffed by northern schoolteachers, who brought with them their values, their educational ideas, and their methods. These white educators from northern states had stereotypic notions about the kind of education African Americans should receive. Rather than encouraging educational self-determination, teachers such as Samuel C. Armstrong, the mentor of Booker T. Washington, stressed a version of industrial training and social control that many claim kept African Americans in a subordinate economic position.[52]

Washington: From Slavery to Freedom. Booker T. Washington (1856–1915) was the leading educational spokesperson for African Americans in the half century after the Civil War. As illustrated in his autobiography, *Up From Slavery,* Washington was a transitional figure who was born a slave, experienced the hectic years of Reconstruction, and painfully articulated the outlines of a compromise with the white power establishment.[53]

As a student at Hampton Institute, Washington studied the educational ideas of General Samuel Armstrong, who had established the institute to prepare African American youth for teaching, agriculture, and industry. Armstrong argued that industrial education was an important force in building character and economic competence for African Americans. Washington subscribed to Armstrong's philosophy of moral and economic "uplift" through work.[54]

"Uplift" through work

Tuskegee Institute

In 1881, Washington was named to head the institute that the Alabama legislature had established in Tuskegee. Washington shaped the Tuskegee curriculum according to his perceptions of the living and working conditions of southern African Americans. He felt that they faced the problem of being a landless agricultural class. The remedy, he believed, consisted of creating an economic base — primarily in farming but also in occupational trades — that would provide southern African Americans with some degree of economic security. His curriculum stressed basic academic, agricultural, and occupational skills and emphasized the values of hard work and the dignity of labor. Although he encouraged his students to become elementary school teachers, farmers, and artisans, he discouraged them from careers in medicine, law, and politics. The pur-

[52]James D. Anderson, *The Education of Blacks in the South, 1860–1935* (Chapel Hill: University of North Carolina Press, 1988).

[53]Booker T. Washington, *Up From Slavery* (New York: Doubleday, 1938).

[54]Raymond W. Smock, ed., *Booker T. Washington in Perspective: Essays of Louis R. Harlan* (Jackson: University Press of Mississippi, 1988).

Under the leadership of Booker T. Washington, the Tuskegee Institute emphasized agricultural and vocational training. These students were learning scientific analysis of soil. (© F. B. Johnston/Library of Congress)

suit of these fields, he believed, was premature and would result in strife with the dominant white power structure in the South.

Washington, a popular platform speaker, developed a theory of racial relations that argued that blacks and whites were mutually dependent economically but could remain separate socially. In 1885, Washington summed up his philosophy in an address at the Cotton Exposition in Atlanta, Georgia, when he said, "In all things that are purely social, we can be as separate as the fingers, yet one as the hand in all things essential to mutual progress."[55]

Today, Washington is a controversial figure. Some say he made the best of a bad situation and that, although he compromised on racial issues, he can be viewed as one who preserved and slowly advanced the educational opportunities of African Americans. Critics see Washington as an opportunist whose compromises restricted African Americans' progress. In any event, Booker T. Washington should be judged in terms of the realities in which he lived.

Du Bois: Challenger to the System.   W.E.B. Du Bois (1868–1963) was a sociological and educational pioneer who challenged the established system of education that tended to restrict rather than to advance the progress of African

---

[55]Booker T. Washington, *Selected Speeches of Booker T. Washington* (New York: Doubleday, 1932), p. 34.

Americans.[56] Du Bois challenged what was often called the "Tuskegee machine" of Booker T. Washington. A sociologist and historian, Du Bois called for a more determined and activist leadership than Washington provided.

Unlike Washington, whose roots were in southern agriculture, Du Bois's career spanned both sides of the Mason-Dixon Line. He was a native of Massachusetts, received his undergraduate education from Fisk University in Nashville, did his graduate study at Harvard University, and directed the Atlanta University Studies of Black American Life in the South. Du Bois approached the problem of racial relations in the United States from two dimensions: as a scholarly researcher and as an activist for civil rights. Among his works was the famous empirical sociological study, *The Philadelphia Negro: A Social Study,* in which he examined that city's African American population and made recommendations for the school system.[57] Du Bois's Philadelphia study was the pioneer work on urban African Americans.

Scholar and activist

Du Bois had a long and active career as a leader in the civil rights movement. He helped to organize the Niagara Movement in 1905, which led to the National Association for the Advancement of Colored People (NAACP), established in 1909. From 1910 until 1934, Du Bois edited *The Crisis,* the major journal of the NAACP. In terms of its educational policy, the NAACP position was that *all* American children and youth should have genuine equality of educational opportunity.[58] Du Bois and the NAACP were persistent adversaries of racial segregation in the schools. Their continual efforts led to the series of court cases that culminated in the momentous 1954 decision by the U.S. Supreme Court in **Brown et al. v. Board of Education of Topeka,** which outlawed racial segregation in the U.S. public schools.

Helped organize the NAACP

Desegregation

Unlike Booker T. Washington, who sought change that was evolutionary in nature and did not upset the social order, Du Bois demanded immediate change. Du Bois believed in educated leadership for African Americans, and he developed a concept referred to as the "talented tenth," according to which 10 percent of the African American population would receive a traditional college education in preparation for leadership. Both men believed strongly in the dignity of work, but Du Bois was especially adamant that a person's vocational calling should be dictated by ability and choice, not by race. Unafraid to challenge the traditional views of both blacks and whites on social and educational issues, W.E.B. Du Bois set the stage for the changes in American race relations that have taken place since the mid-1950s.

Challenged the system

Bethune: Educational Activist.   Mary McLeod Bethune (1875–1955) was a distinguished African American educator and administrator. The daughter of a South Carolina sharecropper, Bethune attended Scotia Seminary in Concord, North Carolina. She then attended Moody Bible Institute in Chicago. After completing her formal education, she returned to the South and established a pri-

---

[56]Virginia Hamilton, *W.E.B. Du Bois: A Biography* (New York: Crowell, 1972).

[57]W.E.B. Du Bois, *The Philadelphia Negro: A Social Study* (Philadelphia: University of Pennsylvania Press, 1899).

[58]W.E.B. Du Bois, *Dusk of Dawn: An Essay Toward an Autobiography of a Race Concept* (New York: Harcourt, Brace & World, 1940).

Getting to the Source ⟶●⟶

The Education of W. E. B. Du Bois

DUSK OF DAWN

AN ESSAY TOWARD
AN AUTOBIOGRAPHY
OF A RACE CONCEPT

BY

W. E. Burghardt Du Bois

HARCOURT, BRACE AND COMPANY, NEW YORK

William E. B. Du Bois (1868–1963) was a leader in the civil rights movement and the campaign to achieve equality of educational opportunity for African Americans. Du Bois was born in and received

his elementary and secondary education in Great Barrington, Massachusetts. From 1885 to 1890, he attended Fisk University, an historically black institution in Tennessee. The following reading describes reactions that Du Bois, a northern African American, had to racism and segregation in the South. Du Bois would later earn his doctorate from Harvard University and devote his life to writing, teaching, and advocating equality for all races and peoples.

[My] three years at Fisk [University] were years of growth and development. I learned new things about the world. My knowledge of the race problem became more definite. I saw discrimination in ways of which I had never dreamed; the separation of passengers on the railways of the South was just beginning; the race separation in living quarters throughout the cities and towns was manifest; the public disdain and even insult in race contact on the street continually took my breath; I came in contact for the first time with a sort of violence that I had never realized in New England; I remember going down and looking wide-eyed at the door of a public building, filled with buck-shot, where the editor of the leading daily paper had been publicly murdered the day before. I was astonished to find many

mary school in Daytona, Florida. In 1904 she founded the Daytona Normal and Industrial School, which is now Bethune-Cookman College.

Education and upward mobility

Bethune was convinced that education was the surest means of winning equality of opportunity and upward mobility for America's African American population. As an educator, she combined certain aspects of Booker T. Washington's program of academic, vocational, and religious education with a more activist civil rights stance that resembled Du Bois's strategy. Bethune, however, tended to work within the political system. She became an adviser to President Franklin D. Roosevelt during the New Deal era of the 1930s and early 1940s. President Roosevelt appointed her director of the Negro Affairs Division of the National Youth Administration.[59] She was an early opponent of Nazi racism and

---

[59]Mary Frances Berry and John W. Blassingame, *Long Memory: The Black Experience in America* (New York: Oxford University Press, 1982).

of my fellow students carrying fire-arms and to hear their stories of adventure. On the other hand my personal contact with my teachers was inspiring and beneficial as indeed I suppose all personal contacts between human beings must be. Adam Spence of Fisk first taught me to know what the Greek language meant. In a funny little basement room crowded with apparatus, Frederick Chase gave me insight into natural science and talked with me about future study. I knew the President, Erastus Cravath, to be honest and sincere.

I determined to know something of the Negro in the country districts; to go out and teach during the summer vacation. I was not compelled to do this, for my scholarship was sufficient to support me, but that was not the point. I had heard about the country in the South as the real seat of slavery. I wanted to know it. I walked out into east Tennessee ten or more miles a day until at last in a little valley near Alexandria I found a place where there had been a Negro public school only once since the Civil War; and there for two successive terms during the summer I taught at $28 and $30 a month. It was an enthralling experience. I met new and intricate and unconscious discrimination. I was pleasantly surprised when the white school superintendent, on whom I had made a business call, invited me to stay for dinner; and he would have been astonished if he had dreamed that I expected to eat at the table with him and not after he was through. All the appointments of my school were primitive: a windowless log cabin; hastily manufactured benches; no blackboard; almost no books; long, long distances to walk. And on the other hand, I heard the sorrow songs sung with primitive beauty and grandeur. I saw the hard, ugly drudgery of country life and the writhing of landless, ignorant peasants. I saw the race problem at nearly its lowest terms.

Questions

1. How did the problem of racial discrimination become a reality for Du Bois?

2. How was Du Bois's education different from that which Booker T. Washington had prescribed for African Americans?

3. Based on Du Bois's narrative, describe the conditions of African American education in the rural South at the turn of the century.

Source: W. E. Burghardt Du Bois, *Dusk of Dawn: An Essay Toward an Autobiography of a Race Concept* (New York: Schocken, 1968), pp. 30–31. First published in 1940. Cover from the 1940 edition published by Harcourt, Brace and Company, New York, 1940. Copyright © 1984 Transaction Publishers. Reprinted with permission.

was appointed to the United Nations as a delegate by President Truman when World War II ended.

Women's rights

Bethune was not only active in educational affairs; she was also an able advocate for women's and human rights. For example, she organized the National Council of Negro Women and the Southern Conference on Human Rights.[60] As an adviser to presidents Roosevelt and Truman, she became an important spokesperson for human rights in general and black rights in particular.

The Civil Rights Movement.   After World War II, the Commission on Civil Rights, appointed by President Harry S. Truman, recommended in its 1947 re-

---

[60]Harvard Sitkoff, *A New Deal for Blacks: The Emergence of Civil Rights as a National Issue*, vol. 1, *The Depression Decade* (New York: Oxford University Press, 1978).

Brown *decision*

port, *To Secure These Rights,* that legislation be enacted to prohibit segregation in schooling on the basis of race, religion, or national origin. The NAACP, through a series of court cases, sought to overturn the "separate but equal" doctrine that permitted segregation of schools, based on race, in seventeen border and southern states. In 1954, in the *Brown* decision, the U.S. Supreme Court held that racially segregated schools generated "a feeling of inferiority" and that "separate educational facilities are inherently unequal."

After the mid-1950s, the movement for civil and educational equality accelerated. Martin Luther King, Jr., emerged as the leader of a national nonviolent civil rights movement, which worked to increase educational opportunities for African Americans and other minority groups. At the same time that civil rights advocates were mobilizing throughout the nation, recalcitrant segregationists sought to evade compliance with the *Brown* decision. In 1957, President Eisenhower ordered federal troops to Little Rock, Arkansas, to enforce the Supreme Court's antisegregation decision.

Civil Rights Act

The enactment of the Civil Rights Act of 1964 further involved the federal government in efforts to end racial discrimination. The act authorized federally initiated lawsuits to compel compliance with desegregation in schools. It also authorized the withholding of federal funds from school districts that continued to discriminate. Efforts were made to end de facto segregation policies based on residence patterns. Some school districts embarked on busing programs in which students were transported from one attendance area to another in order to achieve racial balance and integration.

African American progress from a condition of slavery to the full enjoyment of civil, political, and educational rights has been slow and often torturous. While differing as to strategies, leaders such as Booker T. Washington, W.E.B. Du Bois, and Mary McLeod Bethune pursued a vision to, as Martin Luther King, Jr., eloquently asserted, make African American people "free at last." An important weapon in the march to freedom has been educational access and opportunity. Although African American secondary school completion rates and participation in higher education still lag behind those of whites, there has been a steady improvement since the *Brown* decision ended racial segregation in 1954. For example, the rates of high-school completion for African Americans increased dramatically from 1965 to 1987. In 1965 the rate of high-school completion was 22 percentage points lower than for whites; in 1987 the completion rate was 83 percent, only three percentage points lower.[61]

Native Americans

The educational institutions of the original inhabitants of North America were tribal. Young people were immersed in the culture and traditions of their own society. Tribal education involved vocational training: young men learned to hunt, fish, or trap, and young women learned to weave, prepare food, and care for children. Through the inculcation of religious rituals and folkways, chil-

Tribal education

---

[61]Laurence T. Ogle, ed., *The Condition of Education 1990,* vol. 1, *Elementary and Secondary Education* (Washington, D.C.: U.S. Government Printing Office, 1990), p. 22.

From 1890 to the 1930s, the Bureau of Indian Affairs operated boarding schools for Native American youngsters that stressed a basic curriculum of reading, writing, arithmetic, and vocational training. (© The University of Oklahoma Western History Collections)

dren were brought into participation in tribal life. Education was designed to perpetuate and transmit the cultural heritage of the particular tribe.

Efforts by the settlers of the New World to "educate" the indigenous people were fueled largely by the desire to spread western European ideas. In the Mississippi Valley, French missionaries, especially Jesuits, accompanied the explorers, fur traders, and soldiers attempting to create New France in the North American continent. The missionaries sought to convert the Native Americans to Catholicism. They also brought with them the French language and culture. In conjunction with their missionary efforts, the French attempted some rudimentary educational activities. In the Southwest, which was controlled by Spain, Franciscan missionary priests attempted to alleviate the exploitation of the Native Americans by the Spanish landlords. The Franciscans established missions to convert the Native Americans, and some of the children learned religion, reading, and writing in mission schools.

In the English colonies, Church of England missionaries established some schools under the auspices of the Society for the Propagation of the Gospel in Foreign Parts. English missionary and educational activities among the Native Americans were sporadic, however, and never took place on a large scale. Noteworthy educational efforts were also made by Moravians, a German religious group who were followers of the Bohemian bishop and educational reformer John Amos Comenius. The Moravians, who regarded education as an instrument for bringing peace to the world, went out to teach the Native American tribes. The Moravians translated the Bible and religious tracts into the Indian

Missionary educational efforts

languages spoken in Pennsylvania, North Carolina, and Ohio. Among the early Native American educators was Sequoyah, a Cherokee, who devised an alphabet in his native language. His alphabet, completed in 1832, made the Cherokees, a literate people, the first Native American tribe to have a written language.

After the United States gained its independence, the Native American tribes were pushed westward as the frontier expanded.[62] Eventually, the majority of Native Americans were resettled on reservations, usually against their will, in areas of the Great Plains and the Southwest. In the late nineteenth century, the federal government, assisted by well-intentioned reformers, established a policy designed to assimilate Native Americans into the larger white society. This policy attempted to erode tribal traditions by inculcating individualistic values into what was traditionally a cooperative society.

Assimilationist education

From 1890 to the 1930s, as the Bureau of Indian Affairs (BIA) pursued this educational policy of "forced assimilation," a foremost agency of assimilation was the **Native American boarding school.** In these institutions, Native American youngsters were removed from their tribal environments and cultures. Governed by strict military discipline, they were forbidden to speak their native languages and were forced to use English. The boarding schools stressed a basic curriculum of reading, writing, arithmetic, and vocational training.[63]

Boarding schools

Since the demise of the boarding-school concept in the 1930s, Native American society and education have undergone considerable change. The total population of Native Americans increased slowly, from an estimated 248,000 in 1890 to 357,000 in 1950, and then grew rapidly to 1,959,000 in 1990.[64] Many Native Americans have left the reservations to relocate in large urban centers, particularly inner cities. Children living on reservations attend a variety of schools: schools maintained by the Bureau of Indian Affairs, tribal schools, and other kinds of public and private institutions.[65] Native American children living in cities usually attend public schools.

Contemporary Native American schooling

Although assimilation is no longer an official U.S. government policy, prejudice against Native Americans and their cultural heritage remains, and this results in the alienation of many Native American youth from the educational system. Although 44 percent of Native Americans are under twenty years of age — compared to 32 percent of the national population — their participation in schooling is far lower than average. Because of a very high dropout rate, the level of Native American high-school completion is 67 percent below that of the U.S. population at large.[66]

---

[62]Robert M. Utley, *The Indian Frontier of the American West, 1846–1890* (Albuquerque: University of New Mexico Press, 1984).

[63]Robert A. Trennert, Jr., *The Phoenix Indian School: Forced Assimilation in Arizona, 1891–1935* (Norman: University of Oklahoma Press, 1988). Also see Trennert, "Corporal Punishment and the Politics of Indian Reform," *History of Education Quarterly* (Winter 1989), pp. 595–617.

[64]U.S. Department of Commerce, Bureau of the Census, *We, the First Americans* (Washington, D.C.: U.S. Government Printing Office, n.d.), p. 3; U.S. Bureau of the Census, *Statistical Abstract of the United States, 1991* (Washington, D.C.: U.S. Government Printing Office, 1991), p. 22.

[65]*We, the First Americans*, pp. 9–10.

[66]Ibid., pp. 4–5.

Hispanic Americans

Various Hispanic peoples and cultures

Hispanic Americans comprise the fastest growing minority group in the United States, although the African American population is larger. "Hispanic" is a collective term used to identify Spanish-speaking persons whose ethnic origins can be traced to Mexico, Puerto Rico, Cuba, or other Latin American countries. Whereas Hispanic Americans may speak Spanish as a common language and share many general Spanish traditions, each national group has its own distinctive culture.

Policy of Americanization

Among Hispanic Americans, Mexican Americans are the most numerous. Many of today's Mexican Americans are descendants of people who became U.S. citizens at the end of the Mexican-American War in 1848, when Mexico ceded to the United States large chunks of territory incorporated in the present states of California, Arizona, Texas, Colorado, and New Mexico.[67] In these southwestern states, the public schools followed the general pattern of assimilation used throughout the United States. Under a practice known as **Americanization,** the children of non-English-speaking groups such as Mexican Americans followed a curriculum in which English was the sole language of instruction and which reflected the English or Anglo-Saxon heritage and Protestant values. Mexican American children were taught in English, rather than their vernacular Spanish, and their own cultural heritage was ignored. Consequently, schooling imposed a negative self-image, treating Mexican American children as the conquered people of an inferior culture.[68]

Cultural heritage ignored

Few educational opportunities

In later years, the Mexican American population swelled as immigrants crossed the Mexican border to find work in the United States. Since Mexicans provided cheap labor on ranches, in railroad gangs, and especially as migrant farm workers, their entry was often encouraged. Their wages were low, their housing was frequently squalid, and their working conditions were harsh. Children of the migrant workers, even if they were not working in the fields with their parents, had few or no educational opportunities. Although many of the migrant workers eventually returned to Mexico, others stayed in the United States, either legally or illegally.

Chicano movement

Since World War II the Mexican American population has spread from the Southwest to other states, often to the industrial cities of the Northeast and Midwest. Today, approximately 90 percent of Mexican Americans live in urban communities. By the 1960s a Chicano movement emerging as a counterpart to the African American civil rights movement sought to improve the social, economic, and educational conditions of Mexican Americans. Led by César Chávez, Rudolpho González, José Guitiérrez, and others, this movement has raised national awareness of Mexican American concerns. In terms of education, however, Mexican Americans continue to show the effects of their long struggle for social and educational equality. Although some have entered higher education and the professions, their degree of participation in these areas remains below the national average.

---

[67]Leonard Dinnerstein and David M. Reimers, *Ethnic Americans: A History of Immigration and Assimilation* (New York: Harper & Row, 1982), pp. 88–89.

[68]Julian Nava, *Mexican Americans: A Brief Look at Their History* (New York: Anti-Defamation League of B'nai B'rith, 1970), p. 31. Also see Richard Griswold del Catillo, *The Treaty of Guadalupe Hidalgo* (Norman: University of Oklahoma Press, 1990).

*Common schools in
Puerto Rico*

The history of Puerto Rican Americans, another large Hispanic group, dates to the Spanish-American War of 1898, when the United States acquired the island of Puerto Rico. In 1917 Puerto Ricans were granted American citizenship. U.S. officials replaced the Spanish colonial system of education with the American common school. Although some classes continued to be taught in Spanish, English was made a compulsory language to further the process of Americanization. American educators also trained Puerto Rican teachers in U.S. instructional methods. The result was to create students who lived in two cultures, the Hispanic culture of their island and the American culture of the continental United States.

Dropout rates

Since the early decades of the twentieth century, there has been continuous Puerto Rican immigration to the mainland. Today, more than two million Puerto Rican Americans live in the large urban centers of the United States, such as New York, Chicago, and Philadelphia.[69] Economically and educationally, Puerto Rican Americans have often been disadvantaged. Their family median income is below the national average, and compared to the society as a whole, more families live below the poverty line; high-school dropout rates are high and college attendance rates are low. Throughout the 1980s, however, Puerto Rican Americans have made progress in improving their economic and educational position and have become more politically active and organized, especially in New York and Chicago. Programs such as ASPIRA have been established to encourage Puerto Rican American youth to complete high school and attend college.

Cuban Americans are among the most recent groups of Hispanic immigrants to the United States. Beginning in the 1960s, refugees fleeing the communist regime of Fidel Castro formed the first of several large waves of Cuban immigrants. Many Cubans entering the United States have been well-educated professionals; others, however, have been poor and unskilled. Although children from the wealthier families have generally adapted quickly to American schooling and culture, the economically disadvantaged have faced many of the same problems as other Hispanic Americans.

Bilingual Education Act

The passage of the Bilingual Education Act in 1968 was a watershed for all Hispanic Americans. That act, along with the 1974 Supreme Court decision in *Lau* v. *Nichols,* has led to the spread of bilingual education (see Chapter 11). Public schools have now abandoned the old system of assimilation and Americanization. Moreover, the recent movement toward multiculturalism has helped people recognize the contributions of the various racial, ethnic, and language groups that comprise the U.S. population.

Asian Americans

Entry on West Coast

Whereas European immigrants entered the United States by way of the East Coast, principally New York City, Asian Americans came by way of the West Coast, especially the cities of Los Angeles and San Francisco. For these geographical reasons, the Asian American population was concentrated historically in the western states bordering the Pacific Ocean. From there Asian Americans

[69]Dinnerstein and Reimers, *Ethnic Americans,* p. 102.

moved eastward. The first Asian people to settle in the United States were Chinese and Japanese. More recent Asian immigrant groups include Filipinos, Indians, Thais, Koreans, Vietnamese, Laotians, and Cambodians.

The first Chinese immigrants were merchants or laborers who arrived in California during the gold rush of 1849. In the following years, Chinese immigrants worked as miners, farm workers, and railroad construction workers.[70] Some also founded small businesses, such as grocery stores and laundries, in the cities of the West Coast. Japanese immigration began somewhat later, reaching a peak between 1880 and 1920.[71] From 1882 to 1924, however, the U.S. Congress enacted a number of laws to reduce or ban further immigration of Chinese or Japanese and prevent them from becoming U.S. citizens. For the immigrants who had arrived before these laws took effect, educational and economic opportunities were often limited by hostility and racial discrimination. In 1906, for example, the San Francisco Board of Education began a policy of segregating students of Asian ethnicity from other students. Only diplomatic protests from the Japanese government persuaded the board to rescind its policy.[72] Before World War II, few Chinese or Japanese Americans attained sufficient levels of education to enter the professions.

School segregation

For Japanese Americans, World War II — in particular the Japanese attack on Pearl Harbor — brought ethnic prejudice to the surface. Responding to fears that Japanese in the United States would aid the enemy, the U.S. government interned 110,000 people of Japanese heritage, most of whom were American citizens, in relocation camps. Located in remote areas, the camps lacked basic services and amenities. Although camp schools were eventually established for the young people, the internment experience produced both physical hardship and psychological alienation. The government's repressive action was based on unfounded fears, since not a single act of sabotage was committed by a Japanese American. Not until the 1980s did the federal government admit its wartime violation of civil liberties and provide compensation to those it had interned.[73]

Japanese American internment

A substantial number of Filipinos had also migrated to the mainland United States by the start of World War II. Because the Philippines was a U.S. commonwealth, Filipinos did not experience the immigration restrictions applied to other Asians. Many Filipino men served in the U.S. Navy and afterwards settled with their families on the West Coast. Others, especially in the 1930s, came to the mainland as farm workers.[74]

After World War II the economic and educational status of Chinese, Japanese, and Filipino Americans improved substantially. The McCarran-Walter Act of 1952, while retaining limited quotas, repealed the ban on Asian immigration and citizenship. Asian immigration then increased dramatically, and many of the newcomers were professionals with advanced education. Their arrival sparked a rise in higher education among Asian Americans generally. The

McCarran-Walter Act

Rise in higher education

---

[70]Dinnerstein and Reimers, *Ethnic Americans*, p. 25.

[71]Ibid., pp. 25, 34.

[72]Ibid., p. 52.

[73]Roger Daniels, Sandra C. Taylor, and Harry H. L. Kitano, *Japanese Americans: From Relocation to Redress* (Seattle: University of Washington Press, 1991).

[74]Dinnerstein and Reimers, *Ethnic Americans*, p. 63.

change has been particularly notable for Japanese Americans, who now enjoy more participation in higher education than either the white majority of Americans or any other minority group. Nearly 90 percent of third-generation Japanese Americans attend colleges or universities.

The post–World War II era also showed an increase in immigration by other Asian groups, especially Koreans, who usually located in large cities and often found success as small business people and merchants. Following the collapse of American-supported governments in Southeast Asia in the 1970s, Vietnamese, Cambodians, Laotians, and Hmongs have arrived in substantial numbers. *New Asian immigrants* These newest Asian immigrants have differing educational backgrounds. For example, among the South Vietnamese are former military officers, government officials, businessmen, and professionals. The Hmongs, by contrast, come from a rural culture that does not have a written language. Some recent Asian immigrants, called "boat people" because they fled political repression or civil war in rafts and sampans, have few possessions and little education that would be considered useful in Western technological society.

For all of these Asian American groups, as with the other minorities we have discussed, American schools must strive to eliminate the vestiges of discrimination, meet the needs of students from diverse backgrounds, and give full scope to the students' aspirations and talents. The next section surveys trends in American education since World War II, including efforts to promote equal educational opportunity.

TRENDS IN THE POSTWAR ERA

The civil rights movement, with its stress on expanding educational opportunities for minorities, was part of a general trend following World War II to extend the benefits of education to more and more Americans. This trend began even before the war concluded, with the 1944 passage of the Servicemen's Readjustment Act, better known as the G.I. Bill. To help readjust the society and the economy to peacetime and to reintegrate returning servicemen and servicewomen into American domestic life, the G.I. Bill provided federal funds to veterans to continue their educations. Tuition, fees, books, and living expenses were subsidized, and between 1944 and 1951, 7,800,000 veterans used the bill's assistance to attend technical schools, colleges, and universities. The effect was to double the nation's population of college students. The G.I. Bill ushered in the era of rapid growth of colleges and universities that would continue until the early 1970s.[75]

Debate about federal aid Although the Servicemen's Readjustment Act was a great success, the overall issue of federal financing of education proved problematic and has remained so to this day. Between 1945 and 1958, there was intense debate about federal aid to elementary and secondary schools. Special interests and unique political dynamics blocked the enactment of federal aid legislation. But in 1957 the po- *The space race* litical situation changed when the Soviet Union, the rival of the United States

---

[75]Diane Ravitch, *The Troubled Crusade: American Education, 1945–1980* (New York: Basic Books, 1983), pp. 3–14.

in the Cold War, successfully orbited *Sputnik,* a space satellite. The Soviet space success and well-publicized American space failures induced a climate of national crisis. In explaining America's slippage in the space race, critics pointed to the deficiencies of American students in mathematics and science. In response, Congress passed the National Defense Education Act (NDEA) of 1958, which appropriated federal funds to improve curricula and instruction in those areas considered crucial to national defense and security: mathematics, science, and foreign languages.

NDEA passed

The enactment of the Elementary and Secondary Education Act of 1965 (ESEA), a program related to President Lyndon B. Johnson's "War on Poverty," increased federal financial involvement still further, but in a different way. Whereas the NDEA emphasized science and mathematics, the ESEA was a federal response to the significant social change taking place in American society. Despite the *Brown* decision of 1954, many African American students as well as members of other minority groups, especially in inner-city areas, were educationally disadvantaged because of social and economic conditions. Stressing educational innovations, the ESEA encouraged special programs for children of low-income families and funded pilot programs to supplement the offerings of local school districts.[76] Johnson's "Great Society," especially through ESEA and the Economic Opportunity Act of 1964, created a range of early childhood educational programs for economically and culturally disadvantaged children. Known as Operation Head Start, these programs had an impact on early childhood education not only for minority children but for all children.

ESEA and the War on Poverty

Several important events of the 1970s had a direct effect on schooling. Title IX of the 1972 Education Amendments to the Civil Rights Act prohibited discrimination against women in education programs receiving federal assistance. This legislation, and later acts such as the Women's Educational Equity Act of 1974, evolved out of the extension of the civil rights movement to incorporate women's rights and concerns. Three years after Title IX, in 1975, Congress passed the Education for All Handicapped Children Act (PL 94-142). Like Head Start and bilingual education, PL 94-142 improved opportunities for a group of children who had previously lacked full access to a quality education. In this case, the new law established a national policy that children with handicaps would receive an "appropriate public education." An important provision of PL 94-142 was that, whenever possible, students with handicaps were to be "mainstreamed" into regular classrooms.

Title IX

Education for All Handicapped Children Act

The 1970s also witnessed the creation of the U.S. Department of Education. The new Department of Education had the status of being an independent agency of the federal government whose secretary was a member of the President's cabinet. Prior to the establishment of the Department in 1970, earlier Departments of Education were subordinate parts of other agencies, such as the Department of Interior or Department of Health, Education, and Welfare. Proponents of a Department of Education had argued that education was so important to the national welfare that it should be represented by a cabinet-level department. Opponents contended that the proposed department would involve

Creation of U.S. Department of Education

---

[76]Hugh Davis Graham, *The Uncertain Triumph: Federal Education Policy in the Kennedy and Johnson Years* (Chapel Hill: University of North Carolina Press, 1984), pp. 80–84, 98–112, 146–159.

the federal government in what historically was a prerogative of the states and local school districts. After considerable debate, and with the support of President Jimmy Carter, legislation establishing the new department passed in 1979. During the 1980s, however, the growth of federal involvement in education was reversed. The administration of President Ronald Reagan reduced federal financial support for education, transferring much of the responsibility to state governments.

National reports

Throughout the 1980s, the condition of American education became, once again, a hotly debated topic. A series of national reports, especially *A Nation at Risk,*[77] spotlighted failures in American schooling, much as the critics of the *Sputnik* era had done. The loss of U.S. dominance in the world economy was blamed on educational deficiencies, particularly in mathematics and science. Stimulated by *A Nation at Risk* and similar reports, many states initiated reform legislation to improve academic achievement in mathematics, science, and English. The reforms of the 1980s stressed academic standards, subject-matter courses, and improved school discipline. There was also an increased focus, as indicated in Chapter 1, on the competency of teachers and the changes needed to raise the level of teaching professionalism.

Trends in the 1990s

During the 1990s, curriculum is being shaped by emphasis on subject-matter competencies in English, mathematics, and basic sciences. Computer literacy, computer-assisted instruction, and other technologies in school programs reflect the nation's transition to a high-tech information society. There is a strong concern about the impact of foreign competition on the U.S. economy and a recognition that the competencies of the American workforce need to be improved. Private business and industry are taking a larger initiative to stimulate school reform and to design their own learning and training systems. Private and parochial schools are also educating a greater proportion of the nation's students than they did in the 1970s and 1980s. The debate about school funding continues, and the relative responsibilities of federal, state, and local agencies have yet to be fully resolved.

All of these trends will be discussed further in later chapters. As this chapter has demonstrated, educational issues have been at the core of American culture since the colonial era. Whatever new trends may unfold during the 1990s, the role of education will continue to be a central one for the evolution of American society.

WHAT IS UNIQUE ABOUT AMERICAN EDUCATION?

In contrast to Chapters 3 and 4, which traced many of our educational ideas and practices to earlier cultures and internationally known pioneers, this chapter has concentrated on the history of education in the United States. Although it's important to see our educational system in light of its historical roots, we should also recognize that some features of the national experience have made the American educational system unique.

---

[77]National Commission on Excellence in Education, *A Nation at Risk: The Imperative for Educational Reform* (Washington, D.C.: U.S. Department of Education, 1983), p. 14.

Encounters between different peoples and cultures

1. The history of the United States is characterized by continuing encounters between peoples of different races, cultures, and languages. The initial encounter, beginning in the fifteenth century, was between Europeans and Native Americans. While this encounter was often followed by hostility and outright war, there was also considerable cultural interchange and borrowing. The trend continued when later immigrants, including northern Europeans, eastern and southern Europeans, Hispanics, and Asians, provoked similarly problematical, yet often enriching, encounters. Particularly formative for the United States was the encounter between African Americans and white society, culminating in the civil rights movement and the struggle for equal educational opportunity. After a long period of trying to assimilate and "Americanize" minorities, the public schools now recognize and cultivate our legacy of cultural pluralism.

Influence of frontier

2. Much of American history was influenced by the westward-moving frontier. As the frontier shifted westward, institutions that reflected the political, social, economic, and educational life of the new republic moved with it. In American schooling, the frontier movement helped foster an emphasis on practical education and useful skills for everyday life, as opposed to the traditional focus on classical subjects.

Common schools

3. A number of factors, including the frontier movement, industrialization, and the need to educate citizens capable of participating in a self-governing society, spurred the development of the common school, one of the world's first systems of locally controlled, publicly supported, and almost universally accessible education. The common school philosophy, articulated by Horace Mann and others, was fundamentally democratic in concept. Over time, the egalitarian promises voiced by the common school founders have been increasingly fulfilled in the public schools.

Educational ladder

4. Public educational institutions in the United States are linked in such a way that American children can proceed from the elementary school, through secondary schools such as the middle school and high school, to complete their formal education in state colleges and universities. Thus all students have the opportunity to progress to higher education. This feature of the American system differs from the dual-track system, based on socioeconomic class, that has characterized education in many other countries.

Summing Up

1. The origins of American schooling in the colonial era were based on elitist and religiously oriented European antecedents. When the English colonists settled in North America, they brought with them the conventional European educational institutions based on a rigid social-class pattern. Primary or vernacular schools for the lower socioeconomic strata of society provided a basic curriculum of reading, writing, arithmetic, and religion. Preparatory schools, such as the Latin grammar school, and the colonial colleges were reserved for the upper class males. Offering a classical curriculum, Latin grammar schools and colleges were elitist and prepared the sons of favored families for leadership roles in church, state, and society. Although girls could attend the elementary vernacular schools, their formal educational opportunities were limited to the basic skills taught in primary schools.

2. After the United States won its independence, the forces of democracy, social mobility, and frontier egalitarianism eroded the elitist educational struc-

tures imported from Europe. The American common school arose as the educational institution designed to supply basic civic and skill competencies. The common or public school movement led to the establishment of elementary schools open to all children, both boys and girls.

3. The emergence of the public high school in the nineteenth century contributed to the growing inclusiveness of public schooling in the United States. The rise of state colleges and universities and the enactment of the Morrill Act in 1862 created the final step of an educational ladder that replaced the vestiges of the exclusive European dual-track system.

4. At the beginning of the twentieth century, the American public school system embraced elementary, secondary, and higher institutions. By the mid-twentieth century, concerted efforts were being made to bring equality of educational opportunity to the children of minority groups, especially African Americans, Native Americans, and Hispanic Americans. The major educational problem of the present lies in reforming schools into genuinely multicultural institutions that serve all Americans equally well, regardless of race, sex, or socioeconomic class.

5. The Americanization ideology of the late nineteenth and early twentieth centuries stressed assimilation into a homogeneous cultural pattern. This idea was replaced beginning in the mid-1960s by a pluralistic philosophy that values multicultural contributions of all American people, including those of hitherto neglected minority groups.

6. The recent trends in American education have been to include more groups in the mainstream of American schooling and to emphasize greater academic achievement in the face of technological change.

Key Terms

dual-track system of schools *(152)*

town school *(155)*

hornbook *(155)*

Latin grammar school *(156)*

academy *(160)*

monitorial method *(164)*

common school *(165)*

normal school *(167)*

McGuffey readers *(171)*

educational ladder *(172)*

high school *(173)*

Committee of Ten *(174)*

Commission on the Reorganization of Secondary Education *(175)*

junior high school *(176)*

middle school *(176)*

land-grant colleges *(177)*

Brown et al. v. *Board of Education of Topeka (181)*

Native American boarding school *(186)*

Americanization *(187)*

Discussion Questions

1. How has American education become more inclusive over time?

2. What has been the influence of the Puritan ethic on American culture and education?

3. Is Jefferson's concept of political education adequate for the needs of contemporary American society?

4. In terms of the history of American secondary education, why is the purpose of the high school so frequently a subject of controversy?

5. Compare and contrast the impacts of "Americanization" and cultural pluralism on the education of minorities in the United States.

6. Based upon an assessment of contemporary educational history, what major trends are affecting American schools?

Suggested Readings

Anderson, James D. *The Education of Blacks in the South, 1860–1935.* Chapel Hill: University of North Carolina Press, 1988.

> *A leading historian of the African American educational experience documents the role that stereotypic thinking played in the model of schooling imposed on African Americans in the South.*

Cohen, Ronald D. *Children of the Mill: Schooling and Society in Gary, Indiana, 1906–1960.* Bloomington: Indiana University Press, 1990.

> *Cohen's book offers much information about the impact of schooling on southern and eastern European ethnics and African Americans in a northern industrial city.*

Gutek, Gerald L. *An Historical Introduction to American Education.* 2nd ed. Prospect Heights, Ill.: Waveland Press, 1991.

> *This book provides a general narrative history of the development of key educational institutions in the United States as well as primary source readings.*

Herbst, Jurgen. *And Sadly Teach: Teacher Education and Professionalization in American Culture.* Madison: University of Wisconsin Press, 1989.

> *This book examines the history of U.S. teacher education as it relates to efforts to create a teaching profession.*

Kaestle, Carl, et al. *Literacy in the United States: Readers and Reading since 1880.* New Haven, Conn.: Yale University Press, 1991.

> *This book provides a historical perspective on the reading habits and literacy rates of Americans.*

Labaree, David F. *The Making of an American High School: The Credentials Market and the Central High School of Philadelphia, 1838–1939.* New Haven, Conn.: Yale University Press, 1988.

> *Labaree's book, acclaimed by the History of Education Society as the Outstanding Book of 1989, uses historical analysis to examine the functioning of an effective high school.*

Tyack, David, and Elisabeth Hansot. *Learning Together: A History of Coeducation in American Public Schools.* New Haven, Conn.: Yale University Press, 1990.

> *This book gives a comprehensive history of the policies and practices of gender in American public schools and examines the factors that have shaped coeducation.*

POLITICAL, ECONOMIC, AND LEGAL FOUNDATIONS

The three chapters in Part III deal with the governance and administration of public education, with school finance, and with the legal aspects of education. These chapters provide an overview of political, economic, and legal issues that are most relevant for classroom teachers.

Chapter 6, on governing and administering public education, begins by describing the organization and characteristics of schools and school districts. After delineating local and state roles and responsibilities, the chapter discusses the changing role of the federal government regarding education.

In Chapter 7, we focus on arrangements for financing schools. After describing local, state, and federal contributions to and responsibilities for the finance of public education, we consider a variety of recent trends in school finance, including the accountability movement and the arguments about tuition tax credits and vouchers.

Chapter 8, devoted to the legal aspects of education, discusses the functioning of the court system, teachers' and students' rights and responsibilities, religion and the schools, students and teachers with AIDS, and affirmative action. Teachers obviously must know what their rights and obligations are in order to discharge their responsibilities effectively, and they also must understand the rights and responsibilities of their students. Lack of knowledge regarding important legal issues such as employment contracts, freedom of expression, suspension of students, and religion in the schools not only can place the teacher's job in jeopardy but can cause serious problems in the operation of the educational system.

6

Governing and Administering Public Education

FOCUSING QUESTIONS

How do local, state, and federal governments influence education?

How does the local school board work with the district superintendent in formulating school policy?

Why have many school districts consolidated or decentralized?

What are the different roles and responsibilities of the governor, state legislature, state board of education, state department of education, and chief state school officer in determining school policy?

How has the federal role in education changed in recent years?

ducation in the United States is organized on various governmental levels — local, intermediate, state, and federal. Knowledge of the formal organization of schools and how they are governed is important to people who work in schools. Teachers, or prospective teachers, who know how schools are organized and how they are influenced at different levels of government will be in a better position to make wise choices and realistic decisions about schools and to take appropriate political action. In this chapter, we will examine the various governmental levels and how they affect education.

No national system of education

A national system of education does not exist in this country in the same sense that it does in Great Britain, France, or Japan. Education here is considered a state and/or local function; we have fifty different state systems and many differences among local school systems even within the same state.

State responsibility for public education

The U.S. Constitution makes no mention of public education, but the Tenth Amendment to the Constitution reserves to the states all powers not specifically delegated to the federal government or prohibited to the states by the Constitution. This amendment is the basis for allocating to the states primary legal responsibility for public education. However, responsibility for the practical day-to-day operation of school systems has been delegated by the states to local districts. So we begin our discussion of how schools are governed and administered at the local level.

LOCAL RESPONSIBILITIES AND ACTIVITIES

Every public school in the United States is part of a local school district. The district is created by the state. The state legislature, subject to the restrictions of the state constitution, can modify a local district's jurisdiction, change its boundaries and powers, or even eliminate it altogether. The local district encompasses a relatively small geographical area and operates the schools for children within a specific community. It is the avenue through which local citizens act in establishing districtwide policies in education. However, because a school district operates to carry out a state function, not a local function, local policies must be consistent with policies set forth in the state school code. The local district can be compared to a limited corporation whose powers are granted by state laws; it has only those powers expressly granted to it and those discretionary powers essential to its operation.

Local district like a limited corporation

Local School Boards

Delegated powers from the state

The local boards of education have been delegated powers and duties by the state for the purpose of assuring that their schools are operated properly. Despite the fact that the state limits their prerogatives, **local school boards** have assumed significant decision-making responsibility. School boards have the power for the most part to raise money through taxes. They exercise power over personnel and school property. Some states leave curriculum and student policy very much in the hands of the school board, but others, by law, impose specific requirements. In general, the school board must conform to state guidelines to qualify for state aid, as well as to federal guidelines where U.S. government monies are involved.

Most school boards elected

Methods of selecting board members are prescribed by state law. The two standard methods are election and appointment. Election is thought to make for greater accountability to the public, but some people argue that appointment leads to greater competence and less politics. Election is the most common practice. In 1991, 91 percent of school board members nationwide were elected in nonpartisan elections, 4 percent were elected in partisan elections (as members of a political party), and only 5 percent were appointed. Appointment is more common in large urban districts than in suburban or small-town districts; 11 percent of urban board members in 1991 were appointed.[1] A few states specify a standard number of board members, still others specify a permissible range, and a few have no requirements. Most school boards fall within a seven-to-nine-member range, with the largest school board having nineteen members.

Characteristics of board members

A recent nationwide survey of school board members indicates that the number of women on school boards has increased, from about 33 percent in 1981 to almost 35 percent in 1991. (See Figure 6.1.) Minority representation has declined over the same period from 8.5 percent to 5.5 percent. (Southern states show a higher minority representation on school boards: 11 percent black and 3 percent Hispanic.)[2] School board members tend to be older than the general population (78 percent are over forty); more educated (68 percent have had four or more years of college); wealthier (29 percent have family incomes of $50,000 or more, and 16 percent earn more than $100,000 annually); and more likely to be professionals or managers (50 percent) or owners of their own businesses (12 percent). Interestingly, only 51 percent are parents, and 37 percent have no children in school right now.[3]

The largest one hundred school systems (those enrolling 35,000 or more students) tend to have more heterogeneous boards. A 1991 survey indicates that minority members constitute 28 percent of the school board in these systems; women make up 42 percent.[4]

Types of board meetings

There are three types of board meeting: regular, special, and executive. The first two are usually open meetings and the public is invited. The third type is usually closed to the public and deals with managerial issues or serious problems. Open board meetings obviously enhance school-community relations and allow parents to understand the problems of education as well as air their concerns. The use of closed board meetings to reach major policy decisions is often criticized, but this tactic is occasionally used by central school boards in large cities to minimize conflict and tension. Many school districts have mandated that their meetings be open except under certain specified and rather limited conditions.

---

[1]"Leadership," *American School Board Journal* (December 1991), pp. A10–A12; Nellie C. Weil, "The Significance of Being a School Board Member," *American School Board Journal* (November 1987), pp. 1–4.

[2]"The Demographics of Board Service," *American School Board Journal* (January 1992), pp. 36–37; "School Board Survey: Happily Ever After," *American School Board Journal* (January 1990), pp. 28–33.

[3]"Twelfth Annual Survey of School Board Members: Here's Looking at You," *American School Board Journal* (January 1990), p. 34; "Leadership," pp. A10–A12.

[4]Allan C. Ornstein, "School Superintendents and School Board Members: Who They Are," *Contemporary Education* (Winter 1992), pp. 157–159.

Figure 6.1

Demographics of Local and State School Board Members

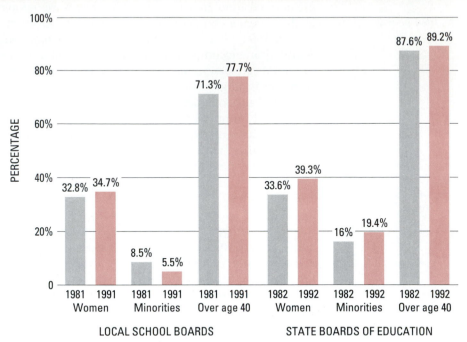

Source: "The Demographics of Board Service," *American School Board Journal* (January 1992), pp. 36–37; "Leadership," *American School Board Journal* (December 1991), pp. A10–A12; "School Board Survey: Happily Ever After," *American School Board Journal* (January 1990), pp. 28–33; Dinah Wiley, *State Boards of Education* (Arlington, Va.: National Association of State Boards of Education, 1983), Tables 1–2, pp. 15–16; and letter from Carolyn Curry, Director of Public Relations, National Association of State Boards of Education, January 22, 1992.

School Board Responsibilities

Schools are big business

    The administration and management of schools is big business, and school board members must have or acquire knowledge of good business practices. Overall, school boards have fiscal responsibility for $215 billion each year and employ more than 4.3 million teachers, administrators, and support staff (such as guidance counselors, librarians, and nurses);[5] this makes them the largest nationwide employer. Board members must be fair and mindful of the law when dealing with students, teachers, administrators, parents, and other community residents. In districts where the school board is elected, board members are subject to the same laws as other elective officials; in many states, each member must file a statement of ethics.

    Board members are expected to govern the school system without encroaching on the authority of the superintendent. Members, in theory, have no au-

[5]*Digest of Education Statistics, 1990* (Washington, D.C.: U.S. Government Printing Office, 1991), Table 78, p. 91.

Political prudence

thority except during a board meeting and while acting as a collective group or board. Board members must be politically prudent because eventually someone will ask for a favor — a friend, a friend of a friend, or a special-interest group — and members must be able to resist this pressure.

School boards as seen by superintendents

The quality of local schools is an important factor in determining a community's reputation, the value of property, and the willingness of businesses to locate nearby. Yet according to a recent survey of sixty-six Illinois school superintendents, school boards have become more political and divisive in recent years; board members are less willing to compromise on major issues, and there is a greater tendency among candidates to represent coalitions or special-interest groups. In short, at least in the view of school superintendents, the new board members seem more interested in the views of their electors than in the views of other board members or professional educators.[6]

The powers and responsibilities of school boards may be classified as follows:

Responsibilities of school board members

1. *Policy.* School boards set the general rules about what will be done in the schools, who will do it, and how.

2. *Staffing.* Technically the board is responsible for hiring all the employees of the school district. In practice, however, school boards usually confine themselves to recruiting and selecting the school superintendent (the district's chief executive officer) and high-ranking members of the central office staff. Decisions on the hiring and retention of principals and teachers are usually made at lower levels of the hierarchy, after review by professional peers.

3. *Employee relations.* School board members are responsible for all aspects of employee relations, including collective bargaining with teacher unions. Large school districts rely on consultants or attorneys to negotiate with teachers; small school districts may use the superintendent or a school board committee to negotiate.

4. *Fiscal matters.* The board must keep the school district solvent, effect savings when possible, and get the most out of every tax dollar. The school district usually has a larger budget than does any other local public agency; the school superintendent normally makes more money than any other local official, including the mayor, fire chief, and police chief.

5. *Students.* The board addresses questions of student rights and responsibilities, extracurricular activities, attendance, and requirements for promotion and graduation.

6. *Curriculum.* The school board is in charge of developing curriculum — especially as it relates to state law and guidelines — and approving the textbooks to be used.

7. *Community relations.* The school board must be responsive not only to parents but also to other members of the community.

---

[6]David Eisner, "School Boards More Political," *Chicago Tribune*, January 22, 1990, sect. 2, p. 4; Mel Heller and Edward Ransic, "Are We Turning Superintendents into Politicians?," *Illinois School Board Journal* (May-June 1992), pp. 12–13.

8. *Intergovernmental requirements.* Federal and state agencies establish a variety of requirements for local schools, and the school board is responsible for seeing that these mandates are carried out.[7]

The School Superintendent and Central Office Staff

Executive officer of school system

One of the board's most important responsibilities is to appoint a competent **superintendent of schools.** The superintendent is the executive officer of the school system, whereas the board is the legislative policy-making body. Since the school board consists of laypeople who are not experts in school affairs, it is their responsibility to see that the work of the school is properly performed by professional personnel. The board of education often delegates many of its own legal powers to the superintendent and staff, although the superintendent's policies are subject to board approval.

Board reliance on superintendent

One of the major functions of the school superintendent is to gather and present data so that school board members can make intelligent policy decisions. Increasing board reliance on the superintendent and staff is evident as school systems grow in size. The superintendent advises the school board and keeps members abreast of problems; generally, the school board will refuse to enact legislation or make policy without the recommendation of the school superintendent. However, it is common knowledge that when there is continual disagreement or a major conflict over policy between the school board and the superintendent, the latter is usually replaced. The average tenure of superintendents is only approximately three to four years.[8] One 1991 survey reported that 24 percent of the superintendents in the largest one hundred school districts had served in their current positions for one year or less.[9]

The superintendent's powers are broad and his or her duties are many and varied. Besides being an adviser to the board of education, he or she is usually responsible for certain other functions, including the following:

Duties of the superintendent

1. Serves as supervisor and organizer of professional and nonteaching (for example, janitors and engineers) personnel
2. Makes recommendations regarding the employment, promotion, and dismissal of personnel
3. Ensures compliance with directives of higher authority
4. Prepares the school budget for board review and administers the adopted budget
5. Serves as leader of long-range planning
6. Develops and evaluates curriculum and instructional program

---

[7]Eva K. Bascal,"On Being a Board Member," *American School Board Journal* (November 1987), pp. 11–16; Robert S. Ross, "The Role of the Local School Board," *American School Board Journal* (November 1987), pp. 5–10.

[8]William E. Eaton, *Shaping the Superintendency* (New York: Teachers College Press, Columbia University, 1990); Ralph B. Kimbrough and Michael Y. Nunnery, *Educational Administration,* 3rd ed. (New York: Macmillan, 1988).

[9]Ornstein, "School Superintendents and School Board Members."

One of the major functions of the school superintendent is to gather and present data so that school board members can make intelligent policy decisions. (© Carmen Chan/Amstock)

7. Determines internal organization of the school district

8. Makes recommendations regarding school building needs and maintenance

In addition, the superintendent is responsible for the day-to-day operation of the schools within the district and serves as the major public spokesperson for the schools.

Community pressure on superintendents

Superintendents are often under strong pressure from various segments of the community, and much of the superintendent's effectiveness will depend on his or her ability to deal with such pressure groups. In large urban school districts, for example, demands may be made for better facilities for students with handicaps or learning disabilities, for more bilingual programs, or for improved vocational education. In middle-class suburbs, parents may be especially sensitive to student achievement scores, demanding upgraded programs if they feel the education is not as superior as their children deserve. In small or rural districts where enrollments are declining, the superintendent may be pressured, on the one hand, to save money by closing schools and, on the other hand, to keep all schools open to preserve the pride and identity of the community. In nearly all these situations, the superintendent must face either disgruntled parents or organized community groups with their own agendas (sometimes overt, sometimes covert). Only a confident school leader can balance the demands and expectations of parents and community groups with the needs of the students.

A **central office staff** assists the superintendent in fulfilling these responsibilities. In large districts of 25,000 or more students, there may be many levels in the staff hierarchy: a deputy superintendent, associate superintendents, assistant superintendents, directors, department heads, and a number of coordinators and supervisors, each with their own support staffs. Central staff matrices are often built on top of other matrices, each with its own functions that are sometimes jealously guarded. Decisions that should take days or weeks sometimes take months or even years, as each department conducts its own review and adds its own recommendations to be considered by the next level.

The picture is further complicated when a large school district decentralizes its operation into several areas or subdistricts; each area may have a "field" superintendent and staff (as well as other administrators) who report to an associate superintendent in the central office.[10] Although the idea of decentralization is to streamline the system, what often happens is that the school district adds a new bureaucratic layer.

Central office organization

In small school districts, the operation of the central office is less bureaucratic simply because there are fewer layers. Figure 6.2 illustrates a small (and "flat") district of more than 1,000 and fewer than 5,000 students, which represents 35 percent of all districts. Figure 6.3 shows a larger (and "taller") organizational chart of a medium-sized school district with 5,000 to 25,000 students; this is representative of almost 10 percent of the school districts nationwide.[11] The organizational hierarchy of larger school districts is even more cumbersome, and a chart of those with 100,000 or more students would extend off the page.

Critique of bureaucracy

Critics charge that the many-layered bureaucracy of large school districts is inefficient — a waste of the taxpayers' money. In terms of administrator-to-student ratios, however, the largest districts are not necessarily the least efficient. For example, in a 1989 survey of fifty-one school districts with 50,000 or more students, the largest districts (those with over 100,000 students) averaged one manager per 579 students; the districts with enrollments between 50,000 and 99,999 averaged one manager per 561 students. By this measurement, the larger districts were slightly more efficient. Only six school districts had manager–student ratios of 1 per 1,000 or higher; the Granite, Utah, school district reported the most efficient ratio of 1 manager per 1,650 students.[12] To be sure, school districts of all sizes should take to heart the lesson learned by many large corporations in the late 1980s: in an era of limited resources, streamlining of the top layers may be crucial to survival. Of course, some administration of school systems is vital, in order to provide consistent educational services for children and leadership for the staff. However, school districts of all sizes should take to heart the need to trim the fat and save money, especially in an era of retrenchment and downsizing (small cars, small homes, less savings).

The Principal and the School

Small vs. large schools

Usually, each school has a single administrative officer, a **principal,** who is responsible for school operations. In small schools, the principal may teach part time as well; in large schools, there may be one or more assistant or vice principals. The administrative hierarchy may also consist of a number of department chairpersons, a discipline officer (e.g., dean of boys, dean of girls), a director of

---

[10]Daniel J. Brown, *Decentralization and School-Based Management* (New York: Falmer Press, 1990); Sherry Keith, *Education, Management, and Participation* (Needham Heights, Mass.: Allyn and Bacon, 1991).

[11]*Digest of Education Statistics, 1990,* Table 85, p. 96.

[12]Allan C. Ornstein, "Administrator-Student Ratios in Large School Districts," *Phi Delta Kappan* (June 1989), pp. 806–808.

Typical Small-sized School District (More Than 1,000 and Fewer Than 5,000 Students)

Figure 6.2

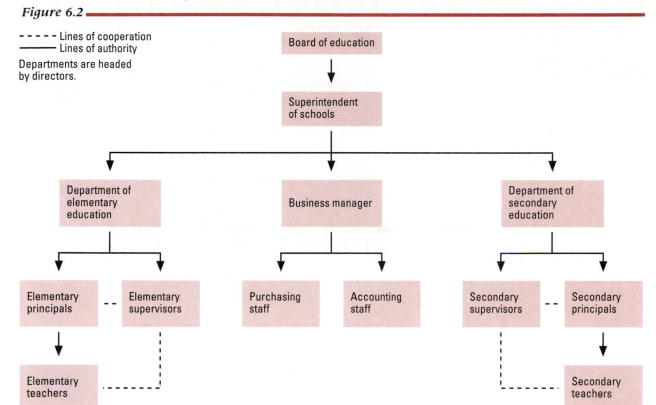

- - - - - Lines of cooperation
———— Lines of authority
Departments are headed
by directors.

guidance, and so on. Furthermore, it is common practice for the principal to work with some type of community group for the improvement of the school; this group is often a parent-teacher association or an advisory school-community committee.

The principal's role

Probably the most important aspect of the principal's job is the role of manager: dealing with the day-to-day operation of the school, the meetings, paperwork, phone calls, and other everyday tasks. However, principals are also expected to exert leadership in curriculum and instruction. Some authorities recommend that principals spend from 50 to 75 percent of their time improving curriculum and instruction;[13] but as principals point out, their numerous managerial tasks often make this impossible. In general, secondary school principals tend to see themselves primarily as general managers, whereas elementary school principals view themselves as leaders in curriculum and instruction.[14] The

[13]Daniel L. Duke, *School Leadership and Instructional Improvement* (New York: Random House, 1987); Thomas J. Sergiovanni, *The Principalship: A Reflective Practice Perspective,* 2nd ed. (Needham Heights, Mass.: Allyn and Bacon, 1991).

[14]Dale L. Brubaker and Lawrence H. Simon, "How Do Principals View Themselves, Others," *NASSP Bulletin* (January 1987), pp. 72–78; Laura A. Cooper, "The Principal as Instructional Leader," *Principal* (January 1989), pp. 13–16; Allan C. Ornstein, "The Principal as Leader," *American Secondary Education* (No. 2, 1991), pp. 16–21.

Typical Medium-sized School District (5,000 to 25,000 Students)

Figure 6.3 ━━

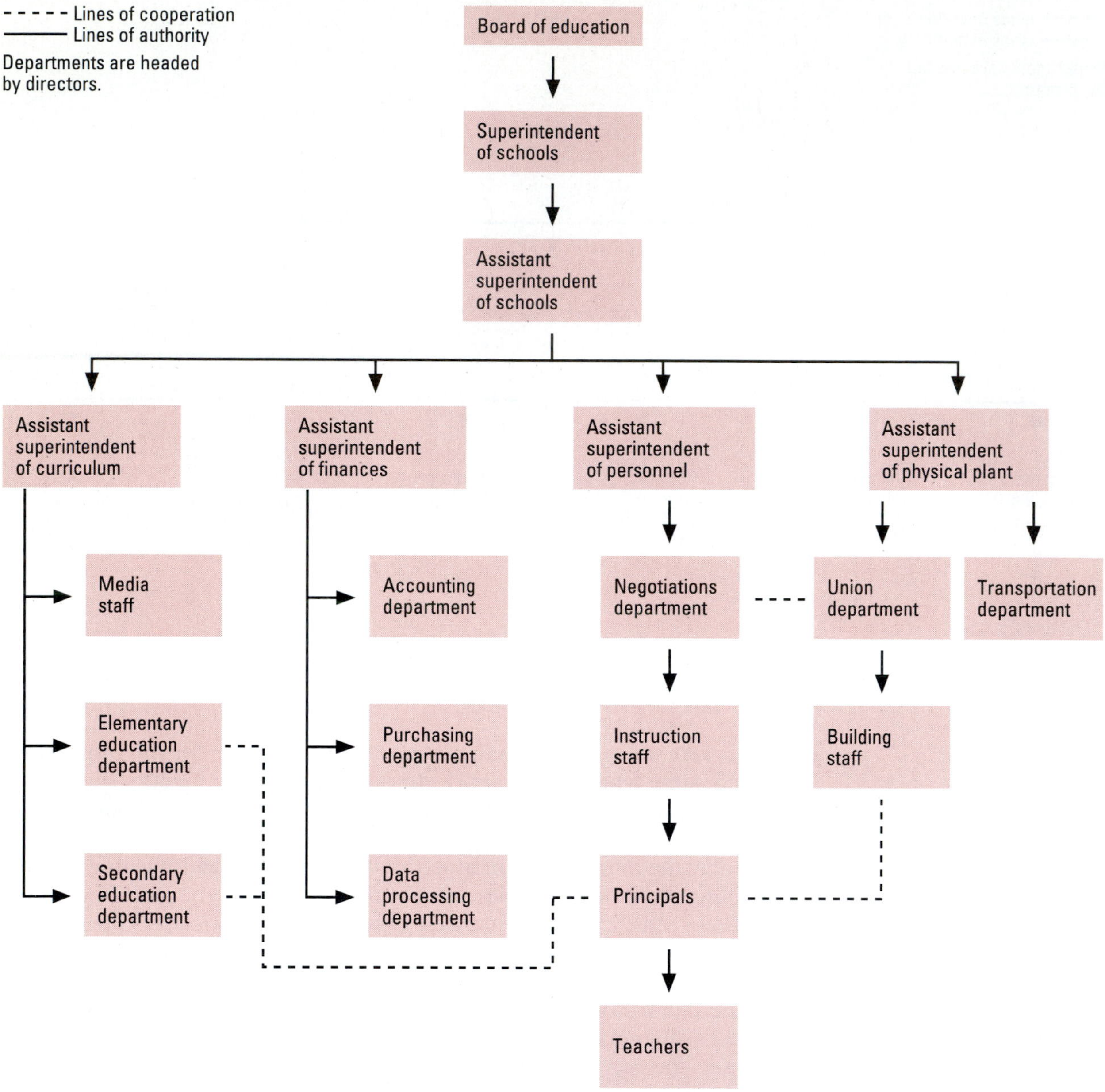

- - - - - Lines of cooperation
─────── Lines of authority
Departments are headed
by directors.

```
                                    Board of education
                                          │
                                          ▼
                                    Superintendent
                                    of schools
                                          │
                                          ▼
                                    Assistant
                                    superintendent
                                    of schools
```

Assistant superintendent of curriculum	Assistant superintendent of finances	Assistant superintendent of personnel	Assistant superintendent of physical plant
Media staff	Accounting department	Negotiations department ---- Union department	Transportation department
Elementary education department	Purchasing department	Instruction staff	Building staff
Secondary education department	Data processing department	Principals	
		Teachers	

reason for this difference may be that the larger size of secondary schools creates more managerial work for the principal. Moreover, secondary school principals are usually assisted by chairpersons in various subject areas who handle curriculum and instructional activities; elementary school principals rarely have such assistance.

Traditionally, authority concerning school policies has proceeded in a top-down fashion, from the school board through the superintendent and central

In general, secondary school principals tend to see themselves primarily as general managers, whereas elementary school principals view themselves as leaders in curriculum and instruction. (© Carmen Chan/Amstock)

School-based management

New role for principals

office staff to the principal. In some districts, however, as explained in Chapter 2, the practice of school-based management has brought more decision-making power to the level of the individual school. This allows principals and teachers increased responsibility for such matters as curriculum, staff development, teaching assignments, and even budgeting. The principal's function therefore changes to some degree; rather than simply managing from above, the principal collaborates with teachers and other school staff to create school policies. This arrangement calls for a more participatory leadership style than is traditional for school principals.[15] Between 750 and 1,000 school districts experimented with such collaboration between 1987 and 1992; interest has been especially strong in the larger states, such as California, Florida, Illinois, Michigan, and New York.

Parent and Community Involvement

Many programs for school-based management go beyond collaboration among principals and teachers; they give important roles to parents and other community members as well. In doing so, they build on a movement for increased parent and community involvement that has been evident for two decades or more.

---

[15]Larry E. Frase and R. Gerald Melton, "Manager or Participatory Leader? What Does It Take?" *NASSP Bulletin* (January 1992), pp. 17–25; Peter Murphy, "Collaborative School Management: Implications for School Leaders," *NASSP Bulletin* (October 1991), pp. 63–66.

*Reasons for
parent involvement*

Many educators have promoted parent involvement for the most basic of reasons: research indicates that it pays off in higher student test scores, better grades, and improved attitudes toward learning.[16] This may be particularly true for inner-city and minority students.[17] Across the nation, polls indicate that the public overwhelmingly supports the idea of parent involvement and believes that parents play a major role in children's education.[18]

Uninvolved parents

Nevertheless, few parents take full advantage of existing opportunities to involve themselves with their children's schooling. According to one survey of 1,270 parents and 3,700 teachers, the majority of parents had neither the time nor the inclination to participate deeply in school matters. More than 75 percent never helped teachers in the classroom or participated in school functions.[19] In 1991 only 32 percent of parents with eighth-grade children reported that they belonged to a parent-teacher organization, and only 36 percent had attended one or more school meetings.[20]

*Types of community
involvement*

Despite such lack of participation from individual parents, the pressure for reform has produced formal arrangements that give parents and other community members a voice in local educational decisions. Usually the community members merely offer advice, but in a few cases they have been granted substantial control over the schools. For purposes of discussion, we can divide the types of community involvement into three broad categories: community participation, community control, and community education.

Community Participation.   The usual form of **community participation** involves advisory committees at either the neighborhood school or central board level. These committees are usually appointed by school officials; in only a few cases are the advisory groups elected by the community. Although the committees offer help and advice, the school board maintains its authority, and the advisory groups must abide by the rules and regulations of the system. Citizen

*Areas of community
participation*

groups provide advice and assistance to educators in many areas: (1) identification of goals, priorities, and needs; (2) selection and evaluation of teachers and principals; (3) development of curricula and extracurricular programs; (4) community support and financing for schools; (5) recruitment of volunteers; and (6) assistance to students in school and in "homework hotline" programs.[21]

---

[16]Lloyd Campbell, "Parents and Schools Working for Student Success," *NASSP Bulletin* (April 1992), pp. 1–4; Anne Henderson, *The Evidence Continues to Grow: Parent Involvement Improves Student Achievement* (Columbia, Md.: National Committee for Citizens in Education, 1987).

[17]James P. Comer, "Empowering Black Children's Educational Environment," in H. P. McAdoo and J. L. McAdoo, eds., *Black Children* (Beverly Hills, Calif.: Sage, 1985), pp. 114–139; Comer, "Parent Participation in the Schools," *Phi Delta Kappan* (February 1986), pp. 442–446; and Barbara L. Jackson and Bruce S. Cooper, "Involving Parents in Urban Schools," *NASSP Bulletin* (April 1992), pp. 30–38.

[18]Frank E. Nardine, "Parent Involvement in the States," *Phi Delta Kappan* (January 1991), pp. 363–366.

[19]Joyce L. Epstein, *Study of Teacher Practices of Parent Involvement* (Baltimore, Md.: Center for Social Organization of Schools, Johns Hopkins University, 1983).

[20]*Digest of Education Statistics, 1990,* Table 22, p. 29; "Parent Involvement," *NEA Today* (March 1991), p. 12.

[21]Don Davies, "Schools Reaching Out: Family, School and Community Partnerships," *Phi Delta Kappan* (January 1991), pp. 376–382; Izona Warner, "Parents in Touch: District Leadership for Parent Involvement," *Phi Delta Kappan* (January 1991), pp. 372–375.

Late in 1989, more than 6,000 members of Chicago's first local school councils were sworn into their posts and began the task of implementing school reform in the nation's third-largest school district. (© AP/ Wide World Photos)

Shared power

Community Control. In a system of **community control,** an elected community council or board does more than offer advice — it shares decision-making power with the central school board. Systems of this sort evolved in New York City and Detroit in the 1970s, but bitter disputes soon erupted between African American and white members and between militant community representatives and professional educators.[22] Detroit ultimately rescinded the powers of the community school boards in the early 1980s. In New York City, community control has persisted, but disputes about exactly who represents the community are frequent. In 1990 Chicago instituted a form of community control as part of local educational reform; parent and community groups were given significant input regarding matters such as recruitment and retention of the school principal, curriculum, and budgets. At the present, the Chicago plan seems to be gaining momentum.[23]

Many educational agencies

Community Education. Since the early 1980s, the school has come to be seen as one, but only one, of the educational agencies within the community. Museums, libraries, parks, businesses, private foundations, labor unions, religious institutions, health care centers, and self-help groups, among others, perform important educational functions. The school serves as a partner — or possibly as a coordinating institution — in developing various community

---

[22]Bernard Bell, "The Battle for School Jobs: New York's Newest Agony," *Phi Delta Kappan* (May 1972), pp. 553–558; Martin Schiff, "The Educational Failure of Community Control in Inner-City New York," *Phi Delta Kappan* (February 1976), pp. 375–378; and telephone conversation with Anthony Alvarado, Superintendent of District #2, New York City Board of Education, August 9, 1991.

[23]G. Alfred Hess, *School Restructuring, Chicago Style* (Newbury Park, Calif.: Corwin Press, 1991).

Taking Issue ◄●─────────────────────────────

The Politics of Community Control

In the 1960s and 1970s, community control became a catchword of the Black Power movement and was seen as one way for African Americans to exert some influence over the neighborhood schools their children attended. By the 1980s this idea had lost ground as the less radical alternative of community participation in schools gained momentum. Recently, however, under the heading of "school reform," the idea of community control has resurfaced as a thorny political issue.

Question: Will increased community control of schools improve education?

Arguments PRO

1 Community control will make teachers and administrators accountable to parents and community residents, where the authority truly belongs.

2 Community control will lead to greater educational innovation and help streamline existing school bureaucracies.

3 Community control will lead to greater public participation in the schools, especially from the parents of children who are failing.

4 Only strict community control will compel local school boards to hire qualified principals and superintendents who can relate to the children they are serving.

5 Under community control schools will develop instructional programs that raise student achievement and increase cultural pride among minority groups.

6 Community control will increase participatory democracy and the power of the people.

Arguments CON

1 It is questionable whether community groups, who often have their own hidden agendas, can objectively assess the performance of teachers and administrators.

2 Community school boards are too focused on politics and self-interest to take the necessary steps required for educational innovation.

3 Most people, including parents, have little time as it is to participate in school affairs. The increased responsibility demanded by community control will discourage parental involvement.

4 Community control will result in hiring and promotion patterns based on race and ethnicity rather than on merit.

5 Community control may actually hinder student achievement by favoring cultural programs over academic programs.

6 Community control leads to extremism, vigilantism, and separatism among people.

educational, social, recreational, and cultural activities. This concept has been referred to as **community education.**[24]

Because the school is part of a community system, it avoids duplicating services provided by other local agencies. The delivery system is open to all consumers: students, parents, childless adults, and aging populations.[25] The notion

[24]Mario D. Fantini, Elizabeth L. Loughren, and Horace B. Reed, "Toward a Definition of Community Education," *Community Education Journal* (April 1980), pp. 11–33; Bruce L. Wilson and Gretchen B. Rossman, "Collaborative Links with the Community: Lessons from Exemplary Secondary Schools," *Phi Delta Kappan* (June 1986), pp. 708–711.

[25]Dan Conrad and Diane Hedin, "School-Based Community Service: What We Know From Research and Theory," *Phi Delta Kappan* (June 1991), pp. 743–749; Allan C. Ornstein, "Redefining

Lifelong education

of lifelong education, and the education of diverse learners of various age groups, is an integral part of community education. In Flint, Michigan, for example, some fifty schools offer a host of educational, recreational, family, and community services to local citizens, including a wide range of preschool programs for three- and four-year-olds and their parents, as well as adult sports and drama, exercise, recreational, and vocational programs.[26]

Needs of diverse groups

As part of the community education plan, schools share their personnel (such as teachers, counselors, and specialists) and facilities (such as portions of the building, yard, or stadium, and buses) with other community agencies or businesses; open their physical plant to a larger segment of the community; and offer programs and services to meet the growing needs of diverse population groups (such as working mothers, businesspeople, and retirees). This sharing process takes place not only after school hours, on weekends or holidays, but also during school hours and school days — whenever underutilized space (say a conference room, auditorium, or pool), equipment, or personnel may be shared for a portion of the day. In return, the schools may expect to share in the facilities, equipment, and personnel of other community agencies and local businesses and may expect increased private and public support for their programs and people. This type of sharing is especially important in a period of retrenchment and school budget cutbacks.

Size of Schools and School Districts

Educators have long debated the question of size: How large should a school be? How many students should be enrolled in a single district? Over thirty years ago, James Conant argued that the most effective high schools were the ones large enough to offer comprehensive and diversified facilities.[27] More recently, however, other educators have contended that small schools are more effective.

Ideal school size

Advantages of small schools

In 1987, after reviewing several studies, two researchers concluded that high schools should have no more than 250 students. Larger enrollments, according to this analysis, result in a preoccupation with control and order, and the anonymity of a large school makes it harder to establish a sense of commitment among students, teachers, and parents.[28] Sociological data also suggest that in large high schools the students and teachers may become psychologically distant from each other; in this situation many "average" students may be overlooked. Large schools foster less identification and sense of belonging than do small schools.[29] Furthermore, since many smaller schools are located in towns where the school serves as a hub of the community's social life, the close relationships among teachers, parents, and neighbors may be a substantial impetus to students' achievement.

Parent and Community Involvement," *Journal of Research and Development in Education* (Summer 1983), pp. 37–45.

[26]Ibid.

[27]James B. Conant, *The American High School Today* (New York: McGraw-Hill, 1959).

[28]Thomas B. Gregory and Gerald R. Smith, *High Schools as Communities: The Small School Reconsidered* (Bloomington, Ind.: Phi Delta Kappa, 1987).

[29]Philip A. Cusick, *Inside High School* (New York: Holt, 1973); Joyce L. Epstein and Nancy I. Karweit, eds., *Friendships in School* (New York: Academic Press, 1983); and Peter McLaren, *Life in Schools* (New York: Longman, 1988).

Getting to the Source

The Problems of Small Schools / James Conant

THE **AMERICAN HIGH SCHOOL TODAY**

A First Report to Interested Citizens
by **JAMES BRYANT CONANT**

McGRAW-HILL BOOK COMPANY, INC.
New York   Toronto   London

***P**robably the most influential educator of the midtwentieth century, James Conant rose to the presidency of Harvard University by age forty. His history-making studies of American schools and teachers have helped to shape educational policy for over a quarter century. In the following selection, he sets* forth the basis of his argument for consolidating or reorganizing school districts in order to eliminate small high schools. Some of these ideas are controversial today.

The enrollment of many American public high schools is too small to allow a diversified curriculum except at exorbitant expense. The prevalence of such high schools — those with graduating classes of less than one hundred students — constitutes one of the serious obstacles to good secondary education throughout most of the United States. I believe such schools are not in a position to provide a satisfactory education for any group of their students — the academically talented, the vocationally oriented, or the slow reader. The instructional program is neither sufficiently broad nor sufficiently challenging. A small high school cannot by its very nature offer a comprehensive curriculum. Furthermore, such a school uses uneconomically the time and efforts of administrators, teachers, and specialists, the shortage of whom is a serious national problem.

Financial considerations restrict the course offerings of the small high schools. As the curriculum is narrowed, so is the opportunity for a meaningful program. Unless a graduating class contains at least one hundred students, classes in advanced subjects and separate sections within all classes become impossible except with

Ideal size of districts

The debate about school size parallels similar disputes about the optimum size of school districts. Larger school districts, according to their proponents, offer a broader tax base and reduce the educational cost per student; consequently, these districts are better able to afford high-quality personnel, a wide range of educational programs and special services, and good transportation facilities. Most studies of this subject over the last sixty years have placed the most effective school district size between 10,000 and 50,000 students,[30] although one

[30]Howard A. Dawson, *Satisfactory Local School Units,* Field Study no. 7 (Nashville, Tenn.: George Peabody College for Teachers, 1934); Mario D. Fantini, Marilyn Gittell, and Richard Magat, *Community Control and the Urban School* (New York: Praeger, 1970); A. Harry Passow, *Toward Creating a Model Urban School System* (New York: Teachers College Press, Columbia University, 1967); and

extravagantly high costs. . . . The normal pattern of distribution of academic talent is such that a class of one hundred will have between fifteen and twenty academically talented students — those who can and should study effectively and rewardingly advanced courses in mathematics, science, and foreign languages as well as general education courses in English and social studies. A slightly smaller number of less bright students will, if they work hard, be able to study a somewhat less intensive program. In a class of one hundred, these two groups together will barely provide sufficient enrollment to justify the school's offering advanced academic courses. If the graduating class were much smaller, these two groups together would be too small to warrant a properly organized sequential program in mathematics, science, and foreign languages. The reluctance of academically talented girls to study advanced science and mathematics courses exists also in small high schools and adds to the financial difficulty of offering such courses. . . .

In many of the really small high schools there are only a few teachers. The scope even of the academic program is correspondingly limited. Courses are often not offered in advanced mathematics, physics or chemistry, and foreign languages, or are offered only every other year. Where there are such courses, they are often taught by teachers whose training in the subject-matter area is inadequate and insufficient. Personnel services such as guidance also tend to be nonexistent or to become the additional responsibilities of the administrator or teachers who lack professional training in these fields. To the extent that there are trained specialists, there is waste. There are not enough students to warrant the full-time services of such specialists.

The same waste occurs in the case of teachers in some fields. A properly qualified physics or mathematics teacher has only limited opportunities in a small high school. He is obliged to teach such subjects as general science and biology on the one hand, or general mathematics and business arithmetic on the other, in addition to his field of special competence. Thus a very scarce national asset is squandered.

Questions

1. Do you agree with Conant's description of the disadvantages of small schools? Why or why not?

2. Can modern communications technology help to alleviate some of the problems Conant identifies? How?

3. On the basis of your own experiences in high school, what would you say is the ideal size for a comprehensive high school? Why?

Source: James Bryant Conant, *The American High School Today: A First Report to Interested Citizens* (New York: McGraw-Hill, 1959), cover, pp. 77–79.

classic study by Paul Mort considered the optimum to be 100,000 students per district.[31]

Today, however, small is often considered better, in school districts as well as in individual schools. For instance, some advocates of small school districts argue that districts with a 5,000-student maximum not only are more cost-effective, but also have lower dropout percentages, higher student achievement

Advantages of small districts

Summary of Research on Size of Schools and School Districts (Arlington, Va.: Educational Research Service, 1974).

[31]Paul R. Mort and Francis G. Cornell, *American Schools in Transition* (New York: Teachers College Press, Columbia University, 1941); Paul R. Mort, William S. Vincent, and Clarence Newell, *The Growing Edge: An Instrument for Measuring the Adaptability of School Systems,* 2 vols. (New York: Teachers College Press, Columbia University, 1955).

scores, and higher graduation and college-entry rates than larger districts.[32] Arguments and counterarguments aside, the trend in American education has been toward larger school districts. American schools, we must remember, are an outgrowth of one-room schoolhouses and rural school districts. As late as 1930, nearly 50 percent of American school districts had fewer than 300 students.[33] However, by 1990 almost half of all public school students were in districts containing 10,000 or more students.

As Table 6.1 demonstrates, the big school districts are few in number, but they enroll a disproportionately large share of the nation's students. For example, the largest 179 school districts (enrolling 25,000 or more students) account for 1.2 percent of districts but 28 percent of student enrollment. On the other hand, nearly 4,000 districts enroll fewer than 300 students; they comprise 25 percent of the nation's school districts but only 1.3 percent of enrollment. In most cases, the larger school systems are located in or near cities, the largest being the New York City system with approximately 940,000 students as of 1990, followed by Los Angeles with 590,000 students and Chicago with 395,000. Two other large school systems, Puerto Rico and Hawaii, span an entire territory and state, respectively.[34]

Table 6.1
Distribution of Public School Systems by Size of District, 1990

Size of District (Number of Pupils)	Public School Districts		Public School Students	
	Number	Percentage	Number	Percentage
Total operating districts	15,367	100.0	40,526,050	100.0
25,000 or more	179	1.2	11,347,280	28.0
10,000–24,999	479	3.1	7,173,102	17.7
5,000–9,999	915	6.0	6,443,634	15.9
2,500–4,999	1,937	12.6	6,808,368	16.8
1,000–2,499	3,547	23.1	5,835,744	14.4
600–999	1,801	11.7	1,418,410	3.5
300–599	2,283	14.9	1,013,150	2.5
1–299	3,910	25.4	526,838	1.3
Size not reported	318	2.1	—	—

Source: *Digest of Education Statistics, 1991* (Washington, D.C.: U.S. Government Printing Office, 1992); advance copy, Table 13, p. 18.

[32]*A Critique of North Carolina Department of Public Instruction's Plan to Mandate School District Mergers Throughout the State* (Raleigh, N.C.: North Carolina Boards Association, 1986); Allan C. Ornstein, "School District Size: Is Bigger Better?" *PTA Today* (October 1989), pp. 16–17; and Ornstein, "School Size and Effectiveness: Policy Implications," *Urban Review* (September 1990), pp. 239–245. Also see Robert W. Jewell, "School and School District Size Relationships," *Education and Urban Society* (February 1989), pp. 140–153; Herbert J. Walberg, "District Size and Student Learning," *Education and Urban Society* (February 1989), pp. 154–163.
[33]Newton Edwards and Herman C. Richey, *The School in American Social Order* (Boston: Houghton Mifflin, 1947); David B. Tyack, *The One Best System* (Cambridge, Mass.: Harvard University Press, 1974).
[34]The reader may find a list of the largest school systems in *Digest of Education Statistics, 1990,* Table 88, p. 103.

Figure 6.4

Declining Number of Public School Districts, 1930–1990

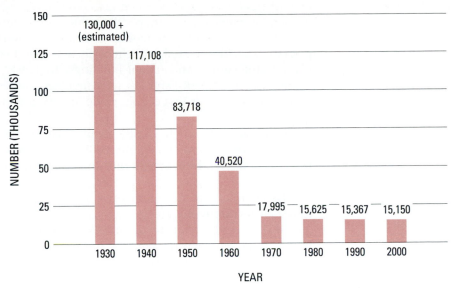

Source: *Digest of Education Statistics, 1990* (Washington, D.C.: U.S. Government Printing Office, 1991), Table 84, p. 96; *Educational Directory: Public School Systems, 1980–81* (Washington, D.C.: U.S. Government Printing Office, 1980), Table 2; Estimate for 2000 is based on authors' projections after speaking with Dr. Vance Grant, specialist in education statistics, Office of Educational Research and Improvement, August 9, 1991.

Combining school districts

Consolidation. The increased size of school districts results both from population growth and from **consolidation,** the combination of a number of smaller school districts into one or two larger ones. As Figure 6.4 illustrates, consolidation has produced a dramatic decline in the overall number of districts, from more than 130,000 in 1930 to slightly more than 15,000 in 1990, with the bulk of the decline taking place in the thirty-year period between 1930 and 1960. The figure also shows a leveling off process since 1970 so that by the year 2000 the number of school districts will remain nearly the same as in 1990. Hence, the era of school consolidation has come to an end, reflecting a bygone era — the rural countryside — that has given way to urban sprawl.

Community resistance

Consolidating districts usually means closing some schools, and this has proved to be a serious and emotional matter, especially in small and rural districts where the local school may be a focal point of the community's identity.[35] In many cases, state school officials, operating under the assumption that consolidation is cost-effective and enhances student opportunity, have clashed with local townspeople who resent the interference of distant bureaucrats.[36]

---

[35]Richard J. Butler and David H. Monk, "The Cost of Public Schooling in New York State," *Journal of Human Resources* (Summer 1985), pp. 361–380; James Guthrie, "Organizational Scale and School Success," *Educational Evaluation and Policy Analysis* (Fall 1979), pp. 17–27.

[36]Allan C. Ornstein, "School District and School Size: An Evolving Controversy," *Clearing House* (December 1989), pp. 156–158.

*Sharing of programs
and personnel*

Whole-grade sharing

*Dividing districts into
smaller units*

White flight

Extent of decentralization

Because of this opposition, officials in many states have searched for ways to obtain the benefits of consolidation without eliminating schools or districts. One method is for neighboring districts to share programs and personnel. Minnesota, for example, encourages this trend by providing up to 75 percent of the cost of shared secondary school facilities and programs.[37] Iowa provides 3 to 50 percent extra funding to local school districts that share course offerings, teachers, administrators, and school buildings. In 1991, 110 Iowa school districts shared superintendents, and 111 were involved in *whole-grade sharing* (programs in which all students in a certain grade are assigned to a single district).[38]

Decentralization.   Ironically, even as consolidation was taking place, the 1960s saw the advent of a countervailing trend, **decentralization.** Decentralization divides a school system into smaller administrative units, often referred to as zones, areas, or regions. Like the various forms of community involvement discussed earlier, decentralization was seen as a way to bring school issues closer to the local community.

In the decades after the Second World War, middle-class and white populations migrated from the cities to the suburbs — in what became known as *white flight* — and the percentages of low-income and minority residents increased in the cities. By the 1960s, members of many inner-city ethnic groups, especially African Americans, began to feel that the schools did not serve their needs. Decentralization, they argued, would give the people greater access to the schools and make the educational system more responsive to the multiethnic student body. Many educators agreed.

Consequently, while small and rural school districts continued the process of consolidation in the 1960s and 1970s, many large urban districts decentralized. By 1980, according to a nationwide survey, 64 percent of school systems with 50,000 or more students reported that they were decentralized.[39] By 1988, however, the proportion reporting decentralization dropped to 31 percent; many of the large districts had halted decentralization to reduce bureaucracy and to save money. Moreover, even those districts claiming to be decentralized tended to have more administrators at the central level than in the field offices or branches.[40] In fact, decentralization did not address the need for responsiveness to the community: in most large urban school districts, decisions regarding curriculum, instruction, staffing and teacher evaluation, graduation requirements, and budgeting continue to be made at the central level — the "downtown office" — rather than at local branch offices.[41] Perhaps this is one reason

[37]Chris Pipho, "Rural Education," *Phi Delta Kappan* (September 1987), pp. 6–7.

[38]*Annual School District Reorganization Report* (Des Moines: Iowa Department of Education, 1987); *Reorganization Feasibility Study: Samples* (Des Moines: Iowa Department of Education, 1987); and telephone conversation with Guy Ghan, Director of School Reorganization, Iowa State Department of Education, August 7, 1991.

[39]Allan C. Ornstein, "Decentralization and Community Participation Policy of Big School Systems," *Phi Delta Kappan* (December 1980), pp. 225–257.

[40]Allan C. Ornstein, "Centralization and Decentralization of Large Public School Districts," *Urban Education* (July 1989), pp. 233–235.

[41]Jack Frymier, *One Hundred Good Schools* (West Lafayette, Ind.: Kappa Delta Pi, 1984); Frymier, "Bureaucracy and the Neutering of Teachers," *Phi Delta Kappan* (September 1987), pp. 9–14.

why the concept of community in Chicago has recently been moved from the back burner to the front burner.

INTERMEDIATE UNITS

Coordination and supplementary services

The term **intermediate unit** or **regional educational service agency (RESA)** refers to an office or agency in a middle position between the state department of education and local school districts. This agency provides coordination and supplementary services to local districts and links local and state educational authorities. The intermediate unit is usually a legal and political extension of the state department of education, generally created by the state legislature. As many as thirty states had some form of intermediate units as of 1989. The average intermediate unit comprised twenty to thirty school districts and covered about 50 square miles, and the number of intermediate units in a state ranged from one in Missouri to more than fifty in California, Maine, Michigan, and Minnesota. In total there are some 1,320 intermediate or regional agencies.[42] In a few states, local school districts themselves form an RESA to provide common services; such districts lack legal, political, and financial support from the state.[43]

Expanded role of intermediate units

Intermediate units are being called on more frequently to regulate and enforce state mandates. In recent years, the intermediate unit has also provided school districts with a wide range of consulting services and resource personnel in such general areas of education as curriculum, instruction, evaluation, and in-service training. Intermediate units have also provided services in more specialized areas, such as education of the gifted and talented as well as children with handicaps, bilingual education, prekindergarten education, vocational education, and data processing and computer education. In 1990, 20 to 25 million students were receiving some kind of service from established intermediate units or regional educational service agencies.

Reliance on grant money

Especially during the 1980s, many intermediate agencies actively sought outside funding as a way of expanding their services. In some cases, local educators became concerned about the growth of these units, especially when district budgets were shrinking, feeling that the resources could have gone directly to their schools. Also, heavy reliance on short-term grants not only reduced the continuity in services and programs; it put these agencies in a difficult bind when cutbacks in educational funding became widespread.[44] These problems can be reduced, even eliminated, by state action that defines more clearly the scope and functions of intermediate units. It is important that they receive their funding from the state, not from other sources, and that it be allocated by the

[42] *Digest of Education Statistics, 1990,* Table 86, p. 97.

[43] William A. Firestone, Gretchen B. Rossman, and Bruce L. Wilson, *The Study of Regional Educational Service Agencies* (Philadelphia: Research for Better Schools, 1983); Firestone and Rossman, "Exploring Organizational Approaches to Dissemination and Training," *Knowledge* (March 1986), pp. 303–330.

[44] William A. Firestone, *The Politics of Technical Assistance: Regional Educational Service Agencies in Their State Context* (Philadelphia: Research for Better Schools, 1983); William A. Firestone, "Regional Educational Service Agencies in Their State Context," *Education and Urban Society* (February 1984), pp. 189–206.

state legislature. This will reduce tensions between intermediate units and local school districts. It is also important that the intermediate agencies serve the needs of the school districts and that local educators perceive those services as useful.

Another bureaucratic layer?

Since a number of states get along without intermediate units, some educators have asked why other states cannot do the same. Aren't the intermediate units merely another bureaucratic layer? Other educators respond, however, that an intermediate unit covering several districts can economically provide services that many small or financially strapped school districts could not afford on their own. This support may enable some small districts to avoid consolidation into larger ones.

City-suburban school plans

Intermediate units can also aid in establishing city-suburban school plans. Over the last several decades many large city school districts have declined in student population, grown more racially segregated, and suffered an erosion of their financial base. Meanwhile, many surrounding suburban districts, often predominantly white, have thrived. Reformers have therefore emphasized the need for a city-suburban connection in which the educational needs of the entire metropolitan area are considered. If empowered to do so by the courts or state legislature, the intermediate unit can help set up a metropolitan-area desegregation plan and distribute important services fairly across the entire region.

STATE RESPONSIBILITIES AND ACTIVITIES

Legal responsibility for education

Every state, by constitution, statute, and practice, assumes that education is one of its primary functions, and federal and state court decisions have supported this interpretation. Each state has legal responsibility for the support and maintenance of the public schools within its borders. Local school boards, as we have seen, are considered creatures of the state that have been devised for the purpose of running a system of schools. Being responsible for the schools, the state enacts legislation; determines school taxes and financial aid to local school districts; sets minimum standards for the training, recruitment, and salaries of personnel; decides on the curriculum (some states also establish "approved" textbook lists); makes provisions for accrediting schools; and provides special services (such as student transportation and free textbooks).

Mandatory and permissive laws

The **state school code** is the collection of laws that establish ways and means of operating schools and conducting education in the state. The state, of course, cannot enact legislation that is contrary to, or conflicts with, the federal Constitution. State statutes can be divided into two groups: *mandatory laws* that establish the minimum program of education and *permissive laws* that define the functions delegated to the school district under appropriate conditions.

Although state constitutions and statutes may simply direct state legislators to provide for the establishment and maintenance of a uniform system of schools, provisions in many states are quite detailed concerning methods of operation. The typical state and local organization, and their respective educational hierarchies, are shown in Figure 6.5.

Structure of a Typical State School System

Figure 6.5

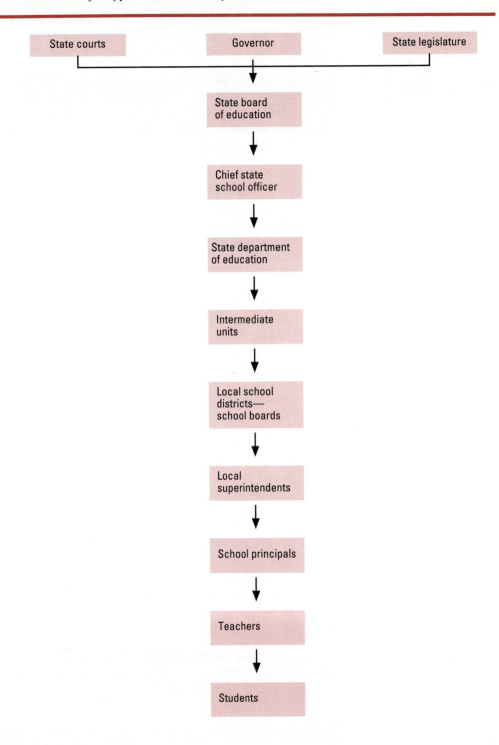

The Governor and State Legislature

Powers of the governor

Although the powers of governors vary widely, their authority on educational matters is spelled out in law. Usually a governor is charged with making educational budget recommendations to the legislature. In many states, the governor has legal access to any accumulated balances in the state treasury, and these monies can be used for school purposes. The governor can generally appoint or remove school personnel at the state level. But these powers often carry restrictions, such as approval by the legislature. In a majority of states, the governor can appoint members of the state board of education and, in a few states, the chief state school officer. A governor can cancel educational measures through his or her veto powers or threaten to use the veto to discourage the legislature from enacting educational laws he or she opposes.

*Powers of the
state legislature*

In most states, the legislature is primarily responsible for establishing and maintaining the public schools and has broad powers to enact laws pertaining to education. These powers are not unlimited; there are restrictions in the form of federal and state constitutions and court decisions. The state legislature usually determines the selection process for and duties of the state boards of education and the chief state officer. It specifies the functions of the state department of education, the types of local and regional school districts, and the selection methods and powers of local school boards. The legislature usually decides on the nature of state taxes for schools, the level of financial support for education, and the taxing power for schools to be allocated on a local or municipal level. The legislature may determine what may or may not be taught, how many years of compulsory education will be required, the length of the school day and school year, and whether or not the state will provide community colleges and adult and vocational schools. The legislature may also determine staff and student policies and testing and evaluation procedures, authorize school programs, set standards for building construction, and provide various auxiliary services (for example, student transportation and school lunches). Where the legislature does not enact these policies, they are usually the responsibility of the state board of education.

*New wave of
state legislation*

Legislative powers over education have been particularly evident during the reform movement of the 1980s and 1990s. Nationwide, more than 1,200 state statutes pertaining to school reform were enacted between 1983 and 1990 alone.[45] These statutes addressed matters ranging from curriculum to teaching qualifications, from class size to graduation requirements. Not since the wave of school reform that followed the Soviet launch of *Sputnik* in 1957 have state legislatures played such a prominent role in educational policy.

The State Board of Education

The **state board of education** is usually the most influential and important state education agency. Almost all states have some sort of state board of

---

[45]Linda Darling-Hammond and Barnett Berry, *The Evolution of Teacher Policy* (Santa Monica, Calif.: Rand Corporation, 1988); Allan C. Ornstein, "Reforming American Schools: The Role of the States," *NASSP Bulletin* (October 1991), pp. 46–55; and Thomas B. Timar and David Kirp, *Managing Educational Excellence* (New York: Falmer Press, 1988).

education, which is dependent on the state legislature for appropriations and authority and serves an advisory function for the legislature. (New York's Board of Regents is perhaps the strongest and most respected state board of education.) In addition, most states have a separate governing board for state colleges and universities; thus there are often two separate state boards, one for elementary and secondary education and another for higher education.

Two separate state boards

With the exception of Wisconsin, all states have boards of education. As of 1991, thirty-two were appointed by the governor of the state, twelve were elected by popular vote (this method has increased during the last twenty years), and five combine appointed members with elected members. The number of members of state boards ranges from seven in the states of Alaska, Colorado, Delaware, Idaho, and Montana to nineteen in Ohio, with an eleven-member board occurring most frequently.[46] (An odd number of members eliminates tie votes.)

Whereas state boards were originally dominated by white males, their demographic composition has changed dramatically in recent decades. A survey of board members conducted in 1967 showed that only 18 percent were women and 3 percent were members of minority groups.[47] By 1982, 34 percent of board members were women, and 16 percent were members of minority groups, and by 1992 the corresponding percentages had risen to 39 percent and 19 percent.[48] (See Figure 6.1 on page 202.) This trend toward greater heterogeneity is important; it broadens the perspectives of board members and ensures that boards reflect a wide range of social and educational concerns.

Characteristics of state school board members

One survey of state boards showed that most members tend to be older (88 percent were forty or older) and well educated (99 percent had at least some postsecondary education). The voluntary nature of service on a state board means that the members must have the time and resources to participate. As a result, the survey found that most board members who were in the workforce described their occupation as "managerial" (25 percent) or "professional" (50 percent); and those not in the paid workforce were either retired (11 percent) or homemakers (12 percent) with a history of voluntary service.[49]

The precise duties and functions of state boards of education vary, but generally the boards are charged with the following:[50]

Duties of state boards of education

1. Adopting and enforcing policies, rules, and regulations necessary to implement legislative acts related to education

---

[46]*State Policy Data Book* (Arlington, Va.: State Policy Research, 1986); telephone conversation with Brenda Welburn, Director of Public Affairs, National Association of State Boards of Education, August 9, 1991.

[47]Gerald Sroufe, "An Examination of the Relationship Between Methods of Selection and the Characteristics and Self-Role Expectations of State School Board Members" (Ph.D. diss., University of Chicago Press, 1970).

[48]Letter from Carolyn Curry, Director of Public Relations, National Association of State Boards of Education, January 22, 1992; Dinah Wiley, *State Boards of Education* (Arlington, Va.: National Association of State Boards of Education, 1983), Tables 1–2, pp. 15–16.

[49]Wiley, *State Boards of Education*, Tables 1–2, pp. 15–16.

[50]James W. Guthrie and Rodney J. Reed, *Educational Administration and Policy,* 2nd ed. (Englewood Cliffs, N.J.: Prentice-Hall, 1991); *State Boards of Education in an Era of Reform*, Final Report of the National Association of State Boards of Education (Alexandria, Va.: National Association of State Boards of Education, 1987).

2. Establishing qualifications and appointing personnel to the state department of education

3. Setting standards for teacher and administrative certificates

4. Establishing standards for accrediting schools

5. Managing state funds earmarked for education

6. Keeping records and collecting data needed for reporting and evaluating

7. Adopting long-range plans for the development and improvement of schools

8. Creating advisory bodies as required by law

9. Acting as a judicial body in hearing disputes arising from state policies

10. Representing the state in determining policies on all matters pertaining to education that involve relationships with other agencies (including the federal government)

11. Advising the governor or legislature on educational matters

12. In some states, appointing the chief state school officer, setting minimum salary schedules for teachers and administrators, and adopting policies for the operation of institutions of higher learning

The State Department of Education

Functions of state departments of education

The **state department of education** usually operates under the direction of the state board of education and is administered by the chief state school officer. Traditionally, the primary function of state departments of education was to collect and disseminate statistics about the status of education within the state. Since the 1950s, they have enlarged their services and functions to include (1) accrediting schools, (2) certifying teachers, (3) apportioning funds, (4) overseeing student transportation and safety, (5) monitoring state regulations, and (6) conducting research, evaluating programs, and issuing reports.[51] Since the 1960s, they have expanded their functions to include (1) monitoring compliance with federal regulations and (2) identifying and improving programs to meet the needs of special students (for example, bilingual students and students with handicaps).

During recent decades, the state departments have had to grapple with controversial issues such as desegregation, compensatory education, student rights and unrest, school finance reform and fiscal crisis, aid to minority groups, collective bargaining, accountability, student assessment, and competency testing. The federal government, the courts, and active interest groups joined the fray and wrestled with many educational or school issues — forcing governors and legislators to increase the staff budget and functions of state departments of education. As a result, state departments of education, once nearly invisible,

[51]Fred C. Lundenburg and Allan C. Ornstein, *Educational Administration: Concepts and Practices* (Belmont, Calif.: Wadsworth, 1991).

Professional staff

ECIA

Added pressure

doubled and tripled in size. By 1985, five states (California, Michigan, New Jersey, New York, and Texas) had professional staffs of more than 1,000.[52]

The leadership role of the state departments of education expanded in the 1980s. The 1981 Education Consolidation and Improvement Act (ECIA) presented states with a broad number of options for spending federal monies. Not only did ECIA give the states more responsibility for determining how and where to spend federal money for education, but it also reduced federal funding, which put more importance on state financial support. Considering that over the last decade citizens' groups have become more aggressive and astute in making their demands felt at the state level, state departments of education in the 1990s face considerable pressure to provide real assistance and leadership to local school districts.

The Chief State School Officer

Chief executive

The **chief state school officer** (sometimes known as the state superintendent or commissioner of education) serves as the head of the state department of education and is also the chief executive of the state school board. He or she is usually a professional educator.

The office is filled in one of three ways: in 1991, eight states filled the position through appointment by the governor, twenty-seven states through appointment by the state board of education, and fifteen states by popular election.[53] As of 1990, only one chief state school officer was African American; however, there were nine female chief officers — a notable increase from earlier decades.[54] The greater number of women in the position represents a departure from the "old-boy network" that once dominated the upper echelons of educational administration.

Decline of "old-boy network"

The duties of the chief state school officer and the relationship between that position and the state board and state department vary widely. Generally an elected chief officer has more independence than one who is appointed. But however they are selected, most chief officers have the following basic responsibilities:[55]

Functions of the chief state school officer

1. Serving as the chief administrator of the state department of education and of the state board of education

2. Selecting personnel for the state department of education

---

[52]Fenwick W. English, *Educational Administration: The Human Science* (New York: Harper Collins, 1992); Thomas J. Sergiovanni et al., *Educational Governance and Administration*, 2nd ed. (Needham Heights, Mass.: Allyn and Bacon, 1992); and telephone conversation with Anna Santiago, Assistant to the Executive Director of the National Association of State Boards of Education, January 27, 1992.

[53]*Directory of Chief State School Officers 1991* (Washington, D.C.: Council of Chief State Officers, 1991); "State Board of Education, 1991," Paper prepared by the Association of State Boards of Education, February 1991.

[54]*Directory of Chief State School Officers 1991.*

[55]Roald Campbell et al., *The Organization and Control of American Schools*, 6th ed. (Columbus, Ohio: Merrill, 1990); Lundenburg and Ornstein, *Educational Administration: Concepts and Practices.*

3. Recommending improvements in educational legislation and educational budgets

4. Ensuring compliance with state educational laws and regulations

5. Explaining and interpreting the state's school laws

6. Deciding impartially controversies involving the administration of the schools within the state

7. Arranging the studies, committees, and task forces as deemed necessary to identify problems and recommend solutions

8. Reporting on the status of education within the state to the governor, legislature, state board of education, and the public

State Courts

State courts are subject to constitutional restrictions and may be overruled by federal district courts or by the U.S. Supreme Court. Even though state courts may serve to set a precedent, decisions rendered in one state are not binding in another. Moreover, there are instances (in matters dealing with teacher tenure, teacher strikes, and student rights, for example) in which a decision in one state appears to be in conflict with a decision in another state. In spite of areas of apparent conflict, on major issues relating to control of schools there has been consistency among the state courts.

*Education as
state function*

State courts have repeatedly held that public education is a function of the state and that the ultimate control of school affairs is vested in the law-making power of the state. The state courts have also made it clear that the state controls the schools for the fulfillment of the public good, not for the benefit of the individual. The state courts have taken the position that a local public school has no inherent powers of government, and its boundaries may be changed or its district abolished at the will of the state legislature, unless prohibited by the state constitution. State courts have upheld the power of the legislatures to levy taxes for school purposes, to confer upon other governmental units (municipalities, counties, towns, or school districts) such taxing power, and to allocate monies to schools.

THE FEDERAL ROLE IN EDUCATION

The role of the federal government can be considered in four parts: (1) the federal agencies that promote educational policies and programs; (2) the trend that has moved many educational decisions from the federal government to the state governments; (3) federal financing of education; and (4) the Supreme Court's decisions concerning education. Here we will focus on the first two parts. Federal spending will be examined in Chapter 7, and court decisions will be discussed in Chapter 8.

Federal Educational Agencies

For the first 150 years of the nation's history, between 1787 and 1937, Congress enacted only fourteen major educational laws. In the last 55 years, however, more than 110 major laws have been passed.[56] Traditionally, the major organizations of teachers and administrators, such as the American Federation of Teachers, the National Education Association, and the National School Boards Association, have preferred that the federal government offer financial aid and special services but refrain from interfering in educational policy. But there is growing support for the idea that the federal government should provide a clear statement of mission and specific kinds of guidance — as well as funds — to state and local agencies that are struggling to improve the schools.[57]

Desire for federal leadership

Although many different federal agencies are now involved in some type of educational program or activity, the **U.S. Department of Education** is the major federal educational agency.

The U.S. Department of Education. When the Department of Education was founded in 1867, its commissioner had a staff of three clerks and a total of $18,600 to spend. From these humble beginnings the department has grown to about 4,800 employees and annual expenditures of more than $22.4 billion in 1990.[58] The department presently administers over 120 separate programs. Although only one of fourteen departments in the federal government, it receives 45 percent of all federal funds for education.[59]

The original purpose of the department was to collect and disseminate statistics and facts and to promote the cause of education throughout the country. Even though it was known as the Department of Education, the commissioner was not a member of the president's cabinet. In fact, the department was attached to the Department of the Interior in 1868 and given the status and name of a bureau.

In 1929 the title Office of Education was adopted, and ten years later the office was transferred to the Federal Security Agency. Then, in 1953, the Office of Education was transferred again, this time to the newly formed Department of Health, Education and Welfare. The Office of Education continued to perform its original functions, and responsibilities were added by various acts of Congress or by order of the president. In particular, it assumed new responsibilities of (1) administering grant funds and contracting with state departments of education, school districts, and colleges and universities; (2) engaging in educational innovation and research; and (3) providing leadership, consultative, and clearing-house services related to education.

Enlarged responsibilities

In 1979, after much congressional debate and controversy, a department of education was signed into law by President Carter, who declared that the creation of the department was the "best move for the quality of life in America for the future." A secretary of education was named, with full cabinet-level status, and the department officially opened in 1980.

Cabinet-level status

---

[56]*Digest of Education Statistics, 1992* (Washington, D.C.: U.S. Government Printing Office, 1992).

[57]*A National Imperative: Educating for the 21st Century* (Washington, D.C.: National School Boards Association, 1989); Allan C. Ornstein, "The National Reform of Education," *NASSP Bulletin* (May 1992), in press; and Marshal S. Smith, Jennifer O'Day, and David K. Cohen, "National Curriculum, American Style," *American Educator* (Winter 1990), pp. 10–17.

[58]*Digest of Education Statistics, 1990,* Table 325, p. 336.

[59]Ibid., Table 326, pp. 337–340.

The establishment of the Department of Education (DOE) with full cabinet status had long been a goal of a number of professional organizations (especially the National Education Association). The secretary of education has widespread visibility and influence. This cabinet official can exert persuasion and pressure in political and educational circles and manages educational policy and the promotion of programs to carry out those policies. To be sure, the last two heads of DOE, William Bennett and Lamar Alexander, have asserted their position and have been in the limelight, pushing their brand of reform — considered conservative by some observers.

Office of Educational Research and Improvement.   The **Office of Educational Research and Improvement** (OERI), established in 1985, is part of the Department of Education. It replaced the National Institute of Education (NIE), which had been established in 1972, and also assumed the functions of the Center for Educational Statistics (which published many of the government surveys and projections in education) and the National Assessment of Educational Programs (which analyzed and reported student progress). Like the old NIE, OERI's primary focus is on research and development as well as on library programs and programs to improve educational practices; but OERI is bureaucratically more streamlined than its predecessor.

Focus on research and development

The early years of OERI have been difficult. Many members of Congress have been disappointed by the agency's lack of direction and action; many also feel that educational research has produced little of value. Similar problems plagued the NIE and led to its eventual demise. The lack of confidence in educational research, combined with a desire to transfer many educational responsibilities to the states, has made it hard for OERI to build support in the political community. In line with other federal cutbacks in the human and educational sectors, OERI has had its budget requests pared down in real dollars.[60]

Difficulties in building support

Even among educators, OERI has not received much support. The agency has not overcome the communication gap between researchers and practitioners, and few people in schools and universities even realize that OERI exists. There has been little discussion of the agency in the professional literature. It is possible that the increased recent national concern with education will spill over to research in education and thus assist OERI in its mission.

The New Federalism of the 1980s and 1990s

Although the federal role in education has expanded dramatically since the 1930s, the 1980s and 1990s were an era of retrenchment. Under presidents Reagan and Bush, a dramatic shift occurred in federal policy. Driven by a belief that the federal government was too intrusive, the Reagan administration in the 1980s reduced federal funding, activities, and regulations — in education as well as in other sectors of society. In what was known as a "new federalism," funds for education were slashed, and more monetary and program responsibilities were shifted to state (and local) agencies. Federal rules and regulations govern-

Shift in federal policy

---

[60]Telephone conversation with Tom Brown, Director of Operations, Office of Educational Research and Improvement, January 6, 1990.

ing education were revoked or more loosely enforced. The powers of the Department of Education were restricted, and the overall scope of the federal role in education was narrowed.[61]

The Bush administration

President Bush took office in 1989 with the pledge to become the "Education President," and his administration outlined a number of national programs to boost achievement in education. By 1991, for example, the Bush administration had promoted magnet schools, alternative certification of teachers, teacher excellence awards, student excellence in science and math, drug-free schools, and endowments for black colleges. However, these programs continued the Reagan administration's tendency to minimize federal spending and shift responsibilities to the local schools.[62] The budget for the Department of Education, though increasing, did not keep up with inflation.

Less equalitarianism?

Along with the reluctance to spend federal funds for education, the new federalism seems to have brought less emphasis on equalitarianism as a national policy. Even while spokespersons were placing new emphasis on national needs in such fields as math and science education and high technology, the government was cutting back programs for big-city schools, especially those for minority and low-income groups. For example, in the late 1980s, only 25 percent of Chapter 2 block-grant monies (funds earmarked by the federal government for the states) were dedicated to compensatory and basic skills programs, compared to the earlier Title I monies of the 1960s and 1970s — when 100 percent of the funds were earmarked for such programs and went directly to the local schools.[63] As a result, many people have become concerned that urban schools, which educate the children of most of the nation's low-income families, have been shortchanged.

Debate on federal role

Many liberal and equalitarian groups would like the federal government to return to the activism in educational matters that it demonstrated in the 1960s and 1970s. Conservative groups contend that such federal involvement is neither appropriate nor affordable. These debates about the proper federal role in education promise to continue for some time.

NONPUBLIC SCHOOLS

Although this chapter has focused on public education, nonpublic schools are not exempt from some of the governmental influences we have discussed. In particular, education laws passed by state legislatures often apply to private and parochial schools as well as to public institutions. These laws pertain to health

---

[61]David L. Clark, Terry A. Astuto, and Paula M. Rooney, "The Changing Structure of Federal Education Policy in the 1980s," *Phi Delta Kappan* (November 1983), pp. 188–193; Larry Cuban, "Four Stories About National Goals for American Education," *Phi Delta Kappan* (December 1990), pp. 265–271.

[62]"Bush Calls for New Programs," *AASA Leadership News,* April 15, 1989, pp. 1–2; Bruce Joyce, "The Doors to School Improvement," *Educational Leadership* (May 1991), pp. 59–62; and Joe Nathan and Jim Kiesmeier, "The Sleeping Giant of School Reform," *Phi Delta Kappan* (June 1991), pp. 738–742.

[63]*Digest of Education Statistics, 1990,* Table 329, p. 345. Also see Nancy A. Madden et al., "Success for All," *Phi Delta Kappan* (April 1991), pp. 593–599.

State aid for nonpublic schools

standards, building codes, welfare of children, student codes, and so forth. In addition, legislative bodies in many states have passed laws to benefit private schools and, at public expense, provide aid in such areas as student transportation, health services, dual enrollment or shared-time plans, school lunch services, purchasing of books and supplies, student testing services, teacher salary supplements, student tuition, and student loans. Although the courts have generally held that the legislature may pass laws providing for the supervision of nonpublic schools, rarely has a state legislature enacted comprehensive regulatory requirements — and where such laws do exist on the books, they are not strictly enforced.

Catholic school enrollments

As indicated in Chapter 1, nonpublic schools now account for over 11 percent of total enrollments in U.S. elementary and secondary schools. Catholic schools still enroll the greatest number of private-school students, although their enrollment has declined from 85 percent of all private-school students in 1969 to 45 percent in 1991. Nearly half of Catholic school enrollments are concentrated in five states; in rank order they are New York, Pennsylvania, California, Illinois, and Ohio. Catholic school enrollments also tend to be concentrated in certain dioceses that correspond to major cities and their surrounding suburbs. In 1991 the leading four dioceses — all with over 100,000 students — were in Chicago, Philadelphia, New York, and Los Angeles.[64]

Other Christian schools

Nonreligious, independent schools have increased their share of students from 8 percent of private-school enrollments in 1969 to as much as 21 percent by 1991. Evangelical and fundamentalist Christian schools have also grown dramatically in number and student population, reflecting the increased influence of conservative Protestants who seek schools that emphasize God, discipline, and faith in community and country.[65] If Christian school enrollments continue to build, the core of public-school support, which is mainly Protestant, may begin to erode.

Bright flight

Cooperation between public and private schools

Educators worried about the growth of nonpublic schools have coined the term "bright flight" to describe the tendency of the private and parochial schools to skim off many of the nation's able students. Many commentators see the relationship between the public and private sectors as one of competition for students and for funds. Other educators, however, prefer to think in terms of potential cooperation between public and nonpublic schools.[66] Given the growing percentage of students who need special, remedial, or bilingual programs that strain school resources — and the difficulty of raising those resources from an aging population in budget-conscious times — the pressure is on all schools, both public and private, to fight for the necessary support. Moreover, the distinction between public and private is being blurred by government regulation of private schools and by the expanding choices within the public-school sector.

---

[64]Allan C. Ornstein, "The Growing Nonpublic School Movement," *Educational Horizons* (Spring 1989), Table 3, p. 73; *United States Catholic Elementary and Secondary Schools 1991–92* (Washington, D.C.: National Catholic Education Association, 1991), Tables 5, 16–17, pp. 7, 17–18.

[65]*Digest of Education Statistics, 1990*, Tables 53, 56, pp. 68, 70; Allan C. Ornstein, "The Growing Popularity of Private Schools," *Clearing House* (January 1990), pp. 210–213; and Charles Park, "The Religious Right and Public Education," *Educational Leadership* (May 1987), pp. 5–11.

[66]Robert L. Cord, "Church-State Separation and the Public Schools: A Re-evaluation," *Educational Leadership* (May 1987), pp. 26–32; Eagan Hunter, "Public and Private Education?" *NASSP* (January 1987), pp. 79–83; and Arthur G. Powell, "A Glimpse at Teaching Conditions in Top Private Schools," *American Educator* (Winter 1990), pp. 28–34.

In the final analysis, both public and private schools perform a public service — educating children and youth and satisfying family and societal needs.

Summing Up

1. The enterprise of education is organized on various government levels: local, intermediate (in most states), state, and federal. Knowledge of this formal organization is important to people who work in schools or who are studying to become teachers.

2. Schools are organized into school districts; today there are over 15,000 public school systems operating in the United States.

3. At the local level, the school board, the school superintendent, the central office staff, and school principals all take part in governing and administering the schools.

4. Educators have made a number of efforts to increase the involvement of parents and community members in the schools. Programs for school-based management often include a greater role for parents and community members. Other forms of public involvement are community participation, community control, and community education.

5. Educators have long debated the optimum size for schools and school districts. Many have come to believe that increases in size do not mean increases in efficiency or effectiveness.

6. Whereas small and rural school districts have undergone a great deal of consolidation since the 1930s, many large urban districts have followed the contrary trend of decentralization.

7. More than half of the states have one or more intermediate units that support local school districts and exercise limited regulatory powers.

8. With the exception of Wisconsin, all states have state boards of education. Operating under the state boards are the state departments of education, headed by the chief state school officer.

9. The federal role in education has dramatically expanded since the 1930s. The 1980s and early 1990s, however, witnessed reduced federal involvement relative to the preceding two decades.

Key Terms

local school boards *(200)*

superintendent of schools *(204)*

central office staff *(205)*

principal *(206)*

community participation *(210)*

community control *(211)*

community education *(212)*

consolidation *(217)*

decentralization *(218)*

intermediate unit *(219)*

regional educational service agency *(219)*

state school code *(220)*

state board of education *(222)*

state department of education *(224)*

chief state school officer *(225)*

U.S. Department of Education *(227)*

Office of Educational Research and Improvement *(228)*

Discussion Questions

1. How can teachers effect changes at the federal, state, and local levels of education?

2. What are the advantages and disadvantages of an elected or appointed state board of education? A local board of education?

3. Why have school districts consolidated? Why have they decentralized? What are the advantages and disadvantages of each trend?

4. Explain the ways in which community control, community participation, and community education differ. Which alternative do you prefer? Why?

5. What are the arguments for and against shifting educational responsibilities from the federal government to the states?

Suggested Readings

Campbell, Roald F., Luvern, L. Cunningham, Raphael O. Nystrand, and Michael D. Usdan. *The Organization and Control of American Schools,* 6th ed. Columbus, Ohio: Merrill, 1990.

> *An important work on the organization of American schools, including a detailed discussion of the federal, state, and local governments' impact on school districts.*

Gregory, Thomas B., and Gerald R. Smith. *High Schools as Communities: The Small School Reconsidered.* Bloomington, Ind.: Phi Delta Kappa, 1987.

> *A powerful discussion of the need for small schools and the importance of school ethos and school-community relations.*

Guthrie, James W., and Rodney J. Reed. *Educational Administration and Policy,* 2nd ed. Englewood Cliffs, N.J.: Prentice-Hall, 1991.

> *A fresh look into the governing structure of the American schools, including an analysis of school boards and school administrators.*

Kimbrough, Ralph B., and Michael Y. Nunnery. *Educational Administration,* 3rd ed. New York: Macmillan, 1988.

> *An analysis of schools and school districts and their relationship to local, state, and federal governments.*

Lundenburg, Fred C., and Allan C. Ornstein. *Educational Administration: Concepts and Practices.* Belmont, Calif.: Wadsworth, 1991.

> *An up-to-date discussion on how to improve schools in the context of the political structure.*

Wirt, Frederick, and Michael W. Kirst. *Schools in Conflict: The Politics of Education,* 2nd ed. Berkeley, Calif.: McCutchan, 1989.

> *An analysis of the federal and state governments' influence on educational policy at the local level.*

7

Financing
Public Education

FOCUSING QUESTIONS

What proportion of school revenues do the local, state, and federal governments contribute?

What is wrong with relying on property taxes as revenue sources for schools?

What particular fiscal problems characterize urban schools?

Why are there significant differences among and within states in spending for education?

What major steps have been taken to reform school finance?

How does public opinion about schools influence financial support of schools?

What financial considerations will most affect school management in the next decade?

E ducation in the United States is big business. As of 1990, more than $215 billion was being spent annually for public education (K–12), and elementary and secondary education represented 4 percent of the nation's annual gross national product (the value of all goods and services produced in the United States).[1] Because most school-related costs have increased more rapidly than inflation in recent years, the business of schooling is in deep financial trouble. Indeed, there is no longer any guarantee that all the nation's schools will be able to open up on time each September, finish the full school year, and still pay all their bills. Since the mid-1980s, school board members, who are the people closest to the problem of school financing, have consistently ranked "lack of financial support" as the number one challenge they face.[2] Of the top five problems ranked by school superintendents in 1991, three were related to school finance (lack of financial resources, overcrowded facilities, and increased property taxes).[3]

Number one problem

Major revenue sources

There are three major sources of revenue or financial support for public schools: the local, state, and federal governments. State and local money remains the basic source. Table 7.1 shows that although revenues from federal sources steadily increased from 0.4 percent in 1929–30 to a high of 9.8 percent in 1979–80, the percentage then began to fall, sinking to 6.2 percent in 1990–91. In contrast, contributions by the states have rapidly increased from 16.9 percent in 1929–30 to 49.3 percent in 1990–91. Estimates for 1995 put state revenue contributions at approximately 55 percent — to make up for federal and local shortfalls in revenues. Local revenue sources have decreased from 82.7 percent in 1929–30 to less than 45 percent in the 1980s and early 1990s. It is expected that local revenue contributions will continue slightly downward, especially in large urban areas that are under financial pressure and in some suburban areas where the population contains fewer school-age children.

In addition to a decreased percentage of federal funding, today's educators must deal with budget constraints at the state and local levels, the question of equity in school financing, taxpayer resistance, and various plans to restructure the system of financial support. This chapter will explore these issues and their implications for the future.

TAX SOURCES OF SCHOOL REVENUES

The operation of public schools relies primarily on revenues generated from taxes, especially the property tax at the local level and sales and income taxes at

[1]*Digest of Education Statistics, 1990* (Washington, D.C.: U.S. Government Printing Office, 1990), Table 27, p. 32.

[2]"Sixth Annual Survey of School Board Members," *American School Board Journal* (January 1984), pp. 24–27, 40; "Tenth Annual Survey of School Board Members," *American School Board Journal* (January 1988), pp. 17–19 ff. Also see Daniel M. Seaton, "The Burden School Board Presidents Bear," *American School Board Journal* (January 1992), pp. 32–36.

[3]Allan C. Ornstein, "Problems Facing School Superintendents and School Board Presidents of Large School Districts," *Urban Review* (September 1991), pp. 207–214.

Table 7.1

Revenue Receipts of Public Elementary and Secondary Schools by Government Source, 1929–30 to 1990–91

School Year	Amount in Thousands of Dollars				Percentage of Total School Revenues		
	Total	Federal	State	Local	Federal	State	Local
1929–30	$ 2,088,557	$ 7,334	$ 353,670	$ 1,727,553	0.4	16.9	82.7
1939–40	2,260,527	39,810	684,354	1,536,363	1.8	30.3	68.0
1949–50	5,437,044	155,848	2,165,689	3,115,507	2.9	39.8	57.3
1959–60	14,746,618	651,639	5,768,047	8,326,932	4.4	39.1	56.5
1969–70	40,266,923	3,219,557	16,062,776	20,984,589	8.0	39.9	52.1
1979–80	96,880,944	9,503,537	45,348,814	42,028,593	9.8	46.8	43.4
1980–81	105,904,908	9,808,007	50,207,192	45,809,709	9.3	47.4	43.3
1990–91	217,980,540	13,495,427	107,550,102	96,935,011	6.2	49.3	44.5

Source: *The Condition of Education, 1987* (Washington, D.C.: U.S. Government Printing Office, 1987), Table 1.13, p. 36; *Digest of Education Statistics, 1982* (Washington, D.C.: National Center for Education Statistics, 1982), Table 66, p. 75; *Digest of Education Statistics, 1983–84* (Washington, D.C.: National Center for Education Statistics, 1984), Table 62, p. 77; and *Estimates of School Statistics, 1990–91* (Washington, D.C.: National Education Association, 1991), pp. 6–7 (used with permission).

Criteria for evaluating taxes

the state level. Some kinds of taxes are considered better than others. Most people today accept the following criteria for evaluating taxes:

1. *A tax should not cause unintended economic distortions.* It should not alter economic behavior, change consumer spending patterns in favor of one good or service for another, negatively affect a taxpayer's willingness to work, or cause the relocation of business, industry, or people.

2. *A tax should be equitable.* It should be based on the taxpayer's ability to pay. Those with greater incomes or with property worth more money should pay more taxes than those with less income or less desirable property. Taxes that are not equitable and that require lower-income groups to pay a higher proportion of their income than higher-income groups are called **regressive taxes.** In contrast, taxes that require high-income groups to pay higher percentages of their income are called **progressive taxes.**

3. *A tax should be collected easily.* This requires that the tax be collected with minimum costs to the taxpayer or government; it also means that it should be difficult to evade and should have no loopholes.

4. *The tax should be responsive to changing economic conditions.* During inflation (when government costs and expenditures rise), the tax revenue should also rise; in a recession, the tax revenue should decrease.[4] Responsive taxes are *elastic;* those that are not responsive are *inelastic.*

---

[4]James Guthrie and Rodney J. Reed, *Education Administration and Policy,* 2nd ed. (Needham Heights, Mass.: Allyn and Bacon, 1991); Donald E. Orlosky et al., *Educational Administration Today* (Columbus, Ohio: Merrill, 1984).

LOCAL FINANCING OF PUBLIC SCHOOLS

Although education is the responsibility of the states, traditionally they have delegated much of this responsibility to local school districts. As indicated earlier, the local contribution to school financing has decreased over the last several decades, whereas the state contribution has increased. Nevertheless, local funding remains a crucial part of public school financing.

Property Tax

The **property tax** is the main source of revenue for local school districts, accounting for 74 percent of local funding nationwide. In eleven states, including all six of the New England states, property taxes make up more than 95 percent of local school revenues.[5] The property tax has been used to support education in this country ever since the colonial period.

How property tax is calculated

Property taxes are determined by first arriving at the *market value* of a property — the amount the property would likely sell for if it were sold. Then the market value is converted to an *assessed value* using a predetermined index or ratio, such as one-fourth or one-third; for example, a property with a market value of $80,000 might have an assessed value of only $20,000. The assessed value is always less than the market value in order to protect the owner and to avoid controversies and appeals. Finally, the local tax rate, expressed in mills, is applied to the assessed value. A **mill** represents one-thousandth of a dollar; thus, a tax rate of 25 mills amounts to $25 for each $1,000 of assessed value.

The property tax does not rate well on the criterion of equity. Because of different assessment practices and lack of uniform valuation, people owning equivalent properties may pay different taxes. This results in unequal treatment of equal property. Also, the property tax does not always distribute the tax burden according to the ability to pay. A retired couple may have a home whose market value has increased substantially, along with their taxes, but because they live on a fixed income they cannot afford the increasing taxes. In this respect, it can be argued that the property tax is regressive.

A regressive tax

In addition, the property tax is not immediately responsive to changing economic conditions. In some states, properties are reassessed every one to two years, but in others, reassessments occur only every three to four years. Thus, a property's assessed value and actual tax are often based on old market conditions. If property values have risen since the last reassessment, then the municipal government is losing potential tax income; if property values have decreased, property taxes may be overburdensome, thereby causing a declining neighborhood to deteriorate further.

Finally, the property tax is not always easy to collect. Collection depends on the efficiency of the local tax collection department. Wealthy individuals and businesses that contest their property taxes often receive abatements.

[5]*Government Finances in Year 1989* (Washington, D.C.: U.S. Government Printing Office, 1990), Table 4, p. 14; *Recent Changes in State, Local, and State-Local Tax Levels* (Denver: National Conference of State Legislatures, 1991), Table 7, p. 15.

Most states specify the basic minimum property tax rate that local school districts can levy. An increase in the tax rate beyond this minimum is common but usually requires voter approval at the local level. Since the mid-1970s, local school districts have had difficulty getting voter approval for raising taxes.

Other Local Taxes and Fees

In addition to the property tax, school districts can gather revenues through special income taxes and other taxes or fees. Some municipalities, especially small villages and towns, depend on such sources as traffic fines and building permits to help raise money for schools.

Rise in user fees

User fees, which are fees charged specifically to the people who use a certain facility or service, are the most common type of special assessment. User fees can be levied on bus service, textbooks, athletic and recreational activities, nursery classes, and after-school centers. Thirty-four states now permit schools to assess user fees on students, and more than two-thirds of the school districts in these states impose such fees.[6] In Ohio, for example, 94 percent of the school districts charge students for various services or materials; the most common charges in rank order are damage to books, laboratory fees, payments for workbooks, damage to books or equipment, and club fees.[7] Because they are not based on ability to pay, user fees are considered a regressive tax.

Local Resources and Disparities

Large differentials in resources

Despite state and federal aid, some school districts are much less able than others to support education. A school district located in a wealthy area or an area with a broad tax base can obviously generate more revenue than can poor school districts. As a result, in the majority of states today, total expenditures per student are frequently two to four times greater in the five wealthiest school districts than in the five poorest school districts.[8] As we discuss later in this chapter, state courts and legislatures have attempted to reduce these great disparities through reforms in the system of educational finance. In most states, however, substantial disparities in funding persist.

Municipal overburden

Though financial problems affect many rural and suburban districts, the greatest financial troubles are usually found in the large cities. Cities are plagued by what is commonly called **municipal overburden,** or severe financial demands for public functions due to population density and the high proportion of disadvantaged and low-income groups. The result is that the large cities cannot devote as great a percentage of their total tax revenues to the schools as suburban and rural districts can. For example, in the late 1980s, Cleveland,

---

[6]Jay Goldman, "User Fees to the Rescue?" *School Administrator* (October 1991), pp. 30–32, 34.

[7]Roger W. Hamm and Sandra Crosser, "School Fees: A Review of Policies in Ohio Public Schools," *American Secondary Education* (Fall 1991), pp. 13–16.

[8]See John Coons, "A Decade After Rodriguez," *Phi Delta Kappan* (March 1983), pp. 479–480; Richard J. Murnane and Edward W. Pauly, "Lessons from Comparing Educational and Economic Indicators," *Phi Delta Kappan* (March 1988), pp. 509–513; and Allan Odden and Lori Kim, "Finance Reform Topples Old Structures," *School Administrator* (October 1991), pp. 8–12.

Detroit, Gary, Newark, and New York City spent less than 30 percent of all local tax revenues for school purposes, whereas the rest of their respective states were able to spend 45 to 50 percent of local taxes for schools.[9]

Educational overburden   Then there is the issue of educational overburden. A large percentage of the student population in city schools is in technical, vocational, and trade programs, which cost more per student than the regular academic high-school program. Similarly, there is a greater proportion of special-need students — namely bilingual and low-income students and students with handicaps — in the city schools than in suburban or rural schools. These students require remedial programs and services, which cost 50 to 100 percent more per student than basic programs.[10] Moreover, the need for additional services tends to increase geometrically with the concentration of poverty. City schools, therefore, have to spend more educational resources per student than a similar-size school district or group of school districts comprising middle-class students. City schools also

Higher operating costs   have higher vandalism costs, lunch costs, desegregation costs, insurance costs, and maintenance costs (their buildings are older than suburban buildings). Both city and rural school districts spend more than suburban districts on transportation.

High city taxes   Finally, despite their dire need for more revenues, cities often cannot realistically raise taxes further. In many cities, the property taxes are already 30 percent higher per capita than in adjacent suburbs. The situation is particularly difficult in the Frostbelt cities of the Northeast and Middle West, where local taxes are 60 to 70 percent higher on average than in most Sunbelt cities.[11] Iron-

Cycle of decline   ically, tax hikes can contribute to the decline of urban schools because they cause businesses and middle-income residents to depart for the suburbs. The city's tax base is thus undermined, which forces the local government to cut city services, including education, to balance the budget. These cuts in turn drive away more middle-class persons and businesses and more tax revenues. Thus the cycle reinforces itself. Financing has become a major problem for city schools, and many recommendations for cutting costs and reducing wasteful programs have become important to consider.[12]

STATE FINANCING OF PUBLIC SCHOOLS

As we noted in Chapter 6, the state is primarily responsible for and has jurisdiction over public schools. Throughout the years, the states have delegated many

[9]E. Blaine Liner, "Shadows on Metropolitan Financing in the '90s," *Urban Institute Research Papers* (July 1990); Allan Odden, "Sources of Funding for Educational Reform," *Phi Delta Kappan* (January 1986), pp. 335–340; and Allan C. Ornstein, "School Finance Trends for the Year 2000," *Educational Horizons* (Fall 1990), pp. 59–64.

[10]Harold Hodgkinson, "Reform versus Reality," *Phi Delta Kappan* (September 1991), pp. 8–16; Mary Jean LeTendre, "Improving Chapter 1 Programs: We Can Do Better," *Phi Delta Kappan* (April 1991), pp. 576–581. Also see Anne M. Ligas, "The Money Gap," *Pioneer Press* (Winnetka, Ill.), January 31, 1991, p. 8.

[11]Allan C. Ornstein, "The Urban Setting: Frostbelt/Sunbelt Differences," *Phi Delta Kappan* (October 1982), pp. 102–107; Rudolph Ponner, "Fiscal Policy in the Short and Long Run," *Urban Institute Research Papers* (January 1991), pp. 1–15.

[12]Keith Baker, "Yes, Throw Money at Schools," *Phi Delta Kappan* (April 1991), pp. 628–630;

powers and responsibilities to local school districts; nevertheless, each state remains legally responsible for educating its children and youth. Since many local school districts are having trouble financing their schools through property taxes, states will probably assume greater financial responsibility for and control over the schools.

Rising taxes

To assume this greater responsibility, however, states will likely have to raise their taxes—a controversial proposition. In recent years state taxes have increased significantly, and the related problems of taxation and educational finance (as well as medical costs) are among the top policy issues confronting state governments.[13] In this section we will look at the principal types of state taxes used to finance education, the variations in school funding from state to state, the methods by which state aid is apportioned among local districts, and the role of state courts in promoting school finance reform.

State Revenue Sources

The **sales tax** and **personal income tax** are the two major sources of revenue for states. Since states currently pay about 60 percent of the cost of education, these two taxes are important elements in the overall support of public education.

Sales Tax.   As of 1990, as many as forty-six states had statewide sales taxes, with such taxes making up 33 percent of state revenues.[14] Measured against the four criteria for evaluating taxes, the sales tax rates fairly high. It may cause some economic distortions, however, where the difference in the tax rates makes it worthwhile to travel to a low-tax state to purchase expensive items. Despite this distorting effect, the sales tax meets the criterion of equity if food and medical prescriptions are removed from the tax base. If the tax is placed on all goods, however, low-income groups are penalized since they spend a large portion of their incomes on basic goods such as food and drugs.

Easy to administer and collect

The sales tax is easy to administer and collect; it does not require periodic valuations or entail legal appeals (as the property tax does) by owners or corporations that feel their taxes are too high. The burden of collection is put on the retailer. A problem does arise with interstate sales, however, because the state cannot levy a tax on sales to be delivered outside the state or easily collect the tax on purchases made by its residents in another state.

Elastic

The sales tax is elastic, because the revenue derived from it tends to parallel the economy. The trouble is that when the state (or nation) is in a recession, sales tax revenues decrease sufficiently to reduce the state's income. But the tax is useful because relatively small increases in the rate result in large amounts of revenue, which can reduce or eliminate deficits.

Increase in median rate

In 1970, the median sales tax was 3 percent, and only one state had a rate as high as 6 percent. By 1991 the median was 5.25 percent, and twelve states

---

Odden, "Sources of Funding for Educational Reform"; and Allan C. Ornstein, "Urban Demographics for the 1980s," *Education and Urban Society* (August 1984), pp. 477–496.
[13] *State Budget and Tax Actions 1990–91* (Denver: National Conference of State Legislatures, 1991).
[14] *Recent Changes in State, Local, and State-Local Tax Levels.*

had rates of 6 percent or higher.[15] Moreover, many states have recently expanded sales taxes to include a wider range of products and services, such as legal and accounting services, hotel lodging, property-tax transfers, disposable paper products, long-distance phone calls, parking, mail-order sales, and periodicals. Yet the states have increasingly exempted food and drugs from the tax base.[16]

Personal Income Tax. The personal income tax is the second largest source of tax revenue for the states, representing 31 percent of state revenues in 1990. Only four states do not levy a personal state income tax.[17] Just as the sales tax rate varies among states, from 2 to 8 percent, the state income tax (based on a percentage of personal income) also varies.

An equitable tax   A properly designed income tax should cause no economic distortions. Assuming no loopholes, it rates very high in terms of equity. In theory, the personal income tax is supposed to reflect the taxpayer's income and ability to pay. The income tax is also more equitable than other taxes since it considers special circumstances of the taxpayer, such as dependents, illness, moving expenses, and the like, and uses tax deductions or credits to take into account these variations. It becomes less equitable only if the taxpayer owns many properties or other depreciable items that minimize the tax. In general, state income taxes have become more progressive because of increased standard deductions and personal exemptions. Between 1985 and 1990, fifteen states that formerly imposed taxes on poor families eliminated them, and several others lightened the tax burden on poor and middle-class families.[18]

Easy to collect   The personal income tax is relatively easy to collect. In most cases, it is collected through payroll deductions. Even so, tax evasion is a perennial problem in the United States, although the use of computers has made evasion more difficult. The personal income tax is also very elastic; it allows the state government to vary rates according to the economy. On the other hand, the elasticity of the income tax makes it vulnerable to recession because the revenue derived from it declines at a faster rate than revenue from other tax sources.

Other State Taxes. Other state taxes contribute limited amounts to education. These taxes include (1) excise taxes on motor fuel, liquor, and tobacco products; (2) estate and gift taxes; (3) severance taxes (on the output of minerals and oils); and (4) corporate income taxes. Of this group, the severance tax is most controversial: certain states in the South and West tax user states for oil, gas, timber and other such natural commodities on the basis that these resources are depletable.

There has also been a trend to establish state lotteries to support education. Although this was a major purpose of the early lotteries, funds have been diverted to meet other social priorities, such as geriatric care, health care, social

[15]*Recent Changes in State, Local, and State-Local Tax Levels; State Budget and Tax Actions 1990–91.*

[16]*Significant Features of Fiscal Federalism, 1990* (Washington, D.C.: U.S. Advisory Commission in Intergovernmental Relations, 1990); *State Budget and Tax Actions 1990–91.*

[17]*Recent Changes in State, Local, and State-Local Tax Levels.*

[18]*State Budget and Tax Actions 1990–91; State Deficit Management Strategies; State Fiscal Conditions,* Legislative Finance Paper No. 55 (Denver: National Conference of State Legislators, 1986).

State lotteries

welfare agencies, and road construction. The result, in most of the twenty-six states where lotteries currently exist, is that the lottery contributes less than 2 percent of the state's total revenue for education.[19] In nine states, however, the lottery is used strictly or mainly for education purposes (California, Florida, Illinois, Michigan, Montana, New Hampshire, New Jersey, New York, and Ohio).[20] These taxes are somewhat regressive because low-income people play the lottery in a greater proportion than high-income people do and spend larger percentages of their annual income on it. (This is also true of taxes on fuel, tobacco, and alcoholic beverages.)

The Ability of States to Finance Education

Geographic accident

Some students are more fortunate than others, simply by geographic accident. State residence has a lot to do with the type and quality of education a child receives. In 1990–91, Connecticut, New Jersey and New York spent more than $8,000 per student (calculated on the basis of average daily attendance), and Alaska spent nearly $7,000. In contrast, as shown in Figure 7.1 and Table 7.2, Arkansas, Idaho, Mississippi, and Utah spent less than $3,500 per student.

It is incorrect to assume from these figures that the education priorities of some states are more than twice as high as the priorities of other states. We must ask what the states can afford, and this has a lot to do with the personal incomes of the states' inhabitants; then we must ask what the states spend on all other services and functions, such as housing, transportation, and medical care.

Education spending and per capita income

For example, in 1990–91, Mississippi spent $3,322 per student — the third-lowest figure nationwide and far short of the national average of $5,208 — yet this amount represented 3.8 percent of Mississippi's per capita income (average income for each person living in the state). The national average was 2.9 percent of per capita income, which made Mississippi's percentage higher than the percentages of twenty-six other states. The wealthier states of California, Washington, and Virginia each spent between $4,826 and $5,335 per student, but in percentage terms the expenditures in these states fell between 2.3 and 2.7 percent of per capita income — less than in Mississippi.[21]

State educational priorities

As another illustration, consider Utah and Idaho, which spent the lowest amounts on education per student in the 1987–88 school year. Utah spent $2,455 per student that year, and Idaho $2,555, compared to a national average of $3,870. As a percentage of spending for all services and functions, however, these amounts represented 26.3 percent for Utah and 24.6 percent for Idaho; the national average was only 24.2 percent (with a range of 17.4 to 28.3). Hence Utah ranked fourteenth highest and Idaho twenty-fourth highest in terms of the priority assigned to education funding. In contrast, in the two states that spent the most per student that year — Alaska and New York — education ranked second and ninth lowest in spending for all services and functions.[22]

---

[19] *Significant Features of Fiscal Federalism, 1990,* Table 72, p. 129.

[20] Fax communication from Chris Pipho, Director of the Information Clearing House, Education Commission of the States, Denver, November 7, 1991; *Significant Features of Fiscal Federalism, 1990,* Table 72, p. 129.

[21] *Estimates of School Statistics, 1990–91,* p. 7; Table 9, p. 37.

[22] *Digest of Education Statistics, 1990,* Table 32, p. 37; *Estimates of School Statistics, 1986–87* (Washington, D.C.: National Education Association, 1987), p. 7.

State Education Expenditures per Student, 1990–91

Figure 7.1

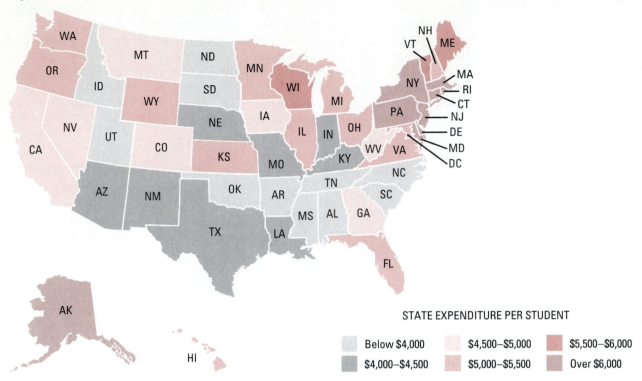

Source: Adapted from *Estimates of School Statistics, 1990–91* (Washington, D.C.: National Education Association, 1991), p. 7. State expenditures are based on average daily attendance and include federal, state, and local revenues.

Table 7.2

Revenues and Expenditures of States for Public Education, 1990–91

	Percentage of Total School Revenues by Source			State Expenditure per Student[a]
	Federal	State	Local	
50 states and D.C.	6.2	49.3	44.5	$5,208
New England (Northeast)				
Connecticut	1.9	47.7	50.4	8,455
Maine	2.6	56.7	40.7	5,894
Massachusetts	3.1	38.9	58.0	6,351
New Hampshire	2.2	7.5	90.3	5,474
Rhode Island	2.2	46.0	51.8	6,989
Vermont	3.0	39.0	58.0	5,740
Mideast (Northeast)				
Delaware	2.3	71.8	25.9	6,016
Maryland	2.9	40.3	56.8	6,184
New Jersey	2.1	43.2	54.7	8,451
New York	2.9	45.5	51.6	8,680
Pennsylvania	2.8	45.9	51.3	6,534

(Cont.)

Great Lakes (Midwest)

Illinois	4.4	39.7	55.9	5,062
Indiana	1.7	62.8	35.5	4,398
Michigan	2.9	37.1	60.0	5,257
Ohio	2.8	45.8	51.4	5,269
Wisconsin	2.2	42.5	55.3	5,946

Plains (Midwest)

Iowa	2.4	54.5	43.1	4,877
Kansas	2.8	45.6	51.6	5,044
Minnesota	1.9	56.3	41.8	5,360
Missouri	3.3	39.9	56.8	4,479
Nebraska	4.2	24.8	71.0	4,080
North Dakota	6.6	52.1	44.3	3,685
South Dakota	7.5	28.7	63.8	3,730

Southeast (South)

Alabama	2.8	77.9	19.3	3,648
Arkansas	3.3	64.9	31.8	3,419
Florida	2.5	56.9	40.6	5,003
Georgia	2.2	65.4	32.4	4,852
Kentucky	2.0	76.8	21.2	4,390
Louisiana	3.9	58.2	37.9	4,041
Mississippi	5.5	64.9	29.6	3,322
North Carolina	3.6	52.1	44.3	3,685
South Carolina	3.5	56.2	40.3	3,843
Tennessee	4.4	53.0	42.6	3,707
Virginia	3.2	36.3	60.8	5,335
West Virginia	2.2	71.0	26.8	4,695

Southwest (South)

Arizona	2.8	45.5	51.7	4,196
New Mexico	1.6	86.5	11.9	4,446
Oklahoma	2.5	67.6	29.9	3,835
Texas	4.2	46.8	49.0	4,326

Rocky Mountain (West)

Colorado	3.2	42.2	54.6	4,702
Idaho	2.6	65.1	32.3	3,211
Montana	3.3	62.4	34.3	4,794
Utah	2.6	60.5	36.9	2,767
Wyoming	2.3	56.3	41.4	5,255

Far West (West)

Alaska	3.5	66.0	30.5	6,952
California	2.0	72.6	25.4	4,826
Hawaii	0	99.9	0.1	5,008
Nevada	2.3	39.1	58.6	4,677
Oregon	4.3	28.5	67.2	5,291
Washington	1.2	78.2	20.6	5,042

[a]Calculated on the basis of average daily attendance.

Source: Adapted from *Estimates of School Statistics, 1990–91* (Washington, D.C.: National Education Association, 1991), p. 7. Used with permission. Federal, state, and local percentages have been calculated by the authors.

Aging population

Educational Support and the Graying of America.   Another factor influencing states' abilities to finance public education is the aging of the population. The median age of the U.S. population has risen steadily since 1900. The proportion of people over 65, which increased from 4.1 percent in 1900 to 13 percent in 1990, is expected to reach 20 percent or more by 2030.[23] Correspondingly, the proportion of households with children has declined in recent decades, from 40 percent in 1970 to 30 percent in 1984 to an estimated 25 percent in 1995.[24] Older people who no longer have children in school are generally more resistant to taxes that support the schools. They are less likely than younger people to vote for school budget increases; and in areas where they form a major segment of the population, their influence will be felt on the priorities of state and local officials. This effect can be seen in recent changes in government spending patterns. Through the 1980s educational spending per student outpaced inflation by about 30 percent; yet by the late 1980s it began to decline. At the same time, government medical and health expenditures — a large proportion of which go to older people — increased.[25]

Graying of the Frostbelt

The increase in average age is a nationwide trend; however, some parts of the country are "graying" faster than others. Many states of the Frostbelt — for example, mid-Atlantic states such as New York and Pennsylvania and Midwest states such as Illinois and Michigan — have lost sizable numbers of young people to the Sunbelt. The effects are especially noticeable in large cities, where for decades much of the young middle-class population has migrated to the suburbs. Elderly, less affluent people left behind in the cities, often concentrated in "geriatric ghettoes," are neither able nor very willing to support urban school systems. Even the suburbs have begun to feel the pinch; the suburbanites who arrived from the cities in the 1950s and 1960s have aged, and many of their children have moved elsewhere.

Better prospects in Sunbelt

Many Sunbelt states, in contrast, are experiencing a boom in student enrollments. The parents of these students provide a solid base of political and financial support for schools, helping to offset the growing influence of older age groups. When it becomes necessary to raise taxes to support education spending, states with rising student enrollments should have less difficulty (all other things being equal) than states with declining enrollments.

State Aid to Local School Districts

States use four basic methods to finance public education. Some states have financial strategies that combine methods.

Oldest, simplest, and most unequal

1. *Flat grant model.* This is the oldest, simplest, and most unequal method of financing schools. State aid to local school districts is based on a fixed amount multiplied by the number of students in attendance. It does not consider the special needs of students (bilingual students are more expensive to educate than are native English speakers), special programs (vocational programs are more

---

[23]Allan C. Ornstein, "Regional Population Shifts: Implications for Educators," *Clearing House* (February 1986), pp. 284–290; Harold G. Shane, "Improving Education for the Twenty-first Century," *Educational Horizons* (Fall 1990), pp. 11–15.

[24]"The Changing Family," *NASSP Bulletin* (December 1987), p. 43.

[25]*Digest of Education Statistics, 1990,* Table 30, p. 35.

expensive than regular programs), or the wealth of the school districts (wealthy school districts have more to spend than do less wealthy school districts).

In most states, the distribution of education funds is based on some type of equalization plan designed to provide extra money for less wealthy school districts. The remaining three methods each seek to bring about greater equality of educational opportunity by allocating more funds to the school districts in greatest need of assistance.

A minimum per student

2. *Foundation plan.* This is the most common approach, and its purpose is to guarantee a minimum annual expenditure per student for all school districts in the state, irrespective of local taxable wealth. However, the minimum level is usually considered too low by reformers, and wealthy school districts are well able to exceed it. School districts with a high percentage of children from low-income families suffer from this plan.

Inverse ratio to wealth

3. *Power-equalizing plan.* Many of the states have adopted some form of this more recent plan. The state pays a percentage of the local school expenditures in inverse ratio to the wealth of the district. Although the school district has the right to establish its own expenditure levels, wealthier school districts are given fewer matching state dollars. The program is constrained by lower and upper limits, and the matching dollars are insufficient for poor school districts. In the end, the equalization effect is usually insufficient.

Student characteristics and programs

4. *Weighted student plan.* Students are weighted in proportion to their special characteristics (that is, handicapped, disadvantaged, and so forth) or special programs (for example, vocational or bilingual) to determine the cost of instruction per student. For example, a state may provide $4,000 for each regular student, 1.5 times that amount ($6,000) for vocational students, and 2 times that amount ($8,000) for students with handicaps.

The Courts and School Finance Reform

Serrano

Efforts to use state funding to equalize educational opportunities among school districts within a state have been spurred by a series of court decisions that have fundamentally changed the financing of public education in most states. The 1971 landmark decision in *Serrano* v. *Priest* radically altered the way California allocated education funds. California, like nearly all the states, depended on local property taxes to support the schools, and plaintiffs argued that this system of financing resulted in unconstitutional disparities in expenditures between wealthy and poor school districts. The California Supreme Court agreed, stating the following: "We have determined that . . . [the California] funding scheme invidiously discriminates against the poor because it makes the quality of a child's education a function of the wealth of his parents and neighbors."

Rodriguez

Following the *Serrano* decision, more than thirty similar cases were filed in other states. One of these, *San Antonio Independent School District* v. *Rodriguez,* was taken to the U.S. Supreme Court after a federal court ruled that school finance arrangements in Texas were unconstitutional. By a five-to-four vote, the Supreme Court ruled in 1973 that expenditure disparities based on differences in local property taxes between school districts in a state were not unconstitutional under the federal constitution but might be unconstitutional under state constitutions, depending on the situation and the wording of the laws in a given

Getting to the Source

Equality in School Funding: The **Serrano** *Case*

PACIFIC REPORTER

Second Series

Volume 487 P.2d

Cases Argued and Determined
in the Courts of

ALASKA   MONTANA
ARIZONA   NEVADA
CALIFORNIA   NEW MEXICO
COLORADO   OKLAHOMA
HAWAII   OREGON
IDAHO   UTAH
KANSAS   WASHINGTON
               WYOMING

ST. PAUL, MINN.
WEST PUBLISHING CO.
1971

The California Supreme Court's decision in the case of Serrano v. Priest *set the tone for many later court cases on the issue of school finance reform. By discriminating against the poor, the court ruled, the system of financing schools through local property taxes violated the Fourteenth Amendment to the U.S. Con-*

stitution, which guarantees all citizens equal protection of the law. The following is an excerpt from the court's opinion.

We are called upon to determine whether the California public school financing system, with its substantial dependence on local property taxes and resultant wide disparities in school revenue, violates the equal protection clause of the Fourteenth Amendment. We have determined that this funding scheme inviduously discriminates against the poor because it makes the quality of a child's education a function of the wealth of his parents and neighbors. Recognizing as we must that the right to an education in our public schools is a fundamental interest which cannot be conditioned on wealth, we can discern no compelling state purpose necessitating the present method of financing. We have concluded, therefore, that such a system cannot withstand constitutional challenge and must fall before the equal protection clause.

. . . Plaintiff children attend public elementary and secondary schools located in specified school districts in Los Angeles County. This public school system is maintained throughout California by a financing plan or scheme which relies heavily on local property taxes and causes substantial disparities among individual school districts in the amount of revenue available per pupil for the districts' educational programs. Conse-

state. The *Rodriguez* decision placed the issue of inequities in school finance in the hands of the state courts and legislatures.

Since *Rodriguez* a number of state courts have ruled that school financing arrangements are unconstitutional if they result in large disparities in per-pupil expenditures based on wealth differences among school districts. The three most visible recent cases were in Kentucky, Texas, and New Jersey. The Kentucky Supreme Court ruled in *Rose v. Council for Better Education* (1989) that the state failed to provide an "efficient system" of schooling. The court declared the entire system unconstitutional and instructed the legislature to create a new and more efficient one. The court struck down the property-tax basis for funding schools and required a much higher student spending base for all school districts. Within two years, the Kentucky legislature hiked average education spending some 30 percent (by means of corporate and sales taxes, and new local taxes), implemented preschool programs for all "at risk" four-year-old students, and grouped elementary students according to educational progress, not age. Most contro-

Kentucky case

quently, districts with smaller tax bases are not able to spend as much money per child for education as districts with larger assessed valuations. . . .

The need for an educated populace assumes greater importance as the problems of our diverse society become increasingly complex. The United States Supreme Court has repeatedly recognized the role of public education as a unifying social force and the basic tool for shaping democratic values. The public school has been termed "the most powerful agency for promoting cohesion among a heterogeneous democratic people . . . at once the symbol of our democracy and the most pervasive means for promoting our common destiny." . . .

[But] so long as the assessed [property] valuation within a district's boundaries is a major determinant of how much it can spend for its schools, only a district with a large tax base will be truly able to decide how much it really cares about education. The poor district cannot freely choose to tax itself into an excellence which its tax rolls cannot provide. Far from being necessary to promote local fiscal choice, the present financing system actually deprives the less wealthy districts of that option. . . .

By our holding today we further the cherished idea of American education that in a democratic society free public schools shall make available to all children equally the abundant gifts of learning. This was the credo of Horace Mann, which has been the heritage and the inspiration of this country. "I believe," he wrote, "in the existence of a great, immortal immutable principle of natural law, or natural ethics, — a principle antecedent to all human institutions, and incapable of being abrogated by any ordinance of man . . . which proves the *absolute right* to an education of every human being that comes into the world, and which, of course, proves the correlative duty of every government to see that the means of that education are provided for all. . . ."

Questions

1. Do you agree that school financing should be equalized throughout all the school districts in a state? If so, how would you define equality?

2. Some researchers have argued that the amount of funding has little or no direct impact on the quality of education. If this is true, is school finance reform unnecessary?

3. Did the *Serrano* decision undermine the concept of local control of schools?

Source: Serrano v. *Priest,* 487 P.2d 1241 (1971).

---

versial, the state now offers bonuses of up to $1,000 per professional for schools, that improve in achievement, attendance, and other factors. The state can declare schools that slip in "crisis" and can develop its own "rescue" plan — including putting all teachers and the principal on probation.[26]

Texas case

Also in 1989, the Texas Supreme Court in *Englewood Independent School District* v. *Kirby* overturned that state's method of financing schools. The court pointed out that differences in spending between the bottom fifty and top fifty school districts averaged $4,000 per student, even though the vast majority of some 1,052 districts spent close to the state average. In a second decision in 1991, the court required that portions of the revenues collected in wealthy

---

[26]Ronald Henkoff, "Four States: Reform Turns Radical," *Fortune,* October 21, 1991, pp. 137–144, ff; Peter Hong, "The Money Questions That Have Schools Stumped," *Business Week,* June 4, 1990, pp. 98–99.

school districts be used to fund poor ones.[27] However, the Texas court did not demand a complete restructuring of the educational system, and some vestiges of the local funding method remained. Once the state had equalized local funds at a required level, the court decided, local communities could enact additional property taxes to supplement their educational funding.[28]

New Jersey case

In a New Jersey case, *Abbott* v. *Burke* (1990), after examining the poorest twenty-eight school districts (mainly city districts), the state court found the state's system of school finance unconstitutional. The court required that spending be equalized at the level of the highest-spending districts. The outcome of the decision moved more than $100 million annually from wealthy districts (about 350) to poor districts (about 250) to help pay for smaller classes in early grades, full-day kindergartens, after-school study programs, guidance counseling, reading programs, and parent literacy programs.[29]

State takeovers

The New Jersey reform provisions also allow the state to intervene, as in Kentucky, to unseat local school boards or take over a school district characterized by chronic academic failure, often called **academic bankruptcy.** As of 1992, fourteen other states had similar provisions.[30] State takeovers generally occur only after local districts have been given repeated warnings and chances to improve their performance. Only five school districts across the nation have been declared academically bankrupt — two in New Jersey, two in Kentucky, and one in Iowa.

Trend toward finance reform

More than twenty-five states have reformed their school finance laws since the *Rodriguez* case in 1973. In these states the state share of public-school revenues has increased from an average of 43 percent in 1973–74 to 53 percent in 1990–91, and poorer school districts are receiving substantially more money.[31] Nevertheless, as we noted earlier, many disparities remain, and the litigation will undoubtedly continue. As of 1990, suits similar to the ones in Kentucky, Texas, and New Jersey had been filed in seventeen other states.

Issues in school finance reform

At the heart of the debate lies the equity issue — the belief that students in poor school districts "have the right to the same educational opportunity that money buys for others."[32] Yet some critics of school finance reform have argued that money alone makes little difference in the quality of education; twenty-five years of research have shown that money does not necessarily equate with ed-

---

[27]Stan Karp, "Rich Schools, Poor Schools, and the Courts," *Substance* (January 1991), pp. 8–9; Martha M. McCarthy, "The Courts as Educational Policy Makers," *Educational Horizons* (Fall 1990), pp. 4–9.

[28]Lonnie Harp, "Split Texas Court Debates over Finance," *Education Week,* March 6, 1991, p. 22; "Texas Judge Supports New Law on Financing for Poorer Schools," *The New York Times,* April 16, 1991, p. A12.

[29]Robert Hanley, "New Jersey Shifts Approach in Helping 'At Risk' Students," *The New York Times,* October 6, 1990, p. 9; Michael Newman, "Finance System for N.J. Schools Is Struck Down," *Education Week,* June 13, 1990, pp. 1, 18.

[30]Fax transmittal from Chris Pipho, Director, Education Commission of the States, Denver, November 7, 1991; telephone conversations with Chris Pipho, November 26, 1991, and January 14, 1992.

[31]*Estimates of School Statistics 1990–91* (Washington, D.C.: National Education Association, 1991), pp. 6–7.

[32]Newman, "Finance System for N.J. Schools Is Struck Down," p. 18.

Taking Issue ━━●━

Expanding State Funding for Education

Education is in deep financial trouble for many reasons. Not only are new taxes, such as user fees, being levied in many areas, but the argument about the proper level of funding from state and federal sources has taken on new urgency. Embattled local districts look to higher levels of government to help them out; but states have their own financial difficulties, and the federal role in education remains a thorny political issue.

Question: Should state contributions to educational funding be substantially increased to make up for federal shortfalls and thus reduce the percentage of funds derived from local sources?

Arguments PRO

1 The federal government has shifted much of the responsibility for educational funding to the states. The states must accept this responsibility and raise their contributions accordingly.

2 State funding can be used to reduce or eliminate the discrepancies between poor and wealthy districts. Such discrepancies are unfair to students in poorer areas. In fact, in many state court decisions, financing systems that foster inequalities in funding have been ruled unconstitutional.

3 State financing will be free of the parochial judgments and petty politics that often plague local decision making. Higher levels of government are better equipped to solve financing problems professionally.

4 A common obstacle in local funding is the need for voters to approve any substantial change in the way schools are financed. State governments can levy taxes, such as income and sales taxes, that do not require public referenda.

5 State governments do not need to ask for large tax hikes for education. They can raise sufficient amounts through the combined total of numerous small taxes. Thus, their taxing will not be seen as excessive.

Arguments CON

1 The federal government needs to restore its financial commitment to education. Most states are financially burdened, unable to tax their residents further without squeezing the middle class or inciting tax rebellion.

2 More money for poorer districts will not necessarily improve educational performance; the problems are not mainly financial. Moreover, more state money will bring more state regulations, and educational priorities will be set at the state level. Ordinary people will have little influence on the schools their children attend.

3 State governments are no strangers to favoritism and pork barreling. Politics will be just as evident at the state level, and there will be less accountability to the local taxpayer and little concern for local interests.

4 The solution to financial problems lies not in easier ways to tax but in reducing the schools' burden of responsibilities. We must decide which responsibilities can be returned to other social institutions, such as the family, the church, and community agencies.

5 Taxpayer revolts derive from feelings that citizens no longer control their own financial fate. People cannot be fooled for long. State tax hikes, even if spread over many varieties of tax, will eventually provoke resistance.

ucational achievement.[33] These critics contend that significant improvement in the schools demands commitment and responsibility on the part of students, teachers, and parents.[34] Moreover, many claim, unless we address a variety of social and cognitive factors, especially family structure, most of our spending reform efforts may be useless or even wasteful. The shifting of financial resources to poorer districts also tends to anger middle-class and suburban parents, who often feel that they are being made to bear the tax burden while their own children's problems are neglected. With all of these issues unresolved, school finance reform will continue to be a hotly debated topic throughout the 1990s.

FEDERAL EDUCATIONAL FUNDING

Education a state responsibility

Until the middle of the twentieth century, the federal government gave very little financial assistance to the states (or local schools) for the education of American students. This attitude was in line with the majority belief that the federal government should have little to do with education and that education is a state responsibility. One might characterize federal programs and activities as passive and uncoordinated during this period. This is not to say that the federal government had no influence on American education. National laws and federal programs had a significant impact on the way education developed in the United States. We will be discussing the most important of these programs in the pages that follow. But what must be kept in mind is that these programs and acts were uncoordinated; they were not part of a broadly conceived national plan for education. After Sputnik (1957), however, as national policy became more closely linked to education, federal funding dramatically increased and steadily involved specific educational targets.

National policy and education

History of Federal Aid to Education

Morrill Act

Grants for Schools and Colleges.   As we saw in Chapter 5, the Northwest Ordinances of 1785 and 1787 are the first instances of federal assistance to education. As a result of these ordinances, thirty-nine states received over 154 million acres of land from the federal government for schools.[35] Seventy-five years were to pass before a second major federal educational program was enacted, this time for institutions of higher learning. In the Morrill Act of 1862, federally owned lands were set aside for each state (a total of 30,000 acres for each senator or representative in Congress) with the provision that the income

---

[33]Eric A. Hanushek, "The Impact of Differential Expenditures in School Performance," *Educational Researcher* (May 1989), pp. 45–51; LeTendre, "Improving Chapter 1 Programs: We Can Do Better"; and Herbert J. Walberg and William S. Fowler, "Expenditure and Size Efficiency of Public School Districts," *Educational Researcher* (October 1987), pp. 5–15.

[34]Richard L. Colvin, "School Finance: Concerns in an Age of Reform," *Educational Researcher* (January–February 1989), pp. 11–15; Fred M. Newmann, "Linking Restructuring to Authentic Student Achievement," *Phi Delta Kappan* (February 1991), pp. 458–463; and Allan C. Ornstein, "The Evolving Accountability Movement," *Peabody Journal of Education* (Spring 1988), pp. 12–20.

[35]Ellwood P. Cubberley, *Public Education in the United States*, rev. ed. (Boston: Houghton Mifflin, 1934).

from the sale or rental of these lands be used to establish colleges for the study of agriculture and mechanical arts. A total of 6 million acres of federal lands was given to the states. These "people's colleges" or land-grant institutions were to become the great multipurpose state universities that now enroll students from all segments of society. The Morrill Act demonstrated that the federal government would take action on education for the welfare of the nation; it also marked the beginning of meaningful federal influence on higher education.

Smith-Hughes Act

Vocational Education Acts. The third phase of federal activity in public education came with the conditional grants for highly specific purposes in public secondary schools. The Smith-Hughes Act of 1917 provided money grants for vocational education, home economics, and agricultural subjects. The original act called for federal appropriations to be matched by state or local educational agencies. It was extended by various acts between 1929 and 1984; the 1984 legislation, called the Perkins Vocational Education Act, extended funding to people with handicaps, single parents, homemakers, and the incarcerated.

The 1917 federal vocational act marked the federal government's first annual appropriation for public secondary education. The 1963 federal vocational act appropriated $235 million for vocational training, quadruple the annual appropriations of the original Smith-Hughes Act.[36] By 1980 the annual federal funding for vocational programs had reached $1.1 billion; since then federal funding has begun to decline in real dollars. By 1990, it was $1.2 billion, but adjusted for inflation it has decreased 50 percent from its high point.[37]

Great Depression

Relief Acts. The fourth phase of federal activity emerged during the Great Depression. Federal interest in schools at that time was only incidental to greater concerns for the welfare of unemployed youth from ages sixteen to twenty-five. The Civilian Conservation Corps (CCC) was organized in 1933 for unemployed males seventeen to twenty-three. More than half of the youth who joined had never finished grade school, and a substantial number were practically illiterate. The act provided federal appropriations for the education and vocational training of more than 3 million youth until it was abolished in 1943. Almost a generation passed before the CCC idea was brought back as a part of the Job Corps in the mid-1960s.

Other federal programs of the depression era included the National Youth Administration (1935), which provided welfare and training programs for unemployed youth ages sixteen to twenty-five, as well as financial aid for needy students attending secondary schools and colleges; the Federal Emergency Relief Administration (1933), which allocated funds for the employment of unemployed rural teachers; and the Public Works Administration (1933) and Works Progress Administration (1935), both of which provided federal money for school plant construction and repairs. All federal relief agencies were terminated by the mid-1940s. Although some educators were concerned about possible federal domination of public schooling during the 1930s, these fears subsided, and

[36]*The Condition of Education, 1983* (Washington, D.C.: National Center for Education Statistics, 1983), Table 3.8, p. 152.
[37]*Digest of Education Statistics, 1990*, Table 34, p. 39; Table 327, p. 343.

the communities that had participated in these programs were in a better position to meet the classroom shortage that occurred after World War II.[38]

War Acts.   The fifth phase of federal activity took place during World War II and the immediate postwar period. Three major bills were passed at this time.

World War II

1. The Lanham Act (1941) provided aid for construction and maintenance of local schools in areas where military personnel resided or where there were extensive federal projects.
2. The Occupational Rehabilitation Act (1943) provided educational and occupational assistance to disabled veterans.
3. The Servicemen's Readjustment Act (1944), commonly called the G.I. Bill, provided funds for the education of veterans and enabled hundreds of thousands of Americans to attend institutions of higher learning or special training schools.

G.I. Bill

The benefits of the G.I. Bill were extended to veterans of the Korean and Vietnam conflicts. Direct aid, totaling more than $10 billion, has helped more than 7,500,000 veterans to attend institutions of higher learning or special training schools. The G.I. Bill, along with the baby boom, was a major factor in the growth and expansion of American colleges, including community colleges. In 1990 more than $690 million in tuition assistance was granted to veterans.[39]

National Defense Education Act.   The Cold War and the Soviet launching of *Sputnik* in 1957 increased pressure for better American schools and federal funding. This led to the sixth phase of federal education legislation, particularly the National Defense Education Act (NDEA) of 1958. The act spelled out the importance of education to the national defense, and funding was earmarked for educational programs that enhanced "the security of the nation . . . and [developed] the mental resources and technical skills of its young men and women."

Sputnik

This broad act emphasized improvement of instruction in science, mathematics, foreign languages, and other critical subjects. It provided college and university student loans and scholarships; funded numerous teacher-training programs, including those for teaching the disadvantaged; stimulated guidance and counseling programs; and promoted curriculum reform and programs in vocational and technical education. By 1960 the federal government was spending nearly $240 million annually on NDEA programs; in the mid-1960s the act was extended to include history, geography, English, and reading as critical subjects.[40]

Compensatory Education Acts.   The 1960s and 1970s brought a new emphasis on equality in education. With the War on Poverty and the spread of the

---

[38]Marvin Lazerson, *American Education in the Twentieth Century* (New York: Teachers College Press, Columbia University, 1987); Joel Spring. *The American School: 1642–1990* (New York: Longman, 1990).

[39]*Digest of Education Statistics, 1990,* Table 326, p. 339.

[40]S. Alexander Rippa, *Education in a Free Society,* 6th ed. (New York: Longman, 1988); Paul Woodring, *The Persistent Problems of Education* (Bloomington, Ind.: Phi Delta Kappa, 1983).

Title IX of the 1972 Education Amendments to the Civil Rights Act outlines what schools and colleges must do to prevent sex discrimination in hiring and to make sports programs and facilities available to women. (© Sven Martson/ Comstock)

civil rights movement, national policy became linked to education, as the government targeted specific groups — namely, minorities and the poor — and created specific policies to improve their educational opportunities. The federal government took on an active and coordinated posture with reference to education as it substantially increased its contributions to a variety of targeted programs and increased its regulations over specific policies.

Elementary and Secondary Education Act

The most important act of this period was the Elementary and Secondary Education Act (ESEA) of 1965, part of President Lyndon Johnson's Great Society. It focused on compensatory programs for minority and low-income students, immediately providing $1 billion for the first year. In 1980, at the height of its funding, monies totaled $3.5 billion, or about $300 per child; from 1965 to 1980, $30 billion had been appropriated. (Appropriations fluctuated between $3.1 and $4.6 billion from 1981 to 1990.[41] Considering inflation, this was a drop in real dollars that reflected the general cutbacks in education by the federal government during this period.)

[41]*Digest of Education Statistics, 1983–84* (Washington, D.C.: U.S. Government Printing Office, 1983), Table 144, p. 174; *Digest of Education Statistics, 1990,* Tables 326–327, pp. 337, 343.

Desegregation and Minority Groups. From the mid-1960s through the 1970s, the full force of the federal government came into play to enforce U.S. Supreme Court decisions on school desegregation, first in the South and then in the North and West. The impetus came from the Civil Rights Act of 1964, which provided that all programs supported by federal funds — including those allocated to public education — must be administered and operated without discrimination. If clear evidence of intent to desegregate and to operate in a nondiscriminatory fashion was not provided, all federal funds were to be withheld.

Withholding federal funds

In addition to these desegregation efforts, the educational needs of minority groups received considerable attention and funding from the mid-1960s to the late 1970s. Groups such as bilingual students, African Americans, Native Americans, low-income students, and students with handicaps were targeted for special programs. Although programs and funding for minority groups received less emphasis in the 1980s, the 1991 civil rights bill should increase affirmative action and direct aid to minority groups.

Programs for minorities

Women's educational concerns were addressed by Title IX of the 1972 Education Amendments to the Civil Rights Act, along with later acts such as the Women's Educational Equity Act of 1974 and a host of affirmative action rulings enforced by the Office of Civil Rights. These acts and rulings have bolstered women's educational rights and funding for women's programs. For example, Title IX outlines what schools and colleges must do to prevent sex discrimination in hiring and to make sports programs and facilities available to women.

Educational equity for women

Current Federal Aid to Education

The 1980s brought a new conservatism at the federal level, and federal spending for education decreased in the early years of the decade, taking inflation into consideration (Table 7.3). By mid-decade federal spending was rising again in absolute dollars, although the federal contribution represented a smaller percentage of total school financing (compare Table 7.3 with Table 7.1).

During the 1980s the method of school funding also changed. **Categorical grants** (funds for specific groups and designated purposes) gave way to **block grants** (funds for a general purpose without precise categories). Categorical grants had been an important feature of federal involvement in education during the 1970s. But Chapter 2 of the federal Education Consolidation and Improvement Act (ECIA) of 1981 replaced categorical grants for twenty-eight separate education programs with one block grant that state and local education agencies could use for broadly defined educational purposes. (Categorical grants for bilingual students and students with handicaps were saved.) This move was part of a *new federalism,* which as we saw in Chapter 6, shifted responsibility for many federal social and educational programs from the national to the state governments.

Education Consolidation and Improvement Act

Observers have cited a number of advantages of the block grant approach for education programs. It has reduced the amount of paperwork required to get a grant (from 20–30 pages for a $50,000 program to 4–6 pages), simplified the administration of grant monies, and enabled school districts to cut down the bureaucracy devoted to grants. Instead of submitting applications to several different federal agencies, a school district now has to deal only with its own state's education agency. The block grant approach has also enhanced the role

Simplified procedures

Table 7.3
Federal Funds for Elementary, Secondary, and Higher Education, 1970–1990

Year	Amount (billions)	Amount Adjusted for Inflation (billions)
1970	$ 9.2	$ 6.8
1972	11.9	7.7
1974	13.1	8.7
1976	19.6	11.8
1978	21.6	12.0
1980	27.5	13.1
1982	26.8	11.6
1984	30.5	12.3
1986	33.7	13.9
1988	37.5	14.4
1990	45.3	15.3

Note: As a result of the Education Consolidation and Improvement Act in 1981, many programs and funds were shifted among various federal departments; the base of comparison has not been exactly the same since then.

Source: *Digest of Education Statistics, 1980* (Washington, D.C.: National Center for Education Statistics, 1980), Table 160, pp. 184–186; *Digest of Education Statistics, 1982* (Washington, D.C.: National Center for Education Statistics, 1982), Tables 153–154, pp. 171–172; and *Digest of Education Statistics, 1990* (Washington, D.C.: National Center for Education Statistics, 1990), Table 327, p. 343. Amounts adjusted for inflation have been calculated by the authors on the basis of *Consumer Price Index: 1913–1990* (Washington, D.C.: Bureau of Labor Statistics, U.S. Department of Labor, 1990), pp. 1–3. Also see *Digest of Education Statistics, 1990,* pp. 332–333.

of local administrators in determining how resources will be used. Finally, under the old system some school districts were continually unsuccessful at competing for federal grants, whereas others became very skillful at the process. Block grants, according to their supporters, have reduced this kind of competition among districts.[42]

Winners and losers

On the other hand, critics have pointed out that the states have failed to pick up some of the programs formerly funded by the federal government. Many states have chosen to distribute funds to local schools on a per child basis rather than on the basis of need. The "winners" under the block grant approach have included small-town and rural school districts; the "losers" have often been urban districts with high percentages of minority and low-income students. Districts under court-ordered desegregation that previously received federal funds also have taken large cuts. Many critics point out that the federal government began providing its services and programs in the first place because the states refused to. For example, before block grants went into effect, the Council of Great City Schools (a coalition that includes the largest urban school districts)

---

[42]Anne H. Hastings, "Snipping the Strings: Local and State Administrators Discuss Chapter 2," *Phi Delta Kappan* (November 1983), pp. 194–198; Michael S. Knapp and Rhonda A. Cooperstein, "Early Research on the Federal Education Block Grant," *Educational Evaluation and Policy Analysis* (Summer 1986), pp. 121–137; and Maria Raynes, Martha Snell, and Wayne Sailor, "A Fresh Look at Categorical Programs for Children with Special Needs," *Phi Delta Kappan* (December 1991), pp. 326–331.

depended on Washington for 16 percent of school revenues, compared to a national average of 8 percent. This need for federal funds, some critics argue, derived from the states' lack of attention to the problems of big-city schools.[43]

Uses of block grant funds

However, the intense interest in winners and losers seems to be waning, and educators now seem more concerned with the variety of the block grant's contributions to local schools and the way funds are distributed from the state to the local level. At present, urban schools (with large percentages of minority and low-income children) overwhelmingly use block grant money for reading and language programs, whereas rural and suburban schools tend to use the money for books and materials as well as computer hardware and software.[44]

SCHOOL FINANCE TRENDS

By the early 1990s, state revenue shortfalls, rising costs, and other budgetary problems had placed many school districts in a bleak fiscal situation. Although the state of the U.S. economy was less than optimistic, concern for reforming schools and meeting economic challenges abroad created the atmosphere for corporate investment in education, as well as another round of finance reform. As we examine the current trends affecting school finance, keep in mind that equal educational opportunity is no longer the only focus of attention. Today

Today's watchwords

the watchwords are educational *excellence, efficiency, performance, accountability,* and *productivity.* At the very least educators are being asked to show proof of a direct relationship between increased spending and student achievement.

Taxpayer Resistance

Beginning in the late 1970s, a tax revolt swept the country, putting a damper on the movement for school finance reform. In California a taxpayer initia-

Taxpayer initiatives

tive called Proposition 13, passed in 1978, set a maximum tax of 1 percent on the fair market value of a property and limited increases in assessed valuation to 2 percent a year. Similar measures were passed in Idaho in 1978 and Massachusetts in 1980, and by 1990 forty-five more states had imposed property tax

Caps on school spending

limitations or direct controls on school spending. A few states put absolute caps on the amount school districts could spend, regardless of local willingness to impose higher taxes; other states permitted voters to recall school boards if expenditures exceeded specified levels.[45]

As a result, average property taxes declined from $4.17 per $100 of personal income in 1977 to $3.38 in 1989. In addition, twenty-one states have intro-

---

[43]Barbara Means and Michael S. Knapp, "Cognitive Approaches to Teaching Advanced Skills to Educationally Disadvantaged Children," *Phi Delta Kappan* (December 1991), pp. 282–289; telephone conversation with Michael Casserly, Legislative and Research Associate, Council of Great City Schools, January 13, 1992; and Arthur E. Wise, "The Two Conflicting Trends in School Reform: Legislated Learning Revisited," *Phi Delta Kappan* (January 1988), pp. 328–332.

[44]Baker, "Yes, Throw Money at Schools"; *Congressional Record—House,* April 13, 1988, pp. H1488–1608; and Allan C. Ornstein, *Strategies for Effective Teaching* (New York: Harper Collins, 1990).

[45]John Augenblick, *School Finance: A Primer* (Denver: Education Commission of the States, 1991).

duced *circuitbreaker* programs that give selected populations (such as older persons and first-time homeowners) a credit for property taxes paid.[46] All of these measures reduce the potential funding base for public schools. Property tax levels increased dramatically in 1990 — rising 12.9 percent from 1989 — primarily because of the new wave of court-based school finance reform. Although these reform efforts were aimed at reducing disparities largely caused by the reliance on property taxes for school financing, the recent result has been to increase property taxes overall. If these new tax levels continue, another round of **taxpayer resistance** may break out, particularly because taxpayers believe "the property tax is the least fair tax of any federal, state, or local tax."[47]

The educational reform movement of the 1980s and 1990s has emphasized the need to improve the quality of education, and the public seems willing to support increased education spending for that purpose. Yet taxpayers remain wary. In the current social and economic climate, there is much interest in results: what are we getting for the dollars we spend? This concern has led the public to begin to hold educators accountable for their use of public funds.

The Accountability Movement

Although definitions of **accountability** vary, the term generally refers to the notion that teachers, administrators, school board members, and even students themselves must be held responsible for the results of their efforts. Teachers must meet some standard of competency and schools must devise methods of relating expenditures to outcomes.

The accountability movement stems from a number of factors. In recent years, more parents have realized that schooling is important for success and that their children are not learning sufficiently well. Because the cost of education has increased, parents demand to know what they are paying for. The general taxpayer, who wants to keep the lid on school spending, wishes to hold educators responsible for the outcomes of instruction and the consequences of any school program. The educational reform movement has also helped to trigger increased demand for program evaluation, performance indicators, cost-effectiveness studies, and greater competence among teachers.

A majority of states have taken the position that accountability should be mandatory, leaving the specifics to the discretion of local school districts. The state legislation ranges in content from very explicit laws to broad and vague guidelines. Some call for assessment of students, some require management goals and methods of evaluation, many require evaluation of teachers, and a few require citizen involvement. Some thirty-seven states have introduced their own statewide assessment programs, and forty-three states use the national assessment testing program to measure students' performance and the cost-effectiveness of teaching.[48] Some states have passed laws calling for the unseating of

New increase in property taxes

Responsibility for results

Reasons for accountability movement

Variation among states

[46]*Recent Changes in State, Local, and State-Local Tax Levels,* Tables 5–6, pp. 12–13.
[47]U.S. Advisory Commission on Intergovernmental Relations, *Changing Public Attitudes on Governments and Taxes* (Washington, D.C.: Government Printing Office, 1991), p. 7.
[48]Telephone conversation with Steven Gorman, Project Director, National Assessment of Educational Progress, November 7, 1991.

school board members and the replacement of school administrators if test scores and other achievement indicators do not measure up. Other states are comparing school district test scores and using the results to cut funding or reward districts with additional monies. The provisions mentioned earlier for state takeovers of "academically bankrupt" districts also pertain to the demand for accountability; fourteen states as of 1991 had adopted "rescue plans" to take over bankrupt or low-achieving districts.[49]

Focus on teachers

Often, the main focus is on teachers. The trend toward testing of teachers and prospective teachers is part of this movement; by 1989 twenty-four states required testing for admission to teacher-education programs, and twenty-one required tests on exit from teacher education.[50] Also related is the decision of some states to issue certificates for only three to five years; the teacher must present positive evaluations or proof of further university work in order to be recertified.

Avoiding simplified concepts

Most people agree that everyone, in education as in other fields, should be held accountable for his or her work. What many educators fear is a simplified concept of accountability that places responsibility solely on the teacher or principal, ignoring the roles of parents, community residents, school board members, taxpayers, and the students themselves. The difficulty of equating students' progress with test scores or of distinguishing superior teachers from average or mediocre teachers must be realized. Although accountability is a desirable goal, legislators and educators should understand that neither the costs nor the results of schooling lend themselves to quick fixes.

Tuition Tax Credits

In addition to taxpayer resistance and the accountability movement, the growth of interest in tuition tax credits has been a barometer of popular dissatisfaction with the public schools. **Tuition tax credits** allow parents to claim a tax reduction for part of the tuition fees they pay to send their children to private schools. By 1991 tuition tax credits were a fact in Minnesota, and in ten other states tax credits, tax deductions, or both were on the legislative agenda.[51] The tax-credit movement is part of the continuing quest of nonpublic schools for support and for increased opportunities for choice by the public; but the issue has been brought to the fore by the wavering of public faith in public institutions, especially the city schools.

Opponents

Debates over tuition tax credits for nonpublic students have been vigorous and emotional. Opponents have argued that such credits would provide unconstitutional support for church-related schools; would aid the rich; would un-

[49]Allan C. Ornstein, "National Reform and Instructional Accountability," *High School Journal* (October–November 1990), pp. 51–56; telephone conversation with Chris Pipho, Director, Education Commission of the States, Denver, November 6, 1991.

[50]Olive Elliott, "The Use of Tests," *American School Board Journal* (February 1991), pp. 33–34; Richard M. Jaeger, "Legislative Perspectives on Statewide Testing," *Phi Delta Kappan* (November 1991), pp. 239–242; Allan C. Ornstein, "Reforming American Schools: The Role of the States," *NASSP Bulletin* (October 1991), pp. 46–55; and Ornstein, "The Evolving Accountability Movement."

[51]Telephone conversation with Chris Pipho, Director, Education Commission of the States, Denver, November 6, 1991.

dermine the public school system by supporting and encouraging the movement of students to nonpublic schools; would result in a large drain on the federal and state treasuries; would reduce the likelihood of obtaining voter support for public school tax increases; and would contribute to additional racial and socio-economic segregation and isolation of low-status students in the city public schools.[52]

Supporters

Supporters of tuition tax credits argue that such credits are not unconstitutional and would not seriously reduce federal revenues or hamper public-school tax levy efforts. They also argue that tax credits would provide wider opportunity for students to attend schools outside the inner city; thus, tax credits would not contribute to, and might even reduce, racial and socioeconomic isolation. In addition, many supporters believe that tax credits not only would provide parents with a choice in selecting schools but would also stimulate improvement in the public schools.[53]

Probably the biggest worry is that the quest for tax credits may directly conflict with the desire that originally fueled the establishment of public schools in the United States; that students share in a common educational experience. A program of increased aid to nonpublic schools is likely to divert funds from public schools, and any benefits of greater public assistance to private schools must be weighed against the possible loss in benefits to public schools. Since political and financial support for education are linked, we also need to consider what effect increased financial support for private schools would have on the political support for public schools.

Educational Vouchers and School Choice

Use of **educational vouchers** is another trend associated with school finance reform. Under a voucher system, parents of school-age children are given a voucher or flat grant representing their children's estimated educational cost or portion of school budget. Children then use this voucher to attend any school, public or private, that they and their parents choose. Like tuition tax credits, vouchers represent a loss of public confidence in public schools, and they have stimulated a similar controversy. The NEA, the AFT, and other educational organizations have taken a dim view of both vouchers and tax credits, arguing that such plans would increase segregation, split the public along socioeconomic lines, and reduce financial support for the public schools.[54]

Opposition to vouchers

Proponents of vouchers generally link the issue with the concept of **school choice,** which is discussed in detail in Chapter 16. By widening the average

---

[52]Daniel U. Levine and Robert J. Havighurst, *Society and Education,* 8th ed. (Needham Heights, Mass.: Allyn and Bacon, 1992); Mary Anne Raywid, "Public Choice, Yes; Vouchers, No!" *Phi Delta Kappan* (June 1987), pp. 762–769; and Raywid, "The Evolving Effort to Improve Schools," *Phi Delta Kappan* (October 1990), pp. 139–142.

[53]Donna Hulsizer, "Public Education on Trial," *Educational Leadership* (May 1987), pp. 12–16; Daniel D. McGarry, "The Advantages and Constitutionality of Tuition Tax Credits," *Educational Freedom* (February 1982), pp. 1–52; and John Weisman, "Revolutionary Steps to Better Education," *Fortune,* October 21, 1991, pp. 128–129.

[54]"Deleterious Programs," *NEA Handbook 1990–91* (Washington, D.C.: NEA, 1991), p. 213; Albert Shanker, "The End of the Traditional Model of Schooling," *Phi Delta Kappan* (January 1990), pp. 344–357.

Widening choices

person's choices for schooling, the supporters contend, we can increase competition among schools and raise the overall level of educational quality. The idea is to depend on education to follow the laws of the marketplace: if students and parents can choose schools, the effective schools will stay in operation and the less desirable ones will either go out of business or improve.[55] Some choice plans allow students to pick any public school they like, and others permit the use of state vouchers in private schools as well. Plans of the latter sort are clearly the most controversial. The AFT, for example, accepts the concept of choice among public schools but opposes the use of vouchers for private schools.

Milwaukee choice plan

One instance frequently cited is the Milwaukee choice plan, which allows students to attend private nonsectarian schools with public-funded vouchers. As of 1990–91, some 550 students were enrolled in the program. However, many established private schools refused to participate because their tuition was higher than the $2,500 voucher. New experimental private schools have sprung up, but many of them operate on a shoestring; some have already filed for bankruptcy.[56]

Despite these problems, the Bush administration proposed a nationwide choice plan that would offer $30 million in grants for states to design school choice programs, and an additional $200 million to aid at-risk students who participate.[57] The plan would have allowed public financing to cover student tuition at private and even parochial schools. The proposal encountered fierce resistance in Congress. Whatever actions Congress may take, controversy about the issues of school choice and educational vouchers should continue throughout the 1990s.

National debate

Streamlining School Budgets

In an era of taxpayer wariness, demands for school accountability, and strain on state budgets, school boards are being pressed to eliminate unnecessary spending before recommending tax increases. Not only must school outcomes measure up to expected standards, but the budget must stand up to close scrutiny. Because of the competing demands for public money — especially from a "graying" U.S. population — coupled with the reduced number of households with children in schools, educators are forced to reduce their budget expectations and do more with less money.

Close scrutiny of school budgets

Businesses and corporations have had to slim down in many ways — by selling off unprofitable enterprises, closing old plants, cutting corporate and regional staff — and in some respects life in the "minimalist" corporation is tougher but simpler.[58] With smaller staffs, decisions can be made more quickly,

Virtues of streamlining

---

[55]William L. Boyd and Herbert J. Walberg, eds., *Choice in Education* (Berkeley, Calif.: McCutchan, 1990); John E. Coons and Stephen B. Sugarman, *Education by Choice — The Case for Family Control* (Berkeley: University of California Press, 1978); and Joseph Murphy, ed., *The Educational Reform Movement of the 1980s* (Berkeley, Calif.: McCutchan, 1990).

[56]Elliott Negin, "Beyond the Rhetoric," *Agenda* (Fall 1991), pp. 50–53; Walter Shapiro, "Tough Choice," *Time,* September 16, 1991, pp. 50–60.

[57]Shapiro, "Tough Choice."

[58]Thomas Moore, "Goodbye, Corporate Staff," *Fortune,* December 21, 1987, pp. 65, 68, 76. Thomas A. Stewart, "Competitiveness: The New American Century," *Fortune* (Spring 1991) Special Issue, pp. 12–23.

Competing demands for public money coupled with the reduced number of households with children in school have led educators to reduce their budget expectations and do more with less money. (© Howard Dratch/The Picture Cube)

accountability is clearer, and many people seem to work harder. The same principles are being applied to the public schools. Corporate leaders often serve on school boards, and the gospel of streamlining and efficiency has had considerable impact on American education — often without questioning whether what has been cut out is "fat" or "protein." We should continue to see the following significant trends.

1. *Class size.* Although many commentators preach the virtue of small classes, reasons of economy have kept average class size at seventeen students per teacher since 1990.[59] The budgetary reasons are reinforced by research studies that suggest no significant differences between achievement in small classes and in large classes — unless class size is reduced so much (in most studies below five students) that the teacher can use different instructional methods.[60]

2. *Modernization of older buildings.* Rather than build new schools, many districts are choosing to save money by maintaining and modernizing their older buildings. Although proper maintenance of older buildings is expensive, it is often less costly than starting from scratch. This is especially the case in the

Maintaining older facilities

---

[59]*Digest of Education Statistics, 1990,* Table 58, p. 72.
[60]Harris M. Cooper, "Does Reducing Student to Instructor Ratios Affect Achievement?" *Educational Psychologist* (Winter 1989), pp. 79–88; Eric A. Hanushek, "The Impact of Differential Expenditures on School Performance," *Educational Researcher* (September 1989), pp. 45–51; Allan C. Ornstein, "In Pursuit of Cost-Effective Schools," *Principal* (September 1990), pp. 28–30; and Robert E. Slavin, "Class Size and Student Achievement: Small Effects of Small Classes," *Educational Psychologist* (Winter 1989), pp. 99–110.

Northeast and Midwest, where the costs of land and labor and the need to en-close and insulate space make the total cost of new construction twice that in the rural South or Southwest.[61]

Building smaller schools

3. *Smaller schools.* Large schools, with big cafeterias, auditoriums, and gym-nasiums, require major outlays for fuel, lighting, insurance, and maintenance. These facilities add to construction costs and remain unoccupied for a large por-tion of the day and year. In many areas the trend is toward smaller school build-ings, which make more efficient use of space and require fewer administrators.[62]

Layoffs in some communities

4. *Teacher layoffs.* Although the era of large-scale teacher layoffs has passed, layoffs will persist in areas that are experiencing school consolidation and de-creasing student enrollments. Whereas school officials are hiring in Arizona, Florida, and other parts of the Sunbelt, districts in Ohio and Oklahoma are still laying off teachers.[63]

Streamlining central staffs

5. *Administrative reductions.* Many districts are finding it possible to operate with smaller central staffs. When administrative staffs are reduced for budget reasons, there is much less outcry than when the teaching force is cut. In some instances, a reduced school-district bureaucracy can function more efficiently. Although the ratio of central administrators to students averages 1 to 561 na-tionwide, about 5 percent of school districts find they can operate with admin-istrator/student ratios of 1 to 1,000 or higher.[64]

Reducing energy costs

6. *Energy economies.* Some schools have learned to dial down temperatures, delay warming up the school before classes each morning, or reduce heat in the hallways and underutilized spaces. Other schools have installed insulation or other energy-saving features, and still others are bypassing utility companies to buy energy directly from gas and oil distributors. All of these economies save precious funds, and when the next energy crisis arrives, more schools will be forced to take similar measures.

School Infrastructure and Environmental Problems

The nation's **school infrastructure** is in a state of critical disrepair. By infrastructure, we mean the basic physical facilities of the school plant (plumb-ing, sewer, heat, electric, roof, masonry, carpentry, and so on). Building experts estimate that schools in the United States are deteriorating at a faster rate than they can be repaired, and faster than most other public facilities. Plumbing, elec-trical wiring, and heating systems in many schools are dangerously out of date;

Deterioration of physical facilities

---

[61]William Brubaker, "Building for Tomorrow," *American School Board Journal* (April 1988), pp. 31–33, 66; Allan C. Ornstein, "School Budgets in the 1990s," *Education Digest* (February 1990), pp. 15–16; and Sally B. Zakariya, "School Construction Is a Hot, New Board Game," *American School Board Journal* (April 1988), pp. 27–30.

[62]Allan C. Ornstein, "Trimming the Fat, Stretching the Meat for 1990 Budgets," *School Adminis-trator* (October 1989), pp. 20–21.

[63]*The Condition of Education, 1990,* Vol. 1 (Washington, D.C.: U.S. Government Printing Office, 1990), Table 1.28, p. 92; *Projections of Education Statistics to 2001* (Washington, D.C.: U.S. Gov-ernment Printing Office, 1989), Tables 34–35, pp. 58–59; and Allan C. Ornstein, "Teacher Sal-aries in Social Context," *High School Journal* (December–January 1990), pp. 129–132.

[64]Allan C. Ornstein, "Administrator/Student Ratios in Large School Districts," *Phi Delta Kappan* (June 1989), pp. 806–807.

roofing is below code; and exterior materials (brickwork, stone, and wood) are chipped or cracked. The cost of deferred expenditures currently runs to over $100 million each in Los Angeles, Detroit, Chicago, Seattle, and Miami's Dade County, with an enormous bill of $680 million for the New York City schools. The accumulated cost to repair the public schools, according to knowledgeable sources, can now be conservatively placed at $20 to $35 billion.[65]

Greatest problems in the Frostbelt

Schools in cities and in the Frostbelt suffer the greatest infrastructure problems because they are the oldest and the most decayed. Nearly 35 percent of the schools in the older industrial cities of the Northeast and Midwest were built before 1930; a large number were constructed before 1900. For example, nearly half of Chicago's 597 school buildings were built before 1930, and as many as 80 schools still in existence in 1991 were built before 1900. In Akron, Buffalo, Kansas City (Mo.), and Portland, more than 50 percent of the schools were built before 1930.[66]

Nationwide, 25 percent of school buildings are considered in "inadequate" condition, 33 percent are "adequate," and 42 percent are "good." Leading the list of inadequate buildings are Connecticut (60 percent), California (55 percent), Washington, D.C. (50 percent), Illinois (50 percent), and Rhode Island (40 percent). Of the buildings that are inadequate, 61 percent need major repairs, 43 percent are obsolete, 42 percent have environmental hazards, 25 percent are overcrowded, and 13 percent are structurally unsound.[67] Many, of course, have multiple problems.

Asbestos cleanup is costly

Environmental hazards in school buildings are a special problem. For example, the Environmental Protection Agency (EPA) has ordered government and commercial property owners, including school districts, to clean up buildings laden with asbestos. Although the costs are hard to calculate, one estimate placed the bill for schools at $3.1 billion, which would cover some 45,000 schools in 31,000 districts.[68] Another nationwide study placed the figure at $2.1 billion overall or $25,244 per school.[69] It is a serious matter. Between 15 and 20 million children and 1.5 million school employees are subject to daily asbestos exposure, yet there is much debate about the proper methods of dealing with the problem. According to recent data, the dangers of asbestos are minimal as long as it remains inert and does not become airborne.[70] In some cases, therefore, the "cure" — if it involves ripping out asbestos in ceilings, walls, floors,

[65]"The Maintenance Gap: Deferred Repair and Renovation in the Nation's Elementary and Secondary Schools" (A Joint Report by the American Association of School Administrators, Council of Great City Schools, and National School Boards Association, Washington, D.C., January 1983); and Allan C. Ornstein and Robert C. Cienkus, "The Nation's School Repair Bill," *American School Board Journal* (June 1990), pp. 2A–4A.

[66]Ornstein and Cienkus, "The Nation's School Repair Bill"; telephone conversation with Michael Spring, Publisher, *American School and University Magazine*, May 13, 1988.

[67]Ann Lewis, *Wolves at the Schoolhouse Door: An Investigation of the Condition of Public School Buildings* (Washington, D.C.: Education Writers Association, 1989).

[68]Louis S. Richman, "Why Throw Money at Asbestos?" *Fortune*, June 6, 1988, pp. 155–170.

[69]Ornstein and Cienkus, "The Nation's School Repair Bill."

[70]Michael D. Lemonick, "An Overblown Asbestos Scare?" *Time*, January 29, 1990, p. 65; Andrew Trotter, "Reassessing the Asbestos Risk," *Executive Educator* (June 1990), pp. 10A–10B; Allan C. Ornstein and Robert C. Cienkus, "Asbestos Removal from Schools: How Much Will It Cost?" *Transaction* (January/February 1991), pp. 2–3.

and basements — may be worse than the "disease." One EPA study indicates that as much as 75 percent of school asbestos cleanup had been done improperly as of 1985.[71]

Radon problems

Radon gas is another environmental concern. Preliminary EPA tests found that radon, now considered the second-leading cause of lung cancer, was present at dangerously high levels in 54 percent of the 130 schools randomly checked.[72] The naturally occurring gas seeps into buildings from the underlying soil and rock. The cost per school for reducing radon to a safe level may range from $1,000 for a simple ventilation adjustment to $50,000 or more if special subventilation is needed.

Indoor air quality

Further environmental problems may affect schools in coming years. For example, experts are studying the health effects of poor indoor air quality. Carpets and plastics emit formaldehyde and other gases; copy machines give off ozone; even drywall, paint, and cleaning fluids produce fumes that may be harmful.[73] Schools may suffer from all of these problems, plus the effects of specific pollutants ranging from chemicals in the science labs and paint in the art rooms to ordinary chalk dust. Still another potential concern is the effect of

Electromagnetic fields

electromagnetic fields. Although the consequences for health are not well understood, initial studies suggest that high-power lines running through many communities — often close to schools and playgrounds — may emit dangerous levels of electromagnetic radiation.[74] Even small electrical devices such as computers, televisions, air conditioners, and fluorescent lights are suspect as a source of harmful electromagnetic fields.[75]

School budgets eventually will have to address these existing infrastructure and environmental problems. Compared to other public sectors, education has physical-plant needs that rank among the most serious in the nation.

Summing Up

1. Schools are supported by the federal, state, and local governments, with the greatest share derived from state sources and the smallest share from federal sources. Since the early twentieth century, state support has increased dramatically and local support has been reduced; the percentage of federal support grew until the 1980s and then began to decline.

2. Although the property tax is the main local source of school revenue, it is considered a regressive tax.

3. There is wide variation in the financial ability among states and within states (at the local district level) to support education. Poorer school districts tend to receive more money from their respective states than do wealthier school

---

[71]Telephone conversation with Robert Garratt, Staff Specialist, Environmental Protection Agency, Region 5, June 7, 1989; Trotter, "Reassessing the Asbestos Risk."

[72]*Radon in Schools,* Bulletin No. 520 (Washington, D.C.: U.S. Government Printing Office, 1989); Hugh Wright, "Radon Gas New Threat in Schools," *USA Today,* April 21, 1989, p. 1A.

[73]Dana Dunn, "Environmental Health Hazards Move Indoors," *Midwest Real Estate News* (November 1990), pp. 1–5.

[74]Casey Burke, "Jury Out on Risk from Power Lines," *Chicago Tribune,* May 26, 1991, p. 19.

[75]"Electromagnetic Fields: Are They a Cause for Concern?" *Winnetka Report* (June 1991), pp. 1–2.

districts, but the amount rarely makes up for the total difference in expenditures.

4. School finance reform, initiated by the courts and carried forward by state legislatives, has attempted to reduce or eliminate funding disparities between poor and wealthy districts. The basic goal is to equalize educational opportunities and give less wealthy districts the means to improve their performance. Some reform plans allow states to take over districts that fail to improve.

5. Since the *Sputnik* era, federal funding of education has become increasingly linked to national policy. Federal aid generally has been coordinated to coincide with national policy goals. But since the 1980s, responsibility for educational funding has shifted from the federal government to the individual states.

6. Controversies over accountability, tuition tax credits, educational vouchers, and school choice reflect public dissatisfaction with the educational system.

7. Taxpayer resistance, especially to increases in property taxes, results in strong pressure to streamline school budgets.

8. Crumbling school infrastructure and environmental dangers pose significant problems for many schools, especially in many cities of the Northeast and Midwest.

Key Terms

regressive taxes *(235)*

progressive taxes *(235)*

property tax *(236)*

mill *(236)*

user fees *(237)*

municipal overburden *(237)*

sales tax *(239)*

personal income tax *(239)*

academic bankruptcy *(248)*

categorical grants *(254)*

block grants *(254)*

taxpayer resistance *(257)*

accountability *(257)*

tuition tax credits *(258)*

educational vouchers *(259)*

school choice *(259)*

school infrastructure *(262)*

Discussion Questions

1. Why do city schools have more fiscal problems than suburban or rural schools?

2. What are the major reasons for the historical rise in state support of education?

3. What are the major reasons for minimal financial support of education at the federal level?

4. What are the primary reasons for taxpayers' resistance to school taxes?

5. Why is school infrastructure becoming a serious problem? Given the public attitude toward saving money, how can people be motivated to pay for school repairs and renovation?

Suggested Readings

Augenblick, John. *School Finance: A Primer.* Denver: Education Commission of the States, 1991.

> *This book examines various existing methods and approaches to financing schools and proposes alternatives.*

Boyd, William L., and Herbert J. Walberg. *Choice in Education.* Berkeley, Calif.: McCutchan, 1990.

> *The authors discuss the advantages and disadvantages of school choice, as well as various choice plans in major cities.*

Guthrie, James W., Walter I. Garms, and Lawrence C. Pierce. *School Finance and Education Policy.* Englewood Cliffs, N.J.: Prentice-Hall, 1988.

> *This is a comprehensive examination of various methods for distributing resources and services for public schools.*

Odden, Allen R., and Lawrence O. Picus. *School Finance: A Policy Perspective.* New York: McGraw-Hill, 1992.

> *This is an examination of school productivity formulas, fiscal policy, and fiscal federalism.*

State Fiscal Outlook for 1991. Denver: National Conference of State Legislatures, 1991.

> *This provides an outlook on declining state revenues and state tax increases.*

Swanson, Austin D., and Richard A. King. *School Finance: Its Economics and Politics.* New York: Longman, 1991.

> *These authors discuss the hows and whys of school finance decisions.*

Ward, James G., and Patricia Anthony. *Who Pays for Student Diversity?* Newbury, Calif.: Sage/Corwin Press, 1992.

> *School finance policy can be a source for social justice and equity funding for students at risk.*

8

Legal Aspects
of Education

FOCUSING QUESTIONS

How do state and federal laws affect school district policies and classroom teaching?

What legal rights and responsibilities do teachers have?

What are the legal rights of students?

Can religious activities be conducted in the public schools? Can the government assist nonpublic schools?

Must the public schools accept students with AIDS?

How does affirmative action affect education?

D uring the past forty years, the courts have frequently been asked to resolve issues relating to public education in the United States. The growing role of the courts in this regard, particularly the federal courts, is evident from the total number of state and federal education-related court cases. In the 107 years from 1789 to 1896, there were only 3,096 such cases; in the 10 years from 1947 to 1956, there were 7,091. The growth of the federal role in settling educational disputes is particularly evident since 1967. Increased educational litigation reflects the fact that education has assumed an importance in our society that it did not have just a few decades ago. This growth in litigation has been paralleled, and to some extent spurred on, by an enormous increase in state and federal legislation affecting education.[1]

Legal decisions have had a significant impact on teachers' and students' behavior, on teachers' employment relationships with their school districts, and on curriculum and instruction. This chapter presents a general overview of the U.S. court system and examines the legal topics and court decisions that have had the most important effects on today's schools and teachers. The major topics considered are the rights and responsibilities both of teachers and of students, religion and the schools, students and teachers with AIDS, and affirmative action and educational equity.[2]

THE COURT SYSTEM

Cases involving education-related issues can be heard either in federal or state courts, depending on the allegations of the **plaintiffs** (the persons who sue). Federal courts decide cases that involve federal laws and regulations or constitutional issues. State courts adjudicate cases that involve state laws, state constitutional provisions, school board policies, or other nonfederal problems. Most cases pertaining to elementary and secondary education are filed in state courts. However, to keep from further overburdening crowded calendars, both federal and state courts usually require that prospective **litigants** (the parties in a lawsuit) exhaust all administrative avenues available for resolution before involving the court system.

Most cases filed in state courts

State Courts

There is no national uniformity in state court organization. The specific details of each state's judicial system are found in its constitution. At the lowest level, most states have a court of original jurisdiction (often called a municipal or superior court) where cases are tried. That is, the facts are established, evidence is presented, witnesses testify and are cross-examined, and appropriate

[1]David Tyack, Thomas James, and Aaron Benavot, *The Law and the Shaping of Public Education, 1785–1954* (Madison: University of Wisconsin Press, 1987); David Tyack, "'Restructuring' in Historical Perspective: Tinkering Toward Utopia," *Teachers College Record* (Winter 1990), pp. 17–31; and Michael Imber and Gary Thompson, "Developing a Typology of Litigation in Education," *Educational Administration Quarterly* (May 1991), pp. 225–244.
[2]Other chapters of this book also discuss selected legal issues in education. For court decisions regarding school finance, see Chapter 7; desegregation law is explained in Chapter 11.

Appeals process

legal principles are applied in rendering a verdict. The losing side may appeal adverse decisions to the next higher level, usually an intermediate appellate court. This court reviews the trial record from the lower court and additional written materials submitted by both sides. In hearing an appeal, the goals of the appellate court are to ensure that appropriate laws were properly applied, that they fit with the facts presented, and that there was no deprivation of constitutional rights.

Should one side still not be satisfied, another appeal may be made to the state's highest court, often called its supreme court. A state supreme court decision is final unless a question involving the U.S. Constitution has been raised. The side wishing to appeal further may then petition the U.S. Supreme Court to consider the case.

Federal Courts

Federal courts are organized into a three-tiered system (see Figure 8.1). The jurisdiction and powers of these courts are set forth in the Constitution and are subject to congressional restrictions. The lowest level, district court, holds trials. For appeals at the next federal level, the nation is divided into twelve regions called circuits. The circuit courts handle appeals only from district courts within their particular geographic area. Unsuccessful litigants may request that the U.S. Supreme Court review their case. If four of the nine justices agree, a writ of certiorari (request for the transcripts of a case) is granted. Refusal to grant certiorari means the appellate court ruling stands.[3]

Federal appeals

Conflicting rulings

Decisions of courts below the U.S. Supreme Court have force only in the geographic area served by that particular court. For this reason, it is possible to find conflicting rulings in different circuits. Judges often look to previous case law for guidance in rendering decisions, and they may find precedent for a variety of legally defensible positions on a single issue.

Although education is considered a responsibility of the states, much federal litigation concerning educational issues has arisen, particularly in connection with the First and Fourteenth Amendments. The First Amendment concerns freedom of religion, speech, press, and assembly, and the right "to petition the government for redress of grievances." Many First Amendment cases have dealt with the role of religion in public education and with the extent of protection guaranteed to expression by students and teachers. The First Amendment has two clauses that are often cited in lawsuits: the **establishment clause,** which prohibits the establishment of a nationally sanctioned religion, and the **free exercise clause,** which protects rights of free speech and expression.

First Amendment

For review of cases under the establishment clause, courts use a three-pronged test first stated in 1971 by the U.S. Supreme Court in *Lemon* v. *Kurtzman:* (1) the act or policy must have been adopted with a secular purpose; (2) the primary effect must neither advance nor inhibit religion; and (3) the law or policy must not result in an excessive entanglement of government and

---

[3]Some case citations in this chapter include the term "cert. denied." This means that the losing parties petitioned the U.S. Supreme Court for review, but their request was denied. See David A. Splitt, "The High Court's Silence Can Speak Volumes," *The Executive Educator* (January 1992), pp. 4, 47.

Figure 8.1 ━━

The Federal Court System

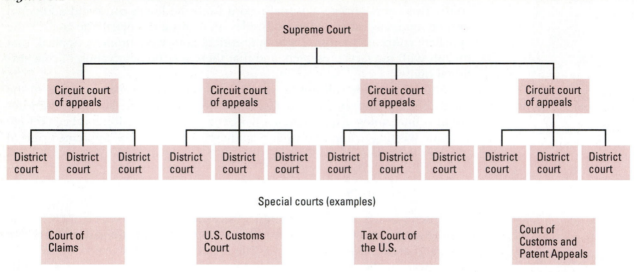

religion.[4] Review under the free exercise clause has a two-pronged test: (1) the plaintiffs must prove that their beliefs are sincerely held and that the protested government action truly injures the exercise of those beliefs; and (2) the government must prove that a truly compelling public necessity requires restricting that free exercise and that no less restrictive means are available.

Fourteenth Amendment

Court cases involving the Fourteenth Amendment often focus on the **equal protection clause,** which says that no state shall "deprive any person of life, liberty, or property, without due process of law; nor deny to any person within its jurisdiction the equal protection of the law." Fourteenth Amendment cases in the past have addressed the issue of school desegregation as well as suspension and expulsion of students.

Liberty and property interests

Litigants citing the Fourteenth Amendment must show that a liberty or property interest is a major element in the case. A liberty interest is involved if "a person's good name, reputation, honor or integrity is at stake"[5] because of action(s) taken by the defendant. A property interest, as defined in *Board of Regents of State Colleges* v. *Roth* (1972), arises from legal guarantees granted to tenured employees under the laws, rules, regulations, and contracts of the state.[6] For instance, teachers beyond the probationary period have a property interest in continued employment. Similarly, students have a property interest in their education. If either a liberty or a property interest is claimed, then a school district must provide due process to those whose rights it may attempt to restrict.

---

[4]*Lemon* v. *Kurtzman,* 91 S. Ct. 2105. See Mark G. Yudof, David L. Kirp, and Betsy Levin, *Educational Policy and the Law,* 3rd ed. (St. Paul, Minn.: West, 1991).

[5]*Goss* v. *Lopez,* 419 U.S. 565 (1975).

[6]*Board of Regents of State Colleges* v. *Roth,* 408 U.S. 564 (1972).

TEACHERS' RIGHTS AND RESPONSIBILITIES

Employment rights

Court decisions have clarified both the rights and the responsibilities of teachers in carrying out their jobs. As pointed out in Chapter 2, until quite recently teachers were vulnerable to dismissal by local boards of education for virtually any reason and without recourse. Collective negotiation statutes, tenure laws, mandatory due process procedures, and the like have been established to curb such abuses and to guarantee teachers certain employee rights. Along with rights come responsibilities, and many of these, too, have been written into law.

Testing and Investigation of Applicants for Certification or Employment

Background checks

Almost everywhere in the United States, persons who wish employment as teachers must possess teaching certificates, which are most often granted by the state. Many states require FBI background checks for teacher certification or employment, particularly in order to identify potential child abusers. Large school districts often check for previous criminal records, and small districts tend to rely on references and informal sources.[7]

Nondiscrimination requirements

Nearly all the states now require prospective teachers to pass one or more competency tests for certification and, in some cases, for continued employment. In states where minority passing rates are considerably lower than those for nonminority candidates, several lawsuits have been filed charging that specific tests discriminate against minority applicants. To answer such a lawsuit, employers must be able to specify the characteristics that a test is being used to measure, establish that these characteristics are necessary in carrying out the job, and demonstrate that the test is either predictive or meaningfully correlated with the work behavior in question.[8] Most lawsuits charging that teacher tests are discriminatory either have not been successful or have been withdrawn because available data did not demonstrate a clear pattern of discrimination.[9]

Drug Testing. Some school districts have attempted to require drug testing of prospective or current employees, especially since passage of the federal Drug-Free Workplace Act of 1988. While the federal legislation neither requires nor prohibits drug testing, these districts have included testing as part of an overall plan to combat use and abuse of drugs. In some of these districts drug-testing policies have been accepted by teachers through collective bargaining; in several others they have been challenged in court.

The New York State Supreme Court has ruled that teachers can be tested only if there is "reasonable suspicion" of illegal drug use, and a federal judge

---

[7]Alan Baas, "Background Checks on School Personnel," *ERIC Digest Series* (Number EA 55, 1990), pp. 1–2; "Background Checks Too Costly, District Says," *The Executive Educator* (April 1992), p. 4.

[8]S. E. Phillips, "Extending Teacher Licensure Testing" (Paper presented at the Annual Meeting of the American Educational Research Association, Chicago, April, 1991).

[9]Blake Rodman, "Arkansas Union Drops Suit over Teacher Tests," *Education Week*, November 25, 1987, p. 10; Hal E. Hagen, "The Legal Environment for Planning," in Robert V. Carlson and Gary Awkerman, eds., *Educational Planning* (White Plains, N.Y.: Longman, 1991), pp. 143–161.

Individualized suspicion

has ruled in favor of teachers' union objections to a Georgia law that required drug testing of applicants for public-school positions and state government jobs. Citing previous cases that permit drug testing only when there is "individualized suspicion" of employees in specified job categories or evidence of a compelling state interest in testing all employees, Judge Robert Hall concluded that the Georgia legislation violated privacy rights guaranteed under the Fourth and Fourteenth Amendments. Although the U.S. Supreme Court has never ruled directly on the constitutionality of random or general drug testing of public-school employees, lower court decisions suggest that such unlimited testing is unlikely to withstand constitutional scrutiny.[10]

Employment Contracts and Tenure

Adherence to regulations

In choosing which teachers to hire, local school boards must comply with laws that prohibit discrimination with respect to age, sex, race, religion, or national origin. Upon appointment, the teacher receives a written contract to sign. The contract may specify that the teacher adhere to school board policies and regulations. If the school district has negotiated with a teacher organization, the provisions of that agreement apply as well.

Damages possible

Contracts are binding on both parties. When one side fails to perform as agreed, the contract is broken. This is referred to as **breach of contract.** In such instances, the party that breached the contract may be sued for damages. Some states permit a teacher's certificate to be revoked if he or she breaches the contract. On the other hand, if a school district breaks a contract, teachers may be awarded damages or reinstatement to their former positions.

Terms of tenure

Nearly every state has some type of tenure law. **Tenure** provides job security for teachers by preventing their dismissal without cause. What constitutes "cause" is defined by each state; the usual reasons include incompetency, immorality, insubordination, and unprofessional conduct. In addition, as explained in the next section, the school district must follow due process if it wishes to dismiss a tenured teacher.

History of tenure

The concept of tenure was developed about a century ago as part of an effort to replace political patronage with a merit system for filling government positions, including teaching jobs. Academic freedom (discussed later in this section) is another important reason for tenure. From its inception, though, there has been uneasiness with the notion of tenure. On the one hand, it helps school districts attract and keep good teachers; on the other hand, it can sometimes provide protection for indifferent, lazy, or ineffective teachers. Tenure laws do contain mechanisms for dismissing the latter group, but the process is often laborious.

Continuing employment

Once tenure has been granted, many teachers do not sign a contract annually. Instead, they are said to be employed under a **continuing contract.** The term means that their re-employment for the next year is guaranteed unless school officials give notice by a specific date that the contract will not be renewed.

[10]Karen Diegmueller, "Federal Judge Strikes Down Ga.'s Drug-Testing Law," *Education Week,* October 3, 1990, p. 5.

Probationary period

Most states have a probationary period before teachers achieve tenure. Moreover, many tenured teachers who change districts lose their tenure and must serve another period of probation. The probationary period often consists of three years of consecutive, satisfactory service plus the offer of a contract for the fourth year. Many probationary contracts allow the teacher to be discharged at the end of the contract term for any reason and without explanation. No due process is required. However, if the teacher can demonstrate that his or her dismissal involves a constitutionally guaranteed liberty or property interest, due process would then be required. Some state laws have been interpreted to mean that probationary teachers judged unsatisfactory must be given a reasonable chance to improve their performance.[11]

Due Process in Dismissal of Tenured Teachers

Fairness a core element

Due process refers to those legal rules and principles that have been established to protect the rights of the accused. The core element of due process is "fairness." Most states have laws describing a teacher's rights and the applicable time limitations for due process proceedings, which the state must follow exactly. Although the requirements vary from state to state, certain elements of due process in cases of teacher dismissal are generally recognized:

1. The teacher must be given timely, detailed, written notice of the charges.
2. The teacher must be accorded a hearing and sufficient time to prepare.
3. The teacher has a right to be represented by legal counsel.
4. The teacher may present written and oral evidence including witnesses.
5. The teacher may cross-examine witnesses and challenge evidence.
6. The hearing is to be conducted before an impartial body. The U.S. Supreme Court has ruled (in *Hortonville District* v. *Hortonville Education Association*) that under the U.S. Constitution a school board may be that impartial body unless bias can be proven.[12]
7. The teacher is entitled to a written transcript of the proceedings.
8. The teacher has the right to appeal an adverse ruling to a higher legal authority, usually the state court system.

Example of insubordination

Firing a teacher for incompetence frequently requires documentation of prior efforts to assist that person in improving. Such documentation can be very burdensome for everyone involved. For example, an Arizona teacher rated unsatisfactory by his principal was required to meet daily with the principal to review his lesson plans, with the aim of improving his teaching performance. After a number of these meetings the teacher balked at attending more, contending they were unproductive and merely a scheme designed to foster his

---

[11]"Dismissed Teacher Denied Chance to Improve, Nevada Ruling Says," *Education Week*, January 27, 1988, p. 3; "A Tenure Primer," *School and Community* (Spring 1991), pp. 18–19; and Allan S. Vann, "Preparing Probationary Teachers for Tenure," *Principal* (March 1992), pp. 42–44.

[12]*Hortonville District* v. *Hortonville Education Association*, 426 U.S. 482 (1976); Louis Fischer, David Schimmel, and Cynthia Kelly, *Teachers and the Law*, 3rd ed. (White Plains, N.Y.: Longman, 1991).

Taking Issue ⎯◆⎯

Tenure for Teachers

At one time, many teaching positions in large cities were controlled by political patronage. In some cities, principalships were available for a certain price at the ward committeeman's office, and teaching jobs were won or lost on the basis of precinct work. In general, teachers were afraid to contradict an administrator or an influential parent. Tenure was introduced partly in order to stop these abuses and to allow teachers independence in and out of the classroom. However, some educators now contend that the tenure system has outlived its usefulness.

Question: Should the tenure system for teachers be maintained?

Arguments PRO

1 Teaching is, by its nature, controversial. A good teacher cannot help but offend someone at some level. Without the academic freedom that tenure helps to protect, teachers could not do their jobs properly.

2 A tenure system does not protect incompetence. There are procedures for removing a teacher who is clearly ineffective. The responsibility for teacher incompetence lies with lax state licensing procedures and with administrators who are too reluctant to dismiss teachers during probationary periods.

3 Teachers must cope with pressure from a bewildering array of sources: parents, other community members, administrators, and legislators, among others. A complaint from any one of these parties might lead to a teacher's dismissal. For this reason, teachers need — and deserve — the special protection offered by tenure.

4 Tenure was originally a response to serious political and administrative abuses, especially in large cities. The same forces that caused these problems still exist, and they will create similar abuses if the protection of tenure is ever removed.

Arguments CON

1 Some teachers use their positions to advance personal, social, or political views under the guise of controversial discussion. Other teachers are simply lazy or incompetent. Often it is these marginal teachers — not the good teachers — whom the tenure system protects.

2 The procedures for removing a tenured teacher are often so complex and arouse so much resentment among other teachers that administrators are discouraged from trying. Furthermore, even if screening methods are upgraded, many ineffective teachers will continue to slip through. The only solution is to give school officials, like private employers, the right to fire an unproductive employee.

3 The many sources of pressure actually enhance a teacher's security. Active parents and community members often use their influence to protect good teachers. The layers of school administration offer avenues of appeal if a teacher's position is threatened. Thus, even without a tenure system, competent teachers will be secure in their jobs.

4 Teachers now have powerful professional organizations that shield them from undue political and administrative interference. With these organizations looking after teachers' rights, the tenure system has become an anachronism.

Less formal procedures

dismissal. His termination, based on insubordination, was upheld. The court said he showed "willful disregard of a reasonable order."[13]

Administrators sometimes use less formal procedures for separating incompetent teachers from their school districts. Some of these procedures include counseling incompetent teachers out of the profession, suggesting and financing early retirement, and allowing the teacher to resign. According to a study by Edwin Bridges, proceedings to dismiss incompetent faculty are increasing. The increase in these cases may be related to recent national concern with teacher competency. Nevertheless, it is still true that very few tenured teachers are dismissed for incompetency or other reasons. For example, only four of 5,850 tenured teachers employed in Delaware in 1988–89 were dismissed.[14]

Negotiation and Strikes

Negotiation allowed in most states

Teachers have the right to form and belong to unions and other professional organizations. Since the 1960s, teacher groups have lobbied for state legislation to permit school boards to negotiate agreements with them. This effort has been successful in a majority of states; however, a few, such as North Carolina and Virginia, continue to prohibit negotiations between teachers and school boards. The laws enacted vary widely, but they usually allow the two sides to bargain collectively or, at least, to "meet and confer." Some states specify the procedure that must be followed if the two sides fail to agree (for example, fact-finding in Kansas; binding arbitration in Maryland).

Penalties for striking

Education is considered to be a vital public service for which the law prohibits strikes by employees. (A few states condone the withholding of services by teachers under specific conditions written into state law.) However, teachers sometimes do strike despite the legal prohibitions. In such instances, school officials are empowered to seek court injunctions ordering teachers to return to their classrooms. Defiance of a court order can result in penalties imposed in accordance with state law. Florida and Minnesota, for example, prohibit striking teachers from receiving salary increases for one year after a strike, New York law allows striking teachers to be penalized two days' pay for each day on strike, and Michigan permits dismissal of striking teachers.

Expenditure of Union Dues

Agency fees

Many teachers have objected to use of their union dues for political or other activities with which they disagree. In *Lehnert* v. *Ferris Faculty Association*, a group of professors at Ferris State College challenged the use of union dues that they were required to pay as "agency fees" collected through a collective bargaining agreement. The U.S. Supreme Court ruled that public employees who must pay dues but are not union members cannot be required under the First Amendment to support lobbying or other political activities unrelated to the agreement. How-

---

[13]*Siglin* v. *Kayenta Unified School District No. 27*, 655 P. 2d 353 (Ariz. Ct. App. 1982); James H. VanSciver, "Teacher Dismissals," *Phi Delta Kappan* (December 1990), pp. 318–319; and Steven R. Staples and Glen I. Earthman, "Ready, Document, Fire," *The Executive Educator* (February 1992), pp. 40–41.

[14]Edwin M. Bridges, *Managing the Incompetent Teacher*, 2nd ed. (Eugene, Ore.: ERIC Clearinghouse on Educational Management, 1990).

Dues and free speech

ever, though they can withhold portions of their dues used in this way, they still must pay to support contributions to the national and state organizations with which their local is affiliated, and for other activities unrelated to the bargaining agreement that do not violate their free speech rights.[15] Since the Supreme Court vote was 5 to 4 and the justices differed among themselves on details, it is not entirely clear what activities can be funded through required dues payments.[16]

Pregnancy and Employment

The rights of pregnant teachers have been established by the courts, by federal and state law, and by school district policies. In a landmark decision in 1974, the U.S. Supreme Court decided *Cleveland Board of Education* v. *LeFleur.*[17] Jo Carol LeFleur, a junior high teacher, had challenged her board's policy, which required all pregnant teachers to take unpaid leaves of absence beginning five months before the expected birth. Return to work was not permitted until the child was at least three months old. The Court found these rules rigid and concluded that there were less arbitrary ways of meeting the board's classroom continuity needs. Boards of education may establish leave policies designed to assure continuity of classroom instruction by requiring teachers to notify the districts early in their pregnancies so that school needs may be anticipated; however, such policies may not contain arbitrary leave and return dates. In addition, school districts, like other employers, may go beyond minimum legal protections and provide special benefits for pregnant teachers.[18]

Traditional policies overturned

Protection Against Assault

Victimized personnel

In recent decades, physical assault on teachers and administrators has become an important problem at some schools, particularly secondary schools in big cities. Two legal scholars who examined recent suits brought by victimized school personnel report that courts generally have convicted defendants whose behavior violated either educational statutes prohibiting assault or general state criminal codes. These analysts concluded that "administrators can help protect themselves and their fellow employees by vigorously pressing criminal charges and assisting with civil suits for assault and battery."[19]

Freedom of Expression

A protected freedom

Courts have tended to uphold teachers' rights to express themselves in public or in school. However, in determining whether the expression is "protected"

---

[15]*Lehnert* v. *Ferris Faculty Association,* 89-1217 S. Ct. (1991); "Good-Bye to All That," *National Review,* May 11, 1992, pp. 14–15.

[16]Debra B. Blum, "Both Sides See Gain in Court Decision on Union Dues," *The Chronicle of Higher Education,* June 5, 1991, pp. A11–A14.

[17]*Cleveland Board of Education* v. *LeFleur,* 414 U.S. 632 (1974).

[18]Thomas N. Jones, "Supreme Court Upholds Pregnancy Leave Law," *NOLPE Notes* (January 1987), p. 1; Kern Alexander and M. David Alexander, *American Public School Law,* 3rd ed. (St. Paul, Minn.: West, 1991).

[19]Perry A. Zirkel and Ivan B. Gluckman, "Assaults on School Personnel," *NASSP Bulletin* (March 1991), p. 10.

under the First Amendment, a number of factors are pertinent: effects on the operation of the school and on the teacher's performance, on teacher-superior relationships, and on co-workers; and appropriateness of time, place, and manner of remarks.

Examples of court decisions

Marvin Pickering was a tenured high school teacher whose letter to the editor criticizing the board and superintendent about bond proposals and expenditures was published in a local newspaper. The letter resulted in his termination. In *Pickering* v. *Board of Education,* the U.S. Supreme Court held that publication of the letter did not impede the "proper performance of his daily duties in the classroom or . . . [interfere] with the regular operation of schools generally."[20] For this reason, Pickering's dismissal was found to be improper.

On the other hand, two teachers in Alaska were dismissed for writing a letter that was highly critical of their superintendent and contained many false allegations. Reaction to the letter was immediate and prolonged. As a result the teachers were terminated. The Alaska Supreme Court held that the teachers' effectiveness had been impaired by their remarks and that their ability to work closely with colleagues had been diminished.[21]

Behavior itself not at issue

A comparison of these cases indicates that the behavior itself was not the sole basis for the decision. Rather, what happened as a result had a bearing on whether the behavior was judged to have impeded the "proper performance" of a teacher's work or to have disrupted the "regular operation" of the schools. These cases also illustrate the three-step analysis the courts have developed for assessing teachers' rights to freedom of expression: (1) Did the teacher's expression of opinion involve a public matter of political, social or other concern to the community? (2) If yes, courts still must weigh First Amendment rights against the employer's responsibility to promote a productive and harmonious climate for the delivery of education. Finally, (3) the teacher is entitled to judicial relief only if his or her expression of opinion can be shown to be a motivating factor in dismissal or other punitive action.[22]

Nonpublic staff not necessarily protected

It should be noted that *Pickering* and similar decisions would not be applicable to private- or parochial-school teachers because those schools are not publicly funded. Private- and parochial-school teachers do not necessarily have the civil rights protections guaranteed public-school teachers (tenure, freedom of expression, due process, and the like). Their rights depend primarily on the terms of their individual contracts with the school.[23]

Verbal Abuse of Students. Teachers' rights to freedom of expression do not extend, of course, to verbal abuse of students. Teachers can be suspended or dismissed for engaging in such behavior. A teacher who also served as a basketball and football coach in northern California was accused of using terms such as "Tontos" in dealing with American Indian students and "jungle bunnies" in referring to African American students. Although allowed to continue

---

[20] *Pickering* v. *Board of Education,* 391 U.S. 563 (1968).

[21] *Watts* v. *Seward School Board,* 454 P. 2d 732 (Alaska 1969), cert. denied, 397 U.S. 921 (1970).

[22] Benjamin Sendor, "Is Speaking Out Cause for Dismissal?" *The American School Board Journal* (March 1990), pp. 8, 46.

[23] Michael W. LaMorte, *School Law: Cases and Concepts,* 2nd ed. (Englewood Cliffs, N.J.: Prentice-Hall, 1987).

Overview 8.1 ━━━●

Selected U.S. Supreme Court Decisions
Affecting Teachers' Rights and Responsibilities

Case	Summary of Decision
Pickering v. *Board of Education* (1968)	Teachers may speak their opinions as long as the school's regular operation is not disrupted.
Board of Regents of State Colleges v. *Roth* (1972)	After the probationary period, teachers have a property interest in continued employment.
Cleveland Board of Education v. *LeFleur* (1974)	Boards of education may establish leave policies for pregnant teachers, but these policies may not contain arbitrary leave and return dates.
Hortonville District v. *Hortonville Education Association* (1976)	In a due process hearing a school board may be the impartial body conducting the hearing.
Washington v. *Davis* (1976)	Underrepresentation of a group in the workforce does not, in itself, prove unconstitutional employment discrimination, but the employer in this situation must prove that hiring has not been discriminatory.
Steelworkers v. *Weber* (1979)	Employers (including school districts) may use affirmative action plans to increase the number of minority employees.
Firefighters v. *Stotts* (1984)	In affirmative action programs, government units may not ignore seniority unless the minority candidates who benefit have personally experienced discrimination.
School Board of Nassau County v. *Arline* (1987)	Dismissing a teacher because of a physical impairment or contagious disease is unconstitutional.
Lehnert v. *Ferris Faculty Association* (1991)	Employees who are not union members cannot be required to pay dues used for political purposes unrelated to collective bargaining agreements.

Abusers dismissed

teaching elementary-school science and physical education, he was suspended from coaching for unprofessional conduct as a first step toward possible later dismissal. Other teachers have had their employment terminated for directing obscene curses at students they perceived as troublesome or for persistently using sarcasm and ridicule to pressure or embarrass students. Courts have tended to uphold such dismissals on the grounds that school officials are in an appropriate position to determine whether the facts in a particular situation constitute adequate "cause" for termination. Teachers also can be sued under civil liability or criminal statutes by parents who believe their children have been injured by verbal abuse.[24]

Academic Freedom

Library and classroom materials

Academic freedom refers to the teacher's freedom to choose subject matter and instructional materials relevant to the course without interference from administrators or outsiders. During the 1990 and 1991 school years there were more than two hundred incidents in which parents or other persons tried to remove or restrict use of public-school materials, including allegedly immoral works such as *Little Red Riding Hood, Snow White,* and *Huckleberry Finn.*[25] Several courts have ruled that materials can be eliminated on the basis of vulgarity but not censorship of ideas.[26] Although the U.S. Supreme Court has not provided definitive rulings, it has emphasized that school officials must take account of the First Amendment in exercising their discretion. Teachers should consider the objections of parents who do not want their children to study specific materials, but they also must work with administrators to ensure that legitimate materials are not removed entirely from classrooms and libraries.[27]

Rulings not definitive

Teachers upheld

After some citizens demanded that a seventh-grade teacher in Michigan be tarred and feathered for showing films on human reproduction to students whose parents had signed permission slips, the teacher was suspended with pay, but an appeals court reversed this decision and awarded the teacher $321,000 in damages. The U.S. Supreme Court upheld the reversal but not the damage award.[28] Similarly, other appeals courts have upheld a high-school teacher's right to assign a magazine article containing "a vulgar term for an incestuous son"[29] and another teacher's use of a film in which citizens of a small town randomly killed one person each year.[30]

Restrictions upheld

On the other hand, decisions of school officials in restricting teachers' use of materials and methods sometimes have been upheld. For example, a West Virginia art teacher was suspended for (unwittingly) distributing sexually explicit cartoons (e.g., *Fritz the Cat*),[31] and an Ohio English teacher was prohibited from assigning the books *One Flew Over the Cuckoo's Nest* and *Manchild in the Promised Land* to juvenile students unless their parents provided knowledgeable

---

[24]Jane Gross, "High School Coach Is Suspended Over Slurs," *The New York Times,* September 30, 1991, p. A11; Perry A. Zirkel and Ivan B. Gluckman, "Verbal Abuse of Students," *Principal* (May 1991), pp. 51–52.

[25]*Attacks on the Freedom to Learn* (Washington, D.C.: People for the American Way, 1991); "Beleaguered Reading Books Under Attack Again," *The Executive Educator* (January 1992), pp. 9–10.

[26]For example, see *Bicknell* v. *Vergennes Union School Board of Directors,* 638 F. 2d 438 (2d Cir. 1980).

[27]*Board of Education* v. *Pico,* 102 S. Ct. 2799 (1982); Donna Hulsizer, "Taking on the Book Banners," *Teacher Magazine* (January 1990), pp. 78–79; and "Censors Target School Libraries," *Teacher Magazine* (March 1992), p. 9.

[28]*Memphis Community School District* v. *Stachura,* 106 S. Ct. 2537 (1986).

[29]*Keefe* v. *Geanakos,* 418 F. 2d 359 (1st Cir. 1969).

[30]*Pratt* v. *Independent School District No. 831,* 670 F. 2d 771 (8th Cir. 1982).

[31]*DeVito* v. *Board of Education,* 317 S.E.2d 159 (W. Va. 1984).

Governing considerations

consent.[32] In general, judicial deliberations and decisions regarding such issues include consideration of (1) age and grade level of the students, (2) the relevancy of the questioned material to the curriculum, (3) duration of the material's use, (4) the general acceptance of a disputed teaching method within the profession, (5) the prior existence of board policy governing selection of materials and teaching techniques, and (6) whether materials are required or optional.

Teacher as Exemplar

Chapter 2 quoted a number of rules governing teacher conduct in Wisconsin in 1922. Teachers' lives were regulated because communities believed they should be examples to their students of high moral standards and impeccable character, conservative dress and grooming, and polished manners. Despite the fact that these standards have relaxed over the years, in some places teachers remain vulnerable to dismissal under immorality statutes for such activities as living unmarried with members of the opposite sex or professed homosexuality. Recent teacher dismissals sometimes have resulted from seemingly less-weighty behaviors such as engaging in a water fight in which a student suffered mild skin irritations.[33]

Immorality standards

Although many cities and counties have specifically affirmed the rights of homosexuals in employment and housing, teaching positions are governed by state laws. Only a few states have laws protecting the rights of homosexual teachers. James Gaylord, a high-school teacher in Tacoma, Washington, lost his job because he was adjudged a "known homosexual."[34] The school district demonstrated to the court's satisfaction that knowledge of his lifestyle impaired his teaching effectiveness and that his retention might signal "adult approval of his homosexuality" to students. The U.S. Supreme Court refused to review this case, thereby affirming the lower court decisions dismissing Gaylord.

Homosexual teacher released

In New York, a sixth-grade teacher admitted to putting his arm around and kissing some of the girls in his class, giving them a "pat on the behind," and allowing obscene jokes to be told in his classroom as well as the use of profanity. The state commissioner of education found him unfit to teach, and that decision was upheld by the New York Appellate Court. The court noted the "potentially harmful effect upon the young minds entrusted" to his care. Similarly, the Third Circuit Court of Appeals upheld the dismissal of a Pennsylvania teacher whom police had charged with displaying pornography and corrupting a minor.[35]

Obscenity potentially harmful

Beginning in the late 1960s, courts were asked to decide a number of cases where teachers' dress and grooming conflicted with school district policies or traditions. A California court ruled that Paul Finot's wearing of a beard was symbolic expression protected by the First Amendment as well as a liberty right

Dress and grooming cases

---

[32]*Grosser* v. *Woollett*, 341 N.E. 2d 356 (Ohio Cm. Pl. 1974).

[33]*Everett Area Sch. Dist.* v. *Ault*, 548 A. 2d 1341 (Pa. Cmwlth. 1988); Perry A. Zirkel, "Weeding Out Bad Teachers," *Phi Delta Kappan* (January 1992), pp. 418–421.

[34]*Gaylord* v. *Tacoma School District No. 18*, 88 Wash. 2d 286, 559 P. 2d 1340, cert. denied, 434 U.S. 879 (1977).

[35]*Katz* v. *Ambach*, New York Appellate Division, *Education Law Reporter*, April 5, 1984; *Peiffer* v. *Lebanon School District*, 848 F. 2d 44 (3rd Cir. 1988).

protected under the Fourteenth Amendment.[36] On the other hand, when Max Miller's contract was not renewed because of his beard and long sideburns, the circuit court upheld the dismissal. The judges said that if a school board decided a "teacher's style of dress or plumage" adversely affected students, "the interest of the teacher is subordinate to the public interest."[37] Similarly, an appeals court

Miniskirts and neckties

upheld the dismissal of a high-school French teacher who wore miniskirts to school.[38] When an English teacher was reprimanded for not wearing a necktie, the court denied his claim that his rights of free speech and privacy had been infringed. "As public servants in a special position of trust," the judges stated, "teachers may properly be subjected to many restrictions in their professional lives which would be invalid if generally applied."[39]

Religious garments

Recently the issue of attire took on another dimension when a Philadelphia teacher was fired for insisting that her Muslim religious beliefs required her to wear a head scarf and long, loose dresses. Her behavior conflicted with a century-old Pennsylvania law prohibiting religious attire in the classroom. Her suit charging violation of her First Amendment rights was rejected by a federal appeals court. A similar challenge by a Sikh teacher in Oregon was denied by that state's Supreme Court. However, the U.S. Supreme Court has never reviewed such a case.[40]

Role models expected

In summary, then, restraints on teachers' behavior and attire are not as stringent as in earlier times, but teachers are still expected to behave in exemplary ways and serve as role models for their students. When the issue is raised in court, a major concern is whether the behavior in question seriously impairs the teacher's classroom effectiveness.

Tort Liability and Negligence

Torts are civil wrongs. Under tort law, individuals who have suffered because of the improper conduct of others may sue for damages. For example,

Student injuries

educators may be found guilty of negligence in instances where students are injured during classes, on the playground, or elsewhere, where injury resulted from failure to take appropriate preventive action. This does not mean that a case will be filed every time a child is accidentally injured. It does mean that when injury results from negligent or intentional action, legal remedies could be pursued where state law permits. Tort law has usually been based on "reasonableness."

A generation ago, nearly every school district was immune from tort liability. This immunity had its origins in English common law, where the king, as sovereign, could not be sued. Since 1960, more than half the states have eliminated or modified this view of governmental immunity. In states where suits are permitted, the parties sued may include the school district as well as specific school administrators and teachers. For example, school districts can be held

Decline of immunity

---

[36]*Finot* v. *Pasadena City Board of Education,* 58 Cal. Rptr. 520 (1976).

[37]*Miller* v. *School District No. 167 of Cook County, Illinois,* 495 F. 2d 65 (7th Cir. 1974).

[38]*Tardif* v. *Quinn,* 545 F. 2d 761 (1st Cir. 1976).

[39]*East Hartford Education Association* v. *Board of Education,* 562 F. 2d 838 (1977).

[40]R. Gustar Niebuhr, "Teachers Wearing Religious Attire Face School Ban," *The Wall Street Journal,* February 8, 1991, p. B6.

liable for the negligent or malicious action (such as sexual abuse or harassment) of their employees if school officials have provided little or no supervision or ignored persistent complaints.[41]

Negligence is decided by courts after examining the evidence. A finding of negligence in educational settings usually involves demonstration of each of the following:

Standards for negligence

1. Existence of a legal "standard of care" requiring educators to protect students from harm.

2. Demonstrated failure by a statutorily responsible person to discharge that duty.

3. Proof that there is a substantial relationship between the educator's conduct and the injury that occurred (in other words, without the educator's conduct the injury probably would not have happened); this is known as **proximate cause.**

4. Tangible loss or damage from the injury.

Proximate cause must be determined on a case-by-case basis. Suppose, for example, that a group of middle-school students are given dangerous chemicals to handle while completing a required class experiment, but no instruction is provided in how to properly work with those chemicals. Several students are injured. The teacher's failure to instruct students in the safe handling of these chemicals could be called the "proximate cause" of their injuries.

Proximate cause

Reasonable and prudent

Teachers are required by law to protect their students from injury or harm. In nearly all states, the traditional standard of care is what a reasonable and prudent person would do under similar circumstances. In one case, a kindergarten teacher was charged with negligence when a child fell from a playground structure while the teacher was attending to other children. The court ruled that the teacher was not required to have all children in sight at all times. Her presence in the immediate area was sufficient to establish that the teacher was fulfilling her duty. The New York State Supreme Court reached a similar conclusion in overturning a jury award to an injured high-school athlete, on grounds that school officials had exercised "reasonable care" in operating their school's football program.[42]

Foreseeability

An important principle is whether the injury could have been foreseen and, thus, prevented. An overweight student expressed concern to her physical education teacher about a class requirement to perform a back somersault. The teacher insisted the somersault be done; the student's neck snapped in the attempt. The court said the teacher showed utter indifference for the student's safety and the jury awarded $77,000 in damages. Similarly, school personnel were found negligent when a student died in a blizzard during a school-sponsored expedition to climb Mount Hood. Plaintiffs' lawyers pointed out that prob-

---

[41]David A. Splitt, "School Law," *The Executive Educator* (June 1990), p. 10; David A. Splitt, "Drawing a Line on Liability," *The Executive Educator* (March 1992), pp. 13, 42.

[42]*Clark* v. *Furch,* 567 S.W. 2d 457 (Mo. App. 1978); "School Sports-Injury Award Upset," *The New York Times,* June 9, 1989, p. 18; and Louis Fischer and Gail P. Sorenson, *School Law* (White Plains, N.Y.: Longman, 1991).

lems should have been foreseen in placing a group of schoolchildren in a dangerous situation.[43]

Parental consent forms

School districts require parents to sign consent forms when students are involved in activities such as field trips or athletic competition. The form as often written has two purposes: to inform parents of their children's whereabouts and to release school personnel from liability in case of injury. However, parents may not waive a child's right to sue for damages should an injury result from negligent supervision, so these forms actually serve the first purpose only. Obtaining a parental waiver does not release teachers from their legal obligations to protect the safety and welfare of students in their care.

Strict liability

Recent years have brought what some observers describe as an "explosion" in litigation related to liability and negligence. In addition, rather than accepting the exercise of reasonable precautions as a defense against negligence, recent judicial decisions have frequently emphasized "strict liability."[44] In this situation, teachers cannot be too careful, for there are numerous places in the school setting where negligence might occur. Physical education instructors, sponsors of extracurricular activities, and shop and laboratory teachers must take special care. Prudent safeguards include a clear set of written rules, verbal warnings to students, regular inspection of equipment, adherence to state laws and district policies regarding hazardous activities, thoughtful planning, and diligent supervision.

Liability insurance

As educators' immunity has waned and the number of lawsuits has increased, teacher and school administrator organizations have begun to offer liability insurance to their members. These organizations also may provide legal assistance to members who are sued.

Reporting Child Abuse

During recent years, child abuse has become a national issue. Increased media attention has prompted state legislatures to review and stiffen existing abuse laws.[45] Because a high percentage of abuse is directed at school-age children, schools thus play an important role in protecting them. In most states, educators

Requirements to report

are required by law to report suspected cases of child abuse to authorities or designated social services agencies. As a result, increasing numbers of school districts have written policies describing how teachers should proceed when they suspect abuse.

In some communities where school personnel have been trained to identify the signs of child abuse, teachers have become the single best source for uncovering abuse cases. Because teachers are so vital in detecting and reporting sus-

Legal penalties

pected abuse, legal penalties exist for failure to discharge this responsibility.

---

[43]*Landers* v. *School District No. 203, O'Fallon,* 383 N.E. 2d 645 (Ill. App. Ct. 1978); Associated Press, "Jury Finds School Negligent in Death of Student Climber," *The New York Times,* April 7, 1990, p. 9.

[44]Michele Galen, "How the Courtroom Became a Casino," *Business Week,* May 31, 1991, p. 121; Peter Kahn, "The Flawed Vision," *The American Prospect* (Summer 1991), pp. 43–54.

[45]Robert Rothman, "Survey Reveals Wide Latitude in Reporting Abuse," *Education Week,* February 28, 1990, pp. 1, 28; Lisa Feder-Feitel, "Teachers Against Child Abuse," *Creative Classroom* (January/February 1992), pp. 55–62.

Under West Virginia law, for example, failure to report suspected cases of child abuse is a misdemeanor punishable by ten days in jail or a $100 fine. In Georgia, teachers must report their suspicions if there is "reasonable cause to believe" that a pupil is being abused. Failure to report is a misdemeanor typically punished with fines up to $5,000 and a year in prison.[46]

Educational Malpractice

Malpractice is a concept we tend to associate with medicine or law, not education. Within the last two decades, however, suits have been filed against school boards alleging negligence as the root cause for an individual student's failure to achieve in school. Thus far, each case has been dismissed, but these attempts raise interesting issues that educators cannot ignore simply because plaintiffs have been unsuccessful.[47]

Alleged educational negligence

One student filed suit against the San Francisco Unified School District charging negligence because he was graduated from high school despite reading achievement at only the fifth-grade level. In tort law the burden of proof is on the plaintiff. The court, in dismissing this action, noted the difficulty of establishing a link between Peter W.'s low reading achievement and allegedly negligent actions of the school district. Similarly, a federal judge rejected the suit of a parent who sued school officials on the grounds that her daughter's reading problems were caused by their failure to provide appropriate, individualized help. The judge concluded that the courts do not have the authority to "oversee" implementation of educational policy when parents and school officials disagree about students' learning problems.[48]

Of the cases filed, *Hoffman* v. *Board of Education of City of New York*[49] appeared to have the best chance to succeed. When Hoffman was five years old, a school psychologist administered the Stanford-Binet Intelligence Test. A portion of this test requires verbal responses, but Hoffman had a severe speech defect. He scored well below the national average of 100 and was placed in a class for mentally retarded students. Included in the psychologist's report was the recommendation that he be re-evaluated within two years. Hoffman spent the next eleven years in special classes and graduated from high school without ever being retested.

Failure to retest student

When Hoffman turned eighteen, Social Security Administration regulations required an IQ test score to demonstrate his need for continued payments. He scored over 100 and became ineligible for either financial assistance or training programs for the retarded. He sued the school board, charging negligence. The

[46]Alex Molnar and Christine Gliszczinski, "Child Abuse: A Curriculum Issue in Teacher Education," *Journal of Teacher Education* (September–October 1983), pp. 39–41; Ann Hagedorn, "Prosecution of Child-Molestation Cases Is More Cautious in Wake of Failed Cases," *The Wall Street Journal,* April 15, 1991, pp. B1, B10.

[47]Perry A. Zirkel and Ivan B. Gluckman, "Educational Malpractice," *Principal* (September 1991), pp. 61–62.

[48]*Peter W.* v. *San Francisco Unified School District,* 131 Cal. Rptr. 854 (1976); *Smith* v. *Philadelphia School District,* 679 F. Supp. 479 E.D. Pa. (1988). See Perry A. Zirkel and Ivan B. Gluckman, "A Legal Brief," *NASSP Bulletin* (October 1991), pp. 110–114.

[49]*Hoffman* v. *Board of Education of City of New York,* 424 N.Y.S. 2d 376 (1979). See Ruth Axman Childs, *Legal Issues in Testing* (Washington, D.C.: American Institutes for Research, 1990).

jury awarded $750,000; the appellate court reduced the award to $500,000, and New York's highest court reversed the lower courts' decisions and dimissed the case. In a 4–3 decision the majority said, "Courts of this state may not substitute their judgment, or the judgment of the jury, for the professional judgment of educators and government officials actually engaged in the complex and often delicate process of educating the many thousands of children in our schools."

Standards not clear

Four points emerge from decisions in these malpractice cases. First, no standard of care could be determined; second, in the opinion of the judges, no clear-cut reasons for failure to learn could be definitively established; third, the monetary value of the harm was indeterminable; and fourth, judges feared that a successful suit would occasion a flood of similar suits, which would severely strain the resources of both the public schools and the court systems.

Copyright Laws

A copyright gives authors and artists control over the reproduction and distribution of works they create; consequently, permission for reproduction usually must be obtained from the owner. The widespread use of copying machines has bred serious and regular violations of copyright laws. Congress amended the original 1909 copyright laws in 1976 to include, among other concerns, photocopying and the educational use of copyrighted materials. In addition, a committee of librarians, publishers, authors, and educators developed "fair use" guidelines. **Fair use** is a legal principle that allows use of copyrighted materials without permission from the author under specific, limited conditions. A summary of restrictions on copying for classroom use or for other educational purposes follows:[50]

Fair use guidelines

Copying of prose is limited to excerpts of no more than 1,000 words.

A poem may be copied if it is less than 250 words, and an excerpt of no more than 250 words may be copied from a longer poem.

Distribution of copies from the same author more than once a semester or copying from the same work or anthology more than three times during the semester is prohibited.

Teachers may make one copy per student for class distribution; if charges are made, they may not exceed actual copying costs.

It is illegal to create by photocopying anthologies or other compilations as substitutes for purchasing the same or similar materials.

Consumable materials

Consumable materials, such as workbooks, may not be copied.

Under the fair use doctrine, single copies of printed materials may be made for personal study, lesson planning, research, criticism, comment, and news reporting.

Most magazine and newspaper articles may be copied freely. However,

---

[50]Thomas J. Flygare, "Photocopying and Videotaping for Educational Purposes: The Doctrine of Fair Use," *Phi Delta Kappan* (April 1984), pp. 568–569; Association of American Publishers, "How to Request Copyright Permissions," *The Chronicle of Higher Education* (September 4, 1991), p. R23.

items in weekly newspapers and magazines designed for classroom use by students may not be copied without permission.

Individual teachers must decide, independently, to copy material; they may not be directed to do so by higher authorities.

There are three categories of material for which copies may be freely made: writings published before 1978 that have never been copyrighted, published works for which copyrights are more than seventy-five years old, and U.S. government publications.

Plays and musical productions

Plays and musical productions usually are copyrighted by their authors. Therefore, school presentation of such works requires permission from the author or the author's agent. Payment of a royalty is often necessary to secure permission. Whether or not admission is charged can affect the amount of the royalty payments.

Videotapes

Videotapes also fall within the fair use guidelines of the copyright laws. These guidelines specify that educational institutions may not keep the tapes they make of copyrighted television programs for more than forty-five days without a license. During the first ten days, an individual teacher may use the tape once, and may show it once again after that period when "instructional reinforcement is necessary." After forty-five days the tape must be erased. Videotaping may occur only when a faculty member requests it in advance; thus, it may not be done on a regular basis in anticipation of faculty requests.

Anthologies

Copyright disputes have been particularly prominent in connection with the practice of preparing, duplicating, and distributing anthologies of material that replace or supplement course textbooks, without obtaining copyright owners' permission and/or paying appropriate royalties. A major legal challenge to this practice occurred when a group of publishers sued a chain of stores (Kinko's) which frequently duplicate such anthologies. In 1991 a U.S. District Court judge determined that the company's practice violated the fair use standards specified above. The company — as well as other "anthologizers" — will have to obtain permission to use any copyrighted material included in a duplicated collection.[51]

Computer Ethics

Hackers

Computer technology has spawned many new abuses. For instance, "hackers" have cracked codes permitting entry into school record-keeping systems, and some have used school-owned equipment to tamper with the computerized files of banks and other businesses. In an attempt to curb abuses, many states now have laws covering computer crime. Computing systems in public schools and universities are particularly vulnerable to unauthorized entry because many of these systems emphasize accessibility to encourage learning. Some observers say that schools should teach computer ethics as well as computer literacy.

Schools vulnerable

Computer programs copyrighted

Computer software is subject to the same fair use restrictions as other copyrighted materials. For example, teachers may not copy protected computer programs and distribute them for use on school computers. The University of Ore-

---

[51]Debra E. Blum, "Copyright Ruling on Anthologies May Spur Vigilance," *The Chronicle of Higher Education,* April 10, 1991, p. A14; "In Box," *The Chronicle of Higher Education,* January 8, 1992, p. A15.

gon paid $130,000 to settle one suit charging that programs had been illegally copied for the university's computers.[52]

STUDENTS' RIGHTS AND RESPONSIBILITIES

Decline of in loco parentis

During the 1960s, students increasingly began to challenge the authority of school officials to control what they perceived as constitutionally protected behavior. Before these challenges, students' rights were considered to be limited by their status as minors and by the concept of *in loco parentis,* according to which school authorities assumed the powers of the child's parents during the hours the child was under the school's supervision. Use of this concept has declined, however, and the courts have become more active in identifying and upholding students' constitutional rights. Concurrently, there has been progress toward recognition of student responsibilities — that is, toward the understanding that the educational rights of students are tied in with responsibilities on the part of both students and educators to ensure effective operation of the school.[53]

The following sections summarize some of the most important court decisions involving student rights and responsibilities. These apply primarily to public schools. As with teachers, students in nonpublic schools may not enjoy all the constitutional guarantees discussed in this chapter. Unless a substantial relationship between the school and the government can be demonstrated, private school activity is not considered action by the state; therefore it does not invoke state constitutional obligations. However, the movement toward school choice plans that provide public funds for students attending nonpublic schools may blur this distinction.[54]

Freedom of Expression

Tinker case

John Tinker, fifteen, his sister Mary Beth, thirteen, and friend Dennis Eckhardt, sixteen, were part of a small group planning to wear black armbands to school as a silent, symbolic protest against the war in Vietnam. Hearing of this plan and fearing problems, administrators responded by adopting a policy prohibiting the wearing of armbands; the penalty was suspension until the armbands were removed. The Tinkers and Eckhardt wore armbands as planned, refused to remove them, and were suspended. Their parents filed suit. In finding for the plaintiffs the U.S. Supreme Court outlined the scope of student rights, and this case, *Tinker* v. *Des Moines Independent Community School District,* became the standard for examining students' freedom of speech guarantees. To justify prohibition of a particular expression of opinion, the Court ruled, school officials must be able to show that their actions were caused by "something more than

---

[52]David L. Wilson, "U. of Oregon Pays $130,000 to Settle Software-Copying Suit," *The Chronicle of Higher Education,* September 4, 1991, pp. A27–A30.

[53]David P. Ericson and Frederick S. Ellett, Jr., "Taking Student Responsibility Seriously," *Educational Researcher* (December 1990), pp. 3–10.

[54]Richard D. Strahan and L. Charles Turner, *The Courts and the Schools* (New York: Longman, 1988); William Celis 3d, "Nonpublic Schools Target in Oregon," *The New York Times,* November 4, 1990, p. 17.

a mere desire to avoid the discomfort and unpleasantness that always accompany an unpopular viewpoint." Student conduct that "materially disrupts classwork or involves substantial disorder or invasion of the rights of others" could be prohibited. In the absence of such good reasons for restraint, the students' constitutional guarantees of free speech would apply.[55]

Nondisruptive expression protected

Limits to expression

There are, however, limits to free expression in public schools. In *Bethel School District No. 403* v. *Fraser,*[56] the U.S. Supreme Court confirmed that students may be punished for offensive or disruptive speech. At a student assembly, Matthew Fraser, seventeen, nominated a friend for a student council office. His speech was laden with sexual innuendo. Students in the audience reacted with hooting, hollering, and some suggestive gestures. Fraser was suspended for two days, and his name was removed from a list of possible graduation speakers. He sued, charging his First Amendment right of free speech had been violated. Chief Justice Warren Burger, writing for the majority, said, "The schools, as instruments of the State, may determine that the essential lessons of civil, mature conduct cannot be conveyed in a school that tolerates lewd, indecent, or offensive speech or conduct such as that indulged in by this confused boy."

Student publications

Regulation of the content and distribution of student publications has generated considerable conflict between school officials and students. District policies requiring administrative review and approval prior to publication or distribution are a major area of difficulty. In these "prior restraint" cases the burden of proof is on the district to show that its actions have been fairly imposed and that regulation is necessary for maintaining order.

Hazelwood case

For example, school policy required the principal to review each proposed issue of *The Spectrum,* the school newspaper written by journalism students at Hazelwood East High School in St. Louis County, Missouri. The principal objected to two articles scheduled to appear in one issue. The first article concerned the personal stories of three teenage students who had become pregnant, the reactions of their parents, their future plans, and details about the sex life of each girl. The second story discussed the effect of divorce on children and quoted from interviews with students. Neither article used real student names, although the problems of a few of the students were known to some of their peers. As a result of the principal's objections the articles were deleted. The principal claimed the articles were deleted not because of the subject matter but because he did not consider them well written and there was not enough time to rewrite them before the publication deadline.

Three student journalists sued, contending their freedom of speech had been violated. This case, *Hazelwood School District* v. *Kuhlmeier,* reached the U.S. Supreme Court, which upheld the principal's action. The justices found that *The Spectrum* was not a public forum but rather a supervised learning experience for journalism students.[57] As long as educators' actions were related to "legitimate pedagogical concerns," they could regulate the newspaper's contents in any reasonable manner. The ruling further stated that a school could disassociate itself not only from speech that directly interfered with school activities, but also from

Legitimate regulation

---

[55]*Tinker* v. *Des Moines Independent Community School District,* 393 U.S. 503 (1969).
[56]*Bethel School District No. 403* v. *Fraser,* 106 S. Ct. 3159 (1986).
[57]Jan C. Robbins, *Public Schools as Public Forums* (Bloomington, Ind.: Phi Delta Kappa, 1990).

Students enjoy constitutional guarantees of freedom of speech, but conduct that "materially disrupts classwork or involves substantial disorder or invasion of the rights of others" can be prohibited by school officials. (© Kenneth Martin/Amstock)

speech that was "ungrammatical, poorly written, inadequately researched, biased, prejudiced, vulgar or profane, or unsuitable for immature audiences." This 1988 decision was a clear restriction on student rights as previously understood.[58]

Written rules help withstand scrutiny

The controversies concerning publications written or distributed by students have prompted many school boards to develop written regulations that can withstand judicial scrutiny. Generally, these rules specify a time, place, and manner of distribution; a method of advertising the rules to students; a prompt review process; and speedy appeal procedures. Students may not distribute literature that is obscene by legal definition, that is libelous, or that is likely to cause the substantial disruption specified in *Tinker*. In recent years growing student activism has led to increased attention to these issues.[59]

Dress Codes and Regulations. Many courts have had to determine whether dress codes and regulations constitute an unconstitutional restriction on students' rights to free expression. In some instances, as in a Louisiana case dealing with requirements that football team members shave their moustaches, judges have ruled that the Constitution allows school boards to impose dress and grooming codes to advance their educational goals. Similarly, a U.S. district court upheld a ban on boys' earrings as part of a policy prohibiting display of

---

[58]*Hazelwood School District* v. *Kuhlmeier*, 86-836 S. Ct. (1988). See Winifred Conkling, "The Big Chill," *Teacher Magazine* (November/December 1991), pp. 47–53.
[59]Mark Walsh, "Student Activism Forces Schools to Revisit Free-Speech Policies," *Education Week*, February 6, 1991, pp. 1, 12.

Mixed decisions

gang emblems. In other cases, however, judges have ruled that prohibitions against long hair were arbitrary and unreasonable, and that girls' wearing of pantsuits or slacks could not be prohibited. Much depends on the arguments and evidence regarding the educational purposes served by such restrictions and the extent to which they can be viewed as reasonably intended to accomplish a valid constitutional goal. The U.S. Supreme Court has not provided definitive guidance on this issue.[60]

Suspension and Expulsion

Nine students received ten-day suspensions from their Columbus, Ohio, secondary schools for various alleged acts of misconduct. The suspensions were imposed without hearings but in accordance with state law. The school board had no written procedure covering suspensions. The students filed suit, claiming deprivation of their constitutional rights.[61] In defense, school officials argued that since there is no constitutional right to education at public expense, the due process clause of the Fourteenth Amendment did not apply.

When this case, *Goss* v. *Lopez*, reached the Supreme Court in 1975, a majority of the Court disagreed with the school officials, reasoning that students had a legal right to public education. In other words, students had a property interest in their education that could not be "taken away for misconduct without adherence to the minimum procedures" required by the due process clause. Further, the justices said that "students facing suspension [up to ten days] . . . must be given some kind of notice and afforded some kind of hearing. . . . The student first [must] be told what he is accused of doing and what the basis of the accusation is." The student then must be "given an opportunity to explain his version of the facts." Also, "as a general rule notice and hearing should precede removal of the student from school." Finally, the Court commented that longer suspensions or expulsions might require more elaborate due process procedures.

Minimum due process procedures

High schoolers expelled

Tenth graders Peggy Strickland and Virginia Crain spiked the punch at a school-related party. For this they were suspended and then expelled from school for the balance of the semester. The school board took this action without affording the girls any of the due process requirements to which they were entitled. The families filed suit. School board members indicated they were not aware of the specific requirements in expulsion cases. The justices ruled in *Wood* v. *Strickland* that ignorance of the law was no excuse and that school board members could be liable for monetary damages if they knew or should have known that actions they took would deprive a student of constitutional rights.[62]

Another Supreme Court ruling has limited school officials' authority to suspend students with handicaps who are disruptive or violent. In the case of *Honig* v. *Doe*, the Court ruled that students with handicaps must be retained in their current placement pending the completion of official hearings as specified in the Education for All Handicapped Children Act (Public Law 94-142).[63]

[60]David A. Splitt, "School Law," *The Executive Educator* (February 1991), p. 13.
[61]*Goss* v. *Lopez*, 419 U.S. 565 (1975).
[62]*Wood* v. *Strickland*, 420 U.S. 308 (1975).
[63]Mitchell L. Yell, "Honig v. Doe," *Exceptional Children* (September 1989), pp. 60–69; Laura F. Rothstein, "Colleges Must Review Policies on Students, Professors, and Staff Members With Disabilities," *The Chronicle of Higher Education*, September 4, 1991, pp. B3, B10.

Current requirements and procedures

In response to recent court decisions, numerous school districts have developed written policies governing suspensions and expulsions. Such policies usually distinguish between short- and long-term suspensions.[64] Short-term suspension rights typically include oral or written notice describing the misconduct, the evidence on which the accusation is based, a statement of the planned punishment, and an opportunity for the student to explain his or her version or refute the stated facts before an impartial person. Expulsions require full procedural due process similar to those necessary for teacher terminations.[65]

Search and Seizure

Lawfully issued search warrants commonly are required to conduct searches. But because of rising drug use in schools and accompanying acts of violence, school officials at some locations (particularly big-city high schools) have installed metal detectors or x-ray machines to search for weapons. They have banned beepers (frequently used in drug sales), required students to breathe into alcohol-analysis machines, searched students' book bags and systematically examined their lockers, and taken other steps to prevent school-related crime.[66] When such practices have been challenged in court, the issue usually has centered on whether searches by school authorities were conducted *Fourth Amendment rights* in violation of the Fourth Amendment, which states: "The right of the people to be secure in their persons, houses, papers, and effects, against unreasonable searches and seizures, shall not be violated, and no warrants shall issue, but upon probable cause, supported by oath or affirmation, and particularly describing the place to be searched, and the person or things to be seized."

Searches usually are conducted because administrators have reason to suspect that illegal or dangerous items are on the premises. For legal purposes, suspicion exists in differing degrees. Where searches have been upheld, courts *Reasonable cause* have said "reasonable" cause was sufficient for school officials to act. By way of contrast, police are held to the higher standard of "probable" cause — some reason for believing it is more probable than not that evidence of illegal activity will be found.

A teacher discovered two girls in a school restroom smoking cigarettes. This was a violation of school rules, and the students were taken to the vice principal's office and questioned. One of the girls admitted smoking, but T.L.O., age fourteen, denied all charges. The vice principal opened T.L.O.'s purse and found *Purse emptied* a pack of cigarettes. While reaching for the cigarettes he noticed some rolling papers and decided to empty the purse. The search revealed marijuana, a pipe, some empty plastic bags, a large number of dollar bills, and a list entitled, "People who owe me money." T.L.O.'s mother was called; the evidence was turned over to the police. T.L.O. confessed to the police that she had been selling marijuana at school.

---

[64]Lisa Jennings, "Los Angeles Task Force Urges Stiff Expulsion Policy," *Education Week,* April 4, 1990, pp. 8–9.

[65]Perry A. Zirkel and Ivan B. Gluckman, "Due Process for Student Suspensions," *NASSP Bulletin* (March 1990), pp. 95–98.

[66]Michael Marriott, "Drug Detection Methods Raise Pupil Rights Issues," *The New York Times,* January 10, 1990, p. 23.

Criteria for searching

After she was sentenced to one year's probation by the juvenile court, T.L.O. appealed, claiming the vice principal's search of her purse was illegal under the Fourth Amendment.[67] In finding for school authorities in *New Jersey* v. *T.L.O.,* the U.S. Supreme Court set up a two-pronged standard to be met for constitutionally sanctioned searches: (1) whether the search is justified at its inception, and (2) whether the search, when actually conducted, is "reasonably related in scope to the circumstances which justified the interference in the first place." Using these criteria, the Court found the search of T.L.O.'s purse justified because of the teacher's report of smoking in the restroom. This information gave the vice principal reason to believe that her purse contained cigarettes. Since T.L.O. denied smoking, a search of her purse was needed to determine her veracity. When the vice principal saw the cigarettes and came across the rolling papers, he had reasonable suspicion to search her purse more thoroughly.

Use of dogs in searching

For two and one-half hours junior and senior high-school students in Highland, Indiana, waited in their seats while six officials using trained dogs searched the 2,780 students for drugs. A school official, police officer, dog handler, and German shepherd entered the classroom where Diane Doe, thirteen, was a student. The dog went up and down the aisles sniffing students. The dog reached Diane, sniffed her body, and repeatedly pushed its nose on and between her legs. The officer understood this behavior to be an "alert" signaling the presence of drugs. Diane emptied her pockets as requested, but no drugs were found. Still the dog kept sniffing her. Finally, Diane was taken to the nurse's office and strip-searched. No drugs were found. Diane had played with her own dog before school. Her dog was in heat, and this smell remaining on her body had alerted the police dog.

Diane Doe vindicated

The Does filed suit. Both the district court and the appeals court concluded that the only thing done improperly that day was the strip-search of Diane. The court of appeals said, "It does not require a constitutional scholar to conclude that a nude search of a thirteen-year-old child is an invasion of constitutional rights of some magnitude. More than that: It is a violation of any known principle of human decency."[68] Diane was awarded $7,500 damages. But the sniffing of student lockers and cars was not considered a search because it occurred when the lockers and cars were unattended and in public view.

In sum, when conducting warrantless searches the following guidelines seem appropriate:[69]

Standards for searches

1. Searches must be particularized. There should be reasonable suspicion that *each student* being searched possesses specific contraband or evidence of a particular crime.

2. Lockers are considered school property and may be searched if reasonable cause exists. Dogs may be used to sniff lockers and cars.

---

[67]*New Jersey* v. *T.L.O.,* 105 S. Ct. 733 (1985). Similar reasoning and conclusions are reported in *Wynn* v. *Board of Education,* 508 So. 2d 1170 (Ala. 1987), and *People in Interest of P.E.A.,* 754 P.2d 382 (Colo. 1988). See Perry A. Zirkel and Ivan B. Gluckman, "Search of Student Automobiles," *NASSP Bulletin* (November 1991), pp. 116–120.

[68]*Doe* v. *Renfrou,* 635 F. 2d 582 (7th Cir. 1980), cert. denied, 101 U.S. 3015 (1981).

[69]"Don't Search That Locker Without Good Reason," *The Executive Educator* (September 1991), pp. 16–17.

3. Generalized canine sniffing of students is permitted only where the dogs do not touch them.

4. Strip-searches are unconstitutional and should never be conducted.

Classroom Discipline and Corporal Punishment

"Time out" arrangements

A sixth grader was placed in a "time out" area of the classroom whenever his behavior became disruptive to the educational process. The student had a history of behavioral problems, and the teacher had tried other methods of discipline without success. While in "time out" the boy was allowed to use the restroom, eat in the cafeteria, and attend other classes. His parents sued, charging that the teacher's actions (1) deprived their son of his property interest in receiving a public education; (2) meted out punishment disproportionate to his offense in violation of his due process rights; and (3) inflicted emotional distress.[70]

Broad authority to enforce standards of conduct

The district court said that school officials possess broad authority to prescribe and enforce standards of conduct in the schools, but this authority is limited by the Fourteenth Amendment under which deprivation of a property interest without due process is prohibited. In this case the student remained in school and thus was not deprived of a public education. "Time out" was declared to be a minimal interference with the student's property rights. The court noted that the purpose of "time out" is to modify the behavior of disruptive students and to preserve the right to an education for other students in the classroom. All of the student's charges were dismissed.

A particularly controversial method of classroom discipline is corporal punishment, which has a long history in American education dating back to the colonial period. It is unacceptable to many educational theorists and practitioners, although it enjoys considerable support within some segments of the community and is administered more frequently than educators like to admit. Recent surveys indicate that more than one million children are spanked or paddled each school year, and more than 10,000 sustain injuries that require medical attention.[71]

Prohibitions on corporal punishment

A number of state legislatures have prohibited all corporal punishment in public schools. Where state law is silent on corporal punishment, local boards have wide latitude in implementing disciplinary policies, including banning physical punishment. However, where a state statute explicitly permits corporal punishment, local boards may regulate but not prohibit its use. Numerous local school boards have elected to develop detailed policies restricting the use of corporal punishment. Violations of policy can lead to dismissal, and legal charges are possible for excessive force, punishment based on personal malice toward the student, or unreasonable use of punishment.[72]

Restrictions

---

[70]*Dickens* v. *Johnson County Board of Education*, 661 F. Supp. 155 (E.D. Tenn. 1987).

[71]"Spare the Rod and Spoil the Child?" *Wellness Letter* (March 1991), p. 7; Daniel Gursky, "Spare the Child?" *Teacher Magazine* (February 1992), pp. 17–19.

[72]*Deskbook Encyclopedia of American School Law 1990* (Rosemount, Minn.: Data Research, 1990); Irwin A. Hyman, *Reading, Writing, and the Hickory Stick* (Lexington, Mass.: Lexington Books, 1990); and William Celis 3d, "Michigan Eases Ban on Punishment," *The New York Times*, March 11, 1992, p. A16.

Getting to the Source

Corporal Punishment / Ingraham v. Wright

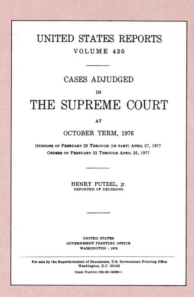

UNITED STATES REPORTS

VOLUME 430

———

CASES ADJUDGED

IN

THE SUPREME COURT

AT

OCTOBER TERM, 1976

Opinions of February 23 Through (in part) April 27, 1977
Orders of February 23 Through April 25, 1977

———

HENRY PUTZEL, Jr.
REPORTER OF DECISIONS

———

UNITED STATES
GOVERNMENT PRINTING OFFICE
WASHINGTON : 1979

For sale by the Superintendent of Documents, U.S. Government Printing Office
Washington, D.C. 20402
Stock Number 028-001-00099-1

In a Florida junior high school James Ingraham was paddled for not responding to a teacher's instructions. His parents sued school officials on the grounds that paddling violated the Eighth Amendment's constitutional prohibition of "cruel and unusual punishments." In the opinion excerpted below, the U.S. Supreme Court ruled that corporal punishment in

schools is not automatically unconstitutional because the Eighth Amendment was constructed to protect the rights of incarcerated prisoners, not school-age children who can be protected by other means. The Ingraham decision means that in states that allow corporal punishment, it is not unconstitutional for teachers to use physical punishment "reasonably necessary" to discipline a student; complaining students or parents have the burden to demonstrate that the teacher's actions went beyond reasonable necessity.

Petitioners acknowledge that the original design of the Cruel and Unusual Punishments Clause was to limit criminal punishments, but urge nonetheless that the prohibition should be extended to ban the paddling of school children. Observing that the Framers of the Eighth Amendment could not have envisioned our present system of public and compulsory education, with its opportunities for noncriminal punishments, petitioners contend that extension of the prohibition against cruel punishments is necessary lest we afford greater protection to criminals than to schoolchildren. It would be anomalous, they say, if schoolchildren could be beaten without constitutional redress, while hardened criminals suffering the same beatings at the hands of their jailors might have a valid claim under the Eighth Amendment. . . .

Florida law allows corporal punishment. In 1977 the U.S. Supreme Court, in *Ingraham* v. *Wright,* ruled on the constitutionality of this law from two federal perspectives: (1) whether use of corporal punishment was a violation of the Eighth Amendment barring cruel and unusual punishment, and (2) whether prior notice and some form of due process were required before administering punishment. James Ingraham and Roosevelt Andrews were junior high school students in Dade County, Florida.[73] Because Ingraham had been slow to respond to the teacher's instructions, he received twenty paddle swats administered in the principal's office. As a consequence, he needed medical treatment and missed a few days of school. Andrews was also paddled, but less severely.

The justices reviewed the history of the Eighth Amendment and determined that the intent of its inclusion in the U.S. Constitution was to protect those convicted of crimes. For this reason, the Eighth Amendment was deemed inappli-

———

[73]*Ingraham* v. *Wright,* 430 U.S. (1977). Also see Perry A. Zirkel, "You Bruise, You Lose," *Phi Delta Kappan* (January 1990), pp. 410–411.

Whatever force this logic may have in other settings, we find it an inadequate basis for wrenching the Eighth Amendment from its historical context and extending it to traditional disciplinary practices in the public schools.

The prisoner and the schoolchild stand in wholly different circumstances, separated by the harsh facts of f criminal conviction and incarceration. The prisoner's conviction entitles the State to classify him as a "criminal," and his incarceration deprives him of the freedom "to be with family and friends and to form the other enduring attachments of normal life." . . .

The schoolchild has little need for the protection of the Eighth Amendment. Though attendance may not always be voluntary, the public school remains an open institution. Except perhaps when very young, the child is not physically restrained from leaving school during school hours; and at the end of the school day, the child is invariably free to return home. Even while at school, the child brings with him the support of family and friends and is rarely apart from teachers and other pupils who may witness and protest any instances of mistreatment.

The openness of the public school and its supervision by the community afford significant safeguards against the kinds of abuses from which the Eighth Amendment protects the prisoner. In virtually every community where corporal punishment is permitted in the schools, these safeguards are reinforced by the legal constraints of the common law. Public school teachers and administrators are privileged at common law to inflict only such corporal punishment as is reasonably necessary for the proper education and discipline of the child; any punishment going beyond the privilege may result in both civil and criminal liability. As long as the schools are open to public scrutiny, there is no reason to believe that the common law constraints will not effectively remedy and deter excesses such as those alleged in this case.

We conclude that when public school teachers or administrators impose disciplinary corporal punishment, the Eighth Amendment is inapplicable.

Questions

1. Assuming corporal punishment is desirable in a particular situation, how does one determine whether a given punishment may be reasonably necessary and thus not excessive?

2. How is it possible for the Supreme Court to decide that the First Amendment applies to elementary and secondary students (as in *Tinker* v. *Des Moines*) but the Eighth Amendment does not?

3. Could or should a student who is to be paddled demand the right to "return home" to escape this punishment?

Source: *Ingraham* v. *Wright*, 97 S. Ct. 1401 (1977).

Eighth Amendment inapplicable

cable to corporal punishment of schoolchildren. As to due process, the Court said, "We conclude that the Due Process clause does not require notice and a hearing prior to the imposition of corporal punishment in the public schools, as that practice is authorized and limited by common law."

Despite ruling for the school officials in the *Ingraham* case, the Court commented on the severity of the paddlings. In such instances, the justices stated, school authorities might be held liable for damages to the child. Moreover, if malice were shown, the officials might be subject to prosecution under criminal statutes. In a later action the Court also indicated a role for the due process clause. By declining to hear *Miera* v. *Garcia*, the Court let stand a circuit court ruling that "grossly excessive" corporal punishment may constitute a violation of the student's due process rights.[74]

Possible liability

---

[74]*Miera* v. *Garcia*, 56 USLW 3390 (1987); Christopher Grasso, "Court Lets Corporal Punishment Stand, Accepts Child Abuse Case," *Education Daily*, March 22, 1988, pp. 3–4.

Overview 8.2 ◄●──

Selected U.S. Supreme Court Decisions
Affecting Students' Rights and Responsibilities

Case	Summary of Decision
Tinker v. *Des Moines Independent Community School District* (1969)	Students are free to express their views except when such conduct disrupts class work, causes disorder, or invades the rights of others.
Goss v. *Lopez* (1975)	Suspension from school requires some form of due process for students.
Wood v. *Strickland* (1975)	A school board's ignorance of the law regarding due process is no excuse for not following it.
Ingraham v. *Wright* (1977)	Corporal punishment is not cruel or unusual punishment and is permitted where allowed by state law.
New Jersey v. *T.L.O.* (1985)	To be constitutional, searches of students and students' property must meet a two-pronged test.
Bethel School District No. 403 v. *Fraser* (1986)	Schools do not have to permit offensive or disruptive speech.
Hazelwood School District v. *Kuhlmeier* (1988)	A school newspaper is not a public forum and can be regulated by school officials.
Honig v. *Doe* (1988)	Disabled students who are disruptive must be retained in their current placement until official hearings are completed.

No cattle prods

Lower courts have ruled against teachers or administrators who used cattle prods to discipline students, slammed students' heads against the walls, or spanked students so hard they needed medical attention. The Supreme Court will probably continue to uphold such rulings. Overall, recent judicial decisions, together with the ever-present possibility of a lawsuit, have made educators cautious in using corporal punishment.[75]

Sexual Harassment or Molestation of Students

The Supreme Court's decision in *Ingraham* v. *Wright* regarding the physical punishment of students strengthened prohibitions against sexual harassment

[75]William Celis 3d, "Debate over School Paddling Grows amid Rising Concerns," *The New York Times*, August 16, 1990, pp. A1, A12.

and molestation. Definitions of "sexual harassment" and "sexual molestation" vary, but for many purposes in education these terms are defined broadly to include not only sexual contact that calls into question the teacher's role as exemplar, but also unwelcome sexual advances or requests for favors, particularly when the recipient may believe that refusal will affect his or her academic standing. Some research indicates that sexual harassment along the latter lines may be a more widespread problem at the precollegiate level than is commonly thought. Contemporary standards for behavior both inside and outside the school make it increasingly incumbent on teachers to avoid behaviors that may constitute or be perceived as constituting sexual harassment or molestation.[76]

Unwelcome sexual advances

Problems may be widespread

Student Records and Privacy Rights

Until 1974, most school records were closed to examination by students and their parents. Yet prospective employers, government agencies, credit bureaus, and certain other external agents were allowed access. As might be guessed, abuses occurred. The **Family Educational Rights and Privacy Act** (also called either FERPA or the **Buckley amendment**) was passed by Congress in 1974 to curb possible abuses in institutions receiving federal funds.

FERPA (Buckley amendment)

Parents' rights

The Buckley amendment requires public school districts to develop policies allowing parents access to their children's official school records. The act prohibits disclosure of these records to most third parties without prior parental consent (in cases of students under eighteen years of age). Districts must have procedures to amend records if parents challenge the accuracy or completeness of the information they contain. Hearing and appeal mechanisms regarding disputed information also must be available. Parents retain rights of access to their children's school records until the child reaches the age of eighteen or is enrolled in a postsecondary institution.

Exceptions to general rules

The Buckley amendment allows several exceptions. Private notes and memoranda of teachers and administrators (including grade books) are exempt from view. Records kept separate from official files and maintained for law enforcement purposes (for example, information about criminal behavior, special education records) cannot be disclosed. Nothing may be revealed that would jeopardize the privacy rights of other pupils. Lastly, schools may disclose directory-type information without prior consent; however, students or their families may request that even this information be withheld.[77]

Hatch Amendment

Student privacy policies also are affected by the Hatch Amendment to the federal General Education Provisions Act of 1978. The Hatch Act specified that instructional materials used in connection with "any research or experimentation program or project" are to be "available for inspection" by participating students' parents and guardians, and that no student shall be required to participate in testing, psychological examination, or treatments in which "the primary

---

[76]Dan H. Wishnietski, "Reported and Unreported Teacher-Student Sexual Harassment," *Journal of Educational Research* (January/February 1991), pp. 164–168; Mark Walsh, "Unwelcome Advances," *Teacher Magazine* (February 1992), pp. 12–13; and "Students Can Collect Damages for Sexual Harassment, Supreme Court Rules," *The Executive Educator* (April 1992), p. 6.

[77]Fischer, Schimmel, and Kelly, *Teachers and the Law;* Lisa Jennings, "Privacy Rights and Public-Safety Concerns," *Education Week,* June 21, 1989, pp. 1, 8–9; and William Celis 3d, "As Fewer Students Drink, Abuse of Alcohol Persists," *The New York Times,* December 31, 1991, pp. A1, A8.

purpose is to reveal information" concerning political affiliations, sexual behaviors or attitudes, psychological or mental problems, income, and other personal matters. It has been difficult to define terms such as "instructional materials" and "research program," and many parents have used the Hatch Act to object to school activities that focus on the affective domain or probe students' feelings or beliefs. Consequently, teachers must consider carefully whether collection of information on students' background or beliefs serves a legitimate goal.[78]

Access to information on crimes

Much recent debate concerning students' privacy rights involves policies that have been interpreted as prohibiting distribution of information about criminal conduct, even when this means that teachers are not alerted to potentially dangerous students who have been charged with violent crimes. In 1991 a federal judge ruled that colleges and universities cannot prevent the public from having access to information on campus crimes.[79]

Compulsory Attendance and Home Schooling

Every state has a law requiring children to attend school, usually from age six or seven to age sixteen or seventeen. In the past two decades these compulsory attendance laws have received increased attention because of a revival of interest in home schooling. A growing number of parents who object to some subject matter taught in public schools, the teaching methods used, or the absence of religious activities have chosen to teach their children at home. Most states allow home schooling subject to varying restrictions.[80]

Most states allow home schooling

Parents upheld

Where home-schooling parents have been brought before courts as violators of compulsory attendance laws, they usually must demonstrate that the home program is essentially equivalent to that offered in public schools with respect to subject matter covered, adequacy of texts used, and number of hours of daily instruction provided. They also must show through standardized test results that the education provided their children is comparable to that of school-educated peers. Parents have tended to prevail in court decisions where state or case law supported their actions and where they demonstrated to judicial satisfaction that the education their children received was at least equal to education in the public schools. However, courts consistently have upheld the right of state legislatures to impose restrictions and requirements such as those indicated above.[81]

Compulsory attendance issues have also been prominent in several states that recently passed legislation stating that young adults cannot receive a driver's license unless they graduated from high school or dropped out due to circumstances beyond their control. A sixteen-year-old in West Virginia sued state officials because they rejected his request for a license after he left school to work

[78]Edward B. Jenkinson, *Student Privacy in the Classroom* (Bloomington, Ind.: Phi Delta Kappa, 1990); "Controversy: Use of Lunch Data," *Effective Schools News* (February 1992), p. 3.

[79]Katherine Bishop, "Judge Orders Release of Campus Crime Reports," *The New York Times,* March 15, 1991, p. B9.

[80]J. Gary Knowles, Stacey E. Marlow, and James Muchmore, "From Pedagogy to Ideology," *American Journal of Education* (March 1991); Robert Rothman, "Court Strikes S.C. Testing Requirement for Home Schoolers," *Education Week,* January 8, 1992, pp. 31, 36.

[81]Naomi Gitins, ed., *Religion, Education, and the U.S. Constitution* (Alexandria, Va.: National School Boards Association, 1990).

Most states allow home schooling subject to various restrictions on subject matter covered, adequacy of texts used, and number of hours of daily instruction provided; parents also must show through standardized test scores that the education provided their children is comparable to that of school-educated peers. (© AP/Wide World Photos)

in his father's garage. The state supreme court ruled against him, indicating that state laws in this case constituted a valid attempt to improve the effectiveness of education.[82]

Need for Balance in Rights and Responsibilities

Need for discipline in schools

During the past several decades, as courts have upheld the constitutional rights of students and placed restrictions on school officials, many educators and parents have decided that the legal process is out of balance. The courts, they believe, place too much emphasis on student rights and too little on the need for school discipline. For example, AFT president Albert Shanker has commented:

A whole series of legal decisions defining students' rights have made it all but impossible to get rid of the few kids who can change a school into a holding tank. The decisions were made for what looked like the best possible reasons. . . . But no

[82]*Means* v. *Sidiropolis*, 401 S.E. 2d 447 (W.Va 1990).

matter how well meaning . . . the result is schools where little or no learning goes on because teachers have to assume the role of warden.[83]

Some scholars believe, however, that since the mid-1980s the Supreme Court has begun to redress the balance. According to Phi Delta Kappa Executive Secretary Lowell Rose, the Court's decisions in *T.L.O.* (1985), *Bethel/Fraser* (1986), and *Hazelwood/Kuhlmeier* (1988) place less burden on school officials than the 1969 *Tinker* decision. Rather than demonstrating that certain rules are necessary for school safety or effectiveness, school officials now need only show that the rules are reasonable. This new emphasis on reasonableness indicates that the Court "is placing considerable confidence in school officials," trusting those officials to maintain a proper balance between student rights and the school's needs.[84]

Reduced burden on school officials

RELIGION AND THE SCHOOLS

The framers of our Constitution were acutely aware of religious persecution and sought to prevent the United States from experiencing the serious and often bloody conflicts that had occurred in Europe. As noted at the beginning of this chapter, the First Amendment, adopted in 1791, prohibits the establishment of a nationally sanctioned religion (the establishment clause) and government interference with individuals' rights to hold and freely practice their religious beliefs (the free exercise clause). The position of government toward religion was succinctly stated by Judge Alphonso Taft over one hundred years ago: "The government is neutral, and while protecting all, it prefers none, and it disparages none."[85]

First Amendment

Prayer, Bible Reading, and Blessings

Students in New Hyde Park were required to recite daily this nondenominational prayer composed by the New York State Board of Regents: "Almighty God, we acknowledge our dependence upon thee, and we beg thy blessings upon us, our parents, our teachers and our Country." Although exemption was possible upon written parental request, the U.S. Supreme Court in *Engle* v. *Vitale* (1962) ruled the state-written prayer unconstitutional. The decision created a storm of protest that has not subsided to this day. The justices wrote:

State prayer unconstitutional

Neither the fact that the prayer may be denominationally neutral nor the fact that its observance on the part of students is voluntary can serve to free it from the lim-

---

[83]Albert Shanker, "Discipline in Our Schools," *The New York Times,* May 19, 1991, p. E7.

[84]Lowell C. Rose, "Reasonableness—The Court's New Standard for Cases Involving Student Rights," *Phi Delta Kappan* (April 1988), pp. 589–592. Also see Lawrence F. Rossow and Janice A. Hiniger, *Students and the Law* (Bloomington, Ind.: Phi Delta Kappa, 1991).

[85]Quoted by Justice Tom Clark in *School District of Abington Township* v. *Schempp,* 374 U.S. 203 (1963).

Violation of neutrality

itations of the Establishment Clause. . . . It is neither sacrilegious nor antireligious to say that each separate government in this country should stay out of the business of writing or sanctioning official prayers and leave that purely religious function to the people themselves and to those the people choose to look to for religious guidance.[86]

Bible reading

A year later the Court again prohibited religious exercises in public schools. This time, the issue involved oral reading of Bible verses and recitation of the Lord's Prayer. These were clearly religious ceremonies and "intended by the State to be so," even when student participation was voluntary.[87]

The Supreme Court also has ruled against invocations and benedictions that open or close public-school ceremonies or events with blessings a clergyman addresses to a deity. In a 1992 decision, the Court concluded that such blessings violate *Lemon* v. *Kurtzman* standards that prohibit the government from advancing religion. However, Justice Anthony Kennedy's majority opinion in this 5–4 decision also noted that state actions implicating religion are not necessarily unconstitutional because some citizens may object to them, and that the decision was not meant to require a "relentless and pervasive attempt to exclude religion from every aspect of public life."[88] One effect of the decision was to postpone constitutional review of several important questions such as whether schools can implement "moment of silence" policies that allow silent prayer on a voluntary basis, and whether it is permissible to allow religiously oriented invocations that are spoken by a lay person and are not addressed to a deity.[89]

Display of Religious Symbols

Meaning of "secular" not always clear

Display in public schools of religious symbols (such as a cross or a menorah) in a manner that promotes a particular religion is clearly unconstitutional. However, the Supreme Court has ruled that such religiously oriented artifacts as a Nativity scene can be displayed in public settings if the overall atmosphere is largely secular. Recent controversies involving the definition and interpretation of such terms as "secular" and "government promotion" of religion culminated in a U.S. Supreme Court decision that banned a Nativity scene in front of the Allegheny County (Pa.) Courthouse because it had not been "junked up" (in the words of a county official) with Santa Claus figures or other secular symbols associated with Christmas. Following the Allegheny County decision, a federal judge required the removal of a crucifixion painting from facilities in the Schuylerville (N.Y.) School District, on the grounds that the painting lacked "any meaningful neutralizing or negating features" to render it partially secular.[90]

---

[86]*Engle* v. *Vitale*, 370 U.S. 421 (1962).

[87]*School District of Abington Township* v. *Schempp* and *Murray* v. *Curlett*, 374 U.S. 203 (1963).

[88]Perry A. Zirkel and Ivan B. Gluckman, "Invocations and Benedictions at School Events," *NASSP Bulletin* (January 1991), pp. 105–109; Linda Greenhouse, "Justices Affirm Ban on Prayers in Public School," *The New York Times*, June 25, 1992, pp. A1, A1b.

[89]David Bernstein, "Why Johnny Can't Pray," *Reason* (February 1992), pp. 56–66.

[90]Michael McGough, "Menorah Wars," *The New Republic*, February 5, 1990, pp. 12–13; Sam Howe Verhovek, "School Ordered to Remove Crucifixion Mural," *The New York Times*, August 30, 1990, p. B12.

Access to Public Schools for Religious Groups

Bible club refused access

Bridget Mergens, a high-school senior in Omaha, organized a group of about twenty-five students who requested permission to meet on campus before school every week or so to read and discuss the Bible. Although similar Bible clubs were allowed to meet at other schools, administrators refused the request, partly to avoid setting a precedent for clubs of Satanists, Ku Klux Klanists, or other groups the school would find undesirable. Bridget's mother brought suit, and in June 1990 the U.S. Supreme Court found in her favor. Public high schools, the Court ruled, must allow students' religious, philosophical, and political groups to meet on campus on the same basis as other extracurricular groups. Permitting such meetings, the Court stated, does not mean that the school endorses or supports them.[91]

Problems in definition

There is a great deal of uncertainty about the implications of the *Mergens* case. Schools apparently have to choose between allowing practically any student group to meet and dropping all extracurricular activities. A third option would be to permit meetings only by groups whose activities are related directly to the curriculum, but difficult problems then arise in defining such activities.[92]

Discrimination against religious organizations not allowed

On a related issue, a circuit court of appeals ruled that a Pennsylvania school district could not prohibit a subsidiary of Campus Crusade for Christ from renting school facilities for a magic show that concluded with a religious testimonial. The Supreme Court's refusal to review this decision means that schools cannot refuse the use of school facilities to religious organizations if they rent them to secular groups.[93]

Pledge of Allegiance

Religious objections

Several Jehovah's Witnesses went to court over a West Virginia requirement that their children recite the pledge of allegiance at school each morning. The parents' objection was based on religious doctrine. The court ruled that the children could be exempted from this requirement because it conflicted with their religious beliefs.[94] Using this ruling as precedent, federal judges have concluded that students who refuse to stand and recite the pledge cannot be compelled to do so if participation violates their religious or other personal beliefs.[95] Recent decisions have provided further support for this conclusion, leading experts on school law to advise that school officials devise an effective system for excusing students who do not want to participate in the pledge.[96]

---

[91] *Board of Education of the Westside Community Schools* v. *Mergens,* 88 S. Ct. 1597 (1990).

[92] Mark Walsh, "Effects of Decision on Extracurriculars Raise Thorny Issues," *Education Week,* June 13, 1990, pp. 1, 12.

[93] Mark Walsh, "Church Group's Access to Public Schools Upheld," *Education Week,* August 1, 1990, p. 9.

[94] *West Virginia State Board of Education* v. *Barnette,* 319 U.S. 624 (1943).

[95] *Lipp* v. *Morris,* 579 F. 2d 834 (3rd Cir. 1978); Eugene F. Provenzo, Jr., and Asterie Baker Provenzo, "Columbus and the Pledge," *The American School Board Journal* (October 1991), pp. 24–25.

[96] Perry A. Zirkel and Ivan B. Gluckman, "Pledge of Allegiance," *NASSP Bulletin* (September 1990), pp. 115–117.

The Changing Face of American Education

American education today is a reflection of some important demographic changes in American society. The student population is more diverse than ever before. From bustling inner-city classrooms to small rural schools, today's educators work in a multitude of different environments and with students of many different cultural, economic, and family backgrounds.

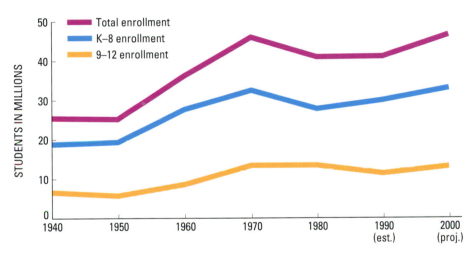

Figure 1 Public School Enrollment, 1880–2000
Total public school enrollment peaked in the early 1970s, then declined with the end of the post–World War II baby boom. Enrollment will rise again, first in elementary schools and later in secondary schools, as the baby boomers themselves have children.

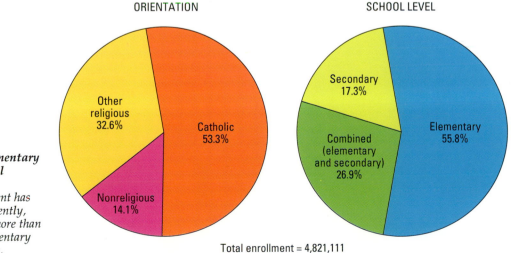

Figure 2 Private Elementary and Secondary School Enrollment, 1991
Private-school enrollment has risen since 1980. Currently, private schools enroll more than 11 percent of U.S. elementary and secondary students.

ORIENTATION

Other religious 32.6%

Catholic 53.3%

Nonreligious 14.1%

SCHOOL LEVEL

Secondary 17.3%

Elementary 55.8%

Combined (elementary and secondary) 26.9%

Total enrollment = 4,821,111

Growing Ethnic Diversity

Particularly in urban areas, minorities make up a substantial and growing proportion of public school enrollment.

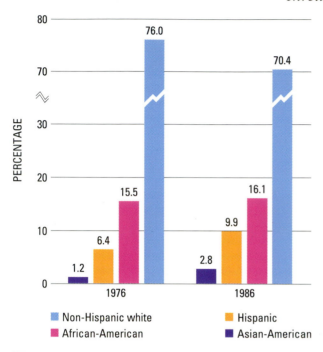

Figure 3 Racial/Ethnic Distribution of Students, 1976 and 1986 (as Percentage of Total Public School Enrollment)

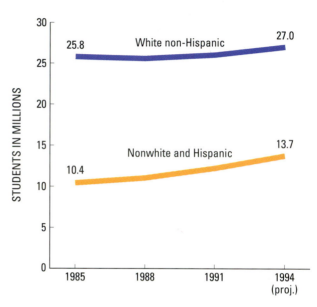

Figure 4 Public School Enrollment by Race/Ethnicity, 1985–1994 (projected) (as Percentage of Total Public School Enrollment)

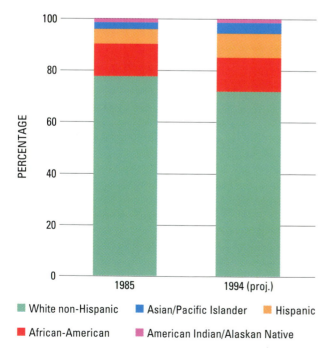

Figure 5 Public High School Graduates by Race/Ethnicity, 1985 and 1994 (projected) (as Percentage of all Children 5 Years and Over)

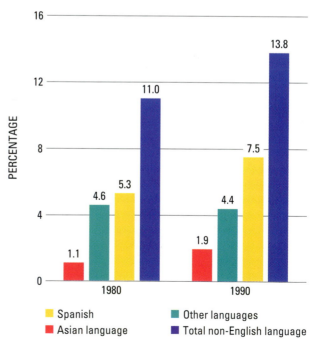

Figure 6 Children 5 Years and Older from Homes Where a Language Other Than English Is Spoken, 1980 and 1990

Figure 7 Sources of U.S. Immigration, 1982–1990

During the 1980s, 84 percent of immigrants to the United States came from either Latin America or Asia.

BY REGION

BY COUNTRY

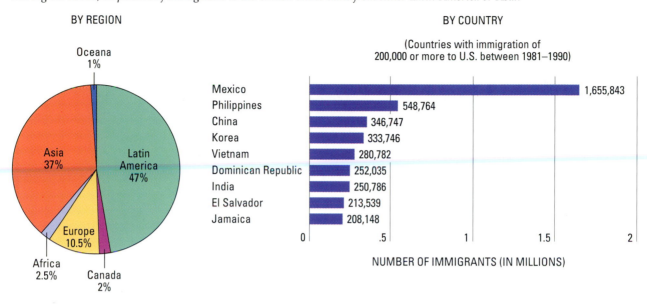

(Countries with immigration of
200,000 or more to U.S. between 1981–1990)

Oceana 1%

Mexico	1,655,843
Philippines	548,764
China	346,747
Korea	333,746
Vietnam	280,782
Dominican Republic	252,035
India	250,786
El Salvador	213,539
Jamaica	208,148

Asia 37%

Latin America 47%

Europe 10.5%

Africa 2.5%

Canada 2%

NUMBER OF IMMIGRANTS (IN MILLIONS)

Total immigration = 7,337,030

Figure 8 Immigrants to the United States, 1820–1990

Immigration to the United States during the 1980s was at a near-record high (second only to the years 1901–1910).

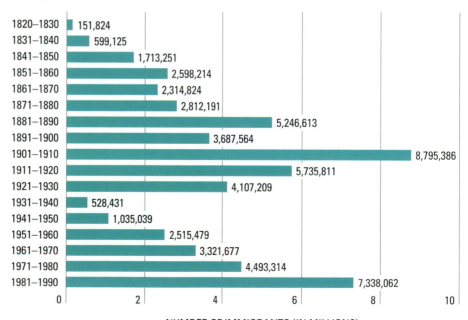

Period	Immigrants
1820–1830	151,824
1831–1840	599,125
1841–1850	1,713,251
1851–1860	2,598,214
1861–1870	2,314,824
1871–1880	2,812,191
1881–1890	5,246,613
1891–1900	3,687,564
1901–1910	8,795,386
1911–1920	5,735,811
1921–1930	4,107,209
1931–1940	528,431
1941–1950	1,035,039
1951–1960	2,515,479
1961–1970	3,321,677
1971–1980	4,493,314
1981–1990	7,338,062

NUMBER OF IMMIGRANTS (IN MILLIONS)

Total immigration = 56,994,014

The Changing American Family

Figure 9 Single-Parent Households, 1976–1991 (as Percentage of All Households with Children Under 18)

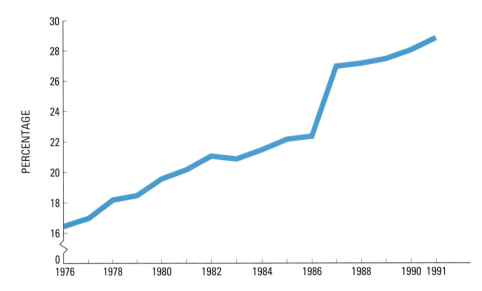

The dramatic rise in single-parent households and the changing make-up of single-parent families have had long-lasting effects on the student population. Many educators believe that such changes in family life influence the way students respond to school.

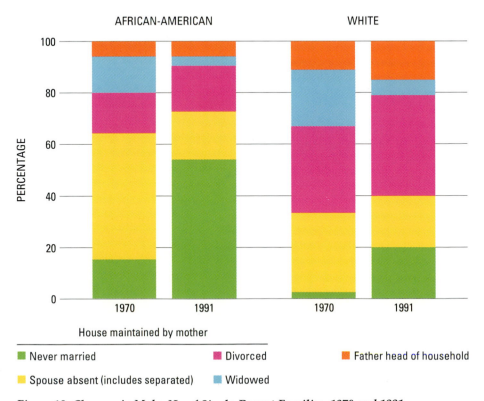

Figure 10 Changes in Make-Up of Single-Parent Families, 1970 and 1991

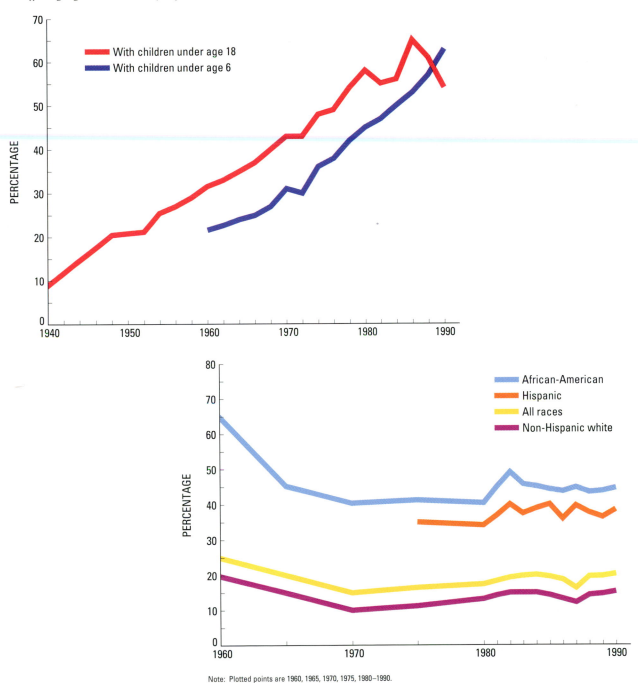

Figure 11 Working Mothers, 1940–1990
Because of the rapidly increasing percentage of mothers who work outside the home, schools are offering a greater number of day-care and after-school programs.

Note: Plotted points are 1960, 1965, 1970, 1975, 1980–1990.

Figure 12 Percentage of Children Under 18 in Poverty, by Race/Ethnicity, 1960–1990
The percentage of children living in poverty substantially decreased during the 1960s but currently is at its highest point in over twenty-five years.

The Changing Teacher Population

Figure 13 Teacher Characteristics, 1976 and 1991
As a group, teachers now are somewhat older and have more teaching experience than in the 1970s. Women still represent over two-thirds of the workforce.

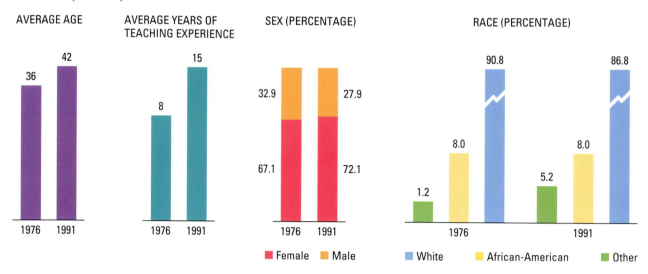

AVERAGE AGE

AVERAGE YEARS OF TEACHING EXPERIENCE

SEX (PERCENTAGE)

RACE (PERCENTAGE)

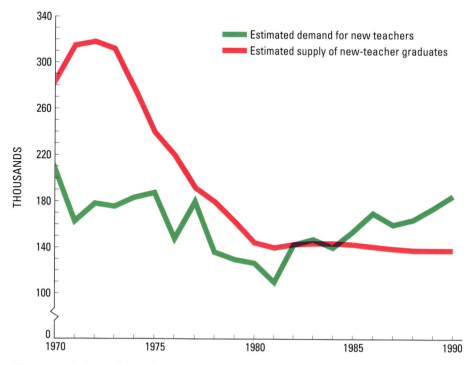

Figure 14 Estimated Supply and Demand for New Teacher Graduates, 1970–1990
According to many projections, job opportunities for new teachers are improving because the demand for additional teachers has begun to exceed the supply.

Federal judges have concluded that students who refuse to stand and recite the pledge of allegiance cannot be compelled to do so if participation violates their religious or other personal beliefs. (© Kenneth Murray/Photo Researchers, Inc.)

Religious Objections Regarding Curriculum

Fundamentalist Christian parents brought suit against the Hawkins County (Tenn.) School District charging that exposure of their children to the content in the Holt, Rinehart and Winston basal reading series was offensive to their religious beliefs. The parents believed that "after reading the entire Holt series, a child might adopt the views of a feminist, a humanist, a pacifist, an anti-Christian, a vegetarian, or an advocate of a one-world government." The district court held for the parents, reasoning that the state could satisfy its compelling interest in the literacy of Tennessee schoolchildren through less restrictive means than compulsory use of the Holt, Rinehart and Winston series.[97] However, an appellate court reversed this decision, stating that no evidence had been produced to show that students were required to affirm their belief or disbelief in any idea mentioned in the Holt books. The textbook series, the court said, "merely requires recognition that in a pluralistic society we must 'live and let live.'"[98]

Basal readers challenged

A similar challenge to curricular materials was mounted in Alabama. Fundamentalist Christians contended that forty-four history, social studies, and home economics textbooks unconstitutionally advanced the religion of secular humanism[99] and excluded "history of the contributions of Christianity to the American way of life." The district judge, W. Brevard Hand, concluded that secular humanism was indeed a religion and that the books at issue discriminated against theistic religions by omitting relevant facts. Judge Hand therefore banned

Secular humanism

[97]*Mozert* v. *Hawkins County Board of Education,* 86-6144 (E.D. Tenn. 1986).
[98]*Mozert* v. *Hawkins County Board of Education,* 87-5024 (6th Cir. 1987).
[99]Secular humanism is a philosophy that excludes religious considerations in its emphasis on the dignity and worth of human beings and their capacity for self-realization through reason.

use of the texts by the Mobile County Public Schools.[100] This decision was reversed by a federal appeals court, which held that the textbooks did not endorse secular humanism or any other religion, but rather attempted to instill such values as independent thought and tolerance of diverse views. The appeals court noted that if the First Amendment prohibited mere "inconsistency with the beliefs of a particular religion there would be very little that could be taught in the public schools."[101]

Creationism

In 1987 the U.S. Supreme Court considered *Edwards* v. *Aguillard*, a case that challenged Louisiana's Balanced Treatment for Creation-Science and Evolution-Science Act. Creation science, or creationism, is the belief that the development of life has proceeded from divine intervention or creation rather than by non-directed biological evolution. The 1982 Louisiana act required that creation science be taught wherever evolution was taught, and that appropriate curriculum guides and materials be developed.[102] The Supreme Court ruled this law unconstitutional. By requiring "either the banishment of the theory of evolution . . . or the presentation of a religious viewpoint that rejects evolution in its entirety," the Court reasoned, the Louisiana act advanced a religious doctrine and violated the establishment clause of the First Amendment.[103]

Texas and California developments

The controversy has continued. For instance, the Texas and California boards of education have both contended with protests from creationists; the California board compromised by referring to evolution as a "theory" rather than simply a "fact." In recent years some parents have also raised constitutional objections to materials designed to improve students' thinking skills; certain of these materials, the parents argued, embodied "New Age" religious practices. Some school districts have responded by eliminating the materials in question.[104]

Teaching About Religion

Promoting understanding of religious traditions

Guarantees of separation between church and state do not mean that public schools are prohibited from teaching about religion as part of studies of local or foreign cultures or other appropriate segments of the curriculum. Stressing the potential importance of teaching about religion in a manner that maintains the constitutional neutrality of government, a number of states and school districts have been moving to strengthen approaches for developing understanding of religious traditions and values while neither promoting nor detracting from any particular religious or nonreligious ideology.[105] In addition, scholars have been

---

[100] *Smith* v. *Board of School Commissioners of Mobile County*, 87-7216 (11th Cir. 1987).

[101] Ibid. Also see Eugene F. Provenzo, Jr., *Religious Fundamentalism and American Education* (Albany: State University of New York Press, 1990).

[102] Donald L. Ecker, *Dictionary of Science and Creationism* (Buffalo, N.Y.: Prometheus, 1990).

[103] *Edwards* v. *Aguillard*, 197 S. Ct. 2573 (1987).

[104] Seth Mydans, "Correction: California Calls Evolution 'a Fact and a Theory,'" *The New York Times*, November 14, 1989, p. 12; Robert Rothman, "Scientists, Creationists Each Claim Victory in Texas Evolution Vote," *Education Week*, March 22, 1989, pp. 1, 14; Debra Viadero, "Parents in S.C. Attack Alleged 'New Age' Program," *Education Week*, January 30, 1991, p. 8; and Thomas R. McDaniel, "On Trial: The Right to Think," *Educational Leadership* (January 1992), p. 85.

[105] Kenneth L. Woodward, "The Fourth R," *Newsweek*, June 10, 1991, pp. 56–57.

preparing materials that can be helpful in constitutionally acceptable teaching about religion.[106]

Government Regulation and Support of Nonpublic Schools

In 1925 *Pierce* v. *Society of Sisters* established that a state's compulsory school attendance laws could be satisfied through enrollment in a private or parochial school.[107] Attention then turned to the question of how much control a state could exercise over the education offered in nonpublic schools. A 1926 case, *Farrington* v. *Tokushige*, allowed nonpublic schools "reasonable choice and discretion in respect of teachers, curriculum and textbooks."[108] Within that framework, however, states have passed various kinds of legislation to regulate nonpublic schools. Some states have few regulations; others require the employment of certified teachers, specify the number of days or hours the school must be in session, or insist that state accreditation standards be met. One current controversy involves the application of state standards for special education.[109]

States can regulate

On the other side of the coin, states have offered many types of support for nonpublic schools, including transportation, books, and health services. In the 1947 case *Everson* v. *Board of Education of Erving Township*, the Supreme Court considered a provision in the New Jersey Constitution that allowed state aid for transportation of private and parochial students. The Court held that where state constitutions permitted such assistance, there was no violation of the U.S. Constitution.[110] Since then, the distinction between permissible and impermissible state aid to nonpublic schools has usually been based on the **child benefit theory.** That is, aid that directly benefits the child is permissible, whereas aid that primarily benefits the nonpublic institution is not.

State aid for transportation

In *Wolman* v. *Walter* (1977) the Supreme Court went further. Addressing particular kinds of state support for nonpublic schools permitted by the Ohio Constitution, the Court decided each specific question by applying the three-pronged test mentioned early in this chapter: (1) whether the statute had a secular purpose, (2) whether the primary effect neither advanced nor inhibited religion, and (3) whether the law refrained from excessive government entanglement with religion. The Court's decisions in *Wolman* v. *Walter* were as follows:[111]

Wolman decisions

1. Providing for the purchase or loan of secular textbooks and standardized tests is constitutional.

[106]For example, see Charles C. Haynes, *Religion in American History* (Alexandria, Va.: Association for Supervision and Curriculum Development, 1990).

[107]*Pierce* v. *Society of Sisters*, 268 U.S. 510 (1925). See William Bentley Ball, "False Assumptions on Voucher Programs and the Law," *Education Week*, February 12, 1992, p. 31.

[108]*Farrington* v. *Tokushige*, 273 U.S. 284 (1926).

[109]Debra Viadero, "Certification for Spec.-Ed. Teachers Sparks Debate in 2 States," *Education Week*, September 26, 1990, p. 8.

[110]*Everson* v. *Board of Education of Erving Township*, 330 U.S. 1 (1947).

[111]*Wolman* v. *Walter*, 433 U.S. 229 (1977).

Overview 8.3 ◄─●─►

Selected U.S. Supreme Court Decisions Affecting Nonpublic Schools and Religious Involvement in Public Schools

Case	Summary of Decision
Pierce v. *Society of Sisters* (1925)	Enrollment at a private or parochial school satisfies compulsory attendance laws.
Farrington v. *Tokushige* (1926)	Nonpublic schools have latitude in selecting teachers, curriculum, and texts.
Everson v. *Board of Education of Erving Township* (1947)	Public transportation of parochial school students is permitted where the state constitution allows it.
Engle v. *Vitale* (1962)	Public schools may not require students to recite prayers.
Lemon v. *Kurtzman* (1971); *Wolman* v. *Walter* (1977)	States may provide educational services to nonpublic-school students if the state law meets a three-pronged test.
Edwards v. *Aguillard* (1987)	Public schools may not be required to teach creationism because such teaching would advance religious doctrine.
Board of Education of the Westside Community Schools v. *Mergens* (1990)	Public high schools must allow students' religious, philosophical, and political groups to meet on campus on the same basis as other extracurricular groups.

---

2. Providing speech, hearing, and psychological diagnostic services at the nonpublic school site is constitutional.

3. Providing remedial services offered by public employees "at a neutral site off the premises of the nonpublic schools is permissible."

4. Providing for the purchase and loan of other instructional materials and equipment such as projectors, science kits, maps and globes, charts, record players, and so on was ruled unconstitutional because this involves excessive government entanglement with religion.

5. Providing funds for field trips was unconstitutional because "where the teacher works within and for a sectarian institution, an unacceptable risk of fostering religion is an inevitable byproduct. . . . Moreover, the public school authorities will be unable adequately to insure secular use of the field trip funds without close supervision of the non-public teachers. This would create excessive entanglement."

Current laws seem muddled

The conclusions in *Wolman* v. *Walter* show why many legal scholars believe that constitutional law regarding religion and the schools is something of a muddle. Why should government purchase of textbooks and tests for nonpublic schools be constitutional but not purchase of maps, globes, charts, and record players? Why can government-supported psychological services be provided at nonpublic schools, whereas remedial services must be provided at a neutral site? Although the Court gave reasons to support these conclusions, many observers view its overall decision as convoluted and difficult to explain to the average person.

Recent decisions

Since *Wolman* v. *Walter,* the U.S. Supreme Court has issued decisions in several cases involving support for nonpublic schools.[112] For example, the Court invalidated a San Francisco School District program that leased church buildings to provide remedial help for parochial students, a Grand Rapids, Michigan, program in which full-time public-school teachers offered remedial instruction at parochial schools,[113] and a New York City program that used federal funds for low-income students to send public-school teachers to parochial schools.[114] But the Court upheld arrangements through which the state of Washington provided financial assistance to help a student with disabilities to attend a Christian college.[115] Other courts have approved government assistance for students with disabilities who receive help in portable classrooms. These and other recent cases have not provided much clarification regarding applicability of the three-pronged test.

Three-pronged test

A related issue concerns practice teaching. At St. Cloud University in Minnesota, education majors could choose to do their practice teaching in either a public school or a private or parochial school. As in many other locales, the school was paid for participating in the program. A professor challenged this arrangement as unconstitutional. Applying the three-pronged test, an appeals court agreed. Although the placement of student teachers had the secular purpose of training them, the court reasoned, payment to participating religious schools had the primary effect of advancing religion.[116] Moreover, the university's failure to specify how the payments could be spent might communicate state approval of the schools' religious messages. State-funded teacher-training institutions must consider this issue in placing student teachers in nonpublic schools.

STUDENTS AND TEACHERS WITH AIDS

The rapid spread of AIDS (acquired immunodeficiency syndrome) and AIDS-related conditions, and the public's growing awareness of their deadly consequences, have brought up a number of legal questions regarding the rights of infected students and teachers.[117] Three brothers, all hemophiliacs, tested

---

[112]Eugene T. Connors, *Religion and the Schools: Significant Court Decisions in the 1980s* (Bloomington, Ind.: Phi Delta Kappa, 1988).

[113]*Grand Rapids School District* v. *Ball,* 105 S. Ct. 3216 (1985); Mark Walsh, "Court Curbs Schools from Providing Chapter 1 Aid on Church Grounds," *Education Week,* January 15, 1992, p. 8.

[114]*Aguilar* v. *Felton,* 105 S. Ct. 3232 (1985); Mark Walsh, "Court Upholds Rule on Chapter 1 Aid to Religious School," *Education Week,* June 5, 1991, p. 5; and Dennis Doyle, "The Challenge, the Opportunity," *Phi Delta Kappan* (March 1992), pp. 511–520.

[115]*Witters* v. *Washington Department of Service for the Blind,* 106 S. Ct. 748 (1986); Steven Huefner, "The Establishment Clause as Antiremedy," *Phi Delta Kappan* (September 1991), pp. 72–77.

[116]*Stark* v. *St. Cloud State University,* 802 F.2d 1046 (8th Cir. 1986).

[117]Sally Reed, "Children with AIDS," *Phi Delta Kappan* (January 1988), pp. K1–K12; Daniel Gursky, "Keeping AIDS a Secret," *Teacher Magazine* (November/December 1990), pp. 58–59.

positive for the AIDS virus. Their parents volunteered this information to school authorities, who responded by barring the boys from school. Home-bound classes or isolated in-school classes were the options presented the parents. The family sued to get the boys back into regular classrooms. After reviewing the information available about AIDS and the boys' conditions, the judge allowed them to return to classes but set the following guidelines:[118]

Court sets conditions

1. A committee consisting of school officials, medical personnel, and the family would determine the boys' continued attendance in regular classes.

2. The boys were responsible for "stringently complying" with class guidelines regarding their conduct.

3. The boys must keep all sores and lesions covered at all times, and must maintain an "elevated standard of hygiene."

4. Contact sports were to be avoided.

5. All incidents where blood could flow or bodily fluids could be exchanged were to be avoided. The judge also specified that the boys receive "complete, clear sexual education as it pertains to the transmission of this disease through sexual contact."

Elsewhere when families have brought suit to have AIDS-infected children admitted to school, courts also generally have upheld the right of these children to attend public schools. However, a judge in Florida permitted school officials to reject a kindergarten student who tested positive for AIDS-related complex and was not yet toilet-trained.[119]

Tuberculosis precedent for teachers

In 1987 the U.S. Supreme Court decided *School Board of Nassau County* v. *Arline,*[120] the case of a teacher dismissed because she had recurring tuberculosis. The teacher sued under Section 504 of the Rehabilitation Act of 1973 and won. The Supreme Court said that allowing discrimination based on the contagious effects of a physical impairment would be inconsistent with the underlying purpose of Section 504.[121] This precedent has been cited in controversies involving the employment of teachers with AIDS. However, few cases regarding teachers with AIDS have gotten as far as the courts. In the first such case, a district in California released a teacher of hearing-impaired students after he had been diagnosed as having AIDS. A federal judge ruled that he must be reinstated and awarded compensation for emotional distress associated with his firing. Additional protection for teachers afflicted with AIDS has been provided in recent federal legislation that prohibits employment discrimination against AIDS victims at institutions that receive federal funds.[122]

---

[118]*Ray* v. *School District of De Soto County,* 666 F. Supp. 1524 (M.D. Fla. 1987).

[119]*Doe* v. *Dolton Elementary School District No. 148,* 694 F. Supp. 440 (N.D. Ill. 1988); "U.S. Appeals Court Rules Against Glass Booth for AIDS Student," *Education Week,* January 11, 1989, p. 5; and "Court Strikes Down Exclusionary Policy," *Rethinking Schools* (October/November 1991), p. 15.

[120]*School Board of Nassau County* v. *Arline,* 55 U.S.L.W. 4245 (1987).

[121]*Doe* v. *Orange County Board of Education,* No. 87-6418 (9th Cir. Nov. 1987).

[122]Steven A. Holmes, "Rights Bill for the Disabled Sent to Bush," *The New York Times,* July 14, 1990, p. 7.

AFFIRMATIVE ACTION AND EDUCATIONAL EQUITY

Affirmative action generally refers to active steps intended to ensure that disadvantaged individuals receive equal opportunity in employment and education. In general, affirmative action requirements are associated with the Fourteenth Amendment, which guarantees all citizens equal protection under the law. Titles VI and VII of the Civil Rights Act of 1964 and the Civil Rights Restoration Act of 1987 specifically prohibit discrimination in federally assisted educational programs on the basis of race, color, religion, national origin, or sex. These laws also prohibit employment discrimination on the basis of any of these criteria. Section 504 of the Rehabilitation Act of 1973 and other legislation extend similar protection to persons with handicaps (see Chapter 11).[123]

Legislation outlaws discrimination

Much litigation since passage of the 1964 Civil Rights Act has involved definitions of discrimination and of the meaning of obligations to overcome past discrimination. In 1976 the U.S. Supreme Court ruled in *Washington* v. *Davis* that "disproportionate impact" alone does not prove the existence of unconstitutional discrimination.[124] For example, the fact that minority groups or women are underrepresented among employees in a school district or college is not by itself sufficient to prove an equal protection violation. However, the Court also ruled that such disproportionate impact is enough to shift the burden of justification to the defendant. Thus if a school-district test for teacher hiring disproportionately eliminates minority candidates, the district must prove that the test has some valid relationship to performance on the job.[125]

Obligations for affirmative action

During the 1970s, federal regulations required that educational institutions receiving federal funds set and meet specific targets for hiring minority applicants and women—in other words, establish quotas. Similar policies were being developed for admission of minority students to colleges. But in 1978 the Supreme Court prohibited this approach. In *Regents of the University of California* v. *Alan Bakke*, the Court ruled that setting aside a specific number of places for minority applicants to a medical school was unconstitutional. On the other hand, the Court encouraged affirmative action policies *not* based on firm quotas—for example, a general preference for applicants whose background (such as membership in a minority group) reflected qualities that the institution wished to have more fully represented.[126] The next year, in *Steelworkers* v. *Weber*, the Court upheld such affirmative action plans that offered minorities preferential treatment

Quotas not constitutional

Affirmative action encouraged

---

[123]Nathan Glazer, "The Affirmative Action Stalemate," *The Public Interest* (Winter 1988), pp. 99–114; Ward Weldon, "Effects of the 1987 Civil Rights Restoration Act on Educational Policy and Practice," *Journal of Negro Education* (Spring 1990), pp. 155–163; and Deborah A. Stone, "Race, Gender, and the Supreme Court," *The American Prospect* (Winter 1992), pp. 63–73.

[124]*Washington* v. *Davis*, 426 U.S. 229 (1976).

[125]Dinesh D'Souza, "Knowing the Score in America," *The Washington Post National Weekly Edition*, September 2–8, 1991, p. 25; Michael Kinsley, "Quota Bill?" *The New Republic*, April 15, 1991, p. 4; and Catharine R. Stimpson, "It Is Time to Rethink Affirmative Action," *The Chronicle of Higher Education*, January 15, 1992, p. A48.

[126]*Regents of the University of California* v. *Alan Bakke*, 438 U.S. 265 (1978); Scott Jaschik, "Scholarships Set Up for Minority Students Are Called Illegal," *The Chronicle of Higher Education*, December 12, 1990, pp. A1, A20; and Milo Geyelin, "Court Rejects Scholarship Aid for Blacks Only," *The Wall Street Journal*, February 5, 1992, pp. B1–B2.

in employment. Employees thus can take vigorous steps to overcome the effects of past discrimination.[127]

Reduction in force and seniority

Affirmative action becomes a contentious issue when school districts reduce their teaching forces because of declining enrollment or financial problems. In most districts the agreements negotiated with teacher organizations require termination in reverse order of seniority: the most recently hired are the first fired. However, some employers, including school districts, have exempted minority employees from this provision as long as the unit is below its target for minority employment. In 1984 in *Firefighters* v. *Stotts,* the Supreme Court ruled that this policy violated civil rights laws unless the minority employees who benefited from it had personally experienced overt discrimination.[128] Later, however, the Court upheld such minority exemptions if they were part of a negotiated agreement.[129]

The legal basis for affirmative action became even more complex in 1989, when the Supreme Court issued several rulings that seemed to reopen issues previously thought to be settled. For example, in *Wards Cove Packing* v. *Antonio,* a case involving the disproportionate impact of employment testing, the Court shifted the burden of proof. Rather than requiring the employer to demonstrate that a test was necessary, the Court said the plaintiffs who alleged discrimination must prove the test unnecessary. Although the Court claimed it was not retreating from Congress's intent to forbid discrimination, many observers were not so sure. Concern and uncertainty about the 1989 decisions ignited national controversies which finally were resolved (at least temporarily) when Congress passed legislation strengthening and clarifying several of the policies the Court had found questionable.[130]

Recent controversies

Chapter 11 will discuss desegregation law and other issues of educational equity for minority and non-English-speaking students and children with handicaps. Before leaving the subject of legal guarantees, however, we should consider the impact of federal laws and regulations on educational opportunities for women. As the next chapter points out, opportunities for women have been limited in part by socialization practices in the home and the larger society. Some of these limitations, though, can be reduced through appropriate actions within the educational system. Such actions have been stimulated by the **Women's Educational Equity Act** (WEEA) of 1974. Among the most important activities conducted under the WEEA have been the following:[131]

---

[127]*Steelworkers* v. *Weber,* 443 U.S. 193 (1979). Also see Louis Fischer, "Voluntary Race-Conscious Affirmative Action Plans," *Equity and Excellence* (Spring 1987), pp. 81–84, and Stephen L. Carter, *Reflections of an Affirmative Action Baby* (New York: Basic Books, 1991).

[128]*Firefighters* v. *Stotts,* 52 U.S.I.W. 4757 (1984).

[129]*International Association of Firefighters* v. *City of Cleveland,* 54 I.W. 5005 (1986). See Ronald Dworkin, "The Reagan Revolution and the Supreme Court," *The New York Review of Books,* July 18, 1991, pp. 23–28.

[130]Linda Greenhouse, "A Changed Court Revises Rules on Civil Rights," *The New York Times,* June 18, 1989, p. E2; Louis Fischer, "Patterson v. McLean Credit Union," *Equity and Excellence* (Summer 1990), pp. 59–62; and Adam Clymer, "Senate Approves Rights Bill Ending Bitter Job-Bias Shift," *The New York Times,* October 31, 1991, p. A10.

[131]Joy R. Simonson and Jeffrey A. Menzer, *Catching Up: A Review of the Women's Educational Equity Act Program* (Washington, D.C.: Citizens Council on Women's Education, 1984); Daniel U. Levine and Robert J. Havighurst, *Society and Education,* 8th ed. (Needham Heights, Mass.: Allyn and Bacon, 1992).

Improving opportunity for girls and women

- Opening math, science, and technology courses and careers to more women and girls
- Reducing sex stereotyping in curriculum materials
- Removing admission restraints and encouraging females to enroll in "non-traditional" vocational education courses, as well as lowering barriers to female entry into apprenticeship training
- Attempting to increase the number of women in school administration
- Encouraging greater participation by females in athletics

Athletic participation improved

Federal regulations require that equitable opportunities for athletic participation be provided to women in secondary schools and postsecondary institutions. The activities fostered by WEEA and the federal regulations have helped improve women's athletic participation rates. Today, more than 1 million young women take part annually in secondary school athletics, compared with only 295,000 in 1970–71. However, observers disagree on whether significant progress has continued to occur in recent years and how much additional change can or should take place in the future.[132]

Summing Up

1. Education-related court cases have significantly increased in the last few decades. Such cases can be heard in both federal and state courts depending on the issues involved. Only decisions of the U.S. Supreme Court apply nationally.

2. Tenure protects teachers from dismissal except on such specified grounds as incompetency, immorality, insubordination, and unprofessional conduct. Teachers accused of such conduct are entitled to due process protections.

3. Teachers have the right to form and belong to unions and other professional organizations, but most states prohibit teachers from striking.

4. Teachers' rights regarding freedom of expression, academic freedom, and censorship depend on a balance between individual and governmental interests. Teachers have rights guaranteed to individuals under the Constitution, but school boards have obligations to ensure the "proper" and "regular" operation of the schools, taking into account the rights of parents, teachers, and students.

5. Restraints on teachers' behavior outside school and on their dress and grooming are not as stringent as they once were in the United States, but teachers still are expected to serve as role models and to behave in an exemplary manner.

6. Schools must uphold definite standards to avoid legal suits charging negligence when students are injured. In addition, teachers must obey copyright laws.

---

[132]Susan Oberlander, "Advocates for Women's Sports Say 1988 Civil Rights Act Has Not Brought Hoped-for Equity With Men," *The Chronicle of Higher Education,* June 21, 1989, pp. A23–A24; "Across the Nation," *Education Week,* October 9, 1991), p. 2; and Laura Mansnerus, "Women Take to the Field," *The New York Times Education Life,* January 5, 1992, pp. 40–41.

7. The courts have clarified and expanded such students' rights as freedom of expression, due process in the case of suspension or expulsion, prohibition against bodily searches in the absence of specific grounds, limitations on corporal punishment, and privacy of records.

8. Organized and mandated prayer and Bible reading are not allowed in public schools. School curricula do not automatically constitute unconstitutional discrimination against religion when they ignore religious points of view or explanations.

9. The legal basis for government support for nonpublic schools is mixed. For example, government may provide textbooks, tests, and psychological services for students at nonpublic schools, but it may not provide funds for field trips, projectors, science kits, or maps. Providing the latter is thought to entangle church and state.

10. In general, public schools must admit students with AIDS, but they must take steps to protect the health of other children.

11. Federal laws prohibit discrimination in educational employment and programming on the grounds of race, color, religion, national origin, and sex. School districts and teachers have an obligation to act affirmatively in providing equal opportunity for minorities and women.

Key Terms

plaintiffs *(268)*

litigants *(268)*

establishment clause *(269)*

free exercise clause *(269)*

equal protection clause *(270)*

breach of contract *(272)*

tenure *(272)*

continuing contract *(272)*

due process *(273)*

academic freedom *(279)*

torts *(281)*

proximate cause *(282)*

fair use *(285)*

in loco parentis *(287)*

Family Educational Rights and Privacy Act (Buckley amendment) *(297)*

child benefit theory *(305)*

affirmative action *(309)*

Women's Educational Equity Act *(310)*

Discussion Questions

1. What are the teacher tenure regulations in your state? How long is the probationary period?

2. Should teachers be required to meet higher or different standards of personal morality than other citizens? Why or why not?

3. What are the signs of child abuse? What reporting procedures do districts in your area follow?

4. Discuss the wisdom or lack of wisdom of the legal decisions on educational malpractice. What types of malpractice suits might be successful in the future?

5. Debate the pros and cons of prayer, Bible reading, and religious observances in public schools.

Suggested Readings

LaMorte, Michael W. *School Law: Cases and Concepts,* 2nd ed. Englewood Cliffs, N.J.: Prentice-Hall, 1987.

In this comprehensive text for the study of school law, the author uses excerpts from judicial opinions to convey important legal principles.

Menacker, Julius. *School Law: Theoretical and Case Perspectives.* Englewood Cliffs, N.J.: Prentice-Hall, 1987.

This book places a useful emphasis on concepts and dilemmas of fairness and justice in the application of school law.

Provenzo, Eugene F., Jr. *Religious Fundamentalism and American Education.* Albany: State University of New York, 1990.

This book describes and analyzes major Supreme Court decisions dealing with church and state censorship, family rights and education, and related issues.

Robbins, Jan C. *Public Schools as Public Forums.* Bloomington, Ind.: Phi Delta Kappa, 1990.

The rights of citizens, students, and teachers are explained with respect to free speech and public forum issues.

Rossow, Lawrence F., and Janice A. Hiniger. *Students and the Law.* Bloomington, Ind.: Phi Delta Kappa, 1991.

This slim "Fastback" includes chapters on freedom of speech, student publications, search and seizure, drug testing, religious activity, discipline in special education, and expulsions and suspensions.

Wills, Garry. "H. R. Clinton's Case," *The New York Review of Books,* March 5, 1992, pp. 3–5.

This article describes new legal theories developed by attorney Hillary Rodham Clinton with respect to protecting the rights of children and adolescents in schools and other institutions.

SOCIAL FOUNDATIONS

*E*ducational systems are established to serve specific purposes in the societies in which they operate. For this reason, it is not possible to understand the way schools and other components of an educational system function without knowing something about the larger society and the ways in which it influences and is reflected by the educational system.

Chapter 9 looks at how students are prepared to participate in our schools and our society and describes the major forces that mold student behavior. The chapter discusses several of the central socializing agents in contemporary society — the family, the peer group, the school, and television — and then deals with sex roles in school and in society and with sex differences in educational achievement. The chapter concludes with an examination of adolescent and youth problems.

In Chapter 10, we examine the relationships among social class, race, and school achievement. After reviewing recent data indicating that working-class students tend to be much lower in achievement than middle-class students, the chapter points out that there is little relationship between minority status and school performance once students' economic disadvantages are taken into account. The problem of low school achievement is most severe among underclass students in concentrated poverty neighborhoods.

Chapter 10 then discusses possible reasons for low school achievement, including a home environment that does not provide good preparation for success in the traditional school, possible hereditary handicaps, and obstacles in the classroom. We report that the influence of heredity does not appear to be well established in any precise way, and that many achievement problems stem from the home environment and from ineffective instruction. Chapter 10 also examines research on the extent to which the educational system provides equal opportunities for students with low socioeconomic status.

Chapter 11 concentrates on the issue of equal educational opportunity. A discussion of desegregation concludes that although much progress has been made in providing desegregated schooling in smaller towns and cities, particularly in the South, most minority students in big cities attend segregated schools. The chapter then examines compensatory education to overcome the educational deficits of economically disadvantaged students. Recent research indicates that compensatory education may be having some positive but limited impact.

Chapter 11 also discusses multicultural education, putting particular emphasis on cultural pluralism and on multicultural instruction that recognizes and responds to students' diverse learning styles and language backgrounds. The chapter concludes with a discussion of educational opportunities for students with disabilities, particularly with reference to classification and labeling of students, mainstreaming, and the disproportionate placement of students from minority backgrounds in programs for the mentally retarded.

9

Culture, Socialization, and Education

FOCUSING QUESTIONS

In what ways does education function to transmit cultural patterns?

What cultural patterns influence instruction in elementary and secondary schools?

How do sex roles and sex differences influence learning and achievement?

How does the culture of the schools socialize the young?

How have television and other mass media affected students?

How do aspects of youth culture affect the schools?

A society ensures its unity and survival by means of culture. The attitudes, behaviors, and understandings that individuals learn in groups — the culture of a large group or society and the subcultures of smaller groups — are what enable people to communicate with one another and to function within a set of common rules. To provide for transmission of culture and to allow society to function satisfactorily, children must be acculturated (learn the concepts, values, and behavior patterns of individuals sharing a common culture) and socialized (prepared to function first as young people and then as adults) so that they can participate effectively in groups and in the larger society.

Many individuals and institutions play a part in helping to acculturate and socialize children and youth. The family, of course, is most important for young children, but in modern societies formal institutions also help determine what a child learns and how well he or she is prepared to function in society. The school has been created for just this purpose, but other institutions also mold the attitudes, behaviors, and understandings of young people.

Chapter 9 provides an overview of some of the most important focal points in the **acculturation** and **socialization** of children and youth in our complex, technological society. Emphasis throughout the chapter will be on how the culture of socializing institutions affects young people's development and achievement. We also consider the ways in which schools are influenced by the conditions and problems created by other social institutions.

CULTURE AND EDUCATION

The term **culture** has been broadly defined to encompass all the continually changing patterns of ''acquired behavior'' transmitted among the members of a society.[1] Anthropologist Ruth Benedict put it another way when she said, ''Culture is that which binds men together.''[2] Culture is a way of thinking and behaving; it is a group's knowledge and customs, its traditions, memories, and written records, its shared rules and ideas.[3] Neither a single individual, nor a group, nor an entire society can be understood without reference to culture.[4] Habits of dress, of diet, of daily routine — the countless small details of ordinary life that seem to require little reflection — all this constitutes a sweeping cultural identity. That culture is responsible for generating wide differences in behavior

Aspects of culture

[1]Harry F. Wolcott, ''Propriospect and the Acquisition of Culture,'' *Anthropology & Education Quarterly* (September 1991), pp. 251–273.

[2]Ruth Benedict, *Patterns of Culture* (Boston: Houghton Mifflin, 1983), p. 14. Also see Christopher Herbert, *Culture and Anomie* (Chicago: University of Chicago Press, 1991).

[3]Susan Florio-Ruane, *Social Organization of Classes and Schools* (East Lansing, Mich.: National Center for Research on Teacher Education, 1989); E. Eugene Clark and William Ramsey, ''Making Schools Work: Why Families Matter,'' *The Family in America* (January 1992), pp. 1–8.

[4]Clyde Kluckhohn, *Mirror for Man* (New York: McGraw-Hill, 1949); George A. De Vos and Marcelo Suarez-Orozoco, eds., *Status Inequality: The Self in Culture* (Newbury Park, Calif.: Sage, 1990).

and attitudes across societies has been recognized at least since the fifth century B.C., when the Greek historian Herodotus noted:

> The Egyptians appear to have reversed the ordinary practices of mankind. Women attend markets and are employed in trade, while men stay at home and do the weaving. . . . Men in Egypt carry loads on their heads, women on their shoulders. . . . To ease themselves they go indoors, but eat outside on the streets, on the theory that what is unseemly but necessary should be done in private, and what is not unseemly should be done openly.[5]

In modern societies, the school serves as perhaps the major institution (other than the family) devised by the adult generation for maintaining and perpetuating the culture. It imparts the tools necessary for survival and ensures the transmission of knowledge and values to future generations. In effect, the school provides us with a sense of the continuity and experience of our culture; it is a highly formal system for educating the young, an institution children are required to attend in order to be acculturated and socialized. In school the values, beliefs, and **norms** (rules of behavior) of the society are upheld and passed on, not only as the subject matter of the lesson but also as embodied in the very structure and operation of the educational system itself.

Education not synonymous with schooling

Most Americans tend to regard education as synonymous with schooling. Actually, a society may have no schools, but it still educates its young through family customs or special rituals and training.[6] In nontechnical societies, all members may become proficient in the entire range of knowledge necessary for survival. In technological societies, formal schooling becomes more important, for people must acquire different proficiencies and abilities; no individual can acquire the entire body of complex knowledge available or expect to be proficient in all areas of learning.

In a diverse society such as our own, schools are responsible for helping young people learn to participate in a national culture, but they also must be sensitive to cultural differences and must make sure that students from minority groups have equal opportunities to succeed in education. The challenges posed by this imperative are analyzed and discussed in the sections of Chapter 11 on multicultural education.

AGENTS OF SOCIALIZATION

Major socializing institutions

A number of social institutions function in transmitting culture to children and youth. For many societies, the most important historically have been the church, the peer group, the school, and of course the family. Some of these institutions, such as the church, have become less influential in Western societies, while oth-

---

[5]Quoted in Christine Hobson, *The World of the Pharaohs* (New York: Thames and Hudson, 1987), p. 23.
[6]Howard Gardner, "The Difficulties of School: Probable Causes, Possible Cures," *Daedalus* (Spring 1990), pp. 85–113.

ers, such as the mass media, have emerged as a socializing force. In this section we discuss several issues concerning the influence of family patterns on education. We then go on to consider the socializing role and educational implications of the peer group, the culture of the school, and the influence of television.

The Family

Although its organization varies, the family is the major early socializing agent in every society. As such, it is the first medium for transmitting culture to children. Because the family is the whole world to very young children, its members teach a child what matters in life, often without realizing the enormous influence they wield. Desires to achieve popularity, expectations about how boys and girls should behave, motivations to excel scholastically — numerous beliefs and values are passed from parent to child. The behaviors adults encourage and discourage and the ways in which they provide discipline also affect a child's orientation toward the world.

Home environment and preparation for school

Many children do well in school because their home and family environment has provided them with good preparation for succeeding in the traditional classroom. Others do poorly in part because they have not been well prepared, and the schools generally have not made successful adjustments to overcome this disadvantage.[7] (Possibilities for modifying instruction and otherwise acting to help unsuccessful students are described in later chapters.) Contemporary changes in the nature of the family have important implications for children's educational development and success in school. This section discusses several of the most important of these changes and their implications for education.

Increase in Working Mothers. The percentage of working mothers with children under eighteen has been increasing steadily in the United States since 1950. In that year, 18 percent of women with children were working; by 1992, more than two-thirds were working. (See color insert.) There are several reasons for this increase in the percentage of mothers in the work force: better employment opportunities for women, rising divorce rates, family financial pressures that require a second income, and changes in traditional cultural attitudes that dictated mothers stay home.[8]

Child-care arrangements

As mothers have gone to work, concomitant changes have occurred in child-care arrangements. By 1992, only about one-fourth of the young children of working mothers were cared for in their homes, as compared with 57 percent in 1958. Researchers do not yet have a complete picture of the average quality of day-care arrangements for preschool children, but as we point out later in this chapter, it is certain that such arrangements are less than satisfactory for

---

[7]Earl S. Schaefer, "Goals for Parent and Future-Parent Education: Research on Parental Beliefs and Behavior," *The Elementary School Journal* (January 1991), pp. 239–248; "The Child Care Market Today," *The Urban Institute Policy and Research Report* (Winter/Spring 1992), pp. 11–12.

[8]Sally B. Kammerman, "What We Owe to Children Under Three," *The American Prospect* (Winter 1991), pp. 64–73; Sue Shellenbarger, "Women with Children Increase in Work Force," *The Wall Street Journal*, February 12, 1992, p. B1.

Contemporary changes in the nature of the family — more working mothers, single-parent families, and children and women living in poverty — have important implications for children's educational development and success in school. (© David S. Strickler/Click, Chicago)

Latchkey children

many of them.[9] Highly problematical is the phenomenon of **latchkey children,** who return to empty homes after school either to sit by the television or to roam the streets.[10] National data indicate that there may be as many as 10 million latchkey children between the ages of five and thirteen.[11] Those who propose expanding government assistance and supervision for latchkey children argue that valuable services could be provided for them through the schools and other institutions. They point out that many children are "losing their child-

---

[9]Kathleen McCartney and Elizabeth Jordan, "Parallels Between Research on Child Care and Research on School Effects," *Educational Researcher* (January 1990), pp. 24–27; Bryce J. Christensen, "Day-Care Defiance," *The Family in America New Research* (March 1992), p. 2.

[10]Bickley Townsend, "How We Live," *American Demographics* (January 1984), p. 6; *Speaking of Kids* (Washington, D.C.: National Commission on Children, 1991).

[11]*Who's Minding the Kids?* (Washington, D.C.: U.S. Government Printing Office, 1990).

hood" because they have to fend for themselves or take care of siblings while parents work.[12]

Effects of maternal employment

The relationship between maternal employment and children's school performance is not well established or understood.[13] Some analysts who reviewed the research on this topic found little evidence to indicate that the preponderant effects of maternal employment on achievement are either positive or negative.[14] However, others have concluded that maternal employment probably does have some negative effects on children's intellectual functioning, social behavior, and/or school performance.[15]

Single-Parent Families. A trend related to the increase in working mothers is the very rapid rise in the percentage of single-parent households, mostly headed by a never-married, divorced, or separated woman. (See color insert.) Much of this increase has been due to the growing divorce rate, which approximately quadrupled in the United States between 1960 and 1990.[16] Some observers therefore conclude that modern marriage is a roulette game as likely as not to leave children at some point in single-parent families.[17]

Increase in single-parent families

Data on national trends further indicate that the percentage of children growing up in families characterized by divorce, separation, or death of a parent rose rapidly after 1960 among both whites and blacks. For example, of all white children under eighteen years of age, only 70 percent were living in two-parent households in 1990, compared with 91 percent in 1960. The figures for African American children and youth are more startling: only 39 percent were living in two-parent households in 1990, compared with 67 percent in 1960. In addition, about half of all young people under eighteen have been in a single-parent family for some part of their childhood.[18]

Conflicting research

Researchers have reported conflicting results when studying the impact of marital disruption or family structure on children's development and achieve-

[12]Anne Bridgman, "Schools Urged to Seek Solutions to Troubles of Latchkey Children," *Education Week,* May 30, 1984, p. 10; Deborah L. Cohen, "Hawaii Program for After-School Care Irks Private Firms," *Education Week,* March 14, 1990, pp. 1, 23.

[13]Lois W. Hoffman, "Effects of Maternal Employment in the Two-Parent Family," *American Psychologist* (February 1989), pp. 283–292.

[14]National Academy of Sciences, *Families That Work: Children in a Changing World* (Washington, D.C.: National Academy Press, 1982); Daniel U. Levine and Robert J. Havighurst, *Society and Education,* 8th ed. (Needham Heights, Mass.: Allyn and Bacon, 1992).

[15]Ann M. Milne, David E. Meyers, Alvin Rosenthal, and Alan Ginsburg, "Single Parents, Working Mothers, and the Educational Achievement of School Children," *Sociology of Education* (July 1986), pp. 125–139; Sonalde Desai, P. Lindsay Chase-Lansdale, and Robert T. Michael, "Mother or Market? Effects of Maternal Employment on the Intellectual Ability of 4-year-old Children," *Demography* (November 1989), pp. 545–561; and Bryce J. Christensen, "A Steadying Influence," *The Family in America New Research* (December 1991), p. 4.

[16]Richard Vedder and Lowell Gallaway, "Youthanasia: The Plight of the Rising Generation," *The Family in America* (July 1990), pp. 1–8; Bryce J. Christensen, "Getting Ahead, Falling Behind," *The Family in America New Research* (February 1992), p. 1.

[17]Alan C. Carlson, "By the Decades: The Troubled Course of the Family, 1945–1990 . . . and Beyond," *The Family in America* (May 1990), pp. 1–8; D. Stanley Eitzen, "Problem Students: The Sociocultural Roots," *Phi Delta Kappan* (April 1992), pp. 584–590.

[18]Randall D. Day and Wade C. Mackey, "The Mother-State-Child Family," *The Family in America* (March 1988), pp. 1–8; Linda J. Rubin and Sherry B. Borgers, "The Changing Family: Implications for Education," *Principal* (September 1991), pp. 11–13; and *State of Black America* (Washington, D.C.: Urban League, 1992).

ment. Much of this research has concentrated on identifying the specific influences on children of growing up in a home where the father is absent. Some studies conclude that there is little measurable impact on children,[19] but others find a variety of negative effects, including a greater likelihood that families will fall into poverty and that children will suffer serious emotional and academic problems.[20] The major reason this research has not been more conclusive is that it is so difficult to control for the effects of social class. A large percentage of families that "lost" a father also declined in social class, and this change in status makes it difficult for researchers to identify the separate effects of each factor.[21]

General conclusions

Recent studies have tried to adjust for such complexities. Teams of researchers in the United States and Great Britain, after analyzing longitudinal data on tens of thousands of families, concluded that divorce or separation has little independent effect on either boys or girls. Children whose parents reported marital problems but remained together subsequently experienced emotional and academic problems about as frequently as children whose parents divorced or separated. The researchers therefore concluded, "At least as much attention needs to be paid to the processes that occur in troubled, intact families as to the trauma that children suffer after their parents separate."[22] In addition, Judith Wallerstein and her colleagues, who have been periodically interviewing a group of persons whose parents divorced, found that serious problems such as depression, low academic performance, and negative interpersonal relationships frequently did not become apparent until ten or more years later.[23]

Recommendations for schools

In an attempt to help educators respond to the trend toward single-parent families, the National Committee for Citizens in Education has made the following recommendations:[24]

Send copies of report cards and other communications to the noncustody parent.

---

[19]Diane Scott Jones, "Family Influences on Cognitive Development and School Achievement," in Edmund W. Gordon, ed., *Review of Research in Education 11* (Washington, D.C.: American Educational Research Association, 1984); Sonalde Desai, P. Lindsay Chase-Lansdale, and Robert T. Michael, "Mother or Market?" *Demography* (November 1989), pp. 545–561.

[20]Deborah A. Dawson, "Family Structure and Children's Health and Well-being" (Paper presented at the Annual Meeting of the Population Association of America, Toronto, May 1990); Elaine C. Kamarck and William Galston, *Putting Children First* (Washington, D.C.: Progressive Policy Institute, 1990); and Bryce J. Christensen, "Saving the Unions," *The Family in America* (March 1992), pp. 1–8.

[21]E. A. Blechman, "Are Children with One Parent at Psychological Risk? A Methodological Review," *Journal of Marriage and the Family* (February 1982), pp. 179–195; Alan C. Acock and K. Jill Kiecolt, "Is It Family Structure or Socioeconomic Status?" *Social Forces* (December 1989), pp. 553–571; and Bryce J. Christensen, "No More Progress," *The Family in America New Research* (March 1992), p. 4.

[22]Andrew J. Cherlin et al., "Longitudinal Studies of Effects of Divorce on Children in Great Britain and the United States," *Science* (June 7, 1991), p. 1388; Joannie M. Schrof, "Wedding Bands Made of Steel," *U.S. News and World Report*, April 6, 1992, pp. 62–63.

[23]Judith S. Wallerstein, *Second Chances* (New York: Ticknor and Fields, 1989); Jane E. Brody, "Children of Divorce: Actions to Help Can Hurt, Studies Find," *The New York Times*, July 23, 1991, pp. B1, B9; and Judith S. Wallerstein, "The Long-Term Effects of Divorce on Children: A Review," *Journal of the American Academy of Child and Adolescent Psychiatry* (May 1991), pp. 349–360.

[24]P. A. Clay, *Single Parents and the Public Schools* (Columbia, Md.: National Committee for Citizens in Education, 1981). Also see Carolyn L. Wanat, "Of School, Single Parents, and Surrogates," *Education Week*, May 8, 1991, p. 25.

Include representation of single-parent families in the curriculum.

Add library materials that show varied lifestyles and help children cope with divorce.

Cooperate with other agencies in improving child-care arrangements before and after school.

Conduct workshops to help teachers avoid any negative expectations they may have developed for children from single-parent families.

Poverty-Level Children and the Feminization of Poverty. Because of the substantial increase in single-parent families, which typically have much lower income than those with two or more employed adults, the percentage of children and youth growing up below the poverty line also has increased. The poverty rate among children and youth under age eighteen fluctuated around 15 percent in the late 1960s, but then increased to more than 20 percent in the second half of the 1980s. Poverty rates are particularly high for children from minority groups, who are disproportionately likely to be in single-parent families: nearly 50 percent of African American youngsters and more than one-third of Hispanic youth are growing up in families below the poverty line. The rising poverty rates among children and youth are also connected with what many observers have called the **feminization of poverty.** More than 40 percent of families headed by a single female parent are below the poverty line, compared to only 10 percent of families with two parents.[25] (See color insert.)

Increase in child poverty rates

Day Care and the Public Schools. In light of the large increase in maternal employment, provision of day-care arrangements for young children has become an important issue in U.S. society.[26] Concerned with the inadequacy of day care, many state governments have acted to limit child-adult ratios, require more training for staff, and otherwise tighten requirements for licensing of day-care centers.[27] In addition, an increasing number of employers have begun to sponsor or subsidize day-care services for the children of their employees.[28]

Controversies over day care focus on a few major questions: whether government should encourage maternal employment through subsidization or provision of services, whether day care — even high-quality day care — has a positive or negative effect on children, whether day care should be provided through the public schools, and what types of programs should be offered. As for the first question, some "profamily" groups believe that maternal employment and day care are undermining the responsibility of the family and sub-

Effects of day care

---

[25]Mary Jo Bane and David T. Ellwood, "One Fifth of the Nation's Children: Why Are They Poor?" *Science*, September 8, 1989, pp. 1047–1053; Jason DeParle, "Fueled by Social Trends, Welfare Cases Are Rising," *The New York Times*, January 10, 1992, pp. A1, A9.

[26]Chris Raymond, "Scientists Urge Federal Standards for Child Care," *The Chronicle of Higher Education*, March 21, 1990, p. A7; Deborah L. Cohen, "Complex Set of Pieces Needed to Fill In School-Readiness Puzzle," *Education Week*, February 12, 1992, pp. 1, 14–15.

[27]Deborah I. Gold, "States Tightening Child-Care Rules," *Education Week*, December 2, 1987, p. 7; Tamar Lewin, "Panel Asks At Least $15 Billion to Improve Child Care in U.S.," *The New York Times*, March 15, 1990, p. A24.

[28]Irene Recio, "Beyond Day Care," *Business Week*, May 20, 1991, p. 142; Ellyn E. Spragins, "On-Site, Low-Cost Day Care, " *INC.* (March 1992), p. 97.

jecting very young children to negative social influences.[29] Indeed, some observers believe that compared to children cared for at home, children who attend day care develop less secure and more aggressive personalities and are more likely to acquire severe communicable diseases.[30] Although early research on day care tended to support the conclusion that its effects on children generally are positive, recent research has increased concern that infant day care frequently may be reducing children's sense of orderliness in the world while increasing hyperactivity and peer aggression.[31]

Support for expansion

Support for expansion and improvement of day care has been growing along with widespread concern for the welfare of low-income children whose parents cannot afford good nursery schools and who are "at risk" in that they are poorly prepared for school and later have low achievement and high dropout rates. Officials of the American Federation of Teachers have stated that we now have a "state of emergency" regarding the education of children growing up in difficult environments. The Committee for Economic Development's major reports titled *Children in Need* and *The Unfinished Agenda* have recommended that the federal government fund national prevention programs to provide preschool education and assistance for all at-risk children through the age of five.[32] This initiative would involve not just day care but a large expansion of preschool programs such as Head Start (see Chapter 11).[33]

Decline in Fertility Rates. The birthrate in the United States and other Western societies substantially declined during the past two centuries. The total fertility rate (the number of children per 1,000 women of childbearing age) fell from 704 in 1800 to 248 in 1970. Since the early 1970s, the U.S. fertility rate has been below the population replacement level of 211. Decline in the average number of children per family has made it easier for mothers to seek employment outside the home.[34]

Positive effects

The decline in the fertility rate probably has had an overall positive effect on the educational system. It is true that decreasing enrollments associated with this trend have produced many problems for educators, but some social scientists have reported that children in small families (particularly first- and second-

[29]Bryce J. Christensen, "Day Care: Thalidomide of the 1980s?" *The Family in America* (November 1987), pp. 1–8; Paul Taylor, "Ideology and the Baby Sitter," *The Washington Post National Weekly Edition,* September 2–8, 1991, pp. 31–32.

[30]Wendy and William Dreskin, "Where Have All the Liberals Gone?" *The Family in America* (September 1990), pp. 1–8.

[31]Thomas E. Ricks, "Day Care for Infants Is Challenged by Research on Psychological Risks," *The Wall Street Journal,* March 3, 1987, p. 35; Betty Holcomb, "Where's Mommy?" *New York,* April 13, 1987, pp. 73–87; and J. Craig Peery, "Children at Risk: The Case Against Day Care," *The Family in America* (February 1991), pp. 1–10.

[32]Committee for Economic Development, *Children in Need: Investment Strategies for the Educationally Disadvantaged* (New York: Committee for Economic Development, 1987); Committee for Economic Development, *The Unfinished Agenda* (New York: Committee for Economic Development, 1991); and "Money for Children Sought," *The New York Times,* February 12, 1992, p. B6.

[33]Deborah Burnett Strother, "Preschool Children in the Public Schools: Good Investment? Or Bad?" *Phi Delta Kappan* (December 1987), pp. 304–308; Victor R. Fuchs and Mary Coleman, "Small Children, Small Pay," *The American Prospect* (Winter 1991), pp. 74–79.

[34]*Monthly Vital Statistics Report 39* (Washington, D.C.: National Center for Health Statistics, 1990); Christiana Jeffrey, "Restoring the Balance," *The Family in America* (February 1992), pp. 1–8.

born children) benefit in intellectual growth; on the average, they may receive more attention from their parents than do children in large families.[35] Some research also indicates that, other things remaining equal, youth in a small cohort have more opportunities than those in a larger cohort, particularly when they enter the labor market.[36] Gains in family income supplied by mothers who have time to work outside the home also may benefit children.[37]

"Super babies"

Pressures on Children.   Awareness of the growing importance of education in contemporary society apparently has stimulated many parents to overemphasize early learning. The desire to raise so-called super babies appears to be particularly prevalent among middle-class parents for whom the "ABCs of babyhood" frequently center on "Anxiety, Betterment, [and] Competition."[38] To meet the demands of such parents, many preschool and primary classrooms may be focusing so systematically on formal instruction that they are "losing the developmental potential of early childhood education in a misplaced effort to mass-produce little Einsteins."[39] The concern that many youngsters feel too much pressure to excel at an early age also extends to art, music, and other educational areas.[40] Some developmental psychologists have viewed the apparent increase of such parental pressure as constituting a type of "miseducation" that creates **hurried children** and deprives young people of childhood.[41] Some responses to the perception that too much pressure is being placed on too many children at too young an age have included raising the age for enrolling in kindergarten and retaining five-year-olds who are not ready to advance to first grade for an additional year in kindergarten.[42]

---

[35]Robert B. Zazonc and Gregory B. Markus, "Birth Order and Intellectual Development," *Psychological Review* (January 1975), pp. 74–88; Robert B. Zazonc and Gregory B. Markus, "Family Factors and Intellectual Test Performance," *Review of Educational Research* (Fall 1986), pp. 365–371; Judith Blake, *Family Size and Achievement* (Berkeley: University of California Press, 1989); and Martha Farnsworth Riche, "The Future of the Family," *American Demographics* (March 1991), pp. 44–46.

[36]Richard Easterlin, *Birth and Fortune: The Impact of Numbers on Personal Welfare* (New York: Basic Books, 1980); Wayne J. Howe, "Education and Demographics: How Do They Affect Unemployment Rates?" *Monthly Labor Review* (January 1988), pp. 3–9; and Bryce J. Christensen, "Boardroom Blunder," *The Family in America* (March 1990), pp. 1–8.

[37]Frank P. Stafford, "Women's Work, Sibling Competition, and Children's School Performance," *The American Economic Review* (December 1987), pp. 972–980; Arlie Hochschild, "The Fractured Family," *The American Prospect* (Summer 1991), pp. 105–115.

[38]Lynn Langway, "Bringing Up Superbaby," *Newsweek*, March 28, 1983, pp. 62–68.

[39]Mary Hatwood Futrell, "Public Schools and Four-Year-Olds," *American Psychologist* (March 1987), pp. 251–252. Also see Chris Raymond, "New Study Reveals Pitfalls in Pushing Children," *The Chronicle of Higher Education*, November 1, 1989, pp. A4–A6; and Sharon L. Kagan, "Readiness 2000," *Phi Delta Kappan* (December 1990), pp. 272–279.

[40]Carol Lawson, "Studying Vivaldi, and Art, in Diapers," *The New York Times*, November 2, 1989, pp. 13, 17; Otto Weininger, "From the Fast Track, to the Fast Lane, to What?" *International Journal of Early Childhood* (no. 1, 1991), pp. 43–58.

[41]David Elkind, *The Hurried Child: Growing Up Too Fast* (New York: Addison-Wesley, 1981); David Elkind, *Miseducation: Preschoolers at Risk* (New York: Knopf, 1987); Janet Elder, "The Super Baby," *The New York Times*, January 8, 1989, pp. Educ 30–36; and Diane C. Burts et al., "Frequencies of Observed Stress Behaviors in Kindergarten Children" (Paper presented at the Annual Meeting of the American Educational Research Association, Boston, April 1990).

[42]Anne Pavuk, "Legislatures, Districts Move to Raise Age for Kindergarten," *Education Week*, June 24, 1987, pp. 1, 17; Deborah L. Cohen, "Va. Bill Would Set Two-Tiered Entry-Age Policy for School," *Education Week*, February 28, 1990, pp. 16–17; and Robert Suro, "Holding Back to Get Ahead," *The New York Times Education Life*, January 5, 1992, pp. 30–31.

Overindulged Children. Whereas many children may be pressured to meet overly compulsive parental demands for early learning, many others may be overindulged by parents who provide them with too many material goods or who protect them from challenges that would facilitate their emotional growth. (Of course, some children may be simultaneously overpressured and overindulged.) Some observers believe that overindulgence is a growing tendency, particularly among young middle-class parents who are trying to provide their children with more advantages than is good for their personal development. In presenting this argument, some psychologists have argued that overindulgence is an "epidemic" afflicting as many as 20 percent of the children in the United States, that these "cornucopia kids" will not be prepared to endure frustration or otherwise face reality when they grow up, and that "fast-track" parents are particularly likely to be overindulgent because they feel guilty about spending too little time with their children.[43]

Overindulgence may be increasing

Child Abuse. As we noted in Chapter 8, educators have a major responsibility to report any evidence that a student has been abused. Our society has become more aware of the extent and consequences of child abuse; the number of children reported as victims of abuse and neglect increased from about 1.2 million in 1981 to nearly 2.5 million in 1990. More than half these cases involved neglect of such needs as food, clothing, or medical treatment, about one-seventh involved sexual mistreatment, and approximately one-fourth involved beatings or other physical violence.[44] Many child-welfare agencies have been overburdened by the extent of the problem and frequently are unable to take corrective action.[45]

Reports of victims increasing

Research on the consequences of child abuse indicates that its victims subsequently tend to experience serious problems in emotional and social development. When they become adults, they have relatively high rates of alcohol and drug abuse, criminal behavior, and psychiatric disturbance.[46] However, this research is difficult to interpret because a relatively high proportion of abuse victims are low-income children. Since poverty also is correlated with developmental problems and subsequent delinquent and criminal behavior, it is not easy to identify a separate connection between abuse and later problems. The relationship is by no means simple, since many abused children do not experience serious emotional and behavioral problems in later years.[47]

Subsequent emotional and social problems

In any case, educators hardly can fail to recognize that students who are physically abused or seriously neglected not only may have a difficult time learn-

---

[43]Bruce A. Baldwin, *Beyond the Cornucopia Kids* (New York: Direction Dynamics, 1988); Andree Aelion Brooks, *Children of Fast-Track Parents* (New York: Viking Penguin, 1989).

[44]Lisa Jennings, "Child-Abuse Reports in 1989 Up 10% Over '88, State-by-State Survey Finds," *Education Week* (April 11, 1990), p. 8; Nicholas Lemann, "The Vogue of Childhood Misery," *The Atlantic Monthly* (March 1992), pp. 119–124.

[45]Millicent Lawton, "Child-Abuse Reports Up 31% in Five Years," *Education Week*, April 24, 1991, p. 8; "Accuracy of Child Abuse Statistics," *The Urban Institute Policy and Research Report* (Winter/Spring 1992), p. 25.

[46]Ralph H. Turner and James F. Short, Jr., eds., *Annual Review of Sociology* (Palo Alto, Calif.: Annual Reviews, 1985); Ellen Flax, "Health," *Education Week*, September 5, 1990, p. 14.

[47]Daniel Goleman, "Sad Legacy of Abuse: The Search for Remedies," *The New York Times*, January 24, 1989, pp. 19–33; "Battered Babies," *The Family in America New Research* (January 1990), p. 2.

ing but also may exhibit behavior that interferes with other students' learning. Although the actual incidence of serious child abuse may be significantly inflated in various national reports and statistics,[48] there is no doubt that abuse and neglect constitute serious problems for many students.[49] For this reason, professional organizations such as the Children's Television Workshop and the National Education Association have developed materials to help teachers deal with abused children and are working with other agencies to alleviate abuse and neglect.[50]

Materials to help educators

Homelessness and Runaways. Economic recession in the early 1980s, rising real estate values and prices, "deinstitutionalization" of mentally ill persons, and other factors have led to a significant increase in the homeless population in the United States. Today's homeless population is more diverse than in previous decades, as one observer describes:

More diverse population

> The homeless seem to be everywhere. Some are obviously homeless, like the bag-ladies, the shopping-cart people, the disheveled who huddle in doorways, and others who seem to wander aimlessly in streets and alleys. Those whose homelessness is apparent, however, and who look as though they fit the long-held stereotypes of bums, derelicts, winos, or the insane, are only the tip of the iceberg. There are also the invisible ones, many of whom are indistinguishable from the rest of us, and who "pass" during the day, roaming shopping malls or university hallways. At night they try to rest in rat- and roach-infested movie theaters, in lonely schoolyards, in their cars, on subways, or in the cold restrooms of public buildings. Most of the contemporary homeless are in fact difficult to detect because of their diversity and "invisibility."[51]

More families and children are homeless now than in the past. In fact, in some metropolitan areas, families with children may constitute one-third of the homeless population.[52] Several studies indicate that homeless children disproportionately suffer from child abuse and physical ill-health as well as relatively low school achievement and attendance.[53] The federal government, confronted

Homeless children

[48]Douglas J. Besharov, "Unfounded Allegations — A New Child Abuse Problem," *The Public Interest* (Spring 1986), pp. 18–33; Robert I. Emans, "Abuse in the Name of Protecting Children," *Phi Delta Kappan* (June 1987), pp. 740–742; Leslie Wayne, "Caring for Children, Men Find New Assumptions and Rules," *The New York Times,* August 5, 1990, pp. 1, 16; and Thomas Sowell, "The New Conformity," *Forbes,* January 20, 1992, pp. 86–87.

[49]"The Battered Child," *The New Republic,* March 20, 1989, pp. 7–8; Joseph F. Delfico, *Child Abuse Prevention* (Washington, D.C.: U.S. General Accounting Office, 1991); and "Teacher Alert," *Creative Classroom* (January/February 1992), p. 54.

[50]*How Schools Can Help Combat Child Abuse and Neglect* (Washington, D.C.: National Education Association, 1987); Lisa Feder-Feitel, "Teachers Against Child Abuse," *Creative Classroom* (January/February 1992), pp. 55–62.

[51]Richard H. Ropers, "The Rise of the New Urban Homeless," *Public Affairs Reports* (October–December 1985), p. 1. Also see Daniel J. Rothman, "The Rehabilitation of the Asylum," *The American Prospect* (Fall 1991), pp. 117–128, and Betsy Streisand, "Gimme Shelter," *U.S. News and World Report,* February 3, 1992, p. 17.

[52]Bryce J. Christensen, "On the Streets: Homeless in America," *The Family in America* (June 1990), pp. 1–8; "School Project for Homeless Children," *The Executive Educator* (February 1992), pp. A13–A15.

[53]Ellen L. Bassuk, "Homeless Families," *Scientific American* (December 1991), p. 66; Kirsten Goldberg, "Many Homeless Children Reported out of School" *Education Week,* March 25, 1987, p. 6.

with a severe budget deficit, has done relatively little to provide for homeless adults and children, and many local governments have been unwilling or unable to provide much assistance. However, many schools are striving to provide appropriate help by employing a full-time person to coordinate services with shelters for homeless families, sponsoring after-school programs, and hiring additional counselors.[54]

Runaways

A special category of homelessness applies to young people who flee from intolerable family situations and frequently wind up in temporary accommodations or on the streets in big cities. The numbers are difficult to estimate, but some observers believe that a million or more teenagers run away from their homes in any given year. Not surprisingly, runaways are at risk for drug abuse and AIDS infection, are very likely to be the victims or instigators of crime, and rarely complete high school.[55]

Children in Foster Care. Among the fallout associated with single-parent families, homelessness, child abuse, and the feminization of poverty has been a rapid increase in the number of children in foster-care homes and institutions. The U.S. House of Representatives Committee on Children, Youth, and Families has reported that more than one-third of a million children are now in foster

Inadequate system

care. Committee chairman George Miller has stated that inadequate financing and operation of the foster-care system means that "we are devastating" hundreds of thousands of children, who are "becoming candidates for long-term dependency" on social-welfare agencies.[56] Inasmuch as the achievement level of children in foster care is far below average even after they have been in care for several years, it is apparent that the guardians and teachers of these children are not providing them with adequate preparation to succeed in school and in adult careers.[57]

Assessment of Trends Related to the Family. The interrelated trends discussed above — more working mothers and single-parent families, declining fertility, the clamor for quality day care — have helped bring about a significant change in the structure and function of families in the United States. These

Diverse effects of family change

trends are associated, on the one hand, with improvements in women's educational and occupational attainment (described later in this chapter) and, on the other hand, with a decline in economic power among many families headed by

[54]John J. DiIulio, Jr., "There But for the Fortunate," *The New Republic* (June 24, 1991), pp. 27–35; Robert Pear, "Homeless Children Challenge Schools," *The New York Times,* September 9, 1991, p. A9; and Paul Taylor, "Recession-Pinched States Are Taking It Out on the Very Poor," *The Washington Post National Weekly Edition,* December 30, 1991–January 5, 1992, p. 32.

[55]Patricia Hersch, "Coming of Age on City Streets," *Psychology Today* (January 1987), pp. 28–37; Mark D. Janus et al., *Adolescent Runaways: Causes and Consequences* (New York: Lexington, 1987); and Frances X. Archambault et al., "Some Findings on the Nature of Physical Abuse Runaways Experience on the Streets" (Paper presented at the Annual Meeting of the American Educational Research Association, Chicago, April 1991).

[56]Associated Press, "Children Pour into Foster Care," *Newsday,* December 12, 1989, p. 15; Jane Gross, "Collapse of Inner-City Families Creates America's New Orphans," *The New York Times,* March 29, 1992, pp. 1, 20.

[57]Deborah L. Cohen, "Foster Youth Said to Get Little Help With Educational Deficits," *Education Week,* June 12, 1991, p. 8.

Getting to the Source

The Problems of Modern Families /
Urie Bronfenbrenner

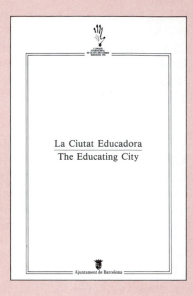

La Ciutat Educadora
The Educating City

Ajuntament de Barcelona

Problems in raising children and maintaining supportive family arrangements are apparent throughout the world. Urie Bronfenbrenner reviewed many of these problems as part of an address given at an international conference on "The Educative City." Bronfenbrenner is perhaps best known for his analysis of results of preschool programs for poverty children in the United States and his comparisons of child-raising institutions in the United States and the former Soviet Union.

It is not only the poor . . . for whom developmental processes are now at risk. In today's world, the well-educated and the well-to-do are no longer protected; in the past other highly vulnerable contexts have evolved that cut across the domains of class and culture. Recent studies reveal that a major disruptive factor in the lives of families and their children is the increasing instability, inconsistency, and hecticness of daily family life. This growing trend is found in both developed and developing countries, but has somewhat different origins in these two worlds. Yet the debilitating effect on child rearing processes and outcomes is much the same. I begin with an example from my own

society, since, in this respect, the United States is probably—and regrettably—a world leader.

In a world in which both parents usually have to work, often at a considerable distance from home, every family member, through the waking hours from morning till night, is "on the run." The need to coordinate conflicting demands of job and child care, often involving varied arrangements that shift from day to day, can produce a situation in which everyone has to be transported several times a day in different directions, usually at the same time—a state of affairs that prompted a foreign colleague to comment, "It seems to me that, in your country, most children are being brought up in moving vehicles."

Other factors contributing to the disruption of daily family life include long "commutes" to and from work; jobs that require one or the other parent to be away for extended periods of time; the frequent changes in employment; the associated moves for the whole family or those that leave the rest of the family behind waiting till the school term ends, or adequate housing can be found; and, last but far from least, the increasing number of divorces, remarriages, and re-divorces. (Incidentally, the most recent evidence suggests that the disruptive effects of remarriage on children may be even greater than those of divorce.)

What are the developmental consequences of family hecticness? Once again, the observed outcomes are educational impairment and behaviour problems, including long-term effects that now also encompass children of the well-educated and the well-to-do.

Questions

1. What is "family hecticness"? What changes in policies or customs might reduce its negative effects?

2. In what ways were children in earlier generations better off than they may be today?

3. Who or what is most responsible for overcoming contemporary problems that make it difficult to raise children?

Source: Urie Bronfenbrenner, "Cities Are for Families," in *La Cuitat Educadora* (Barcelona: Ajuntament de Barcelona, 1990), cover, pp. 545–546. Reprinted with permission of the author.

women with low incomes. Research does not conclusively establish that the overall results are permanently damaging to children; in some respects, maternal employment and smaller family size probably reflect some gains for children. However, some research indicates that maternal employment and life in a single-parent or divorced family have detrimental effects for many children.

Grounds for worry

Looked at historically, there probably are reasonable grounds for worrying about the effects of family change on the socialization and achievement of children and youth in the schools. Many historians believe that our system of universal education drew fundamental support from the development of the **nuclear family** (two parents living with their children) that grew to prominence in Western societies during the last two centuries. That period ended in the United States when the divorce rate began to skyrocket after World War II. Edward Shorter and other historians describe the nuclear family as being highly child centered, devoting many of its resources to preparing children for success in school and later in life.[58] With the decline of the nuclear family the tasks confronting educators may grow increasingly difficult.

"Postnuclear" family

David Popenoe has examined developments involving the family in Western societies, paying particular attention to trends in highly industrialized countries such as Sweden and the United States. Popenoe concluded that these trends are creating a "postnuclear" family in which emphasis is placed on "individualism" (individual self-fulfillment, pleasure, self-expression, and spontaneity), as contrasted with the child-centered "familism" of the nuclear family.[59] Adults, Popenoe further concluded, "no longer need children in their lives, at least not in economic terms. The problem is that children . . . still need adults . . . who are motivated to provide them with . . . an abundance of time, patience, and love."[60]

Many changes in the family appear to have had a destructive impact on the socialization of children and youth. Among the consequences that social scientists have been most worried about are the following:

1. Some research indicates that the "total contact time" between parents and children has declined as much as 40 percent during the past few decades.[61]

Agencies overloaded

2. Many social agencies established to help children and youth are too overloaded with problems to provide services effectively. William Zinsmeister has described how "many child-protection agencies are now doing little more than preventing murder, and sometimes they fail even to do that." For example, one Maryland social worker, when asked why a six-year-old had

[58]Edward Shorter, *The Making of the Modern Family* (New York: Basic Books, 1975). Also see Bryce Christensen, "Why the Family?" *The Family in America* (March 1987), pp. 1–8; Lawrence Stone, *Road to Divorce: England 1537–1987* (New York: Oxford University Press, 1991); and William Raspberry, "Rescuing Marriage Before It's Too Late," *The Washington Post National Weekly Edition*, January 20–26, 1992, p. 29.

[59]David Popenoe, "Family Decline in the Swedish Welfare State," *The Public Interest* (Winter 1991), pp. 65–77. Also see "The Law and the Individual," *The Family in America New Research* (January 1992), p. 3.

[60]David Popenoe, *Disturbing the Nest* (New York: Aldine de Gruyter, 1988), pp. 329–330. Also see David Hamburg, *Today's Children: Creating a Future for a Generation in Crisis* (New York: Times Books, 1992).

[61]Sylvia Ann Hewlett, *When the Bough Breaks: The Cost of Neglecting Our Children* (New York: Basic Books, 1991).

not been removed from a known crack house run by his mother, responded that there were "twenty similar cases on his desk, and that he didn't have time to go through the time-consuming process of taking a child from a parent" unless there was an immediate emergency.[62]

National Commission on Children

Responding to numerous concerns about the status of American children and families, the National Commission on Children, appointed by the president and Congress, recently issued a report calling for comprehensive (and expensive) improvements in health care, education, income security, and various other services. While recognizing that most American children are "healthy, happy, and secure," the commission acknowledged the many children "in jeopardy." Even children who are free from extreme misfortune, the report pointed out,

> confront circumstances and conditions that jeopardize their health and well-being. They too attend troubled schools and frequent dangerous streets. The adults in their lives are often equally hurried and distracted. . . . The combined effects are that too many children enter adulthood without the skills or motivation to contribute to society.[63]

The Peer Group

Functions of peer groups

Family relationships may constitute a child's first experience of group life, but peer-group interactions soon begin to make their powerful socializing effects felt. From play group to teenage clique, the peer group affords young people many significant learning experiences — how to interact with others, how to be accepted by others, and how to achieve status in a circle of friends.[64] Peers are equals in a way parents and their children or teachers and their students are not. A parent or a teacher sometimes can force young children to obey rules they neither understand nor like, but peers do not have formal authority to do this; thus the true meaning of exchange, cooperation, and equity can be learned more easily in the peer setting.[65] Peer groups increase in importance as the child grows up and reach maximum influence in adolescence, by which time they sometimes dictate much of a young person's behavior both in and out of school.[66]

Increasing importance

Several sources of information indicate that the peer group has grown more important in the socialization of children and youth. For example, Suzanne Boocock collected data on the daily activities of children in several communities and found that children spend much of their time with friends "fooling around" or

[62]William Zinsmeister, "Growing Up Scared," *The Atlantic Monthly* (June 1990), p. 67; Allan Wolfe, "The New American Dilemma," *The New Republic,* April 13, 1992, pp. 30–37.

[63]National Commission on Children, *Beyond Rhetoric: A New American Agenda for Children and Families* (Washington, D.C.: U.S. Government Printing Office, 1991), pp. xvii–xviii.

[64]Donna Eder and Stephen Parker, "The Cultural Production and Reproduction of Gender," *Sociology of Education* (July 1987), pp. 200–213; Steven R. Asher and John D. Coie, eds., *Peer Rejection in Children* (New York: Cambridge University Press, 1990).

[65]William A. Corsaro, "Routines in the Peer Culture of American and Italian Nursery School Children," *Sociology of Education* (January 1988), pp. 1–14.

[66]Thomas J. Berndt, "Relations of Friendships and Peer Acceptance to Adolescents' Self-Evaluations" (Paper presented at the Annual Meeting of the American Educational Research Association, Boston, April 1990).

watching television. She concluded that in comparison with earlier historical periods, relatively few children have strong linkages with the larger society. Other studies indicate a decline in the influence of family and church relative to the peer group, and many researchers believe that some children turn to their friends because they have little close contact with their parents.[67]

Importance of friends

Peer Culture and the School. Educators are particularly concerned with the workings and influence of the peer group and associated characteristics of student culture within the school. A landmark 1961 study by James Coleman examined the functioning of adolescent society in high schools and found that favored activities among students included eating with friends in school and "hanging around" with friends outside of school. Students gained the esteem of their peers by a combination of friendliness and popularity, athletic prowess, an attractive appearance and personality, or possession of valued skills and objects (cars, clothes, records). In general, the peer culture hindered rather than reinforced the school's academic goals. Reflecting on these results forty years later, Coleman expressed the opinion that peer "suppression of academic activity" still constitutes a negative force in many schools and classrooms.[68]

Suppression of academic activity

"A Study of Schooling"

More recent research continues to support the conclusion that **peer culture** constitutes a major socialization experience.[69] "A Study of Schooling," conducted by John Goodlad and his colleagues, collected data from 17,163 students and 1,350 teachers and made detailed observations in more than 1,000 classrooms in thirty-eight representative elementary and secondary schools. Junior and senior high-school students were asked to respond to the question, "What is the one best thing about this school?" As shown in Table 9.1, "my friends" was by far the most frequent response.

Popular students

Respondents also were asked to identify the types of students they perceived to be most popular. Only 14 percent of junior high respondents and 7 percent of senior high respondents selected "smart students"; instead, 60 percent of the junior high students and 79 percent of the senior high students selected either "good looking students" or "athletes."[70] Pondering these data, Goodlad concluded that "physical appearance, peer relationships, and games and sports" are not just concerns carried into the school; these phenomena "appear to prevail" there. Noting that Coleman and others reported similar findings in earlier decades, he further wondered "why we have taken so little practical account of them in schools."[71]

---

[67]Suzanne S. Boocock, *Students, Schools, and Educational Policy* (Cambridge, Mass.: Aspen Institute, 1976), p. 10; Francis A. Ianni, *The Search for Structure* (New York: Macmillan, 1989).

[68]James S. Coleman, *The Adolescent Society* (New York: Free Press, 1961); James S. Coleman, "Reflections on Schools and Adolescents," in Derek L. Burleson, ed., *Reflections* (Bloomington, Ind.: Phi Delta Kappa, 1991), p. 64.

[69]Kenneth A. Tye, *The Junior High School* (Lanham, Md.: University Press of America, 1985); Dale H. Schunk, "Peer Models and Children's Behavioral Change," *Review of Educational Research* (Summer 1987), pp. 149–174; Penelope Eckert, *Jocks and Burnouts* (New York: Teachers College Press, 1989); and Moshe Smilansky, *Friendship and Adolescence in Young Adulthood* (Gaithersburg, Md.: Psychological and Educational Publications, 1991).

[70]John I. Goodlad, *A Place Called School* (New York: McGraw-Hill, 1984), pp. 76–77.

[71]Ibid., p. 75.

Table 9.1
*Secondary Students' Responses to the Question, "What Is the **One** Best Thing About This School?"*

	My Friends	Sports	Good Student Attitudes	Nothing	Classes I'm Taking	Teachers	Other
Junior high respondents	37%	15%	10%	8%	7%	5%	18%
Senior high respondents	34	12	12	8	7	3	24

Source: Compiled from data in John I. Goodlad, *A Place Called School* (New York: McGraw-Hill, 1984), pp. 76–77.

Suggestions for teachers

The implications of these studies are quite evident: teachers should take account of the fact that peer relationships strongly determine what happens in the school and the classroom.[72] Specialists in cooperative learning make the following recommendations to teachers who want to help develop and reinforce positive peer relationships conducive to learning:[73]

Conduct activities that encourage students to learn cooperatively.

Make sure that cooperative tasks are doable.

Stress joint rather than individual work whenever possible.

Teach interpersonal and small-group skills.

Incorporate interesting things in cooperative activities.

Assign children responsibility for the welfare of their peers.

Encourage students to support and accept their classmates.

Provide experience with success in cooperative work.

Structure opportunities for prosocial activities.

Counteract peer pressure for antisocial behavior.

Encourage older children to interact with younger children.

Encourage students to exchange information with peers.

Participation in Extracurricular Activities.   Polls continually show that students consider their involvement with friends and classmates in extracurricular activities to be a highlight of their school experience. Many educators believe this participation is a positive force in the lives of many students.

Positive impacts

However, investigators have had difficulty determining whether participation in extracurricular activities really does benefit students in other aspects of their personal and academic development. The difficulty is in determining

---

[72]Thomas Lickona, "Four Strategies for Fostering Character Development in Children," *Phi Delta Kappan* (February 1988), pp. 419–423; Shirley B. Heath and Leslie Mangiola, *Children of Promise* (Washington, D.C.: National Educational Association, 1991); and Adele M. Brodkin and Steven R. Asher, "Why Some Kids Are Better At Making Friends," *Creative Classroom* (February 1992), pp. 15–16.

[73]David W. Johnson and Roger T. Johnson, *Cooperation and Competition* (Hillsdale, N.J.: Erlbaum, 1990); Susan S. Ellis and Susan F. Whalen, "Keys to Cooperative Learning," *Creative Classroom* (February 1992), pp. 34–37.

To overcome "peer suppression of academic activity," specialists in cooperative learning recommend that teachers help students develop positive peer relationships conducive to learning. (© Tony Velez/The Image Works)

Correlation between participation and grades

whether participation is a cause or an effect of such development. It is known, for example, that students who participate in many extracurricular activities generally have higher grades, other things being equal, than those who do not participate.[74] It may also be true, however, that students with higher grades are more likely to participate than are those with lower grades. Despite these interpretive difficulties, research does tend to support the conclusion that participation — especially in athletics, service, leadership activities, and music — fosters students' aspirations to higher educational and occupational attainment (for example, more years of school completed later). The research also suggests that these effects probably result from peer associations, contacts with teachers, and encouragement from parents.[75]

These conclusions regarding the effects of extracurricular activities may have great significance for educators. Participation outside the academic curriculum probably is more "manipulable" (alterable by the school) than most other factors related to educational outcomes. For example, the home environment of students is related to their aspirations, but it is rarely possible for educators to

Participation relatively alterable

---

[74]David A. Sweet, "Extracurricular Activity Participants Outperform Other Students," *OERI Bulletin* (September 1986), pp. 1–4; Anne Hafner et al., *A Profile of the American Eighth Grader* (Washington, D.C.: U.S. Department of Education, 1990).

[75]Luther B. Otto, "Extracurricular Activities," in H. Walberg, ed., *Improving Educational Standards and Productivity* (Berkeley, Calif.: McCutchan, 1982), pp. 217–227; Alyce Holland and Thomas Andre, "Participation in Extracurricular Activities in Secondary Schools," *Review of Educational Research* (Winter 1987), pp. 437–466; and B. Bradford Brown, Diane Kohrs, and Cary Lanzarro, "The Academic Costs and Consequences of Extracurricular Participation in High School" (Paper presented at the annual meeting of the American Educational Research Association, Chicago, April 1991).

change the home environments of students who have low or unrealistic aspirations. They can, however, encourage and facilitate student participation in extracurricular activities, and this may be one of the most effective actions teachers and administrators can take.

Causes of bullying

Research on Bullies. In recent years, research has begun to address the problems caused by "bullies" — antisocial youngsters who severely harass their peers either inside or outside the school. Some psychologists describe bullies as aggressive children and youth who appear to gain satisfaction from harming others physically or psychologically. Among the factors frequently cited as causing some children to behave this way are neglect and abuse in their homes, the influence of television, and a lack of social skills that leads to a cycle of aggressive behavior and dislike by peers.[76] Educators are concerned about not only the harm bullies do to others but also the tendency of bullies to exhibit criminal behavior as adults. Some approaches for modifying the behavior of bullies include behavioral contracts, instruction in peaceful conflict resolution, parental involvement in supervising behavior, and school behavioral guidelines.[77]

The Culture of the School

Education in school, compared with learning experiences in the family or peer-group context, is carried on in relatively formal ways. Group membership is not voluntary but is determined by age, aptitudes, and sometimes sex. Students are tested and evaluated; they are told when to sit, when to stand, how to walk through hallways, and so on. The rituals of school assemblies, athletic events, and graduation ceremonies — as well as the school insignia, songs, and cheers — all convey the culture of the school and socialize students.[78]

Aspects of school culture

What typical behavior patterns are exhibited by students and teachers in U.S. elementary and secondary schools? What student role behaviors are generally expected and demanded by teachers? A number of scholars have addressed these kinds of questions, and have described the cultural patterns that have prevailed in our schools during the twentieth century.

Student Roles and the Hidden Curriculum. Gita Kedar-Voivodas has examined the research on teacher expectations for student roles (that is, desired student behaviors and characteristics) within the social system of the elementary classroom. Despite what she found to be a "rather voluminous literature" on this topic, she was able to identify three main types of expected student role: the pupil role, the receptive learner role, and the active learner role.

Three major student roles

The *pupil role* is one in which teachers expect students to be "patient, docile, passive, orderly, conforming, obedient and acquiescent to rules and regulations,

[76]Deborah Franklin, "Charm School for Bullies," *Hippocrates* (May–June 1989), pp. 75–77.
[77]Leonard D. Eron et al., "Aggression and Its Correlates Over 22 Years," in D. H. Crowell, ed., *Childhood Aggression and Violence* (New York: Plenum, 1987); Michael Tony, "Putting an End to Schoolyard Terror," *Network for Public Schools* (September 1990), p. 3.
[78]Edgar Z. Friedenberg, *Coming of Age in America* (New York: Random House, 1965); Edward Wynne, *Growing Up Suburban* (Austin: University of Texas Press, 1977); and Susan Moore Johnson, *Teachers at Work* (New York: Basic Books, 1990).

receptive to and respectful to authority, easily controllable, and socially adept."[79] The *receptive learner role* requires students to be "motivated, task-oriented, . . . good achievers, and as such, receptive to the institutional demands of the academic curriculum."[80] This role also requires that students work independently and efficiently despite distractions and adequately perform homework and class assignments. In the *active learner role*, according to Kedar-Voivodas, students go "beyond the established academic curriculum both in terms of the content to be mastered and in the processes" of learning; traits of the active learner include "curiosity, active probing and exploring, challenging authority, an independent and questioning mind, an insistence on explanations."[81] She noted that many educational philosophers, John Dewey and Maria Montessori among them, have claimed that the active learner role is a desired outcome of the educational enterprise.

Kedar-Voivodas also found, however, that students exemplifying the active learner role sometimes are rejected by teachers, despite the presumed desirability of curiosity, exploration, and independent questioning. Citing several studies, she concluded that many teachers apparently are negative about children who are active, independent, and assertive.[82] Kedar-Voivodas discussed the implications of these findings in terms of the difference between the school's "academic" curriculum, which demands successful mastery of cognitive material, and its "hidden" curriculum, which demands "institutional conformity."[83]

Hidden curriculum

The **hidden curriculum** is what students learn, other than academic content, from what they do or are expected to do in school. In addition to teaching children to conform passively in the classroom, the hidden curriculum may be preparing students with economic disadvantages to be docile workers later in life. It can communicate negative racial and sexual stereotypes through material included in (or omitted from) textbooks. By putting too much emphasis on the competition for grades, the hidden curriculum may also teach students that "beating the system" is more important than anything else.[84]

Culture of the Classroom. Philip Jackson examined previous research and observed classroom processes in elementary schools. He reported that there is a "constancy" in elementary schools, which he described as follows:

Classroom routines

> The daily schedule . . . is commonly divided into definite periods during which specific subjects are to be studied or specific activities engaged in. . . . Despite the diversity of subject matter content, the identifiable forms of classroom activity are not great in number. The labels: "seatwork," "group discussion," "teacher demonstration," and "question-and-answer period" . . . are sufficient to categorize most of the things that happen. . . . These major activities are performed according to rather

---

[79]Gita Kedar-Voivodas, "The Impact of Elementary Children's School Roles and Sex Roles on Teacher Attitudes: An Interactional Analysis," *Review of Educational Research* (Fall 1983), p. 417. Also see Jeremy D. Finn and Deborah Cox, "Participation and Withdrawal Among Fourth-Grade Pupils," *American Educational Research Journal* (Spring 1992), pp. 141–162.

[80]Kedar-Voivodas, "The Impact of Elementary Children's School Roles and Sex Roles," p. 417.

[81]Ibid., p. 418.

[82]Ibid., p. 428.

[83]Ibid., p. 418.

[84]William Bigelow, "Inside the Classroom: Social Vision and Critical Pedagogy," *Teachers College Record* (Spring 1990), pp. 437–448.

well-defined rules . . . [such as] no loud talking during seatwork . . . [and] raise your hand if you have a question. . . . [Throughout the day the teacher serves as a] combination traffic cop, judge, supply sergeant, and time-keeper . . . [in] a place where things often happen not because students want them to, but because it is time for them to occur.[85]

Emphasis on orderliness

Jackson's portrayal of elementary classrooms provides a detailed picture of how rules and regulations help make up the culture of the school. The "rules of order that characterize most elementary school classrooms," he concluded, focus on prevention of disturbances.[86] Thus, the prevailing socialization pattern in the culture of the school and classroom is one that places greatest emphasis on what Kedar-Voivodas described as the obedient pupil role.[87]

Typical patterns

Other studies have reached essentially the same conclusion as did Jackson. For example, "A Study of Schooling" conducted by John Goodlad and his colleagues described the following general patterns, which appeared so widespread that Goodlad referred to them as constituting an "extraordinary sameness of instructional patterns" typical of the varied schools and grade levels in the study.[88]

1. The "dominant pattern of classroom organization is a group" that the teacher treats as a whole. This pattern seems to arise from the need to "maintain orderly relationships among from 20 to 30 or more persons in a relatively small space." Socialization into this pattern is "rather thoroughly achieved" by the end of the primary grades.

Enthusiasm controlled

2. "Enthusiasm and joy and anger are kept under control." As a result, the general emotional tone is "flat," or "neutral."

3. Most student work involves "listening to teachers, writing answers to questions, and taking tests and quizzes," in all subjects at all grade levels. Students rarely learn from one another. Little use is made of audiovisual equipment, guest lecturers, or field trips. Except in physical education, vocational education, and the arts, there is little "hands-on activity." Textbooks and workbooks generally constitute the "media of instruction."

4. These patterns become increasingly rigid and predominant as students proceed through the grades.

Emphasis on information

5. Instruction seldom goes beyond "mere possession of information" to emphasize "the ability to think rationally, the ability to use, evaluate, and accumulate knowledge . . . [or arousal] of students' curiosity." This is true even in science and the social studies, subjects that should, in many people's opinion, emphasize such themes.

Summarizing the overall results of "A Study of Schooling," Goodlad wrote: "Students listened; they responded when called on to do so; they read short

---

[85]Philip W. Jackson, *Life in Classrooms* (New York: Holt, 1968), pp. 8–9, 13. Also see Philip W. Jackson, *The Practice of Teaching* (New York: Teachers College Press, Columbia University, 1986), and Daniel W. Rossides, *Social Stratification* (Englewood Cliffs, N.J.: Prentice-Hall, 1990).

[86]Jackson, *Life in Classrooms*, pp. 104, 33.

[87]Also see Donald J. Willower and William L. Boyd, *Willard Waller on Education and Schools* (Berkeley, Calif.: McCutchan, 1989), and Reba N. Page, "Cultures and Curricula," *Educational Foundations* (Winter 1990), pp. 49–76.

[88]Goodlad, *A Place Called School*, pp. 123–124, 236, 246.

Passive learning

sections of textbooks or chose from among alternative responses in quizzes. . . . [But] they rarely planned or initiated anything, read or wrote anything of some length, or created their own products. And they scarcely ever speculated on meanings."[89]

As we discuss elsewhere in this book, such systematic emphasis on passive learning by rote is in opposition to much research on productive learning, to contemporary ideas on what education should accomplish, and to educational goals stressed in preservice and in-service teacher education. Why, then, do so many classrooms so often function in a way that seems incompatible with many educators' views of desirable practice? This exceedingly important question needs careful consideration if change is to be brought about in elementary and secondary schools.[90] Philip Jackson and other observers of classroom life have

Regularities of schooling

tried to explain why the "regularities" of schooling persist despite myriad proposals and recommendations for encouraging more active learning in the classroom.[91] Some of the major reasons for the persistence of these patterns follow.

1. *Institutional requirements to maintain order.* As Jackson emphasizes, a multitude of routines are devised to govern the interactions between twenty or thirty students and a teacher. Jackson, John Goodlad, and other observers use terms

Institutional realities

such as "institutional realities" and classroom "organizational dynamics" to describe the forces that result in an emphasis on passive learning in accordance with institutional rules and regulations.[92]

2. *Student preferences for passive learning.* The degree to which many students resist engagement in active learning should not be underestimated. Walter Doyle has summarized some of the dynamics behind this type of reaction in a paper analyzing academic work in elementary and secondary schools:

Restricting output

> Students restrict the amount of output they give to a teacher to minimize the risk of exposing a mistake. In addition, restricted output can elicit assistance from others in a classroom . . . [as in a] case in which first-grade pupils hesitated in giving answers until either the teacher or another student answered for them. . . . [As one older student said] "Yeah, I hardly do nothing. All you gotta do is act dumb and Mr. Y will tell you the right answer. You just gotta wait, you know, and he'll tell you."[93]

3. *Accommodations, bargains, and compromises between students and teachers.* Institutional constraints on teachers and students frequently interact with stu-

---

[89]John I. Goodlad, "A Study of Schooling: Some Findings and Hypotheses," *Phi Delta Kappan* (March 1983), p. 468. Also see Ana Maria Villegas, *Culturally Responsive Teaching* (Princeton, N.J.: Educational Testing Service, 1991).

[90]Larry Cuban, "A Fundamental Puzzle of School Reform," *Phi Delta Kappan* (January 1988), pp. 341–344; Linda Darling-Hammond and Ann Lieberman, "The Shortcomings of Standardized Tests," *The Chronicle of Higher Education,* January 29, 1992, pp. B1–B2.

[91]Also see William A. Reid, "Institutions and Practices," *Educational Researcher* (November 1987), pp. 10–15, and Judith W. Little, "The Persistence of Privacy," *Teachers College Record* (Summer 1990), pp. 509–536.

[92]Goodlad, "A Study of Schooling," pp. 469–470; Barbara B. Tye, "The Deep Structure of Schooling," *Phi Delta Kappan* (November 1987), pp. 281–284; and Mary Haywood Metz, "How Social Class Differences Shape Teachers' Work," in Milbrey W. McLaughlin, Joan E. Talbert, and Nina Bascia, eds., *The Contexts of Teaching in Secondary Schools* (New York: Teachers College Press, 1990), pp. 40–110.

[93]Walter Doyle, "Academic Work," *Review of Educational Research* (Summer 1983), pp. 184–185. Also see Walter Doyle, "Classroom Knowledge as a Foundation for Teaching," *Teachers College Record* (Spring 1990), pp. 347–360, and Martin Haberman, "The Pedagogy of Poverty Versus Good Teaching," *Phi Delta Kappan* (December 1991), pp. 290–294.

Getting to the Source ──◄●►──

Authority and Subversion / Willard Waller

THE SOCIOLOGY OF
TEACHING

BY
WILLARD WALLER, Ph.D.

NEW YORK
RUSSELL & RUSSELL

Willard Waller (1899–1946) is remembered mostly for essays examining the balance of freedom and order in the classroom. Published originally in 1932, his Sociology of Teaching *was an influential work*

that helped create a new field of study—the sociology of education. Waller believed it desirable to emphasize active participation and creativity in the learning process, but he was pessimistic about the prospects for doing this. In his view, the culture of classrooms and schools tends to encourage teacher domination that in turn produces alienation among students.

The teacher-pupil relationship is a form of institutionalized dominance and subordination. Teacher and pupil confront each other in the school with an original conflict of desires, and however much that conflict may be reduced in amount, or however much it may be hidden, it still remains. The teacher represents the adult group, ever the enemy of the spontaneous life of groups of children. The teacher represents the formal curriculum, and his interest is in imposing that curriculum upon the children in the form of tasks; pupils are much more interested in life in their own world than in the desiccated bits of adult life which teachers have to offer. The teacher represents the established social order in the school, and his interest is in maintaining that order, whereas pupils have only a negative interest in that feudal superstructure. Teacher and pupil confront each other with attitudes from which the underlying hostility can never be altogether removed. Pupils are the ma-

Treaties between students and teachers

dents' preference for passive learning and with other forces to produce low-level *accommodations* or *bargains* through which teachers and students *compromise* on the establishment of minimal standards and nonchallenging education. The widespread existence of such "A, B, C's" has been documented in a number of major studies conducted in the 1980s.[94] Michael Sedlak and his colleagues, who studied these phenomena in several high schools, reported that many students "invest their time and energy outside the school in activities that reward them financially, offer them some semblance of adult responsibility, or treat them as valued consumers," while simultaneously "disengaging" themselves from academic opportunities. This disengagement helps to generate "a complex, tacit conspiracy to avoid rigorous, demanding academic inquiry."[95]

[94]For examples, see Theodore R. Sizer, *Horace's Compromise* (Boston: Houghton Mifflin, 1984); Arthur Powell, Eleanor Farrar, and David Cohen, *The Shopping Mall High School* (Boston: Houghton Mifflin, 1985); Robert I. Hampel, *The Last Little Citadel* (Boston: Houghton Mifflin, 1986); and Samuel G. Freedman, *Small Victories* (New York: Harper, 1990).
[95]Michael W. Sedlak et al., *Selling Students Short* (New York: Teachers College Press, 1986), pp.

terial in which teachers are supposed to produce re-sults. Pupils are human beings striving to realize themselves in their own spontaneous manner, striving to product their own results in their own way. Each of these hostile parties stands in the way of the other; in so far as the aims of either are realized, it is at the sacrifice of the aims of the other.

Authority is on the side of the teacher. The teacher nearly always wins. In fact, he must win, or he cannot remain a teacher. Children, after all, are usually docile, and they certainly are defenceless against the machinery with which the adult world is able to enforce its decisions; the result of the battle is foreordained. Conflict between teachers and students therefore passes to the second level. All the externals of conflict and of authority having been settled, the matter chiefly at issue is the meaning of those externals. Whatever the rules that the teacher lays down, the tendency of the pupils is to empty them of meaning. By mechanization of conformity, by "laughing off" the teacher or hating him out of all existence as a person, by taking refuge in self-initiated activities that are always just beyond the teacher's reach, students attempt to neutralize teacher control. The teacher, however, is striving to read meaning into the rules and regulations, to make standards really standards, to force students really to conform.

This is a battle which is not unequal. The power of the teacher to pass rules is not limited, but his power to enforce rules is, and so is his power to control attitudes toward rules.

Questions

1. Are students today more or less interested than their counterparts sixty years ago in "life in their own world," as contrasted with "desiccated bits of adult life" offered by teachers?

2. Is it still true that children "are usually docile" and are "defenceless against the machinery with which the adult world is able to enforce its decisions"? Has anything happened that might suggest a modification in this observation?

3. Have you ever participated in an activity undertaken to "neutralize teacher control"? What will you do if your own students some day initiate similar activities?

Source: **Willard Waller,** *The Sociology of Teaching* (New York: Russell & Russell, 1961), cover, pp. 195–196. Copyright © by Russell & Russell. Reprinted by permission of John Wiley & Sons.

Difficulties in helping students

4. *Teachers' allocation of attention.* Many teachers feel compelled to give the largest share of their time and attention to a limited number of students. In some cases, these will be the slowest students — whomever the teacher perceives as most in need of his or her help. In many other cases, however, attention goes primarily to the brightest students, who frequently are perceived to benefit the most from extra attention. This attitude is particularly prevalent if there are so many "slow" students that the task of helping all of them seems virtually impossible.

Helen Gouldner and her colleagues found these latter dynamics to be present in their study of an innner-city elementary school enrolling a large proportion of students from low-income home environments that did not prepare them to function well in the classroom. The few students who were well prepared (and who generally were from families with relatively high status in the all-

13, 2–5. Also see Walter Doyle, "Classroom Tasks," in Michael S. Knapp and Patrick W. Shields, eds., *Better Schooling for the Children of Poverty* (Berkeley, Calif.: McCutchan, 1991), pp. 235–256, and Dennis Sparks, "A 'Friendly Conversation' with Ted Sizer," *Journal of Staff Development* (Winter 1991), pp. 42–46.

*Pets, nobodies,
and troublemakers*

black, predominantly working-class school studied) were the "pets" — teachers helped them throughout their school careers. The largest group (the "nobodies") consisted of students who received relatively little teacher attention and generally were neither disruptive nor particularly successful. The remaining students, a small group of "troublemakers," were unable or unwilling to conform to the routine demands of the classroom.[96] These patterns were well in line with the school's "sorting and selecting" function because the teachers, most of whom were African American, could feel they were promoting success for at least some black students in a difficult learning environment.[97]

5. *Lack of practical knowledge on how to improve instruction.* Until recently, relatively little was known about how to change instruction so as to promote more active, independent learning.[98] Educators also knew relatively little about how to carry on the process of change in the schools. It is true that many thousands of studies have been conducted on such varied topics as homogeneous grouping (designed in part to meet individual differences), methods of teaching subject matter, and use of television and other technology. Unfortunately, the research frequently indicated that no particular approach was better than any other, that a suggested approach failed as often or more often than it worked, and that innovations proposed to improve learning did not seem to make much difference. These results are not surprising inasmuch as new or different approaches for improving instruction typically are poorly implemented and seldom involve adequate teacher training, leadership, and other resources.[99]

*Innovative methods
usually have not succeeded*

Given this situation, it has been difficult for educators to move successfully away from traditional practices that appear to be antithetical to productive learning of higher-order skills. About all that a critic of traditional practice could do was describe and bewail negative learning environments found in the schools and plead with teachers to individualize instruction, provide for more active learning, and concentrate on improving students' thinking skills. Limited largely to this kind of rhetorical pep talk, criticisms frequently were perceived as personal attacks from people who did not "know" what teaching is like. (See subsequent chapters, especially Chapter 16, for recent approaches suggested for improving instruction in thinking skills.)

Realities in society

6. *Requirements that students learn to conform.* Underlying institutional forces in the school that impel teachers to emphasize passive learning are the realities that require children and youth to learn to function within other social institutions outside the school. Since most people in contemporary society must be able to cope with large institutions that have been organized to carry out economic, political, and social functions, children must be socialized to follow rou-

---

[96]Helen Gouldner, *Teachers' Pets, Troublemakers, and Nobodies* (Westport, Conn.: Greenwood, 1978), pp. 133–134.

[97]This self-fulfilling prophecy and the way it operated at the school studied by Gouldner and her colleagues are described at greater length in Ray C. Rist, *The Urban School: A Factory for Failure* (Cambridge, Mass.: MIT Press, 1973).

[98]Beau F. Jones and Lorna Idol, eds., *Dimensions of Thinking and Cognitive Instruction* (Hillsdale, N.J.: Erlbaum, 1990); Daniel U. Levine and Allan C. Ornstein, "Implications for Secondary Schools of International and NAEP Achievement Analyses," *NASSP Bulletin* (1993, in press).

[99]Stanley Pogrow, "Good Statistics from Bad Programs Tell Little," *Educational Leadership* (October 1991), p. 93; Stanley Pogrow, "Armchair Reformers," *Hotstuff* (March 1992), p. 4.

tines and regulations that make organized activity possible. Philip Jackson has summarized this part of the school's socialization mission as follows:

> It is expected that children will adapt to the teacher's authority by becoming "good workers" and "model students." . . . Most students learn to look and listen when told to and to keep their private fantasies in check. . . . Moreover, this skill . . . is doubly important because the student will be called upon [to use it later]. . . . The transition from classroom to factory or office is made easily by those who have developed "good work habits" in their early years.[100]

Demands on teachers

7. *Teacher overload.* It is difficult for teachers to provide active, meaningful learning experiences when they must cope with the demands of large classes and class loads, a variety of duties and tasks outside their classrooms, pressures to "cover" a very wide range of material and skills, and other responsibilities of elementary and secondary teaching.[101] Many of these demands have been described in detail by Stuart Palonsky, a college professor who obtained a two-year position teaching in a local high school. Palonsky summarized the job of the high-school teacher as typically requiring the production of 900 "shows" (classes) a year.[102] In sections titled "A Difficult, Demanding Job" and "Feeling Unsupported and Vulnerable," Palonsky pointed out that it is hard for teachers to provide students with individual attention or to work with other teachers to improve instruction while interacting frequently with multitudes of students and carrying out many other responsibilities assigned by administrators. As we document elsewhere in this book, there is growing recognition of the heavy burdens teachers characteristically experience in elementary and secondary schools, and many reformers are working to substantially reduce teacher loads and assignments.

Institutional constraints

Many additional reasons could be elaborated to explain why instructional patterns in the classroom have been relatively unaffected by contemporary learning theory, but most of them in some way implicate institutional constraints that favor passive, rote learning and the difficulties inherent in implementing different approaches in the face of these constraints.[103] To provide students with sufficient assistance to ensure active mastery of progressively more difficult skills, for example, requires profound change both in institutional realities and in the fundamental cultural patterns of the traditional school. Changes of this magnitude require more than stressful adaptations on the part of teachers and students; organizational and pedagogical innovations must also occur to make change possible. Several recent efforts to introduce such innovations, sometimes with considerable success, will be described in Chapter 16.

---

[100]Jackson, *Life in Classrooms,* p. 32.

[101]Linda M. McNeil, *Contradictions of Control* (New York: Routledge and Kegan Paul, 1986); Thomas B. Corcoran, "Schoolwork," in Milbrey W. McLaughlin, Joan E. Talbert, and Nina Bascia, eds., *The Contexts of Teaching in Secondary Schools* (New York: Teachers College Press, 1990), pp. 142–166; and Lee Sherman Caudell, "The Jobs of Teaching," *The Northwest Teacher* (January 1992), pp. T3–T4.

[102]Stuart B. Palonsky, *900 Shows a Year* (New York: Random House, 1986). Also see Edward Pauly, *The Classroom Crucible* (New York: Basic Books, 1991).

[103]Other frequently cited reasons include the tendency for teachers to teach the way they were taught, and lack of adequate preservice and in-service training.

*Passive learning most
prevalent in
working-class schools*

Before concluding this discussion, we should mention that research indicates that passive, rote learning is more likely to be systematically emphasized in schools with low-achieving, working-class students than in schools with high-achieving, middle-class students. To study this topic, Jean Anyon examined five elementary schools that differed markedly in social class.[104] Anyon found that instruction in the two predominantly working-class schools in her sample emphasized mostly mechanical skills such as punctuation and capitalization. In contrast, instruction in the mixed-status school emphasized following directions to figure out the right answers; instruction in the "affluent professional" school emphasized working independently to "express and apply ideas and concepts"; and instruction in the predominantly middle-class school emphasized development of analytical and conceptual skills.

Positive outcomes

Since much of this section has focused on negative aspects of school culture, we should emphasize that many positive statements can be made about elementary and secondary schools in the United States. Most schools provide an orderly learning environment, and most students learn to read and compute at a level required to function in our society. The large majority of students receive a high-school diploma and proceed to some form of postsecondary education. Successful aspects of the U.S. system of education are described in Chapters 10 and 16 and elsewhere in this book.

Television and Other Media

The "first curriculum"

Some social scientists refer to television as the "first curriculum" because it appears to be affecting the way children develop learning skills and orient themselves toward the acquisition of knowledge and understanding.[105] According to this viewpoint, television's curriculum is designed largely to maintain interest; the school's curriculum must accomplish other purposes, such as moral development and mastery of abstract thinking skills that may not be very interesting to children.[106] Because watching television requires little of the viewer in the way of effort and skills, educators face a formidable challenge in maintaining students' interest and motivation in schoolwork. This task is particularly daunting because many children spend more time watching television than they do in school; as shown in Figure 9.1, the average eighth grader spends nearly three times as much time viewing television as doing homework and reading outside school.[107]

---

[104]Jean Anyon, "Social Class and the Hidden Curriculum of Work," *Journal of Education* (Winter 1980), pp. 67–92, reprinted in Gerald Handel, ed.; *Childhood Socialization* (New York: Aldine de Gruyter, 1990). Also see Marshall S. Smith and Jennifer R. O'Day, "Educational Equality: 1956 and Now," in D. A. Verstesen and J. G. Ward, eds., *Spheres of Justice in Education* (New York: HarperCollins, 1990), pp. 53–100.

[105]Neil Postman, *Teaching as a Conserving Activity* (New York: Delacorte, 1979); Carolyn A. Stroman, "Television's Role in the Socialization of African American Children and Adolescents," *Journal of Negro Education* (Summer 1991), pp. 314–326.

[106]Jane M. Healy, "Why Sesame Street Is 'Bad News for Reading,'" *Education Week*, September 19, 1990, pp. 32, 26.

[107]Robert MacNeil, "Is Television Shortening Our Attention Span?" *National Forum* (Fall 1987), pp. 21–23; Jane M. Healy, "Chaos on Sesame Street," *American Educator* (Winter 1990), pp. 22–27, 39.

Figure 9.1

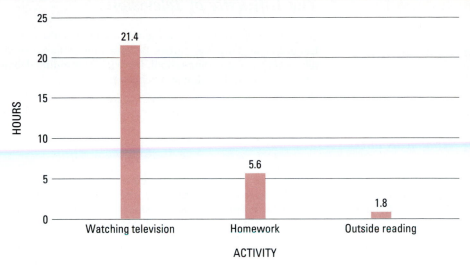

Average Hours per Week the Typical Eighth Grader Spends on Homework, Reading Outside School, and Watching Television

Source: Anne Hafner, Steven Ingels, Barbara Schneider, and David Stevenson, *A Profile of the American Eighth Grader: NELS: 88 Students Descriptive Summary* (Washington, D.C.: U.S. Department of Education, 1990), p. 48.

Television and school achievement

Research on school achievement related to television viewing indicates that there is a relationship, but the nature of the relationship is not entirely clear. The studies have been limited primarily to reading achievement. Some studies suggest that viewing television may reduce students' reading activities, but this conclusion is not well documented. It is difficult to separate cases in which television "causes" reduced attention to reading activities from those in which low-performing students turn to television or other nonacademic activities for escape. In addition, studies of viewing have found that although watching television more than a few hours a day is associated with low achievement in reading, mathematics, and writing across all social-class groups, television viewing is positively associated with achievement for students low in social class, as long as they spend less than three or four hours a day in this manner.[108] But despite the absence of conclusive data, many educators are very concerned that watching television may lower achievement for large numbers of students.

General mass media effects

Apart from their possibly negative effects on school achievement, television and other mass media such as the movies and the music industry deeply influence the acculturation and socialization of children and youth. The mass media both stimulate and reflect fundamental changes in the attitudes and behaviors that prevail in our society, from recreation and career choices to sexual rela-

[108]*Survey of Sixth Grade School Achievement and Television Viewing Habits* (Sacramento: California State Department of Education, 1982); Karen DeWitt, "Low Scores Renew Debate on TV," *The New York Times*, August 28, 1991, p. B7.

Taking Issue ━●●━━━━━━━━━━━━━━━━━━━━━━━━━━━━━━━━━━

The Influence of Television

Television is a fixture in almost every home; its influence is so pervasive that it has been called another parent. Because most children spend more time watching television than attending school, there is a continuing debate about television's effect on student learning and behavior.

Question: Is television's influence on students generally a benefit to the teacher?

Arguments PRO

1 Television enriches the background knowledge of students so that they can understand much instruction more readily. By taking advantage of what students already have learned from TV, teachers can accelerate the presentation of subject matter.

2 In addition to providing useful information, television awakens interest in a wide range of topics. Drawing on the interests that television arouses, teachers can involve students more deeply in many parts of the curriculum.

3 Television assists teachers by making learning palatable at an early age. Programs such as "Sesame Street" and "Mister Rogers' Neighborhood" have increased student achievement in the early years by showing children that learning can be fun.

4 Television provides a catharsis for feelings of hostility and anger. By watching television dramas, children can work out potentially violent impulses that might otherwise be directed at classmates, parents, or teachers.

5 Television can provide a good socializing experience. Research has shown that programs like "Sesame Street" can increase cooperative behavior among children. Furthermore, many children's shows offer their viewers a welcome relief from the world of adults.

Arguments CON

1 Most often, the information students gain from television is a superficial collection of facts, not useful background knowledge. Moreover, TV may delude students into thinking that these scattered facts represent genuine understanding.

2 Although television may provoke a fleeting interest in a topic, it accustoms students to learning through passive impressions rather than thoughtful analysis. Thus, it creates mental habits that teachers must try to counteract.

3 Early exposure to "fun" learning often raises false expectations about school. The teacher cannot be as entertaining as Big Bird, nor can schoolwork be as effortless as watching Mister Rogers. The need to compete with such TV shows makes the teacher's job more difficult.

4 Research on modeling indicates that many children, confronted with a situation parallel to one they have seen on TV, respond with the same behavior used by the television characters. In other words, violent TV programs often encourage violent behavior.

5 For every "Sesame Street," there are dozens of TV programs that tend to alienate children from the values of the school and the wider society. For example, some programs reinforce negative peer attitudes toward social institutions; some present simplistic or distorted notions of right and wrong; and many encourage dangerous fantasies.

tionships and drug use.[109] Unfortunately, there are no conclusive data to determine just how much the media affect children and youth or whether overall effects are positive or negative (depending, of course, on what one values as positive or negative). For example, twenty-four-hour-a-day rock-music programming on cable television has been viewed both as a means to keep young people off the streets and as the beginning of the end of Western civilization.[110] Although most observers would agree on the vast influence of the mass media, data to assess their effects more precisely are very limited.[111]

*Aggressive
behavior promoted*

Many adults are particularly worried that television and other media may encourage aggressive or violent behavior.[112] The average child now witnesses more than 8,000 murders and about 100,000 other violent acts by the time he or she completes elementary school. Reviews of research have found that the effects of television on children's aggression are largely dependent on situational factors such as the child's degree of frustration or anger, similarities between the available target and the target in the television portrayal, potential consequences such as pain or punishment, and opportunity to perform an act of violence.[113] A committee of behavioral scientists has reviewed the research and concluded that "television violence is as strongly correlated with aggressive behavior as any other behavioral variable that has been measured." The American Academy of Pediatrics and the American Psychological Association also have concluded that repeated exposure to violence on TV promotes a tendency to engage in violent behavior.[114]

Positive aspects

It also is true, however, that television can be an important force for positive socialization.[115] This conclusion has been supported by research indicating that the program "Sesame Street" has helped both middle-class and working-class youth academically, and that children can become more cooperative and nurturant after viewing programs emphasizing these behaviors. Research also in-

[109]Leo N. Miletich, "Rock Me with a Steady Roll," *Reason* (March 1987), pp. 20–27; John Rockwell, "Why Rock Remains the Enemy," *The New York Times*, January 21, 1990, p. 24; and John Nordheimer, "How Do I Love Thee? First Let Me Worry," *The New York Times*, February 12, 1992, pp. B1, B7.

[110]Allan Bloom, *The Closing of the American Mind* (New York: Simon and Schuster, 1987); Edward Hoffman, "Pop Psychology and the Rise of Anti-Child Psychology," *The Family in America* (August 1991), pp. 1–10.

[111]Jon Pareles, "As the Volume Rises in the Labeling Debate, Distortion Rules," *The New York Times*, April 1, 1990, p. 32.

[112]Nancy Carlsson-Paige and Diane E. Levin, "Young Children and War Play," *Educational Leadership* (December 1987–January 1988), pp. 80–84; Mark Walsh, "Media," *Education Week* (February 7, 1990), p. 8; and Eugene Provenzo, *Video Kids* (Cambridge, Mass.: Harvard University Press, 1992).

[113]Aimee Dorr, *Television and Children* (Newbury Park, Calif.: Sage, 1986); Peter Plagens, "Violence in Our Culture," *Newsweek* (April 1991), pp. 41–52.

[114]U.S. Department of Health and Human Services, *Television and Human Behavior: Ten Years of Scientific Progress and Implications for the Eighties*, Vol. 1, Summary Report (Washington, D.C.: U.S. Government Printing Office, 1982), pp. 6, 38–39; Paul Simon, "Reducing Violence on Television," *Education Week*, October 4, 1989, p. 28; and *Big World, Small Screen* (Washington, D.C.: American Psychological Association, 1992).

[115]Dorr, *Television and Children*; Peter Hellman, "Street Smart," *New York*, November 23, 1987, pp. 48–53; Peggy Charen, "What's Missing in Children's TV," *World Monitor* (December 1990), pp. 28–34; and Fred D'Ignazio, "Why Should You Teach with TV?" *Instructor* (March 1992), pp. 40–42.

dicates that "Square One TV" can help elementary students improve in mathematics.[116]

Recognizing both the good and the damaging effects that the media can have on children and youth, many individuals and groups have been working to bring about improvements. The Parent-Teacher Association has made reform of television — particularly reduction in sex and violence during prime time — one of its major national goals, and organizations such as the National Citizens Committee for Broadcasting and Action for Children's Television have been established to collect information and lobby for change.[117] But the situation in recent years appears to have grown worse: "A typical afternoon of kidvid these days can be a mind-numbing march of cartoon superheroes like He-Man, Brave-Star and the Defenders of the Earth," and many programs insistently instruct children to demand another trip to the nearest toy store.[118] Critics classify some popular children's shows as little more than extended commercials.[119]

Reform of television

SEX ROLES AND SEX DIFFERENCES

Not only does society demand conformity to its fundamental values and norms; it also assigns specific roles to each of its members, expecting them to conform to certain established behavioral patterns. Socialization is particularly forceful regarding **sex roles** — that is, ideas about the ways boys and girls and men and women are "supposed" to act. Sex roles vary from culture to culture, but within a given culture they are rather well defined, and they are developed through an elaborate schedule of selective reinforcement. For example, a preschool boy may be ridiculed for playing with dolls, and young girls may be steered away from activities considered too physically rough. Robert Havighurst has summarized early development of sex roles as follows:

Sex roles vary with culture

> By age 3, there is a noticeable difference in behavior between boys and girls. Males show more initiative and are more active. Females are more dependent and are more nurturant. . . . [Research on toy preferences indicates] that five and six-year old children use [even] more sex-role stereotypes in explaining toy preferences. Thus, there is an increase of sex-stereotypes used by children as they grow older.[120]

---

[116]David A. England, *Television and Children* (Bloomington, Ind.: Phi Delta Kappa, 1984); Eleanor Blau, "Making Mathematics Come Alive," *The New York Times,* March 26, 1990, p. B3; and Peggy Charen, "Kidvid Doing Battle with G.I. Joe," *The New York Times,* January 26, 1992, p. H29.

[117]Richard Zoglin, "Zapping Back at Children's TV," *Time,* November 30, 1987, pp. 99–101; Edmund L. Andrews, "F.C.C. Adopts Limits on TV Ads Aimed at Children," *The New York Times,* April 10, 1991, p. C6.

[118]Zoglin, "Zapping Back at Children's TV," p. 99; Harry F. Waters, "Watch What Kids Watch," *Newsweek,* January 8, 1990, pp. 50–52.

[119]Bryce J. Christensen, "Sell Out: Advertising's Assault on the Family," *The Family in America* (February 1990), pp. 1–8; Nancy Carlsson-Paige and Diane E. Levin, "Saturday Morning Pushers," *Utne Reader* (January/February 1992), pp. 68–70.

[120]Robert J. Havighurst, "Sex Role Development," *Journal of Research and Development in Education* (Winter 1983), p. 61. Also see Gerard Duveen and Barbara Lloyd, *Social Representations and the Development of Knowledge* (New York: Cambridge University Press, 1990).

Problems Reflected in the Schools

Disadvantages for boys

When children go to school they discover it is dominated by traditional norms of politeness, cleanliness, and obedience. Teachers generally suppress fighting and aggressive behavior.[121] This can be a problem for boys because, as research indicates, on the average they are more aggressive than girls almost from the time they are born, which probably is related to hormone differences.[122] After reviewing research supporting the conclusion that teachers tend to reward passive behavior and discourage aggressiveness, some scholars have concluded that this practice probably helps account for boys' relatively high rates of failure and violation of school rules. Boys receive many more reprimands from teachers than do girls, and by the time students enter the secondary grades, boys greatly outnumber girls in remedial classes and in classes for the emotionally impaired.[123]

Disadvantages for girls

By way of contrast, the problems that girls experience in the educational system generally reflect their socialization for dependence rather than assertiveness. Until recently, most girls were not encouraged to prepare for or enter high-status occupations such as law or medicine or high-paying occupations requiring technical skills and training beyond high school. Instead they were expected to prepare for roles as wives and homemakers. The few occupations women were encouraged to consider, such as elementary teacher, social worker, and nurse, tended to have relatively low pay and low status. This type of socialization did not motivate girls to acquire skills that might contribute to later economic success. Furthermore, verbal skills of the kind in which girls tend to excel did not prepare them for success in mathematics and science. The result was that girls were excluded from many educational opportunities.[124]

Cooperative girls and competitive boys

The emphasis placed on dependency in socializing females meant that girls were expected to be cooperative and even docile. In contrast, boys were taught to be competitive and to exercise leadership in overcoming obstacles.[125] Socialization in the elementary school frequently is intended to make boys obedient and cooperative, but in high school the emphasis placed on athletics means that boys receive more opportunities to learn leadership and competitive skills that may be useful in later life. Girls traditionally have had relatively little encour-

[121]Ray H. Bixler, "Nature Versus Nurture: The Timeless Anachronism," *Merrill-Palmer Quarterly* (April 1980), pp. 153–159; Susan F. Chipman, "Far Too Sexy a Topic," *Educational Researcher* (April 1988), pp. 46–49.

[122]Diane McGuiness, "How Schools Discriminate Against Boys," *Human Nature* (February 1979), pp. 87–88. Also see Mellissa Keys and Margaret Nash, "Sex Role Stereotyping and Students at Risk" (Paper presented at the Annual Meeting of the American Educational Research Association, Chicago, April 1991).

[123]Kedar-Voivodas, "The Impact of Elementary Children's School Roles and Sex Roles"; Pamela Keating, "Striving for Sex Equality in Schools," in John I. Goodlad and Pamela Keating, eds., *Access to Knowledge* (New York: College Entrance Examination Board, 1990), pp. 91–106.

[124]Susan L. Gabriel and Isaiah Smithson, eds., *Gender in the Classroom* (Urbana: University of Illinois Press, 1990); Katrinka Moore, "Girls Boot Up," *Creative Classroom* (January/February 1992), pp. 42–43.

[125]Susan F. Klein, ed., *Handbook for Achieving Sex Equity Through Education,* 2nd ed. (Baltimore, Md.: Johns Hopkins University Press, 1990).

agement or opportunity to learn these skills, and those who did were perceived as violating "proper" norms for female behavior in American society.[126]

Elementary peer groups and gender roles

Raphaela Best studied the peer-group behavior of boys and girls, and found that peer groups in the schools also help teach a sex-role curriculum that communicates traditional expectations for boys and girls.[127] Best reported that boys' peer groups stress "canons" such as "Be First," "Be Strong," and "Don't Associate with a Sissy," whereas girls' peer groups place relatively more emphasis on having fun rather than winning and on cooperation rather than competition. Best also reported that as the students she studied grew older, they made some progress in overcoming stereotypes that limited the aspirations of girls and restricted the emotional growth of boys.

Sex Differences in Achievement and Ability

Reading and mathematics

Recent studies in the United States indicate that sex differences in achievement have been narrowing. For example, data on the reading performance of nine-, thirteen-, and seventeen-year-olds indicate that although females scored 3 or 4 percent higher than males in 1988, this gap was significantly smaller than in 1971. Conversely, among seventeen-year-olds, males scored slightly higher than females in higher-order mathematics achievement, but this difference was much smaller than it had been in 1973; among nine- and thirteen-year-olds, there was no meaningful difference in mathematics scores for females and males.[128] Research also indicates that female gains in mathematics probably are due in part to greater participation in math courses during the past few decades.[129]

Mathematics ability

Controversies concerning possible sex differences in ability frequently focus on the question of whether a larger proportion of males than females have unusually strong innate ability for higher-order mathematics or abstract thinking in general. Research on this topic indicates that there is more variability in ability among males than among females; males are more likely to be either very high or very low in ability. The greater number of males low in ability appears to be due at least partly to the fact that young boys are more vulnerable to childhood maladies than are girls.[130]

---

[126]Beverly Fagot, "Using Knowledge from Play Research to Expand Sex-Typing Options" (Paper presented at the Annual Meeting of the American Educational Research Association, Chicago, April 1991).

[127]Raphaela Best, *We've All Got Scars: What Boys and Girls Learn in Elementary School* (Bloomington: Indiana University Press, 1983). Also see Barrie Thorne, "Children and Gender: Construction of Differences," in Deborah L. Rhode, ed., *Theoretical Perspectives on Sexual Difference* (New Haven, Conn.: Yale University Press, 1990), pp. 100–113.

[128]John A. Dossey et al., *The Mathematics Report Card* (Princeton, N.J.: Educational Testing Service, 1988); Ina V. S. Mullis and Lynn B. Jenkins, *The Reading Report Card, 1984–88* (Princeton, N.J.: Educational Testing Service, 1989); and Paul E. Barton and Richard J. Coley, *Performance at the Top* (Princeton, N.J.: Educational Testing Service, 1991).

[129]Laura Horn, *Trends in High School Math and Science Course Taking* (Berkeley, Calif.: MPR Associates, 1990).

[130]E. E. Maccoby and C. N. Jacklin, *Psychology of Sex Differences* (Palo Alto, Calif.: Stanford University Press, 1974); Julian C. Stanley, "We Need to Know Why Women Falter in Math," *The Chronicle of Higher Education*, January 10, 1990, p. B4; and Boyce Rensberger, "The Fragile X Chromosome Marks the Spot," *The Washington Post National Weekly Edition*, December 30, 1991–January 5, 1992, p. 38.

Possible differences in brain functioning

Those who believe that ability differences between the sexes are present at birth point to differences that have been found in the brain functioning of boys and girls. Research indicates that for most people, the left hemisphere of the brain specializes in verbal tasks, whereas the right hemisphere specializes in nonverbal functions. Research also indicates, however, that among right-handed persons, females appear to handle spatial functions more with the left hemisphere (relative to males), whereas males have less hemispheric specialization in spatial functions. Females also have more right-hemispheric processing in verbal functions. Laboratory research also suggests that sex hormones play a part in influencing the growth and development of the brain.[131]

Differences are small

Other observers, however, argue that differences in experience and expectations account for most or all of the learning differences between boys and girls. For example, one observer who reviewed evidence on sex differences in ability concluded that "when one examines the limited amount of the cognitive differences between the sexes, one is struck by their inconsequential nature, at least in terms of any kind of evidence that would warrant advising boys and girls to pursue different courses or careers on the basis of sex differentials in ability."[132] Similar conclusions have been reached by researchers who analyzed the performance of boys and girls on the Iowa Tests of Basic Skills.[133]

Socialization aspects

Particular attention has been given in recent years to the possibility that the relatively poor performance of some women in math (and therefore in science and other fields dependent on math) is due to socialization practices that make them anxious and fearful about mathematical analysis.[134] A related line of argument is that women fear success in traditionally male activities and occupations because succeeding would violate sex stereotypes and thereby invite ridicule and create identity problems. Several reviews of research have concluded that although such considerations still depress achievement among females, the situation is complex, and few overall generalizations can be made concerning the degree to which various factors cause sex differences in ability and achievement.[135]

---

[131]Richard M. Restak, "The Other Difference Between Boys and Girls," *Educational Leadership* (December 1979), pp. 232–235; C. Sue Carter and William T. Greenough, "Sending the Right Sex Messages," *Psychology Today* (September 1979), p. 112; Doreen Kimura, "Male Brain, Female Brain: The Hidden Difference," *Psychology Monthly* (March 1988), pp. 77–82; Sandra Blakeslee, "Men's Test Scores Linked to Hormone," *The New York Times*, November 14, 1991, p. A1; and Denise Grady, "The Brains of Gay Men," *Discover* (January 1992), p. 29.

[132]Julia A. Sherman, "Sex-Related Cognitive Differences: A Summary of Theory and Evidence," *Integrateducation* (January–February 1978), p. 40. Also see Linsday A. Tartre, "Special Skills, Gender, and Mathematics," in Elizabeth Fennema and Gilah C. Leder, eds., *Mathematics and Gender* (New York: Teachers College Press, 1990).

[133]Elizabeth A. Witt, Stephen B. Dunbar, and H. D. Hoover, "A Multivariate Perspective on Sex Differences in Achievement" (Paper presented at the Annual Meeting of the American Educational Research Association, Chicago, April 1991).

[134]Shelia Tobias and Carol S. Weissbrod, "Anxiety and Mathematics: An Update," *Harvard Educational Review* (February 1980), pp. 63–70; Jacquelynne S. Eccles, "Gender-Roles and Women's Achievement," *Educational Researcher* (June–July 1986), pp. 15–19; and Susan Chira, "Bias Against Girls Is Found Rife in Schools, With Lasting Damage," *The New York Times*, February 12, 1992, pp. A1, B6.

[135]Elizabeth Fennema, "Overview of Sex-Related Differences in Mathematics," (Paper presented at the Annual Meeting of the American Educational Research Association, New York, March 1982); Lindsay Tartre and Elizabeth Fennema, "Mathematics Achievement and Gender" (Paper presented at the Annual Meeting of the American Educational Research Association, Chicago, April 1991); and Christine Gorman, "Sizing Up the Sexes," *Time*, January 20, 1992, pp. 42–51.

Only recently have girls been encouraged to prepare to enter high-status occupations such as law or medicine or high-paying occupations requiring technical skills and training beyond high school. (© Sven Martson/ Comstock)

Educational and Occupational Attainment of Women

Changing attitudes

Attitudes regarding sex roles have changed substantially in the United States since the 1960s. Women's attitudes in particular became much less traditional as they developed more favorable views toward equal home and work roles for both sexes.[136] Throughout most of U.S. history, women had completed fewer years of schooling than did men. This difference diminished, however, and by 1977 the average years of education completed for both men and women were 12.6. In 1979, females for the first time outnumbered males among college freshmen. In 1991, more than half of all bachelor's and master's degrees were awarded to women — up from less than 40 percent in 1962; and 38 percent of all doctoral degrees were earned by women, compared with 11 percent in 1962.[137]

Educational gains

Occupational gains

Related gains were registered in the occupational status of women. For example, in 1950 only 15 percent of accountants were female, compared to 50 percent in 1990; the comparable percentages for female lawyers were 4 percent in 1950 and 20 percent in 1990. Very large recent increases in the percentage of female students in medicine, business administration, and other professional fields should increase the number of women employed in high-status positions in the future. Affirmative action in employment and education (see Chapter 8),

---

[136]Cheryl Russel, "The New Homemakers," *American Demographics* (October 1985), pp. 23–27; Bickley Townsend and Kathleen O'Neil, "Women Get Mad," *American Demographics* (August 1990), pp. 26–32.

[137]"Fact File," *The Chronicle of Higher Education*, October 16, 1991, p. A20; *Projections of Education Statistics to 2002* (Washington, D.C.: U.S. Government Printing Office, 1992).

encouragement of girls to attend college and prepare for the professions, efforts to eliminate sexism from school curricula, and other actions to equalize opportunity are having an impact in the schools and the wider society.[138]

Much still to be accomplished

Nevertheless, much remains to be achieved, and improvements of various kinds should continue to occur. Despite recent gains, women still tend to be concentrated in low-paying, low-status occupations, and there is a higher proportion of female workers in clerical and service jobs now than in 1910. Although the number of female scientists and engineers with doctoral degrees more than doubled between 1973 and 1990, in the latter year they still constituted only 20 percent of the total. In 1991 the average female worker earned only 72 percent of the annual income of the average male. (This gap is substantially less when account is taken of experience and number of hours worked.) The increase in the educational and occupational attainment of women is associated with growth in the percentage of working mothers and single-parent families; as we saw earlier, these trends may have a negative impact on children and the schools, but they also signify greater equalization of opportunity and may serve to improve the social class and income of many families.[139]

Scholars associated with the Wellesley College Center for Research on Women and the American Association of University Women recently provided a comprehensive analysis of possibilities for improving equity for women. In a report that identifies the enhancement of educational opportunities for women as a means of addressing the feminization of poverty and the precarious U.S. economic situation, the authors offer such recommendations as:[140]

■ Provide increased teacher training dealing with gender issues.

■ More rigorously enforce civil rights laws.

■ Increase efforts to involve girls in math and science studies.

■ Attend more closely to gender equity in vocational education.

■ Eliminate bias in standardized tests, and reduce the role of these tests in college admissions.

■ Ensure a central role for women and girls in school reform efforts.

■ Improve educational programs dealing with health and sexuality.

■ Reduce sex stereotyping and increase the representation of females in instructional materials.

■ Protect the rights of pregnant girls and teenage parents.

■ Introduce "gender fair" multicultural curricula that accommodate differences in learning styles.

---

[138]Sara E. Rix, ed., *The American Woman, 1987–88* (New York: Norton, 1987); Sylvia Nasar, "Women's Gains Will Keep Coming," *U.S. News and World Report,* April 2, 1991, p. 45; and "Contrasting Wage Gaps by Gender and Race," *The Urban Institute Policy and Research Report* (Winter/Spring 1992), pp. 7–8.

[139]Gary S. Becker, "Working Women's Staunchest Allies: Supply and Demand," *Business Week,* December 2, 1991, p. 18; Millicent Lawton, "Schools' 'Glass Ceiling' Imperils Girls, Study Says," *Education Week,* February 12, 1992, pp. 1, 17.

[140]*How Schools Shortchange Women: The A.A.U.W. Report* (Washington, D.C.: American Association of University Women, 1992).

ADOLESCENT AND YOUTH PROBLEMS

In primitive and traditional cultures, the young are usually initiated into adult life after puberty. This initiation sometimes takes place through special rites and rituals designed to test and prove the young person's worthiness to assume adult roles. In such societies one is either a child or an adult; there is only a brief gap between the two — if there is any gap at all.

Separate stage of life

In modern technological societies the young are forced to postpone their adulthood for a period of time called adolescence or youth. A major reason for this is that modern society no longer has an economic need for young people in this age group, and an unfortunate result is that youth have become more and more isolated from the rest of society. In recent decades, this isolation has made many youth-centered problems — drug use and drinking, suicide, pregnancy, delinquency — more intense and has hampered efforts by the schools and other social institutions to prepare young people for adulthood.[141]

Drugs and Drinking

Decline in drug use

General usage of drugs and alcohol among youth has grown markedly over the past half-century. However, use of most drugs has declined significantly in recent years partly due to increased concern about health and to reduced peer pressure to use illicit substances.[142] Recent surveys on substance use and abuse among high-school seniors can be summarized as follows:[143]

Cigarettes. The percentage of high-school seniors who smoked cigarettes in the previous month declined from 39 percent in 1976 to 29 percent in 1990.

Marijuana. The percentage of high-school seniors who had used marijuana during the previous year declined from 54 percent in 1978 to 27 percent in 1990.

Tranquilizers. Annual use on a nonmedical basis declined from 11 percent in 1978 to less than 5 percent in 1990.

Heroin. Less than 2 percent of seniors had used heroin or other opiates within the previous month in 1990.

Cocaine. Annual use of cocaine increased from 7 percent in 1975 to 13 percent in 1985, but then declined to 6 percent in 1990. The percentage of seniors who reported they could obtain cocaine (including crack cocaine) fairly easily declined from 54 percent in 1989 to 42 percent in 1990.

Amphetamines. Less than 9 percent of seniors had used amphetamines without medical supervision in 1990.

Alcohol. Regular use of alcohol has remained fairly stable, with less than 5 percent of seniors reporting daily use in 1990. However, the percentage reporting "occasional binge drinking" (five or more drinks in a row at least

[141]James S. Coleman, "Families and Schools," *Educational Researcher* (August–September 1987), pp. 32–38; Aaron H. Esman, *Adolescence and Culture* (New York: Columbia University Press, 1990).

[142]"Drug Awareness Rises," *ISR Newsletter* (Spring, 1991), pp. 3–4; Jean Seligmann, "The New Age of Aquarius," *Newsweek*, February 3, 1992, pp. 66–67.

[143]Data are summarized largely from annual surveys conducted by the University of Michigan Institute for Survey Research.

once in the previous two weeks) declined from 40 percent in the mid-1980s to 32 percent in 1990. On the other hand, research indicates that use of alcohol has been increasing among students less than fifteen years old, that an alarming number of teenagers frequently drink alone when they are bored or upset, and that laws prohibiting sale of alcohol to minors are widely violated.[144]

Implications of drug use

Concern about young people's use of alcohol, marijuana, and other relatively mild drugs arises in part because it may reinforce or stimulate alienation from social institutions or otherwise impede the transition to adulthood. Although there is reason to believe that drug use as often follows from as causes negative outcomes such as low academic performance, rebelliousness, and criminal activity, many young people are using drugs and alcohol to escape from problems they encounter in preparing for life.[145] Contrary to much earlier opinion, some authorities now believe that mild drugs such as marijuana frequently are a steppingstone to stronger drugs such as cocaine and heroin.[146] Young people themselves believe that drugs and alcohol are a negative influence in their lives. The results of national surveys consistently have shown that most high-school students cited either drugs or alcohol as the "single worst influence" in their lives.[147] Recent decline in drug use has been encouraging, but usage rates among U.S. youth still are higher than in any other industrialized nation. Teenagers' use of hallucinogenic drugs increased substantially in 1990 and 1991, and widespread use of crack cocaine has been particularly worrisome.[148]

Suicide

Large increase in suicide rate

Educators have become more concerned about suicide among young people. The data indicate that the suicide rate among children and youth more than tripled between 1950 and 1990, and some surveys suggest that as many as one in ten school-age youth may attempt suicide.[149] Reasons for this increase appear

[144]Felicity Barringer, "With Teens and Alcohol, It's Just Say When," *The New York Times,* June 23, 1991, pp. E1, E4; Ellen Flax, "Teenage-Drinking Study Spurs Questions," *Education Week,* June 19, 1991, p. 13.

[145]National Institute on Drug Abuse, *Marijuana and Health* (Washington, D.C.: U.S. Government Printing Office, 1977); Michael J. Wargo et al., *Rural Drug Abuse* (Washington, D.C.: U.S. Government General Accounting Office, 1990).

[146]Carol J. Mills and Harvey I. Noyes, "Patterns and Correlates of Initial and Subsequent Drug Use Among Adolescents," *Journal of Consulting and Clinical Psychology* (April 1984), pp. 231–243; Lisa Feder-Feitel, "How to Talk About Substance Abuse," *Creative Classroom* (September 1991), pp. 107–115.

[147]"Today's Youth Edge Back to Tradition," *U.S. News & World Report,* April 9, 1984, p. 16; Joseph B. Treaster, "Cocaine Use on the Way Down Among U.S. Youths," *The New York Times,* January 15, 1991, pp. A1, A12.

[148]Joshua Fischman, "The Ups and Downs of Teen Drug Use," *Psychology Today* (February 1986), pp. 68–69; Richard Hawley, "The Bumpy Road to Drug-Free Schools," *Phi Delta Kappan* (December 1990), pp. 310–314; and Michael Isikoff, "What Was Down Came Back Up," *The Washington Post National Weekly Edition,* December 30, 1991–January 5, 1992, p. 33.

[149]Judy Folkenberg, "To Be or Not to Be: Prevention Legislation," *Psychology Today* (April 1984), p. 9; Millicent Lawton, "More Than a Third of Teens Surveyed Say They Have Contemplated Suicide," *Education Week,* April 10, 1991, p. 5; and "Demographics," *The Atlantic Monthly* (March 1992), p. 18.

to include a decline in religious values that inhibit suicide, failed relationships with peers, and pressures or despondency associated with divorce or other problems in the family.[150]

Deborah Strother has reviewed research on suicide among young people and discussed its implications for school personnel. Strother concluded her discussion by pointing out that educators should help their "school community become aware of changes in a student's level of functioning and involvement. Young people who are deeply troubled will show it, and observers who notice the symptoms can direct such young people to appropriate sources of help." Warning signs that can alert teachers to potentially suicidal behavior include the following: changes in eating and sleeping habits; withdrawal from friends, family, and regular activities; violent or rebellious behavior; running away; alcohol or drug abuse; unusual neglect of personal appearance; radical change in personality; persistent boredom; difficulty in concentrating; decline in the quality of schoolwork; emotion-related symptoms such as headaches and stomachaches; and inability to tolerate praise or rewards.[151]

Warning signs

Teenage Pregnancy

Although the number and rate of births among teenagers fell substantially during the 1970s and early 1980s due to availability of contraceptives, abortion, and other causes, the pregnancy rate per thousand women fifteen-to-nineteen years of age has increased substantially, and the percentage of out-of-wedlock births among teenagers has increased explosively from 15 percent in 1960 to nearly 75 percent in 1991.[152] Researchers who examined these trends have identified problems such as the following:[153]

Increase in out-of-wedlock birth percentage

Families headed by young mothers are seven times as likely as other families to live below the poverty line.

Teenage mothers are much less likely to receive prenatal care than are older mothers.

Billions of dollars are expended each year to support the children of teenage mothers.

Children of teenage mothers tend to have poor health and to perform poorly in school.

[150]Alina Tugend, "Suicide's 'Unanswerable Logic,'" *Education Week,* June 18, 1986, pp. 15–19; *Suicide* (Eugene, Ore.: ERIC Clearinghouse on Educational Management, 1991); and Colette Dowling, "Rescuing Your Child from Depression," *New York,* January 20, 1992, pp. 44–53.

[151]Deborah Strother, "Suicide Among the Young," *Phi Delta Kappan* (June 1986), p. 759. Also see Maxine Seibel and Joseph N. Murray, "Early Prevention of Teenage Suicide," *Educational Leadership* (March 1988), pp. 48–51, and Melissa Etlin, "How to Help a Suicidal Student," *NEA Today* (May/June 1990), p. 6.

[152]Stephen J. Caldas, "Understanding Teenage Pregnancy and Childbearing in the United States" (Paper presented at the Annual Meeting of the American Educational Research Association, Chicago, April 1991); Robert Pear, "Bigger Number of New Mothers Are Unmarried," *The New York Times,* December 4, 1991, p. A11; and E. J. Dionne, Jr., "Lies, Damned Lies and Politics," *The Washington Post National Weekly Edition,* February 3–9, 1992, pp. 23–24.

[153]Select Committee on Children, Youth, and Families, *Teen Pregnancy: What Is Being Done* (Washington, D.C.: U.S. Government Printing Office, 1986); Janet B. Hardy and Laurie S. Zabin, *Adolescent Pregnancy in an Urban Environment* (Washington, D.C.: Urban Institute Press, 1991); and "Wanting Children," *American Journal of Public Health* (March 1992), pp. 341–343.

Reasons for increase

Research indicates that teenage births constitute a substantially higher percentage of births in the United States than in other industrialized nations. Social scientists who have analyzed fertility data for the United States and other countries have concluded that the increase in out-of-wedlock births among teenagers has resulted from such interrelated factors as greater social acceptance of teenage sexuality and illegitimacy, earlier and more frequent sexual intercourse, decrease in "early" marriages, decline in community and parental influence over the young, and assumption by social agencies of responsibility for helping younger mothers.[154] Research also indicates that teenage pregnancy and birth rates are even higher among disadvantaged minority youth than they are for the youth population as a whole.[155]

Schools' responses

As teenage pregnancy rates have escalated, educators have become increasingly concerned with problems thereby created for young people and for society. Schools have responded by establishing school-based clinics and expanding courses focusing on sex education, health, personal development, and family life. Data on the effectiveness of clinics established in the 1970s and early 1980s generally were negative, but recent studies indicate that school-based clinics can be effective in preventing or alleviating problems associated with teenage pregnancy.[156] In addition, data on a project conducted by Girls, Inc. (formerly the Girls Clubs of America) indicate that a long-range approach that concentrates on providing girls with a combination of assertiveness training, health services, communications skills, personal counseling, and information about sexuality can substantially reduce the incidence of teenage pregnancies.[157]

Recommendations and controversies

The National Education Association has published a book describing pregnancy-prevention approaches and recommending that the schools further expand sex education, initiate antidropout programs for pregnant adolescents, and offer appropriate prenatal care and support services. The National Research Council has issued a major report recommending widespread distribution of inexpensive contraceptives, expansion of abortion services for teenagers, establishment of more school-based clinics, and greater emphasis on sex education and life-planning courses for younger students. The Education Commission of the States also has disseminated information nationally on ways to alleviate problems associated with teenage pregnancy.[158] Controversy over the school's role in

---

[154]Kingsley Davis, "A Theory of Teenage Pregnancy in the United States," in Catherine S. Chilman, ed., *Adolescent Pregnancy and Childbearing* (Washington, D.C.: U.S. Government Printing Office, 1980). Also see Philip J. Hilts, "Birth-Control Backlash," *The New York Times Magazine* (December 16, 1990), pp. 41, 55, 70–74, and Bryce J. Christensen, "Fewer Brides — More Illegitimate Babies," *The Family in America New Research* (March 1992), p. 4.

[155]Andrew Hacker, "American Apartheid," *The New York Review of Books,* December 3, 1987, pp. 26–33; Naomi Farber, "The Significance of Race and Class in Marital Decisions Among Unmarried Adolescent Mothers," *Social Problems* (February 1990), pp. 51–63; and Bryce J. Christensen, "More — And Less," *The Family in America New Research* (March 1992), pp. 3–4.

[156]Dean F. Miller, *The Case for School-Based Health Clinics* (Bloomington, Ind.: Phi Delta Kappa, 1990).

[157]Jane E. Brody, "Helping Teen-agers Avoid Pregnancy," *The New York Times,* October 2, 1991, p. A8.

[158]Nancy Compton, Mara Duncan, and Jack Hruksa, *Student Pregnancy* (Washington, D.C.: National Education Association, 1986); Panel on Adolescent Pregnancy and Childbearing, *Risking the Future: Adolescent Sexuality, Pregnancy, and Childbearing* (Washington, D.C.: National Research Council, 1986); and *Reducing Risks of Learning Impairment During Pregnancy and Infancy* (Denver, Colo.: Education Commission of the States, 1990).

dealing with teenage pregnancy has focused particularly on whether clinics should be operated inside or outside the schools and whether school-based clinics should provide services involving contraceptives and abortion.[159]

Delinquency and Violence

Long-term increase

Juvenile delinquency has increased in recent decades, paralleled by related increases in the size of the youth group, the influence of peer culture, the use of drugs and alcohol, and the growth of low-income neighborhoods in big cities. In 1988, young people aged eighteen to twenty-four accounted for 31 percent of all arrests although they made up only 11 percent of the population. Problems connected with violence and delinquency are particularly acute among young African American males, whose rate of death from homicide increased by more than two-thirds in the late 1980s and early 1990s. Even among young white males, however, homicide rates are more than twice as high as in any other industrialized country.[160]

Research on delinquency and violence among youth has supported a number of generalizations, among them the following:

Significant delinquency rates are found among youth of all social classes. However, violent delinquency is much more frequent among working-class than middle-class youth.[161]

Although a large proportion of crimes are committed by persons under twenty-five, most delinquents settle down to a productive adult life.[162]

Violent delinquency is in part a reflection of participation in a violent subculture.[163]

Violence and gangs

Increase in gangs has helped generate greater violence among youth in the past two decades.[164]

Delinquency is associated with unemployment. As Daniel Glaser has observed, "To combat youth crime is largely futile unless an effort is also made to assure legitimate employment for youths." From this point of view, de-

---

[159]Bill Montague, "Battles Waged over In-school Clinics," *Education Week,* June 11, 1986, pp. 4, 15; Michael Marriott, "As Students Come to Class Less Healthy, School Clinics Try to Offer More," *The New York Times,* January 30, 1991, p. B8.

[160]Edward Wynne and Marcia Hess, "Long-term Trends in Youth Conduct and Revival of Traditional Value Patterns," *Educational Evaluation and Policy Analysis* (Fall 1986), pp. 294–308; Joe Schwartz and Thomas Exter, "Crime Stoppers," *American Demographics* (November 1990), pp. 24–30; and Fox Butterfield, "U.S. Expands Its Lead in the Rate of Imprisonment," *The New York Times,* February 11, 1992, p. C18.

[161]James R. Wetzel, *American Youth: A Statistical Snapshot* (Washington, D.C.: William T. Grant Foundation, 1987); Mercer L. Sullivan, *Getting Paid* (Ithaca, N.Y.: Cornell University Press, 1990).

[162]Jonathan Rieder, "Adventure Capitalism," *The New Republic,* November 19, 1990, pp. 36–40; Christopher Jencks, *Rethinking Social Policy* (Cambridge, Mass.: Harvard University Press, 1992).

[163]Millicent Lawton, "Why Are Children Turning to Guns?" *Education Week,* November 6, 1991, pp. 1, 14–15.

[164]Joan Gaustad, "Gangs," *ERIC Digest Series* (Number EA 52, 1990), pp. 1–2; Jerome H. Skolnick, "Gangs in the Post-Industrial Ghetto," *The American Prospect* (Winter 1992), pp. 108–120.

linquency is a partial response to the restricted opportunity available to some young people in modern society.[165]

Family characteristics related to delinquency include lack of effective parental supervision and lack of family cohesiveness.[166]

Delinquency and violent crime rates for girls have been increasing much more rapidly than those for boys.[167]

Related to learning disabilities

Delinquency is related to learning disabilities and associated low levels of school performance.[168]

Perceived certainty of punishment is inversely related to delinquency.[169]

Crime and delinquency may reflect genetic dispositions, such as high aggressiveness, that culture channels into antisocial outlets.[170]

One of the strongest predictors of delinquency is influence of peers, but this influence interacts with the family, the school, the neighborhood, and other causal factors.[171]

Youth Culture Problems Reflected in the Schools

Drugs and antisocial behavior

As we have seen, young people do not simply leave larger cultural patterns behind when they enter the schoolhouse door. Like the other topics discussed in this chapter, the characteristics of youth culture have enormous consequences for the U.S. educational system. The most direct problems are drugs and alcohol in the school, and violence, theft, and disorder on school grounds. Indicators of antisocial behavior in and around the schools have been a continuing topic of debate during the past thirty years. In almost all the annual Gallup Polls of public opinion on education conducted since 1968, "discipline" and "drugs" have been most frequently cited as the most serious problems in the schools.[172]

[165]Daniel Glaser, "Economic and Sociocultural Variables Affecting Rates of Youth Unemployment," *Youth and Society* (September 1979), p. 79; Terry M. Williams, *The Cocaine Kids* (Reading, Mass.: Addison-Wesley, 1989); and Arnold P. Goldstein, *Delinquents on Delinquency* (Champaign, Ill.: Research Press, 1990).

[166]James Q. Wilson, *Thinking About Crime* (New York: Basic Books, 1983); Edward J. Loughran, "Refocusing on Prevention of Delinquency," *Education Week,* March 21, 1991, p. 32; and "Violent Teens," *The Family in America New Research* (January 1992), p. 3.

[167]Danielle Crittenden, "You've Come a Long Way, Moll," *The Wall Street Journal,* January 25, 1990, p. A14; Felicia R. Lee, "For Gold Earrings and Protection, More Girls Take Road to Violence," *The New York Times,* November 25, 1991, pp. A1, A16.

[168]Delbert S. Elliott, David Huizinga, and Suzanne S. Ageton, *Explaining Delinquency and Drug Use* (Newbury Park, Calif.: Sage, 1985); Peter E. Leone, ed., *Understanding Troubled and Troubling Youth* (Newbury Park, Calif.: Sage, 1990).

[169]Christopher Jencks, "Is Violent Crime Increasing?" *The American Prospect* (Winter 1991), pp. 97–109.

[170]Christopher Jencks, "Genes and Crime," *The New York Review of Books,* February 12, 1987, pp. 33–41; "How Criminals Are Made," *The New York Times,* February 2, 1992, p. E7.

[171]LeGrande Gardner and Donald J. Shoemaker, "Social Bonding and Delinquency," *The Sociological Quarterly* (Fall 1989), pp. 481–500; Roberto Rodriguez, "Understanding the Pathology of Inner-City Violence," *Black Issues in Higher Education,* April 23, 1992, pp. 18–20.

[172]Stanley M. Elam, "The Gallup Education Surveys: Impressions of a Poll Watcher," *Phi Delta Kappan* (September 1983), pp. 26–32; Stanley M. Elam, Lowell C. Rose, and Alec M. Gallup, "The 23rd Annual Gallup Poll," *Phi Delta Kappan* (September 1991), pp. 41–56.

*Recent increase in
school violence*

Data on violence and vandalism in the schools indicate that these problems became much more serious in the 1960s and 1970s and reached alarming proportions by about 1975, particularly in urban schools. Violence and other antisocial behavior by students increased again in the late 1980s. Although violence and vandalism are most common at low-income schools in big cities, they are serious problems at many schools outside the inner city that also are afflicted by teenage and young-adult gangs, by crime connected with substance abuse and drug sales, and by infiltration of school buildings by trespassers.[173]

*Social service personnel
in schools*

In response to the numerous problems of children and youth in contemporary society, schools now employ many more counselors, social workers, and other social service personnel than was typical in earlier decades. Recent studies of urban high schools, for example, have found that they utilize the services of such specialized personnel as guidance and career counselors, psychologists, security workers, nurses and other health workers, truant officers, and home-school coordinators. Many of these specialists help conduct programs that target alcohol and drug abuse, teenage sex, school dropout, suicide, intergroup relations, and parenting skills. The authors of some studies have concluded that these multiple services and programs are frequently too fragmented and uncoordinated to help students trying to cope with the negative forces that impede learning.[174] The final chapter of this book examines some further possibilities for improving school effectiveness in this area.

Summing Up

1. Changes in the family may be having a detrimental influence on children's behavior and performance in school. Although the situation is complicated and research is inconclusive, increases in single-parent families and in the number of working mothers appear to be having a negative effect for many students, whereas the decline in the fertility rate and in family size may be having a positive effect.

2. The peer culture becomes more important as children proceed through school, but it has an important influence on education at all levels of schooling. Educators should be aware of the potentially positive effects for students of participation in extracurricular activities.

3. The culture of the school (that is, "regularities" in school practice) appears to stress passive, rote learning in many elementary and secondary schools, particularly in working-class schools and mixed-class schools with relatively large numbers of low-achieving students. This happens in part because schools are institutions that must maintain orderly environments; because

---

[173]Julius Menacker, Ward Weldon, and Emanuel Hurwitz, "Community Influences on School Crime and Violence," *Urban Education* (April 1990), pp. 68–80; Dennis Smith, *Caught in the Crossfire* (Washington, D.C.: Center to Prevent Handgun Violence, 1990); Daniel Foley, "Danger: School Zone," *Teacher Magazine* (May 1990), pp. 57–63; and Tom Morganthau, "It's Not Just New York," *Newsweek*, March 9, 1992, pp. 27–29.

[174]Eleanor Farrar and Robert I. Hampel, "Social Services in American High Schools," *Phi Delta Kappan* (December 1987), pp. 297–304; Samuel G. Freedman, *Small Victories* (New York: Harper, 1990); and Grace Pung Guthrie and Larry F. Guthrie, "Streamlining Interagency Collaboration for Youth at Risk," *Educational Leadership* (September 1991), pp. 17–22.

many students prefer passive learning; because teachers generally cannot adequately attend to the learning needs of all students; because little practical knowledge has been available on how to change this situation; and because students must learn to function within institutions.

4. Television probably increases aggressiveness and violent behavior among some children and youth, and it may detract from achievement — particularly in reading — among some children.

5. Girls traditionally have not been encouraged to seek education that prepares them for full participation in the larger society, and both girls and boys have experienced sex-role pressures in the school. Even so, educational and occupational opportunities for women have been improving rapidly. Although sex differences in school achievement have been declining, some differences in ability may persist in verbal skills (favoring females) and advanced mathematics (favoring males).

6. In some ways, youth has become a separate stage of life marked by immersion in a number of discernible subcultures. Teenage drug use and drinking, suicide, pregnancy, delinquency, and violence raise serious concerns about the development of adolescents and youth both inside and outside the school.

Key Terms

acculturation *(318)*

socialization *(318)*

culture *(318)*

norms *(319)*

latchkey children *(321)*

feminization of poverty *(324)*

hurried children *(326)*

nuclear family *(331)*

peer culture *(333)*

hidden curriculum *(337)*

sex roles *(348)*

Discussion Questions

1. Compare and contrast the socialization experiences of urban adolescents in the United States with those of youth living in a rural setting.

2. How do changes in social values affect the role and functioning of the schools?

3. How does schooling differ from education? How should one define each term? What are the implications of this type of analysis?

4. How do adolescents gain high status within their peer group? What types of students are most popular? Why? How does the social composition of the school affect the status positions of peer groups?

5. What can the schools do to alleviate the problems of drug use, violence, and teenage pregnancy? What should they do?

Suggested Readings

Best, Raphaela. *We've All Got Scars: What Boys and Girls Learn in Elementary School.* Bloomington: Indiana University Press, 1983.

This book gives detailed observations of gender-related behaviors in the elementary grades, analyzes why relatively more boys than girls are poor readers, and examines the differences in boys' and girls' participation in the academic curriculum and the hidden curriculum.

Burleson, Derek L., ed. *Reflections*. Bloomington, Ind.: Phi Delta Kappa, 1991.

Many of the thirty-three distinguished educators who describe their careers in this book of essays focus on changes they have seen in the family, peer groups, the media, and other social institutions.

Gordon, Edmund W., ed. *Review of Research in Education 11*. Washington, D.C.: American Educational Research Association, 1984.

The chapters by Diane Scott-Jones and Ann M. Clarke provide comprehensive reviews of research on the family environment as it relates to socialization, social class, and child development.

Lortie, Dan C. *Schoolteacher*. Chicago: University of Chicago Press, 1975.

This is a seminal analysis of the role and functioning of teachers within the culture of elementary and secondary schools.

Sedlak, Michael W., Christopher W. Wheeler, Diana C. Pullin, and Philip Cusick. *Selling Students Short*. New York: Teachers College Press, Columbia University, 1986.

This work describes and assesses classroom "bargains" that result in low-level learning and analyzes the weaknesses of bureaucratic school reform that takes little account of these classroom realities.

Spindler, George, and Louise Spindler. *The American Cultural Dialogue and Its Transmission*. New York: Falmer, 1990.

The authors summarize decades of observation and analysis they have provided on topics relating culture and education.

10

Social Class, Race, and School Achievement

FOCUSING QUESTIONS

What is the relationship between social class and success in the educational system?

After accounting for social class, are race and ethnicity associated with school achievement?

What are the major reasons for low achievement among students with low socioeconomic status?

What is the role of home and family environment in encouraging or discouraging high achievement?

Do environment and heredity interact to cause low achievement?

How does the relationship between social class and school achievement affect the national goal of providing equal educational opportunities for all students?

T his chapter begins by providing a brief explanation of social class and examining relationships among students' social class, racial/ethnic background, and performance in the educational system. We go on to discuss why students with low social status, and disadvantaged minority students in particular, typically rank low in educational achievement and attainment. The chapter concludes by examining the implications of these relationships within the context of our nation's historic commitment to equal educational opportunity.

SOCIAL CLASS AND SUCCESS IN SCHOOL

American society is generally understood to consist of three broad classes: working, middle, and upper. It is well known that there is a strong relationship between social class and educational achievement. Traditionally, working-class students have not performed as well as middle- and upper-class students. As you read the analysis in this section, you should ask yourself why it has been so difficult to improve the achievement of working-class students and what can be done to improve their achievement in the future.

Categories of Social Class

Social-class groups

Most social scientists believe that populations can be classified according to social-class groups, which differ in their economic, social, and political interests and characteristics. One of the most commonly used classifications for social-class groups in the United States was developed in the 1940s by W. Lloyd Warner and his colleagues. They used four main variables (occupation, education, income, and housing value) to classify individuals and families in five groups: upper class, upper middle class, lower middle class, upper lower class, and lower lower class.[1] Individuals very high in occupational prestige, amount of education, income, and housing value are high in **socioeconomic status (SES);** they are viewed by others as upper-class persons and are influential and powerful in their communities. Conversely, persons low in socioeconomic status are viewed as low in prestige and power.

Today, the term *working class* is more widely used than *lower class,* but social scientists still use measures of occupation, education, and income to describe three to six levels of SES, ranging from upper class at the top to lower working class at the bottom. The **upper class** is usually defined as including very wealthy persons having substantial property and investments; the **middle class** includes professionals, managers, and small-business owners (upper middle) as well as technical workers, technicians, sales personnel, and clerical workers (lower middle). The **working class** is generally divided into upper working class (including skilled crafts workers) and lower working class (unskilled manual workers). Skilled workers may be either middle class or working class, de-

[1]W. Lloyd Warner, Marcia Meeker, and Kenneth Eells, *Social Class in America* (Chicago: Science Research Associates, 1949). Also see Delbert C. Miller, *Handbook of Research Design and Social Measurement,* 5th ed. (Newbury Park, Calif.: Sage, 1991).

pending on their education, income, and other considerations such as the community in which they live.

In recent years, a number of observers also have identified an underclass group within the working class. The **underclass** generally resembles the lower working class, but as the term implies, many of its members are the third or fourth generation to live in poverty and are dependent on public assistance to sustain a relatively meager existence. Usually concentrated in the inner slums of cities or in deteriorated areas of rural poverty, members of the underclass frequently have little or no hope that their economic and social situation will ever improve.[2]

Intergenerational poverty

We also should note that poverty is closely associated with family structure. As pointed out in the preceding chapter, there has been a large increase in single-parent families headed by women with low incomes. Poverty rates among two-parent families and among the elderly substantially declined during the past three decades, but a large proportion of female-headed households have remained in poverty.

Research on Social Class and School Success

"Middletown" studies

One of the first systematic studies investigating the relationship between social class and achievement in school was Robert and Helen Lynd's study of "Middletown" (a small midwestern city) in the 1920s. The Lynds concluded that parents, regardless of social class, recognize the importance of education for their children; however, many working-class children do not come to school equipped to acquire the verbal skills and behavioral traits required for success in the classroom. The Lynds' observations of social class and the schools were repeated by W. Lloyd Warner and his associates in a series of studies of towns and small cities in New England, the Deep South, and the Midwest. Hundreds of studies have since documented the close relationship between social class and education in the United States and, indeed, throughout the world.[3]

NAEP

For example, a clear picture of this relationship has been provided by the **National Assessment of Educational Progress (NAEP),** and other agencies that collect achievement information from nationally representative samples of students. As shown in Table 10.1, mathematics and reading proficiency scores of fourth graders and eighth graders vary directly with their social class: students whose parents are well educated (one primary measure of social class) score considerably higher than students whose parents have less education. This holds to such an extent that average scores for fourth graders whose parents completed college are about the same as those for eighth graders whose parents have not completed high school.

---

[2]Ken Auletta, *The Underclass* (New York: Random House, 1982); Christopher Jencks and Paul E. Peterson, eds., *The Urban Underclass* (Washington, D.C.: The Brookings Institution, 1991); and *The State of Black America, 1992* (Washington, D.C.: Urban League, 1992).

[3]Robert S. Lynd and Helen M. Lynd, *Middletown: A Study in American Culture* (New York: Harcourt, Brace & World, 1929); Marlaine E. Lockheed, "Accounting for School Effects in Five Developing Countries" (Paper presented at the Annual Meeting of the American Educational Research Association, Chicago, April 1991).

Table 10.1

Average Mathematics and Reading Proficiency Scores of Fourth and Eighth Graders, by Parental Education and Type of Community, 1988 and 1990

	Eighth-Grade Mathematics (1990)	Eighth-Grade Reading (1988)	Fourth-Grade Reading (1988)
Parental Education			
Not graduated high school	241	245	204
Graduated high school	250	256	226
Some college	261	269	241
Graduated college	263	273	241
Type of Community			
Disadvantaged urban	243	247	208
Rural	253	271	228
Advantaged urban	271	274	248

Note: The National Assessment of Educational Progress defines community type as follows: *advantaged urban*, communities located in or around cities with a population of 200,000 or more, and a "high proportion of the residents are in professional or managerial positions"; *rural*, communities located in areas with population below 10,000, and many of the residents are farmers or farm workers; *disadvantaged urban*, communities located in or around cities of 200,000 or more, and a "high proportion of the residents are on welfare or are not regularly employed."

Source: Judith A. Langer, Arthur N. Applebee, Ina V. S. Mullis, and Mary A. Foertsch, *Learning to Read in Our Nation's Schools* (Princeton, N.J.: Educational Testing Service, 1990), pp. 106, 109; Ina V. S. Mullis, John A. Dossey, Eugene H. Owen, and Gary W. Phillips, *The State of Mathematics Achievement Executive Summary* (Princeton, N.J.: Educational Testing Service, 1991), p. 24.

Type of community and achievement

School achievement also is correlated with type of community, which reflects the social class of persons who reside there. As shown in Table 10.1, the average mathematics and reading scores of students in "advantaged" urban areas (with a high proportion of residents in professional or managerial occupations) are much higher than those of students in "disadvantaged" areas (with a high proportion of residents who receive public assistance or are unemployed). Fourth graders in the advantaged communities perform about as well as eighth graders in disadvantaged areas.

Concentrated poverty schools

Further evidence of the relationship between social class and school achievement can be found in studies of poverty neighborhoods in very large cities. Data on the performance of students in such neighborhoods have provided a bleak picture of schooling over the past three decades. For example, Levine and his colleagues examined sixth-grade achievement patterns at more than a thousand predominantly low-income schools (which they called concentrated poverty schools) in seven big cities and reported that all but a few had average reading scores more than two years below the national average. They also pointed out that at least one-fourth of the students at these schools cannot read well enough to be considered functionally literate when they enter high school. This pattern can be found at concentrated poverty schools in big cities throughout the United States.[4]

[4]Daniel U. Levine and Robert J. Havighurst, *Society and Education*, 8th ed. (Needham Heights, Mass.: Allyn and Bacon, 1992). Also see Carlos Martinez, "Schools Not Successful with Low-income Students," *Substance* (November 1991), pp. 7, 15, and Nathan Glazer, "The Real World of Public Education," *The Public Interest* (Winter 1992), pp. 57–75.

Rural poverty

Many educators also are concerned about the achievement of rural students, especially those who live in low-income regions and pockets of rural poverty. Although the average achievement of rural students is generally at about the national average, research indicates that poverty and inequality hamper their achievement, and that two-thirds of rural educators believe the academic performance of their low-income students either is in "great need" or "fairly strong need" of improvement.[5]

Unusually effective schools

We also should emphasize, however, that there are methods for improving the achievement of students with low socioeconomic status. In particular, the "effective schools" movement that came to prominence in the 1980s demonstrated that appropriate schoolwide efforts to enhance instruction can produce sizable gains in the performance of disadvantaged students, even in concentrated poverty schools in big cities and rural schools in poor areas. It is easier today than only ten or fifteen years ago to find schools that have improved the achievement of low-income students. The effective schools movement and other efforts to improve the performance of disadvantaged students are described in subsequent chapters, particularly Chapter 16.

Social Class and College Attendance. Social class is associated with many educational outcomes in addition to achievement in reading, math, and other subjects. On the average, working-class students not only have lower achievement scores, but also are less likely than middle-class students to complete high school or to enroll in and complete college. Only about 10 percent of high-school students from the lowest socioeconomic quartile (measured in terms of family income) subsequently enter college and attain a postsecondary degree, compared with more than 50 percent of high-school graduates in the highest quartile.[6]

Social class and college attendance

However, because social class is correlated with test scores and one would not expect students with low test scores to succeed in college to the same extent as those with high scores, assessments of the relationship between social class and college attendance should take account of students' test scores. Data of this kind are given in Table 10.2, which shows the relevant information for high-school graduates in 1980 who entered postsecondary institutions during the next six years. As one might expect, students who scored higher in reading achievement are more likely to attend postsecondary institutions than are those who scored lower, and this is true at each socioeconomic level. Similarly, at each achievement level above the bottom quartile, students with higher socioeconomic status are more likely to attend postsecondary institutions than are those with lower socioeconomic status. Overall, only 57 percent of students in the

[5]Jane H. Arends, *Building on Excellence: Regional Priorities for the Improvement of Rural, Small Schools* (Washington, D.C.: Council for Educational Development and Research, 1987); Jonathan Weisman, "Rural America Is Quietly 'Hurting,' Educators Warn," *Education Week*, October 10, 1990, p. 10; and Deborah L. Cohen, "Conditions 'Bleak' for Rural Children, C.D.F. Finds," *Education Week*, January 8, 1992, p. 3.

[6]Thomas G. Mortenson, *Equity of Higher Educational Opportunity for Women, Black, Hispanic, and Low-Income Students* (Iowa City: American College Testing Program, 1991); Thomas G. Mortenson, "Equity of Higher Education Opportunity," *Postsecondary Education Opportunity* (March 1992), pp. 1–6.

Students with higher socioeconomic status are more likely to attend postsecondary institutions than are those with lower socioeconomic status. (© Ulrike Welsch/Photo Researchers, Inc.)

bottom two socioeconomic quartiles (not shown in the table) enrolled in post-secondary institutions, compared with 82 percent of those in the top half. Due to limitations in federal financial aid and other causes, this discrepancy has been growing in recent years.[7]

---

[7]Thomas G. Mortenson, *The Impact of Increased Loan Utilization Among Low Family Income Students* (Iowa City: American College Testing Program, 1990); Gerald W. Bracey, "Why Blacks Are Not Going to College," *Phi Delta Kappan* (February 1992), p. 494.

Table 10.2

Percentage of 1980 High School Graduates Who Entered a Postsecondary Institution by 1986, by Ability Level and Socioeconomic Status Level

Reading Achievement Level	Socioeconomic Status		
	Lowest Fourth	*Middle Half*	*Highest Fourth*
Lowest fourth	42	44	66
Middle half	58	70	86
Highest fourth	78	90	97

Note: Socioeconomic status is a composite score based on parental education, family income, father's occupation, and selected household characteristics.

Source: Cecilia Ottinger, *College Going, Persistence, and Completion Patterns in Higher Education* (Washington, D.C.: American Council on Education, 1991), p. 2. Reprinted with permission.

RACE/ETHNICITY AND SCHOOL SUCCESS

Race and ethnicity

Patterns of social class and educational achievement in the United States are further complicated by the additional factors of race and ethnicity. The term **race** identifies groups of people with common ancestry and physical characteristics. The term **ethnicity** identifies people who have a shared culture. Members of an **ethnic group** usually have common ancestry and share language, religion, and other cultural traits. Since there are no "pure" races, some scholars prefer to avoid reference to race and instead discuss group characteristics under the heading of ethnicity.

As we saw in Chapter 5, the population of the United States is a mix of several races and ethnicities. It is well established that racial and ethnic minorities in this country experience social and economic oppression *as a group* despite the accomplishments of individuals. The nation's largest racial minority group — African Americans — is, on the whole, much lower in socioeconomic status than is the white majority. Other major ethnic minority groups, such as Mexican Americans and Puerto Ricans, are also disproportionately low in socioeconomic status. An ongoing concern for educators is the fact that these racial and ethnic minority groups are correspondingly low in academic achievement, high-school and college graduation rates, and other measures of educational attainment.[8] (See color insert.)

Eighth-grade sample

The close association among social class, race or ethnicity, and school performance is shown in Table 10.3, which presents average math and reading scores attained by nationally representative samples of eighth graders. As shown in the table, African American students have the lowest SES scores (as measured by family income), the lowest math scores, and the second-lowest reading scores; non-Hispanic whites are high on all of these measures. In general, school

---

[8]Howard M. Bahr, Bruce A. Chadwick, and Joseph H. Strauss, *American Ethnicity* (Lexington, Mass.: D.C. Heath, 1979); Robin M. Williams, Jr., and Gerald D. Jaynes, *A Common Destiny* (Washington, D.C.: National Academy Press, 1989); Nicholas Lemann, *The Promised Land* (New York: Knopf, 1991); and Peter Schmidt, "La Raza Details Hispanics' Low Level of Education," *Education Week*, February 12, 1992, p. 11.

Table 10.3

Indicators of School Performance and Attainment and Socioeconomic Background, by Racial and Ethnic Group

Racial/Ethnic Group	Percent of Eighth Graders Below Basic Math Level, 1990	Percent of Eighth Graders Below Basic Reading Level, 1988	Percent of Eighth Graders from Families with Income Below $15,000, 1988
African American	70	24	47
Asian American	22	15	18
Hispanic	58	21	37
Native American	44	27	42
Non-Hispanic White	26	10	14

Note: The Asian American category includes students with Pacific Islands origins. The Native American category includes American Indians and students with Alaskan origins. The "basic math level" represents "partial mastery of knowledge and skills" designated as standard for eighth graders by the National Education Goals Panel. The "basic reading level" is defined in terms of literal comprehension as assessed in the National Educational Longitudinal Study of 1988.

Source: Ann Hafner et al., *A Profile of the American Eighth Grader: National Educational Longitudinal Study of 1988, Student Descriptive Summary* (Washington, D.C.: Government Printing Office, 1990), pp. 3, 6, 29.

achievement scores parallel scores on socioeconomic status; the higher the SES score, the higher the achievement scores.[9]

Minority reading gains

However, data collected by the NAEP also indicate that African American and Hispanic students have registered gains in reading, math, and other subjects. As shown in Figure 10.1, gains in reading have narrowed the gap between white students on the one hand and African American and Hispanic students on the other. Some observers attribute these improvements partly to the effects of the federal Chapter 1 program and/or to some increase in desegregation.[10] (See Chapter 11 for discussions of Chapter 1 and desegregation.) On the other hand, African American and Hispanic students still score far below whites in reading and other subjects, and black and Hispanic seventeen-year-old students still have average reading scores only a little above the average white thirteen-year-old.

Dropout rates

In line with the data shown in Table 10.3, non-Hispanic white and Asian students (other than Vietnamese Americans) are much more likely to complete high school than are African American and Hispanic students. As Figure 10.2 shows, the high-school completion rate for African American students has been

[9]Further analysis of these and other data also indicates considerable variation within broad racial/ethnic classifications. For example, among Hispanics, Cuban Americans have much higher SES and achievement scores than do Mexican American and Puerto Rican students.

[10]Daniel Koretz, *Educational Achievement: Explanation and Implications of Recent Trends* (Washington, D.C.: Congressional Budget Office, 1987); "Equality in Education: Progress, Problems, and Possibilities," *CPRE Policy Briefs*, July 6, 1991, pp. 1–11; and *Testing in American Schools* (Washington, D.C.: Congress of the United States Office of Technology Assessment, 1992).

Average Reading Proficiency Scores of African American, Hispanic, and White Students, 1971 to 1988

Figure 10.1

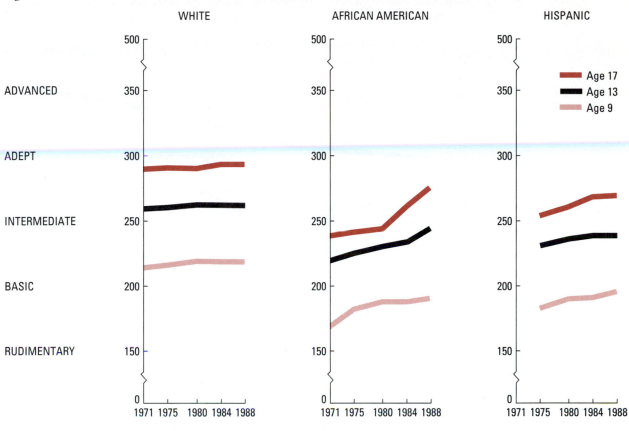

SCHOOL YEAR ENDING

Source: Ina V. S. Mullis and Lynn B. Jenkins, *The Reading Report Card, 1971–88* (Princeton, N.J.: Educational Testing Service, 1990), pp. 54, 58, 62.

rising since 1975, but it is still significantly below the rate for whites, and the rate for Hispanic students has not improved. In addition, high-school dropout rates are still extremely high among African American and Hispanic students in big-city poverty areas. Knowledgeable observers estimate that dropout rates range from 40 to 60 percent in some big cities and sometimes exceed 75 or 80 percent at schools enrolling mostly underclass students. Inasmuch as high-school dropouts have rapidly diminishing opportunities to succeed in the economy, the high dropout rate of urban schools has become a major problem for American society.[11]

---

[11]*States and Communities on the Move: Policy Initiatives to Create a World-Class Workforce* (Washington, D.C.: William T. Grant Foundation Commission on Work, Family and Citizenship, 1991); Roberto Suro, "Generational Chasm Leads to Cultural Turmoil for Young Mexicans in U.S.," *The New York Times*, January 20, 1992, p. A11.

*High-School Completion Rates for 19- and 20-Year-Olds, by Race/Ethnicity,
1975 to 1990*

Figure 10.2

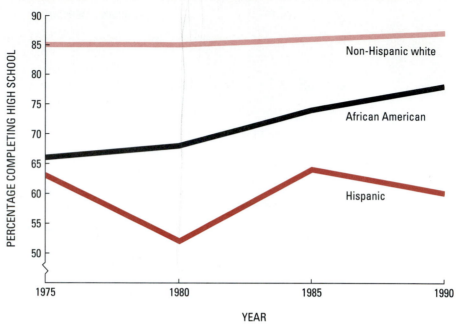

Source: *The National Education Goals Report* (Washington, D.C.: National Education Goals
Panel, 1991), p. 8.

College enrollment

African American and Hispanic students are also less likely to enter and complete college and other postsecondary institutions. Postsecondary enrollment rates for African American and Hispanic high-school graduates have increased only a little since 1975, whereas rates for whites have increased markedly. As a result, the percentage of African American students in the college population declined from almost 10 percent in the mid-1970s to slightly under 9 percent in the early 1990s. African American enrollments in graduate and professional schools also have declined relative to white enrollment. Among the causes cited for these negative trends have been the following:[12]

Many higher education institutions have reduced or eliminated special recruiting and assistance programs.

Shifts in federal aid from grants to loans have combined with rising tuition to exclude disadvantaged students.

Many students may have concluded that higher education will not help them obtain better employment.

---

[12]Denise K. Magner, "Hispanics Remain 'Grossly Underrepresented' on Campuses, Report Says," *The Chronicle of Higher Education,* January 23, 1991, p. A2; Thomas G. Mortenson, *Equity of Higher Educational Opportunity;* Richard C. Richardson, Jr., "Promoting Fair College Outcomes," *Policy Perspectives* (May 1991), pp. 7B–8B; and Mary Jordan, "2 Steps Forward, 1 Step Nowhere," *The Washington Post National Weekly Edition,* February 10–16, 1992, p. 38.

More African American youth may be joining the military to acquire lower-cost education.

Participation in drug cultures may have disabled many minority youth.

Calls for improvement

Reports published by the Education Commission of the States have referred to the rate of minority enrollment in higher education as "shockingly low" and have called for federal, state, and higher education officials to make a larger commitment to ensuring fuller participation rates among minority students. Similarly, a report issued by the State Higher Education Executive Officers pointed out that the nation's self-interest requires that a high priority be placed on expanding minority enrollment. The report concluded that colleges and universities should take a variety of steps to increase minority enrollment. The American Council on Education also has issued reports concluding that declines in minority enrollment have been "intolerable."[13]

The Effect of Minority Status Plus Poverty

As documented above, educational achievement generally is distressingly low at schools in poor inner-city neighborhoods. We also pointed out that although high-school completion rates for African American students have been rising nationally, the dropout problem is still severe in big cities. These problems reflect the fact that the inner cores of large urban areas in the United States have increasingly become segregated communities populated by working-class and underclass African American and Hispanic residents. Some of the causes and results of this socioeconomic and racial/ethnic stratification include the following:

Segregated inner cities

1. *The African American population of the United States has become more economically polarized.* The overall socioeconomic status and income of this population have increased substantially since 1950, as opportunities for African Americans improved and many joined the middle class. However, many other African Americans still live in urban poverty, in neighborhoods in which a large majority of families are headed by single women and in which rates of crime, delinquency, drug abuse, teenage pregnancy, and other indicators of social disorganization are all very high.[14]

Polarization among African Americans

2. *Both the number and the percentage of low-income minority persons residing in urban poverty areas have increased substantially.* Although the overall population of the fifty largest cities in the United States has declined since 1970, the number of low-income African Americans living in poverty areas has increased by more than one-third. In addition, low-income persons in these areas are further below the poverty line than they were in the 1960s. In a related trend, more than two-thirds of the students in many big-city school districts, such as Chicago, Detroit,

Increasing concentration

---

[13]Scott Jaschik, "State Leaders Urged to Intensify Colleges' Efforts to Enroll and Graduate More Minority Students," *The Chronicle of Higher Education*, July 15, 1987, pp. 1, 15; Richard C. Richardson, Jr., *Promoting Fair College Outcomes* (Denver: Education Commission of the States, 1991); and *Tenth Annual Status Report on Minorities in Higher Education* (Washington, D.C.: American Council on Education, 1992).

[14]Bart Landry, *The New Black Middle Class* (Berkeley: University of California Press, 1987); William J. Wilson, *The Truly Disadvantaged: The Inner City, the Underclass, and Public Policy* (Chicago: University of Chicago Press, 1987); "More Than Economics," *The Family in America New Research* (March 1992), pp. 2–3.

and New York, are now from low-income families, and more than 80 percent are minority students.[15]

3. *Social institutions such as the family, the school, and the law enforcement system frequently appear to have become dysfunctional in the inner city.* Parents find it increasingly difficult to control their children, and law enforcement agencies are unable to cope with rising rates of juvenile delinquency and adult crime.[16]

Increasing social isolation

4. *Concentration of low-income minority populations in big-city poverty areas has increased their isolation from the larger society.* In contrast to the urban slums and ghettos of fifty or one hundred years ago, today's concentrated poverty areas are larger geographically, and in many cases their residents are more homogeneous in (low) socioeconomic status. Unskilled and semiskilled jobs are more difficult to obtain, and many jobs have moved to the suburbs where they are practically inaccessible to central-city residents. Andrew Hacker observed that the contemporary "mode of segregation, combining poverty and race, is relatively new. To reside amid so many people leading desultory lives makes it all the harder to break away."[17]

Problems for young males

5. *The problems experienced by young black males have escalated enormously.* Some knowledgeable observers believe that the plight of young males in inner-city poverty areas is at the root of a series of other serious problems: very high rates of out-of-wedlock births, the persistence of welfare dependency, and violent crime and delinquency. The growth in female-headed families in urban poverty areas is directly related to the high rates at which young African American men drop out of the labor force, are incarcerated in prisons, enter the military, or otherwise are excluded or exclude themselves from mainstream institutions. The result is a great reduction in the pool of males available to participate in stable families and accumulate resources for upward mobility.[18]

Whether the assessment emphasizes poverty, segregation, or social disorganization, educational achievement and attainment levels of inner-city children and youth are tragically low in part because poverty schools in big cities typically are overloaded with problems that make them dysfunctional and ineffective for many students. The extent of this ineffectiveness has been underlined in an analysis of achievement data for high schools in the Milwaukee metropolitan area.

City/suburban disparity

At city high schools in the study, an average of 40 percent of tenth graders had

[15]John Herbers, "Poverty of Blacks Spreads in Cities," *The New York Times*, January 26, 1987, pp. A1, A27; Lynne Duke, "The Black Money Gap Grows," *The Washington Post National Weekly Edition*, August 25–31, 1991, p. 37; and Alan Wolfe, "The New American Dilemma," *The New Republic*, April 13, 1992, pp. 30–37.

[16]Karl Zinsmeister, "Growing Up Scared," *The Atlantic* (June 1990), pp. 49–66; William R. Prosser, "The Underclass: Assessing What We Have Learned," *Focus* (Summer 1991), pp. 1–18; and Jason DeParle, "Cultivating Their Own Gardens," *The New York Times Magazine*, January 5, 1992, pp. 22–23, 32, 42–48.

[17]Andrew Hacker, "American Apartheid," *The New York Review of Books*, December 3, 1987, pp. 32–33; Andrew Hacker, "Black Crime, White Racism," *The New York Review of Books*, March 3, 1988, pp. 36–41; Andrew Hacker, "Playing the Racial Card," *The New York Review of Books*, October 24, 1991, pp. 14–18; and Andrew Hacker, *Two Nations* (New York: Scribner's Sons, 1992).

[18]Wilson, *The Truly Disadvantaged*; Ronald B. Mincy, "No Underclass Solution Can Ignore Young Males," *The Urban Institute Policy and Research Report* (Fall 1990), p. 28; Barbara Vobejda, "A Good Man Is Even Harder to Find," *The Washington Post National Weekly Edition*, November 18–24, 1991, p. 34; and "Pressing the Higher Education Agenda," *Black Issues in Higher Education*, February 13, 1992, pp. 17–20.

reading and math scores above the national average, whereas the average for the eleven suburban high schools was 64 percent. All but two of the suburban high schools enrolled less than 12 percent low-income students; the city high schools enrolled an average of almost 40 percent low-income students. None of the suburban high schools had minority enrollment higher than 14 percent, compared with minority percentages ranging from 32 percent to 55 percent at the city high schools.[19] (Due to an extensive desegregation plan, there is relatively less segregation in Milwaukee's city high schools than in those of many other urban communities.) Comparable patterns differentiating city and suburban schools undoubtedly would be found in most metropolitan areas.

The Influence of Social Class

Social-class influence

Because social class, race/ethnicity, and school achievement are so closely interrelated, researchers frequently ask whether race and ethnicity are associated with performance in the educational system even after one takes into account the low socioeconomic status of African Americans and other disadvantaged minority groups. In general, the answer has been that social class accounts for most of the variation in educational achievement by race and ethnicity. That is, if one knows the social class of a group of students, one can predict with a good deal of accuracy whether their achievement, ability scores, and college attendance rates are high or low; information about their racial or ethnic group does little to improve such a prediction. This also means that working-class white students as a group are low in achievement and college attainment, whereas the average middle-class minority student ranks relatively high on these variables.

Analyses such as those we have presented support the conclusion that one of the central problems faced by disadvantaged minorities in the United States is that minority persons are still disproportionately working class and underclass and that their children are much less successful in the educational system than are the children of the middle class. Moreover, because education is an important channel for gaining access to the job market, minority students with low socioeconomic status have relatively less opportunity for economic success later in their lives. From this point of view, the ineffectiveness of the schools in educating students from working-class homes helps to perpetuate the current class system — and the burden of poverty and low achievement falls disproportionately on the nation's racial and ethnic minority groups.

REASONS FOR LOW ACHIEVEMENT AMONG LOW-STATUS STUDENTS

Over the past forty years, much research has been aimed at understanding and overcoming the academic deficiencies of low-achieving students in general and low-achieving students from working-class or poor families in particular. Although the explanations researchers advance are not necessarily mutually ex-

---

[19]Levine and Havighurst, *Society and Education*; John Witte and Daniel J. Walsh, "A Systematic Test of the Effective Schools Model," *Educational Evaluation and Policy Analysis* (February 1990), pp. 188–218.

clusive, we will group them under the following major factors: home environment, heredity versus environment, and obstacles in the classroom.

Home Environment

Chapter 9 pointed out that the family and home environment is the most important agent in the early socialization and education of the child. We also noted that characteristics of the home environment closely reflect the family's social class. Thus, social-class differences in home environment are associated with the level of educational performance and attainment that students achieve.

Types of differences

One way to categorize the home environment in terms of how well it prepares children to succeed in school is to look at differences in knowledge and understandings, cognitive and verbal skills, and values and attitudes. Regarding *knowledge and understandings*, middle-class children are more likely than working-class children to acquire a wide knowledge of the world outside the home and immediate neighborhood through greater access to books and cultural institutions (for example, museums), parental teaching, and exploration of diverse environments. Knowledge and understandings acquired through exposure to the wider world are helpful to children when they enter school.[20]

Ordinary/formal language

Students' *cognitive and verbal skills* also reflect social-class differences in family language environments.[21] Basil Bernstein has found that although both middle- and working-class children develop adequate skills with respect to "ordinary" or "restricted" language, middle-class children are superior in the use of "formal" or "elaborated" language. Ordinary, restricted language is grammatically simple and relies on gestures and further explanations to clarify meaning. Elaborated, formal language is grammatically complex and provides greater potential for organizing experience within an abstract meaning system.[22] Many scholars believe that facility in using elaborated language helps middle-class children excel in cognitive development. Catherine Snow and her associates have also reported that working-class mothers are less likely than middle-class mothers to establish productive conversational routines and to provide responsive talk that helps children improve in abstract language. The authors believe that this difference may be due to family differences in both resources and philosophies.[23]

---

[20]Annette Lareau, "Social Class Differences in Family-School Relationships: The Importance of Cultural Capital," *Sociology of Education* (April 1987), pp. 73–85; Annette Lareau, *Home Advantage* (London: Falmer, 1989); Earl S. Schaefer, "Goals for Parent and Future-Parent Education," *Elementary School Journal* (January 1991), pp. 239–248; and Annette Lareau, "Red-Shirting and Retention: Class Differences in Parent Involvement in Schooling" (Paper presented at the Annual Meeting of the American Educational Research Association, San Francisco, April 1992).

[21]Shirley B. Heath and Milbrey W. McLaughlin, "A Child Resource Policy," *Phi Delta Kappan* (April 1987), pp. 576–580; Sharon Lynn Kagan, ed., *The Care and Education of America's Young Children* (Chicago: University of Chicago Press, 1991); and Willard L. Boyd, "Museums as Centers of Learning" (Paper presented at the Annual Meeting of the American Educational Research Association, San Francisco, April 1992).

[22]Basil Bernstein, *Class, Codes, and Control* (London and Boston: Routledge & Kegan Paul, 1975); Basil Bernstein, "Codes, Modalities, and the Process of Cultural Reproduction: A Model," *Language and Society* (December 1981), pp. 327–363; and Basil Bernstein, *The Structuring of Pedagogic Discourse* (New York: Routledge, 1990).

[23]Catherine E. Snow, Clara Dubber, and Akke De Blauw, "Routines in Mother-Child Interaction," in Lynne Feagans and Dale Clark Farran, eds., *The Language of Children Reared in Poverty*

Regarding *values and attitudes*, children from lower socioeconomic backgrounds are at a disadvantage because their socialization appears to emphasize obedience and conformity, whereas middle-class families stress independent learning and self-directed thinking.[24] Differences along these lines undoubtedly reflect the fact that many working-class environments are relatively dangerous for children; other differences arise from parents' education, resources, and knowledge of what practices help children develop intellectually. Although the child-raising methods of working-class families probably are becoming more like those of middle-class families, and although they may be superior in preparing children to function in a hostile environment, socialization practices in many working-class homes do not prepare children to function independently in the school and classroom.[25] Based on intensive study of 700 families in Nottingham, England, John and Elizabeth Newson have summarized these different socialization patterns as follows:

> Parents at the upper end of the social scale are more inclined on principle to use democratically based, highly verbal means of control, and this kind of discipline is likely to produce personalities who can both identify successfully with the system and use it for their own ends later on. At the bottom end of the scale . . . parents choose on principle to use a highly authoritarian, mainly non-verbal means of control, in which words are used more to threaten and bamboozle the child into obedience than to make him understand the rationale behind social behavior. . . . Thus the child born into the lowest social bracket has everything stacked against him including his parents' principles of child upbringing.[26]

The importance of the home and family environment for general intellectual development also has been documented in studies by J. McVicker Hunt, Martin Deutsch, Benjamin Bloom, and other researchers. These studies generally indicate that environmental stimulation in working-class homes is less conducive to intellectual development, on the average, than it is in middle-class homes. (Hunt and Deutsch helped stimulate the trend toward *compensatory education,* which attempts to remedy the effects of environmental disadvantages through enrichment programs, especially in preschool years.) Hunt summarized hundreds of studies indicating that environment is important in shaping intellectual performance. Deutsch outlined a number of factors, such as lack of productive visual and tactile stimulation, that detract from readiness to learn among many dis-

(New York Academic Press, 1982); Catherine E. Snow, "The Theoretical Basis of the Home-School Study of Language and Literacy Development" (Paper presented at the Annual Meeting of the American Educational Research Association, Chicago, April 1991); and "Teachers, Culture, and Power," *Rethinking Schools* (March/April 1992), pp. 14–16.

[24]Victor Gerkas, "The Influence of Social Class on Socialization," in Wesley R. Burr et al., eds., *Contemporary Theories About the Family* (New York: Free Press, 1979); Melvin L. Kohn et al., "Position in the Class Structure and Psychological Functioning in the United States, Japan, and Poland," *American Journal of Sociology* (January 1990), pp. 964–1008.

[25]James D. Wright and Sonia R. Wright, "Social Class and Parental Values for Children: A Partial Replication and Extension of the Kohn Thesis," *American Sociological Review* (June 1976), pp. 527–537; Duane F. Alwin, "Changes in Qualities in Children Valued in the United States," *Social Science Research* (September 1989), pp. 195–236; and Carolyn Cody, "Teachers Need Help, Not Accusations," *Black Issues in Higher Education,* January 2, 1992, p. 22.

[26]John Newson and Elizabeth Newson, *Seven Years Old in the Home Environment* (London: Allen & Unwin, 1976), p. 406. Chapter 3 in *Society and Education* by Levine and Havighurst describes in detail the advantages of emphasizing obedience in a working-class environment, particularly in the inner city.

The most rapid development of many human characteristics — including cognitive skills — occurs during the preschool years; home environment therefore is crucial to cognitive development. (© Elizabeth Crews/The Image Works)

Home environment factors

advantaged children. Deutsch and others have developed indexes of environmental disadvantage that correlate more closely with IQ scores and school success than do social-class indicators.[27]

The environmental disadvantage theory holds that early years of development are more important than later years. As pointed out by Benjamin Bloom, Richard Restak, and other researchers, the most rapid development of many human characteristics, including cognitive skills, occurs during the preschool years. Home environment therefore is crucial, because of the large amount of cognitive development that has already taken place before the child enters the first grade.[28] Furthermore, the child's intellectual development is affected even during the prenatal stages by the mother's general health, her diet, her alcohol intake and drug usage, and biochemical changes related to stress and other emotional factors. This does not mean that remediation of learning deficits associated

Early cognitive development

[27]Martin Deutsch, "The Role of Social Class in Language Development and Cognition," in A. H. Passow, M. I. Goldbery, and A. J. Tannenbaum, eds., *Education of the Disadvantaged* (New York: Holt, 1967), pp. 214–224; J. McVicker Hunt, *Intelligence and Experience* (New York: Ronald Press, 1961); J. McVicker Hunt, "Psychological Development: Early Experience," *Annual Review of Psychology* (1979), pp. 103–143; and Bettye M. Caldwell, "Continuity in the Early Years," in Sharon Lynn Kagan, ed., *The Care and Education of American's Young Children* (Chicago: University of Chicago Press, 1991), pp. 69–90.

[28]Benjamin S. Bloom, *Stability and Change in Human Characteristics* (New York: Wiley, 1964), p. 88; Cheryl D. Hayes, John L. Palmer, and Martha J. Zaslow, eds., *Who Cares for America's Children?* (Washington, D.C.: National Academy Press, 1990); Kevin R. Hopkins, "A Plague of Numbers," *Business Week*, November 25, 1991, pp. ED6–ED73; and David Hamburg, *Today's Children* (New York: Times Books, 1992).

with disadvantaged home environments is impossible. But it does imply that it is more difficult to produce changes for older children and that a more powerful environment is needed to bring about these changes.[29]

Social class and home environment not synonymous

It is important to emphasize that socialization differentials such as the foregoing reflect average differences across social-class groups, not universal patterns that distinguish all middle-class families from all working-class families. Thus, many families with low socioeconomic status do provide a home environment that is conducive to achievement, and the great majority of low-income parents try to provide their children with a positive learning environment. Similarly, many children from working-class families do well in school, and many middle-class children do not. Nevertheless, children from low-income, working-class homes are disproportionately likely to grow up in an environment that does not adequately prepare them to succeed in schools as they are presently operated.

The Heredity Versus Environment Debate

Role of heredity

During the past century, there has been heated controversy about whether intelligence is determined primarily by heredity or environment. When IQ tests were undergoing rapid development early in the twentieth century, many psychologists believed that intelligence was determined primarily by heredity. They thought they were learning to assess innate differences in people's capacity through IQ tests and other measures of cognitive development. Since economically disadvantaged populations and some minority groups such as African Americans scored considerably below middle-income populations and nonminority groups, the hereditarians believed that low-income populations and minority groups were innately inferior in intellectual capacity.

Stress on compensatory help

Environmentalist View.   By the middle of the twentieth century, numerous published studies had counteracted the hereditarian view, and most social scientists took the position that environment is as important as or even more important than heredity in determining intelligence. The preceding section discussed the views of some noted proponents of the **environmentalist view of intelligence** — J. McVicker Hunt, Martin Deutsch, and Benjamin Bloom. Environmentalists generally stress the need for compensatory programs on a continual basis beginning in infancy. Many also criticize the use of IQ tests on the grounds that these tests are culturally biased. Many environmentalists attribute the differences in IQ scores between African Americans and whites, for example, to differences in social class and family environment and to systematic racial discrimination.

Sandra Scarr and Richard Weinberg studied differences between African American children growing up in biological families and those growing up in

---

[29]Benjamin S. Bloom, *Human Characteristics and School Learning* (New York: McGraw-Hill, 1976); Benjamin S. Bloom, *All Our Children Learning* (New York: McGraw-Hill, 1981); Benjamin S. Bloom, "Helping All Children Learn in Elementary School — and Beyond," *Principal* (March 1988); Lucile F. Newman and Stephen L. Buka, "Clipped Wings," *American Educator* (Spring 1991), pp. 27–33, 42; and Kevin R. Hopkins, *Another Country: Poverty in the United States* (Washington, D.C.: Cato Institute, 1992).

IQ gains in the twentieth century

adopted families. They concluded that the effects of environment outweigh the effects of heredity. Thomas Sowell examined IQ scores collected for various ethnic groups between 1920 and 1970. He found that the scores of some groups such as Italian Americans and Polish Americans have substantially improved. Other studies indicate that the test scores of African Americans and Puerto Ricans have risen more rapidly than scores in the general population in response to such environmental improvements as better teaching and improvements in living conditions.[30]

Similar data on other countries have been collected by James Flynn, who found that "massive" gains have occurred during the twentieth century in the IQ scores of the population in fourteen nations. Flynn's analysis of the data indicates that the major cause of these improvements is not genetic improvement in the populations tested but rather environmental changes that led to improvement in the kinds of skills assessed by IQ tests. Torsten Husen and his colleagues also have reviewed large amounts of data indicating that improvements in economic and social conditions, and particularly in the availability of schooling, can produce substantial gains in average IQ from one generation to the next.[31]

Gains associated with schooling

In general, educators committed to improving the performance of low-achieving students should be encouraged by these studies. In this regard, Stephen Jay Gould has reviewed evidence documenting an increase in IQ scores of the U.S. population during the past half-century and has concluded:

> This general gain can hardly be ascribed to genetic causes; it reflects whatever improved literacy, earlier access to information through radio and television, better nutrition, and so forth have wrought in just thirty-five years. When we recognize that the average black-white difference is 15 points, and that gains of up to two thirds this amount have occurred in certain age groups as a result of general changes in environment not specifically directed toward this end, then why should we be ready to conclude that group differences are ineluctable?[32]

Hereditarian View.   The **hereditarian view of intelligence** underwent a major revival in the 1970s and 1980s, based particularly on the writings of Arthur Jensen, Richard Herrnstein, and a group of researchers who have been conducting the Minnesota Study of Twins. Summarizing previous research as well as their own studies, these researchers concluded that heredity is the major factor in determining intelligence — accounting for up to 80 percent of the vari-

---

[30]Sandra Scarr and Richard A. Weinberg, "I.Q. Test Performance of Black Children Adopted by White Families," *American Psychologist* (July 1976), pp. 726–739; Thomas Sowell, "Race and IQ Reconsidered," in Thomas Sowell, ed., *American Ethnic Groups* (Washington, D.C.: Urban Institute, 1978); and Thomas Zuckerman, "Some Dubious Premises in Research and Theory on Racial Differences," *American Psychologist* (December 1990), pp. 1297–1303.

[31]James R. Flynn, "Massive Gains in 14 Nations," *Psychological Bulletin* (vol. 101, 1987), pp. 171–191. Also see Torsten Husen and Albert Tujinman, "The Contribution of Formal Schooling to the Increase in Intellectual Capital," *Educational Researcher* (October 1991), pp. 17–25.

[32]Stephen Jay Gould, "Jensen's Last Stand," *The New York Review of Books,* May 1, 1980, p. 43. Also see James R. Flynn, *Asian Americans: Achievement Beyond IQ* (Hillsdale, N.J.: Erlbaum, 1991).

Jensen's conclusions

ance.[33] The most widely publicized of these studies was described in Jensen's lengthy article in the Winter 1969 issue of the *Harvard Educational Review,* which presented the following conclusions:

1. African Americans average about 15 points below the white score on IQ tests; this is due to a genetic difference between the two races in learning abilities and patterns.

2. African Americans as a group and students with low socioeconomic status in general have more difficulty than do others in abstract reasoning.

3. Conversely, African Americans and students with low socioeconomic status tend to do well in tasks involving rote learning.

4. Compensatory education has failed and will continue to fail because it is trying to compensate children of limited intellectual talents with learning approaches that are geared to students of average or above average talent.

Criticism of Jensen

The most comprehensive critical analysis of Jensen's conclusions appeared as responses in the next issue of the *Review.* Most of the responders supported the view that environment plays a larger role in determining IQ scores than Jensen had allowed. Their main points included the following:[34]

1. Jensen's research was based on relatively small samples.

2. The environment-heredity interaction is impossible to separate and measure.

3. IQ outcomes are affected by a host of environmental variables, such as malnutrition and prenatal care, which are difficult to measure.

4. Racial prejudice could account for any differences in IQ that might exist between African Americans and whites.

5. IQ tests are biased, and the scores do not necessarily measure intelligence.

After publication of his 1969 article, Jensen was under severe criticism in the professional literature; his classes were disrupted, he and his family were threatened, he was denied the opportunity to address many professional audiences, and on some occasions he was prevented from finishing his lectures.[35] Jensen has continued to cite data that he believes indicate that intelligence is

[33]Arthur R. Jensen, "How Much Can We Boost IQ and Scholastic Achievement?" *Harvard Educational Review* (Winter 1969), pp. 1–123; Arthur R. Jensen, *Bias in Mental Testing* (New York: The Free Press, 1980); Richard J. Herrnstein, "IQ Testing and the Media," *The Atlantic Monthly* (February 1982), pp. 68–74; Richard J. Herrnstein, "IQ and Falling Birthrates," *The Atlantic Monthly* (May 1989), pp. 73–79; and Thomas J. Bouchard, Jr., et al., "Sources of Human Psychological Differences: The Minnesota Study of Twins Reared Apart," *Science,* October 12, 1990, pp. 223–228. Also see Daniel Seligman, *The IQ Debate* (New York: Carol, 1992).

[34]"How Much Can We Boost IQ and Scholastic Achievement: A Discussion," *Harvard Educational Review* (Spring 1969), pp. 273–356. Contributors were Jerome S. Kagan, J. McVicker Hunt, James F. Crow, Carl Bereiter, David Elkind, Lee J. Cronbach, and William F. Brazziel. Also see Flynn, "Massive IQ Gains in 14 Nations," and Charles Locurto, *Sense and Nonsense About IQ* (Westport, Conn.: Praeger, 1991).

[35]Part of the criticism of Jensen focused on his use of data on twins, which had been collected by a distinguished British psychologist (Sir Cyril Burt). Many scholars now believe that these data were fabricated to support hereditarian conclusions. See Leon J. Kamin, *The Science and Politics of IQ* (Potomac, Md.: Erlbaum, 1974), and Arthur R. Jensen, "IQ and Science," *The Public Interest* (Fall 1991), pp. 93–106.

determined primarily by heredity, and critics respond with evidence that environment and, in particular, schooling have a major influence on IQ.[36]

Synthesizers' View.   Although hundreds of studies have investigated the relationship of heredity and of environment to intelligence, scientists still disagree vigorously on the interpretation of those studies.[37] A number of social scientists have taken a middle, or "synthesizing," position in the controversy. The **synthesizers' view of intelligence** holds that both heredity and environment contribute to differences in measured intelligence. For example, Christopher Jencks and his colleagues reviewed a large amount of data and divided the IQ variance into .45 due to heredity, .35 due to environment, and .20 due to interaction between the two (i.e., particular abilities thrive or wither in specific environments). Robert Nichols reviewed all these and other data and concluded that the true value may be anywhere between .40 and .80 but that the exact value has little importance for policy. In general, Nichols and other synthesizers maintain that the best way to conceptualize the contribution of heredity to a trait such as intelligence is to think of heredity as determining the fixed limits of a range; the interaction of both components yields the individual's intelligence. Even if we cannot specify exactly how much of a child's intelligence is the result of environmental factors, teachers (and parents) should provide each child with a productive environment in which to realize her or his maximum potential.[38]

Intermediate position

Interaction effects crucial

Obstacles in the Classroom

Certain school and classroom dynamics help bring about very low achievement among working-class students in the United States and other countries. We already have noted that the home and family environment of many working-class students lacks the kind of educational stimulation that adequately prepares students for success in the classroom. The following list highlights some of the most important classroom obstacles to overcome in order to redress the educational disadvantages of students from these backgrounds.[39]

1. *Inappropriate curriculum and instruction.* Curriculum materials and instructional approaches in the primary grades frequently assume that students are familiar with vocabulary and concepts to which working-class students have

---

[36]Arthur R. Jensen, "g: Artifact or Reality?" *Journal of Vocational Behavior* (December 1986), pp. 330–331; Elaine Mensh and Harry Mensh, *The IQ Mythology* (Carbondale: Southern Illinois University Press, 1991).

[37]John Raven, "The Raven Progressive Matrices: A Review of National Norming Studies and Ethnic and Socioeconomic Variation Within the United States," *Journal of Educational Measurement* (Spring 1989), pp. 1–16; Robert Cancro, ed., *Intelligence: Genetic and Environmental Influences* (New York: Grune & Stratton, 1991).

[38]Robert C. Nichols, "Policy Implications of the IQ Controversy," in Lee S. Shulman, ed., *Review of Research in Education* (Itasca, Ill.: Peacock, 1978); Christopher Jencks, "Genes and Crime," *The New York Review of Books,* February 12, 1987, pp. 33–41; Robert Plonim, "Environment and Genes," *American Psychologist* (February 1989), pp. 105–111; Robert M. Hauser, Gerald D. Jaynes, and Robin M. Williams, Jr., "Understanding Black-White Differences," *The Public Interest* (Spring 1991), pp. 110–119; and Marilee C. Rist, "Genes and Behavior," *Executive Educator* (December 1991), pp. 16–21.

[39]The discussion in this section is based in part on material in Levine and Havighurst, *Society and Education,* Chapter 8.

had little or no exposure. As students proceed through school, terminology and concepts become increasingly abstract, and many students fall further behind because their level of mastery is too rudimentary to allow for fluent learning. After grade three, much of the curriculum requires reading skills that many working-class students have not yet acquired; hence they fall further behind in other subject areas.[40]

Curriculum increasingly abstract

Students' perceptions

2. *Lack of previous success in school.* Lack of academic success in the early grades not only detracts from learning more difficult material later; it also damages a student's perception that he or she is a capable learner who has a chance to succeed in school and in later life. Once students believe that they are inadequate as learners and lack control over their future, they are less likely to work vigorously at overcoming learning deficiencies.[41]

3. *Difficulty of teaching conditions in working-class schools.* As students fall further behind academically and as both teachers and students experience frustration and discouragement, behavior problems increase in the classroom and teachers find it still more difficult to provide a productive learning environment. One frequent result is that some teachers eventually give up trying to teach low achievers or leave the school to seek less frustrating employment elsewhere.[42]

Difficult for teachers

4. *Differences in teacher/student backgrounds.* Teachers from middle-class backgrounds may have difficulty understanding and motivating disadvantaged pupils. Particularly in the case of white teachers working with disadvantaged minority students, differences in dialect and language background may make it difficult for middle-class teachers to communicate effectively with their students. Because teachers in this situation may reject students who have different habits of dress, physical mannerisms, or expressive styles, many educators believe it is desirable for school faculties to include minority teachers whose cultural backgrounds can help in establishing positive relationships with disadvantaged minority students.[43]

Language and other cultural differences

5. *Teacher perceptions of student inadequacy.* Many teachers in working-class schools may observe low achievement in their classrooms and conclude that large numbers of their students are incapable of learning. This view easily becomes a self-fulfilling prophecy because teachers who question their students' learning potential are less likely to work hard to improve academic performance, particularly since improvement requires an intense effort that quickly consumes virtually all of a teacher's energy. Since students are influenced by their teachers'

Self-fulfilling prophecy

[40]Michael S. Knapp and Patrick M. Shields, eds., *Better Schooling for the Children of Poverty* (Berkeley, Calif.: McCutchan, 1991).

[41]Thomas I. Good, "Two Decades of Research on Teacher Expectations," *Journal of Teacher Education* (July–August 1987), pp. 32–47; James A. Beane, "Sorting Out the Self-Esteem Controversy," *Educational Leadership* (September 1991), pp. 25–30.

[42]Reba Page and Linda Valli, eds., *Curriculum Differentiation* (Albany: State University of New York Press, 1990); Stanley Pogrow, "What to Do About Chapter 1," *Phi Delta Kappan* (April 1992), pp. 624–630.

[43]Jacqueline Jordan Irvine, "Teacher Race as a Factor in Black Student Achievement" (Paper presented at the Annual Meeting of the American Educational Research Association, New Orleans, April 1988); Josie G. Bain and Joan L. Herman, eds., *Making Schools Work for Underachieving Minority Students* (New York: Greenwood, 1990); and Bob Peterson, "Reform vs. Scapegoating," *Rethinking Schools* (March/April 1992), pp. 1, 9–11.

perceptions and behaviors, low teacher expectations generate further declines in students' motivation and performance.[44]

6. *Ineffective homogeneous grouping.* Educators faced with large groups of low achievers frequently address the problem by setting them apart in separate classes or subgroups in which instruction can proceed at a slower pace without detracting from the performance of high achievers. Unfortunately, both teachers and the students themselvers tend to view concentrations of low achievers as "slow" groups for whom learning expectations are low or nonexistent. Ray Rist studied this type of arrangement, called **homogeneous grouping,** at a working-class school in St. Louis and offered the following description of its effects on instruction.

Low expectations for "slow" groups

> The class was divided into groups: those expected to succeed ("fast learners") and those expected to fail ("slow learners"). . . . This categorization had the following results:
>
> (1) Differential treatment was accorded the two groups in the classroom, the group designated as "fast" learners receiving the most teaching time, rewards, and attention from the teacher. Those designated as "slow learners" were taught infrequently, subjected to more control, and received little if any support from the teacher.
>
> (2) The interactional patterns between the teacher and the various groups in her class became increasingly rigidified, taking on caste-like characteristics, during the course of the school year. . . .
>
> (3) The consequence of the differential experiences of the children within the same kindergarten classroom was that they were differentially prepared for the first grade. The first grade teacher grouped the children according to the amount of "readiness" material they had completed in kindergarten.[45]

Differential preparation

Implications of this analysis of homogeneous grouping of low achievers are not entirely clear. Individualized instruction in heterogeneous classes might make it possible for each student to make continual progress at his or her own rate, but individualization is extremely difficult to implement effectively and probably requires such costly and systematic change in school practices as to constitute a virtual economic impossibility. Thus, teachers confronted with heterogeneous classes in schools with mostly low-income students generally have not been able to work effectively with the large numbers of low achievers in their classrooms.[46] One solution is to group low achievers homogeneously for blocks of reading and language arts instruction, but to make sure that the groups are small and are taught by highly skilled teachers who are enthusiastic about working with such students. This alternative is well in line with recent research indicating that "restrictive" school settings (that is, separate arrangements for low achievers) may have either positive or negative outcomes, depending on

Practical implications unclear

Restrictive settings

[44]Charles M. Payne, *Getting What We Ask For* (Westwood, Conn.: Greenwood, 1984); Good, "Two Decades of Research on Teacher Expectations"; Hersholt C. Waxman et al., eds., *Leadership, Equity, and School Effectiveness* (Newbury Park, Calif.: Sage, 1992).

[45]Ray C. Rist, *The Urban School: A Factory for Failure* (Cambridge, Mass.: MIT Press, 1973), p. 91. Also see Daniel L. Duke and Robert L. Canaday, *School Policy* (New York: McGraw-Hill, 1991).

[46]Michael Scriven, "Problems and Prospects for Individualization," in Harriet Talmage, ed., *Systems of Individualized Education* (Berkeley, Calif.: McCutchan, 1975), pp. 199–210; Michael S. Knapp et al., *What Is Taught, and How, to the Children of Poverty* (Washington, D.C.: U.S. Department of Education, 1991).

Taking Issue ━━●▶

Homogeneous Grouping

Many schools and classrooms group students by ability in specific subjects, separating the slower from the faster learners or the more advanced from the less advanced. Advocates of homogeneous grouping argue that it is both fair and effective, but critics have charged that it harms students, particularly low achievers.

Question: Is homogeneous grouping of students by ability a generally effective approach for classroom instruction?

Arguments PRO

1　In a large, heterogeneous class with students at many different levels, the teacher cannot give the slowest learners the special attention they need. In fact, students who struggle to master the lesson may come to be seen as "problems," and quicker students may become favorites. Therefore, it makes sense to separate students into ability groups for specific subjects.

2　For high-achieving students who are capable of learning quickly, it is unfair to slow the pace of instruction to meet the needs of the average student. The high achievers may become bored and discouraged unless they are separated into groups that can proceed at a faster rate.

3　Homogeneous grouping encourages the growth of an esprit de corps among group members. With co-operation and friendly competition, students at similar levels can spur each other forward.

4　Many teachers are more effective with certain kinds of students than with others. Homogeneous grouping allows teachers to spend more time with groups they enjoy teaching and are best suited to teach.

5　Homogeneous grouping indicates to parents that the school recognizes differences in learning styles. The school is seen as making a commitment to each child's individual needs.

Arguments CON

1　Research has shown that ability grouping tends to stereotype slower learners and hamper their progress. The instruction offered to such groups is often inferior. Because little is expected of them, they are seldom challenged, and thus they fall further behind the more advanced students. In general, slower learners will do better in heterogeneous classes.

2　Although high-achieving students may be hindered somewhat in a heterogeneous setting, they will remain motivated as long as they sense that the teacher appreciates their talents. It is important for them to learn, moreover, that students of all academic levels have something of value to contribute.

3　A group spirit may develop among high achievers who feel a special honor in being placed together. But low achievers will feel stigmatized, and their attitudes as a group will often be negative. They may become increasingly alienated from school and society.

4　Only a few very special teachers have the skill, patience, and enthusiasm needed to work effectively with an entire group of low achievers. Teachers assigned to such groups may become frustrated and demoralized.

5　Parents of low achievers are rarely pleased at seeing their children separated from others. A heterogeneous setting is the best indication that the school cares about all its students.

what one does to make instruction effective.[47] The issue of homogeneous grouping is discussed further in Chapter 16.

7. *Delivery-of-service problems.* The problems we have described suggest that it is very difficult to deliver educational services effectively in classes or schools with a high percentage of low achievers. If, for example, a teacher in a working-class school has ten or twelve very low achieving students in a class of twenty-five, the task of providing effective instruction is many times more difficult than

Multiplied difficulties

that of a teacher who has only four or five low achievers in a middle-class school. Not only may teachers in the former situation need to spend virtually all their time overcoming low achievers' learning problems, but the negative dynamics that result from students' frustration and misbehavior make the task much more demanding.[48] Administrators, counselors, and other specialized personnel in working-class schools experience the same predicament: so much time is taken up with addressing learning and behavior problems that little may be

Overload widespread

left for working on delivery of improved services for all students. In such **overloaded schools** the high incidence of serious problems makes it very difficult for educators to function effectively.

8. *Overly large classes.* As suggested above, one reason instruction is ineffective for many low-achieving students is that classes frequently are too large for teachers to provide sufficient help to overcome learning problems. This is particularly true with respect to critical thinking, reading comprehension, mathematics problem solving, and other higher-order skills. Acquisition of complex

Complex-skill learning hampered

skills among low achievers appears to require systematic "mediated" assistance in small groups or individually.[49]

Tennessee STAR Project

This conclusion has been supported by a major study of student performance in Project STAR classes in eighty schools in Tennessee. From kindergarten through third grade, students were assigned randomly to classes respectively classified as "small" (13 to 17), "regular" (22 to 25), or "regular plus a full-time teacher aide." Contrasting their results with earlier studies, which frequently have been ambiguous as to the impact of small classes, researchers assessing Project STAR found that students in the small classes scored substantially higher in reading and math in kindergarten and first grade than did students in regular classes, and then maintained their advantage through the third grade. Effects were particularly impressive at inner-city schools, which enrolled large proportions of students from low-income minority backgrounds.[50]

---

[47]Gaea Leinhardt and Allan Pallay, "Restrictive Educational Settings: Exile or Haven?" *Review of Educational Research* (December 1982), pp. 557–558; Daniel U. Levine and Lawrence W. Lezotte, *Unusually Effective Schools* (Madison, Wis.: National Center for Effective Schools Research and Development, 1990).

[48]Eugene E. Eubanks and Daniel U. Levine, "Administrative and Organizational Arrangements and Considerations," in Dorothy S. Strickland and Eric J. Cooper, eds., *Educating Black Children* (Washington, D.C.: Howard University, 1987), pp. 19–32; Barbara Smey-Richman, "At-Risk, Low-Achieving Students," *Equity and Excellence* (Fall 1991), pp. 25–29.

[49]Lorna Idol and Beau Fly Jones, eds., *Educational Values and Cognitive Instruction* (Hillsdale, N.J.: Erlbaum, 1991); Barbara Z. Presseisen, "Mediated Learning" (Paper presented at the Annual Meeting of the American Educational Research Association, San Francisco, April 1992).

[50]Jeremy D. Finn and Charles M. Achilles, "Answers and Questions About Class Size: A Statewide Experiment," *American Educational Research Journal* (Fall 1990), pp. 557–577; Barbara Miner, "Students Learn Best in Small Classes," *Rethinking Schools* (January–February 1992), p. 15.

9. *Low standards of performance.* By the time low-achieving working-class students reach the upper elementary grades or the high school, many of them are required to accomplish very little — low performance has become acceptable to their teachers. Whether in a poverty or working-class school or a mixed-status school, many such students make little or no effort to meet demanding academic requirements by the time they reach the secondary level. Julia Wrigley has summarized the way in which student-teacher interactions reinforce low performance requirements as follows:

Students feel defeated

> Educational ambivalence is essential to the functioning of many ghetto schools; if the students lose faith entirely, they become impossible to control, yet the teachers do not want to foster hopeless illusions about their students' possible success. Thus, students are praised for work that might actually be below par, even while a climate of failure and misdirected application hangs over the entire school.[51]

10. *Negative peer pressure.* Several researchers have studied peer influences in predominantly working-class schools and reported that academically oriented students frequently are ridiculed and rejected for accepting school norms. Paul Willis and Robert Everhardt found that this pattern was prominent among working-class students in England and the United States, respectively. John Ogbu and Signithia Fordham have described negative peer influences as being particularly strong among working-class African American students, many of whom exemplified a "coping lifestyle" that is frequently present when students have failed in the classroom and thereafter are unwilling to exert themselves in educational activities that might result in still more failure. At inner-city schools where significant numbers of students react in this way, high achievers who work hard are labeled as "brainiacs" and accused of "acting white."[52] (Some researchers have reported that such attitudes appear to be much less prevalent among black students who are middle class or who attend desegregated schools.[53]) Commenting on the negative effects of these phenomena, an African American professor at Fordham University concluded that the "notion that someone with a hunger for knowledge would be regarded as a 'traitor to his race' . . . would seem like some kind of sinister white plot. In a society where blacks had to endure jailings, shootings, and lynchings to get an education, it

Coping lifestyle

---

[51]Julia Wrigley, "A Message of Marginality: Black Youth, Alienation, and Unemployment," in Harry F. Silberman, ed., *Education and Work* (Chicago: University of Chicago Press, 1982), p. 245. Also see Mary McCaslin and Thomas L. Good, "Compliant Cognition," *Educational Researcher* (April 1992), pp. 4–17.

[52]Paul Willis, *Learning to Labour* (Westmead, England: Saxon House, 1977); Robert Everhardt, *Reading, Writing and Resistance* (Boston: Routledge & Kegan Paul, 1983); John U. Ogbu, *Minority Education and Caste* (New York: Academic Press, 1978); Signithia Fordham, "Racelessness as a Factor in Black Students' School Success: Pragmatic Strategy or Pyrrhic Victory?" *Harvard Educational Review* (February 1988), pp. 54–84; Seth Mydans, "Black Identity vs. Success and Seeming White," *The New York Times* (April 25, 1990), p. 36; John Ogbu, "Minority Status and Literacy in Comparative Perspective," *Daedalus* (June/July 1990), pp. 141–165; Signithia Fordham, "Racelessness in Private Schools," *Teachers College Record* (Spring 1991), pp. 470–484; Margaret A. Gibson and John U. Ogbu, *Minority Status and Schooling* (New York: Garland, 1991); and Michel Marriott, "Blacks in Science Program Shatter Stereotypes," *The New York Times*, March 18, 1992, p. B7.

[53]Alan Peshkin and Carolyn J. White, "Four Black American Students: Coming of Age in a Multiethnic High School," *Teachers College Record* (Fall 1990), pp. 21–39.

seems utterly unbelievable that some black youngsters now regard . . . academic failure as a sign of pride."[54]

However, recent research by Lois Weis suggests that antischool peer pressures among working-class students lessen as they realize that education is important for future success. Weis observed and interviewed students at "Freeway" High School. More than in previous research, the boys in her study perceived schooling as offering "utilitarian opportunities" for acquiring skilled jobs and thus were willing to "put in their time" in school and even go to college. She also found that girls were more likely than earlier studies suggested to reject the traditional "patriarchal premise" that "woman's primary place is in the home-family sphere."[55]

11. *Incompatibility between classroom expectations and students' behavioral patterns and learning styles.* Numerous analysts have concluded that the behavioral patterns and learning styles of many working-class students and some groups of minority students are different from those of middle-class or nonminority students, and that these differences frequently lead to school failure. Traditional classroom expectations may be geared to high-achieving, middle-class students.

For example, some research has suggested that many African American students tend to be energetic (i.e., have high "activation" levels) and do not perform well if teachers require them to sit in one place for extended periods of time or prohibit impulsive responses; that some low-income African American students tend to become confused when teachers do not act forcefully and "authoritatively"; and that African American and Hispanic students may tend to be "field dependent" — that is, they do not learn well when instruction begins with abstract, "decontextualized" concepts that the student examines independently.

Based on this type of analysis, various observers have recommended that teachers should allow more physical movement and help low achievers learn step-by-step how to function appropriately. They should present concrete material before moving to abstract analysis, avoid treating students as "buddies," provide opportunities for students to learn in pairs or cooperative groups, and take other steps that accommodate different behavioral patterns and learning styles.[56]

It should be emphasized that research has not conclusively established the existence of distinctive behavioral patterns or learning styles among working class or minority students; to the extent that some African American, Hispanic, or other minority students do learn differently from nonminority students, differences may be attributable to socioeconomic status, not to race or ethnicity. However, numerous studies do support the conclusion that teachers who adjust

---

[54]Mark Naison, "Blacks Blocking the School Door," *Newsday* (April 2, 1990), pp. 40, 42. Also see Roslyn A. Mickelson, "The Attitude-Achievement Paradox Among Black Adolescents," *Sociology of Education* (January 1990), pp. 48–61.

[55]Lois Weis, "The 1980s: De-Industrialization and Change in White Working Class Male and Female Youth Cultural Forms," *Metropolitan Education* (Fall 1987), pp. 93, 114; Lois Weis, *Working Class Without Work* (New York: Routledge, 1990).

[56]Manuel Ramirez and Carlos Castaneda, *Cultural Democracy, Bicognitive Development, and Education* (New York: Academic Press, 1974); Janice Hale-Benson, "Vision for Children: Educating Black Children in the Context of Their Culture," in Kofi Vomotey, ed., *Going to School* (Albany: State University of New York Press, 1990), pp. 209–220; Jacqueline J. Irvine, *Black Students and School Failure* (Westport, Conn.: Greenwood, 1990); and Nancy J. Protheroe and Kelly J. Barsdate, "Culturally Sensitive Instruction," *National Association of Elementary School Principals Streamlined Seminar* (March 1992), pp. 1–4.

for different learning styles can help improve the performance of their low-achieving students.[57] Such alternative teaching practices are discussed in the next chapter in the section on multicultural education.

Substantial learning gains possible

The preceding analysis makes it clear that many students are not only economically disadvantaged but also experience educational disadvantages in our schools and classrooms. Recent research indicates that disadvantaged students can be much more successful in the educational system than they are now. Mastery learning research, for example, indicates that disadvantaged low achievers can make substantial gains when they have adequate time to learn and receive appropriate assistance in the classroom.[58] But the discouraging facts of achievement and social class have led some to question whether schools do indeed make a difference — whether they help at all in counteracting the disadvantages students experience. The rest of this chapter presents interpretations of and disagreements over this issue. Later chapters, particularly Chapter 16, will discuss ways to bolster student achievement by improving the organization and delivery of instruction.

DO SCHOOLS EQUALIZE OPPORTUNITY?

The research discussed in the preceding sections indicates that disproportionate numbers of students from low-income backgrounds enter school poorly prepared to succeed in traditional classrooms, and in later years rank relatively low in achievement and other indicators of success such as high-school completion, entry into postsecondary institutions, and, consequently, acquisition of skills required for rewarding employment. If equal opportunity is defined in terms of overcoming the disadvantages associated with family background so that students on the average perform equally well regardless of socioeconomic status, one must conclude that the educational system has not been very successful in equalizing opportunity.

Lack of success in overcoming disadvantages

Equal opportunity study

The issue of equal educational opportunity has received considerable attention since the publication in 1966 of a massive national study conducted by James Coleman and his colleagues. Titled *Equality of Educational Opportunity*, this federally supported study collected data on approximately 600,000 students at more than 4,000 schools. Congressional sponsors of the study expected it would show that low achievement among students with low socioeconomic status was due to low expenditures on their education, thus providing a basis for increased funding of the schools they attend.

---

[57]Madge G. Willis, "Learning Styles of African American Children: A Review of the Literature and Interventions," *The Journal of Black Psychology* (Fall 1989), pp. 47–65; Patrick M. Shields and Debra M. Shaver, *The Mismatch Between the School and Home Cultures of Academically At-Risk Students* (Menlo Park, Calif.: SRI, 1990); and Maxine L. Clark, "Social Identity, Peer Relations, and Academic Competence," *Education and Urban Society* (November 1991), pp. 41–52.

[58]Daniel U. Levine and Beau Fly Jones, "Mastery Learning," in Richard Gorton, Gail Schneider, and James Fischer, eds., *Encyclopedia of School Administration and Supervision* (Phoenix: Oryx, 1988); Thomas R. Guskey, "Integrating Innovations," *Educational Leadership* (February 1990), pp. 11–15; and Glenn M. Hymel, "The Essential Literature in Outcomes-Based Education and Mastery Learning" (Paper presented at the Annual Meeting of the American Educational Research Association, San Francisco, April 1992).

Getting to the Source ━━━━◆━

The Effects of Schools on Achievement /
James S. Coleman

EQUALITY OF EDUCATIONAL OPPORTUNITY

By James S. Coleman, Johns Hopkins University
and
Ernest Q. Campbell, Vanderbilt University
Carol J. Hobson, U.S. Office of Education
James McPartland, U.S. Office of Education
Alexander M. Mood, U.S. Office of Education
Frederic D. Weinfeld, U.S. Office of Education
Robert L. York, U.S. Office of Education

U.S. DEPARTMENT OF HEALTH, EDUCATION, AND WELFARE
John W. Gardner, *Secretary*
OFFICE OF EDUCATION, Harold Howe II, *Commissioner*

James S. Coleman is a sociologist who has devoted much of his research to issues involving the behavior and achievement of students in different types of schools. *In the 1960s he led a team of researchers who conducted a massive study of achievement in public elementary and secondary schools. The resulting report,* Equality of Educational Opportunity, *is still cited widely in discussions on how to improve our schools.*

Of the many implications of this study of school effects on achievement, one appears to be of overriding importance. This is the implication that stems from the following results taken together:

1. The great importance of family background for achievement;

2. The fact that the relation of family background to achievement does not diminish over the years of school;

3. The relatively small amount of school-to-school variation that is not accounted for by differences in family background, indicating the small independent effect of variations in school facilities, curriculum, and staff upon achievement;

4. The small amount of variance in achievement explicitly accounted for by variations in facilities and curriculum;

Influence of school social class

Coleman and his colleagues reported that, as expected, achievement was highly related to students' socioeconomic background and that schools with high proportions of working-class and underclass students generally were not as well funded as middle-class schools. However, they also found that expenditures for reduced class size, laboratories, libraries, and other aspects of school operation were fundamentally unrelated to achievement after taking account of (1) a student's personal socioeconomic background and (2) the social-class status of other students in the school. Many readers incorrectly interpreted the data to mean that schools cannot be successful in improving the performance of economically disadvantaged students, but the results did support two conclusions: (1) simply spending more on education for disadvantaged students should not be expected to improve their achievement substantially, and (2) placing students who previously attended mostly working-class schools in schools with middle-class students could improve achievement.[59]

─────────

[59]James S. Coleman et al., *Equality of Educational Opportunity* (Washington, D.C.: U.S. Govern-

5. Given the fact that no school factors* account for much variation in achievement, teachers' characteristics account for more than any other—[but] teachers tend to be socially and racially similar to the students they teach;

6. The fact that the social composition of the student body is more highly related to achievement, independently of the student's own social background, than is any school factor;

7. The fact that attitudes such as a sense of control of the environment, or a belief in the responsiveness of the environment, are extremely highly related to achievement, but appear to be little influenced by variations in school characteristics.

Taking all these results together, one implication stands out above all: That schools bring little influence to bear on a child's achievement that is independent of his background and general social context; and that this very lack of an independent effect means that the inequalities imposed on children by their home, neighborhood, and peer environment are carried along to become the inequalities with which they confront adult life at the end of school. For equality of educational opportunity through the schools must imply a strong effect of schools that is independent of the child's immediate social environment, and that strong independent effect is not present in American schools.

Questions

1. What are some of the reasons why the relationship between family background and achievement does not diminish as a group of low-income students proceeds through the grades?

2. In what ways does the socioeconomic composition of the student body as a whole influence a student's achievement level?

3. In what way can findings from *Equality of Educational Opportunity* be used to support the conclusion that low-income students attending inner-city poverty schools should be transferred to predominantly middle-class schools?

*School factors analyzed in the study included facilities and instructional materials, class size, expenditures per student, curricula, characteristics of the teachers, and the social and educational backgrounds of the other students.

Source: James S. Coleman et al., *Equality of Educational Opportunity* (Washington, D.C.: U.S. Government Printing Office, 1966), cover, p. 325.

Similar conclusions were widely disseminated in the following decade after the publication of two influential books by Christopher Jencks and his colleagues. After analyzing numerous data sets collected by the U.S. Census Bureau, reanalyzing data available from *Equality of Educational Opportunity*, Project Talent, and other large studies of U.S. schools, and examining many other relevant sources, Jencks and his colleagues concluded that:[60]

Jencks studies

1. School achievement depends substantially on students' family characteristics.

2. The schools accomplish little in terms of reducing the achievement gap between students with higher and lower socioeconomic status.

ment Printing Office, 1966); Frederick Mosteller and Daniel P. Moynihan, eds., *On Equality of Educational Opportunity* (New York: Random House, 1972); and James S. Coleman, *Equality and Achievement in Education* (Boulder, Colo.: Westview, 1990).

[60]Christopher Jencks et al., *Inequality* (New York: Basic Books, 1972); Christopher Jencks et al., *Who Gets Ahead?* (New York: Basic Books, 1979).

3. Family background accounts for nearly half the variation in adult occupational status and between 15 percent and 35 percent of the variation in adult earnings, depending on the data set analyzed and the statistical method researchers employ. Individuals from families with high status are relatively successful economically in part because they acquire more education and skills than individuals from families with low status.

Problem is international

Conclusions similar to these are apparent from numerous studies in other countries. For example, scholars at the World Bank reviewed several decades of research on education internationally and reported that family background has an "early and apparently lasting influence" on achievement, particularly when alternate measures of social class are used to take account of differences between countries. Regarding relationships between social-class background, amount of schooling, and later economic success, a review of studies in Great Britain concluded that schools there have served as "mechanisms for the transmission of privileges from one generation of middle-class citizens to the next"; analyses of data collected in France, Germany, Great Britain, Hungary, Ireland, Poland, Scotland, Sweden, and other nations also support the conclusion that education importantly helps children from middle-class families attain financially rewarding employment more frequently than it helps children from working-class families.[61]

Privileges transmitted across generations

Many students succeed

This does not mean, however, that all or even most students from low-income families will be unsuccessful as adults or that the schools should be viewed as mostly unsuccessful in helping provide worthwhile opportunities for students with diverse socioeconomic backgrounds. Research supports the following general conclusions:

1. *Although students with low socioeconomic status tend to perform poorly in school and subsequently have restricted employment opportunities, a substantial proportion of working-class children and some from families living in poverty do eventually attain middle-class status.* For example, although about two-thirds of men in the U.S. labor force grew up in working-class families or on a farm, nearly half are in middle- or high-status jobs; nearly 40 percent are in upper-middle-class jobs even though less than 25 percent were raised in upper-middle-class families. Socioeconomic mobility of this kind has been present throughout U.S. history. It appears to have increased somewhat in recent decades because technological and economic change has been creating high-status jobs and eliminating unskilled jobs.[62]

Socioeconomic mobility

2. *The educational system has played an important part in helping many persons rise in status beyond that of their parents.* Its role in promoting socioeconomic mo-

---

[61]John H. Goldthorpe, *Social Mobility and Class Structure in Modern Britain*, 2nd ed. (Oxford: Clarendon Press, 1987); Marlaine E. Lockheed, Bruce Fuller, and Ronald Nyirongo, *Family Background and School Achievement* (Washington, D.C.: The World Bank, 1988), p. 23; Gordon Marshall, *In Praise of Sociology* (London: Unwin Hyman, 1990), p. 37; and Annemette Sørensen, "Educational Systems Matter," *Educational Researcher* (March 1992), p. 36.

[62]David L. Featherman and Robert M. Hauser, *Opportunity and Change* (New York: Academic Press, 1978); Michael Hout, "More Universalism, Less Structural Mobility: The American Occupational Structure in the 1980s," *American Journal of Sociology* (May 1988), pp. 1358–1400; and Daniel H. Krynowski, "The Process of Status Attainment Among Men in Poland, the United States, and West Germany," *American Sociological Review* (February 1991), pp. 46–59.

bility has grown more central as middle- and high-status jobs have become more complex and increasingly require specialized educational skills and credentials.[63]

College increasingly important

3. *As education increasingly determines socioeconomic status and mobility, college attendance and graduation constitute a kind of "dividing line" differentiating persons who are likely to attain high socioeconomic status and those who are not.* Enrollment in high school probably was the best educational indicator of socioeconomic status one hundred years ago, and high-school graduation constituted the clearest dividing line fifty or sixty years ago. Today attendance at postsecondary institutions is almost a prerequisite for middle- or high-status jobs. A college degree already is required for many high-status jobs, and probably will become an even more widespread requirement in the future.[64]

4. *Educational, social, and economic opportunities are not sufficiently available to overcome the disadvantages of the underclass population.* Children who attend low-achieving poverty schools are disproportionately likely to remain very low in socioeconomic status.

TRADITIONAL VERSUS REVISIONIST INTERPRETATIONS

Growing recognition of the strong relationship between social class and school achievement has led to a fundamental disagreement between two groups of observers of education in the United States. Briefly, according to the **traditional view of schools,** the educational system successfully functions to provide economically disadvantaged students with meaningful opportunities for social and economic advancement. The **revisionist view of schools,** by way of contrast, holds that the schools fail to provide most disadvantaged students with a meaningful chance to succeed in society. Many revisionists also believe that schools are not even designed to accomplish this purpose, but instead are established and operated to perpetuate the disadvantages experienced by working-class students.[65] The term **critical theory** or **critical pedagogy** is often used as a synonym for the revisionist view. The following sections explore the ramifications of these two arguments.

Critical pedagogy

The Revisionist View and Critical Pedagogy

Revisionists contend that through control of the schools, elite groups have channeled disadvantaged students into second-rate secondary schools and pro-

---

[63]Goldthorpe, *Social Mobility and Class Structure;* Hout, "More Universalism"; Ronald E. Kutscher, "The Mismatch Revisited," *Work America* (April 1990), pp. 9–11; and Dick Youngblood, "U.S. Education Needs Abrupt Change for the Better," *Congressional Record,* January 22, 1992, p. 5130.

[64]Frank Levy and Robert C. Michel, *The Economic Future of American Families* (Washington, D.C.: The Urban Institute, 1991); Iver Peterson, "Why Older People Are Richer Than Other Americans," *The New York Times,* November 3, 1991, p. E3; and Jean Evangelauf, "Enrollment Projections Revised Upward in New Government Analysis," *The Chronicle of Higher Education,* January 22, 1992, pp. A1, A36.

[65]Some of the revisionists frequently are referred to as neo-Marxists because they believe that the capitalist system must be abolished or fundamentally changed if schools are to provide truly equal opportunity for all students.

grams, third-rate community colleges, and fourth-rate jobs. Many critical pedagogists also believe that the educational system has been set up specifically to produce disciplined workers at the bottom of the class structure.[66] This is accomplished in part by emphasizing discipline in working-class schools, just as the working-class family and the factory labor system emphasize discipline. According to this point of view, the schools are based on a correspondence principle, whereby the social relations of the factory are replicated in the socialization and education of children and youth. Samuel Bowles has summarized this argument as follows:

Correspondence principle

> [The] division of labor . . . gives rise to distinct class subcultures. The values, personality traits, and expectations characteristic of each subculture are transmitted from generation to generation through class differences in family socialization and complementary differences in the type and amount of schooling ordinarily attained by children of various class positions.[67]

Much recent analysis in critical pedagogy has been referred to as **resistance theory,** which attempts to explain why some students with low socioeconomic status refuse to conform to school expectations and do not comply with the demands of their teachers. Resistance arises partly because school norms and expectations contradict the traditional definitions of masculinity and femininity such students hold, and because an "oppositional peer life" stimulates students to resist what they perceive as irrelevant middle-class values disseminated by their teachers. Resistance theorists also have concluded that the "hegemonic" traditional curriculum marginalizes the everyday knowledge of such students, thereby reinforcing anti-intellectual tendencies in working-class cultures.[68]

Oppositional peer life

Critical theorists have been devoting considerable attention to what educators can or should do to improve opportunities for students with low socioeconomic status. Using a variety of related terms and concepts such as "critical discourse," "critical engagement," and "critical literacy," they have emphasized the importance of teachers' becoming "transformative intellectuals" who take comprehensive action to make education more meaningful for such students.[69]

Critical discourse

---

[66]Major writings of the revisionist scholars and critical pedagogists include the following: Martin Carnoy, ed., *Schooling in a Corporate Society* (New York: McKay, 1975); Joel H. Spring, *The Sorting Machine* (New York: McKay, 1976); Paul C. Violas, *The Training of the Urban Working Class* (Chicago: Rand McNally, 1978); Richard H. deLone, *Small Futures* (New York: Harcourt Brace Jovanovich, 1979); Samuel Bowles and Herbert Gintis, *Schooling in Capitalist America* (New York: Basic Books, 1976); Michael W. Apple and Lois Weis, eds., *Ideology and Practice in Schooling* (Philadelphia: Temple University, 1983); Henry A. Giroux and David Purpel, eds., *The Hidden Curriculum and Moral Education* (Berkeley, Calif.: McCutchan, 1983); Michael W. Apple, *Education and Power* (Boston: Ark, 1985); Martin Carnoy and Henry M. Levin, *Schooling and Work in the Democratic State* (Stanford, Calif.: Stanford University Press, 1985); David W. Livingston et al., *Critical Pedagogy and Cultural Power* (South Hadley, Mass.: Bergin and Garvey, 1987); and Henry A. Giroux, *Cultural Workers and the Politics of Education* (New York: Routledge, 1991).

[67]Samuel Bowles, "Unequal Education and the Reproduction of the Social Division of Labor," in Carnoy, ed., *Schooling in a Corporate Society,* p. 58.

[68]Robert W. Connell et al., *Making the Difference* (Boston: George Allen & Unwin, 1982); Henry A. Giroux and Roger I. Simon, eds., *Popular Culture, Schooling and Everyday Life* (Granby, Mass.: Bergin and Garvey, 1989); and Gene Maeroff, "Focusing on Urban Education in Britain," *Phi Delta Kappan* (January 1992), pp. 352–358.

[69]Henry A. Giroux, *Teachers As Intellectuals* (Granby, Mass.: Bergin and Garvey, 1988); Michael W. Apple, *Ideology and Curriculum,* 2nd ed. (New York: Routledge, 1990).

The Traditional View

Proponents of the traditional view acknowledge the relationships among social class, educational achievement, and economic success, but they emphasize the opportunities that exist and the data indicating that many working-class youth do experience social mobility through the schools and other social institutions. Most traditionalists believe that our educational and economic institutions balance a requirement for excellence with provision of opportunity. From this perspective, each individual who works hard, no matter how socially or economically disadvantaged, is afforded the opportunity to succeed in elementary and secondary schools and to go to college.

Traditionalists point out that the U.S. educational system is designed to allow the individual more chances to attend college than are the educational systems of most other countries (see Chapter 15). Students in this country are not confronted with an examination that at age eleven or twelve shunts them into one of several educational tracks that is virtually impossible to escape. Even if American students do poorly in high school, they can go to a community college and subsequently transfer to a university. Furthermore, admission standards at many four-year colleges permit open enrollment of any high-school graduate.

Traditionalists admit that schools serve as a screening device to sort different individuals into different jobs, but they do not believe that this screening is as systematically based on race, ethnicity, or income as the revisionists contend. Instead, they believe, the better educated get the better jobs primarily because they have been made more productive by the schools. Additional years of schooling constitute an indication of this greater productivity. The employer has to use some criteria to decide whom to hire, and in a democratic society that values unimpeded mobility and equal opportunity, it is largely the quality of education that counts — not the applicant's family connections, race, ethnic origin, or social class.

An Intermediate Viewpoint

This chapter began by providing data indicating that working-class students as a group perform more poorly in the educational system than do middle-class students. After examining some of the reasons that have been offered to account for this difference, we summarized several decades of research concluding that elementary and secondary schools frequently fail to overcome the disadvantages that working-class students bring to school. Although several recent studies indicate that some schools have succeeded in this regard, the overall pattern suggests that there is significant research support for some of the revisionists' conclusions.

On the other hand, it is not true that all working-class students or all minority students fail in the schools or that all middle-class students succeed. An accurate portrayal of the relationships between social class and achievement lies somewhere between the revisionist and the traditional views. Schools do not totally perpetuate the existing social-class structure into the next generation, nor do they provide sufficient opportunity to break the general pattern wherein a great many working-class students perform at a predictably low level in the schools. Levine and Havighurst have reviewed the research on each side of the debate over educational opportunity and have offered an intermediate view that stresses the following:[70]

Schools help create mobility

■   Although no data allow us to pinpoint the exact percentage of working-class students who succeed in the schools or who utilize their education to advance in social status, the schools do serve as an important route to mobility for many economically disadvantaged children and youth.

■   Although many working-class students attend predominantly working-class schools in which their initial disadvantages are frequently reinforced through ineffective delivery of instruction, many others attend mixed-status schools in which teaching and learning conditions are somewhat more conducive to high performance.

Lowest class positions more "frozen"

■   Research on social mobility in the United States indicates that it is mainly at the bottom level that people tend to be "frozen" into the social-class position of their parents. That is, there is considerable intergenerational movement up and down the socioeconomic ladder from upper working class to upper middle class, but large proportions of Americans from lower-working-class and underclass backgrounds do not improve their status beyond that of their parents.[71]

Education implicated in perpetuating low status

■   Social and demographic trends have concentrated many children in low-income urban and rural communities whose schools are very low on achievement measures. A disproportionately high percentage of students in these schools are from racial or ethnic minority groups. For a large proportion of these children, education is implicated in the transmission of low status and disadvantage across generations.[72]

Historic commitment to equal opportunity

Historically, educational leaders such as Horace Mann worked to establish and expand the public school system partly because they felt this would help give all American children and youth an equal chance to succeed in life, regardless of the circumstances of their birth. The data cited in this chapter, which tend to be compatible with the revisionist view and critical theory or with an intermediate view, suggest that the traditional public-school function of providing equal educational opportunity has taken on a more charged meaning. Provision of equal educational opportunity now significantly depends on improving the effectiveness of instruction for children — particularly children from minority backgrounds — who attend predominantly poverty schools. This issue will be discussed further in succeeding chapters.

Summing Up

1. Social class is related both to achievement in elementary and secondary schools and to entry into and graduation from college. Students with low socioeconomic status tend to be low in educational attainment; middle-class

---

[70]Levine and Havighurst, *Society and Education.*

[71]Featherman and Hauser, *Opportunity and Change;* Hout, "More Universalism."

[72]Spring, *The Sorting Machine;* Ann Bastian et al., *Choosing Equality* (Philadelphia: Temple University, 1986); and William L. Boyd, "What Makes Ghetto Schools Succeed or Fail," *Teachers College Record* (Spring 1991), pp. 331–362.

students tend to be high. Low achievement is particularly a problem in poverty areas of large cities.

2. Low-income minority groups generally are low in educational achievement, but there is little or no independent relationship between race or ethnicity and achievement after taking account of social class.

3. Major reasons for low achievement include the following: (a) students' home and family environments do not prepare them well for success in the traditional school; (b) genetic considerations (that is, heredity) may interact with environment in some cases to further hamper achievement; and (c) traditionally organized and operated schools have not provided effective education for economically disadvantaged students.

4. Many problems in the schools tend to limit achievement: inappropriate curriculum and instruction, difficult teaching conditions, differences in teacher/student backgrounds, teacher perceptions of student inadequacy, ineffective homogeneous grouping, delivery-of-service problems, overly large classes, low standards and expectations for students, negative peer pressures, and incompatibility between classroom expectations and students' behavioral patterns and learning styles.

5. Until recently, research in the United States and elsewhere indicated that schools seldom succeeded in overcoming the problems experienced by economically disadvantaged students. However, research during the past ten years indicates that schools can be much more successful if they take appropriate steps to improve instruction.

6. To some extent, research on social class and education has supported the revisionist view that schools help perpetuate the existing social-class system. This contrasts with the traditional view that U.S. society and its educational system provide children and youth with equal opportunity to succeed regardless of their social-class background.

7. Because recent research indicates that the schools can be much more effective, the ideal of equal opportunity may be attained more fully in the future.

Key Terms

socioeconomic status *(364)*

upper class *(364)*

middle class *(364)*

working class *(364)*

underclass *(365)*

National Assessment of Educational Progress (NAEP) *(365)*

race *(369)*

ethnicity *(369)*

ethnic group *(369)*

environmentalist view of intelligence *(379)*

hereditarian view of intelligence *(380)*

synthesizers' view of intelligence *(382)*

homogeneous grouping *(384)*

overloaded schools *(386)*

traditional view of schools *(393)*

revisionist view of schools *(393)*

critical theory (critical pedagogy) *(393)*

resistance theory *(394)*

Discussion Questions

1. How does social class influence school performance? Discuss several different kinds of school performance.

2. What can teachers and schools do to overcome each of the school-related problems that contribute to low achievement among economically disadvantaged students?

3. In addition to those listed in this chapter, what considerations help account for inadequate achievement among students from low-income backgrounds?

4. Which revisionist arguments are the most persuasive? Which are most vulnerable to criticism?

5. You have been hired as a new teacher in a school with a racial, economic, and linguistic composition different from that with which you are acquainted. What can you do, and whom can you turn to for assistance?

Suggested Readings

Bowers, C. A. *Elements of a Post-Liberal Theory of Education.* New York: Teachers College Press, Columbia University, 1987.
> *This is a careful consideration of revisionist writing in the context of classical works by John Dewey, B. F. Skinner, and others.*

Fussell, Paul. *Class.* New York: Summit, 1983.
> *Fussell illustrates and examines social-class patterns in housing, dress, recreation, and other areas.*

Gould, Stephen Jay. *The Mismeasure of Man.* New York: Norton, 1981.
> *This is a relatively nontechnical discussion of material on the hereditarian-environmentalist controversy.*

Herndon, James. *The Way It Spozed to Be.* New York: Bantam, 1968.
> *Herndon's book is a classic account of the way education works, or doesn't work, in inner-city schools.*

Jencks, Christopher, and Paul E. Peterson, eds. *The Urban Underclass.* Washington, D.C.: The Brookings Institution, 1991.
> *The authors offer diverse analysis of the origins and status of problems arising from concentrated poverty in urban areas.*

Levine, Daniel U., and Robert J. Havighurst. *Society and Education,* 8th ed. Needham Heights, Mass.: Allyn and Bacon, 1992.
> *A text on the sociology of education, this pays special attention to issues of social class, race/ethnicity, and school achievement.*

Ogbu, John U. *Minority Education and Caste.* New York: Academic Press, 1978.
> *Obgu gives a detailed description and analysis of how minority racial status interacts with social class to affect opportunities in education and society.*

Payne, Charles M. *Getting What We Ask For.* Westport, Conn.: Greenwood, 1984.
> *This is an outstanding case study of an inner-city high school and the forces that generate low expectations and performance among students and teachers.*

11

Providing Equal Educational Opportunity

FOCUSING QUESTIONS

What are the rationales for desegregation, compensatory education, multicultural education, and education of all children with disabilities?

What is the situation regarding desegregation of schools? What have been the major obstacles and approaches in desegregating the schools?

What are the major approaches to compensatory education? What does research say about their effectiveness?

What is multicultural education? What forms does it take in elementary and secondary schools? What are its major benefits and dangers?

What does the law say about providing education for students with disabilities? What are the major issues involving their education?

P rovision of equal educational opportunity has been a central theme of the U.S. educational system. Through the efforts of Horace Mann and other reformers, our public school system became the first in the world to aim at providing all students with educational opportunity through high school and postsecondary levels. Nonetheless, as Chapter 10 indicated, in all too many cases effective education is not being extended to economically disadvantaged and minority students. Stimulated by the civil rights movement of the 1960s, many people have recognized that educational opportunity should be improved not just for disadvantaged students but also for students with disabilities. There has been widespread realization that providing all citizens with equal opportunity, in education as in other areas, is a moral and political imperative for our society.

In this chapter, we examine desegregation, compensatory education for economically disadvantaged students, multicultural education (including bilingual education), and education for students with disabilities. These topics reflect four significant movements that have attempted to enlarge and equalize educational opportunities for students in U.S. schools.

DESEGREGATION

Desegregation and integration

Desegregation of schools is the practice of enrolling students of different racial groups in the same schools. **Integration** describes the situation not only in which students of different racial groups attend schools together, but also in which effective steps have been taken to accomplish two of the underlying purposes of desegregation: (1) to overcome the achievement deficit and other disadvantages of minority students and (2) to develop positive interracial contacts and relationships. Attention has shifted during the past three decades from simply placing students in desegregated schools to bringing about productive integration that provides equal and effective educational opportunity for students of all backgrounds. Much remains to be done, however, to fully achieve both desegregation and integration.

A Brief History of Segregation in American Education

Slaves not full persons

The Declaration of Independence was first published in the July 10, 1776, issue of the *Pennsylvania Gazette*. That same issue carried an advertisement offering to sell a black slave. The U.S. Constitution itself provided for representation of the free population but allowed only three-fifths representation for "all other persons," generally meaning slaves. Discrimination and oppression by race were deeply embedded in our national institutions from their very beginning. In most of the South before the Civil War, it was a crime to teach a slave to read and write.

After the Civil War, the Thirteenth, Fourteenth, and Fifteenth Amendments to the Constitution attempted to extend rights of citizenship irrespective of race. During Reconstruction, some gains were made by African Americans, but after 1877 this progress generally ceased, and blacks throughout the South and in some other parts of the country were separated by legislative action in segre-

Segregated facilities

gated institutions. African Americans were required to attend separate schools, were in certain places barred by law from competing with whites for good employment, and were denied, through various electoral practices, the right to vote.[1] Where dictated by local law, African Americans were required to use separate public services and facilities (for example, transportation, recreation, restrooms, drinking fountains), and frequently had no access at all to private facilities such as hotels, restaurants, and theaters. Similar though generally less virulent discriminatory practices were carried out against Asian Americans, Hispanics, Native Americans, and other minority groups. For example, in some states Chinese Americans were excluded by law from many well-paid jobs, and their children were required to attend separate schools.[2]

Separate and unequal

Much evidence collected during the first half of this century indicated that, on any measure of equality, schools provided for African Americans were seldom equal to schools attended by whites. For example, in the early 1940s school officials in Mississippi spent $52.01 annually per student in white schools but only $7.36 per student in black schools. As for higher education, one study found fewer books in the separate law school the state of Oklahoma provided for African Americans than in that state's penitentiary library. In many cases, African American students had to travel long distances at their own expense to attend the nearest black school, and in some cases there was no black senior high school within a hundred miles or more.[3]

Second-class status

A number of legal suits challenging segregation in elementary and secondary schools were filed in the early 1950s. The first to be decided by the U.S. Supreme Court was a case in which lawyers for Linda Brown asked that she be allowed to attend white schools in Topeka, Kansas. Attacking the legal doctrine that schools could be "separate but equal," the plaintiffs argued that segregated schools were inherently inferior, even if they provided equal expenditures, because forced attendance at a separate school automatically informed African American students that they were second-class citizens. One result, according to such scholars as John Ogbu, was to destroy students' motivation to succeed in school and in society.[4] In a unanimous decision that forever changed U.S. history, the Supreme Court ruled as follows in May 1954, in *Brown* v. *Board of Education:* "In the field of public education the doctrine of separate but equal has no place. . . . We hold that the plaintiffs and others similarly situated . . . are, by reason of the segregation complained of, deprived of the equal protection of the laws guaranteed by the Fourteenth Amendment."

Separate is unequal

---

[1]In this chapter the term "whites" is used to refer to non-Hispanic whites, that is, citizens who are not classified as members of a racial or ethnic minority group for the purposes of school desegregation.

[2]Karl Zinsmeister, "Bittersweet Success," *Reason* (October 1987), pp. 22–31; Benjamin Hooks, "Being Denied," *U.S. News and World Report,* July 22, 1991, p. 9; and Gwen Kin Kead, "Chinatown-1," *The New Yorker,* June 10, 1991, pp. 45–83.

[3]U.S. Commission on Civil Rights, *Fulfilling the Letter and Spirit of the Law: Desegregation of the Nation's Public Schools* (Washington, D.C.: U.S. Government Printing Office, 1976); National Research Council, *Common Destiny* (Washington, D.C.: National Academy Press, 1989); and Hugh Speer, *Funny Things Happened on the Way to the Supreme Court and Back* (Kansas City, Mo.: School of Education, University of Missouri-Kansas City, 1990).

[4]John U. Ogbu, *Minority Education and Caste* (New York: Academic Press, 1978); John U. Ogbu, "Minority Status and Literacy in Comparative Perspective," *Daedalus* (Spring 1990), pp. 141–168; and Lerone Bennett, Jr., "Brown vs. Board of Education," *Ebony* (February 1992), p. 112.

Since 1957, when the National Guard escorted African American students to a formerly all-white public high school in Little Rock, Arkansas, considerable progress has been made in desegregating the country's public schools in medium-sized cities and towns and in rural areas. (© UPI/Bettmann)

Effects of the *Brown* decision soon were apparent in many areas of U.S. society, including employment, voting, and all publicly supported services. After Mrs. Rosa Parks refused in December 1955 to sit at the back of a bus in Montgomery, Alabama, protests against segregation were launched in many parts of the country. Dr. Martin Luther King, Jr., and other civil rights leaders emerged to challenge deep-seated patterns of racial discrimination. Fierce opposition to civil rights demonstrations made the headlines in the late 1950s and early 1960s, as dogs and fire hoses were sometimes used to disperse peaceful demonstrators. After three civil rights workers were murdered in Mississippi, the U.S. Congress passed the 1964 Civil Rights Act and other legislation that attempted to guarantee equal protection of the laws for minority citizens.[5]

Emergence of civil rights movement

Initial reaction among local government officials to the *Brown* decision outlawing government-supported segregation was often negative. Although the Supreme Court ruled in 1955 *(Brown II)* that school desegregation should proceed with "all deliberate speed" and that constitutional guarantees could not be withheld on the grounds that white citizens resisted change, massive resistance occurred. This resistance took such forms as delaying reassignment of African American students to nearby white schools, opening private schools with tuition paid by public funds, gerrymandering school boundary lines to increase segregation, suspending or repealing compulsory attendance laws, and closing desegregated schools. National attention to the problem of attaining desegregation in

All deliberate speed?

---

[5]Patricia M. Lines, "The Denial of Choice and Brown v. Board of Education," *Metropolitan Education* (Spring 1987), pp. 108–127; Gene B. Sperling, "Does the Supreme Court Matter?" *The American Prospect* (Winter 1991), pp. 91–97; and John Egerton, *Shades of Gray* (Baton Rouge: Louisiana State University Press, 1992).

education increased after 1957. That year Arkansas governor Orval Faubus refused to allow school officials at Central High in Little Rock to admit five African American students, and President Dwight Eisenhower called out the National Guard to escort the students to school. As of 1963, only 2 percent of African American students in the South were attending school with whites.

The Progress of Desegregation Efforts

Since the early 1960s, considerable progress has been made in desegregating the country's public schools in medium-sized cities and towns and in rural areas. The South, in particular, has made significant progress and is now the most integrated region of the United States (see Table 11.1). In response to court orders, school officials have been able to reduce African American attendance in racially isolated minority schools (most often defined as 90 percent or more minority).[6] As shown in Table 11.1, the percentage of African American students attending such schools nationwide decreased from 64 percent in 1968 to 33 percent in 1986. Progress has been greatest in the South, where the percentage of African American students in racially isolated schools decreased from 78 percent to 25 percent. Although complete national data have not been collected since 1986, demographers studying desegregation believe that these figures have remained basically the same into the 1990s.[7]

Reduction in segregation

Despite this progress, about one-third of all African American students in the public schools still attend schools 90 percent or more minority. Segregation of minority students has continued or increased in many communities, particularly in larger cities and metropolitan areas where school segregation is associated with housing patterns that separate large groups of minority and non-minority citizens in relatively distant neighborhoods. Thus, progress seems to have occurred in small and medium-sized communities in combating both **de jure segregation** (segregation resulting from laws, government actions, or school policies specifically designed to bring about separation) and **de facto segregation** (segregation resulting from circumstances associated with housing patterns rather than from laws or government policies and practices), but segregation in large metropolitan regions has increased as housing segregation has become more pronounced. Today, the large majority of public-school students in big cities such as Atlanta, Chicago, Detroit, New York, and Philadelphia are minority students, and most attend predominantly minority schools.[8]

Distinctions in segregation

It should be noted that the percentage of Hispanic students attending predominantly minority schools has actually increased in all parts of the United States since 1968. In that year, 55 percent of Hispanics attended schools more

[6]The term "minority" in this context refers to African Americans, Asians, Hispanics, Native Americans, and several other smaller racial or ethnic groups as defined by the federal government.

[7]Harrison Rainie, "Black and White in America," *U.S. News and World Report,* July 22, 1991, pp. 18–21; Gary Orfield and Franklin Monfort, *Status of School Desegregation: The Next Generation* (Washington, D.C.: National School Boards Association, 1992).

[8]Finis Welch and Audrey Light, *New Evidence on School Desegregation* (Washington, D.C.: U.S. Commission on Civil Rights, 1987); Karl Taeuber, "Desegregation of Public School Districts," *Phi Delta Kappan* (September 1990), pp. 18–24; and "The Urban Burden," *Agenda* (Winter 1992), p. 25.

Table 11.1 ━━━━━━━━━━━━━━━━━━━━━━━━━━━━━━━━
**Percentage of African American Students in Racially Segregated Public Schools,
1968 to 1986**

	Percentage of African American Students in Schools 50 Percent or More Minority			Percentage of African American Students in Schools 90 Percent or More Minority		
	1968	*1980*	*1986*	*1968*	*1980*	*1986*
National	77	63	63	64	33	33
9 northeastern states	67	80	73	43	49	50
11 midwestern states	77	70	70	58	44	39
11 western states	72	67	68	51	34	28
6 border states and D.C.	72	59	59	60	37	36
11 southern states	81	57	58	78	23	25

Note: National figures are for the continental United States excluding Alaska and Hawaii. "Minority" refers to Asian, African American, Hispanic, and other racial/ethnic minority groups as defined by the federal government.

Source: Gary Orfield, *Desegregation of Black and Hispanic Students from 1968 to 1980* (Washington, D.C.: Joint Center for Political Studies, 1982), p. 19; Gary Orfield, Franklin Monfort, and Melissa Aaron, *Status of School Desegregation 1968–1986* (Washington, D.C.: National School Boards Association, 1989), pp. 5–6; and Gary Orfield and Franklin Monfort, *Status of School Desegregation: The Next Generation* (Washington, D.C.: National School Boards Association, 1992).

than 50 percent minority; in 1988, nearly 75 percent of Hispanic students (compared with 64 percent of African American students) attended such schools. By 1987, nearly 80 percent of Hispanic students in six states (California, Illinois, New Jersey, New York, New Mexico, and Texas), which represents more than four-fifths of U.S. Hispanic enrollment, were in predominantly minority schools.[9] This trend toward greater segregation among Hispanic students reflects the movement of Hispanic population into inner-city communities in large urban areas, particularly the migration of Mexicans into cities in California and Texas and of Puerto Ricans into New York, Chicago, and other eastern and midwestern cities.

Hispanic segregation

Evolving Desegregation Law

Actions taken to reduce segregation in local school districts have reflected decisions and mandates of the U.S. Supreme Court. Desegregation law has evolved to provide districtwide solutions to segregation problems and to allow for metropolitan or regional solutions that cross school district boundary lines.

Desegregation was greatly accelerated by the Supreme Court's 1968 decision in *Green* v. *County School Board of New Kent County,* in which the Court required segregated districts to devise a desegregation plan that "promises realistically to

────────────

[9]Gary Orfield, Franklin Monfort, and Melissa Aaron, *Status of School Desegregation 1968–1986* (Washington, D.C.: National School Boards Association, 1989); Thomas Exter, "One Million Hispanic Club," *American Demographics* (February 1991), p. 59; and "Hispanic Students Becoming Isolated in Minority Schools," *Education Daily,* January 9, 1992, pp. 1–2.

Removing vestiges

work now." Its 1971 decision in *Swann* v. *Charlotte-Mecklenberg* supported busing of students, revision of attendance zones, or other actions to remove the "vestiges" of state-imposed segregation, as long as a desegregation plan is workable. In 1974 in *Keyes,* which involved the Denver schools, the Court concluded that if a portion of a school district is segregated as a result of official government action, the entire district may have to be desegregated. This decision laid the basis for court orders aimed at districtwide desegregation in Boston, Dallas, Cleveland, San Francisco, and several other large cities.

A series of important Supreme Court decisions also formed the basis for some movement toward metropolitan or regional desegregation. In 1974 the Court rejected metropolitan desegregation for Detroit in *Bradley* v. *Milliken,* stating that the autonomy of existing school districts cannot be disregarded for desegregation purposes unless it can be shown that a constitutional violation in one district has a significant segregative effect in another district. However, the Court later upheld decisions that merged city and suburban districts in Louisville (1975) and in Wilmington, Delaware (1975). In both these cases, one major reason given for metropolitan desegregation was that prior to 1954 suburban black students were required to cross school district boundaries to attend segregated city schools.[10]

Metropolitan desegregation

Metropolitan desegregation has also come about as a result of the *Liddell* case in St. Louis. Twice upheld after appeals to the Supreme Court, federal judges initiated action to stimulate development of a 1983 voluntary plan that encourages suburban districts to accept African American students transferring from city schools and that includes provisions for improvement of segregated city schools. By 1992, more than 13,000 African American students from the city were attending suburban schools, and more than 900 suburban white students were attending city schools.[11]

Obstacles to Desegregation

Given the fact that residential patterns in most metropolitan areas are so highly segregated, a major stumbling block to desegregation of schools has been the desire of most whites, and of many minority parents, to maintain neighborhood schools. In addition, opposition to desegregation has increased in school districts where a high percentage of minority students are from low-income families. Middle-class parents, whether nonminority or minority, are reluctant to send their children to schools with a high proportion of students from low-income families. They generally are quick to withdraw their children from schools in which desegregation has substantially increased the proportion of such students. Involuntary busing, a highly emotional issue, has also generated substantial white withdrawal from many school districts that implement com-

Middle-class withdrawal

[10]David S. Tatel, Kevin J. Lanigan, and Maree F. Sneed, "The Fourth Decade of Brown: Metropolitan Desegregation and Quality Education," *Metropolitan Education* (Spring 1986), pp. 15–35; Donna Harrington-Lueker, "Donald Ingwerson," *The Executive Educator* (October 1990), pp. 14–15, 20.
[11]Susan Uchitelle, "Status of the Voluntary Interdistrict Transfer Plan — Year Four," *Metropolitan Education* (Spring 1987), pp. 89–93; Margaret Gillerman, "St. Louis Magnet Schools Fill Fast," *St. Louis Dispatch,* March 24, 1991, p. 11D.

prehensive desegregation plans.[12] The net result is that city school districts and schools have become increasingly low income and minority in their student composition.[13]

Suburban resegregation

In addition, some suburban public schools are beginning to be resegregated as middle-class minority families move to the suburbs only to find that white enrollment falls as the white population declines or withdraws. The situation in the Cleveland metropolitan area illustrates the growing segregation of minority students in the suburbs: the East Cleveland suburban school district has become nearly all African American. In the Los Angeles metropolitan area, a number of suburban school districts have enrollments of more than half minority.

Desegregation Plans

Plans to accomplish desegregation typically involve one or more of the following actions:[14]

1. Alter attendance areas to include a more desegregated population.
2. Establish **magnet schools** — schools that incorporate specialized programs and personnel in order to attract students throughout a school district.
3. Bus students involuntarily to desegregated schools.
4. Pair schools, bringing two schools in adjacent areas together in one larger zone. For example, School A enrolls all students from grades one through four; School B enrolls all students from grades five through eight.
5. Allow **controlled choice,** a system in which students can select the school they wish to attend as long as such choice does not result in segregation.
6. Provide voluntary transfer of city students to suburban schools.

Milwaukee desegregation

Using means such as these, many small or medium-sized cities have been able to substantially desegregate schools. A good example is Milwaukee. At a time when African American students made up approximately 40 percent of the city's school population, Milwaukee increased the number of its desegregated schools (defined as 25 to 50 percent black) from 14 in 1976 to 101 in 1978. Most of this increase was achieved through (1) establishing magnet schools, (2) implementing a voluntary city-suburban transfer plan, and (3) redrawing school boundaries. By 1992, nearly 6,000 minority students from the city were attending suburban schools, and a court settlement requires substantial future

[12]Christine H. Rossell, *The Carrot or the Stick for School Desegregation Policy* (Philadelphia: Temple University, 1990); Nathan Glazer, "The Real World of Urban Education," *The Public Interest* (Winter 1992), pp. 57–75.

[13]Daniel U. Levine and Eugene E. Eubanks, "The Promise and Limits of Regional Desegregation Plans for Central City School Districts," *Metropolitan Education* (Spring 1986), pp. 36–51; William L. Boyd et al., *Policy Dilemmas in Urban Education* (Washington, D.C.: National Association of State Urban Land Grant Colleges, 1991); and Peter Schmidt, "Palm Springs Shifts Integration Focus to Housing," *Education Week,* February 26, 1992, pp. 1, 9–11.

[14]Carol Ascher, *Using Magnet Schools for Desegregation: Some Suggestions from the Research* (New York: Columbia University Teachers College ERIC Clearinghouse on Urban Education, 1987); Charles V. Wille, "Controlled Choice Avoids the Pitfalls of Choice Plans," *Educational Leadership* (January 1991), pp. 62–64; and Saul M. Yanofsky and Laurette Young, "A Successful Parents' Choice Program," *Phi Delta Kappan* (February 1992), pp. 476–479.

expansion of the city-suburban transfer program. This progress illustrates what can be accomplished through voluntary desegregation in all but the largest, most segregated cities.[15]

Big-city obstacles

In large, central-city districts, however — especially those with 50 percent or higher minority enrollment — desegregated schooling is difficult to attain. For example, in a big city with 80 percent minority students, action to eliminate predominantly single-race schools may involve hour-long bus rides and the transportation of students from one largely minority school to another. Middle-class students and/or nonminority students may leave in the process. Many educators do not believe that this type of desegregation is very helpful.[16]

Emphasis on instruction

For these and similar reasons, desegregation plans in some big cities include little, if any, student reassignment and leave most minority students in predominantly minority schools. Instead of aiming for full desegregation, such plans generally concentrate on trying to improve the quality of instruction. Plans of this type have been approved by courts in such cities as Detroit and Chicago, and the Supreme Court has approved lower court rulings that require state governments to pay half or more of the cost of instructional improvements.[17]

Magnet plans

According to recent research, even large and very segregated cities can benefit from the expansion of magnet schools and other voluntary means of desegregation — more so than from large-scale, involuntary busing that transports students to predominantly minority schools. Districts that operate a substantial number of magnet schools include Boston, Buffalo, Cincinnati, Dallas, Houston, Kansas City, Minneapolis, Rochester, San Diego, and Seattle. The plan in Kansas City, Missouri, for example, uses a variety of magnet themes (shown in Table 11.2) in order to draw nonminority students to schools that are largely minority and minority students to schools that are largely nonminority. To improve the quality and effectiveness of all the district's schools — and also, it is hoped, to make the district more attractive for desegregation — the Kansas City plan further provides for class-size reduction, enhancement of libraries and learning materials, expanded preschool education, renovation of all school buildings in the district, and other improvements related to the instructional program. Between 1986 and 1992, more than $2,000 per student per year was expended for instruction-related improvements as part of the district's court-ordered desegregation plan.[18]

---

[15]David A. Bennett, "The Impact of Court Ordered Desegregation" (Paper presented at the ERIC Conference on Impact of Courts on Schools, 1979); Robert S. Peterkin, "What's Happening in Milwaukee?" *Educational Leadership* (January 1991), pp. 50–52; and John J. Lane and Edgar G. Epps, eds., *Restructuring the Schools: Problems and Prospects* (Berkeley, Calif.: McCutchan, 1992).

[16]William Bradford Reynolds, "Education Alternatives to Transportation Failures," *Metropolitan Education* (Spring 1986), pp. 3–14; Karen De Witt, "The Nation's Schools Learn a 4th R: Resegregation," *The New York Times*, January 19, 1992, p. E5.

[17]Bill Johnston, "School District Merger, Busing, and the Courts," *The Urban Review* (Spring 1987), pp. 49–64; William Celis 3d., "Kansas City Praises Desegregation," *The New York Times*, September 25, 1991, p. B8; and Peter Schmidt, "Desegregation Costs Put Ga., Ohio Officials at Odds with Districts," *Education Week*, March 18, 1992, p. 20.

[18]Eugene E. Eubanks and Daniel U. Levine, "Ancillary Relief Components in Urban School Desegregation," Working paper No. 8 (Chicago: University of Chicago National School Desegregation Project, 1987); Lynn Horsley, "KC School Review Is Requested," *The Kansas City Star*, August 24, 1991, p. C-2; and Dennis Farney, "Crash Course," *The Wall Street Journal*, January 8, 1992, pp. A1, A6.

Table 11.2
Magnet Themes in the Kansas City, Missouri, Public Schools, by Level of School

Senior High	*Middle School*	*Elementary*
Agribusiness	College prep	Communications
Business/communications	Communications	Computers
Engineering	Computers	Environmental science
Environmental science	Environmental science	French/German/Spanish
Health professions	Foreign language	Latin grammar/traditional*
International studies/ languages	Latin grammar/traditional*	Montessori
	Olympic sports	Olympic sports
Law and public service	Performing and visual arts	Performing and visual arts
Naval ROTC	Science/math	Science/math
Olympic sports		
Performing and visual arts		
Science/math/technology		

*"Traditional" refers to schools with strict policies regarding discipline, dress, homework, and other matters.

Source: Phale D. Hale and Daniel U. Levine, *Kansas City, Missouri School District Long-Range Magnet School Plan* (Kansas City: Kansas City Public Schools, 1986), pp. 15–16; Phale D. Hale, "Kansas City, Missouri: A Comprehensive Magnet Plan," in Nolan Ester, Daniel U. Levine, and Donald R. Waldrip, eds., *Magnet Schools* (Austin, Tex.: Morgan, 1990), pp. 143–160.

Nonblack Minorities

Variations in defining desegregation participation

Another aspect of desegregation that deserves special attention is the status of nonblack minority groups. Depending on regional and local circumstances and court precedents, some racial minority groups may or may not be counted as minority for the purposes of school desegregation.[19] For example, in the 1970s, the courts determined that Mexican American students in the Southwest were victims of the same kinds of discrimination as were African American students. However, in some northern cities, the courts have not explicitly designated Mexican American and other Hispanic students to participate as minorities in a desegregation plan, even though many or most attend predominantly minority schools.

The situation is further complicated by the relatively large number of Asian American groups in some big cities. With a rapidly growing population of Filipino, Korean, and Vietnamese students, added to the many students of Chinese and Japanese ancestry, city school districts face considerable uncertainty in devising multiethnic desegregation plans. The court order for San Francisco, for example, has required multiethnic enrollment and busing of four groups: Asian American, African American, Hispanic, and non-Hispanic white.

Resolution of issues difficult

Questions regarding the desegregation of nonblack minority groups will multiply in the future given the continuing in-migration of Asian and Hispanic students to many locales. Resolution of these issues will be difficult because bilingual services that tend to require a concentration of these students will con-

---

[19]However, federal data collection activities are standardized and have required that student enrollments be reported separately for the following groups: "Black," "American Indian," "Spanish-Surnamed American," "Portuguese," "Asian," "Alaskan Natives," "Hawaiian Natives," and "Non-Minority."

Taking Issue ●

Magnet Schools and Desegregation

In recent years, many city school districts have established desegregation plans that rely in part on magnet schools. By offering a specialized program in a particular field of interest, a magnet school can attract students from all parts of a city or region, thereby creating a mix of ethnic and racial groups. Critics have argued, however, that magnet schools often cause more problems than they solve.

Question: Are magnet schools an effective means of promoting desegregation and achieving related school-improvement goals?

Arguments PRO

1 Research in a number of cities has shown that a coordinated plan involving magnet schools can lead to substantial gains in desegregation. Milwaukee and Buffalo, for example, are using magnet schools effectively.

2 Through their specialized, high-level programs, magnet schools attract middle-class and college-bound students to the public school system. In this way, magnets help to reverse the white, middle-class exodus that has long plagued desegregation efforts.

3 In addition to attracting various ethnic and racial groups, magnet schools create a mixture of socioeconomic classes. Working-class and middle-class students are brought together in a setting that encourages beneficial socialization.

4 Because of their concentration of resources, magnet schools can offer a better education than a system of nonspecialized schools. Most important, they make this high-quality education available to everyone, regardless of racial, social, or cultural background.

5 As students gain recognition for academic excellence at the magnet schools, community pride will grow. The schools will become a means of promoting community identity, bringing together all races and classes in a common endeavor.

Arguments CON

1 Only limited evidence supports the idea that magnet schools make a significant contribution to desegregation. Because magnets frequently are expensive to develop and maintain, they may well become unjustifiable financial burdens for school districts.

2 Magnets often "drain away" the best students, leaving other public schools in the district with high concentrations of low achievers. These other schools find it increasingly difficult to maintain teacher and student morale and deliver a good education.

3 In some areas, the conversion of a local school into a magnet has led to increased tension between socioeconomic groups. Local students distrust the "outsiders" (generally of a different social class) who come into the neighborhood to attend the school.

4 Many magnet schools are not really for everyone. Instead, they are selective: students must meet certain achievement standards in order to be admitted. Thus, low-achieving students—the ones most in need of help—are not as likely to benefit from magnet schools as are other students.

5 Because of their elitist nature, magnet schools will not foster a sense of community. More likely, they will provoke resentment among parents whose children are excluded—especially when taxes are raised to support the magnet program.

flict with desegregation goals emphasizing dispersal and mul'iethnic enrollment. Many educators and lay leaders also are very uncertain a' out whether or how to include middle-class Asian American and Hispanic students in desegregation plans. Most of these students perform well academically, and many seem to be very well integrated into U.S. schools and society. Some concerned observers suggest that middle-class minority students should attend schools with low-income minority students in order to reduce the latter group's economic isolation in districts that have few nonminority students.[20]

Effects on Student Performance and Attitudes

Inconsistent data and conclusions

To what extent do students benefit from integrated schools? The voluminous research on this subject is nonetheless somewhat contradictory. Some studies show a positive relationship between desegregation and academic achievement, but other studies show little or no relationship. Several analysts reviewed a large number of these studies and concluded that desegregation seldom detracts from the performance of white students and frequently contributes to achievement among minority students. The latter results are most likely to occur when low-income minority students attend schools with middle-income nonminority students, but only if desegregation plans are well implemented (see below) and substantial action is taken to improve the effectiveness of instruction.[21]

Importance of effective implementation

Similarly, some data show that desegregation has positive effects on interracial attitudes, but some studies indicate no effect or even a negative effect. Positive intergroup attitudes and relationships develop only if desegregation is implemented well and if educators take action to promote equal-status contact between minority and nonminority students.[22] The results of studies on minority students' aspirations are much more consistent; they indicate that desegregation frequently improves the educational aspirations and college enrollment of minority students by making these aspirations more realistic and better informed. Several studies also indicate that desegregated schooling helps minority students enter the mainstream "network" of social and cultural contacts needed for success in later life.[23]

---

[20]Kenneth J. Meier and Joseph Stewart, Jr., *The Politics of Hispanic Education* (Albany: State University of New York Press, 1991); "New Definition Urged," *NSBA News Service,* January 21, 1992, p. 30.

[21]Ronald A. Krol, "A Meta Analysis of the Effects of Desegregation on Academic Achievement," *Urban Review* (December 1980), pp. 211–224; Walter G. Stephan, "School Desegregation," in Harry J. Knopke, Robert J. Norrell, and Ronald W. Rogers, eds., *Opening Doors* (Tuscaloosa: University of Alabama Press, 1991), pp. 100–118; and Daniel U. Levine, "Desegregation," *International Encyclopedia of Educational Research,* 2nd ed. (Oxford: Pergamon, in press).

[22]Maureen T. Hallinan and Ruy A. Teixeira, "Students' Interracial Friendships," *American Journal of Education* (August 1987), pp. 563–583; Janet Schofield, "School Desegregation and Intergroup Relations: A Review of the Literature," in Gerald Grant, ed., *Review of Research in Education 17* (Washington, D.C.: American Education Research Association, 1991), pp. 335–412.

[23]Richard R. Scott and James M. McPartland, "Desegregation as National Policy: Correlates of Racial Attitudes," *American Educational Research Journal* (Winter 1982), pp. 397–414; Jomills H. Braddock, "Social and Academic Consequences of School Desegregation" (Paper prepared for the Conference on Future Designs for Educational Equity, St. Louis, 1987); and Maureen T. Hallinan and Richard A. Williams, "Students' Characteristics and the Peer-Influence Process," *Sociology of Education* (April 1990), pp. 122–132.

Unfortunately, only a few studies focus on schools in which desegregation seems to have been carried out effectively. (Studies examining this type of school avoid the problem typical in educational research of mixing well-implemented examples of an innovation with poorly implemented ones and then concluding that the innovation is universally unsuccessful.) One of the most comprehensive studies of successfully desegregated schools is a report evaluating the Emergency School Aid Act, which provided hundreds of millions of dollars between 1972 and 1982 to facilitate desegregation. This study indicated that desegregation had a favorable impact on the achievement of African American students in schools with four characteristics: resources are focused on attaining goals, administrative leadership is outstanding, parents are more heavily involved in the classroom, and staff systematically promote positive interracial attitudes.[24]

Successfully desegregated schools

Despite the mixed evidence as to how desegregation affects academic achievement and interracial attitudes, perhaps the most compelling reasons for integration are moral and political. Morally, our national education policy must reflect a commitment to American ideals of equality. Politically, two separate societies, separately educated, cannot continue to exist in America without serious harm to the body politic. In the words of Federal Appeals Court Judge Gerald Heaney, because minority students will have to "compete in an integrated society, they must, to the extent possible, be educated in an integrated school system."[25]

Moral and political reasons for desegregation

COMPENSATORY EDUCATION

Another aspect of our nation's commitment to equal educational opportunity is the **compensatory education** movement, which has sought to overcome (i.e., compensate for) disadvantaged background and thereby improve the performance of low-achieving students, particularly those from low-income families. Stimulated in part by the civil rights movement of the 1960s, compensatory education was expanded and institutionalized as part of President Lyndon Johnson's War on Poverty. Compensatory education has been funded largely by the federal government, although some states and local school districts also have set aside funds for this purpose.

Part of the War on Poverty

The Elementary and Secondary Education Act (ESEA) was passed in 1965 and immediately provided $1 billion in Title I funds to supplement and improve the education of economically disadvantaged children. (A disadvantaged student was defined as a student from a family below the government's official poverty line.) In 1981, Title I of ESEA was revised and is now known as **Chapter 1** of ECIA (Educational Consolidation and Improvement Act). By 1992, Chapter 1 funding amounted to nearly $7 billion expended to provide assistance to more than five million students, and many additional students participated in

Chapter 1

[24]J. E. Coulson, *National Evaluation of the Emergency School Aid Act (ESAA): Survey of the Second-Year Studies* (Washington, D.C.: System Development Corporation, 1976). Also see Daniel U. Levine and Robert J. Havighurst, *Society and Education,* 8th ed. (Needham Heights, Mass.: Allyn and Bacon, 1992).

[25]Gerald W. Heaney, "School Desegregation: Results and Prospects," *Metropolitan Education* (Spring 1987), pp. 79–85; Percy Bates, "Desegregation: Can We Get There from Here?" *Phi Delta Kappan* (September 1990), pp. 8–17.

other compensatory programs. Some of the important services of compensatory education include:

Preschool education

1. *Infant education and intervention in family life.* Programs of infant education and parental involvement have ranged from helping parents learn to teach their children to improving family functioning and employability.

2. *Early childhood education.* **Head Start** and **Follow Through** have been the largest programs of this kind. Whereas Head Start generally attempts to help disadvantaged four- and five-year olds achieve "readiness" for the first grade, Follow Through concentrates on sustaining readiness and improving achievement in the primary grades. In 1991 Head Start served almost 600,000 students.

3. *Reading, language, and math skills.* Most Chapter 1 projects have concentrated on improvement in reading, language, and math.

4. *Bilingual education.* Hispanic children constitute the largest group in bilingual programs, but nationwide, bilingual programs have been provided in more than sixty languages. Bilingual programs are discussed in the following section on multicultural education.

5. *Guidance, counseling, and social services.* Various psychological and social services have been provided for disadvantaged students, and social workers have been employed to help bridge gaps between school and home.

6. *Dropout prevention.* Along with vocational and career education, a number of services have aimed at preventing students from dropping out of school, through offering work-study programs, on-the-job training, and financial incentives.

7. *Personnel training.* Many preservice and in-service training programs have been funded to help teachers improve instruction.

8. *Additional school personnel.* The recruitment and training of teacher aides and paraprofessionals have increased, and instructional specialists also have been employed.

Evaluation of Programs

Discouraging early results

The majority of interventions during the first decade of compensatory education appeared to be relatively ineffective in raising achievement levels and cognitive development of participating students. Despite the expenditure of billions of dollars per year, research indicated that students in compensatory education generally were not making long-range academic gains. For example, according to a former director of the U.S. Office of Education Division of Compensatory Education, among more than 1,200 compensatory education projects evaluated between 1970 and 1972, only 10 had solid data that unambiguously demonstrated their success. Longitudinal studies also revealed a "fadeout" process; that is, the early gains made by disadvantaged youngsters at some locations eventually disappeared after a few years of schooling.[26]

[26]Richard I. Fairley, "Accountability's New Test," *American Education* (June 1972), pp. 33–35. Also see Westinghouse Learning Corporation and Ohio University, *The Impact of Head Start*

Improvements in compensatory programs

However, subsequent data on compensatory education have justified a somewhat more positive view. In part, more encouraging recent results can be traced to corrections made to rectify the more serious mistakes of the first decade: (1) the federal and state governments improved monitoring procedures and required school districts to spend a "comparable" amount on disadvantaged and nondisadvantaged students before adding compensatory funds; (2) some states began to provide additional money as part of a systematic plan to improve the performance of disadvantaged students; and (3) the government required more adequate evaluation and initiated studies to improve compensatory education.[27] By the early 1980s, several sources of information supported the conclusion that compensatory education in the preschool and primary grades can improve the cognitive development and performance of disadvantaged students.

Outstanding early childhood programs

In particular, several studies of outstanding early childhood education programs demonstrated that such efforts can have a long-lasting effect if they are well conceived and effectively implemented.[28] For example, Francis Palmer's longitudinal study of inner-city students in a special preschool program in New York showed that participating children scored no higher than control-group children in the first grade. When retested in the fifth grade, however, they scored nine points higher on IQ tests and somewhat higher in reading than did the control group.[29] (This pattern of delayed improvement is called the "sleeper effect.") Positive long-range achievement results also have been reported for disadvantaged students who attended outstanding preschool programs in Ypsilanti, Michigan; Syracuse, New York; and other locations. Analysis of these programs also indicates that they are cost-effective. Participating students are less likely than nonparticipants to be placed later in special education or to repeat grades (both of which are very expensive) and are more likely to graduate from high school and to acquire skills and motivation needed for rewarding employment, thereby increasing tax revenues and reducing subsequent needs for public assistance.[30]

However, it also should be kept in mind that the vast majority of preschool and primary programs have not been as well funded or well implemented and

---

(Washington, D.C.: U.S. Government Printing Office, 1969); Cheryl Hayes, John L. Palmer, and Martha J. Zaslow, *Who Cares for America's Children?* (Washington, D.C.: National Academy Press, 1990); and Douglas J. Besharov, "Why Head Start Badly Needs a Re-Start," *The Washington Post National Weekly Edition,* February 10–16, 1992, pp. 26–27.

[27]Thomas W. Fagan and Camilla A. Heid, "Chapter 1 Program Improvement: Opportunity and Practice," *Phi Delta Kappan* (April 1991), pp. 582–585.

[28]Irving Lazar et al., "Lasting Effects of Early Education," *Monographs of the Society for Research in Child Development* (Nos. 2–3, 1982); The Consortium for Longitudinal Studies, *As the Twig Is Bent: Lasting Effects of Preschool Programs* (Hillsdale, N.J.: Erlbaum, 1983); W. Steven Barnett and Colette M. Escobar, "The Economics of Early Educational Intervention: A Review," *Review of Educational Research* (Winter 1987), pp. 387–414; and Susan Chira, "New Head Start Studies Raise Questions on Help," *The New York Times,* March 4, 1992, p. B9.

[29]Francis H. Palmer, *The Effects of Minimal Early Intervention on Subsequent IQ Scores and Reading Achievement* (Stony Brook, N.Y.: State University of New York, no date).

[30]Margaret Farnsworth, Lawrence J. Schweinhart, and John R. Berrueta-Clement, "Preschool Intervention, School Success, and Delinquency in a High-Risk Sample of Youth," *American Educational Research Journal* (Fall 1985), pp. 445–464; Edward Kennedy, "School Readiness Act," *Congressional Record,* April 24, 1991, pp. S4986–S5009; and Hobart Rowen, "Investing in Our Children," *The Washington Post National Weekly Edition,* February 3–9, 1992, p. 5.

*Many programs
not effective*

have not produced gains as impressive as those researchers have identified as exemplary. On the whole, Chapter 1 programs still do not ensure that most low-achieving students will acquire the academic and intellectual skills necessary for obtaining good jobs in a modern economy. On the one hand, Chapter 1 students typically gain about a year in reading and math achievement for each year of participation in the elementary grades, and thus no longer fall further behind their more advantaged peers. On the other hand, various problems persist: many disadvantaged students receive only one or two years of compensatory services and then frequently decline in relative achievement; comparatively few disadvantaged students are served above the sixth grade; participants who start out far behind national achievement averages usually remain there; and many of the Chapter 1 programs conducted nationally at more than 50,000 schools in more than 14,000 districts are poorly implemented and ineffective.[31]

Comprehensive Ecological Intervention

*Deleterious poverty
environments*

For some children and youth, improvement of opportunities and programs in the schools cannot be expected to overcome extreme disadvantages associated with growing up in a concentrated poverty neighborhood or other particularly deleterious environments. Recognizing the difficulties involved in providing compensatory education for severely disadvantaged young people, policy makers and educators increasingly support **ecological intervention** — comprehensive efforts to improve the family environment of very young children growing up in debilitating circumstances.[32]

Taking note of research on cognitive development during infancy and the frequently disappointing results of Head Start interventions beginning at age four or five, advocates of ecological intervention have stressed the value of intensive psychological, social, and economic support for young children and their parents. In particular, research indicates that comprehensive ecological intervention can be successful when it[33]

*Aspects of ecological
intervention*

■ includes nutrition, health care, and other social services.

■ provides information and guidance on parenting.

■ is carried out by capable staff who provide individualized assistance for participating families, particularly with regard to activities that stimulate children's intellectual development.

[31]Lorin W. Anderson and Leonard O. Pellicer, "Synthesis of Research on Compensatory and Remedial Education," *Educational Leadership* (September 1990), pp. 10–16; Virginia R. L. Plunkett and Benjamin D. Stickney, "Most Assuredly an Achievement Program," *Educational Leadership* (May 1991), pp. 87–89; and Stanley Pogrow, "What to Do About Chapter 1," *Phi Delta Kappan* (April 1992), pp. 624–630.

[32]Lizbeth Schorr, *Within Our Reach* (New York: Anchor Doubleday, 1989); Kenneth R. Hopkins, "The Necessary Revolution," *Business Week,* November 25, 1991, pp. ED62–ED73; and *Pathways to Self-Sufficiency for Two Generations* (New York: Foundation for Child Development, 1992).

[33]Schorr, *Within Our Reach;* Michael F. Kelley and Elaine Surbeck, *Restructuring Early Childhood Education* (Bloomington, Ind.: Phi Delta Kappa, 1991); National Commission on Children, *Beyond Rhetoric* (Washington, D.C.: U.S. Government Printing Office, 1991); and David Hamburg, *Today's Children* (New York: Times Books, 1992).

■ delivers appropriate assistance beginning when children are less than two or three years old.

■ enrolls very young children in educationally oriented day care or preschool classes.

Among the best-known efforts that have begun to report promising outcomes are the following:[34]

Examples of comprehensive interventions

■ The Beethoven Project, which provides coordinated services focused on health, adult education, employment training, parent education, and children's intellectual and psychological development, for all members of families with very young children at a large public-housing project in Chicago

■ The Homebuilder Project, which was initiated to furnish coordinated social services provided by staff with very small caseloads to low-income families in Tacoma, Washington, and since has been expanded to other locations

■ The Giant Step program which enrolls preschool children in New York City and, compared to typical Head Start classes, provides for more intensive parental involvement and assistance, greater staff training, improved adult/student ratios, and comprehensive social and psychological services

Parents as Teachers

■ The Parents as Teachers approach, which began as a State of Missouri project and has expanded to several other states in which specially trained teachers visit the homes of preschool children to help parents learn how to provide supportive learning environments

■ The Parent and Child Education (PACE) program, through which parents of preschool students receive literacy instruction, parenting education, and adult basic education while their children attend classes at numerous Kentucky sites

Unfortunately, analysts report that most efforts have not been as comprehensive and intensive as these successful programs. It also should be acknowledged that use of crack cocaine and increase in crime, delinquency, and other indicators of social disorganization in poverty neighborhoods appear to be making it substantially more difficult to implement comprehensive ecological intervention. For example, drug addiction among women who live in inner cities has reached unprecedented levels, and many babies born to addicted mothers are likely to suffer from long-term intellectual and emotional retardation. Hospitals, social agencies, and other human-service institutions in poverty neighborhoods are overwhelmed with problems that seriously limit their capacity to improve the lives and prospects of severely disadvantaged children.[35]

---

[34]Schorr, *Within Our Reach*, pp. 293–294; Gina Kolata, "Program Helped Underweight Babies, Study Shows," *The New York Times*, June 13, 1990, p. A10; Barbara Dillon Goodson et al., *Working with Families: Promising Programs to Help Parents Support Young Children's Learning* (Cambridge, Mass.: Abt Associates, 1991); and Thomas C. Hayes, "Parents on the Front Line," *The New York Times Education Life*, January 5, 1992, p. 22.

[35]Franklin Frazier et al., *The Urban Underclass* (Washington, D.C.: U.S. Government Printing Office, 1990); Janice Hutchison, "What Crack Does to Babies," *American Educator* (Spring 1991), pp. 31–32; and Donald H. Johnston, "Readiness: Vague Idea, Pressing Need," *Agenda* (Winter 1992), pp. 29–31.

Getting to the Source ●━━━━━━━

Comprehensive Social Services /
Richard Weissbourd

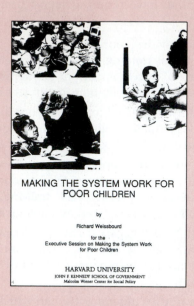

MAKING THE SYSTEM WORK FOR
POOR CHILDREN

by

Richard Weissbourd

for the
Executive Session on Making the System Work
for Poor Children

HARVARD UNIVERSITY
JOHN F. KENNEDY SCHOOL OF GOVERNMENT
Malcolm Wiener Center for Social Policy

In line with many major policy reports and recommendations, numerous projects have been initiated to coordinate the work of social agencies and schools in order to provide comprehensive social services for young people and families. Analysts are trying to de-

termine how services can best be coordinated to fundamentally improve the overall environment for at-risk children and youth. One of the most thoughtful documents has been prepared by Richard Weissbourd, who summarized the results of three years of discussion among a group of concerned practitioners, scholars, and policymakers.

Too often services are driven by legislative, funding, professional and bureaucratic requirements, rather than by the needs of children and families themselves. Because of legislative and bureaucratic requirements, for example, most public institutions and programs today isolate and react rigidly to a narrowly defined need, ducking problems that do not fall neatly within their jurisdictions. Schools deal with school problems. Health agencies deal with health problems. Drug programs treat drug problems. Yet children's needs are commonly untidy, and many children have multiple and interconnected problems. A child's diarrhea, for example, may be connected to an emotional crisis caused by a divorce at home or by a transition to a new school. Further, the problems of children are frequently enmeshed with the problems of their families. A young teenage girl's failure in school may be directly connected to her mother's alcoholism, or her father's sud-

Coordinated Human Services

Collaboration to integrate services

Education, health care, economic assistance, social and psychological support, and other forms of assistance increasingly extend to older disadvantaged children and youth as well. Frequently advocated under such headings as "coordination of human services," "collaboration among schools and social services agencies," and "integration of social and educational services" for young people and their families, coordinated-service approaches have been endorsed by the Council of Chief State School Officers, the National Commission on Children, the National Association of State Boards of Education, and innumerable other groups of educators and civic leaders.[36]

───────────

[36]National Commission on Children, *Beyond Rhetoric;* National Commission on the Role of the School and the Community in Improving Adolescent Health, *Code Blue* (Alexandria, Va.: Na-

den disappearance, or to constant conflict between her mother and her mother's boyfriend at home. Alternatively, this girl may be failing school because she has to stay home to take care of a younger sibling, or because she is unable to get needed reading help at home because both of her parents are illiterate. Yet our current service system tends to treat each family member in isolation—a program for every person, a program for every problem.

This report outlines the shape of a system that would take as its starting point and as its map the interwoven needs of children and families. The model we propose is undergirded by five principles: *prevention, comprehensiveness, continuity, effective accountability,* and *enhancing the dignity and authority of families.* Further, this report describes concrete and far-reaching reforms that flow from these principles. Primarily, we argue that the service system needs to be a good deal more dynamic and flexible at many different levels. Most important, we need to untie the hands of human service workers—teachers, counselors, social workers, health care professionals. To provide preventive and comprehensive services, these workers need the authority, the skills and the support to respond flexibly and improvisationally to children and family needs. Program and city administrators need far more freedom—more freedom, for example, to shift resources into preventive ef-

forts and to change direction when new problems suddenly spring up. This report argues that one promising way of giving city and agency administrators more latitude is "decategorization," providing them with single, flexible grants that pool, for example, child welfare, foster services, Chapter I, Maternal and Child Health, and/or Head Start funds.

Questions

1. Why do various social and educational agencies usually function so separately from one another? How does this history of isolation impede the delivery of services?

2. What particularly might be done to enhance the "dignity and authority of families"?

3. When you become a teacher, what can you do to help coordinate social and educational services for students who are experiencing serious problems at home or in their neighborhoods?

Source: Richard Weissbourd, "Making the System Work for Poor Children," a report of the Executive Session on *Making the System Work for Poor Children* (Cambridge, Mass.: Harvard University, John F. Kennedy School of Government, Wiener Center for Social Policy, 1991), cover and p. i.

Fragmented services ineffective

Many advocates of **coordinated human services** explicitly aim to reach all young people who experience problems growing up in modern society. The greatest emphasis usually is placed on the particularly critical need to help those for whom school-based efforts probably will not be sufficient to counteract the effects of severely damaging environments. Coordination is necessary because numerous forms of help often must be mobilized — and to "expect a youth-in-crisis" and his or her "stressed parents to negotiate, unassisted, the maze of agencies, programs, and eligibility rules in order to get the help they need is to ask the impossible." In many communities, city, county, or regional agreements and taxes make coordinated services possible. Political leaders also are exploring ways to enhance collaboration through youth-service coordinating boards,

tional Association of State Boards of Education, 1990); and Anne C. Lewis, "All Together Now: Building Collaboration," *Phi Delta Kappan* (January 1992), pp. 348–349.

*Characteristics
of successful
collaborative programs*

interagency compacts with schools, and other mechanisms.[37] Scholars report that successful collaborative programs share the following characteristics:[38]

■ They offer a wide array of services and provide an easy entry point.

■ They move beyond crisis intervention by emphasizing prevention and development.

■ They cross bureaucratic and organizational boundaries in order to provide services coherently, often at nontraditional hours in nontraditional settings.

■ They provide staff with the time and training necessary to develop relationships based on trust and respect.

■ They involve teachers and parents in communications loops.

■ They include facilitating staff from the local community.

■ They view the child as part of the family, and the family as part of the community.

Questions About Compensatory Education

Although data collected in the 1980s suggest that compensatory education can be successful for disadvantaged students, there still are many questions and problems concerning its status and effectiveness.

1. *Can compensatory education result in permanent meaningful gains for most disadvantaged students?* In line with conclusions summarized in the preceding sections and in Chapter 10, data on achievement levels in U.S. schools indicate

Achievement still too low

that the performance of many disadvantaged students entering secondary schools is still unacceptably low regardless of whether they have been in Chapter 1 or other compensatory programs. In most big cities, for example, the average reading score of ninth graders at inner-city schools remains at about the seventh-grade level. This means in turn that 50 percent or more of these students are unable to read well enough to succeed in school or rewarding jobs later in life.[39]

2. *How can Chapter 1 be made more effective?* Research indicates that Chapter 1 has been relatively ineffective in many schools in part because most programs

Pullout usually ineffective

utilize a **pullout approach.** This is the practice of taking eligible low achievers out of regular classes for supplementary reading or math instruction. Pullout approaches generally do not work well because they generate much movement of students and attendant confusion throughout the school, and because it is

---

[37]A. I. Melaville and Martin J. Blank, *What It Takes: Structuring Interagency Partnerships to Connect Children and Families with Comprehensive Services* (Washington, D.C.: Education and Human Services Consortium, 1991), p. 7; Michael W. Kirst, "Improving Children's Services," *Phi Delta Kappan* (April 1991), pp. 615–618; and Cindy Wehling, "Leadville's Remarkable Experiment," *Principal* (January 1992), pp. 10–12.

[38]Carol Ascher, "Linking Schools With Human Service Agencies," *Clearinghouse on Urban Education Digest* (February 1990), pp. 1–2; Grace Peng Guthrie and Larry F. Guthrie, "Streamlining Interagency Collaboration for Youth at Risk," *Educational Leadership* (September 1991), pp. 17–22; and *Families in Schools: State Strategies and Policies to Improve Family Involvement in Education* (Washington, D.C.: Council of Chief State School Officers, 1992).

[39]Mary M. Kennedy, *The Effectiveness of Chapter 1 Services* (Washington, D.C.: U.S. Government Printing Office, 1987); Judith A. Langer et al., *Learning to Read in Our Nation's Schools* (Princeton, N.J.: Educational Testing Service, 1990).

difficult to coordinate instruction between Chapter 1 and regular classes. In addition, Chapter 1 frequently has overemphasized learning of "mechanical" sub-skills, such as word recognition in reading and simple computation in math, rather than broader and more functional skills, such as reading comprehension, math problem solving, and "learning-to-learn" strategies.[40]

Recent improvements

In recent years, federal legislation has made it easier to replace Chapter 1 pullout with more feasible schoolwide approaches that allow for coordinated, in-class assistance for low achievers. In addition, staff development has been expanded to help teachers broaden instruction to assist low-achieving disadvantaged students in moving beyond mechanical subskills. Other changes in federal legislation provide for participation of more low-achieving students in Chapter 1 through the secondary level as well as for a variety of improvements in program design and implementation. Data collected during the next few years may make it possible to determine whether these changes are having a positive impact, and to identify additional promising modifications for the future.[41]

Behavioristic vs. cognitive approaches

3. *What type of early instruction should be provided?* Much of the uncertainty regarding instruction for early compensatory education involves the issue of whether programs should utilize a behavioristic direct-instruction approach, which focuses on basic skills such as decoding of words or simple computation in math, or instead should emphasize conceptual development and abstract thinking skills. Some direct-instruction programs have had excellent results through the third grade, but performance levels usually have fallen when participating children enter the middle grades. Results in cognitive-oriented programs stressing independent learning and development of thinking skills generally have not been as good in terms of mastery of "mechanical" skills in the primary grades, but some of the best cognitive approaches have resulted in gains that show up later in basic and conceptual skills. The frequent fall-off in scores as children enter the middle grades is probably partly due to inadequate conceptual development in the primary grades.[42]

4. *What should be done at the secondary school level?* Although most sizable programs of compensatory education have been carried out at the elementary level, some efforts have been initiated in secondary schools, and a few secondary programs have reported promising results. Some success has been achieved in individual classrooms, in "schools within a school," and in "street academies" or store-front schools. However, researchers know relatively little about ap-

---

[40]Joel Meyers et al., "Classroom, Remedial, and Resource Teachers' Views of Pullout Programs," *The Elementary School Journal* (April 1990), pp. 533–545; Michael S. Knapp and Patrick M. Shields, eds., *Better Schooling for the Children of Poverty* (Berkeley, Calif.: McCutchan, 1991); and The National Council on Education Standards and Testing, *Raising Standards for American Education* (Washington, D.C.: U.S. Government Printing Office, 1992).

[41]"Augustus F. Hawkins–Robert T. Stafford Elementary and Secondary School Improvement Amendments of 1988," *Congressional Record—House,* April 13, 1988, pp. H1488–H1608; Mary Jean LeTendre, "Improving Chapter 1 Programs," *Phi Delta Kappan* (April 1991), pp. 577–581; and "ED Proposal Would Ease Chapter 1 Restrictions," *Education Daily,* January 9, 1992, pp. 1, 3.

[42]Bettye M. Caldwell, "Continuity in the Early Years," in Sharon Lynn Kagan, ed., *The Care and Education of America's Young Children* (Chicago: University of Chicago Press, 1991), pp. 69–90; Lawrence J. Schweinhart and Charles F. Hohmann, "The High/Scope K–3 Curriculum," *Principal* (May 1992), pp. 16–19.

proaches for providing successful compensatory education in intermediate and senior high schools.[43]

5. *Is it financially feasible to include most economically disadvantaged students in effective compensatory education programs?* Effective programs for the most economically disadvantaged students tend to be expensive because they require prolonged intervention in the home and family environment. At present, no one can say exactly what proportion of children requires this type of intervention, but the figure is likely to be fairly high, and per pupil costs may run several thousand dollars per year. Effective compensatory education on a national scale will cost significantly more than is now available for this purpose. Some estimates indicate that only about one-third of students eligible for Head Start and 50 percent of those eligible for Chapter 1 currently are served and that it would require billions of dollars a year in added funds to include most eligible children. Whether the public is willing and able to spend such money and what the cost-effectiveness ratio for success might be are difficult to determine.[44]

What is financially feasible?

A Fundamental Issue

Some educators question whether compensatory education, even if designed for maximum effectiveness, can significantly improve a student's chances of succeeding in school and in later life — especially a minority student living in a neighborhood of concentrated poverty. As described in Chapter 10, revisionist critics argue that U.S. public schools have failed and will continue to fail to provide equal opportunity for the poor in the absence of fundamental reforms in society as a whole. For example, many analysts contend that neighborhood, school, or other environmental conditions lead children in poor families to develop feelings of futility and powerlessness that ensure their failure in the classroom. Thus, many observers believe that it may be necessary to improve parents' economic opportunities before children's school achievement will improve at all significantly.[45]

Fundamental reforms in society

It remains to be seen whether further efforts to improve education for disadvantaged students can be sufficiently effective to disprove the skeptics' pessimism. In recent years, the effective schools movement has attempted to bring about improvements in both "regular" and compensatory education for children with low socioeconomic status. The research on effective schools is discussed at length in Chapter 16.

---

[43]Daniel U. Levine, "Educating Alienated Inner City Youth: Lessons from the Street Academies," *Journal of Negro Education* (Spring 1975), pp. 139–149; Daniel U. Levine "Implementation of an Urban School-Within-a-School-Approach," in Hersholt C. Waxman et al., eds., *Students at Risk in At-Risk Schools* (Newbury Park, Calif.: Sage Corwin, 1992).

[44]Terrell H. Bell, "Parting Words of the 13th Man," *Phi Delta Kappan* (February 1988), pp. 400–407; National Commission on Children, *Beyond Rhetoric;* and Kevin R. Hopkins, *Another Country: Poverty in the United States* (Washington, D.C.: Cato Institute, 1992).

[45]Ann Bastian et al., *Choosing Inequality* (Philadelphia: Temple University Press, 1986); John U. Ogbu, "The Consequences of the American Caste System," in Ulric Neisser, ed., *The School Achievement of Minority Children* (Hillsdale, N.J.: Erlbaum, 1986); David Hill, "A Theory of Success and Failure," *Teacher Magazine* (June/July 1990), pp. 40–45; and Andrew Hacker, *Two Nations* (New York: Scribner's Sons, 1992).

Table 11.3

Estimated Population of Major Racial Groups and Hispanics in the 1990 Census

Group	Percentage of Total Population	Percentage Increase in Population Since 1980
African American	12	13
Asian	3	108
Hispanic	9	53
Native American	1	38
White	80	6
Other	4	45

Note: Hispanics may be of any race. For this reason, percentages given above add to over 100 percent. The estimated percentage of non-Hispanic whites in the population in 1990 was 76 percent. Many persons in the "Other" category are reassigned to the major groups specified above after additional analysis. In previous census reassignments, more than 90 percent were classified as White.

Source: Various U.S. Bureau of the Census publications.

MULTICULTURAL EDUCATION

More than most other countries, the United States consists of a large number of ethnic and racial groups with diverse histories and origins. Many of these are considered to be "minority" groups because in one way or another they have been placed at a disadvantage compared with "mainstream" groups whose ancestry and heritage are primarily European.

A multiethnic population

Minority groups in turn include a variety of racial and ethnic subgroups. For example, African Americans include persons whose ancestors were brought here as slaves and persons with other family origins in the Caribbean, Latin America, Africa, and elsewhere. Hispanics (or "Latinos") include Cuban Americans, Mexican Americans, Puerto Ricans, and numerous other subgroups originating in Spanish-speaking cultures in Central and South America and in Spain. Asian Americans include persons from scores of distinct cultures and societies of the Far East (e.g., China, Japan), the Indian subcontinent (e.g., India, Pakistan), Southeast Asia (e.g., Cambodia, Laos, Vietnam), and Hawaii and other Pacific Islands. Native Americans include American Indians from more than two hundred tribal-language groups, and Alaskan Aleuts and Eskimos. Students from all these minority groups are expected to constitute more than one-third of public-school enrollment by the mid-1990s.[46]

Growth in minority population

As we point out in Chapter 10 and elsewhere in this book, many U.S. minority groups and subgroups are disproportionately low in socioeconomic status, and many children and youth from these groups are very low in educational achievement and attainment. Since the minority population of the United States has been growing rapidly in recent years (see Table 11.3), it is increasingly im-

[46]Lee H. Hamilton, "Results of the 1990 Census," *Congressional Record*, October 13, 1991, p. E3517; William P. O'Hare and Judy C. Felt, *Asian Americans: America's Fastest Growing Minority Group* (Washington, D.C.: Population Reference Bureau, 1991); and Peter Brimelow, "The Fracturing of America," *Forbes*, March 30, 1992, pp. 74–75.

portant that the educational system effectively address the problems and accommodate the needs of diverse groups of students.

Multicultural education is a term that refers to the variety of ways in which the schools can take productive account of cultural differences among students and improve opportunities for students with cultural backgrounds distinct from the U.S. mainstream. Some aspects of multicultural education focus on improving instruction for students who have not learned Standard English or who exemplify other cultural differences that place them at a disadvantage in traditional classrooms. Educators also are concerned with the larger implications of multicultural education that make it valuable for *all* students. Thus, multicultural education can address the goals of ensuring positive intergroup and interracial attitudes and contacts, and of enabling all students to function in a culturally pluralistic society. (From this point of view, the movement toward desegregation can be considered a component of multicultural education). Before discussing several major aspects of multicultural instruction, we will review some historical trends in the development of a pluralistic society in the United States.

Multicultural goals for all students

From Melting Pot to Cultural Pluralism

Although the population of the United States always has been pluralistic in its composition, the emphasis throughout much of our history has been to assimilate diverse ethnic groups into the national mainstream rather than to maintain group subcultures. Many social observers now believe that people should not be required to give up their group identity completely in order to participate in the mainstream, but in the early days of nation building it may have been necessary to minimize adherence to cultural patterns that set smaller groups apart from the "Anglo" majority. As early as 1782 St. John de Crèvecoeur commented that the colonists were being "melted" into a "new race" of men. Israel Zangwill's 1908 play *The Melting Pot* popularized this term and called attention to the challenge of "Americanizing" the large streams of immigrants who were entering the United States at the turn of the century. In educating diverse groups of immigrants, the public school system has stressed the development of an American identity. Students learned how "Americans" were supposed to talk, look, and behave, sometimes in classes of fifty or sixty pupils representing the first or second generation of immigrants from ten or fifteen countries.[47]

Historical emphasis on assimilation

From our vantage point today, the schools sometimes may have produced counterproductive results in emphasizing a particular set of behaviors and standards. For example, Mexican American students in the Southwest frequently were alienated from education when they were prohibited from speaking Spanish even on the playground, and insistence on Protestant religious customs in the schools helped stimulate the establishment of Catholic school systems in many big cities.[48] In general, however, the public schools and other institutions

Excessive restrictions and requirements

[47]Joan Strouse, "Continuing Themes in Assimilation Through Education," *Equity and Excellence* (Spring 1987), pp. 105–112; Dinitia Smith, "The Golden Door," *New York,* August 27, 1990, pp. 28–34.

[48]James W. Sanders, *The Education of an Urban Minority* (New York: Oxford University Press, 1977); David B. Tyack and Elizabeth Hansot, *Managers of Virtue: Public School Leaders in America, 1820–1980* (New York: Basic Books, 1982); and William Celis 3d, "Bilingual Teaching: A New Focus on Both Tongues," *The New York Times,* November 27, 1991, p. A11.

were successful in acculturating and socializing the children of generations of immigrants. Except for the most segregated minorities, ethnic groups have been able to achieve substantial socioeconomic mobility. An expanding economy, cheap land on the frontier, free public schools, and other opportunities made it possible for them to enter the mainstream of society, in the process acquiring many of the attitudes and behaviors of the typical American while also enriching American culture with their contributions in language, the arts, food, sports, entertainment, and scholarship.[49]

Enrichment of culture

Nevertheless, beginning in the 1950s and 1960s many scholars and lay-people realized that the melting pot in fact had not totally assimilated its ingredients. Ethnic identity not only was not being completely eliminated; it seemed to be undergoing a resurgence. Andrew Greeley, for example, described how the Irish in the United States maintained themes and practices from their traditional culture, and some studies of major ethnic groups in big cities found that ethnic identification was increasing as a result of four factors: the downgrading of working-class occupational statuses, increased immigration, international events that stimulated an affirmation of ethnicity, and decline in traditional forms of patriotism.[50] Other observers have pointed out that African Americans, Asian Americans, Hispanics, Native Americans, and some European ethnic groups were systematically discriminated against in a manner that revealed the shortcomings of the melting pot concept.[51]

Recognizing ethnic identity and discrimination

In the 1960s, as leaders of the civil rights movement fought to reduce the exclusion of minority groups, emphasis shifted (in some interpretations) from the stress on assimilation to a stress on diversity and cultural pluralism. In place of the metaphor of the melting pot, the concept of **cultural pluralism** introduced new metaphors, such as a "tossed salad" or a "mosaic," that allow for distinctive group characteristics within a larger whole. According to the American Association of Colleges for Teacher Education (AACTE),

Pluralistic metaphors

> to endorse cultural pluralism is to endorse the principle that there is no one model American. . . . [and] is to understand and appreciate the differences that exist among

---

[49]Historical mobility data for some ethnic and racial groups in the United States are reviewed in Alice Kessler-Harris and Virginia Yans-McLaughlin, "European Immigrant Groups," in Thomas Sowell, ed., *American Ethnic Groups* (Washington, D.C.: Urban Institute, 1978), pp. 107–137. Also see Nathan Glazer, ed., *Clamor at the Gates* (San Francisco: Institute for Contemporary Studies, 1985); *Ethnic Identity: The Transformation of White America* (New Haven, Conn.: Yale University Press, 1990); and Christine E. Sleeter, "The White Ethnic Experience in America," *Educational Researcher* (January–February 1992), pp. 33–36.

[50]Nathan Glazer and Daniel P. Moynihan, *Beyond the Melting Pot*, 2nd ed. (Cambridge, Mass.: MIT Press and Harvard University Press, 1970); Harriet Orcutt Duleep and Hal Snider, *The Economic Status of Americans of Southern and Eastern European Ancestry* (Washington, D.C.: U.S. Commission on Civil Rights, 1986); Sam Roberts, "Melting Pot: A Look Back and Beyond," *The New York Times*, May 17, 1990, p. A15; and Peter Schmidt, "Asians Often Face Bigotry in Schools, Report Says," *Education Week*, March 11, 1992, p. 10.

[51]Howard Bahr, Bruce A. Chadwick, and Joseph H. Strauss, *American Ethnicity* (Lexington, Mass.: D.C. Heath, 1979); William J. Wilson, *The Truly Disadvantaged* (Chicago: University of Chicago Press, 1987); John U. Ogbu, "Overcoming Racial Barriers to Equal Access," in John I. Goodlad and Pamela Keating, eds., *Access to Knowledge* (New York: The College Board, 1990), pp. 59–90; and Andrew Hacker, "The New Civil War," *The New York Review of Books*, April 23, 1992, pp. 30–33.

the nation's citizens. It is to see these differences as a positive force. . . . Cultural pluralism is more than a temporary accommodation to placate racial and ethnic minorities. It is a concept that aims toward a heightened sense of being and of wholeness of the entire society based on the unique strengths of each of its parts.[52]

It should be emphasized that acceptance of or stress on cultural pluralism does not mean that one supports a philosophy aimed at cultural, social, or economic separation. Depending on how cultural pluralism is defined, it may or may not stress integration in cultural, social, or economic matters, but generally it lies somewhere between total assimilation and strict separation of ethnic or racial groups. Cultural pluralism is more important than ever before as the United States becomes transformed into what some observers call the first "universal nation."[53]

Balance between assimilation and separation

In response to these trends, educators have been developing ways to build the goals of a constructive pluralism into the school system. The AACTE views this goal as a major educational responsibility because of the fact that schools "play a major role in shaping the attitudes and beliefs of the nation's youth . . . [and in] preparing each generation to assume the rights and responsibilities of adult life." Its statement on cultural pluralism states that multicultural education should be made an "integral part" of education at all levels.[54] Many other observers also view various aspects of multicultural education as constituting an important task for teachers in every subject area.[55]

Constructive pluralism

Multicultural Instruction

One key area in multicultural education concerns instructional approaches for teaching students with differing ethnic and racial backgrounds. Some of the most frequently discussed approaches have to do with student learning styles, recognition of dialect differences, bilingual education, and multiethnic curriculum.

Student Learning Styles.   In the previous chapter we briefly described behavioral patterns and learning styles that appear to be correlated with students' socioeconomic status and, perhaps, with their race or ethnicity. We also discussed recommendations for modifying instruction to accommodate differences in learning styles. One good example of an effort to identify instructional approaches uniquely suited to students' ethnic or racial background was described by Vera John-Steiner and Larry Smith, who worked with Pueblo Indian children

Possible group differences

[52]"No One Model American: A Statement of Multicultural Education" (Washington, D.C.: American Association of Colleges for Teacher Education, 1972), p. 9.

[53]Nicholas Appleton, *Cultural Pluralism in Education* (New York: Longman, 1983); Felicia Barringer, "Census Shows Profound Changes in Racial Makeup of the Nation," *The New York Times,* March 11, 1991, pp. A1, A12; and Lewis Lapham, "Who and What Is America?" *Harper's* (January 1992), pp. 43–49.

[54]"No One Model American."

[55]Edith W. King, "Aspects of Ethnicity and Multicultural Teaching," *Multicultural Teaching* (Spring 1984), pp. 33–35; Appleton, *Cultural Pluralism in Education;* Elizabeth Grugeon and Peter Woods, *Educating All* (New York: Routledge, 1990); and James A. Banks, "Multicultural Education: For Freedom's Sake," *Educational Leadership* (January 1992), pp. 32–36.

in the Southwest. They concluded that schooling for these children would be more successful if it took better account of their "primary learning" patterns (learning outside the school), and thereby emphasized personal communication in tutorial (face to face) situations. Other researchers who have examined learning patterns in Native American classrooms also concluded that taking account of students' cultural patterns and learning styles can enhance instructional effectiveness. For example, Frederick Erickson reported that achievement rose "dramatically" when teachers "interacted with students in ways that were culturally appropriate" in that social control was mostly indirect and teachers avoided putting students in competitive situations. Similarly, several researchers have reported that cooperative learning arrangements are particularly effective with American Indian students whose cultures de-emphasize competition.[56]

Culturally appropriate interaction

KEEP program

Positive data for an approach that modifies instruction to fit students' cultural learning styles also has been reported for the Kamehameha Early Education Program (KEEP) in Hawaii. The KEEP approach combines whole-group direct instruction with individualized work in learning centers. The program addresses the students' cultural backgrounds by emphasizing student-produced stories in language arts, instant feedback, no penalization for "wrong" answers, and discussion of students' responsibilities as group members. Researchers assessing the KEEP approach collected evidence indicating that this attempt to capitalize on the informal interaction characteristic of native Hawaiian culture has had positive effects on student achievement.[57]

Analysts concerned with possible differences in learning styles between minority and nonminority groups also have examined research on the performance of Asian American students. Several observers have concluded that some subgroups of Asian students (e.g., Koreans, Vietnamese) tend to be nonassertive in the classroom, and that this reluctance to participate may hinder their academic growth, particularly with respect to verbal skills.[58]

Nonstandard dialects

Recognition of Dialect Differences. Teachers generally have attempted to teach "proper" or standard English to students who speak nonstandard dialects, but simplistic insistence on proper English frequently has caused students either to reject their own cultural background or to view teachers' efforts to correct them as demeaning and hostile. In recent years, educators have been particularly concerned with learning problems encountered by students who speak Black English. Research shows that Black English is not simply a form of slang

---

[56]Vera John-Steiner and Larry Smith, "The Educational Promise of Cultural Pluralism" (Paper prepared for the National Conference on Urban Education, St. Louis, Missouri, 1978); Frederick Erickson, *Qualitative Methods in Research on Teaching* (East Lansing, Mich.: Institute for Research on Teaching, 1985), p. 55; and Nancy J. Protheroe and Kelly J. Barsdate, "Culturally Sensitive Instruction," *National Association of Elementary School Principals Streamlined Seminar* (March 1992), pp. 1–4.

[57]Kathryn H. Au and Alice J. Kawakami, "Research Currents," *Language Arts* (April 1985), pp. 406–411; "Cultural Differences in the Classroom," *The Harvard Education Letter* (March 1988), pp. 1–4; and Richard C. Anderson, Bonnie B. Armbruster, and Mary Roe, "Improving the Education of Reading Teachers," *Daedalus* (Spring 1990), pp. 187–210.

[58]Ester Lee Yao, "Asian-Immigrant Students' Unique Problems That Hamper Learning," *NASSP Bulletin* (December 1987), pp. 82–88; Janine Bempechat and Miya C. Omori, "Meeting the Educational Needs of Southeast Asian Children," *ERIC Clearinghouse on Urban Education* (August 1990), pp. 1–2.

but that it differs systematically from standard English in grammar and syntax. Because Black English seems to be the basic form of English spoken by many low-income African American students who are not succeeding academically, some educators have proposed that schools use Black English as the language of instruction for these students until they learn to read.

Research on teaching in Black English or other dialects has not provided much support for the conclusion that students will gain academically if initially taught in their own dialect. In addition, there usually is considerable disagreement among members of dialect communities concerning the way in which the school should teach English. In working-class African American communities, for example, many or most parents believe that their children should be taught only in "proper" English. Research also indicates that many students who use Black English in spontaneous speech are able to use standard English in reading and in responding to tests.[59]

Disagreement regarding teaching in dialect

Despite a lack of research indicating the superiority of any particular instructional method, educators should seek constructive ways to overcome the learning problems many students with nonstandard dialects encounter in standard English classrooms. This task became particularly important when a federal judge ruled in 1979 that the Ann Arbor, Michigan, school district must recognize that students who speak Black English may need special help in learning standard English. The district was ordered to implement a plan to identify children who speak Black English and then to take their dialect into consideration in teaching them to read. Although the decision is not binding outside the Ann Arbor schools, it has influenced some other school districts struggling to provide effective multicultural education. Guidelines for doing so stress possibilities for building "associative bridges" between a child's dialect and standard English and for helping children develop skills in appropriately switching to standard English.[60]

Ann Arbor ruling

Bilingual Education. **Bilingual education,** which provides instruction in their native language for students not proficient in English, has been expanding in U.S. public schools. In 1968, Congress passed the Bilingual Education Act, and in 1974 the Supreme Court ruled unanimously in *Lau* v. *Nichols* that the schools must take steps to help students who "are certain to find their classroom experiences wholly incomprehensible" because they do not understand English. Congressional appropriations for bilingual education increased from $7.5 million in 1969 to almost $200 million in 1992. Although the federal and state governments fund bilingual projects for more than sixty language groups speaking various Asian, Indo-European, and Native American languages, the large majority of children served by these projects are Hispanic.

Lau v. **Nichols** *requirements*

---

[59]J. R. Harber and D. N. Bryan, "Black English and the Teaching of Reading," *Review of Educational Research* (Summer 1976), pp. 397–398; Jane W. Torrey, "Black Children's Knowledge of Standard English," *American Educational Research Journal* (Winter 1983), pp. 627–643; and "Teachers, Culture, and Power," *Rethinking Schools* (March/April 1992), pp. 14–16.

[60]Pauline E. Brooks, *Designing and Evaluating Language Programs for African American (Black) Dialect Speakers: Some Guidelines for Educators* (Los Angeles: UCLA Graduate School of Education Center for the Study of Evaluation, 1987); Toya A. Wyatt and Harry N. Seymour, "The Implications of Code-Switching in Black English Speakers," *Equity and Excellence* (Summer 1990), pp. 11–18.

One advantage frequently attributed to bilingual education is its potential for emphasizing comprehension and thinking skills in the students' native language while they are learning to function fluently in English. (© Jeff Thiebauth/Lightwave)

The Supreme Court's unanimous decision in the *Lau* case, which involved Chinese children in San Francisco, did not focus on bilingual education as the only remedy for teaching limited-English-proficient (LEP) and non-English-proficient (NEP) students. Instead, the Court said, "Teaching English to the students of Chinese ancestry is one choice. Giving instruction to this group in Chinese in another. There may be others." In practice, federal regulations for implementing the *Lau* decision have tended to focus on bilingual education as the most common solution, generally suggesting that school districts initiate bilingual programs if they enroll more than twenty students of a given language group at a particular grade. Bilingual programs have proliferated accordingly. Since 1983 the federal government has indicated some willingness to accept English-as-a-second-language (ESL) instruction or other nonbilingual approaches for providing help to LEP and NEP students. Nevertheless, data collected by the Council of Chief State School Officers indicate that large numbers of LEP students are not receiving significant specialized assistance (whether in bilingual or other programs) to help them learn English and other subjects.[61]

Proliferation of bilingual programs

Controversies arise

Controversies over bilingual education have become increasingly embittered. As in the case of teaching through dialect, there are arguments between those who would "immerse" children in an English-language environment and those who believe initial instruction will be more effective in the native lan-

[61]James Crawford, "Bilingual Education," *Education Week,* April 1, 1987, pp. 1–14; Cynthia G. Brown, *The Challenge and State Response* (Washington, D.C.: Council of Chief State School Officers, 1990).

Types of bilingual programs

guage. Residents in some ethnic neighborhoods are fervently divided over proposals to establish bilingual programs in the public schools. Educators and laypeople concerned with LEP and NEP students also argue over whether emphasis should be placed on teaching in the native language over a long period of time, called **first-language maintenance,** or providing intensive English instruction and then proceeding to teach all subjects in English as soon as possible, called **transitional bilingual education.** The latter approach, frequently referred to simply as TBE, has been supported by federal guidelines and by legislation in some states, partly on the grounds that public schools should teach basic skills in languages other than English only until students can learn in English. On the one side are those who favor maintenance because they believe that this will help build or maintain a constructive sense of identity and community among ethnic or racial minorities.[62] On the other side are those who believe that cultural maintenance programs are harmful because they separate groups from one another or discourage students from mastering English well enough to function successfully in the larger society.[63]

Adherents and opponents of bilingual education also differ on related issues. Some critics claim that bilingual programs are advocated primarily as a means of providing teaching jobs for native language speakers and question whether individuals who fill these jobs are competent in English. Observers who favor

Bilingual staff

bilingual/bicultural maintenance tend to believe that the schools need many adults who can teach LEP or NEP students in their own language, whereas some observers who favor transitional or ESL programs feel that very few native language or bilingual speakers are required to staff a legitimate program.

Educators are particularly concerned with the question of whether bilingual education is effective in improving the performance of low-achieving students. Some scholars who have examined the research believe that bilingual education

Conflicting research

has brought about little if any improvement. Several researchers in this group have concluded that "structured immersion" (placement in regular classes with special assistance provided inside and outside of class) and "sheltered immersion" (using principles of second-language learning in regular classrooms) are more successful than TBE.[64] However, other scholars disagree, arguing that well-implemented bilingual programs do improve achievement. For example, Heidi

[62]Leonard C. Pacheco, "Educational Renewal: A Bilingual/Bicultural Imperative," *Educational Horizons* (Summer 1977), pp. 168–176; Lily Wong Fillmore, "Language and Cultural Issues in the Early Education of Language Minority Children," in Sharon Lynn Kagan, ed., *The Care and Education of America's Young Children* (Chicago: University of Chicago Press, 1991), pp. 30–49; and Mary McGroarty, "The Societal Context of Bilingual Education," *Educational Researcher* (March 1992), pp. 7–9, 24.

[63]Noel Epstein, *Language, Ethnicity, and the Schools: Policy Alternatives for Bilingual-Bicultural Education* (Washington, D.C.: George Washington University Institute for Educational Leadership, 1977); Rosalie Pedalino Porter, *Forked Tongue* (New York: Basic Books, 1990); and Linda Chavez, *Out of the Barrio* (New York: Basic Books, 1991).

[64]Russell Gersten and James Woodward, "A Case for Structured Immersion," *Educational Leadership* (September 1985), pp. 75–79; Daniel L. Watson, Linda Northcutt, and Laura Rydell, "Teaching Bilingual Students Successfully," *Educational Leadership* (February 1989), pp. 59–61; Christine H. Rossell, "The Research on Bilingual Education," *Equity and Excellence* (Winter 1990), pp. 29–36; Keith A. Baker, *Bilingual Education* (Bloomington, Ind.: Phi Delta Kappa, 1991); and Rosalie Pedalino Porter, "Language Choice for Latin Students," *The Public Interest* (Fall 1991), pp. 48–60.

Dulay and Marina Burt reviewed a number of studies and reported that bilingual education worked significantly better than monolingual programs. Several subsequent reviews of research also concluded that bilingual programs frequently have had positive effects on student achievement.[65]

A number of researchers have also identified specific characteristics that help make programs for LEP and NEP students successful. These characteristics include continuity in enrollment for a given student, frequent monitoring of progress, and open-ended assistance (rather than the elimination of assistance at an arbitrary point).[66] For bilingual programs in particular, success is more likely if *Active teaching* the program features "active" teaching, communication of high expectations to the students, and coordination of English-language development with academic studies.[67]

Special help needed Despite disagreements on the effects of existing programs, most researchers agree that LEP and NEP students should and must be given special assistance in learning to function in the schools. According to the research, "submersion" approaches, which simply place LEP and NEP students in regular classrooms, without any special assistance or modifications in instruction, frequently result in failure to learn. In addition, numerous researchers have reported that it is critically important to stress cognitive development and higher-order skills when implementing bilingual education; indeed, one advantage frequently attributed to bilingual education is its potential for emphasizing comprehension and thinking skills in the students' native language while they are learning to function fluently in English.[68]

Bilingual education for all students Many scholars believe that bilingual education ideally should be provided for all students, regardless of their ethnic group. Programs to provide education in both English and another language for all students at a multiethnic school sometimes are referred to as "two-way" bilingual immersion. Several groups of

---

[65]Heidi Dulay and Marina Burt, "Bilingual Education: A Close Look at Its Effects," *Focus of the National Clearinghouse for Bilingual Education* (January 1982), pp. 1–4. Also see Ann C. Willig, "A Meta-Analysis of Selected Studies on the Effectiveness of Bilingual Education," *Review of Educational Research* (Fall 1985), pp. 269–317; Ann C. Willig, "Examining Bilingual Education Research," *Review of Educational Research* (Fall 1987), pp. 363–376; and Gary A. Cziko, "The Evaluation of Bilingual Education," *Educational Researcher* (March 1992), pp. 10–15.

[66]Charlene Rivera and Annette Zehler, *Collaboration in Teaching and Learning: Findings from the Innovative Approach Research Project* (Arlington, Va.: Development Associates, 1990); J. David Ramirez, Sandra D. Yuen, and Dena R. Ranney, *Longitudinal Study of Structured English Immersion Strategy, Early-Exit and Late-Exit Transition and Bilingual Education Programs* (San Mateo, Calif.: Aquirre International, 1991).

[67]William J. Tikinoff, *Applying Significant Bilingual Instruction Features in the Classroom* (Roslyn, Va.: Inter-America Research Association, 1985); Thomas P. Carter and Michael L. Chatfield, "Effective Bilingual Schools," *American Journal of Education* (November 1986), pp. 200–232; William J. Tikinoff, "Modifying Instructional Environments" (Paper presented at the annual meeting of the American Educational Research Association, Chicago, April 1991); and Lucinda Pease-Alvarez and Kenji Hakuta, "Enriching Our Views of Bilingualism and Bilingual Education," *Educational Researcher* (March 1992), pp. 4–6, 19.

[68]Kenji Hakuta, *Mirror of Language* (New York: Basic Books, 1986); Kenji Hakuta and Lois J. Gould, "Synthesis of Research on Bilingual Education," *Educational Leadership* (March 1987), pp. 38–45; Judith A. Langer et al., "Meaning Construction in School Literacy Tasks: A Study of Bilingual Students," *American Educational Research Journal* (Fall 1990), pp. 427–471; Claude Goldenberg and Ronald Gallimore, "Local Knowledge, Research Knowledge, and Educational Change," *Educational Researcher* (November 1991), pp. 2–13; and Douglas A. New, "Teaching in the Fourth World," *Phi Delta Kappan* (January 1992), pp. 396–398.

civic leaders have recommended the following emphases to make this type of bilingual education a positive force for education in the future:[69]

■   A strong insistence on full mastery of English.

■   Emphasis on multilingual competence, rather than just on English remediation.

■   Increased attention to the international political and economic advantages of multilingual competence.

Improvements in multicultural programming

Multiethnic Curriculum and Instruction.   Since the mid-1960s, educators have been striving to take better account of cultural diversity by developing and using multiethnic curriculum materials and instructional methods. Many textbooks and supplemental reading lists have been systematically revised to include materials and topics relating to diverse racial and ethnic groups. In-service training has been provided to help teachers learn about multiethnic source materials and approaches and to employ instructional methods that promote multicultural perspectives and positive intergroup relations. Guidelines for designing and delivering instruction frequently have stressed the importance of selecting materials that reflect the diversity of U.S. society.[70]

Changes for Native Americans

Efforts to devise and utilize multiethnic curricula have been particularly vigorous with respect to the education of Native American students. For example, educators at the Northwest Regional Education Laboratory have prepared an entire Indian Reading Series based on Native American culture. Mathematics instruction for Native American students sometimes uses familiar tribal symbols and artifacts in presenting word and story problems, and local or regional tribal history has become an important part of the social studies curriculum in some schools. Many observers believe that incorporation of such materials and methods can help Native American students establish a positive sense of identity conducive to success in school and society.[71]

Importance for all students

However, it should not be inferred that introduction of multiethnic curriculum is intended only to bolster the self-image and enhance the learning of minority students. Among its most crucial purposes is to ensure that each group of students acquires knowledge and appreciation of other racial and ethnic groups. Guidelines for attaining this goal through multiethnic curriculum and instruction typically involve interrelated activities dealing with such skills and understanding as the following:[72]

■   *Human relations skills* involving development of students' self-esteem and interpersonal communications

[69]Academy for Educational Development, "A New Direction for Bilingual Education in the 1980s," *Focus of the National Clearinghouse for Bilingual Education* (March 1982), pp. 1–4; *What Works in Education: A Symposium* (Washington, D.C.: U.S. Government Printing Office, 1990).

[70]Vernay Mitchell, "Curriculum and Instruction to Reduce Racial Conflict," *ERIC Clearinghouse on Urban Education Digest* (April 1990), pp. 1–2; David L. Kirp, "Textbooks and Tribalism in California," *The Public Interest* (Summer 1991), pp. 20–36; and Sara Bullard, "Sorting Through the Multicultural Rhetoric," *Educational Leadership* (January 1992), pp. 8–11.

[71]William A. Gollnick, "The Reappearance of the Vanishing American," *The College Board Review* (Spring 1990), pp. 30–36; Lee Little Soldier, "The Education of Native American Students," *Equity and Excellence* (Summer 1990), pp. 66–69; and *Indian Reading Series* (Portland, Ore.: Northwest Regional Educational Laboratory, 1990).

[72]James A. Banks, *Multiethnic Education* (Needham Heights, Mass.: Allyn and Bacon, 1988; Mi-

■ *Cultural self-awareness* developed through students' research on their ethnic or racial group, family history, and local community

■ *Multicultural awareness* derived in part from historical studies incorporating diverse racial and ethnic points of view

■ *Cross-cultural experiences* including discussions and dialogue with students and adults from different ethnic and racial groups

Recent Controversies. In recent years particular attention has been given to ensuring that curriculum and instruction are not overwhelmingly *Eurocentric* (reflecting the culture and history of ethnic groups of European origin) but instead also incorporate materials and perspectives representing the concerns, culture, and history of ethnic and racial groups of different origins. For example, *Afrocentric* programs focus on the history and culture of African Americans. Afrocentric and related approaches not only introduce materials dealing with the history and status of minority groups, but also involve activities such as community service assignments and cooperative learning tasks that are thought to acquaint students with minority cultures and traditions.[73]

Eurocentric emphasis criticized

Efforts to introduce Afrocentric and other minority-oriented themes have provoked controversy in California, New York, and other states. Related controversies also have arisen in the Portland (Oregon) public schools and other individual school districts. Critics of minority-oriented projects have offered a number of strongly voiced objections:[74]

Separation may be overly emphasized

■ Many of the materials being introduced or recommended embody an overly broad rejection of both the traditional curriculum and of existing efforts to make the school constructively multicultural. In constantly criticizing Europeans and European traditions and concentrating almost entirely on minority themes, Afrocentric and related approaches are encouraging racial and ethnic separation and animosity. For example, Diane Ravitch concluded that some of the new materials espouse a "version of history in which everyone is either the descendant or victim of oppressors," thereby re-creating and fanning "ancient hatreds" and conflicts.

Some materials may be inaccurate

■ Many of the new materials are historically inaccurate. For example, after noting that some of these materials are based on the conclusions that the culture and population of ancient Egypt were predominantly African and that ancient Greece derived much of its culture from Egypt, John Leo reported that classical scholars believe these generalizations exaggerate the extent to which Egypt was primarily African and influenced Greece.

chael Webb, "Multicultural Education in Elementary and Secondary Schools," *ERIC Clearinghouse on Urban Education Digest* (July 1990), pp. 1–2; and Barbara Miner, "Conservatives Attack Anti-Bias Education," *Rethinking Schools* (January/February 1992), p. 3.

[73]Andrew Trotter, "Rites of Passage," *The Executive Educator* (September 1991), pp. 48–49; Marge Scherer, "School Snapshot: Focus on African-American Culture," *Educational Leadership* (January 1992), pp. 17, 19.

[74]Diane Ravitch, "Multiculturalism Yes, Particularism No," *The Chronicle of Higher Education,* October 24, 1990; p. A44; John Leo, "A Fringe History of the World," *U.S. News and World Report,* November 12, 1990, p. 25; Albert Shanker, "The Danger in Multiple Perspectives," *The New Republic,* December 2, 1991, p. 50; Lynne V. Cheney, "Beware the PC Police," *The Executive Educator* (January 1992), pp. 31–34; and Erich Martel, "How Valid Are the Portland Baseline Essays?" *Educational Leadership* (January 1992), pp. 20–23.

- ■ Viewpoints said to encapsulate the beliefs and attitudes of minority racial and ethnic groups are not representative of the diversity of opinions that exist within each group, which vary with group members' political philosophy, degree of assimilation, personal experience, social class, and other factors.

- ■ Emphasis on minority culture and history sometimes is being pursued as a substitute for the difficult actions required to improve minority students' academic performance.

Responding to the kinds of attacks summarized above, supporters of Afrocentric and other related approaches have answered that the criticisms generally have been misguided. Among their rebuttals and counterarguments have been the following:[75]

Western culture not completely rejected

- ■ Few Afrocentric supporters advocate elimination of material on Western culture and history from the curriculum. Molefi Asante of Temple University has stated that the Afrocentric movement is based on the work of scholars who use both Western and African sources and are striving to de-bias the curriculum by adding appropriate Afrocentric materials, not by eliminating Western classics.

Academic achievement not neglected

- ■ Few if any supporters of Afrocentric or related approaches minimize the importance of academic achievement or advocate its de-emphasis in the curriculum. Instead, stress on the history and contributions of one's racial or ethnic group is advocated as a way to enhance motivation while challenging children to perform to their fullest potential.

Initial reports promising

Although the academic effects of emphasizing minority history and culture have not been researched systematically, some initial reports as well as anecdotal accounts suggest that Afrocentric and related approaches may help improve the performance of low-achieving students. For example, educators in some big cities have concluded that inclusion of materials on minority history and culture can help improve students' motivation to learn. Both attendance and reading scores appear to have improved at some Atlanta schools that have introduced Afrocentric themes, and an assessment of college students who participated in an Afrocentric studies program for one year found that their grades improved substantially.[76]

Despite the controversies and uncertainties that exist regarding the design and effects of multiethnic curriculum materials and Afrocentric themes, most

---

[75]Molefi Asante, *The Afrocentric Idea* (Philadelphia: Temple University Press, 1987); Calvin Sims, "World Views," *The New York Times*, November 4, 1990, p. Educ 23; Denise K. Magner, "Ph.D. Program Stirs a Debate on the Future of Black Studies," *The Chronicle of Higher Education*, June 19, 1991, pp. A1, A13; Ed Wiley III, "Afrocentrism," *Black Issues in Higher Education*, October 24, 1991, pp. 1, 20–21; Karen J. Winkler, "Organization of American Historians Backs Teaching of Non-Western Culture and Diversity in Schools," *The Chronicle of Higher Education*, February 6, 1991, pp. A5–A7; Molefi Asante, "Afrocentric Curriculum," *Educational Leadership* (January 1992), pp. 28–31; and Ellen K. Coughlin, "Scholars Confront Fundamental Question," *The Chronicle of Higher Education*, January 29, 1992, pp. A8, A11.

[76]Charles Devarics, "Afro-centric Program Yields Academic Gains," *Black Issues in Higher Education*, December 6, 1990, pp. 1, 34; Isabel Wilkerson, "Blacks Look to Basics," *The New York Times*, November 4, 1990, p. Educ 26; and Gary Putka, "Course Work Stressing Blacks' Role Has Critics but Appears Effective," *The Wall Street Journal*, July 1, 1991, pp. A1, A4.

influential educators believe that there is an urgent need to develop and implement comprehensive multicultural approaches that emphasize and reflect minority experiences and concerns. New York State Commissioner of Education Thomas Sobol summarized much of this imperative as follows:

> Critics ask why we are fretting over multicultural curriculums instead of getting back to the basics. What they miss is the interconnection. . . . If children are to do well academically . . . the child must experience the school as an extension, not a rejection, of home and community. . . . [A central goal] is to develop a shared set of values and a common tradition . . . [while also helping] each child find his or her place within the whole . . . [and understand how Western tradition] has been changed and enriched by the cumulative participation of the sons and daughters of Africa, of Asia, of Central America, of Native Americans.[77]

Opportunities and Dangers in Multicultural Education

Important to avoid fragmentation and overload

General disagreements about multicultural education have followed some of the same lines as the specific arguments about Afrocentric and other minority-oriented curricula. For example, critics contend that multicultural education may divide society by emphasizing ethnic separatism rather than developing citizens who will work together to accomplish common goals. Some believe that multicultural education will fragment and overload the school curriculum, reinforcing tendencies for teachers to stress memorization and regurgitation of disconnected facts and concepts.[78] Furthermore, critics argue that multicultural concerns may be misused to justify second-rate education for economically disadvantaged or minority students. If "ethnic studies" programs do not make great efforts to maintain a high quality of instruction, the diplomas or degrees students receive may be viewed as second-rate.[79]

Guidelines for multicultural programs

To avoid these potential dangers, the director of an institute for civic education has provided some useful guidelines for implementing and evaluating multicultural programs:[80]

> *Maintain openness.* . . . courses should have detailed syllabi available for any citizen to see at any time. A reasonable syllabus would outline the content, indicate the major topics and subtopics . . . and specify the required reading or other activities. . . .

---

[77]Thomas Sobol, "Understanding Diversity," *Educational Leadership* (February 1990), pp. 27–30. Also see Patricia Pickles-Thomas and Cornell Thomas, "Do You Really Understand Your Students?" *Principal* (January 1992), pp. 54–55.

[78]Albert Shanker, "A Curriculum of Fragmentation," *The New York Times,* January 28, 1990, p. E7; Willard A. Hageboom, "America Has Shaped Us More Than We It," *Education Week,* December 4, 1991, pp. 36, 27; and Diane Ravitch, "A Culture in Common," *Educational Leadership* (January 1992), pp. 8–11.

[79]Shanker, "The Danger in Multiple Perspectives"; Eleanor-Armour-Thomas and William A. Profiedt, "Cultural Awareness and 'Learner-Centrism,'" *Education Week,* December 4, 1991, pp. 36, 27; and Albert Shanker, "Courting Ethnic Strife," *The New Republic,* March 30, 1992, p. 13.

[80]Sandra Stotsky, "Cultural Politics," *The American School Board Journal* (October 1991), p. 28; Sandra Stotsky, "Whose Literature? America's!" *Educational Leadership* (January 1992), pp. 53–56.

Find out what positive aspects of Western civilization are being taught. If students are not learning that constitutional government, the rule of law, and the primacy of individual rights are among the hallmarks of Western civilization, then they are not learning the essential features of their heritage. . . .

Find out if students are being taught that racism, sexism, homophobia, and imperialism are characteristics of all cultures and civilizations at some time — not culture-specific evils. . . . America's failings should not be taught in isolation from the failings of other countries — no double standard.

Insist that all students study both Western and non-Western cultures. Students need solid academic courses in Latin American, African, and Asian history, in addition to European history.

Healthy recognition of problems

The concern with multicultural education reflects a healthy recognition that systematic steps must be taken to ensure positive intergroup relationships and provide more effective educational opportunities for all groups of students in a pluralistic society. As with desegregation and compensatory education, educators will disagree among themselves on just what steps are needed. For years to come, however, the goal of attaining equal opportunity through multiculturalism will continue as a prominent theme in U.S. education.

EDUCATION FOR STUDENTS WITH DISABILITIES

One of the major developments in education in the 1970s and 1980s involved schooling for children with disabilities. Large gains have been made in providing and improving special education services for these students. Table 11.4 shows the numbers of students with disabilities served in or through public education in 1977 and in 1989. As indicated, the total number served during this time increased by nearly a half million children. Analysis conducted by the U.S. Department of Education indicates that 69 percent of students with disabilities receive most or all of their education in regular classes (with or without assignment to part-time resource rooms); 25 percent are in self-contained classes; and the rest are in special schools or facilities.[81]

Growth of special education

Influence of Brown decision

The growth of special education has been associated with the civil rights movement and its concern with equal educational opportunity. In 1954 the U.S. Supreme Court in *Brown* v. *Board of Education* said: "In these days, it is doubtful that any child may reasonably be expected to succeed in life if he is denied the opportunity of an education. Such an opportunity, where the state has undertaken to provide it, is a right which must be made available to all on equal terms." Although the *Brown* decision addressed the segregation of African American children in separate schools, it also served as a precedent in establishing the rights of students with disabilities to be provided with equal educational opportunity. This right was explicitly affirmed in 1974 when a U.S. district court ruled

[81]U.S. Department of Education, *"To Assure the Free Appropriate Education of All Handicapped Children"* (Washington, D.C.: U.S. Department of Education, 1990).

Table 11.4

Number of Students Receiving Public Special Educational Services by Type of Disability, 1977 and 1989

Type of Disability	1977	1989
Speech or language impaired	1,302,666	968,908
Mentally retarded	969,547	581,465
Learning disabled	797,213	1,998,422
Emotionally disturbed	283,072	377,295
Other health impaired	141,417	50,349
Hard of hearing and deaf	89,743	57,555
Orthopedically impaired	87,008	47,392
Visually handicapped	38,247	22,743
Deaf-blind and other multihandicapped	NA[a]	86,386
Total	3,708,913	4,190,515

[a]NA = Not an applicable category in 1977.

Source: U.S. Department of Education, *"To Assure the Free Appropriate Education of All Handicapped Children"* (Washington, D.C.: U.S. Department of Education, 1990), Table 1.4, p. 11; other U.S. Department of Education sources.

Pennsylvania decision

in *Pennsylvania Association for Retarded Children, Nancy Beth Bowman et al.* v. *Commonwealth of Pennsylvania, David H. Kurtzman:*

> The Commonwealth of Pennsylvania has undertaken to provide a free public education for all its children between the ages of six and twenty-one years. It is the Commonwealth's obligation to place each mentally retarded child in a free, public program of education and training appropriate to the child's capacity.

The Pennsylvania case and other judicial decisions have reflected federal laws that extended a right to access to educational services to students with disabilities under the Fifth and Fourteenth Amendments to the Constitution. These amendments state that no person can be deprived of liberty and of equal protection of the laws without due process. Federal requirements regarding the education of disabled students were enumerated systematically in the **Education for All Handicapped Children Act (PL 94-142)** of 1975, which set forth as national policy the goal that "free appropriate public education . . . must be extended to handicapped persons as their fundamental right." The basic requirements spelled out in PL 94-142, as well as other laws and judicial interpretations, are as follows:

PL 94-142

Basic requirements in providing special services

1. Testing and assessment services must be fair and comprehensive; placement cannot be based on a single criterion such as an IQ score.

2. Parents or guardians must have access to information on diagnosis and may protest decisions of school officials.

3. Individualized education programs (IEPs) that include both long-range and short-range goals must be provided.

4. Educational services must be provided in the **least restrictive environment,** which means that children with disabilities may be placed in special

Effective mainstreaming of students with disabilities into regular classroom settings requires a variety of special resources, relatively small classes, and educators skilled in and dedicated to creating an effective learning environment and acceptance for all students. (© Will/Deni McIntyre/ Photo Researchers, Inc.)

or separate classes only for the amount of time judged necessary to provide appropriate services. If a school district demonstrates that placement in a regular educational setting cannot be achieved satisfactorily, the student must be provided adequate instruction elsewhere, paid for by the district.

Progress still needed

The number of special education students in public schools now exceeds 4 million, and special education services are now being extended to preschool students with disabilities.[82] Nevertheless, much progress still needs to be made in many school districts that tend to have high percentages of students with mental retardation, learning disabilities, and emotional problems. For example, recent reports presented data indicating that tens of thousands of children with disabilities are on waiting lists for placement in special education programs, and that federal and local monitoring and enforcement activities are weak and inadequate. Various analyses also indicate that PL 94-142 has been implemented much more successfully in some locations than in others, and that implementation in big cities has been particularly inadequate.[83]

---

[82]Maggie Hume, "States Dive into Programs for Disabled Students," *Education Daily,* March 25, 1988, pp. 3–4; Michael deCourcy Hinds, "Nationwide Revolution in Education Is Giving Handicapped a Headstart," *The New York Times,* July 17, 1991, p. 7.

[83]Judith D. Singer and John A. Butler, "The Education for All Handicapped Children Act: Schools as Agents of Social Reform," *Harvard Educational Review* (May 1987), pp. 125–152; Joan L. Buttram and Keith M. Kershner, *A Second Look at Special Education in Urban Districts* (Philadelphia: Research for Better Schools, 1989); Jane Knitzer, Zina Steinberg, and Brahm Fleisch, *At the Schoolhouse Door* (New York: Bank Street College, 1990); and *Youth with Disabilities: How Are They Doing?* (Menlo Park, Calif.: SRI International, 1992).

Classification and Labeling of Students

Difficulties in classifying

Many of the problems associated with improving education for children with disabilities are related to difficulties in identifying students who require special education services. It is very difficult to be certain, for example, whether a child is mentally retarded and could benefit from special services or is simply a slow learner who requires more time and guidance to learn. Similarly, it is difficult to determine whether a child who is working below capacity has brain impairment or some other learning disability or is performing poorly because he or she is poorly motivated or poorly taught. (Of course, all these reasons may be operative for the same child.) Experts in special education disagree among themselves not only on what constitutes a "learning disability" that requires special education services but also on what services should be provided to ameliorate it.[84] Similar problems are encountered in distinguishing between severe and mild emotional disturbances or between partial and complete deafness. Children who fall close to some borderline in disability status (a borderline that may be very fuzzy and ill defined) are especially difficult to classify. Maynard Reynolds, an authority on such classification, has described the overall problem as follows:

> The procedures used to categorize children for special placements are left over in part from practices in the 19th century asylums of Europe. Some adjustments have been made by extending or enlarging the notion of mental retardation to include the educable retarded and the concept of mental illness to include emotionally disturbed and behaviorally disturbed (and disturbing?) children. A poorly defined category, learning disabilities, has been added to fill in the gaps between other categories; the label is applied to children who do not respond to ordinary instruction in the schools and yet do not fit any traditional category.[85]

What are learning disabilities?

Reynolds and other analysts also point out that the vagueness of the learning disabilities (LD) category has encouraged school districts to use this classification because it enables them to obtain federal funds to improve educational services. Since most LD students spend much of their time in regular classes but receive extra assistance in some special classes, LD services are frequently a form of compensatory education for disadvantaged students and low-achieving students who do not qualify for Chapter 1 placement. This helps to explain why the number of students in the LD category has grown so large. Research indicates that half or more of the LD students in the schools do not meet criteria commonly accepted by experts in special education.[86]

---

[84]Barry Franklin, ed., *Learning Disabilities: Dissenting Essays* (Philadelphia: Falmer, 1987); James E. Ysseldyke, Bob Algozinne, and Martha A. Thurlow, *Critical Issues in Special Education*, 2nd ed. (Boston: Houghton Mifflin, 1992).

[85]Maynard C. Reynolds, "Classification of Students with Handicaps," in Edmund W. Gordon, ed., *Review of Research in Education 11* (Washington, D.C.: American Educational Research Association, 1984), p. 89. Also see James J. Gallagher, "New Patterns in Special Education," *Educational Researcher* (June–July 1990), pp. 34–36.

[86]Steven A. Gelb and Donald T. Mizokawa, "Special Education and Social Structure: The Commonality of Exceptionality," *American Educational Research Journal* (Winter 1986), pp. 543–557; Richard L. Allington, "How Policy and Regulation Influence Instruction for At-Risk Learners," in Lorna Idol and Beau F. Jones, eds., *Educational Values and Cognitive Instruction* (Hillsdale, N.J.: Erlbaum, 1991), pp. 273–296.

Dangers in labeling

Uncertainty in accurately classifying students arises with fundamental questions regarding the appropriateness of special educational arrangements. Children placed in special education programs are thereby categorized as having a "learning problem" or as "handicapped" in learning. During the 1950s, a higher percentage of students than in earlier decades were being labeled as handicapped and placed in separate classes. During the 1960s, however, many educators and parents began to question this practice, primarily on the grounds that it isolates children with disabilities from other students. In so doing, critics argue, it fails to prepare them to function in the larger society and it generates feelings of inadequacy. Critics also are concerned with the possibility that handicapped classification may represent a self-fulfilling prophecy. Students labeled as "disturbed," for example, may be more inclined to misbehave because the label makes unruly behavior acceptable and expected.[87]

Problems in evaluation

Researchers concerned with the effects of labeling have tried to determine whether placement in a special class or program really does have a detrimental effect on students. Among the variables they have considered are effects on self-concept, peer acceptance, and postschool outcomes. This type of research is very difficult to conduct because of problems in defining terms, measuring program effects, and allowing for different students' different reactions to a given program. Moreover, the likelihood that labeling may have a negative effect does not mean that placement in a regular class or setting necessarily will be more beneficial.

Overcoming problems in restrictive settings

Some researchers who have reviewed studies on labeling thus concluded that the allegedly overall negative effects of special classes or programs for students with disabilities are not well established. However, neither has it been proved that separate classes or programs are more beneficial, on the average, than is placement in regular classes. Several reviews of research have concluded that for students with mild learning problems, restrictive educational settings need not detract from achievement, provided that effective practices are used to overcome problems such as stigmatization and slow pacing of instruction. Several authors also concluded, however, that less restrictive settings generally are preferable on ethical grounds and because they produce social benefits such as enhancement of students' self-esteem and increased communications between students with and without disabilities.[88]

Mainstreaming

Despite the lack of conclusive data showing detrimental effects of separate classes and settings for students with disabilities, some courts have weighed the

---

[87]Donald I. Macmillan and C. Edward Meyers, "Educational Labeling of Handicapped Learners," in D. C. Berliner, ed., *Review of Research in Education 7* (Washington, D.C.: American Educational Research Association, 1979), pp. 121–194; Gillian Fulcher, "Students with Special Needs," *Education Policy* (October/December 1990), pp. 347–358; and Perry A. Zirkel, "Offensive Parents," *Phi Delta Kappan* (March 1992), pp. 572–574.

[88]Gaea Leinhardt and Allan Pallay, "Restrictive Educational Settings: Exile or Haven?" *Review of Educational Research* (Winter 1982), pp. 557–578; Gaea Leinhardt and William Bickel, "Instruction's the Thing Wherein to Catch the Mind That Falls Behind," *Educational Psychologist* (Spring 1987), pp. 177–207; and Christine Padilla and Thomas Parrish, *A Cost Analysis of Programs for Problem Learners* (Menlo Park, Calif.: SRI International, 1990).

evidence and concluded that separate placement probably does have detrimental effects for many students. This may be particularly true for those classified as having only mild handicaps. Now that PL 94-142 requires that students with disabilities be placed in the least restrictive environment, efforts to accommodate these students in regular class settings, referred to as **mainstreaming,** have been carried out in school districts throughout the country. Mainstreaming is not necessarily intended to eliminate special services or classes for children with exceptional needs. Extra support may include a wide range of services, from consultation by specialists skilled in working with a particular disability to provision of special equipment. Even if a disability is severe and a child needs to spend a substantial amount of time away from the regular classroom, he or she can still be encouraged to take part in activities, such as art or music, that are open to other children.[89]

Mandate for
mainstreaming

Extra support required

Research on mainstreaming has led to conclusions as ambiguous as the results of studies of labeling and separate class placement. Some analysts have concluded that mainstreaming can improve the social acceptance of students with disabilities provided that direct interventions are made to achieve this goal, but they found scant evidence indicating that mainstreaming generally has improved the academic performance of students with disabilities. This finding probably is related to difficulties in defining and measuring various mainstreaming approaches, as well as the separate settings with which they then are compared.[90]

Research ambiguous

Researchers who have reviewed the data on separate class placement and on mainstreaming thus seem to agree that research has not provided conclusive support for either approach. In part, this can be attributed to the probability that neither approach generally is carried out very well; if this is the case, one would expect to find that both are ineffective and neither is superior to the other.[91]

Weak implementation

However, these pessimistic observations should not be viewed simplistically as justifications for complete despair concerning the future of mainstreaming or of other efforts to improve education for students with disabilities. Mainstreaming may prove to be a positive answer to the long tradition of isolating students with disabilities, but in itself it is not a panacea. To be effective, mainstreaming requires a variety of special resources, relatively small classes, and educators who are skilled in and dedicated to creating an effective learning environment

Requirements for success in mainstreaming

[89]Maggie Hume, "Educators Warn of 'Growing Insensitivity' to Handicapped Students," *Education Daily*, June 1, 1987, pp. 3–4; Christine L. Salisbury and Barbara J. Smith, "The Least Restrictive Environment: Understanding the Options," *Principal* (September 1991), pp. 24–27; and Reinhard Nickisch, "Strategies for Integrating Handicapped Students," *Principal* (January 1992), pp. 20–21.
[90]Melvyn I. Semmel, Jay Gottlieb, and Nancy M. Robinson, "Mainstreaming: Perspectives on Educating Handicapped Children in Public Schools," in Berliner, *Review of Research in Education*, pp. 223–279; Maynard C. Reynolds and Jack W. Birch, *Adaptive Mainstreaming* (New York: Longman, 1988); and Andrew R. Brulle, "Appropriate, with Dignity," *Phi Delta Kappan* (February 1991), p. 487.
[91]Allan Gartner and Dorothy Kerzner Lipsky, "Beyond Special Education: Toward a Quality System for All Students," *Harvard Educational Review* (November 1987), pp. 367–395; Andy Hargreaves, "Prepare to Meet Thy Mood" (Paper presented at the Annual Meeting of the American Educational Research Association, Chicago, April 1991).

and acceptance for all students.[92] Thus, one important educational goal is to make the mainstreaming approach now mandated by the federal government more successful than it has been. This overall goal has been supported by a review of mainstreaming research that reached the following conclusions:

No turning back

> There is no support in the research for a retreat from mainstreaming toward self-contained special education classes, except perhaps for very low IQ students in cases where individualized instruction or other supports cannot be used in regular classes. . . . Training programs for regular teachers to help them meet the instructional and socio-emotional needs of academically handicapped students must continue, and teachers should receive training in methods (such as cooperative learning, individualized instruction, or combinations of these) that enable them to meet diverse needs in the same classroom.[93]

Disproportionate Placement of Minority Students

Data on special education placement show that students from some racial minority groups are much more likely to be designated for mental retardation programs than are non-Hispanic white students. For example, the most recent data available in 1991 indicated that African American students are about three times as likely as white students to be in "educable mentally retarded" classes. Many analysts believe that placement in classes for the retarded has been too

Overuse of IQ tests

dependent on intelligence tests, which have been constructed for use with middle-class whites. Some also believe that disproportionate numbers of minority students are shunted into classes for the emotionally disturbed or the retarded mainly to alleviate teachers' problems in dealing with culturally different children and youth. Many educators and parents worry that such placements may constitute a new version of segregation and discrimination by sentencing minority students to special classes with low or nonexistent educational expectations.[94]

Several courts have been sympathetic to this criticism and have issued rul-

Courts intervene

ings to make it less likely that students will be misassigned to special education classes. In the 1970 case *Diana* v. *Board of Education*, for example, a California

---

[92]Madeleine Will, *Educating Students with Learning Problems — A Shared Responsibility* (Washington, D.C.: U.S. Department of Education Office of Special Education and Rehabilitation Services, 1986); Margaret C. Wang, "A 'Promising Approach' for Reforming Spec. Ed.," *Education Week*, May 4, 1988, pp. 36, 28; and Margaret C. Wang, Jane Hill, Nancy Weishew, and Patricia Van Leuvang, "Arrowhead Integrated School," *The Executive Educator* (February 1992), pp. A20–A21.

[93]Nancy A. Madden and Robert E. Slavin, "Mainstreaming Students with Mild Handicaps: Academic and Social Outcomes," *Review of Educational Research* (Winter 1983), p. 560. Also see David R. Adamson, Pat Matthews, and Joan Schuller, "Five Ways to Bridge," *Teaching Exceptional Children* (Winter 1990), pp. 74–77; Robert E. Evans, "Making Mainstreaming Work Through Prereferral Consultation," *Educational Leadership* (September 1990), pp. 73–77; and Joanne Yatvin, "Navigating the Mainstream," *Educational Leadership* (March 1992), pp. 90–91.

[94]R. A. Quantz, "Mild Mental Retardation and Race," *Educational Studies* (Winter 1981–82), pp. 387–393; James Lytle, "Is Special Education Serving Minority Students?" *Harvard Educational Review* (February 1988), pp. 116–120; Sallie Tisdale, "Neither Morons Nor Imbeciles Nor Idiots," *Harper's* (June 1990), pp. 47–56; and Doris Goldberg et al., "Which Newborns in New York City Are at Risk for Special Education Placement?" *American Journal of Public Health* (March 1992), pp. 438–440.

court examined the claim of nine Mexican American children who felt they had been improperly classified as mentally retarded on the basis of an IQ test on which their scores ranged from 52 to 68. When tested by a bilingual psychologist and allowed to respond in Spanish or English, their IQs increased by an average 15 points. The court ruled that (1) all children whose primary language is not English must be tested in both their primary language and English; (2) the tests cannot depend solely on vocabulary, general information, or other experience-based items; and (3) districts that have a disparity between the percentage of Mexican American students in regular classes and in classes for the retarded must be able to show that this disparity is due to valid classification methods. In *Larry P.* v. *Riles*, a California court heard evidence indicating that the dialect and family environment of many African American students produced invalid scores on IQ tests, and then ruled that these students could not be placed in classes for the educable mentally retarded on the basis of IQ tests "as currently administered."[95]

An Optimal Learning Environment?

Requirements of PL 94-142 and related legislation specify that school officials must prepare an individualized educational plan for students with disabilities, including special services to help achieve educational goals specified in the plan. These requirements have frequently been interpreted as implying that an "appropriate" free education for children with disabilities requires whatever services are necessary to help them derive as much benefit from education as do other students — perhaps establishing an optimal learning environment for every student who requires special assistance.

Optimal environments expensive

However, providing an optimal learning environment for students with severe disabilities (or, perhaps, for any student) can be very expensive. Arguments have arisen between school officials, who claim they cannot afford to provide maximally effective education for some students with disabilities, and parents or other advocates who believe that such students have a constitutional right to whatever services are needed to ensure maximum educational gains.[96]

Definition of "benefit"

The issue went to the U.S. Supreme Court in 1982, when the parents of a deaf first grader named Amy Rowley demanded that she be provided with a sign-language interpreter in academic classes. Local educators argued that they had provided an FM hearing aid, a tutor of the deaf, and a speech therapist but could not provide an interpreter. In *Board of Education of Hudson Central School District* v. *Rowley*, the Court ruled that although the law requires the provision of such "supportive services" as "may be required to assist a handicapped child to benefit from public education," it does not require a particular level of benefit above the "basic floor of opportunity . . . [which] consists of access to specialized

---

[95]Ruth Axman Childs, *Legal Issues in Testing* (Washington, D.C.: American Institutes for Research, 1990).

[96]Debra Viadero, "'Medically Fragile' Students Pose Major Dilemma for School Officials," *Education Week*, March 11, 1987, pp. 1, 14; Benjamin Sendor, "Upholding Congress' Preference for the 'Least Restrictive Environment,'" *The American School Board Journal* (October 1991), pp. 16–17; and "Court Supports 'Least Restrictive Environment,'" *Network for Public Schools* (Winter 1992), p. 15.

instruction and related services individually designed" for a child.[97] According to constitutional scholars who have reviewed the *Rowley* decision, "The Court in effect said that school officials will decide whether the additional costs are worth it in terms of the educational payoff for the child."[98] Although *Rowley* requires a program "reasonably calculated to enable the child to receive educational benefits," it does not require "the best program available or possible."[99]

Growing expenditures

High Costs of Special Education.   Even though school districts do not have to provide the best possible learning environment, at a potentially astronomical cost, for students with severe disabilities, special education has consumed a growing percentage of public-school budgets. Mandated by federal law to maintain previous levels of per-pupil expenditure for an increasing number of students identified as disabled (including millions of LD students), many economically distressed school districts have substantially reduced their "regular" budgets while maintaining or increasing outlays for special education.

Recent developments

The Americans with Disabilities Act (1991) and other recent legislative changes have required public-school officials to introduce or expand services for disabled preschool children and for students with traumatic brain injuries, serious emotional problems, and other severe disabilities. So, too, have children's disabilities associated with drug addiction among mothers increased the costs of special education in many districts. Although federal officials promised to repay local districts 40 percent of the costs they incurred after the passage of PL 94-142 in 1975, federal reimbursement has never exceeded 12 percent and in recent years has been well below 10 percent. The growing financial bind thus created in many school districts makes it likely that policies regarding placement, provision of services, and funding for special education students will be systematically re-examined in the future.[100]

Directions for the Future

Legislation to provide equal educational opportunity for students with disabilities has led to expansion of special education services, much of it in the form of mainstreaming with special assistance or some separate classes for designated students. We have seen, however, that research does not provide strong

---

[97]However, the Supreme Court later reaffirmed that certain supportive services might be required to make basic educational opportunities truly available for a handicapped child. In deciding the case of Amber Tatro, an eight-year-old with spina bifida, the Court ruled that school officials must provide intermittent catheterization. On the other hand, a 1991 U.S. appeals court decision interpreted the Rowley ruling as meaning that a school district did not have to pay tuition costs for a severely retarded student's attendance at an expensive private school. See Martha M. McCarthy, "Severely Disabled Children: Who Pays?" *Phi Delta Kappan* (September 1991), pp. 66–71.

[98]Mark Yudof, "Education for Handicapped: Rowley in Perspective," *American Journal of Education* (February 1984), p. 172. Also see Perry A. Zirkel, "Handicapped Parents," *Phi Delta Kappan* (October 1990), pp. 164–166.

[99]David A. Splitt, "School Law," *The Executive Educator* (September 1991), p. 18.

[100]Anne C. Lewis, "Churning Up the Waters in Special Education," *Phi Delta Kappan* (October 1991), pp. 100–101; Theodore O. Cron, "Grasping the Impact of the 'A.D.A. Era,'" *Education Week*, January 22, 1992, pp. 32, 23.

evidence that mainstreaming is more successful on a widespread basis than are separate placements that label and isolate the child.

What should be done, then, to improve education for students with disabilities? Many observers have suggested that less energy should be given to classifying and assisting special education students in distinct groups. Instead, efforts should concentrate on providing more effective schooling — a more optimal learning environment — for all low-achieving students and all students with disabilities except the most severely handicapped, almost entirely as part of regular classroom instruction. This approach, generally referred to either as the **regular education initiative** or as **inclusive education,** would pool most compensatory education funds, special education resources, and other currently separate budget lines with regular per-pupil funding. Combined funds would allow for both implementation of instructional programs based on knowledge of effective schooling and provision of appropriate individualized assistance for all students.[101]

Inclusive education

Advocates of inclusive education believe it not only would avoid the negative effects of labeling but also would benefit all students by eliminating disruptive pullout, which greatly complicates operations in many schools. However, critics and skeptics are dubious about the capacity of teachers and schools to be effective if classrooms become even more heterogeneous because mentally, physically, or emotionally disabled students are assigned there full time. Until 1991, no major educational organization not identified with special education had provided a strong endorsement of such an initiative. In October of that year, however, a National Association of State Boards of Education Study Group issued a report calling for increased incorporation of students with disabilities into regular classrooms and for comprehensive improvements in instruction in order to ensure the success of all students in a system that "unifies" regular and special education.[102]

Reduction in pullout

NASBE endorsement

Summing Up

1. Much desegregation has been accomplished in smaller school districts, but the concentration of minority students and economically disadvantaged students in big-city districts has made it difficult to bring about stable desegregation.

2. Compensatory education seemed to be unsuccessful until evidence accumulating in the 1980s began to justify a more positive conclusion. However, many serious questions remain concerning the degree to which compensatory education can have substantial and lasting results on a large scale.

---

[101]Margaret C. Wang, Jacqueline L. Rubenstein, and Maynard C. Reynolds, "Clearing the Road to Success for Students with Special Needs," *Educational Leadership* (September 1985), pp. 62–67; Maria Raynes, Martha Snell, and Wayne Sailor, "A Fresh Look at Categorical Programs for Children With Special Needs," *Phi Delta Kappan* (December 1991), pp. 326–331; Thomas R. Skrtic, "The Special Education Paradox," *Harvard Education Review* (May 1991), pp. 147–206; and Mara Sapon-Shevin, "Learning to Become a Community," *Rethinking Schools* (January/February 1992), pp. 18–19.

[102]Millicent Lawton, "NASBE Calls for End to Differentiation," *Education Week,* October 16, 1991, p. 4.

3. Efforts to contribute to constructive cultural pluralism through education include multicultural education approaches that take account of student learning styles, recognize differences in dialect, provide for bilingual education, and introduce methods and materials involving multiethnic curriculum and instruction. These approaches can help improve the performance of economically disadvantaged minority students and otherwise contribute to the attainment of a productive pluralistic society.

4. Legislative and court mandates have led to a large expansion in education for students with disabilities. As part of this process, educators are trying to mainstream these students as much as possible in order to avoid the damaging effects of labeling and separation. Although research is not clear concerning the overall gains and losses associated with mainstreaming versus special placement, many observers believe that the underlying problem centers on provision of more effective instruction for all low-achieving students.

5. Desegregation, compensatory education, multicultural education, and education for students with disabilities center on the goal of providing equal educational opportunity for all students. For this reason, all four of these topics also relate to the broader goal of making schools more effective.

Key Terms

desegregation *(400)*

integration *(400)*

de jure segregation *(403)*

de facto segregation *(403)*

magnet schools *(406)*

controlled choice *(406)*

compensatory education *(411)*

Chapter 1 *(411)*

Head Start *(412)*

Follow Through *(412)*

ecological intervention *(414)*

coordinated human services *(417)*

pullout approach *(418)*

multicultural education *(422)*

cultural pluralism *(423)*

bilingual education *(426)*

first-language maintenance *(428)*

transitional bilingual education (TBE) *(428)*

Education for All Handicapped Children Act (PL 94-142) *(435)*

least restrictive environment *(435)*

mainstreaming *(439)*

regular education initiative *(443)*

inclusive education *(443)*

Discussion Questions

1. What educational benefits and problems are associated with school desegregation? (Be sure to discuss academic learning, psychological factors, political factors, and moral factors.)

2. What is the difference between de jure and de facto segregation? What implications do these two types of segregation have for northern and southern regions of the United States?

3. Why is compensatory education an important national issue? What proposals have been made to improve compensatory education in the future?

4. What are some of the major goals and components of multicultural education? What can teachers in predominantly white, middle-class schools do to advance its goals?

5. What can teachers in regular classrooms do to help special education students who are mainstreamed in their classes?

Suggested Readings

Bain, Josie G., and Joan L. Herman, eds. *Making Schools Work for Underachieving Minority Students.* Westport, Conn.: Greenwood, 1990.

> *Wide-ranging chapters deal with instructional methods in compensatory education, bilingual programs, schoolwide intervention, and many other related topics.*

Consortium for Longitudinal Studies. *As the Twig Is Bent: Lasting Effects of Preschool Programs.* Hillsdale, N.J.: Erlbaum, 1983.

> *This work describes the long-lasting effects of unusually well planned and successful preschool programs for disadvantaged students.*

Gibson, Margaret A., and John U. Ogbu, eds. *Minority Status and Schools.* New York: Garland, 1991.

> *In addition to general analysis regarding the experience of minority students in several countries, chapters deal specifically with African American, Hispanic, Korean, Sikh, Ute Indian, and West Indian students in the United States.*

Imhoff, Gary, ed. *Learning in Two Languages.* New Brunswick, N.J.: Transaction, 1990.

> *This book presents information and diverse perspectives on a large variety of issues related to bilingual education.*

Levine, Daniel U., and Robert J. Havighurst. *Society and Education,* 8th ed. Needham Heights, Mass.: Allyn and Bacon, 1992.

> *This text on the sociology of education provides detailed analysis of topics discussed in this chapter.*

Stephan, Walter G., and Joel R. Feagin, eds. *School Desegregation: Past, Present, and Future.* New York: Plenum, 1980.

> *Excellent chapters deal with the status of desegregation, effects of desegregation, "white flight" from desegregated schools, improvement of instruction in desegregated classrooms, and other related topics.*

Van Horne, Winston A., and Thomas V. Tonnesen, eds. *Ethnicity and Language.* Madison: University of Wisconsin Board of Regents, 1987.

> *Here is useful analysis and discussion of multicultural education, Black English, cultural pluralism, language minorities, and related topics.*

PHILOSOPHICAL AND CURRICULAR FOUNDATIONS

*T*his section of the text deals with the philosophy of education, aims and goals of education, and curriculum and instruction. Educational philosophy is the study of the most basic beliefs and values that govern our approach to education and schooling. Aims and goals are the general purposes of education, the end points we strive to reach in our educational endeavors. Curriculum and instruction encompass the specific materials we teach and how we teach them.

Chapter 12 examines some important philosophical questions. How does philosophy influence our view of schools? What philosophies and theories have been most influential in education? We describe the following major approaches: idealism, realism, perennialism, essentialism, pragmatism, progressivism, social reconstructionism, existentialism, and philosophical analysis. The educational philosophies teachers adopt interact with historical as well as contemporary events; it is this relationship that affects the aims of education that prevail during any period.

Chapter 13 explores these aims. It describes the different levels at which educational purposes are formulated and the terminology appropriate to each level. After providing a historical overview on the aims of education, the chapter focuses on the recent national reports that are influencing aims for the future. Throughout the chapter, emphasis is placed on the role of social change in defining our educational purposes.

We begin Chapter 14 by examining the fundamental differences between subject-centered and student-centered curricula, and we discuss several examples of each approach. We also describe a number of important instructional approaches, including individualized instruction, cooperative learning, mastery instruction, critical thinking, computerized instruction, and video and satellite systems. The chapter ends with an examination of future trends in curriculum.

12

Philosophical Roots of Education

FOCUSING QUESTIONS

What is the relationship between philosophy in general and the philosophy of education in specific?

How do philosophers' conceptions of human nature influence their views of education?

How do philosophers of education treat the ethical or value dimension of education?

How do philosophies of education shape the formulation of educational aims, curriculum, and everyday school practice?

What philosophies of education lie behind current proposals for educational reform?

Today American educators face compelling and profound questions about the condition of American education and the future of our nation's schools. Many of the questions have a philosophical dimension. For example, the following questions are essentially philosophical:

1. How does a teacher's educational relationship to students reflect his or her views of human nature?

2. How does a teacher's method of instruction reflect a particular theory of knowledge and human understanding?

3. How is the schools' treatment of student diversity a reflection of how people conceive of a good society?

4. How do educators' views of what is most important or worthwhile in life influence the learning experiences emphasized in the classroom?

These questions pertain to the topic of each chapter in this book, but they are especially relevant to the discussion of the aims of education in Chapter 13 and of curriculum in Chapter 14. Underlying this entire part of the book are some important philosophical questions. What is knowledge? What is education? What is schooling? Who should attend school? How should teaching be carried on? As a future teacher, you will be called upon to answer such questions. This chapter explores them at the most general level. If an answer to a question is stated in its most abstract and general terms, it can transfer to a wide variety of situations.

Philosophical implications of immediate concerns

When you teach, you will face many immediate concerns that derive from the day-to-day problems of classroom management and lesson preparation. These immediate concerns will be specific to a given day, time, or event, but how you choose to deal with them will reveal your educational philosophy. The policies and procedures of the school in which you teach will also reflect an underlying philosophy. An examination of some philosophical ideas that have been elaborated by others can help you develop your own philosophy of education and aid you in understanding how philosophy guides school policy.

In this chapter, we shall examine five educational *philosophies* and four educational *theories.* Although there are similarities between philosophies and theories of education, some distinctions can be made. Traditional philosophies, such as idealism and realism, refer to complete bodies of thought that present a world view of which education is a part. (Other, newer philosophies such as philosophical analysis are primarily methodological. They seek to establish meaning for human experience.) In contrast, educational theories focus on education itself; they are more directly based on the practice of education in organized schools.

Theory arising from practice

There are, however, close links between the general philosophies examined in this chapter and the more specific theories of education. In some ways, the theories are the school-based components of the philosophical approaches. For example, the theory of essentialism is closely related to the overall philosophy of realism. Similarly, the theories of progressivism and reconstructionism both derive from the philosophy of pragmatism.

All of these philosophies and theories have had a major impact on American education, and they are especially important today. To understand current disputes about educational aims and curricula, we need to explore these often conflicting philosophical roots. Before we do so, however, we must define certain terms and areas of philosophy.

SPECIAL TERMINOLOGY

Practitioners in every field of disciplined inquiry develop a special terminology. The philosophy of education employs the basic terms *metaphysics, epistemology, axiology,* and *logic.* Metaphysics deals with the nature of reality. Epistemology deals with the nature of knowledge. Axiology deals with the nature of values. Logic deals with the nature of reasoning.

Reality and existence

Metaphysics examines the nature of ultimate reality. In speculating about the nature of existence, metaphysicians have not arrived at a single agreed-upon definition of reality. Idealists see reality in nonmaterial, or spiritual, terms. Realists see it as an objective order that exists independently of humankind. Pragmatists see it as the result of human experiences with the social and physical environment. In educational philosophy, metaphysics relates to the particular conception of reality reflected in the subjects, experiences, and skills of the curriculum. Much school learning represents the efforts of curriculum makers, teachers, and textbook writers to describe reality to students.

Knowledge and knowing

Epistemology, which deals with knowledge and knowing, is closely related to methods of teaching and learning. Again, different philosophies hold different epistemological conceptions. Idealists see knowing, or cognition, as the recall of ideas that are latent in the mind. For them, the Socratic dialogue is the most appropriate teaching method. Pragmatists, on the other hand, contend that we create knowledge by interacting with our environment; hence problem solving is the appropriate method of teaching and learning.

What is of value?

Axiology seeks to prescribe what is of value. Axiology is divided into *ethics* and *aesthetics.* **Ethics** examines moral values and the rules of right conduct; **aesthetics** addresses values in beauty and art. Idealists and realists subscribe to the objective theory of value, which asserts that the good, true, and beautiful are universally valid in all places and at all times. Pragmatists hold that values are culturally or ethically relative and depend on group or personal preferences that vary with situation, time, and place. Parents, teachers, and societies reward or punish behavior as it conforms to or deviates from their conceptions of what is right, good, and beautiful.

Deductive and inductive thinking

Logic, which is concerned with the requirements of correct and valid thinking, examines the rules of inference that enable us to frame correctly our propositions and arguments. **Deductive logic,** associated with idealism and realism, moves from general statements to particular instances and applications. **Inductive logic,** associated with pragmatism, moves from the particular instance to tentative generalizations that are subject to further verification.

Curriculum and reality

The terminology described above may appear initially to be somewhat removed from what teachers regard as the ''real'' world of the classroom. When teachers begin to confront the reality of their classroom situation, however, they find themselves immersed in metaphysics, epistemology, axiology, and logic. Much of every teacher's work involves introducing students to what is real. Studying the sciences introduces students to the realities of the physical and biological world. Studying the social sciences introduces them to political, economic, and sociological realities. Curriculum makers, as they incorporate the findings of the sciences and social sciences into the curriculum, often face hard choices between competing conceptions of reality. Teachers who find themselves serving on textbook review committees will have to make choices between authors' competing metaphysical interpretations and points of emphasis.

Teaching and epistemology

Whereas metaphysics underlies curriculum choices, epistemological issues are at the heart of what every teacher does in the classroom. Methods of instruction reflect the epistemological question of how human beings know what they know. Teachers who believe that human ideas should conform to what they see as the ordered structure of reality will stress the orderly and sequential teaching of bodies of subject knowledge. In contrast, teachers who believe that the process (*how* we know) is more important than the content (*what* we know) will stress the method of inquiry or of problem solving. Still other teachers will be epistemologically eclectic and stress both content and process. The organization of both the curriculum and instruction are further based upon a conception of logic. Is there something in the subject itself that dictates how material should be organized and presented to students? Or should teachers take their cue from the students, their experiences and their readiness, when deciding how to present subject matter? As you read about various curricular designs in Chapter 14, you will be able to identify their underlying metaphysical and epistemological foundations.

Values and ethical behavior

Finally, the school and the classroom deal with axiology by acting as agents of value transmission and clarification. Teachers and students together examine ethical and aesthetic models through studies in history and literature. The classroom interactions between teachers and students represent the interplay of what is held to be good and right behavior. The very climate of the school and the classroom represents the values of the educational community.

Now that you begin to see the meaning and relevance of this special philosophical terminology, we can go on to discuss nine different philosophies and theories. After describing each one, we will answer the basic questions raised at the beginning of the chapter from the perspective of its adherents.

IDEALISM

Idealism is among the oldest of the traditional philosophies. Plato developed the classic formulation of idealist philosophical principles. The German philosopher Georg W. F. Hegel created a comprehensive philosophical and historical world view based on idealism. In the United States, the transcendentalist philosophers Ralph Waldo Emerson and Henry David Thoreau elaborated on the idealist conception of reality. The founder of the kindergarten, Friedrich Froebel, was an exponent of idealist pedagogy. William Harris, a historically significant American educational leader, used idealism as a rationale for his administration as a U.S. commissioner of education at the end of the nineteenth century.[1]

---

[1]For information on the leading contributors to idealism, see Howard A. Ozman and Samuel M. Craver, *Philosophical Foundations of Education* (Columbus, Ohio: Merrill, 1990), pp. 2–15.

Key Concepts

Metaphysics.   To the idealists, only the mental or the spiritual is ultimately real. For them, the universe is an expression of a highly generalized intelligence and will — a universal mind. The individual's spiritual essence, or soul, is durable and permanent. One's mind, or life force, gives one vitality and dynamism. This world of mind and ideas is eternal, permanent, regular, and orderly. Truth and values are absolute and universal.[2]

Macrocosm and microcosm

Idealists, such as the transcendentalists, have used the concepts of the macrocosm and the microcosm to explain their version of reality. **Macrocosm** refers to the universal mind, the first cause, creator, or God. Regardless of the particular name used, the macrocosmic mind is the whole of existence. It is the one, all-inclusive, and complete self of which the lesser selves are parts. The universal, macrocosmic mind is continually thinking and valuing. The **microcosm** is a limited part of the whole — an individual and lesser self. But the microcosm is of the same spiritual substance as the macrocosm. In educational terms, the student can be conceived of as a spiritual entity that is also a part of the larger spiritual universe. Although there are metaphysical differences among idealists, all agree that the universe is made up of spiritual realities and that individuals are part of the one comprehensive and universal whole.

Epistemology.   Idealist knowledge is based on the recognition or reminiscence of latent ideas that are already present in the mind. Such ideas are **a priori;** that is, they concern knowledge or concepts that exist prior to and independent of human experience about them. Through introspection the individual examines his or her own mind and finds a copy of the macrocosmic mind. What is to be known is already present in the mind. The teacher's task is to bring

Latent knowledge

this latent knowledge to consciousness. Since reality is mental, education is properly concerned with conceptual matters. The learner seeks a broad and general perspective of his or her universe.[3]

The idealist educator prefers the pattern of a subject-matter curriculum that relates ideas and concepts to each other. For example, the liberal arts embrace many conceptual systems, or learned disciplines, such as language, history, mathematics, science, and philosophy. The highest level of knowledge recognizes the relationships among and integrates these subject matters.

The hierarchy of subjects

The idealist curriculum, constituting the cultural heritage of humankind, is hierarchical. At the top are the most general disciplines, philosophy and theology. These more general subjects are abstract; they transcend the limitations of time, place, and circumstance, and they transfer to a wide range of situations. Mathematics is especially valuable because it cultivates the power to deal with abstractions. History and literature also rank high because they are sources of moral and cultural models, exemplars, and heroes. Somewhat lower in curric-

----

[2]For a treatment of wisdom as a unifying educational goal, see William F. Losito, "The Wisdom Theme in Augustine's Writings: A Tradition for Research in Educational Foundations," *Educational Foundations* (Fall 1986), pp. 81–90.

[3]Morris L. Bigge, *Educational Philosophies for Teachers* (Columbus, Ohio: Merrill, 1982), pp. 25–36.

ular priority are the natural and physical sciences, which address particular cause-and-effect relationships. Since it is necessary for communication, language is an essential tool at all levels of learning.

Absolute, eternal, and universal values

   Axiology.   To the idealist, values reflect the good inherent in the universe. They are absolute, eternal, and universal. Ethical conduct grows out of the permanent aspects of our cultural heritage. Since the ethical core is contained within and transmitted by this heritage, philosophy, theology, history, literature, and art are rich value sources. Values education requires that the student be exposed to worthy models, especially the classics — the great works of the human race that have endured over time.

The Basic Questions

   If you were to ask an idealist teacher, "What is knowledge?" he or she would reply that knowledge concerns the spiritual principles that are the base of reality. This knowledge of reality takes the form of ideas. If knowledge is about transcendent and universal ideas, then education is the intellectual process of bringing ideas to the learner's consciousness.

   In answering the question, "What is schooling?" the idealist educator would say that the school is a social agency where students seek to discover and pursue truth. It is an intellectual institution where teachers and students explore the basic ideas that provide answers to the questions Socrates and Plato first asked: What is truth? What is beauty? What is the good life? These answers, although hidden, are present in our minds, and we need to reflect deeply to bring them forth. Nothing should be allowed to distract us from the intellectual pursuit of truth. Educational aims and goals should emphasize intellectual development above all.

Intellectual pursuit of truth

   Who should attend school? To this question the idealist would say everyone. Not all students will demonstrate the same intellectual aptitude, but all need to cultivate their minds to the limits of their capacities. The brightest students will need the greatest intellectual challenges that the teacher can provide. The aim of learning is to develop the creative person.

   How should teaching be carried on? The idealist would say that thinking and learning are names for the process of bringing ideas to consciousness. An appropriate means of doing this is the **Socratic method,** a process by which the teacher stimulates the learner's awareness of ideas by asking leading questions. Another important aspect of idealist methodology is the role of imitation. The teacher should have wide knowledge of the cultural heritage, lead a well-ordered life, and serve as a model worthy of imitation by the students.

Socratic method

High standards

   Idealists assert that the quality of education is safeguarded by the maintenance of high intellectual standards. Teachers should insist on high academic standards. In Plato's *Republic,* for example, the intellectual and academic standards were so high that only a gifted minority entered the ruling elite of philosopher-kings. Today's idealists generally favor defining educational aims in such a way that intellectual capacity becomes a requirement for participating in higher education.

Overview 12.1 ◄●────────────────────────────────

Philosophies of Education

Philosophy	Metaphysics	Epistemology	Axiology	Educational Implications	Proponents
Idealism	Reality is spiritual or mental and unchanging	Knowing is the rethinking of latent ideas	Values are absolute and eternal	A subject-matter curriculum emphasizing the great and enduring ideas of the culture	Berkeley Butler Froebel Hegel Plato
Realism	Reality is objective and is composed of matter and form; it is fixed, based on natural law	Knowing consists of sensation and abstraction	Values are absolute and eternal, based on nature's laws	A subject-matter curriculum stressing humanistic and scientific disciplines	Aquinas Aristotle Broudy Martin Pestalozzi
Pragmatism (experimentalism)	Reality is the interaction of an individual with environment or experience; it is always changing	Knowing results from experiencing; use of scientific method	Values are situational or relative	Instruction organized around problem solving according to the scientific method	Childs Dewey James Peirce
Existentialism	Reality is subjective, with existence preceding essence	Knowing is to make personal choices	Values should be freely chosen	Classroom dialogues designed to stimulate an awareness that each person creates a self-concept through significant choices	Sartre Marcel Morris Soderquist
Philosophical analysis	Reality is verifiable	Knowing involves empirical verification or logical analysis of language	Values are regarded as emotional preferences	Instruction that uses language analysis to clarify communication and to establish meaning	Russell Moore Wittgenstein

Overview 12.2 ◀●▶

Theories of Education

Theory	Aim	Curriculum	Educational Implications	Proponents
Perennialism (rooted in realism)	To educate the rational person	Subject matter that is hierarchically arranged to cultivate the intellect (great books, etc.)	Focus on enduring human concerns as revealed in great works of the Western cultural heritage	Adler Bloom Hutchins Maritain
Essentialism (rooted in idealism and realism)	To educate the useful and competent person	Basic education: reading, writing, arithmetic, history, English, science, foreign languages	Emphasis on skills and subjects that transmit the cultural heritage and contribute to socioeconomic efficiency	Bagley Bestor Conant Morrison
Progressivism (rooted in pragmatism)	To educate the individual according to his or her interests and needs	Activities and projects	Instruction that features problem solving and group activities; teacher acts as a facilitator	Dewey Kilpatrick Parker Washburne
Social reconstructionism (rooted in pragmatism)	To reconstruct society	Social sciences used as reconstructive tools	Instruction that focuses on significant socioeconomic problems	Brameld Counts Stanley

Implications for Today's Classroom Teacher

Idealism, although a broad philosophical perspective, holds a number of significant implications for today's classroom teacher. Most importantly, idealism seeks to set a tone or point of view for conducting instruction. Education is about ideas and is an intellectual undertaking. This perspective rejects the consumerism and vocationalism that often shape attitudes in contemporary society. According to this view, teachers are important agents in helping students to realize their fullest potentials as persons. Teachers are to acquaint themselves and their students with the finest elements of the cultural heritage. Such an immersion in the great ideas of the heritage is designed to make students become participants in and contributors to the heritage.

Cultural heritage

Teachers who subscribe to idealism will see certain subjects as especially powerful in stimulating thinking and identification with the cultural heritage. For example, such a teacher would use mathematics as an instrument to develop students' powers of abstraction. History would be viewed as a means of studying the contributions made by the great women and men of the past. Teachers would expose students to the classics — great and enduring works of art, literature, and music — so that they can experience and share in the values conveyed by these cultural works from generation to generation.

REALISM

Realism, like idealism, stresses objective knowledge and values, but the realist view of metaphysics and epistemology is different. The essential doctrines of realism hold that (1) there is a world of real existence that human beings have not made or constructed; (2) this real existence can be known by the human mind; and (3) such knowledge is the most reliable guide to human conduct, both individual and social.[4] These doctrines provide a convenient starting point for considering the educational implications of realist metaphysics, epistemology, and axiology.

Key Concepts

Metaphysics and Epistemology. For the realist, a material world exists that is independent of and external to the mind of the knower. The basis for understanding reality is found in a world of objects and in the perceptions of these objects.[5] All objects are composed of matter. Matter must be encased in a form and has to assume the structure of a particular object.

Knowing involves sensation and abstraction

Human beings can *know* these objects through their senses and their reason. Knowing is a process that involves two stages: sensation and abstraction. First, the knower sees an object and records the sensory data about it, such as color, size, weight, smell, or sound. The mind sorts these sensory data into those qualities that are always present in the object and those qualities that are sometimes present in the object. By means of abstraction, or identifying the necessary qualities of an object (those that are always present), the learner forms a concept of the object. Conceptualization occurs when the mind has abstracted the form of an object and has recognized the object as belonging to a class. Objects are classified when they are recognized as having qualities that they share with other members of the same class but not with objects that belong to a different class.[6]

The realist theory of knowledge has also been referred to as a "spectator theory." This simply means that people are spectators or onlookers in the world. In their experience people see many objects. Some of them are two-legged creatures like themselves, others are four-legged and other species of the animal kingdom, and still other objects are plants and minerals. As spectators of reality, men and women engage in a process of sorting out these objects according to

---

[4]John Wild, *Introduction to Realist Philosophy* (New York: Harper & Row, 1948).

[5]For a contemporary discussion of realism in the context of critical naturalism, see Roy Bhaskar, *Scientific Realism and Human Emancipation* (London: Verso, 1986), and Roy Bhaskar, *Reclaiming Reality: A Critical Introduction to Contemporary Philosophy* (London: Verso, 1989). An analysis of Bhaskar's conception of realism appears in David Corson, "Educational Research and Bhaskar's Conception of Discovery," *Educational Theory* (Spring 1991), pp. 189–198.

[6]Gerald L. Gutek, *Philosophical and Ideological Perspectives on Education* (Englewood Cliffs, N.J.: Prentice-Hall, 1988), pp. 41–45.

Sorting and classifying objects

their form or structure. They sort objects that are alike into related classifications. Their conception of an object is accurate when it corresponds to the structure of the object in reality.[7]

Like the idealist, the realist believes that a curriculum consisting of organized, separate subject matters is the most effective and efficient way of learning about reality. Organizing subject matter, as scientists and scholars do, is a sophisticated method of classifying objects. For example, the past experiences of humankind can be organized into history. Plants can be studied in a systematic way according to their classifications in the subject matter of botany. Units of political organization such as nations, governments, legislatures, and judicial systems can be organized into the study of political science. For the realist, the way to gain knowledge of reality is to pursue ordered and disciplined inquiry through these compartmentalized bodies of knowledge or subject matters.

Axiology.   Based on the realist's conception of knowledge, certain identified prescriptions govern intelligent behavior. For example, human beings ought

Rational behavior

to behave in a rational way; behavior is rational when it conforms to the way in which objects behave in reality. From their study of the subjects that explain reality, men and women can arrive at theories that are based on natural, physical, and social laws. Since natural laws are universal and eternal, so are the values that are based upon them. The rational person governs his or her behavior in the light of such tested theory.

The Basic Questions

To begin our philosophical cross-examination, we again ask, What is knowledge? Realists would reply that knowledge concerns the physical world in which we live. According to the realists' metaphysics, an objective order of reality exists. When we know something, our knowledge is always about an object. The concepts that we have in our minds are true when they correspond to those objects as they really exist in the world.[8]

Organized bodies of knowledge

Education, the realists would say, is the study of the subject-matter disciplines into which knowledge has been sorted and classified. History, language, science, mathematics — these are organized bodies of knowledge. If we know them, we will know something about the world in which we live. This knowledge is our best guide in conducting our daily affairs.

The school is the institution that has been established to teach students about the objective world. Based on their philosophical orientation, realists would develop educational aims that define the school's role as primarily academic. Students should learn subjects that will help them understand their world so that they can live full and satisfying lives. The realist teacher needs to be able to recognize the basic concepts in the subject and the generalizations that explain their interactions, and to render these into a teachable and learnable order that meets the needs of the learner.[9]

[7]Edward J. Power, *Philosophy of Education: Studies in Philosophies, Schooling, and Educational Policies* (Englewood Cliffs, N.J.: Prentice-Hall, 1982), pp. 89–106.
[8]David Kelley, *The Evidence of the Senses: A Realist Theory of Perception* (Baton Rouge: Louisiana State University Press, 1986).
[9]William O. Martin, *Realism in Education* (New York: Harper & Row, 1969).

Realist educators welcome standards that require students and teachers to demonstrate mastery of academic subject matter. They would argue that genuine quality of education requires teachers who are competent in the subjects that they teach. Teachers, administrators, and school boards should maintain academic standards and encourage a high level of performance and achievement from students.

Implications for Today's Classroom Teacher

In a classroom based on realism, the teacher's primary responsibility is to teach some skill, such as reading, writing, or computation, or some body of disciplined knowledge, such as history, mathematics, or science, to students. Although realist teachers understand that their students are emotional as well as rational persons, they do not permit the classroom to become a therapeutic center for emotional or behavioral adjustment. In fact, realist teachers would oppose those activities that interfere with the school's primary function as a center of academic learning.

School as center of learning

In order to perform their primary educational responsibility, realist teachers need to be knowledgeable in the content of their subject. For example, the teacher of history should be a historian who possesses a thorough background in that discipline. In addition to being competent in a specific subject matter, the realist teacher should have a general education in the liberal arts and sciences; this kind of background will enable the teacher to point out relationships between her or his area of expertise and other subject matter areas. Because of this stress on the teacher's knowledge, realists tend to favor competency testing in teacher-education programs.

Competency of teachers

Realist teachers usually also believe in competency testing of students, for subject-matter knowledge and competency are primary objectives in the realist classroom. To attain this knowledge outcome, realist teachers may employ a wide repertoire of methods, such as the lecture, discussion, demonstration, or experiment. Mastery of content is most important, and methodology is a necessary but subordinate means to the attainment of that goal.

How would a high-school physics teacher with a realist philosophical orientation plan a unit on Isaac Newton's laws of motion? First, the teacher would present a short discussion of Newton's scientific research and contributions; second, the teacher would illustrate the laws of motion in a laboratory demonstration; third, the students would discuss the demonstration and frame the scientific generalization that the demonstration illustrated; finally, students would take a test to demonstrate their understanding of Newton's laws of motion.[10]

PERENNIALISM

Perennialism is an educational theory that draws heavily on the principles of realism. It presents a conservative or traditional view of human nature and education. Perennialists, who agree with Aristotle's statement that human beings are rational, see the school as an institution designed to cultivate human intel-

---

[10]Philip H. Phenix, *Philosophies of Education* (New York: Wiley, 1961), pp. 22–24.

ligence. Based upon their concept of the school as an agency to cultivate rationality, perennialists oppose political, social, and economic movements that seek to use the school as a multipurpose institution. They do not want it to become a therapeutic agency that stresses students' emotional adjustment; nor do they want to transform the school into a training ground for entry into various vocations. Perennialists realize that emotional wellness and vocational competency are necessary for people to function in society. However, they believe that agencies other than schools should attend to these activities. To keep adding new demands on the school is to weaken its central identifying purpose.

The perennialists see the most important educational aims as the search for and the dissemination of truth. Since they believe that truth is universal and unchanging, a genuine education is also universal and constant. The school's curriculum should emphasize the recurrent themes of human life. It should contain cognitive subjects that cultivate rationality and the study of moral, aesthetic, and religious principles to cultivate ethical behavior. Like idealists and realists, perennialists prefer a subject-matter curriculum. The perennialist curriculum includes history, language, mathematics, logic, literature, the humanities, and science. The content of these subjects should come from the classical works of literature and art. Mastering the subject matter of these learned disciplines is regarded as essential for training the intellect.

One of the most articulate perennialist spokespersons was Robert Hutchins, president of the University of Chicago, whose influence as an educational pioneer was examined in Chapter 4. Hutchins described the ideal education as "one that develops intellectual power. . . . The ideal education is not an *ad hoc* education, not an education directed to immediate needs; it is not a specialized education, or a preprofessional education; it is not a utilitarian education. It is an education calculated to develop the mind."[11]

Hutchins based his educational philosophy on two major premises: human nature is rational, and knowledge resides in unchanging, absolute, and universal truths. Since the rationality of human nature is universal, Hutchins stressed that education must also be universal.[12] Since reason is our highest power, the development of the intellect should be education's highest priority. Hutchins advocated a curriculum that consists of permanent, or perennial, studies. He particularly recommended the study of the classics, or the great books of Western civilization. Reading and discussing great books cultivates the intellect and prepares students to think carefully and critically. In addition to these classics, he urged the study of grammar, rhetoric, logic, mathematics, and philosophy.

In general, perennialism represents a conservative theoretical position centered on the authority of tradition and the classics. Among its major educational principles are the following: (1) truth is universal and does not depend on the circumstances of place, time, or person; (2) a good education involves a search for and an understanding of the truth; (3) truth can be found in the great works of civilization; and (4) education is a liberal exercise that develops the intellect.

---

[11]Robert M. Hutchins, *A Conversation on Education* (Santa Barbara, Calif.: The Fund for the Republic, 1963), p. 1. Also see Robert M. Hutchins, *The Learning Society* (New York: Praeger, 1968).
[12]Robert M. Hutchins, *The Higher Learning in America* (New Haven, Conn.: Yale University Press, 1962).

Taking Issue

Education Through Great Books

Throughout the history of education, there have been persistent advocates of the concept that schooling should concentrate on the "great books of Western civilization." For these advocates, among them Hutchins and Adler, the principal aim of education is to develop the student's mind. A "great books" curriculum normally includes traditional subject-matter disciplines with a particular focus on the classics of literature, art, history, and philosophy.

Question: Should education concentrate on the great books of Western civilization?

Arguments PRO

1 The great books contain the best insights into persistent human issues. They discuss problems basic to the human condition. To ignore the insights of Plato, Aristotle, and other great thinkers of the past is to descend into the ignorance of presentism that causes us to constantly reinvent the wheel.

2 Reading and discussion of the great books could provide us with a common background of shared ideas and values. This background would form the best basis for the "cultural literacy" that many educators believe is sorely lacking in the United States.

3 Because of specialization and relativism, the fundamental values of Western civilization have eroded. Many people have little sense of right or wrong, good or bad. Emphasis on the great books will restore these essential and perennial values.

4 The great books once constituted the curriculum of the learned men of society; today, it is possible to share this rich intellectual legacy with all people. Everyone can benefit from the intellectual training that studying the classics provides, and no one should be denied it.

5 The great books stretch the mind. They stimulate the reader (or learner) to reflect, to think, to inquire.

Arguments CON

1 Because education always occurs in a certain context, at a particular time and place, it must be relevant to specific social needs. The great books were once the popular thinking of their particular historical periods. Despite their insights into the human condition, they are not timely enough to be the focus of modern education.

2 Schools should help students develop a process of problem solving that can transfer to a wide range of situations. This process is more important than learning specific ideas from certain books, and it provides a better foundation for a true cultural literacy.

3 Every period of human history is characterized by cultural and social change. Some values are discarded and replaced by new ones. Schools need to emphasize the clarification and reconstruction of values rather than simply transmitting values from the past.

4 The great books approach is based on an elitist and restricted view of knowledge. It assumes that all Americans should be educated in the same manner — a "Western" and classical manner. Democratic education needs a more pluralistic view of truth. Students should be exposed to the ideas of other civilizations as well as important works from outside the cultural mainstream.

5 The great books are based in the past. Too much emphasis on the past will not prepare learners for the future—to think or inquire in an age of electronics and computers.

The Paideia Proposal

A revival of perennialism began in the early 1980s with the publication of Mortimer J. Adler's ***The Paideia Proposal: An Educational Manifesto.***[13] The term *paideia* is a Greek word that means the upbringing, or total educational formation, of a child. Adler argued that there exists a general learning that all human beings should possess. Since American society is a democracy based on political and ethical equality, the same quality of schooling should be provided for all students.

One curriculum for all students

Adler and his Paideia associates advocated a general curriculum for all students. They identified the following organized subject matters as indispensable: language, literature, fine arts, mathematics, natural sciences, history, geography, and social studies. While emphasizing fundamental subjects, the Paideia group did not see subject matter as an end in itself but rather as the context for developing a repertoire of intellectual skills. Among the sought-after intellectual skills were reading, writing, speaking, listening, calculating, observing, measuring, estimating, and problem solving.[14] Together, the fundamental subjects and intellectual skills lead to a still higher level of learning, reflection, and awareness. Through the Socratic dialogue, students can be challenged to enlarge their understanding of ideas and values. For Adler, like Hutchins, the purpose of education is to cultivate an awareness and understanding of significant ideas.

The Basic Questions

Progressive educational critics of perennialism have charged that it fosters educational elitism. In denying this charge, Hutchins and Adler have asserted that their educational proposals are truly democratic. They argue that all persons should have the right to the same education and that this education should be of the highest quality. Students, they contend, should not be grouped or streamed into tracks that would prevent some from acquiring the general education to which they are entitled by their common humanity.

Opposition to tracking

For Hutchins, Adler, and other perennialists, genuine quality of educational opportunity is maintained by providing a learning experience of high intellectual quality for all. To track some students into an academic curriculum and others into a vocational curriculum is to deny the latter genuine equality of educational opportunity. In other words, true equity can be satisfied only by access to a quality education.

The Attack on Cultural Relativism

Perennialism's stress on universal truth and values strongly opposes the view that education should be relative to particular times and places and that ethical questions are relative to situations. Perennialists contend that **cultural relativism** — which is associated with pragmatism, progressivism, and social

---

[13]Mortimer J. Adler, *The Paideia Proposal: An Educational Manifesto* (New York: Macmillan, 1982); also see Mortimer J. Adler, *Paideia Problems and Possibilities* (New York: Macmillan, 1983).
[14]Adler, *Paideia Proposal*, pp. 22–23.

reconstructionism — has eroded the quality of American education by denying the importance of universal truth. According to cultural relativism, our concepts of truth arise from the interactions that people have with changing environments. Since environments change over time and are different from place to place, truth, rather than being universally valid, is a temporary assertion based on human situations. The effect of this relativism has been to deny the need for standards of right and wrong.

Universal standards of truth

A strong example of the antirelativist argument is Allan Bloom's *The Closing of the American Mind*.[15] Like Hutchins, Bloom is concerned about the failure of American education to cultivate in students a desire to search for the good life based on the search for truth. This failure, Bloom contends, is a product of the educational system's relativism, which in the name of a false doctrine of equality rejects universal standards of truth according to which some matters are either right or wrong. Relativism also induces a moral malaise, a refusal to recognize that judgments and actions are either good or bad. Bloom returns to the perennial questions of good and evil that led Socrates and his student Plato on their quest for truth. Just as Socrates and Plato did combat with the Sophists in ancient Athens, Bloom battles against the relativists in the modern university.

To remedy the defects caused by relativism, Bloom contends, as did Hutchins, that it is necessary to reestablish the idea of the educated human being and to re-create the liberal education that would cultivate such a person.[16] Such a liberal education would rest on the critical reading and analysis of the great classics of Western culture.

Implications for Today's Classroom Teacher

Perennialism, like idealism and realism, sees the classroom as a center for the intellectual growth and development of students. In order to serve as competent stimulators of their students' intellectual development, teachers must be liberally educated persons who have a love of and a desire to lead a life based on truth. Indeed, a liberal education would be more important for perennialist teachers than would courses in educational methods.

Need for a liberal education

In the primary grades, the perennialist teacher would stress the learning of the fundamental tools, such as reading, writing, and computation, that contribute to a person's literacy and readiness to begin the lifelong quest for truth. At the secondary level of schooling, perennialist teachers would structure lessons around the enduring human concerns that are explored in the great works of history, literature, and philosophy. Like the idealists, perennialists emphasize the importance of the classics that have captured the interest of people throughout history and across generations.

Emphasis on classics

The perennialist classroom would be part of a school in which administrators, teachers, and students hold high academic standards. Teachers would expect their students to be participants in the quest for truth and to conduct themselves according to standards of civility that make such a quest possible.

---

[15] Allan Bloom, *The Closing of the American Mind* (New York: Simon and Schuster, 1987).
[16] Ibid., pp. 380–381.

ESSENTIALISM

Schooling as skill and subject development

Essentialism is a conservative educational theory that arose in opposition to progressive education. Rooted philosophically in both idealism and realism, essentialism emphasizes an academic subject-matter curriculum and encourages teachers to stress order, discipline, and effort. For essentialists, the important aims of education are: (1) to transmit the basic skills and knowledge found in the cultural heritage; (2) to emphasize the learning of those skills and subjects that can lead learners to still higher level skills and knowledge; and (3) to use education as a civilizing agency that emphasizes continuity between the knowledge and values of the past and the requirements of the present.

Basic skills and academic subjects

For the essentialists, education involves learning the basic skills, arts, and sciences that have been developed in the past.[17] Mastering these skills and subjects prepares the student to function as a member of a civilized society. In addition, the student also should acquire the behavior needed for successful living.

Discipline and hard work

The learning of the essential curriculum requires discipline and hard work. Those who aspire to be teachers should be skilled professionals both in subject matter and in teaching.

Arthur Bestor, an advocate of essentialism, sees the liberal arts and sciences as the core of a general education that will enable all men and women to function intelligently. Bestor and the members of the Council on Basic Education have argued that the intellectual quality of American education has been jeopardized by those professional educators who have weakened academic standards.[18] In the elementary school the essentialists see reading, writing, arithmetic, and research skills as the indispensable studies. In the high school they stress science, mathematics, history, English, and foreign languages. It is the task of the school to channel the accumulated experience of humankind into these organized, coherent, and differentiated disciplines. Only after mastering these basic disciplines can the student be expected to use them to solve personal, social, and civic problems.

Indispensable studies

Basic Education

Revival of essentialism

Since the 1970s a **"back-to-basics" movement** has helped to revive essentialism in American schools.[19] Back-to-basics proponents contend that social experimentation and untested innovations have lowered academic standards. They charge that many children have not mastered basic literary and computational skills and that academic weaknesses at the secondary level have derived from a rejection of prescribed courses in favor of electives and minicourses. The back-to-basics position is that schools should concentrate on the essential skills and subjects that contribute to literacy and to social and intellectual efficiency.

In this view, teachers should be restored to instructional authority. They must be well prepared and held accountable for children's learning. Instruction

---

[17]Gerald L. Gutek, *Basic Education: A Historical Perspective* (Bloomington, Ind.: Phi Delta Kappa Educational Foundation, 1981); Christopher J. Lucas, *Foundations of Education: Schooling and the Social Order* (Englewood Cliffs, N.J.: Prentice-Hall, 1984), pp. 25–70.

[18]Arthur E. Bestor, *The Restoration of Learning* (New York: Knopf, 1955).

[19]Ben Brodinsky, "Back to the Basics: The Movement and Its Meaning," *Phi Delta Kappan* (March 1977), pp. 523–527.

Homework and testing

should be geared to organized learning, often in the form of textbooks. The method of instruction should center on regular assignments, homework, recitations, and frequent testing and evaluation.

Neoessentialism

During the 1980s, a series of national reports on the condition of American education ushered in a period of educational reform that was neoessentialist in character. The term *neoessentialist* is used to indicate that this movement used themes drawn from the essentialists of the 1930s, the critics of the 1950s, and the basic education advocates of the 1970s. These essentialist themes were presented as educational remedies for certain economic and social problems facing the United States.

Five new basics

The neoessentialist philosophical orientation is clearly evident in *A Nation at Risk,* which is examined in Chapter 13. The "five new basics," which the authors of *A Nation at Risk* recommended as the core requirements for high-school students, resembled Bestor's early call for a curriculum based on intellectual disciplines. Only one "new basic," computer science, was really new;[20] the others — English, mathematics, science, and social studies — had all been emphasized by earlier essentialists.

Another national report that echoed neoessentialist arguments was *American Memory: A Report on the Humanities in the Nation's Public Schools.*[21] *American Memory* severely criticized educators who reject or ignore the school's mission in transmitting the nation's cultural heritage, especially as it is found in history and literature. *American Memory* attacked educators who emphasize "process" over content. The report argued that history should be taught as a separate subject and not submerged in the ill-defined social studies. Also, English should be revitalized as the study of literature and not watered down in the language arts. In making the case for history and literature, Lynn V. Cheney, the author of *American Memory,* stated: "We would wish for our children that their decisions be informed not by the wisdom of the moment, but by the wisdom of the ages."[22]

Stress on history and literature

Cultural literacy

In a similar vein, E. D. Hirsch had decried the decline of **cultural literacy** in the United States. For Hirsch, the American people need to possess a core of essential background knowledge. It is this core that contributes to cultural literacy, which in turn is necessary for functional literacy and national discourse and communication. Without the transmission of such a cultural core by education, American society will become increasingly fragmented as a culture. There is, Hirsch insists, a large and necessary body of essential information that needs to be transmitted and mastered if the nation is to be culturally literate.[23]

---

[20]National Commission on Excellence in Education, *A Nation at Risk: The Imperative for Educational Reform* (Washington, D.C.: U.S. Government Printing Office, 1983), pp. 23–31.

[21]Lynn V. Cheney, *American Memory: A Report on the Humanities in the Nation's Public Schools* (Washington, D.C.: National Endowment for the Humanities, 1987).

[22]Ibid., p. 28.

[23]E. D. Hirsch, Jr., *Cultural Literacy: What Every American Needs to Know* (Boston: Houghton Mifflin, 1987).

A neoessentialist philosophy was evident in **A Nation at Risk,** *which recommended "five new basics" for students — English, mathematics, science, social studies, and computer science. (© Sven Martson/Comstock)*

Certain common themes can be found in all variations of the essentialist position. Among them are (1) the elementary school curriculum should aim to cultivate basic skills that contribute to literacy and to mastery of arithmetical computation; (2) the secondary curriculum should cultivate competencies in history, mathematics, science, English, and foreign languages; (3) schooling requires discipline and a respect for legitimate authority; and (4) learning requires hard work and disciplined attention.

The Basic Questions

Since the perennialists and essentialists share many ideas about knowledge, education, schooling, and instruction, their views can be examined as a defense of educational conservatism in a cultural sense. They see historical experience as the surest guide to questions about educational issues. For them, the school is concerned with ideas, knowledge, the cultivation of human intellectuality, and the cultural heritage. The school's task, then, is to civilize human beings.

Traditional conservative view of education

Perennialists and essentialists are suspicious of the argument that the school should be an agency of socialization or of vocationalism. For these culturally conservative educators, the school transmits the cultural heritage to the young. In so doing, it acts as an agency of civilization by bringing those who are culturally immature into contact with the great works of art and literature. In contrast, socialization may simply refer to social adjustment or accommodation. While perennialists and essentialists encourage socialization, the process of acquiring the behaviors of a particular society are raised to a higher dimension when conveyed in the heritage of a great civilization. They claim that such nonintellectual activities detract from and will ultimately destroy the school's intellectual and civilizing roles. Perennialists and essentialists are also suspicious of educational change for the sake of change. They see the teaching-learning relationship as centered on the transmission and mastering of academic subject matter.

Both the essentialists of the past and the more recent neoessentialists believe that the school is an institution designed to teach basic skills and subjects. To ensure a skilled, civil, and literate society, schools need to maintain rigorous academic standards for the mastery of such skills and subjects. Social promotion policies or compensatory programs that weaken mastery of skills and subjects have no place in the school. The competency testing many states require for both students and teachers reflects contemporary essentialist thinking.

Rigorous standards

Implications for Today's Classroom Teacher

The teacher who follows essentialist principles seeks to transmit the cultural heritage to students by means of basic skills and subjects that are organized carefully into units. Essentialist teachers have a well-defined conception of curriculum. In their view, each subject should be organized separately from other subjects. The teacher is to be a specialist in subject-matter content and skilled in organizing it into instructional units. In the essentialist classroom, students devote their energy to learning academic skills and subjects rather than to following short-lived, current fads. Reading, writing, and arithmetic and subject-matter disciplines such as English, foreign languages, mathematics, history, science, and geography are emphasized.

Essentialist curriculum

Much contemporary commentary about "effective schools" is based on an essentialist perspective of what constitutes effectiveness. Schools are judged to be effective when principals and teachers stress high expectations of academic achievement and see the function of the school to be the cultivation of academic competencies. Effective teachers are likewise judged to be those who know their subject, are committed to teaching it as an academic discipline, and succeed in having students score well on examinations designed to measure academic achievement.

Essentialism and effective schools

PRAGMATISM

Pragmatism, a philosophy developed in the United States, stresses the need to test ideas by acting on them. Among its founders were Charles S. Peirce (1839–1914), William James (1842–1910), George Herbert Mead (1863–1931), and John Dewey (1859–1952). Peirce stressed the use of the scientific method in validating an idea; James applied pragmatic interpretations to psychology, religion, and education; and Mead emphasized the development of the child as a learning and experiencing human organism. Dewey, in particular, wrote extensively on education.[24] His work as an educational pioneer was examined in Chapter 4. This chapter will focus on his pragmatic or experimentalist philoso-

Founders of pragmatism

---

[24]John Dewey, *The Child and the Curriculum* (Chicago: University of Chicago Press, 1902); John Dewey, *Democracy and Education* (New York: Macmillan, 1906); John Dewey, *The School and Society* (Chicago: University of Chicago Press, 1923); and John Dewey, *Experience and Education* (New York: Macmillan, 1938).

phy, which was based on change, process, relativity, and the reconstruction of experience.

Dewey was a commanding figure in the field of education. He drew from Charles Darwin's theory of evolution in applying the terms *organism* and *environment* to education. According to Dewey, the human being is a biological and sociological organism possessing drives or impulses that function to sustain life and to further growth and development. Every organism lives in a habitat or environment. In the process of living, the human organism experiences problematic situations that threaten his or her continued existence or that interfere with ongoing activities. The successful human being can solve these problems and add the details of the particular problem-solving episode to his or her general stock of experiences. In Dewey's philosophy of education, *experience* is the key word. Experience can be defined as the interaction of the human organism with its environment. Since living depends on the ability to solve problems, education becomes the means to cultivate problem-solving skills and methods.[25]

Cultivating problem-solving skills

Dewey's concept of experience was a key component of his experimentalist philosophy. Rejecting the a priori foundation of the older idealist, realist, and perennialist philosophical perspectives, Dewey's test of experience meant that human purposes and plans could be validated only by acting on them and judging them by their consequences. The need to judge by consequences also applied to educational programs. Did a particular educational program, curricular design, or methodological strategy achieve its anticipated goals and objectives? For Dewey, the only valid test was to try out the proposal and judge the results.

The test of experience

Whereas idealism, realism, perennialism, and essentialism all emphasized bodies of substantive knowledge or subject-matter disciplines, Dewey stressed the process of problem solving. According to Dewey, learning occurs as the person engages in problem solving. In Dewey's experimental epistemology, the learner, as an individual or as a member of a group, utilizes the scientific method to solve both personal and social problems. For Dewey, the problem-solving method can be developed into a habit that is transferable to a wide variety of situations.[26]

Key Concepts

Metaphysics and Epistemology. Where the more traditional philosophies of idealism and realism had a carefully separated metaphysics and epistemology, pragmatism or experimentalism construed epistemology as a process in which reality is constantly changing.

Environmental interaction and change

The epistemological, or knowing, situation involves a person, an organism, and an environment. The person interacts with the environment in order to live, grow, and develop. This interaction may alter or change the environment, and it may also alter or change the person. Knowing is thus a *transaction* between the learner and the environment. Basic to this interaction is the concept of change. Each interaction may have some generalizable aspects or features that

---

[25]Tom Colwell, "The Ecological Perspective in John Dewey's Philosophy of Education," *Educational Theory* (Summer 1985), p. 257.

[26]Lawrence J. Dennis and George W. Stickel, "Mead and Dewey: Thematic Connections on Educational Topics," *Educational Theory* (Summer–Fall 1981), pp. 320–321.

can be carried to the next interaction, but each episode is somewhat different. Thus, the person is constantly changing, the environment is constantly changing, and the experiences or transactions are also changing.

If reality is continually changing, then a curriculum based on permanent realities such as that of the perennialists or the essentialists cannot be acceptable for the pragmatists. What is needed is a method for dealing with change in an intelligent manner. Since reality is a process of transformation or reconstruction of both the person and the environment, how can the course of change be directed toward desired outcomes? The Deweyites stress problem solving as the most effective and efficient method for dealing with the direction of change. Concepts of unchanging or universal truth, such as the realists and idealists suggest, become untenable. The only guides that human beings have in their interaction with the environment are established generalizations or tentative assertions that are subject to further research and verification. Each time a human experience is reconstructed to solve a problem, a new contribution is added to humanity's fund of experience.

Dealing with change

Axiology and Logic. Pragmatic conceptions of axiology are highly situational. Values are relative to time, place, and circumstance. What contributes to human and social growth and development is regarded as valuable; what restricts or contracts experience is unworthy. It is necessary to test and reexamine value assumptions in the same way that scientific claims are subjected to verification.[27]

The logic used in experimentalist education is inductive and based on the scientific method. Tentative assertions are based on empirical experience and must be tested. Experimentalist logic is suspicious of a priori truths and deductions based on them.

Scientific method

The Basic Questions

The pragmatist answers to questions about knowledge, education, schooling, and instruction are very different from those of the more traditional schools of educational philosophy. For the pragmatists, knowledge is tentative and subject to revision. They are more concerned with the process of using knowledge than with truth as a body of knowledge. In contrast, the traditional philosophers emphasize truth as a permanent body of knowledge.

For the pragmatist, education is an experimental process; it is a method of dealing with and solving problems that arise as people interact with their world. Dewey argued that human beings experience the greatest personal and social growth when they interact with the environment in an intelligent and reflective manner. The most intelligent way of solving problems is to use the scientific method. When you face a problem, the information needed to solve the problem comes from many sources. It is interdisciplinary, rather than located within a single discipline or academic subject. For example, the information needed to

Interdisciplinary approach to solving problems

[27]For a discussion of Dewey's theory of ethics, see William R. Caspary, "Judgments of Value in John Dewey's Theory of Ethics," *Educational Theory* (Spring 1990), pp. 155–169. Also see Robert B. Westbrook, *John Dewey and American Democracy* (Ithaca, N.Y.: Corneil University Press, 1991), pp. 151–156.

define the problem of pollution of the physical environment and to suggest ways of solving it comes from many different sources. The factors that must be considered are historical, political, sociological, scientific, technological, and international. An educated person, in the pragmatic sense, knows how to take information from various sources and disciplines and use that knowledge in an instrumental manner. The more traditional philosophical perspectives represented by idealism, realism, perennialism, and essentialism are suspicious of the interdisciplinary approach in education because they believe that a student must first master organized subject matter before attempting to solve problems.

School as an extension of society

Pragmatists such as Dewey see the school as a specialized environment that is an extension of the more general social environment. For them, no separation exists between school and society. The school has a threefold function: to simplify, purify, and balance the cultural heritage. To simplify, the school selects elements of the heritage and reduces their complexity to appropriate units for learning. To purify, the school selects worthy elements of the cultural heritage and eliminates unworthy ones that limit human interaction and growth. To balance, the school integrates the selected and purified experiences into a harmony. Since many different groups participate in society, the school assists the children of one group in understanding members of other social groups. As a genuinely integrated and democratic learning community, the school should be open to all.

Transmitting the cultural heritage

Sharing of resources

Dewey, in particular, was an advocate of an open and sharing society. For him, quality and equity were not mutually exclusive. A society and its educational system reach their zenith when they provide for the widest possible sharing of resources among all people in the society. Sharing does not diminish quality but enriches it. In Dewey's terms, quality and equity are reciprocal and related social and educational "goods" to be shared by all.

Implications for Today's Classroom Teacher

Unlike the more traditional idealist, realist, perennialist, and essentialist teachers who see the teaching of subject-matter disciplines as their primary responsibility, the pragmatist teacher is more concerned with the process of solving problems intelligently. The pragmatist teacher does not ignore the importance of subject matter but rather uses it instrumentally to fashion solutions to problems. Furthermore, the teacher does not attempt to dominate learning but seeks to guide it by acting as a director or facilitator of the student's research.

Teacher as facilitator

For students in a pragmatist classroom, the main objective is to apply the scientific method to a full range of personal, social, and intellectual problems. Through their use of the problem-solving method, it is expected that the students will learn to apply the process to situations both in and out of school. Further, the problem-solving method is believed to reduce the separation of the school from society.

Classroom as community

Pragmatist teachers work to make the classroom into a community. They consciously encourage students to share their interests, concerns, and problems with each other. Students build a sense of community as they work together to solve common problems. For those who follow Dewey's philosophy, the use of the experimental method in a sharing community of persons, in school and out, is the surest means of making democracy work.

Educational risk taking

Teachers who subscribe to pragmatism have to be risk takers. They see the world and knowledge about that world as indeterminate or open-ended rather than based on the status quo of either belief or opinion. The aims of education, for such teachers, are expressed as ongoing inquiry and action. For Dewey, the most general aim of education is human growth for the purpose of more growth.

PROGRESSIVISM

Part of a larger reform movement

Although progressive education, or the educational theory of **progressivism,** is often associated with John Dewey's pragmatism or experimentalism, the progressive education movement wove together a number of diverse strands. In its origins the progressive education movement was part of the larger sociopolitical movement of general reform that characterized American life in the late nineteenth and early twentieth centuries. Political progressives such as Robert La Follette and Woodrow Wilson wanted to curb powerful trusts and monopolies and to make the system of political democracy truly operative.[28] Social welfare progressives such as Jane Addams worked in the settlement house movement to improve living conditions in Chicago and in other urban areas. Thus, progressive education was part of a more general movement to reform American life and institutions.[29] Progressivism was also derived from educational practice. Educators such as G. Stanley Hall, Francis Parker, and William H. Kilpatrick argued against traditional school practices that stressed mindless routine, rote memorization, and authoritarian classroom management styles. Antitraditional and anti-authoritarian teachers began to develop practices that emphasized students' own interests. The learning communities that they created were flexible, permissive and open-ended. As a theory, progressive education grew out of such grassroots classroom experiences.

Antitraditionalism

Child's interests and needs

Having no central dogma, progressive educators argue that all learning should arise from children's interests and needs. One leading progressive educator described the principles of education as follows:

> We believe the educational program should aim to meet the needs of the growing child. We believe that childhood is for itself and not a preparation for adult life. Therefore, the school program must answer the following questions: What does the child of any particular age need to minister to the health of his body, to preserve the integrity of the intellect, and to keep him sincere and unself-conscious of spirit?
>
> The answers to these questions will constitute the curriculum of the school, and as we grow in understanding of the nature and needs of childhood, the curriculum will change.[30]

---

[28]For the contrasting leadership styles of two progressive presidents, see John M. Cooper, Jr., *The Warrior and the Priest: Woodrow Wilson and Theodore Roosevelt* (Cambridge, Mass.: Belknap Press of Harvard University Press, 1983).

[29]Robert M. Crunden, *Ministers of Reform: The Progressives' Achievement in American Civilization, 1889–1920* (Urbana: University of Illinois Press, 1984).

[30]Marietta Johnson, "The Educational Principles of the School of Organic Education, Fairhope, Alabama," in H. Rugg, ed., *The Foundations and Technique for the Study of Education*, National Society for the Study of Education, Part I (Bloomington, Ind.: Public School Publishing, 1926), p. 349.

School as a pleasant place   Others stressed as well the need to make school a pleasant place for learning.

> Every child has the right to live naturally, happily, and fully as a child. . . . Childhood in itself is a beautiful section of life, and children should be given a chance for free, full living.
>
> We try to make the schools happy, attractive places for children to be in. . . . We believe in colorfulness, coziness, hominess in our classrooms; in an opportunity for spontaneity. We want children to *want* to come to school.[31]

Progressive Principles

The loosely structured Progressive Education Association, organized in 1919, was not united by a single comprehensive philosophy of education. The progressives differed in many of their theories and practices, but they were united in opposition to certain traditional school practices. They generally con-

Criticized traditional school practices

demned the following: (1) the authoritarian teacher, (2) exclusive reliance on bookish methods of instruction or on the textbook, (3) passive learning by memorization of factual data, (4) the four-walls philosophy of education that attempted to isolate education from social reality, and (5) the use of fear or physical punishment as a form of discipline.

Members of the Progressive Education Association also agreed on these positive principles: (1) the child should be free to develop naturally; (2) interest, stimulated by direct experience, is the best stimulus for learning; (3) the teacher should be a resource person and a guide to learning activities; (4) there should be close cooperation between the school and the home; and (5) the progressive school should be a laboratory for pedagogical reform and experimentation.[32]

Progressive education was both a movement within the broad framework of American education and a theory that urged the liberation of the child from the traditional emphasis on rote learning, lesson recitations, and textbooks. Opposing the conventional subject matter of the traditional curriculum, progressives experimented with alternative curricular organization — utilizing ac-

Focus on learner, not on subject

tivities, experiences, problem solving, and the project method. Progressive education focused on the child as the learner rather than on the subject; emphasized activities and experiences rather than verbal and literary skills; and encouraged cooperative group learning activities rather than competitive individualized lesson learning. The use of democratic school procedures was seen as a prelude to community and social reform. Progressivism also cultivated a cultural relativism that critically appraised and often rejected traditional value commitments.[33] The relativist position argues that each generation reconstructs its knowledge and values according to changing circumstances and problems. Cultural relativism can be contrasted with the perennialist defense of enduring truth and values.

---

[31]Carleton Washburne, "The Philosophy of the Winnetka Curriculum," in Rugg, ed., *The Foundations and Technique for the Study of Education,* pp. 222–223.

[32]Stephen I. Brown and Mary E. Finn, eds. *Readings from Progressive Education: A Movement and its Professional Journal* (Lanham, Md.: University Press of America, 1988).

[33]The progressive movement in education has been given an excellent treatment in Lawrence A. Cremin, *The Transformation of the School* (New York: Random House, 1961).

The Basic Questions

Since the progressives were not of a single mind, they gave a variety of
responses to questions about the nature of education, the school, teaching, and
learning. However, they were able to agree on their opposition to traditionalism
and authoritarianism. Whereas some progressives believed that education was
a process intended to liberate children, others were more concerned with social
reform. Child-centered progressives saw the school as a place where children
would be free to experiment, to play, and to express themselves. Those inclined
to a more societal perspective saw the school as a community center or as an
agency of social reform.

*Liberating children and
social reform*

Progressives generally were not interested in using the curriculum to transmit subjects to students. Rather, the curriculum was to come from the child.
Learning could take a variety of forms, such as problem solving, field trips, creative artistic expression, and projects. Above all, progressives saw the teaching-
learning process as active, exciting, and ever changing. Progressive educators
rejected barriers of class, race, or creed that separated people from each other.
They believed that as students work together on projects based on their common
shared experience, they break down the isolation that diminishes the quality of
the human experience.

Implications for Today's Classroom Teacher

Progressive teachers who follow an experimentalist philosophical orientation generally incorporate problem solving, projects, group work, and activities

into their instructional methodology and classroom style.[34] For example, a junior high or middle school teacher might engage students in a social studies unit on the African American contribution to American life. Students might work in groups, with each group expected to contribute to the total project. Among the group projects, there might be the following:

> *Group A* would trace the origins of African Americans to Africa and the slave trade. Such an investigation would involve research and reading in geography, economics, anthropology, and history. Each student in Group A would investigate a particular phase of the problem, and the results would then be integrated into the whole project.

> *Group B* might identify the leading African American contributors to U.S. culture and prepare biographical sketches for class presentations. The group could also arrange an exhibit that included photographs and evidence of each leader's contribution.

> *Group C* might research current achievements, problems, and issues facing African Americans. The students could consult current newspapers and magazines and prepare a scrapbook of clippings.

As the various groups work on their projects, the teacher serves as a resource facilitator. Working with each group individually, he or she suggests sources and helps students discover other ways of pursuing the project.

SOCIAL RECONSTRUCTIONISM

Creation of a new society

Whereas some progressive educators emphasized the individuality of the child, other progressives were vitally concerned with social change. These progressives, called social reconstructionists, argued that progressive education should do more than reform the social and educational status quo; it should create a new society. **Social reconstructionism** will be examined here as a separate educational theory; its origins, however, were part of the progressive movement in education.

Social reconstructionism postulates that humankind is in a state of profound cultural crisis. If schools reflect the dominant social values, as the traditional educational theorists suggest, then, according to the reconstructionists, organized education will merely transmit the social ills that are symptoms of the pervasive problems and afflictions that beset humankind. The reconstructionists generally assert that the only legitimate goal of a truly humane education is to create a world order in which people control their own destiny. In an age of nuclear weaponry, ecological deterioration, and pandemic disease, reconstructionists see education as a means to prevent global catastrophe. They see an urgent need for society to reconstruct itself before it self-destructs.[35]

---

[34]Kathe Jeris and Carol Montag, eds., *Progressive Education for the 1990s: Transforming Practice* (New York: Teachers College Press, Columbia University, 1991).

[35]For an analysis of reconstructionism in a global perspective, see Carole Ann Ryan, "George S. Counts: Dare Educators Inspire World Vision?" in David B. Annis, ed., *Proceedings of the Annual Conference of the Midwest Philosophy of Education Society* (1990–1991), pp. 11–17.

Lag in cultural adaptation

In analyzing the cultural crisis, the reconstructionists contend that although humankind has moved from an agricultural and rural society to an urban and technological society at the level of invention and scientific discovery, there is a serious lag in cultural adaptation. Humankind has yet to reconstruct its values in order to catch up with the changes in the technological order, and organized education has a major role to play in reducing the gap.

Reconstructionist Thinking

Social and economic problems

The reconstructionists recommend that teachers and schools embark on a critical examination of the culture in which they live. They should seek to identify the major areas of controversy, conflict, and inconsistency and seek to explore and to resolve them. For example, certain nations enjoy plenty while other peoples face the constant threat of starvation. While a few people enjoy luxury, many are victims of disease and poverty. Education should expose these social inconsistencies and seek to resolve them so that the people as a whole can determine the distribution of important resources.

The reconstructionists further believe that the technological era is one of tremendous interdependence. Events in one area of the globe will have an impact on other areas. Pollution, for example, is not restricted to a single place or to a single people. In such an interdependent world, the old forms of education that stressed either isolationism or nationalism are obsolete. The reconstructionist generally would seek to internationalize the curriculum so that men and women would learn that they live in a global village.

Human survival depends on education

The social reconstructionists share a common concern that human survival and education are reciprocally related. To ensure the continuation of our species on this planet, we must become social engineers, plotting our course of change and then using our scientific and technological expertise to arrive at the defined goal. A reconstructionist program of education will be one that (1) critically examines the cultural heritage; (2) does not fear to examine the most controversial of social issues; (3) is deliberately committed to bringing about constructive social change; (4) cultivates a planning attitude; and (5) enlists students and teachers in definite programs of social, educational, political, and economic change as a means of total cultural renewal.[36]

The Basic Questions

The social reconstructionists are convinced that a new social order will come about only as educators challenge obsolete conceptions of knowledge, education, schooling, and instruction and initiate carefully planned and directed educational change that will lead to social change. Like the progressives, social reconstructionists see knowledge in instrumental terms. The knowledge areas that are particularly useful are the social sciences — anthropology, economics,

---

[36]Among the most important sources of reconstructionist philosophy are Theodore Brameld, *Toward a Reconstructed Philosophy of Education* (New York: Holt, Rinehart and Winston, 1956); George S. Counts, *Dare the School Build a New Social Order?* (New York: John Day Publishing, 1932); and William O. Stanley, *Education and Social Integration* (New York: Teachers College Press, Columbia University, 1952).

Getting to the Source ➤◆

Dare the School Build a New Social Order? /
George S. Counts

DARE
THE SCHOOL
BUILD A NEW
SOCIAL ORDER?

By
GEORGE S. COUNTS
Author of The American Road to Culture,
The Soviet Challenge to America, *etc.*

New York
THE JOHN DAY COMPANY

George S. Counts (1889–1974) played multiple roles in American education. He was a professor of education at Columbia University's Teachers College, an

expert on Soviet education, a president of the American Federation of Teachers, and an originator of the theory of social reconstructionism. Among his many books, Dare the School Build a New Social Order?, *published in 1932, is frequently cited as an argument that teachers and schools should originate rather than reflect sociopolitical and economic ideas and values. In the following selection, Counts argues that teachers should seek to shape the society and not fear imposing their views in the educational process.*

That the teachers should deliberately reach for power and then make the most of their conquest is my firm conviction. To the extent that they are permitted to fashion the curriculum and the procedures of the school they will definitely and positively influence the social attitudes, ideals, and behavior of the coming generation. In doing this they should resort to no subterfuge or false modesty. They should say neither that they are merely teaching the truth nor that they are unwilling to wield power in their own right. The first position is false and the second is a confession of incompetence. It is my observation that the men and women who

sociology, political science, and psychology. These social sciences provide insights, information, and methods for use in devising strategies for planned social change in contemporary society.

Active problem solving

Education, for the social recontructionists, is designed to awaken students' consciousness about social problems and to engage them actively in the solving of problems. To awaken social consciousness, students are encouraged to question the status quo and to investigate controversial issues in religion, economics, politics, and education. It is by examining controversial issues that the student will develop alternatives to the conventional wisdom.

The school as a social agency is an institution where new suggestions for changing society are to be encouraged, but not as a purely intellectual exercise. Rather, the school is an instrument for creating alternative political, social, and economic institutions and processes. Since it is on the cutting edge of change, the school will be in the center of controversy.

Social reconstructionists are firmly committed to equality in both society and education. For them, barriers of socioeconomic class and racial discrimination need to be identified, examined, and eradicated. In the American context,

have affected the course of human events are those who have not hesitated to use the power that has come to them. Representing as they do, not the interests of the moment or of any special class, but rather the common and abiding interests of the people, teachers are under heavy social obligation to protect and further those interests. In this they occupy a relatively unique position in society. Also since the profession should embrace scientists and scholars of the highest rank, as well as teachers working at all levels of the educational system, it has at its disposal, as no other group, the knowledge and wisdom of the ages. It is scarcely thinkable that these men and women would ever act as selfishly or bungle as badly as have the so-called "practical" men of our generation — the politicians, the financiers, the industrialists. If all of these facts are taken into account, instead of shunning power, the profession should rather seek power and then strive to use that power fully and wisely and in the interests of the great masses of the people.

The point should be emphasized that teachers possess no magic secret to power. While their work should give them a certain moral advantage, they must expect to encounter the usual obstacles blocking the road to leadership. They should not be deceived by the pious humbug with which public men commonly flatter the members of the profession. . . . Moreover, while organization is necessary, teachers should not think of their problem primarily in terms of organizing and presenting a united front to the world, the flesh, and the devil. In order to be effective they must throw off completely the slave psychology that has dominated the mind of the pedagogue more or less since the days of ancient Greece. They must be prepared to stand on their own feet and win for their ideas the support of the masses of the people. Education as a force for social regeneration must march hand in hand with the living and creative forces of the social order.

Questions

1. According to Counts, why should teachers reach for power?
2. How can education be a force for social reconstruction?

Source: George S. Counts, *Dare the School Build a New Social Order?* (Carbondale, Ill.: Southern Illinois University Press, 1978), pp. 26–28. Cover from the 1932 edition, published by The John Day Company, New York.

social reconstructionists have often been political and educational activists who believe that the school should contribute to a greater sharing of the intellectual, social, and material resources of American life.[37]

Implications for Today's Classroom Teacher

For the reconstructionist teacher, the school should be used as an agency to improve the quality of human life. Education should not be defined in exclusively academic terms, as perennialists and essentialists claim, but should be used as an instrument of deliberate social change.

Role of the reconstructionist teacher

In order to proceed with the agenda of creating a new society, teachers would encourage students to diagnose the major problems confronting human beings on planet Earth. Among the problems that threaten human survival are pollution of the environment, warfare, famine, and the spread of epidemic dis-

[37]Gerald L. Gutek, *George S. Counts and American Civilization: The Educator as Social Theorist* (Macon, Ga.: Mercer University Press, 1984).

eases such as AIDS. Reconstructionist teachers do not want to be neutral commentators about world problems. They want to be committed to solving these problems for the betterment of humankind.

Issue-oriented lessons

Reconstructionist teachers, for example, would be eager to explore multicultural issues in the classroom. They would use issue-oriented lessons to expose problems of racism, classism, and sexism that interfere with equality of opportunity or that seek to impose a monolithic cultural pattern on a diverse population. To build a pluralistic cultural community in the classroom, they would encourage projects in which students share their unique cultural heritages. To develop strategies for creating a truly multicultural society, they would build a knowledge base that incorporates the contributions that various ethnic, racial, social, and language groups have made to American society. Their major emphasis would be to demonstrate that the cultural fabric of American life is still unfinished and becomes enriched by cultural diversity.

EXISTENTIALISM

Rather than constituting a systematic philosophy, **existentialism** examines life in a very personal manner. It became popular in the post–World War II period. In some ways, existentialism represents a feeling of desperation, but it also contains a spirit of hope. An education that follows the existentialist orientation will emphasize deep personal reflection on one's commitments and choices.

Self-examination

Key Concepts

The existentialist author Jean-Paul Sartre stated, "Existence precedes Essence." This means that human beings are born and enter the world without being consulted. They simply are here in a world that they did not make or shape. However, they possess volition, or will, which gives them the freedom to make choices and to create their own purposes for existence. As people live, they are thrust into a number of choice-making situations. Some choices are minute and trivial. Other choices, however, deal with the purpose of life. These are decisions that lead to personal self-definition. A person creates his or her own definition and makes his or her own essence. You are what you choose to be.[38]

The existentialist conception of a human being as the creator of his or her own essence differs substantially from that of the idealists and realists, who see the person as a universal category. Whereas the idealist or realist sees the individual as an inhabitant of a meaningful and explainable world, the existentialist believes that the universe is indifferent to human wishes, desires, and plans. Human freedom is total, say the existentialists, who also hold that one's responsibility for choice is total.

Total responsibility for choices

Existentialism also focuses on the concept of *Angst,* or dread. Each person knows that his or her destiny is death and that his or her presence in the world is only temporary. As a conscious being, the individual must carry the knowl-

---

[38]Gutek, *Philosophical and Ideological Perspectives on Education,* pp. 111–133.

edge of ultimate demise every day. It is with this sense of philosophical dread that each person must make choices about freedom and slavery, love and hate, and peace and war. As one makes these choices, a question is always present: What difference does it make that I am here and that I have chosen to be what I am?

Desperation and hope

According to the existentialists, human beings are desperate creatures who realize that life is temporary. They live in a world where others — persons, institutions, and agencies — are constantly seeking to impinge upon and violate their choice-making freedom. But existentialism does see hope behind the desperation. Each person's response to life has to be based on an answer to the question, Do I choose to be a self-determined person or do I choose to be defined by others? Even though desperate, each person has the potential for loving, creating, and being. Each can choose to be an inner-directed, authentic person. An authentic person is one who is free and aware of his or her freedom. Such a person knows that every choice is really an act of personal value creation. The authentic person defines him- or herself and is aware that self-definition is a personal responsibility.[39]

Essence and values

Since existentialists have deliberately avoided systemization of their philosophy, it is difficult to categorize its metaphysical, epistemological, axiological, and logical positions. However, some comments on these areas can illustrate the existentialist point of view. Metaphysically, each person creates his or her own self-definition through the being or essence created by individual choice. Epistemologically, the individual chooses the knowledge that he or she wishes to possess. It is axiology that is most important for existentialists, because human beings create their own values through the choices that they make. Finally, the logic to which a person subscribes is a matter of individual preference.

The Basic Questions

The educational implications of existentialism are many. The existentialist realizes that we live in a world of physical realities and that we have developed a useful and scientific knowledge about these realities. However, the most significant aspects of our lives are personal and nonscientific.[40] So to the questions we have asked about knowledge and education, existentialists would say that the most important kind of knowledge is about the human condition and the choices that each person has to make. For existentialists, the most significant aim of education is to develop human consciousness about the freedom to choose and to illuminate the meaning of choice. Education should be designed to create in us a sense of self-awareness and to contribute to our authenticity as human beings.

Meaning of life, love, and death

An existentialist teacher would encourage students to philosophize about the meaning of the human experiences of life, love, and death. The questioning process would grow into a dialogue between the members of the learning groups. It should be remembered that the answers to these questions would be

---

[39]Maxine Greene, *Landscapes of Learning* (New York: Teachers College Press, Columbia University, 1978); Van Cleve Morris, *Existentialism in Education* (New York: Harper & Row, 1966).

[40]John R. Scudder and Algis Mickunas, *Meaning, Dialogue, and Enculturation: Phenomenological Philosophy of Education* (Lanham, Md.: University Press of America, 1985).

For existentialists, education should help students develop consciousness about the freedom to choose and allow them to experiment with artistic media to dramatize their feelings and insights. (© Roger Malloch/Magnum)

personal and subjective for each individual and could not be measured on standardized tests.

An existentialist curriculum would consist of the experiences and subjects that lend themselves to philosophic dialogue. They would be subjects that vividly portray individual men and women in the act of making choices. Since existentialist choice making is so personal and subjective, those subjects that are emotional, aesthetic, and poetic are appropriate to an existentialist curriculum.[41] Literature and biography are important sources for revealing choice-making conditions. Drama and films that vividly portray the human condition and human decision making ought to be seen and discussed by students. In addition to literary, dramatic, and biographical subjects, students also need to find modes of self-expression.[42] They should be free to experiment with artistic media, to dramatize or make concrete their emotions, feelings, and insights.

Modes of self-expression

The school, for the existentialist educator, is a place where individuals meet to pursue dialogue and discussion about their own lives and choices. Since every person is in the same predicament and has the same possibilities, every individual should have opportunities for schooling. In the school, both teachers and

---

[41]Maxine Greene, *The Dialectic of Freedom* (New York: Teachers College Press, Columbia University, 1988).

[42]For an approach that uses narrative and dialogue to examine philosophical issues in education, see Carol Witherell and Nel Noddings, eds., *Stories Lives Tell: Narrative and Dialogue in Education* (New York: Teachers College Press, Columbia University, 1991).

students should have the opportunity to ask questions, to suggest answers, and to engage in dialogue.

Implications for Today's Classroom Teacher

Teaching from an existentialist perspective is not easy because goals and objectives cannot be specified in advance by the teacher. They are determined by each student as an individual person.

Teacher encourages student awareness

Rather than imposing goals on the student, the existentialist teacher seeks to create an awareness in each student that she or he is ultimately responsible for her or his own education and self-definition. In creating this awareness, the existentialist teacher encourages students to examine the institutions, forces, and situations that tend to limit freedom of choice. Further, existentialist teachers seek to create open classrooms in which freedom of choice is maximized. Within these open learning environments, the method of instruction is a form of self-learning.

Open classrooms

PHILOSOPHICAL ANALYSIS

Language analysis

Philosophical analysis, or language analysis, is a method of examining the language used in making statements about knowledge, education, and schooling and of seeking to clarify it by establishing its meaning. Philosophical analysis is used by educational philosophers who believe our communications about education have grown increasingly confused.[43] To establish meaning, philosophical analysts seek to reduce statements about education to empirical terms.

Empirical analyses

Philosophical analysis does not pretend to be a school of educational philosophy.[44] While idealists, realists, and perennialists describe their philosophies as a world view or universal system, philosophical analysts reject cosmic system building as a speculative exercise that has no real meaning for educators. Such analysts assert that the metaphysical basis of cosmic philosophies cannot be verified in human experience. In addition, they find the expressions of the existentialists to be primarily poetic and emotional, deficient in supplying empirical data to establish meaning in educational issues. Since pragmatists use the scientific method, they are agreeable to the analytical view. But even the pragmatists have failed to use language with precise meaning. For example, Dewey's terms such as "democracy," "growth," "interests," and "experience" have caused much debate among philosophers of education.[45]

Establishing precise meaning

This dissatisfaction with the schools of philosophy led some philosophers to develop a new way of working with ideas and their expression in language. Two

---

[43]Richard Pratte, "Analytic Philosophy of Education: A Historical Perspective," in Jonas F. Soltis, ed., *Philosophy of Education Since Mid-Century* (New York: Teachers College Press, 1981), pp. 17–37.

[44]George F. Kneller, *Movements of Thought in Modern Education* (New York: Wiley, 1984).

[45]For representative presentations of analytical philosophy, see Jonas F. Soltis, *An Introduction to the Analysis of Educational Concepts* (Lanham, Md.: University Press of America, 1985), and Cornel M. Hamm, *Philosophical Issues in Education: An Introduction* (London: Falmer Press, 1989).

major philosophers who led the movement of language analysis were G. E. Moore and Bertrand Russell. Russell in particular sought to identify the logical structure that underlies language usage.

Key Concepts

Although differences exist among analysts, a few generalizations can illustrate their contributions to educational philosophy. For example, we express ourselves in sentences that convey propositions about reality. According to the analysts, only some of these sentences are meaningful communications between persons. Meaningful sentences are either analytically true or empirically true.[46] If we say that 2 + 2 = 4, we have expressed a mathematical statement that is analytically true because the 4 is analyzed out of and means the same as 2 + 2. The statement can be reversed and can be stated as 4 = 2 + 2. Other statements are true in that they can be verified in empirical terms. For example, the statement that water boils at 212° Fahrenheit can be tested empirically.

Meaningful statements

If meaningful statements are either analytically or empirically true, then many other statements are meaningless in scientific communication because they cannot be examined by these two methods. For example, the idealist proposition that "world is mind" cannot be tested. Neither can the existentialist statement that "existence precedes essence." However, it is possible to examine and find meaning in the pragmatist proposition that "experience is the interaction of the human organism with the environment." To verify this statement, it would be necessary to render the words "experience," "human organism," "interaction," and "environment" in terms that can be verified empirically or analyzed logically.

Growing specialization

In many respects, philosophical analysis is a response to the condition of knowledge in the twentieth century.[47] The lives of men and women, their occupations, and their areas of knowledge competency have grown increasingly complicated and specialized as technology has advanced and institutions have been modernized. Each specialization has its own highly specialized language. The use of highly specialized terminologies makes it difficult even for those in the same field to communicate with each other across their specialties. By explaining the language used in a complex technological society, the philosophical analyst can contribute to more meaningful communication.

The Basic Questions

Concern with educational issues

Philosophical analysts do not attempt to provide broad answers to questions about knowledge, education, schooling, and instruction. Quite the contrary, they redefine these questions to specific educational issues. In dealing with knowledge, they focus on those knowledge claims and propositions that can be verified empirically. They have deflated many grandiose educational claims that

---

[46]Albert J. Taylor, *An Introduction to the Philosophy of Education* (Lanham, Md.: University Press of America, 1985).

[47]Israel Scheffler, *Of Human Potential: An Essay in the Philosophy of Education* (Boston: Routledge & Kegan Paul, 1985).

cannot be put to the test of experience. In matters that concern teaching and learning, philosophical analysts give careful attention to the language transactions that take place between the teacher and the learner in the classroom.

The analytical method is particularly applicable in examining statements about educational aims, which often contain polemical, emotive, or ideological language. Analysts seek to render such statements into language that can be verified logically or empirically. If the aim can be expressed in meaningful terms, then we have a better chance of determining whether it has been achieved. The same applies to many arguments about curriculum and teaching methods. State the matter empirically, the analysts say, and its truth can be tested.

Implications for Today's Classroom Teacher

There are many educational issues that need careful definition such as the philosophical analysts propose. As an example, consider the issue of providing equality of educational opportunity. While American educators are committed to the proposition that each person in the United States has the right to "equality of educational opportunity," what does the statement mean in terms of educational policy and school practices? If *equal* means "the same," does this mean that every student should have the same educational experiences? If so, then how would teachers meet students' individual differences and needs? Perhaps we should define *equal* as "equivalent." This would allow teachers to vary practices according to students' needs, but this definition raises a new question: how would educators determine which practices were equivalent? In terms of educational policy and classroom practices, allegiance to a belief in equality of educational opportunity is not the simple matter that it appears to be. In this case, the definition of the word *equality* holds the key to school practice.

In the classroom, philosophical analysis is a tool to clarify and interpret the language used in instruction. It provides a means of reducing misinformation, ambiguity, and confusion. Students, living in a technological society, find themselves involved in communicating about highly specialized terminologies. Language analysis provides help in clarifying these complex terminologies. The classroom is an arena of communications, and language analysis can help to make these communications more effective in advancing teaching and learning.

Summing Up

1. Chapter 12 has attempted to put into perspective traditional philosophies of education, such as idealism and realism, and traditional theories of education, such as perennialism and essentialism. We have also discussed the process-oriented philosophy of pragmatism, or experimentalism, and the theories of progressivism and social reconstructionism. The chapter concluded by describing two approaches to contemporary philosophy of education: existentialism and philosophical analysis.

2. The major concepts of these philosophies and theories are summarized in overview charts 12.1 and 12.2, which appear on pages 455 and 456. The study of these philosophies and theories of education reveals how varied are the aims of education.

3. By studying these philosophical approaches to education, you can appreciate the rich complexity of educational theorizing and can work toward formulating your own philosophy of education. With a knowledge of educational philosophy, teachers can also recognize the underlying philosophical bases of the curriculum found in their schools.

Key Terms

metaphysics *(451)*

epistemology *(451)*

axiology *(451)*

ethics *(451)*

aesthetics *(451)*

deductive logic *(451)*

inductive logic *(451)*

idealism *(452)*

macrocosm *(453)*

microcosm *(453)*

a priori ideas *(453)*

Socratic method *(454)*

realism *(457)*

perennialism *(459)*

The Paideia Proposal (462)

cultural relativism *(462)*

essentialism *(464)*

"back-to-basics" movement *(464)*

cultural literacy *(465)*

pragmatism *(467)*

progressivism *(471)*

social reconstructionism *(474)*

existentialism *(478)*

philosophical analysis *(481)*

Discussion Questions

1. How would you answer the basic philosophical questions about knowledge, education, and schooling? How does your philosophy of education reflect or differ from the philosophies of education treated in this chapter?

2. Suppose you are a realist. How would you assess pragmatism and progressivism?

3. Which of the philosophies of education treated in this chapter has had the greatest impact on American education? Why?

4. Suppose you are a social reconstructionist. Identify the major problems facing American society, construct an educational agenda, and devise a teaching strategy designed to promote the solution of these problems.

5. Which of the philosophies treated in this chapter is most relevant to contemporary education, and which is most irrelevant? Why?

6. Analyze some current proposals for educational reform. Identify the philosophies of education upon which these proposals are based.

Suggested Readings

Bloom, Allan. *The Closing of the American Mind.* New York: Simon and Schuster, 1987.
   In his widely read book, Bloom attacks the effects of relativism on American education.

Brumbaugh, Robert S., and Nathaniel M. Lawrence. *Philosophers on Education: Six Essays on the Foundations of Western Thought.* Lanham, Md.: University Press of America, 1986.
   In this well-reviewed book, the authors examine the educational philosophies of six major thinkers: Plato, Aristotle, Rousseau, Kant, Dewey, and Whitehead.

Goodlad, John I., Roger Soder, and Kenneth A. Sirotnik, eds. *The Moral Dimensions of Teaching.* San Francisco: Jossey-Bass, 1990.

> *The editors have assembled essays by some of the leading authorities in philosophy of education to examine the moral and ethical foundations related to schooling, teaching, and learning.*

Gutek, Gerald L. *Philosophical and Ideological Perspectives on Education.* Englewood Cliffs. N.J.: Prentice-Hall, 1988.

> *The author uses a systems approach to examine leading educational philosophies and ideologies.*

Hirsch, Jr., E. D. *Cultural Literacy: What Every American Needs to Know.* Boston: Houghton Mifflin, 1987.

> *An essentialist notion of what a good education is about and what every young American needs to know about Western culture.*

Jervis, Kathe, and Carol Montag, eds. *Progressive Education for the 1990s.* New York: Teachers College Press, Columbia University, 1991.

> *This contemporary treatment of progressive education approaches the subject from both historical and practical perspectives that can guide schooling, teaching, and learning.*

Knight, George R. *Issues and Alternatives in Educational Philosophy,* 2nd ed. Berrien Springs, Mich.: Andrews University Press, 1989.

> *Knight presents a succinct and clearly written survey of the major philosophies and philosophic issues relevant to education.*

Ozmon, Howard A., and Samuel M. Craver. *Philosophical Foundations of Education,* 4th ed. Columbus, Ohio: Merrill, 1990.

> *In their widely used text, Ozmon and Craver present a well-done introduction to the most important schools of educational philosophy.*

13

Aims of Education

FOCUSING QUESTIONS

How do social forces combine with philosophies of education to shape our educational purposes?

What are the major differences among aims, goals, and objectives?

How are aims, goals, and objectives formulated?

What groups of students have been targeted for special treatment in recent decades? What emphasis has there been on the academically talented and on the economically disadvantaged?

What are the major themes of recent policy reports on education? What aims will be most important in the future?

C ontemporary society changes fundamentally and rapidly. As it changes, we must fit ourselves into the present and project ourselves into the future. We look to the schools to help us cope with the climate of change. As a society, we react to change and social pressures by revising our educational purposes, and the schools respond in turn by changing their programs.

In this continual revision of educational priorities, the basic philosophies and theories examined in Chapter 12 play a strong role. People respond differently to the same events; they appraise, reflect on, and react to the tendencies of the times according to their own philosophies and values. Moreover, certain eras in American education have been dominated by particular philosophical approaches; as times change, the dominant philosophy or theory often changes, and the impact is felt in classrooms across the country.

This chapter demonstrates how philosophies and theories of education interact with social forces to influence the purposes of American schools. After describing the purposes that have prevailed at different times in the history of American education, we examine the important changes of recent years. First, however, the chapter shows how educational purposes are defined in terms of aims, goals, and objectives.

ESTABLISHING AIMS, GOALS, AND OBJECTIVES

Levels of educational purpose

When we talk about the purposes of education, we may be referring to purposes at one or more of the following levels: nation, state, school district, school, subject/grade, unit plan, or lesson plan. Although there is no perfect agreement, most educators use the terms **aims, goals,** and **objectives** to distinguish among levels of purpose — aims being the broadest and objectives being the most specific. The three different terms are all used to describe a direction — what we are seeking to accomplish. Many educators, including Hilda Taba and Ralph Tyler, refer to aims, goals, and objectives as ''ends'' or ''end points'' of education.[1]

Effect of social forces and philosophies

All of these end points, however, are influenced by social forces and by prevailing philosophies or theories of education, as illustrated in Figure 13.1. Social forces and philosophies combine to shape the aims adopted at the national or state level; these aims in turn affect the more specific goals and objectives adopted in particular schools and classrooms. Over time, changes in social forces can also lead to modifications in prevailing philosophies and theories. There are three main types of influential forces: changes in society in general, in developments in knowledge, and in the perceived nature of the learner.[2]

---

[1]Hilda Taba, *Curriculum Development: Theory and Practice* (New York: Harcourt, Brace, 1962); Ralph W. Tyler, *Basic Principles of Curriculum and Instruction* (Chicago: University of Chicago Press, 1949).

[2]The concept of three sources of change is rooted in the ideas of Boyd Bode and John Dewey, writing some seventy-five years ago. These ideas, popularized by Ralph Tyler in 1949, have been developed by contemporary curriculum theorists such as Allan Ornstein, J. Galen Saylor, and Robert Zais.

The Purposes of Education and the Forces That Influence Them

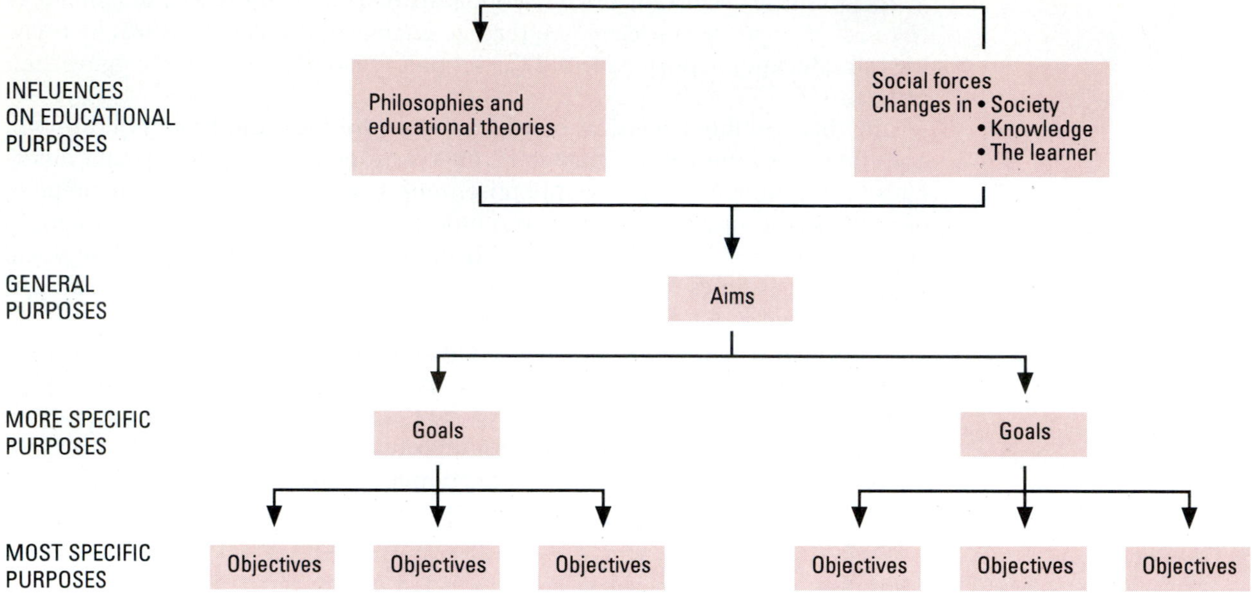

Figure 13.1

INFLUENCES
ON EDUCATIONAL
PURPOSES

| Philosophies and educational theories | Social forces
Changes in • Society
• Knowledge
• The learner |

GENERAL
PURPOSES

Aims

MORE SPECIFIC
PURPOSES

Goals   Goals

MOST SPECIFIC
PURPOSES

Objectives   Objectives   Objectives   Objectives   Objectives   Objectives

Changes in society

Changes in *society* include shifts in emphasis among the various influences examined in Chapters 9 and 10, such as the family, peer groups, and social class. Changes in the economy and in work and leisure environments may also have an effect. For example, many educators now believe the United States should redefine its educational purposes in order to increase the country's economic competitiveness with foreign nations.

Changes in knowledge

Changes in *knowledge* include new developments in science and technology, new methods of processing and storing information, and new methods of defining or organizing fields of study. We can see an obvious illustration in the rapid development of computer technology. Since the computer revolution, the need for "computer literacy" has had a powerful influence on educational purposes.

Changes in the learner

Finally, changes in the perceived nature of the *learner* also produce changes in educational theories. Such problems as delinquency, drugs, and teenage pregnancy can lead educators to alter their ideas of what education can and should accomplish. New theories of learning, growth, and development that change our understanding of the basic learning process may also cause educational purposes to change accordingly.

With these social influences in mind, we can now define the different levels of educational purposes, from the most general aims to the most specific objectives.

Aims

The word *aims* is often used interchangeably with the terms *ultimate objectives* and *broad objectives*. Aims are important guides in education, although they cannot be directly observed or evaluated; they are broad statements that denote a desired and valued competency, a theme or concern that applies to education in

*Aims formulated on
national or state level*

general. Aims are usually formulated at the national level, or sometimes at the state level, by prestigious commissions or task force groups; aims reflect the conditions of society and are intended to guide schools in defining goals. Examples of aims might be "to prepare students for democratic citizenship" and "to prepare students for a vocation."

*Assigning responsibilities
to schools and other
institutions*

In defining aims, we must ask what the responsibilities of the school are in contrast to those that properly belong to the family, community, church, and various social or youth agencies. What responsibilities should the school share with other institutions or agencies? As we attempt to answer these questions, our educational aims evolve. They provide direction for developing programs and organizing schools and classrooms to make the most effective use of the time and abilities of students and teachers.[3]

Clarifying our priorities

In many cases when we speak of aims, however, the language is so general that we cannot agree on the intent. For example, what does the phrase "to prepare students for democratic citizenship" mean? What do people have in mind when they claim that the "schools should stress citizenship preparation?" We must recognize that aims only suggest a direction for people to follow. They are too vague either to tell parents what the schools are attempting to accomplish or to tell teachers what they are expected to teach or what their students are expected to learn. In communicating aims, the schools need to translate them into statements that will coincide more closely with the philosophy and priorities of their own communities.[4] These translations correspond to goals.

Goals

Goals are sometimes called *mission statements* or *intermediate objectives*. They are formulated at the school district level and school level, usually by a committee consisting of a group of administrators, teachers, and/or community members. Goals are derived from the perceived priorities and needs of the local community as well as from the educational aims of the nation or state.

*Goals are derived
from aims*

An example of a goal under our citizenship aim might be, "to be involved in the political and social life of the community." For the aim of vocational preparation, the corresponding goal might read, "to acquire knowledge of personal aptitudes and interests pertaining to career possibilities." These goals in turn serve as guides for developing classroom objectives that are more specific.

School goals expanded

Goals for schools have been so expanded that today's schools may be attempting to achieve too many things for all students and may not be doing many of them well enough. As educators frequently point out, schools have been increasingly burdened with the tasks and responsibilities that other social institutions, especially the family, no longer do well, or care to do.[5] The outcome is

---

[3]Albert Shanker, "The End of the Traditional Model of Schooling," *Phi Delta Kappan* (January 1990), pp. 344–357; Theodore R. Sizer, "No Pain, No Gain," *Educational Leadership* (May 1991), pp. 32–34.

[4]Elliot W. Eisner, *The Educational Imagination*, 3rd. (New York: Macmillan, 1993); Decker F. Walker, *Fundamentals of Curriculum* (San Diego: Harcourt Brace Jovanovich, 1990).

[5]Raymond L. Calabrese, "Alienation: The Secondary School At Risk," *NASSP Bulletin* (February 1989), pp. 72–76; Ronald S. Brandt and Ralph W. Tyler, "Goals and Objectives," in F. W. English, ed., *Fundamental Curriculum Decisions*, 1983 ASCD Yearbook (Alexandria, Va.: Association for Supervision and Curriculum Department, 1983), pp. 40–52; and Allan C. Ornstein, "How Do Educators Meet the Needs of Society?" *NASSP Bulletin* (May 1985), pp. 36–47.

Table 13.1 ——
Major Goals of American Schools

1. *Mastery of basic skills or fundamental process.* In our technological civilization, an individual's ability to participate in the activities of society depends on mastery of these fundamental processes.

2. *Career or vocational education.* An individual's satisfaction in life will be significantly related to satisfaction with her or his job. Intelligent career decisions will require knowledge of personal aptitudes and interests in relation to career possibilities.

3. *Intellectual development.* As civilization has become more complex, people have had to rely more heavily on their rational abilities. Full intellectual development of each member of society is necessary.

4. *Enculturation.* Studies that illuminate our relationship with the past yield insights into our society and its values; further, these strengthen an individual's sense of belonging, identity, and direction for his or her own life.

5. *Interpersonal relations.* Schools should help every child understand, appreciate, and value persons belonging to social, cultural, and ethnic groups different from his or her own.

6. *Autonomy.* Unless schools produce self-directed citizens, they have failed both society and the individual. As society becomes more complex, demands on individuals multiply. Schools help prepare children for a world of rapid change by developing in them the capacity to assume responsibility for their own needs.

7. *Citizenship.* To counteract the present human ability to destroy humanity and the environment requires citizen involvement in the political and social life of this country. A democracy can survive only through the participation of its members.

8. *Creativity and aesthetic perception.* Abilities for creating new and meaningful things and appreciating the creations of other human beings are essential both for personal self-realization and for the benefit of society.

9. *Self-concept.* The self-concept of an individual serves as a reference point and feedback mechanism for personal goals and aspirations. Facilitating factors for a healthy self-concept can be provided in the school environment.

10. *Emotional and physical well-being.* Emotional stability and physical fitness are perceived as necessary conditions for attaining the other goals, but they are also worthy ends in themselves.

11. *Moral and ethical character.* Individuals need to develop the judgment that allows us to evaluate behavior as right or wrong. Schools can foster the growth of such judgment as well as a commitment to truth, moral integrity, and moral conduct.

12. *Self-realization.* Efforts to develop a better self contribute to the development of a better society.

Source: Adapted from John I. Goodlad, *What Are Schools For?* (Bloomington, Ind.: Phi Delta Kappa, 1979), pp. 44–52. Reprinted with permission.

that parents continue to put pressure on schools not to drop any of the goals that have emerged over the past years.

Categorizing goals

John Goodlad and his associates have synthesized the school goals published by local boards of education across the country. From approximately one hundred different goals, Goodlad identified a cluster of twelve that represented the spirit of the total list. Each can be further defined by a rationale statement, as shown in Table 13.1. By and large, these goals have not changed much over the years; rather, the emphasis has varied depending on the school district's or school's philosophy and the way it has interpreted the forces of social change.

Tyler's four questions

In developing goals for our own schools, Ralph Tyler's outline has become a model to follow. Tyler identified four fundamental questions that need to be considered:

1. What educational purposes should the school seek to attain?

Aims, goals, and objectives — which help teachers define educational purposes — are influenced by social forces and prevailing theories of education. (© Robert Finken/ The Picture Cube)

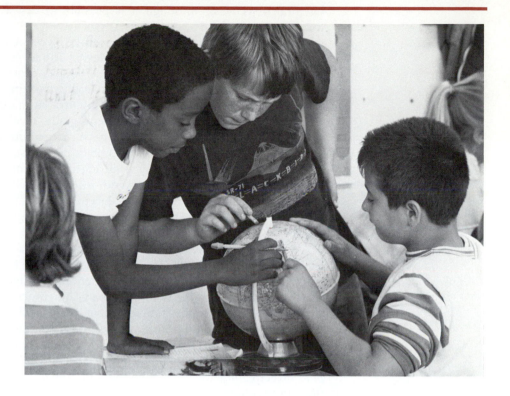

2. What educational experiences can be provided to help attain these purposes?

3. How can these educational experiences be effectively organized?

4. How can we determine whether [and to what extent] the purposes have been attained?[6]

Goals are not behavioral

When translating aims into goals, some educators expect the latter to be narrowly defined and written in terms of specific behaviors. This is not the case. Goals, like aims, are usually written in nonbehavioral terms and are not tied to particular content or subject matter. By describing what the schools intend to accomplish, goals provide a general direction, but they are still too vague for teachers and students to use in the classroom. For classroom use, goals must be translated into more specific objectives.

Objectives

Observing and measuring objectives

Objectives are formulated to organize content and learning experiences in behavioral terms; that is, content and experiences are stated in such a way as to be observed and measured. Consequently, many objectives are also called "be-

---

[6]Tyler, *Basic Principles of Curriculum and Instruction,* p. 1.

havioral objectives," although it is possible to devise "nonbehavioral objectives."[7]

Objectives are generally written at three levels of instruction: subject/grade level, unit plan level, and lesson plan level.[8] The level of specificity increases as we move toward lesson plan objectives. Subject-centered professional associations (such as the National Council of Teachers of English or the National Science Teachers Association) often publish curriculum guides that prescribe subject objectives, sometimes for different grade levels. State departments of education and larger school districts have curriculum departments or committees at the central office that develop objectives by subject and grade level. Occasionally, teachers are employed during the summer to work in committees that devise such objectives, along with recommended content and learning experiences. An example of a subject objective in citizenship for eighth-grade history might be "to discuss how laws protect the rights of all people within a society."

Subject/grade level objectives

Textbook publishers often require their authors to develop unit plan and lesson plan objectives. These objectives may be listed in the front of each chapter or in the teacher's manual. Teachers themselves often develop their own unit plan and lesson plan objectives, which are sometimes evaluated by the teachers' supervisors. An example of an objective in citizenship at the *unit plan* level is "to identify how the U.S. Constitution protects the rights of American citizens." This unit might take two or three weeks to teach, and the content and learning experiences would depend on the grade level and ability of the students. A *lesson plan* objective in citizenship might be "to prepare a chart illustrating the functions of the three branches of government." This lesson would be completed in one class period, 45 to 55 minutes.

Unit plan and lesson plan objectives

Overview 13.1 summarizes the differences among aims, goals, and objectives. Note that as we move from aims to objectives, the examples become more specific — that is, they are easier to measure or observe. To gain a better understanding of how general priorities are translated into specific educational outcomes, we will look at three methods of writing objectives: the educational taxonomy, the Gronlund approach, and the Mager method.

Taxonomy.   One way of translating aims and goals into instructional objectives is to categorize the desired outcomes according to a classification scheme analogous to the systems used to classify books in a library, chemical elements in a periodic table, or members of the animal kingdom. Such a classification system, known as an educational **taxonomy,** establishes standards for classifying objectives and allows educators to communicate better and add precision to their language. Such objectives can be used at the subject/grade and unit plan levels. They can also be used at the lesson plan level, although some educators might argue that they are too general for this purpose.

---

[7]Ronald C. Doll, *Curriculum Improvement: Decision Making and Process,* 8th ed. (Needham Heights, Mass.: Allyn and Bacon, 1992); Allan C. Ornstein and Francis P. Hunkins, *Curriculum: Foundations, Principles, and Issues,* 2nd ed. (Needham Heights, Mass.: Allyn and Bacon, 1993).
[8]George J. Posner and Alan N. Rudnitsky, *Course Design: A Guide to Curriculum Development for Teachers,* 4th ed. (New York: Longman, 1992); Taba, *Curriculum Development.*

Overview 13.1 ◄━●━

Aims, Goals, and Objectives

Ends	Influenced by	Level of Direction	Developed by	Example(s)
Aims of education	Philosophy or theory of education; conditions of society	Nation, state	Commissions, task force groups, broad professional associations	To improve basic literacy skills
Goals of education	Aims of education; conditions of local community	School district, school	Groups of administrators, teachers, and/or community members; broad professional associations	To acquire information and meaning through reading, writing, speaking, and mathematical symbols
Objectives of education	Goals of education	Subject/grade	Subject-centered professional associations; curriculum departments or committees of state departments of education; curriculum departments or committees of large school districts	To improve reading comprehension To appreciate reading whole books
		Unit plan	Textbook authors; teachers	To develop word recognition skills To listen to stories read
		Lesson plan	Textbook authors; teachers	To identify the main ideas of the author To write ten new vocabulary words

The educational taxonomy divides learning into three domains: *cognitive, affective,* and *psychomotor.* Handbooks of objectives for the first two of these domains were developed by the American Educational Research Association.[9] In each domain the taxonomy describes levels of knowledge ranging from the simple to the more advanced. In the cognitive domain, which relates to knowledge and higher intellectual skills, the taxonomy includes six major categories arranged in hierarchical order: (1) *knowledge,* or recall of facts and principles; (2) *comprehension,* which includes translation and interpretation of ideas and methods; (3) *application,* or using principles and abstractions in particular situations; (4) *analysis,* breaking a whole into parts and distinguishing relationships; (5) *synthesis,* putting parts together in a new form; and (6) *evaluation,* judging facts, logic, or evidence.

Cognitive domain

In the affective domain, which includes objectives related to attitudes, feelings, and interests, there are five hierarchical categories: (1) *receiving,* which involves sensitivity to or awareness of stimuli; (2) *responding,* including active attention and willing responses; (3) *valuing,* related to preferences and commitments concerning beliefs and attitudes; (4) *organization,* involving internalization or conceptualization of values; and (5) *characterization,* the formation of a generalized set of values or philosophy of life.

Affective domain

Although the original group of educators never completed work on the psychomotor domain, several scholars and subject-matter specialists have described similar categories for psychomotor objectives. In all three domains the arrangement of particular steps in the hierarchy may be open to argument. For example, is evaluation (what an art or drama critic might do) truly a higher form of cognition than synthesis (what an artist or playwright does when creating a new work)? Nevertheless, the taxonomy provides a useful tool for developing new objectives, categorizing and grouping existing sets of objectives, and formulating test items.

General Objectives and Specific Outcomes.   Norman Gronlund has developed a flexible method for formulating objectives whereby the teacher moves from a general objective to a series of specific learning outcomes.[10] Gronlund recommends that teachers start with generalized objectives because learning is too complex to be described adequately in terms of specific behaviors. He provides a list of general objectives that can be used for nearly any subject or grade;[11] the reason is they are not content oriented.

General objectives

1. Knows basic terminology

2. Understands concepts and principles

3. Applies principles to new situations

---

[9]Benjamin S. Bloom et al., *Taxonomy of Educational Objectives, Handbook I: Cognitive Domain* (New York: McKay, 1956); David R. Krathwohl, Benjamin S. Bloom, and Bertram Masia, *Taxonomy of Educational Objectives, Handbook II: Affective Domain* (New York: McKay, 1964).

[10]Norman E. Gronlund and Robert L. Linn, *Measurement and Evaluation in Teaching,* 6th ed. (New York: Macmillan, 1990).

[11]Ibid., p. 39.

4. Interprets charts and graphs

5. Writes a well-organized theme

6. Demonstrates skill in critical thinking

For each of these general objectives, the teacher would then develop several specific learning outcomes. For example, under general objective 6 (critical thinking), we might write the following specific outcomes:[12]

Specific outcomes

a. Distinguishes between fact and opinion

b. Distinguishes between relevant and irrelevant information

c. Identifies fallacious reasoning in written material

d. Identifies the limitations of given data

e. Formulates valid conclusions from given data

f. Identifies the assumptions underlying conclusions

Specific Objectives.   Robert Mager is more precise in formulating objectives. His objectives have three characteristics: (1) the *behavior* of the learner when demonstrating his or her achievement of the objective, (2) the *conditions* imposed upon the learner when demonstrating the mastery of the objective, and (3) the *minimum proficiency* level that will be acceptable.[13] To write a behavioral objective in American history using Mager's approach, we might state:

> The student is to read the biography of Benjamin Franklin. He or she is then to prepare a 1,000-word oral statement combining three or more important facets of the man's life in a 5-minute presentation to the class to be judged successful by at least three out of five students who have also read the biography.

One more example should suffice, this time in science:

> After studying the unit, the student must be able to complete a 100-item multiple-choice examination on the subject of pollution. Acceptable performance will be 80 items answered correctly within an examination period of 60 minutes.

Debate on specificity of objectives

Some educators strongly advocate this specific approach, claiming that it helps teachers define objectives exactly.[14] Test specialists particularly like objectives to be precise so that student performance is easy to measure. Training specialists in private industry and the military also prefer concise objectives written in tiny steps and sequential form. However, many educators prefer a less specific approach like that of Gronlund's method or the educational taxonomy. They contend that Mager's procedure produces an unmanageable number of objectives, leads to trivia, and wastes time; they also argue that it is difficult to pre-

---

[12]Ibid., p. 40.

[13]Robert F. Mager, *Preparing Instructional Objectives,* rev. ed. (Belmont, Calif.: Fearon, 1984).

[14]Robert M. Gagné, *The Conditions of Learning,* 4th ed. (New York: Holt, Rinehart and Winston, 1985); Robert Kibler, Larry L. Baker, and David T. Miles, *Behavioral Objectives and Instruction,* 2nd ed. (Boston: Allyn and Bacon, 1981); and W. James Popham, *Modern Educational Measurement,* 2nd ed. (Englewood Cliffs, N.J.: Prentice-Hall, 1990).

scribe such specific objectives in advance.[15] Most teachers would agree that a strict adherence to Mager's method would become too mechanistic and rigid.

HISTORICAL PERSPECTIVE

We live in an era when educators and the public at large are questioning the purposes of American education. What is it that our schools should be trying to do? The answers are varied, and the debate has often been heated. To understand this debate, we need to know how educational purposes have developed and changed over the years. As the following sections illustrate, the aims of American education have undergone many transformations.

The Mental Discipline Approach

Value of the mental discipline approach

Prior to the twentieth century, the perennialist theory generally dominated American education. Subject matter was organized and presented as a mere accounting of information. Changes were made largely within the broad framework of existing subjects to improve reasoning and mental faculties. Proponents of the **mental discipline approach** believed that the mind is strengthened through mental exercises, just as the body is strengthened by exercising. Social and psychological concerns of the learner were largely ignored. Traditional subjects, such as Latin and geometry, were valued for their cultivation of the intellect; the more difficult the subject and the more the student had to exercise the mind, the greater the value of the subject.

Three major committees (the Committee of Fifteen on Elementary Education, the Committee of Ten on Secondary School Studies, and the Committee on College Entrance Requirements), organized by the National Education Association (NEA) between 1892 and 1895, strengthened this educational mold for years to come. As Ellwood Cubberley pointed out, "The committees were dominated by subject-matter specialists, possessed of a profound faith in mental discipline. No study of pupil abilities, social needs, interest, capabilities or differential training found a place in their [committee members'] deliberations."[16]

Nine academic subjects

The Committee of Ten's recommendations best illustrate this tough-minded, mental discipline approach. The committee, headed by one of the most influential figures of the time, Harvard University President Charles Eliot, selected nine academic subjects around which to organize the high-school curriculum: (1) Latin, (2) Greek, (3) English, (4) modern languages such as French and German, (5) mathematics, (6) physics, astronomy, and chemistry, (7) natural history (biology, botany, zoology, and physiology), (8) history, civil government, and political economy, and (9) geography, geology, and meteorology.[17]

---

[15]Gordon H. Bower and Ernest R. Hilgard, *Theories of Learning,* 5th ed. (Englewood Cliffs, N.J.: Prentice-Hall, 1981); Robert L. Ebel and David A. Frisbie, *Essentials of Educational Measurement,* 5th ed. (Needham Heights, Mass.: Allyn and Bacon, 1991); and Robert Glaser, ed., *Advances in Instructional Psychology,* vol. 3 (Hillsdale, N.J.: Erlbaum, 1986).

[16]Ellwood P. Cubberley, *Public Education in the United States,* rev. ed. (Boston: Houghton Mifflin, 1947), p. 543.

[17]*Report of the Committee of Ten on Secondary School Studies* (Washington, D.C.: National Education Association, 1894).

The committee's refusal to recognize the value of art, music, physical education, and vocational courses was based on the theory that these subjects had little mental or disciplinary value.

The committee further suggested that all of its nine recommended subjects except Latin and Greek be taught at the elementary school level. Even though less than 5 percent of the students at that time went to college, this college preparatory program established a curriculum hierarchy, from elementary school to college, that promoted academics and ignored the majority of students who were noncollege bound.

Progressive education as a new pedagogy

Gradually, however, demands were made for various changes in the school to meet the needs of a changing social order. The pace of immigration and industrial development led a growing number of educators to question the classical curriculum and the constant emphasis on mental discipline and to oppose the methods of incessant drill. The adherents of the new pedagogy represented the growing and influential progressive voice in education. They emphasized schoolwork and school subjects designed to meet the needs of everyday life for *all* children. By the turn of the twentieth century, the effort to reform the schools along more progressive lines was moving into full swing. Out of this movement came a number of committees and organized groups whose new educational aims are still influential.

Cardinal Principles

Perhaps the most widely accepted list of educational aims in the twentieth century was compiled by the NEA's Commission on the Reorganization of Secondary Education in 1918. Its influential bulletin, which reflected the rise of progressivism, was entitled ***Cardinal Principles of Secondary Education.*** The seven areas of life, or aims of secondary education, designated by the commission are as follows:

1. *Health.* The secondary school should . . . provide health instruction, inculcate health habits, organize an effective program of physical activities, regard health needs in planning work and play, and co-operate with home and community in safeguarding and promoting health interests. . . .

2. *Command of fundamental processes.* The facility that a child of twelve or fourteen years may acquire . . . is not sufficient for the needs of modern life. [Further instruction in the fundamentals is urged.]

3. *Worthy home membership.* Worthy home membership as an objective calls for the development of those qualities that make the individual a worthy member of a family, both contributing to and deriving benefit from that membership. . . .

Broadened aims of education

4. *Vocation.* Vocational education should equip the individual to secure a livelihood for himself and those dependent on him, to serve society well through his vocation, to maintain the right relationships toward his fellow workers and society, and, as far as possible, to find in that vocation his own best development. . . .

5. *Civic education.* Civic education should develop in the individual those qualities whereby he will act well his part as a member of neighborhood, town or city, state, and nation, and give him a basis for understanding international problems. . . .

6. *Worthy use of leisure.* Education should equip the individual to secure from his leisure the recreation of body, mind, and spirit, and the enrichment and enlargement of his personality. . . .

7. *Ethical character.* In a democratic society ethical character becomes paramount among the objectives of the secondary school. Among the means for developing ethical character may be mentioned the wise selection of content and methods of instruction in all subjects of study and the social contacts of pupils with one another and with their teachers.[18]

The aims cited in 1918 are still found in one form or another in statements of major aims of contemporary education, as may be seen from the discussion to follow. The most important aspect of the document is that it emphasized the aim of secondary schools to educate *all* youth for "complete living," not just college-bound youth for mental rigor.

Educate all youth for "complete living"

The Purposes of Education in American Democracy

Twenty years later the Educational Policies Commission of the NEA, which included the presidents of Harvard and Cornell, the U.S. commissioner of education, and a number of progressive pedagogical specialists, issued a report entitled *The Purposes of Education in American Democracy.*[19]

Concerned with the problems of out-of-school youth and unemployment resulting from the Great Depression and with the general need to adjust to daily life patterns, these educators put forth a comprehensive set of four equally important aims (which they called objectives): (1) self-realization, (2) human relations, (3) economic efficiency, and (4) civic responsibility. *Self-realization* pertained to the inquiring mind, speech, reading, writing, numbers, sight and hearing, health knowledge, health habits, public health, recreation, intellectual interests, aesthetic interests, and character formation. *Human relations* concerned respect for humanity, friendship, cooperation with others, courtesy, appreciation of the home, conservation of the home, homemaking, and democracy in the home. *Economic efficiency* encompassed work, occupational information, occupational choice, occupational efficiency, occupational appreciation, personal economics, consumer judgment, efficiency in buying, and consumer protection. *Civic responsibility* related to social justice, social activity, social understanding, critical judgment, tolerance, conservation of resources, social applications of science, world citizenship, law observance, economic literacy, political citizenship, and devotion to democracy.

Aims in the 1930s

Education for All American Youth

During the mid-1940s, the Educational Policies Commission of the NEA continued to modify and formulate the aims of education. Influenced by World War II, it stressed aims related to democracy and world citizenship as well as those related to the general needs of children and youth. Its most influential report, *Education for All American Youth,* listed "Ten Imperative Needs of

Aims in the 1940s

---

[18]Commission on the Reorganization of Secondary Education, *Cardinal Principles of Secondary Education,* Bulletin no. 35 (Washington, D.C.: U.S. Government Printing Office, 1918), pp. 11–15.

[19]Educational Policies Commission, *The Purposes of Education in American Democracy* (Washington, D.C.: National Education Association, 1938).

Underlying the whole-child movement was the view that schools should be concerned with the development of the entire child, not just with selected mental aspects of the child's growth. (© Peter Vandermark/ Stock Boston)

Youth." All youth need to develop skills and/or attitudes that enhance the following: (1) productive work experiences and occupational success, (2) good health and physical fitness, (3) rights and duties of a democratic citizenry, (4) conditions for successful family life, (5) wise consumer behavior, (6) understanding of science and the nature of man, (7) appreciation of arts, music, and literature, (8) wise use of leisure time, (9) respect for ethical values, and (10) the ability to think rationally and communicate thoughts clearly.[20]

Prior to World War I, the aims of education had represented a perennialist philosophy of education and a mental discipline approach to learning. During the period from the 1918 Seven Cardinal Principles to the 1944 Ten Imperative Needs, the aims were dominated by the philosophy of progressivism and by the offshoot science of child psychology. During this period, emphasis was placed

---

[20]Educational Policies Commission, *Education for All American Youth* (Washington, D.C.: National Education Association, 1944).

The whole-child concept

on the *whole child* and on life adjustment; hence, educational aims stressed social, psychological, vocational, moral, and civic responsibilities. Aims related to cognitive or mental growth were not preeminent at this time; they were simply on a par with other important aims of education. The **whole-child concept** and the corresponding growth of child psychology had a tremendous impact on the schools. Underlying this movement was the view that schools had to be concerned with the growth and development of the entire child, not just with certain selected mental aspects of the child's growth.

Focus on the Academically Talented

During the era of the Cold War and the Soviet *Sputnik* flight (1957), international events gave major impetus to the movement to reexamine subject matter. The country was appalled at the notion of losing technological superiority to the Soviets; national pride was challenged; national goals were threatened; and physical survival seemed to be at stake.

Return to academic essentials

The critics claimed that there was too much stress on the whole child and on general education at the expense of intellectual rigor. Influenced by the perennialist and essentialist theories of education, they called for a return to academic essentials and mental discipline. "Concern with the personal problems of adolescents [had] grown so excessive as to push into the background what should be the school's central concern, the intellectual development of its students," stated noted historian Arthur Bestor.[21] Admiral Hyman Rickover wondered why Johnny could not read while Ivan could and did. Rickover demanded a return to the basics, a beefing up of our science and mathematics courses, and a "de-emphasis of life-adjustment schools and progressive educationalists."[22]

National legislation to support our aims

Hard on the heels of *Sputnik* came national legislation to support training, equipment, and programs in fields deemed vital to defense. The major legislation was the National Defense Education Act, which singled out science, mathematics, modern languages, and guidance (often thought of as a way to steer youth into the three former fields and into college if they had the ability). The focus on certain subjects was often couched in terms of a free people surviving in a world threatened by the spread of communism. The scientific community, university scholars, and curriculum specialists were called upon to reconstruct subject-matter content, especially on the high-school level; government and foundation sources provided the funds.[23] John Gardner, president of the Carnegie Corporation, expressed the crucial needs as follows: "It is not just technologists and scientists that we need, though they rank high in priority. We desperately need our gifted teachers, our professional men, our scholars, our critics, and our seers."[24]

---

[21]Arthur Bestor, *The Restoration of Learning* (New York: Knopf, 1956), p. 120.

[22]Hyman G. Rickover, *Education and Freedom* (New York: Dutton, 1959), p. 190.

[23]William Van Til, "In a Climate of Change," in E. F. Carlson, ed., *Role of Supervisor and Curriculum Director in a Climate of Change*, 1965 ASCD Yearbook (Washington, D.C.: Association for Supervision and Curriculum Development, 1965), p. 21.

[24]John W. Gardner, "The Great Talent Hunt," *Annual Report for the Fiscal Year Ended September 30, 1956* (New York: Carnegie Corporation, 1956), p. 12.

Emphasis on academically talented

The new educational climate included an increasing emphasis on providing topnotch education for the academically talented child. In 1952, as chairperson of the Educational Policies Commission, James Conant had endorsed a progressive policy document that urged a student-centered, whole-child approach to schooling. By 1959, after visiting fifty-five high schools with "good reputations" across the country, Conant concluded, "I think one general criticism would be in order: The academically talented student, as a rule, is not being sufficiently challenged, does not work hard enough, and his program of academic subjects is not of sufficient range."[25]

Moderate reform

Conant's influential book, *The American High School Today*, was a blueprint for moderate reform — that is, for upgrading the curriculum in general, especially mathematics, science, and foreign language; requiring more academic subjects; tightening standards and grades; pushing students to their maximum cognitive potential; and grouping students according to their abilities. Although he gave some consideration to slow and average learners, his major emphasis for reform pertained to serving the needs of the highly gifted (the intellectually highest 3 percent of the student population on a national basis) and the academically talented (the top 20 percent in terms of scholastic aptitude).

Focus on Disadvantaged Students

During the 1960s the social conscience of America burst forth, bringing increased concern about poverty, racial discrimination, and equal educational opportunity. Hence, new aims and educational priorities surfaced, often related to the progressive and social reconstructionist theories of education. Educators noted that the majority of students did not go on to college and a large percentage of students dropped out of school or graduated as functional illiterates. Under those circumstances, serious problems could be anticipated if our aims and priorities continued to be narrowly directed toward our most able students.

Excellence and equality

At first the shift in priorities was gradual, and this can be illustrated by John Gardner's concern for both the talented and the underachieving child, for both excellence and equality: "No democracy can give itself over to extreme emphasis on individual performance and still remain a democracy — or to extreme equalitarianism and still retain its vitality. . . . A society such as ours has no choice but to seek the development of human potentialities at all levels."[26] Gardner noted that extreme forms of equalitarianism and proportional representation of groups in school or jobs tend to eliminate both excellence and merit, but that, on the other hand, extreme forms of elitism based on excellence and merit could create a permanent underclass among the less able. He tried to draw a middle position, sounding a note of urgency that other educators would soon echo.

A middle position

In 1961, the same year that John Gardner's book was published, James Conant wrote *Slums and Suburbs*. Only two years before, Conant had advocated academic rigor and upgraded academic subjects, as well as greater attention to

---

[25]James B. Conant, *The American High School Today* (New York: McGraw-Hill, 1959), p. 40.
[26]John W. Gardner, *Excellence: Can We Be Equal and Excellent Too?* (New York: Harper & Row, 1961), pp. 28–29, 77.

Closer attention to the disadvantaged child

the top 20 percent of the high-school graduates. Now he urged educators and policy makers to pay closer attention to the inner-city and disadvantaged child:

> I am concerned we are allowing social dynamite to accumulate in our large cities. I am not nearly so concerned about the plight of the suburban parents [and their children] who have difficulty finding places in prestige colleges as I am about the plight of parents in the slums whose children either drop out or graduate from school without prospects of either future education or employment.[27]

Given the student unrest and urban riots of the 1960s, it was easy to accept the arguments of an impending crisis. Conant's new position was a sign of the times — a shift in educational aims to focus on the disadvantaged. Historically a strong advocate of academic excellence, and a former scientist, he was expressing a new viewpoint: one that would correct the educational discrepancies among students by placing greater emphasis on less able students, especially inner-city students. To some educators, however, it appeared that the new emphasis tended to overlook the average and above-average student — the group that represented what was later to be called "middle America."

Expanded Priorities

The focus on disadvantaged students extended into the 1970s and was expanded to include multicultural and bilingual students and students with disabilities. Our multicultural and bilingual efforts were characterized by increased federal funding for Hispanic, Asian American, and Native American students; by the Bilingual Education Act in 1968, which expanded bilingual programs in American schools; and by the 1974 U.S. Supreme Court ruling in *Lau* v. *Nichols*, which stated that schools must take steps to help students who "are certain to find their classroom experiences wholly incomprehensible" because they do not understand English. The courts, as well as policy makers and educators, took an active role in providing educational opportunities for limited-English-proficient and non-English-proficient students. Despite controversies concerning specific approaches and programs, multicultural and bilingual education are growing in importance and will continue to influence our schools through the 1990s.

Multicultural and bilingual programs

Students with disabilities

During the 1970s and 1980s, much concern surfaced for special education, especially for students with learning disabilities or other handicaps. The cornerstone of these new policies and programs was the Education for All Handicapped Children Act, passed in 1975. As described in Chapter 11, this legislation mandated a free and appropriate public education for all children and youth with disabilities. The Act was amended in 1986 to extend the full rights and protection of this law to children aged 3 through 5. It also permitted the schools to identify these young children as "developmentally delayed" rather than by the category of handicap.[28]

Today, concern for children with disabilities is very much alive, and the courts continue to take an active role in protecting their rights and improving educational opportunities for them. Monies earmarked for these students con-

---

[27]James B. Conant, *Slums and Suburbs* (New York: McGraw-Hill, 1961), p. 2.

[28]Allan C. Ornstein, Daniel U. Levine, and Janet W. Lerner, "Education of Young Handicapped and At-Risk Children," *Illinois School Research and Development* (Fall 1989), pp. 24–32.

tinue to increase in real dollars and in proportion to spending on nonhandi-capped students; morever, an increasing number of students are identified as having disabilities.[29] This increase indicates that educators and policy makers recognize that many students who did not receive help in the past in fact need special help — not that contemporary students have more problems than students of earlier generations.

Students "at risk"

In the 1990s the term "at risk" has begun to replace the older term "disadvantaged," and the definition of students covered by the term has continued to expand. A category of the "new needy" has emerged, including some 250,000 to 500,000 homeless children, 250,000 to 300,000 crack-exposed babies born each year, and some 500,000 to 600,000 children of migrant workers.[30] Latchkey children, which comprise perhaps 60 to 65 percent of all American students, are also held to be potentially at risk because they lack adult supervision after school.[31] Some educators would further expand the at-risk category to include students who fall into any of these groups: (1) prematurely born, (2) abused or neglected, (3) substance addicted, (4) pregnant, (5) gang or cult members, (6) infected with the HIV virus, (7) living in a single-parent family. These educators would also include all children whose parents are (1) school dropouts, (2) teen-aged, (3) HIV infected, (4) divorced, (5) drug- or alcohol-dependent, or (6) incarcerated.[32]

Expansion of the at-risk category

High numbers at risk

Adding all these groups to the categories traditionally used to describe disadvantaged students — low income, minority, immigrant, bilingual, handicapped — we confront a situation in which more than 90 percent of the U.S. student population might be considered at risk and in need of extra assistance in school. Although many would argue that 90 percent is too pessimistic and extreme a number, a figure of that magnitude does help to explain the dramatic decline in U.S. student achievement compared to achievement in other industrialized nations and why our workforce seems unable to compete with other industrialized nations. Whatever the precise definition of "at-risk" that educators adopt, they must face the fact that educational reform efforts may fail if the needs of these students are not addressed.

Concern for the average student

As concern for at-risk students has widened, some educators have increasingly begun to worry that the needs of the "average" student may be neglected. In the last several decades, national priorities for the most part have not focused on the ordinary student who is nonrich, nonpoor, nonminority, nongifted, and nonnewsworthy. There has been very little in the educational literature on the cultural, social, and educational diversity of students in middle America or

---

[29]*Thirteenth Annual Report to Congress on the Implementation of the Education of the Handicapped Act* (Washington, D.C.: U.S. Government Printing Office, 1991).

[30]"The New Needy," *Education Digest* (February 1990), pp. 70–71; Martha R. Burt, "Roots and Remedies of Homelessness," Urban Institute Policy and Research Report (Summer 1991), pp. 1–5; *The Effects of Migration upon Children* (Washington, D.C.: U.S. Office of Education, 1989); and Marilee C. Rist, "The Shadow Children," *American School Board Journal* (January 1989), pp. 19–24.

[31]Lynette Long and Thomas R. Long, "Latchkey Adolescents: How Administrators Can Respond to Their Needs," *NASSP Bulletin* (February 1989), pp. 102–108.

[32]Allan C. Ornstein, "Enrollment Trends in Big-City Schools," *Peabody Journal of Education* (Summer 1989), pp. 64–71; David C. Smith and Edward E. Greene, "Preparing Tomorrow's Principals Today," *Principal* (September 1990), pp. 20–24.

small-town U.S.A. Particularly in larger schools, these students may be over-looked, falling into the cracks in the educational system.[33] The educational reform movement, described in the next section, has brought some attention to these students as part of the national demand for excellence in schools; nevertheless, special programs and services for the average child remain minimal, as do special programs for schools in rural America and in the small towns and suburbs adjacent to the large cities. Most people would hopefully agree that some balance is needed in terms of funding and focusing on various student populations.

THE CALL FOR EXCELLENCE

Now that we have surveyed the ways in which American educational aims have changed over time, we can look more closely at the contemporary demand for reform in the schools. As you read this section, keep the historical background in mind. How do various recent proposals reflect important changes in American educational aims? How well do particular reforms fit your own ideas about the purpose of education?

Overview of Policy Reports

By the early 1980s national attention began to focus on the need for educational excellence and higher academic standards for all students, not just the disadvantaged or the talented. In the years since then, a number of national policy reports, most of them reflecting what has been called a neoessentialist perspective, have called urgently for reforms to improve the quality of education in the United States. To support their proposals, the reports have presented a host of devastating details and statistics indicating a fundamental decline in American education. For example:

Policy reports call for reform

1. Average achievement scores on the Scholastic Aptitude Test (SAT) demonstrated a virtually unbroken decline from 1963 to 1988. Average verbal scores fell 38 points (466 to 428), and mathematics scores dropped 21 points (492 to 471).[34]

Declining test scores

2. In 1991 only 20 percent of eighth-grade students achieved math competency for their grade level; the remaining 80 percent scored below their grade level. Among twelfth-grade students, only 14 percent were capable of performing at grade level and only 2.6 percent were capable of advanced work such as calculus or statistics.[35]

3. International comparisons of student achievement in the last fifteen years revealed that on nineteen academic tests U.S. students were never first or

International comparisons

---

[33]Allan C. Ornstein, "School District and School Size: An Evolving Controversy," *Clearing House* (December 1989), pp. 156–158; Ornstein, "School Size and Effectiveness: Policy Implications," *Urban Review* (September 1990), pp. 239–245.

[34]*Digest of Education Statistics, 1989* (Washington, D.C.: U.S. Government Printing Office, 1989), Table 108, p. 120.

[35]Barbara Kantrowitz and Pat Wingert, "A Nation Running in Place," *Newsweek*, October 14, 1991, p. 54.

second and, in comparison with other industrialized nations, were last seven times. In 1988 they scored last in math (averaging 94 points below first-ranked Korea) and next to last in science (averaging 71 points below first-ranked Korea). U.S. students also scored last in geographical knowledge; more than 33 percent lower than their first-ranked counterparts in Sweden.[36]

Functional illiteracy

4. Some 23 to 25 million U.S. adults are functionally illiterate by the simplest tests of everyday reading and writing. Moreover, about 13 percent of all seventeen-year-olds in the United States are considered functionally illiterate, and this illiteracy rate jumps to 40 percent among minority youth. Twenty-six percent of all American students never graduate high school.[37]

Expensive remedial education

5. Business and military leaders complain that they are required to spend millions of dollars annually on costly remedial education and training programs in the basic skills, or three Rs. Colleges face the same problem: in 1990, 21 percent of college freshmen enrolled in remedial mathematics, 16 percent in remedial writing, and 13 percent in remedial reading. A total of 30 percent of all college freshmen took at least one remedial course, and 74 percent of the nation's colleges and universities offered remedial courses.[38]

Student-teacher ratios

6. These problems have occurred despite a relatively good student-teacher ratio. In 1988 the American ratio of students to teachers was 17 to 1, seventh best in the world. Such countries as Japan and Korea had student-teacher ratios of over 30 to 1. Moreover, our per-pupil expenditures for education K to college were the second highest in the world (only about $300 less than first-ranked Switzerland).[39]

These deficiencies have come to light at a time when the demand for highly skilled military personnel and workers in labor and industry is accelerating rapidly and amidst growing concern that the United States is being overtaken by other nations in commerce, industry, science, and technology.

Ten of the national reports are summarized in Overview 13.2 on pages 506–510. Seven of them emphasize the need to strengthen the curriculum in the core subjects of English, math, science, foreign language, and social studies. The focus is thus on a common curriculum. Technology and computer courses are mentioned often, either as components of science or math or as a separate subject area (sometimes referred to as the fourth R). High-level cognitive and thinking skills are also stressed. Some of the reports are also concerned with programs and personnel for disadvantaged students and students with learning disabilities, although this message is not always loud and clear.

A common curriculum

---

[36]*The Condition of Education, 1989,* Vol. 1 (Washington, D.C.: U.S. Government Printing Office, 1989), Charts 1.3, 1.5, pp. 13, 17; *Digest of Education Statistics, 1989,* Tables 347, 349, pp. 390–391.

[37]*Digest of Education Statistics, 1990* (Washington, D.C.: U.S. Government Printing Office, 1990), Table 94, p. 108; National Commission on Excellence in Education, *A Nation at Risk: The Imperative of Educational Reform* (Washington, D.C.: U.S. Department of Education, 1983).

[38]Allan C. Ornstein, "The National Reports on Education: Implications for Directions and Aims," *Kappa Delta Pi Record* (Winter 1985), pp. 58–64; Mark Pitsch, "74% of Colleges Offer Remedial Courses," *Education Week,* May 22, 1991, p. 11.

[39]*The Condition of Education, 1989,* Chart 1.18, p. 107; *Digest of Education Statistics, 1989,* Table 340, p. 385. Also see John Hood, "Education: Money Isn't Everything," *The Wall Street Journal,* February 9, 1990, p. 14.

Overview 13.2

Selected Recommendations of Ten Reports on Education, 1983–1991

Report and Sponsor	Basic Recommendations	Content Emphasis	School Organization	Government-Business Role
Academic Preparation for College The College Board	Improve student competencies in reading, writing, speaking, listening, reasoning, math, and study skills Raise college entrance standards	English, math, science, computers, foreign language	Stress on study and independent learning Incentives to students	Develop a national standard for academic achievement in secondary education
Action for Excellence Education Commission of the States	Establish minimum competencies in reading, writing, speaking, listening, reasoning, and economics Strengthen program for gifted students Raise college entrance standards	English, math, science, foreign language, history, computer literacy	Consider longer school day Emphasize order and discipline More homework More rigorous grading with periodic testing Independent learning	Foster partnerships between private sector and education Increase federal funds for education
Educating Americans for the 21st Century National Science Foundation	Devote more time to math and science in elementary and secondary schools Provide more advanced courses in science and math Raise college entrance standards	Math, science, technology, computers	Consider longer school day, week, and/or year Twelve-year plan for math and science	With federal input, establish national goals for education Increase NSF role in curriculum development and teacher training

Report and Sponsor	Basic Recommendations	Content Emphasis	School Organization	Government-Business Role
High School Carnegie Foundation for Achievement in Teaching	Stress mastery of language, including reading, writing, speaking, and listening Expand basic academic curriculum Aid student transition to work and further education Strengthen graduation requirements	Core of common learning, including English, history, civics, math, science, technology Computer literacy	Improved working conditions for teachers Use of technology to enrich curriculum Flexible schedules and time allotments One track for all students School-community learning activities Greater leadership role for principal	Make "connections" between school and community, business, and universities Increase parent and community coalitions with and service to schools Utilize retired personnel from business and colleges Give federal scholarships to science and math teachers
Making the Grade Twentieth Century Fund	Improve basic skill programs Improve learning in English, math, and science Initiate general programs for students with learning problems and a voucher program for the disadvantaged	Basic skills English, math, and science Computer literacy	Rewards for teacher performance Special programs for poor, minority, handicapped, bilingual, and immigrant students	Increase federal aid for special programs for disadvantaged student populations Increase federal aid for programs to develop scientific literacy among all students and advanced math and science for academically able secondary students

Overview 13.2 (cont.)

Selected Recommendations of Ten Reports on Education, 1983–1991

Report and Sponsor	Basic Recommendations	Content Emphasis	School Organization	Government-Business Role
A Nation at Risk National Commission on Excellence in Education	Improve textbooks and other instructional materials Provide more rigorous courses in vocational education, arts, and science Strengthen graduation requirements Raise college entrance requirements	Five new basics: English, math, science, social studies, and computer science	Consider seven-hour school day Tighten attendance and discipline More homework More rigorous grading and periodic testing Group students by performance rather than age	Increase federal cooperation with states and localities Meet needs of disadvantaged student populations as well as gifted and talented Establish national standardized tests
First Lessons: A Report on Elementary Education in America The Secretary of Education	Improve basic skills for young children Improve complex learning tasks and abilities for older children Increase knowledge base essential for democratic society and national identity Improve textbook and workbook writing and selection Raise academic standards	Basic skills, especially reading through phonics Problem-solving skills in mathematics and hands-on learning and discovery in science Unified sequence stressing history, geography, and civics Computer literacy and cultural literacy	Longer school day More homework More rigorous testing Parental choice in children's schools Rewards for teacher performance	Increase communitywide and parental responsibility in education Require teacher and school accountability Improve training programs for elementary teachers; emphasize arts and science rather than methods courses

Report and Sponsor	Basic Recommendations	Content Emphasis	School Organization	Government-Business Role
The Disappearing Quality of the Workforce: What Can We Do to Save It? National Alliance of Business	Educate all youth in basic skills Provide students with high-level skills required for information and service society Restructure education; increase financial support Increase the quality of the nation's workforce	Basic skills, critical thinking skills Tutoring programs Raise academic standards and high-school graduation requirements	Increase attendance rates; reduce school dropout rates Increase adopt-a-school programs Teacher-administrative accountability Staff development/mentoring programs	Collaborative efforts between business and education groups Reshape education at state and local levels Involve citizen, parent, political, and business coalitions
Investing in People: A Strategy to Address America's Workforce Crisis U.S. Department of Labor	Commitment to literacy Increase federal and business support for education Upgrade standards for high-school graduation, college entry, and labor market Develop national goals and timetables to improve education and training	Basic skills programs for dropouts Literacy programs for adults Lifetime education and training Combine vocational and technical education	Increase attendance rates; reduce dropout rates Increase parent participation and community and business presence in schools Reduce competitive learning; increase cooperative learning More rigorous teacher training; test new teachers	Partnerships between business, labor, and government at all levels Teacher incentive and performance programs funded by business Increase government training programs to address labor needs Tax credits to private sector for educational and training programs

Overview 13.2 (cont.)

Selected Recommendations of Ten Reports on Education, 1983–1991

Report and Sponsor	Basic Recommendations	Content Emphasis	School Organization	Government-Business Role
National Goals for Education U.S. Department of Education	Focus on all students, with emphasis on at-risk students Equip students with knowledge and skills necessary for responsible citizenship and world of work Ensure readiness for school; upgrade school standards and student achievement Improve adult literacy and lifelong education Provide a safe and drug-free school environment	Basic knowledge and skills Reasoning and problem-solving skills Math, science, English, history, and geography Drug and alcohol prevention programs Citizenship, community service, cultural literacy, and knowledge of the international community	Preschool programs for all disadvantaged learners Parental training for child's early learning; parental choice in children's schools Up-to-date instructional technology Multilayer system of vocational, technical, and community colleges More student loans, scholarships, and work study programs in higher education Upgrade teacher preparation; reward teachers but hold them accountable	Inspire reform at the federal, state, and local levels Enlist assistance of parents, community, business, and civic groups; involve all parts of society Create effective apprenticeships, job training, teacher-employee exchanges, and adopt-a-school programs Increase flexibility, innovation, accountability, and results Targets established for the year 2000

Tougher academic standards

The reports further emphasize tougher standards and tougher courses, and a majority propose that colleges raise their admission requirements. Most of the reports also talk about increasing homework, time for learning, and time in school, as well as instituting more rigorous grading, testing, homework, and discipline. They mention upgrading teacher certification, increasing teacher salaries, increasing the number of and paying higher salaries for science and math teachers, and providing merit pay for outstanding teachers. Overall, the reports stress academic achievement (not the whole child) and increased productivity (not relevancy or humanism).

Schools play too many roles

Most of the reports express concern that the schools are pressed to play too many social roles; that the schools cannot meet all these expectations; and that the schools are in danger of losing sight of their key role — teaching basic skills and core academic subjects, new skills for computer use, and higher-level cog-

The demand for highly skilled workers is accelerating rapidly amid growing concern that the United States is being overtaken by other nations in commerce, industry, science, and technology. (© Elizabeth Crews/Stock Boston)

nitive skills for the world of work, technology, and military defense. Many of the reports, concerned not only with academic productivity but also with national productivity, link human capital with economic capital. Investment in schools would be an investment in the economy and in the nation's future stability. If education fails, so do our workforce and nation. Hence, it behooves business, labor, and government to work with educators to help educate and train the U.S. populace.

In the following sections, we will look more closely at the two most popularized and influential reports: **A Nation at Risk,** published in 1983, and *National Goals for Education,* published in 1990.

A Nation at Risk.   The report by the National Commission on Excellence in Education, compiled by a panel appointed by the Department of Education,

Rising tide of mediocrity

indicates that the well-being of the nation is being eroded by a rising tide of mediocrity.[40] This mediocrity is linked to the foundations of our educational institutions and is spilling over into the workplace and other sectors of society. What was unimaginable a generation ago has begun to occur — other nations are surpassing our educational attainments and industrial output.

The report lists several aspects of educational decline that were evident in the early 1980s: lower achievement scores, lower testing requirements, lower graduation requirements, lower teacher expectations, fewer academic or solid

---

[40]National Commission on Excellence in Education, *A Nation at Risk: The Imperative for Educational Reform.*

Taking Issue ◆━━━━━━

The Intellect Versus the Whole Child

Since World War I, there has been an underlying conflict concerning the aims of American education. One argument states that the schools should emphasize social experiences and personal development as well as academics. This position has been called the whole-child concept of education. The opposing argument insists that schools focus strongly on intellectual competence instead of trying to incorporate nonacademic concerns.

Question: Given the crisis in academic achievement and the strain on school resources, should today's schools concentrate on intellectual training rather than whole-child education?

Arguments PRO

1   Schools are having a hard time maintaining basic academic standards. Many students cannot even read and write acceptably. Devoting school time to personal and social development undercuts attempts to improve achievement.

2   Whole-child education often intrudes into the proper domains of parents, church, and community. A child's moral instruction, for example, should be determined by his or her parents, not by teachers, curriculum planners, or any other agency of government.

3   The whole-child concept is often used to justify unnecessary school activities (such as driver's education) or to guarantee jobs for special interest groups (such as counselors, psychologists, and health educators). The strain on school finances would be reduced if such marginal programs were eliminated.

4   If schools would concentrate on a general humanities curriculum, the needs of the whole child would in fact be served. Virtually every moral, social, or personal dilemma a student might encounter is addressed in the classic and modern works of Western civilization.

Arguments CON

1   Concentration on achievement and basic skills develops only a partial person. Students who do not fit socially, morally, or personally into society will not lead a rewarding life or act as responsible citizens.

2   The modern home and the institutional structures of contemporary society can no longer perform the same roles as in the past. Consequently, children are growing up in a developmental vacuum. The schools seem to be the only institutions able to fill students' needs.

3   Students today grow up faster than ever before. Society hurries them into coping with psychological and social pressures that are difficult even for adults. Specialists like counselors and psychologists therefore play an increasingly vital role in education.

4   To trust academic courses to promote nonacademic development is to divorce thought from action, speculation from experience. Reading great works of moral thought does not necessarily make one a moral person. Students need help in applying ideas to their own lives.

courses, more remedial courses, and higher illiteracy rates. The report states that the United States has compromised its commitment to educational quality as a result of conflicting demands placed on the nation's schools and concludes that the schools have attempted to tackle too many social problems that the home and other agencies of society either will not or cannot resolve.

Longer school day and year

The report calls for, among other things, tougher standards for graduation, including more courses in science, mathematics, foreign language, and the "new basics" such as computer skills; a longer school day and school year; far more homework; improved and updated textbooks; more rigorous, measurable, and higher expectations for student achievement; higher teacher salaries, based on performance, and career ladders that distinguish among the beginning, experienced, and master teacher; demonstrated entry competencies and more rigorous certification standards for teachers; accountability from educators and policy makers; and greater fiscal support from citizens.

National Goals for Education. In 1990, President George Bush announced the establishment of national goals for education to serve as guidelines for state and local education agencies. The overriding theme of the published document is the push for an educated citizenry, well trained and responsible, capable of adapting to a changing world, knowledgeable of its cultural heritage and the world community, and willing to accept and maintain the American leadership position in the next century. It is a nationalistic, upbeat document, and an urgent sense of competitiveness rings throughout it: "America's educational performance must be second to none. . . . [It] is central to our quality of life [and] is at the heart of our economic strength and security."[41]

Stress on maintaining American leadership

The contention is that "sweeping changes" in schools must be made if we are "to maintain our strength and international competitiveness."[42] Educators must be given greater flexibility to devise teaching and learning strategies that serve all students, regardless of abilities or interests; at the same time, educators should be held responsible for their teaching. Parents must become involved in their children's education, especially during the preschool years. Community, civic, and business groups all have a vital role to play in reforming education. Finally, students must accept responsibility for their education, and this means they must work hard in school.

"Sweeping changes" needed

The report outlines six specific goals to be reached by the year 2000:

Six goals for the year 2000

1. *Readiness for school.* All children in America will start school ready to learn.

2. *High-school completion.* The high-school graduation rate will increase to 90 percent.

3. *Student achievement and citizenship.* On tests taken in grades four, eight, and twelve American students will demonstrate competency in math, science, English, history, and geography; all students will learn to be responsible citizens and productive workers.

4. *Science and mathematics.* U.S. students will be first in the world in science and mathematics achievement.

5. *Adult literacy.* Every adult American will be literate and possess the knowledge and skills to compete in a global economy.

6. *Safe, disciplined, and drug-free schools.* Every American school will be free of drugs and violence and will offer a disciplined environment conducive to learning.

Focus on three periods of education

To achieve these national goals, the report focuses on three periods of education. The discussion of *the preschool years* emphasizes the parents' role and

---

[41]*National Goals for Education* (Washington, D.C.: U.S. Department of Education, 1990), p. 1.
[42]Ibid., pp. 1–2.

Getting to the Source ◄ ◆ ►

A Nation at Risk

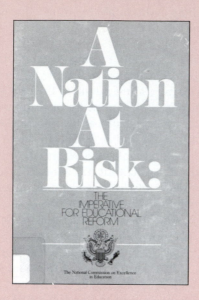

*I*ssued in 1983, the landmark report A Nation at Risk *alerted Americans to the dangers of an inadequate educational system. Stressing the challenge of international economic competition, the report em-*

phasized the need to prepare a skilled workforce for the "information age." Many subsequent reports and commentaries have sounded similar calls for educational reform.

Our Nation is at risk. Our once unchallenged preeminence in commerce, industry, science, and technological innovation is being overtaken by competitors throughout the world. This report is concerned with only one of the many causes and dimensions of the problem, but it is the one that undergirds American prosperity, security, and civility. We report to the American people that while we can take justifiable pride in what our schools and colleges have historically accomplished and contributed to the United States and the well-being of its people, the educational foundations of our society are presently being eroded by a rising tide of mediocrity that threatens our very future as a Nation and a people. What was unimaginable a generation ago has begun to occur — others are matching and surpassing our educational attainments.

If an unfriendly foreign power had attempted to impose on America the mediocre educational performance that exists today, we might well have viewed it

responsibility in the children's early education and suggests that parents need to be trained to fulfill this role. In *the school years,* the emphasis is on restructuring schools, giving parents more public-school choices, utilizing technology, and providing federal, state, and local monies to improve learning. Concern is also for bolstering math and science, assisting students at risk of failing or dropping out of school, and increasing the number of well-qualified teachers in critical subject areas and shortage areas, including rural and urban schools. The section on *the after school years* calls for eliminating adult illiteracy, creating public and private partnerships in education, and improving vocational, technical, and community colleges, as well as apprenticeship programs, job training, and teacher-employee exchanges.[43]

Goals adopted by state governors

These highly idealistic goals have been adopted by the governors of the states through the National Governors' Association (NGA). The implementation

---

[43]*Invest in Our Children Through the National Education Goals* (Washington, D.C.: U.S. Department of Education, 1990); *National Goals for Education.*

as an act of war. As it stands, we have allowed this to happen to ourselves. We have even squandered the gains in student achievement made in the wake of the Sputnik challenge. Moreover, we have dismantled essential support systems which helped make those gains possible. We have, in effect, been committing an act of unthinking, unilateral educational disarmament. . . .

History is not kind to idlers. The time is long past when America's destiny was assured simply by an abundance of natural resources and inexhaustible human enthusiasm, and by our relative isolation from the malignant problems of older civilizations. The world is indeed one global village. We live among determined, well-educated, and strongly motivated competitors. We compete with them for international standing and markets, not only with products but also with the ideas of our laboratories and neighborhood workshops. America's position in the world may once have been reasonably secure with only a few exceptionally well-trained men and women. It is no longer.

The risk is not only that the Japanese make automobiles more efficiently than Americans and have government subsidies for development and export. It is not just that the South Koreans recently built the world's most efficient steel mill, or that American machine tools, once the pride of the world, are being displaced by German products. It is also that these developments signify a redistribution of trained capability throughout the globe. Knowledge, learning, information, and skilled intelligence are the new raw materials of international commerce and are today spreading throughout the world as vigorously as miracle drugs, synthetic fertilizers, and blue jeans did earlier. If only to keep and improve on the slim competitive edge we still retain in world markets, we must dedicate ourselves to the reform of our educational system for the benefit of all — old and young alike, affluent and poor, majority and minority. Learning is the indispensable investment required for success in the "information age" we are entering.

Questions

1. What new skills are needed for the information age? Are they indeed *new*?

2. In your view, what educational reforms are most important for improving our "competitive edge"?

Source: National Commission on Excellence in Education, *A Nation at Risk: The Imperative for Educational Reform* (Washington, D.C.: U.S. Department of Education, 1983), cover, pp. 1–2, 5.

plan consists of twenty-two state strategies for achieving the national education goals. The strategies tend to cluster in four areas: early childhood education, restructuring schools, colleges and universities, and lifelong education.[44]

Assessment and Action

Criticisms of the reports

Criticisms of the reports by the educational community tend to center on three major points: (1) the reports are too idealistic and unrealistic; (2) they put too much emphasis on excellence at the expense of equality and equity; and (3) they are enormously expensive to implement — and they come at a time when the federal government has reduced its support for education. Although it is true that school districts can easily "accomplish" such changes as more rigorous

[44]*Educating America: State Strategies for Achieving the National Education Goals* (Washington, D.C.: National Governors' Association, 1990). Also see Bill Honig, "Target Areas for Reaching National Goals," *Education Week*, February 28, 1990, pp. 31, 56.

homework or graduation requirements by mandating them, the history of school improvement shows that substantial funding is required to initiate and support effective change on a school-by-school basis.

Reform as a complex process

One educator points out that the reports ignore what is known about school change and improvement — the process is complex and involves the cooperation of teachers, administrators, parents, and community members who often have different hidden agendas and ideas about reform.[45] Others say the reports ignore the realities of students' situations. Why talk about raising standards when most at-risk students cannot even meet existing standards because of their difficult social and home environments?[46]

Students' realities

No "magic bullets"

Seasoned educators have learned, sometimes the hard way, that there are no "magic bullets" for reforming schools; there is no one policy or single combination of policies that will automatically transform ineffective schools into effective ones. School life, like human life in general, is much more complicated. Moreover, as two educators note, the education highways are cluttered with reforms that have run out of gas — the "wrecks" of famous bandwagons.[47] Why should today's reform movement be any different?

A new consensus

One reason, according to former NEA president Mary Futrell, is that there seems to be a new consensus on the necessity of providing high-quality education for *all* students. Reflecting this new consensus, coalitions are now being formed among government, corporate, and educational groups.[48] It has taken many years to reach this point of cooperation.

Political and popular backing for reform

Furthermore, as educators assert, the political force driving educational reform is another basis for optimism. Reforms in the past were based on educational ideas that did not necessarily have widespread support from legislators or policy makers, much less the public.[49] With the exception of the years following *Sputnik,* a sense of urgency has not existed. Today, the fear about American decline touches far more people than ever before, and they seem willing to do something about it. People are now making the connection between education and economics, realizing that school failures are tied to economic failures and that it is time to invest in children and youth. There seems to be a guarded willingness on the part of the public to spend money on education, as long as educators show substantive results.

State reform efforts

Overall, the reports have captured national attention, spotlighted concern for the quality of education, and helped to upgrade school standards. In the last decade, nearly all the states have revised their curricula, raised high-school graduation requirements (especially in math and science), established competency

---

[45]Thomas R. Guskey, "Guidelines for School Innovation," *Education Digest* (October 1990), pp. 23–27.

[46]David Hill, "The Federal Role in Education: A Strategy for the 1990s," *Phi Delta Kappan* (January 1990), pp. 398–402; and John O'Neil, "A Generation Adrift?" *Educational Leadership* (September 1991), pp. 4–10.

[47]Ron Brandt, Keynote Address to Washington State Association for Curriculum Development and Supervision, Seattle, February 11, 1983; Allan C. Ornstein, "National Reform and Instructional Accountability," *High School Journal* (October–November 1990), pp. 51–56.

[48]Mary Hatwood Futrell, "Mission Not Accomplished: Education Reform in Retrospect," *Phi Delta Kappan* (September 1989), pp. 1–4.

[49]David S. Seeley, "Carrying School Reform into the 1990s," *Education Digest* (May 1990), pp. 3–6; Walter Shapiro, "Tough Choice: Can This Man Save Our Schools?" *Time,* September 16, 1991, pp. 54–60.

testing for teachers and students, or adopted other well-publicized reform measures. In the view of many educators these reforms merely scratch the surface — although some may be counterproductive. Nevertheless, we may now have the best opportunity in generations for a comprehensive and effective reform of American schools.

SWINGS OF THE PENDULUM

Role of social and economic change

In examining the aims of education from the turn of the twentieth century until today, we see considerable change but also considerable reiteration. As current ideas begin to fade, old ideas reemerge in updated versions. The cycle appears to be linked to the sweep of social and economic change. For example, a stress on rigorous intellectual training, evident in the early twentieth century, reappeared in the 1950s during the Cold War and again in the 1980s as a result of concern over economic competition with foreign countries. Similarly, as the social ferment of the 1960s and 1970s brought increasing concern for the rights and aspirations of low-income and minority groups, the ideas of the early progressive educators resurfaced, and a renewed stress was placed on educating the disadvantaged. Although this concern for disadvantaged or at-risk students remains, the pendulum has now swung closer to the center: our current priorities are more diffuse, and there is growing concern for various kinds of students, including average and academically talented groups.

In looking at the broad sweep of American educational aims, you may ask yourself whether schools are expected to do more than is feasible. The schools are often seen as ideal agencies to solve the nation's problems, but can they do so? Many people throughout society refuse to admit their own responsibility for helping children develop and learn. Similarly, parents and policy makers often expect teachers and school administrators to be solely responsible for school reform. In fact, without significant cooperation from parents and community members, schools cannot do a good job, and reform efforts will fail.

Demands of interest groups

Recall, too, the influence of social pressure and of various interest groups. As society changes, and as different groups seek to promote their own causes, the aims of education must change. Rarely will there be complete agreement on the overall purposes of education, much less on what the schools should teach. But popular rhetoric and slogans of the day, as well as the demands of interest groups, must be balanced by a consideration for the good of the general public. Ideally, our educational priorities should derive from the needs of all portions of our society. To promote a balanced approach, the panels and commissions that attempt to define our educational aims should include representatives from as many groups as possible: parents, students, educators, researchers, community members, the business community, special interest groups, professional educational organizations, and government officials.[50]

Need to involve many groups

Coping with change

Unquestionably, the aims of education must be relevant to the times. If the schools cannot adapt to changing conditions and social forces, how can they expect to produce people who do? Today we live in a highly technical, auto-

[50]Ornstein, "How Do Educators Meet the Needs of Society?"; Ornstein, "The National Reports on Education."

mated, and bureaucratic society, and we are faced with pressing social and economic problems — aging cities, the effects of centuries of racial and sexual discrimination, an aging population, unemployment and a displaced workforce, exhaustion of our natural resources, and the pollution of the physical environment. Whether we allow the times to engulf us, or whether we can cope with our new environment, will depend to a large extent on what kinds of skills are taught to our present-day students — and on the development of appropriate priorities for education.

Summing Up

1. The purposes of education are influenced by changing social forces as well as by educational philosophies and theories.

2. General aims — broad statements of educational purpose — are usually translated into more specific goals by the school district or individual school. These goals, in turn, are developed into even more specific objectives at the subject/grade, unit plan, or lesson plan level. Three popular methods for writing objectives are the educational taxonomy, the Gronlund approach, and the Mager method.

3. Since the turn of the century, American aims of education have gone through at least five periods, each with a different focus of attention: academic rigor and mental discipline; the whole child; academically talented students; disadvantaged and minority students and children with disabilities; and, in the 1980s and 1990s, tougher academic standards for all students.

4. Most of the major reports released since 1983 have emphasized the need for educational excellence and higher standards. Although educators disagree about the usefulness or practicality of the reports' recommendations, most states have already implemented changes based on the reports.

5. We must learn to live with some disagreement about the purposes of schooling. Various groups of people need to work together in formulating future educational priorities.

6. We often expect schools to be a key instrument for solving our technological or social problems and preparing our workforce for the future. The years ahead will severely test this expectation.

Key Terms

aims *(487)*

goals *(487)*

objectives *(487)*

taxonomy *(492)*

mental discipline approach *(496)*

Cardinal Principles of Secondary Education (497)

The Purposes of Education in American Democracy (498)

Education for All American Youth (498)

whole-child concept *(500)*

A Nation at Risk (511)

National Goals for Education (513)

Discussion Questions

1. In terms of aims and goals, why is the question "What are schools for" so complex?

2. Why is the bulletin *Cardinal Principles of Secondary Education* such an important milestone in American education? How did it differ from later approaches or reports? Do the seven principles seem valid today?

3. Are the proposed aims of the Educational Policies Commission, set forth in *The Purposes of Education in American Democracy* and *Education for All American Youth*, desirable for education today? How might you modify them? How would you compare these aims with those discussed in *A Nation at Risk* and *National Goals for Education*?

4. Who should have educational priority: below-average students, average students, or above-average students?

5. Why must the aims of education change as society changes?

Suggested Readings

Bloom, Benjamin S., et al. *Taxonomy of Educational Objectives, Handbook I: Cognitive Domain.* New York: McKay, 1956.
> *This is a classic text on how to write behavioral objectives in the cognitive domain of learning.*

Conant, James B. *The American High School Today.* New York: McGraw-Hill, 1959.
> *Written during the* Sputnik *era, the book focuses on many recommendations for upgrading the high-school curriculum.*

Duke, Daniel, and Robert L. Canady, *School Policy.* New York: McGraw-Hill, 1991.
> *Here is a compact book on federal, state, and local school policy — and on how to formulate, evaluate, and revise aims and goals of education.*

Gardner, John W. *Excellence: Can We Be Equal and Excellent Too?* New York: Harper & Row, 1961.
> *Written about thirty years ago, the book remains relevant today: the questions and issues raised still elicit concern in American schools and society.*

Gronlund, Norman E. *How to Write and Use Instructional Objectives,* 4th ed. New York: Macmillan, 1991.
> *The author shows how to write behavioral objectives for teaching and testing.*

National Commission on Excellence in Education. *A Nation at Risk: The Imperative for Educational Reform.* Washington, D.C.: U.S. Department of Education, 1983.
> *Among the recent reports on American education, this one has had the most political impact.*

National Goals for Education. Washington, D.C.: U.S. Department of Education, 1990.
> *This document proposes six major aims for improving American schools by the year 2000.*

14

Curriculum and Instruction

FOCUSING QUESTIONS

How does curriculum content reflect changes in society?

What forces affect curriculum change?

What are some of the ways in which curriculum may be organized?

How might the use of cooperative learning or mastery learning influence your work as a teacher?

How can computers be used in the classroom to improve instruction?

What are some trends that seem likely to affect curriculum and instruction in the future?

A mericans — perhaps more than the citizens of any other country — have demanded the utmost from their schools. We ask the schools to teach children to think, to socialize them, to alleviate poverty and inequality, to reduce crime, to perpetuate our cultural heritage, and to produce intelligent, patriotic citizens. Inevitably, American schools have been unable to meet all of these obligations. Nonetheless, the demands persist, and it is the **curriculum** — the planned experiences provided through instruction — that is their focal point. Consequently, the curriculum is continuously modified as the aims and goals of education are revised, as student populations change, as social issues are debated, as interest groups are activated, and as society changes.

Historical changes in curriculum

As the historical overview in Chapter 13 demonstrated, the different periods in American education have produced different emphases in curriculum. When the mental discipline approach prevailed in the nineteenth century, the curriculum generally stressed reading, spelling, writing, and arithmetic. Gradually, as the scientific and industrial revolution brought fundamental social and economic change, schools began to teach a wider range of subjects, including advanced mathematics and science, music, art, and physical education. During the progressive movement of the early and mid-twentieth century, the aims of schooling were broadened to stress the everyday needs of all students, including recent immigrants, the urban poor, and other groups not served by the traditional emphasis on mental discipline. Consequently the curriculum often expanded to include courses in citizenship, family living, home economics and health, and vocational education.[1]

Since then, as the aims of education have shifted, as national priorities and social pressures have changed, schools have modified their curricula many times. In this chapter we will look at a number of the major curricular approaches evident in the last several decades. You will see that they are closely related to the philosophies and theories discussed in Chapter 12 and to the various aims and goals of education described in Chapter 13.

Curriculum involves instruction

As we examine curriculum, we will also examine instructional activities that relate to curriculum. To some extent they are intertwined. Teaching a curriculum involves instruction, which is the implementation of a curriculum — its methods and materials. Although some educators argue for a separation, based on theoretical and traditional grounds, other educators recognize that in reality the two realms of knowledge need to be synthesized. As a result, some schools of education offer separate courses in curriculum and instruction, whereas others combine some of them.

CURRICULUM ORGANIZATION

The various types of curriculum organization in American schools can be viewed from two perspectives. One emphasizes the subject to be taught; the other em-

---

[1]See R. Freeman Butts, *The Revival of Civic Learning* (Bloomington, Ind.: Phi Delta Kappa, 1980); Lawrence A. Cremin, *American Education: The National Experience* (New York: Harper & Row, 1980); and Cremin, *The Transformation of the School* (New York: Random House, 1964).

phasizes the student. In the first case, the curriculum is viewed as a body of content, or subject matter, leading to certain achievement outcomes or products. The second approach defines curriculum in terms of the needs and attitudes of the student; the concern is with process — in other words, with the climate of the classroom or school.

Extremes on a continuum

Actually, both views represent the two extremes of a continuum, and most practitioners (and researchers) rely on some curriculum blend within this continuum. Even though most teachers tend to emphasize one approach over the other, they incorporate both choices in the classroom. Very few employ pure cognitive (subject-centered) or pure psychological (student-centered) approaches in the teaching-learning process.

Subject-Centered Curricula

Subject matter is both the oldest and most contemporary framework of curriculum organization. It is also the most common — primarily because it is convenient. In fact, the departmental structure of secondary schools and colleges tends to prevent us from thinking about the curriculum in any other way. Curricular changes usually occur at the departmental level. Courses are added, omitted, or modified, but faculty members rarely engage in comprehensive, systematic curriculum development and evaluation. Even in the elementary schools, where self-contained classrooms force the teachers to be generalists, curricula are usually organized by subjects.

Proponents defend **subject-centered curricula** on four grounds:

1. Subjects are a logical way to organize and interpret learning.
2. Such organization makes it easier for people to remember information for future use.
3. Teachers (in secondary schools, at least) are trained as subject-matter specialists.
4. Textbooks and other teaching materials are usually organized by subject.

Pros and cons of subject matter

Critics, however, claim that subject-centered curricula are fragmented, a mass of facts and concepts learned in isolation. They see this kind of curriculum as deemphasizing life experiences and failing to consider adequately the needs and interests of students. The emphasis, such critics argue, is on the teaching of knowledge, the recall of facts; the teacher thus dominates the lesson, allowing little student input.

The following sections discuss seven variations of subject-centered curricula. These are not the only possible variations, nor do they represent hard-and-fast categories. Many schools and teachers mix these approaches, drawing from more than one of them. Keep in mind that they share a similar focus on a body of content or subject matter.

Subject-Area Curriculum.   The subject area is the oldest and most widely used form of curriculum organization. It has its roots in the seven liberal arts of classical Greece and Rome: grammar, rhetoric, dialectic, arithmetic, geometry, astronomy, and music. Modern subject-area curricula trace their origins to the work of William Harris, superintendent of the St. Louis school system in the

1870s. Steeped in the classical tradition, Harris established a subject orientation that has virtually dominated U.S. curricula from his day to the present. For example, consider Table 14.1, which shows the recommendations of the Committee of Fifteen in 1895. Although the committee's proposal is a century old, the subject categories are quite relevant; students are still introduced to "algebra" and "English grammar," "reading" and "writing," as well as "geography" and "history."

Common, special, and elective content

The modern **subject-area curriculum** treats each subject as a specialized and largely autonomous body of verified knowledge. These subjects can be further organized into three traditional content categories. *Common content* refers to subjects considered essential for all students; these subjects usually include the three Rs at the elementary level and English, history, science, and mathematics at the secondary level. *Special content* refers to subjects that develop knowledge and skills for particular vocations or professions — for example, business mathematics and physics. Finally, *elective content* affords the student optional offerings. Some electives are restricted to certain students, say, advanced auto mechanics for vocational students or fourth-year French for students enrolled in a college-preparatory program. Other electives, such as photography and human relations, are open to all students.

Exploratory subjects

A new term, *exploratory subjects,* has entered the curriculum vocabulary at the middle school level and in some junior high schools. In lieu of a fifth standard subject, students are allowed to choose one subject from a list of courses designed to suit a wide range of learning styles, needs, and interests. These courses, usually arranged in ten- or twelve-week blocks, can include such subjects as study skills, computer science, creative writing, and drama. In this way the school can diversify its subject offerings beyond the usual smattering of electives.[2] Schools that include these exploratory subjects in the curriculum tend to be more progressive in outlook than schools that still favor the traditional core academic subjects.

Subject-Structure Curriculum. Another variation of the subject-centered approach is the **subject-structure curriculum,** which adheres to traditional subject areas but puts a special focus on their internal structure or logic. During the 1950s and 1960s, the National Science Foundation and the federal government devoted sizable sums to the improvement of science and mathematics curricula at the elementary and secondary levels. New curriculum models were formulated according to the structure of each subject or discipline. The subject-structure curriculum rejects memorization, factual information, and rote learning — characteristic of most subject-centered curricula — and stresses those

Unifying concepts and principles

unifying concepts, rules, and principles that define and limit a subject and control the methods of research and inquiry. Structure brings together and organizes a body of knowledge, and it dictates appropriate ways of thinking about the subject and of generating new data. Curriculum models for other subjects quickly followed those for mathematics and the sciences.

Those who advocated this kind of focus on structure nonetheless rejected the idea that knowledge is fixed or permanent. They regarded teaching and

[2]Allan C. Ornstein, *Middle and Secondary School Methods* (New York: Harper & Row, 1992).

Table 14.1

The Elementary School Curriculum Proposed by the Committee of Fifteen in 1895

Branches	1st year	2d year	3d year	4th year	5th year	6th year	7th year	8th year
Reading	10 lessons a week	5 lessons a week						
Writing	10 lessons a week	5 lessons a week		3 lessons a week				
Spelling lists				4 lessons a week				
English grammar	Oral, with composition lessons					5 lessons a week with textbook		
Latin								5 lessons a week
Arithmetic	Oral, 60 minutes a week	5 lessons a week with textbook						
Algebra							5 lessons a week	
Geography	Oral, 60 minutes a week	*5 lessons a week with textbook				3 lessons a week		
Natural science and hygiene	60 minutes a week							
U.S. history						5 lessons a week		
U.S. Constitution								*5 lessons a week
General history	Oral, 60 minutes a week							
Physical culture	60 minutes a week							
Vocal music	60 minutes a week divided into 4 lessons							
Drawing	60 minutes a week							
Manual training or sewing and cooking							One-half day each	
Total hours of recitation	12	12	11	13	16¼	16¼	17½	17½

*Begins in second half of year.

Source: Committee of Fifteen, "Report of the Sub-Committee on the Correlation of Studies in Elementary Education," *Educational Review* (March 1895), p. 284.

learning as continuing inquiry, but they confined such inquiry within the established boundaries of subjects, ignoring or rejecting the fact that many problems cut across disciplines. Instead, they emphasized the students' cognitive abilities. They taught students the structure of a subject and its methods of inquiry so that students would learn how to learn. They tended, however, to dismiss learners'

Social and psychological needs dismissed

social and psychological needs. As Philip Phenix wrote, "There is no place in the curriculum for ideas which are regarded as suitable for teaching because of the supposed nature, needs, and interests of the learner, but which do not belong within the regular structure of the discipline."[3] In making students into young scholars or scientists, critics charged, the subject-structure approach neglected to educate citizens to deal with everyday realities and problems — how to fix a garage door, for example, or how to read a book for enjoyment.

The emphasis on structure led each discipline to develop its own unifying concepts, principles, and methods of inquiry. Learning by the inquiry method in chemistry differed from learning by the inquiry method in physics, for example. Moreover, curriculum planners could not agree on how to teach the structure of the social sciences and fine arts. Today, science and math programs still provide the best examples of teaching according to the structure of a subject. Much of the recent concern about critical thinking and "learning how to learn" is rooted in the subject-structure approach, what some educators might call old-fashioned analysis and problem-solving skills.

Perennialist Curriculum.   Two of the educational theories described in Chapter 12 are fundamentally subject centered: perennialism and essentialism.[4] Believing that the main purpose of education is the cultivation of the intellect — and of certain timeless values concerning work, morality, and family living — the perennialists concentrate their curriculum on the three Rs, Latin,

Latin, logic, and the classics

and logic at the elementary level, adding study of the classics at the secondary level. The assumption of the **perennialist curriculum,** according to Robert Hutchins, is that the best of the past — the so-called permanent studies, or classics — is equally valid for the present.[5]

Great Books

Although it originated in the American colonial period and the Latin grammar school, perennialism is evident in many schools today. The "Great Books" approach, originally designed for college students, has filtered down to the high schools and elementary schools through such programs as the Paideia program, Junior Great Books, Read Aloud, and the Battle of Books.[6] For example, in the Read Aloud curriculum, kindergartners and first graders listen to oral readings by their teachers and by their parents at home; the readings are followed by

---

[3]Philip H. Phenix, "The Disciplines as Curriculum Content," in A. H. Passow, ed., *Curriculum Crossroads* (New York: Teachers College Press, Columbia University, 1962), p. 64.

[4]These two terms were coined by Theodore Brameld in *Patterns of Educational Philosophy* (New York: Holt, 1950).

[5]Robert M. Hutchins, *The Higher Learning in America* (New Haven, Conn.: Yale University Press, 1936). Also see Allan Bloom, *The Closing of the American Mind* (New York: Simon and Schuster, 1987); E. D. Hirsch, *Cultural Literacy: Rediscovering Knowledge in American Education* (Boston: Houghton Mifflin, 1987).

[6]*Introduction to Great Books* (Chicago: Great Books Foundation, 1990); telephone conversation with Carolyn S. Saper, Editorial Coordinator, Great Books Foundation, June 11, 1991.

discussion questions, drawing, and dramatizations. From the second through twelfth grades, the Junior Great Books program follows a list of suggested readings ranging from *Cinderella* and *Jack and the Beanstalk* in early grades to Kant's *Conscience* and Kafka's *A Hungry Artist* in the senior year.[7]

Throughout these programs, the emphasis is not on practice or drill but on thinking about good literature, analyzing ideas, articulating meanings, and evaluating opinions. Rather than teach reading and language through basal readers and isolated words and skills, the programs follow a **whole-language approach;** that is, they integrate language arts throughout the curriculum, emphasizing the ways language is used in real situations. The classrooms also stress questioning and discussion, or "shared inquiry."

Essentialist Curriculum. Essentialists believe that the elementary curriculum must consist of the three Rs, and the high-school curriculum of five major disciplines: English (grammar, literature, and writing), mathematics, the sciences, history, and foreign languages.[8] Adherents of the **essentialist curriculum** believe these subject areas constitute the best way of systematizing and keeping up with the explosion of knowledge. Some recent essentialist advocates would also add geography to the list of important or core academic subjects.

Five major disciplines

Essentialism shares with perennialism the notion that the curriculum should focus on rigorous intellectual training, a training possible only through the study of certain subjects. Although the perennialist sees no need for nonacademic subjects, the essentialist is often willing to add such studies to the curriculum provided they receive low priority. Essentialists are willing to allow minimal play and puzzle activities at the primary level, so long as these activities are cognitively oriented.

Lynn Cheney, Chester Finn, E. D. Hirsch, and Diane Ravitch are among the best known current essentialists. They see a decline in the overall literacy of American students — that is, a decrease in important knowledge that is required for functioning in our society and our world. They argue that mere "basic" skills are an insufficient preparation for life. Students, they claim, need an academic knowledge base — what they call "cultural literacy" or "essential knowledge" — if they are to deal with new ideas and challenges.

Both perennialists and essentialists advocate educational meritocracy. They favor high academic standards and a rigorous system of grading and testing to help schools sort students by ability. The goal is to educate each person to the limits of his or her potential. Today, many parochial schools and academically oriented public schools stress various aspects of the perennialist and essentialist curricula.

Back-to-Basics Curriculum. Despite the fact that many essentialists argue for a cultural literacy that goes beyond mere basic skills, others have focused precisely on those basics. The strong back-to-basics movement among both parents and educators arose in reaction to the general relaxation of academic standards in the 1960s and 1970s and the decline of student standardized test scores

---

[7]*The Junior Great Books Program* (Chicago: Great Books Foundation, 1991).

[8]Arthur Bestor, *The Restoration of Learning* (New York: Knopf, 1956); James B. Conant, *The American High School Today* (New York: McGraw-Hill, 1959).

A back-to-basics curriculum places heavy emphasis on reading, writing, and mathematics. (© James L. Shaffer/Lightwave)

Attacks on the "soft-sell approach"

in reading, writing, and computation. Even the mass media attacked the "soft-sell approach" to education that offered automatic promotion of marginal students, a sometimes dizzying array of elective courses, and textbooks designed as much to entertain as to educate. Between 1976 and 1991, in annual Gallup Polls that asked the public to suggest ways to improve education, "devoting more attention to teaching the basics" and "improving curriculum standards" ranked no lower than fifth in the list of responses.[9]

Proponents of the **back-to-basics curriculum** insist on the need to maintain minimum standards, and much of the state school reform legislation passed in the 1980s and 1990s reflects this popular position. In most states, standardized tests serve a "gatekeeping" function at selected points on the educational ladder. The majority of states also require students to pass a statewide exit test before receiving a high-school diploma.[10]

Statewide testing

Although the back-to-basics movement means different things to different people, it usually connotes an essentialist curriculum with heavy emphasis on

---

[9]See the annual Gallup Polls published in the September or October issues of *Phi Delta Kappan,* 1976 to 1991.

[10]Allan C. Ornstein, "National Reform and Instructional Accountability," *High School Journal* (October–November 1990), pp. 51–56; William E. Webster and J. Daniel McMillin, "A Report on Calls for Secondary School Reform in the United States," *NASSP Bulletin* (February 1991), pp. 77–83.

Solid subjects in all grades   reading, writing, and mathematics. So-called solid subjects — English, history, science, and mathematics — are taught in all grades. History means U.S. and European history and perhaps Asian and African history but does not include Afro-American history or ethnic studies. English means traditional grammar, not linguistics or nonstandard English; it means Shakespeare and Wordsworth, not *Catcher in the Rye* or *Lolita*. Creative writing is frowned upon. Science means biology, chemistry, and physics, not ecology. Mathematics means old math, not new math. Furthermore, these subjects are required. Proponents of the basics consider elective courses in such areas as scuba diving, transcendental meditation, and hiking to be nonsense. Some even consider humanities or integrated social science courses too "soft." They may grudgingly admit music and art into the program, but only for half credit.

Devaluation of diplomas   Proponents of the movement believe that too many illiterate students pass from grade to grade and eventually graduate; that high-school and college diplomas are meaningless as measures of graduates' abilities; that minimum standards must be set; and that the basics (reading, writing, math) are essential for employment. Critics point out that the decline in standardized test scores — a grave concern of the back-to-basics enthusiasts — may be linked less to curriculum than to higher student/teacher ratios, a decrease in the number of low-achieving students who drop out of school, the competing influence of television, and the more permissive attitudes of society. They worry that a focus on *Criticism of back-to-basics* basics will suppress the students' creativity and shortchange other domains of *movement* learning, thereby encouraging conformity and dependence on authority.[11]

Higher Standards Curriculum.   There is a demand today for tougher academics. The demand for higher achievement (not just minimum competency) for all children (not just college-bound students) focuses on the cognitive and academic areas. The ability to think, reason, and solve problems, to take serious subjects such as calculus, physics, and advanced foreign language is stressed. *Upgrading the curriculum* Proponents of the **higher standards curriculum** believe that we must upgrade our definition of minimum competencies to include advanced skills and knowledge, including computer and communication competencies, that will be required for tomorrow's technological world. They believe we must increase the time and quality of instruction, and reestablish the prestige of our teachers, schools, and colleges.[12] As part of this quest for higher academic standards, the National Assessment Governing Board has begun to set performance standards for each of the three grade levels (4, 8, and 12) measured by the National Assessment of Educational Progress (NAEP).[13]

---

[11]Linda Darling-Hammond, "Achieving Our Goals: Superficial or Structural Reforms," *Phi Delta Kappan* (December 1990), pp. 286–295; Bruce R. Joyce, "The Doors to School Improvement," *Educational Digest* (May 1991), pp. 59–62.

[12]Ernest L. Boyer, *College: The Undergraduate Experience in America* (New York: Harper & Row, 1987); Phillip C. Schlechty, *Schools for the 21st Century* (San Francisco: Jossey-Bass, 1990); and Theodore R. Sizer, *Horace's Compromise: The Dilemma of the American High School,* rev. ed. (Boston: Houghton Mifflin, 1985).

[13]John O'Neil, "Drive for National Standards Picking Up Steam," *Educational Leadership* (February 1991), pp. 4–8; Daniel P. Resnick and Lauren B. Resnick, "Understanding Achievement and Acting to Produce It: Some Recommendations for the NAEP," *Phi Delta Kappan* (April 1988), pp. 576–579.

Taking Issue ◄━◆━

State Competency Tests for Students

One feature of the back-to-basics movement has been a rise in statewide testing of students. The failure of many students to master even the most basic skills, especially in reading, writing, mathematics, and history, has prompted state legislators to demand proof that schools are meeting minimum standards. All states now employ statewide testing at one or more stages in the educational process. Many states, in fact, have established minimum-competency tests that students must pass before graduating from high school.

Question: Should every state require students to pass a statewide competency test in order to receive a high-school diploma?

Arguments PRO

1 Statewide testing for high-school graduation forces schools to improve their minimum standards. Students are no longer passed automatically through the system, and every student is taught the skills required for basic literacy.

2 The rise in minimum standards brought about by statewide testing is especially important for students from disadvantaged backgrounds. To break the cycle of poverty and joblessness, these students must be given the skills needed for productive employment.

3 Besides improving minimum standards, statewide testing helps to shift curriculum emphasis back to the basics. All of our students need a firmer grounding in such essential subjects as reading, writing, and mathematics.

4 Testing for graduation shows the public that schools are being held accountable for their performance. The test results help to identify schools that are not doing their jobs properly.

5 Using the data provided by statewide testing, educators can discover where the overall problems lie. Policies can be modified accordingly, and curricula can be designed to address the problem areas.

Arguments CON

1 Statewide testing is cumbersome, costly, and may not lead to much improvement in minimum standards. The effort must come from the local level, where educators know the strengths and weaknesses of their own schools.

2 Statewide tests discriminate against minorities and the urban and rural poor, who fail the tests in disproportionate numbers. This failure stigmatizes them unjustly and further damages their prospects for employment.

3 When schools try to focus on "basics," they often neglect other important elements of education, such as problem solving and creative thinking. These higher-order abilities are increasingly important in a technological society.

4 Test scores by themselves cannot identify ineffective schools, and it is dangerous to use them for that purpose. There are too many complicating factors, such as the students' home environment and socioeconomic background.

5 Most teachers already know where the problems lie. Moreover, soon after a statewide test is established, many teachers begin to "teach the test." Thus, the data obtained from such examinations become meaningless or misleading.

It is easy to argue for greater emphasis and tougher standards in mathematics, science, and foreign language — even for computer literacy. But if students take more courses in these subject areas, observers point out, they will have fewer opportunities to study such areas as culture and the arts, thus raising the question of curriculum balance. It is possible that students not going to college will be overlooked or pushed into poorly equipped classrooms and second-rate programs.[14] Appropriate mathematics, science, and other classes for vocational and non-college-bound students should be developed. Although students should be required to speak fluently at least one foreign language, we must not forget our immigrant and limited-English-speaking students who must learn formal English.

Raising standards costs money

Raising standards will cost money. Teacher salaries, for example, will have to be raised to attract, and retain, teachers in math, science, and foreign language. We will have to improve, and in some cases build, science laboratory facilities. Schools will need to introduce new instructional materials, including updated textbooks, computers, and language laboratories. In addition, research suggests that it is effective to begin instruction in these subject areas in the elementary grades. No one believes a higher standards curriculum will be easy to implement on a large scale, but the impetus in that direction appears to be serious. Governors, legislators, educators, business leaders, and civic groups have all expressed their concern, believing that the nation as a whole must raise its educational standards in order to stay competitive.

Core Curriculum.   The meaning of a core curriculum has changed from the original concept developed in the 1940s and 1950s, which stressed a "flexible curriculum" to meet the "special interests and concerns" of students.[15] Today, proponents of a **core curriculum** focus on the need for students to experience a *common* curriculum — that is, a selected core of subjects that every student would be required to take. Whereas in the past the concept of core curriculum was tied to a progressive philosophy, today it reflects the conservative theories of perennialism and essentialism; its advocates attempt to affirm both equality and excellence in schooling by defining what is central to the education of all students.[16]

Common curriculum for all students

First popularized at Harvard University in the early 1980s, the new idea of core curriculum filtered down to the schools partially as a result of the national task force reports. Ernest Boyer, John Goodlad, and Theodore Sizer are best known for popularizing the idea at the high-school level, and Mortimer Adler is best known for his influence on the elementary schools.

Although Boyer, Goodlad, and Sizer have not defined the exact rubrics of a core curriculum, they believe that the typical secondary school curriculum fails to offer an overall conceptual framework or an appropriately balanced preparation for further academics or for the world of work. Boyer and Sizer contend

[14]Elliot W. Eisner, "What Really Counts in School," *Educational Leadership* (February 1991), pp. 10–17; Kenneth Gray, "Vocational Education in the High School: A Modern Phoenix?" *Phi Delta Kappan* (February 1991), pp. 437–445; and Kenneth A. Sirotnik, "Improving Urban Schools in an Age of 'Restructuring,'" *Education and Urban Society* (May 1991), pp. 256–269.

[15]Roland C. Faunce and Nelson L. Bossing, *Developing the Core Curriculum,* 2nd ed. (Englewood Cliffs, N.J.: Prentice-Hall, 1958), pp. 59–60.

[16]John I. Goodlad, "A New Look at an Old Idea: Core Curriculum," *Educational Leadership* (December 1986–January 1987), pp. 8–16.

Focus on intellect

that high schools should not try to be all-comprehensive; that is, the schools should not offer learning in all domains of life. Rather, high schools should focus on the education of the intellect. Sizer also stresses the importance of education in moral character and responsibility for one's own behavior, meshing these concepts with intellectual development.[17]

Expansion of core courses

Both Boyer and Sizer emphasize the humanities, communication and language skills, science, math, and technology. Boyer asserts that the core units required for graduation should be expanded from one-half of the total curriculum (now the norm) to about two-thirds. Goodlad would like to see about 80 percent of the curriculum devoted to core courses, with only 20 percent reserved for the development of individual talents and interests; the core curriculum would begin at age four and extend to age sixteen. Goodlad would also eliminate the division of students into separate academic and vocational tracks because tracking thwarts the idea of a common curriculum for all students.[18]

Elimination of tracking

Electives postponed

Adler wishes to develop a one-track system of schooling for twelve years, starting at first grade. Electives and specialization would be postponed until the college, technical, or professional level of education. Adler's curriculum emphasizes the domains of organized knowledge, intellectual skills, and the understanding of ideas and values. It is not clear how he would address the needs of less intellectual students.[19]

Along with back-to-basics advocates, the proponents of a core curriculum have helped to bring about changes in subject-matter requirements in many districts throughout the nation. Between 1982 and 1988, according to government estimates, the average number of years of coursework required for high-school graduation increased from 1.6 to 2.3 in mathematics, from 1.5 to 2.0 in science, from 3.6 to 3.9 in English, and from 2.6 to 2.9 in social studies.[20]

Criticisms of core curriculum

The core approach has drawn some of the same criticisms as the higher standards and back-to-basics curricula. It may be argued that the new core curriculum turns the clock back to the turn of the century, when subject-matter emphasis and academic rigor were the order of the day. Compared to 1900, there are more students today who are college bound, and for them the academic core courses may be appropriate; yet there are also more students who graduate from our schools as functional illiterates. It would be advantageous to bring order to our curriculum; but to have value for all students, a core curriculum should take account of student differences.

Student-Centered Curricula

As we have seen, the subject-centered curricula focus on cognitive aspects of learning as represented in traditional subject disciplines. A direct contrast can be found in the many varieties of **student-centered curricula.** The student-

---

[17]Ernest L. Boyer, *High School* (New York: Harper & Row, 1983); Sizer, *Horace's Compromise.*

[18]Boyer, *High School;* Sizer, *Horace's Compromise;* and John I. Goodlad, *A Place Called School* (New York: McGraw-Hill, 1984).

[19]Mortimer J. Adler, *The Paideia Proposal* (New York: Macmillan, 1982); Mortimer J. Adler, *Paideia Problems and Possibilities* (New York: Macmillan, 1983).

[20]*The Condition of Education 1987* (Washington, D.C.: U.S. Government Printing Office, 1987), Table 1.37 B, p. 84; *The Condition of Education 1991*, Vol. 1 (Washington, D.C.: U.S. Government Printing Office, 1991), Tables 1.14-1, 1.4-2, pp. 187–188.

centered approach emphasizes students' interests and needs — the affective aspects of learning. At its extreme the student-centered approach is rooted in the philosophy of Jean Jacques Rousseau, who encouraged childhood self-expression. Implicit in Rousseau's philosophy is the necessity of leaving the child to his or her own devices; Rousseau considered creativity and freedom essential for children's growth. Moreover, he thought children would be happier if they were free of teacher domination, the demands of subject matter, and adult-imposed curriculum goals.

Progressivism and student interests

Progressive education gave impetus to student-centered curricula. Progressive educators believed that when the interests and needs of learners were incorporated into the curriculum, intrinsic motivation resulted. This does not mean that student-oriented curricula are dictated by the whims of the learner. Rather, advocates believe that learning is more successful if the interests and needs of the learner are taken into account. One flaw of student-centered curricula, however, is that they sometimes overlook important cognitive content.

A balanced curriculum

John Dewey, one of the chief advocates of student-centered curricula, attempted to establish a curriculum that balanced subject matter with students' interests and needs. As early as 1902, he pointed out the fallacies of either extreme. The learner was neither "a docile recipient of facts" nor "the starting point, the center, and the end" of school activity.[21] More than thirty years later, Dewey was still criticizing overpermissive educators who provided little education for students under the guise of meeting those students' expressive and impulsive needs.[22] Dewey sought instead to use youngsters' developing interests to enhance the cognitive learning process. In the last decade, many educators have again called for nearly the same synthesis.

There are at least five major types of student-centered curricula.

Child-Centered Curriculum.   The movement from the traditional subject-dominated curriculum toward a program emphasizing student interests and needs began in 1762 with the publication of Rousseau's *Emile*, in which Rousseau maintained that the purpose of education is to teach people to live. By the turn of the next century the Swiss educator Johann Pestalozzi was stressing human emotions and kindness in teaching young children. When Friedrich Froebel introduced the kindergarten in Germany in 1837, he emphasized a permissive atmosphere and the use of songs, stories, and games as instructional materials. Early in the twentieth century, Maria Montessori, working with the slum children of Rome, developed a set of didactic materials and learning exercises that successfully combined work with play. Many of her principles became popular in the United States during the 1960s as part of the compensatory preschool movement.

Permissive atmosphere in kindergartens

Experimental schools

Early progressive educators in the United States adopted the notion of schools with a **child-centered curriculum.** After Dewey's organic school (which he described in *Schools of Tomorrow*), many other private and experimental schools developed — the best known of which were Columbia University's

---

[21]John Dewey, *The Child and the Curriculum* (Chicago: University of Chicago Press, 1902), pp. 8–9.
[22]John Dewey, *Art and Experience* (New York: Capricorn Books, 1934); Dewey, *Experience and Education* (New York: Macmillan, 1938).

Lincoln School, Ohio State's Laboratory School, the University of Missouri Elementary School, the Pratt Play School in New York City, the Parker School in Chicago, and the Fairhope School in Alabama.[23] These schools had a common feature: their curricula stressed the needs and interests of the students. Some stressed individualization; others grouped students by ability or interests.

Many child-centered programs today are carried on in **free schools** or **alternative schools** organized by parents and teachers who are dissatisfied with the public schools. These schools are typified by a great deal of freedom for students and noisy classrooms that sometimes appear untidy and disorganized. The teaching-learning process is unstructured. Most of these schools are considered radical and anti-Establishment, even though many of their ideas are rooted in the well-known child-centered doctrines of progressivism.

Summerhill, a school founded in 1921 by A. S. Neill and still in existence today, is perhaps the best-known free school. Neill's philosophy was to replace authority with freedom.[24] He was not concerned with formal learning; he did not believe in textbooks or examinations. He did believe that those who want to study *will* study and those who prefer not to study will *not*, regardless of how teachers teach. Neill's dual criteria for success were the ability to work joyfully and the ability to live a happy life.

Recent radicals

Although Neill, Edgar Friedenberg, Paul Goodman, and John Holt[25] all belong to an earlier generation of school reformers, other radicals have emerged. They include Paul Freire, Henry Giroux, Ivan Illich, Herbert Kohl, and Jonathan Kozol. These educators stress the need for, and in many cases have established, child-centered free schools or alternative schools.[26]

Criticism of free schools

Critics condemn these schools as places where little cognitive learning takes place. They decry a lack of discipline and order. They feel that the reformers' attacks on establishment teachers and schools are overgeneralized and unfair and that the language of the attack is oversimplified and rhetorical.[27] Opponents do not find the radicals' idea of schooling to be feasible for mass education, and they wish to hold the radicals accountable for irresponsible pedagogical deci-

[23]A number of these early experimental schools are discussed in detail by John Dewey and his daughter Evelyn in *Schools of Tomorrow,* published in 1915. Another good source is the 1930 yearbook of the National Society for the Study of Education, a two-volume work titled *The Foundations of Curriculum* and *Techniques of Curriculum Construction.* Lawrence Cremin's *The Transformation of the School,* published in 1961, is still another good source. Finally, Ohio State's Laboratory School is best summarized in a 1938 book titled *Were We Guinea Pigs?* written by the senior class.

[24]A. S. Neill, *Summerhill: A Radical Approach to Child Rearing* (New York: Hart, 1960).

[25]See Edgar Z. Friedenberg, *The Vanishing Adolescent* (Boston: Beacon Press, 1959); Paul Goodman, *Growing Up Absurd* (New York: Random House, 1960) and *Compulsory Mis-Education* (New York: Horizon Press, 1964); and John Holt, *How Children Fail* (New York: Pitman, 1964) and *How Children Learn* (New York: Delta, 1972).

[26]See Paul Freire, *Pedagogy of the Oppressed* (New York: Herder and Herder, 1970); Henry A. Giroux, *Teachers as Intellectuals* (Granby, Mass.: Bergin and Garvey, 1988); Ivan Illich, *Deschooling Society* (New York: Harper & Row, 1971); Herbert R. Kohl, *The Open Classroom* (New York: Random House, 1969) and *On Teaching* (New York: Schocken Books, 1976); Jonathan Kozol, *Free Schools* (Boston: Houghton Mifflin, 1972) and *Savage Inequalities: Children in America's Schools* (New York: Crown Publishers, 1991).

[27]Diane Ravitch, *The Troubled Crusade* (New York: Basic Books, 1983); Frank Smith, *To Think* (New York: Teachers College Press, Columbia University, 1990).

sions. Proponents counter that children do learn in these child-centered schools, which — instead of stressing conformity — are made to fit the child.

Activity-Centered Curriculum.   This movement, which grew out of the private child-centered schools, has strongly affected the public elementary school curriculum. William Kilpatrick, one of Dewey's colleagues, was its leader. Kilpatrick differed with Dewey's child-centered view; he believed that the interests and needs of children could not be anticipated and therefore a preplanned curriculum was impossible. He attacked the school curriculum as unrelated to the problems of real life; he advocated purposeful activities that were as lifelike as possible and that were tied to a child's needs and interests.[28]

Purposeful activities

During the 1920s and 1930s, many elementary schools adopted some ideas from the **activity-centered curriculum,** perhaps best summarized and first put into practice by Ellsworth Collings, a doctoral student of Kilpatrick's.[29] A host of teaching strategies emerged, including lessons based on life experiences, group games, dramatizations, story projects, field trips, social enterprises, and interest centers. All of these activities involved problem solving and active student participation; they emphasized socialization and the formation of stronger school-community ties.

Recent curriculum reformers have translated ideas from this movement into community and career-based activities intended to prepare students for adult citizenship and work and into courses emphasizing social problems and social responsibility. They have also urged college credit for life experiences. Secondary and college students often earn credit today by working in welfare agencies, early childhood programs, tutoring programs, government, hospitals, and homes for the aged.[30] Schools can also make use of the rich experiences of the business and scientific community, neighborhood libraries, recreational or park district agencies, playhouses, and youth agencies (such as the Scouts). As one educator pointed out, "We take for granted that our schools are communities, when, in fact, they are merely institutions that become communities only when we work at it."[31] Schools employing an activity-centered curriculum envision students as involved citizens rather than just as test takers and future workers. By encouraging hands-on activities and real-life experiences, these schools give students a sense of ownership in the school, a sense of community.

Community-based activities

Relevant Curriculum.   Unquestionably, the curriculum must reflect social change. This point is well illustrated in *The Saber-Tooth Curriculum*, a satiric book on education, written in 1939 by Harold Benjamin, a reconstructionist, under

---

[28]William H. Kilpatrick, "The Project Method," *Teachers College Record* (September 1918), pp. 319–335.

[29]Ellsworth Collings, ed., *An Experiment with a Project Curriculum* (New York: Macmillan, 1923). Another description of the activity-centered program was provided by Harold Rugg and Ann Shumaker, *The Child-Centered School: An Appraisal of the New Education* (Yonkers, N.Y.: World Book, 1928).

[30]Elise Boulding, *Education for the Reconstruction of a Civic Culture* (New York: Teachers College Press, Columbia University, 1987); Mario D. Fantini, *Regaining Excellence in Education* (Columbus, Ohio: Merrill, 1986).

[31]George H. Wood, "Teaching for Democracy," *Educational Leadership* (November 1990), p. 33.

The activity-centered curriculum generated a host of teaching strategies — including lessons based on life experiences, group games, dramatizations, story projects, field trips, social enterprises, and interest centers. (© Elizabeth Crews/The Image Works)

Fish catching, horse clubbing, and tiger scaring

the pseudonym Abner J. Peddiwell.[32] He describes a society in which the schools continued to teach fish catching (because it would develop agility), horse clubbing (to develop strength), and tiger scaring (to develop courage) long after the streams had dried up and the horses and tigers had disappeared. The wise men of the society argued that "the essence of true education is timeless . . . something that endures through changing conditions like a solid rock standing squarely and firmly in the middle of a raging torrent."[33] Benjamin's message was simple: the curriculum was no longer relevant.

The 1960s and 1970s saw a renewed concern for a **relevant curriculum,** but with a somewhat different emphasis. There was less concern that the curriculum reflect changing social conditions and more concern that the curriculum be relevant to students. This shift was part of the Dewey legacy: learners must be motivated and interested in the learning task, and the classroom should build on their real-life experiences.

Relevant to students

The demand for relevance came from both students and educators. In fact, the student disruptions of the 1960s and 1970s were related to this demand. Proponents who advocate this approach today see the following needs: (1) the individualization of instruction through such teaching methods as independent inquiry and special projects; (2) the revision of existing courses and development of new ones on such topics of student concern as environmental protection, drug addiction, urban problems, and cultural pluralism; (3) the provision of educational alternatives (such as electives, minicourses, open classrooms) that allow more freedom of choice; (4) the extension of the curriculum beyond the

---

[32]Harold Benjamin, *The Saber-Tooth Curriculum* (New York: McGraw-Hill, 1939).
[33]Ibid., pp. 43–44.

Credit for life experiences

school's walls through such innovations as work-study programs, credit for life experiences, and external degree programs; and (5) the relaxation of academic standards and admission standards to schools and colleges.[34]

Efforts to relate subject matter to student interests have been largely ad hoc, and many were fragmented and temporary. This has been a source of concern to advocates of relevance. In other cases, changes made in the name of relevance have in fact watered down the curriculum.

Humanistic Curriculum.   Like many other modern curriculum developments, humanistic education began as a reaction to what was viewed as an overemphasis on cognitive learning in the late 1950s and early 1960s. Terry Borton, a Philadelphia schoolteacher, was one of the first to write about this movement. He contended that education had only two major purposes: subject

Subject mastery and personal growth

mastery and personal growth.[35] Nearly every school's statement of goals includes both purposes, but Borton, and later others, asserted that goals related to personal growth, feelings, and the happy life were included only for show.[36] Almost everyone knows, the argument went, how little schools have done to promote learning related to personal insights and the affective domain. In his best-selling book, *Crisis in the Classroom,* Charles Silberman also advocated the humanizing of U.S. schools.[37] He charged that schools were repressive, teaching students

Docility and conformity

docility and conformity.

The humanistic model of education grew out of the human potential movement in psychology. Within education it is rooted in the work of Arthur Jersild, who linked good teaching with knowledge of self and students, and in the work of Arthur Combs and Donald Snygg, who explored the impact of self-concept and motivation on achievement.[38] Combs and Snygg considered self-concept to be the most important determinant of behavior.

A **humanistic curriculum** emphasizes affective rather than cognitive outcomes. Such a curriculum draws heavily on the work of Abraham Maslow and

"Self-actualizing people"

of Carl Rogers.[39] Its goal is to produce "self-actualizing people," in Maslow's words, or "total human beings" as Rogers puts it. The works of both psychologists are laden with such terms as *choosing, striving, enhancing,* and *experienc-*

---

[34]Michael W. Apple and Linda Christian-Smith, *The Politics of the Textbook* (New York: Routledge, 1991); Herbert Kliebard, *The Struggle for the American Curriculum* (Boston: Routledge & Kegan Paul, 1986); and Arthur Powell, Eleanor Farrar, and David Cohen, *The Shopping Mall High School* (Boston: Houghton Mifflin, 1985).

[35]Terry Borton, *Reach, Touch, and Teach* (New York: McGraw-Hill, 1970).

[36]Louise M. Berman and Jessie A. Roderick, eds., *Feelings, Values, and the Art of Growing,* 1977 ASCD Yearbook (Washington, D.C.: Association for Supervision and Curriculum Development, 1977); Elliot W. Eisner, *The Educational Imagination,* 2nd ed. (New York: Macmillan, 1985); and James Herndon, *Notes from a Schoolteacher* (New York: Simon and Schuster, 1985).

[37]Charles A. Silberman, *Crisis in the Classroom* (New York: Random House, 1971).

[38]Arthur T. Jersild, *In Search of Self* (New York: Teachers College Press, Columbia University, 1952); Jersild, *When Teachers Face Themselves* (New York: Teachers College Press, Columbia University, 1955); and Arthur Combs and Donald Snygg, *Individual Behavior,* 2nd ed. (New York: Harper & Row, 1959).

[39]Abraham H. Maslow, *Toward a Psychology of Being* (New York: Van Nostrand Reinhold, 1962) and *Motivation and Personality,* 2nd ed. (New York: Harper & Row, 1970); Carl R. Rogers, *On Becoming a Person* (Boston: Houghton Mifflin, 1961); and Carl Rogers, *Freedom to Learn,* 2nd ed. (Columbus, Ohio: Merrill, 1983).

Humanists attempt to form meaningful relationships between students and teachers, foster student independence and self-direction, and promote greater acceptance of self and others. (© Sven Martson/Comstock)

ing — as well as *independence, self-determination, integration,* and *personal relationships.*

Advocates of humanistic education contend that the present school curriculum has failed miserably by humanistic standards, that teachers and schools are determined to stress cognitive behaviors and to control students *not* for students' good but for the good of adults. Humanists emphasize more than affective processes; they seek higher domains of spirit, consciousness, aesthetics, and morality.[40] Humanists would attempt to form more meaningful relationships between students and teachers; they would foster student independence and self-direction and promote greater acceptance of self and others. The teacher's role would be to help learners cope with their psychological needs and problems, to facilitate self-understanding among students, and to help students develop fully.

Higher domains of consciousness

Values-Centered Curriculum. As social and economic conditions change, so do people and the ideas they value; this is a natural and inevitable process. Yet because of the fast pace of modern society, the breakdown of the nuclear family, and the decline in church influence, people today often suffer from value confusion, the symptoms of which may include apathy, uncertainty, and inconsistency. A **values-centered curriculum** attempts to alleviate the confusion by placing special emphasis on moral and ethical issues.

Value confusion

[40]Elliot Eisner, *The Educational Imagination,* 3rd ed. (New York: Macmillan, 1993); Maxine Greene, *Landscapes of Learning* (New York: Teachers College Press, Columbia University, 1978); Greene, *The Dialectic of Freedom* (New York: Teachers College Press, Columbia University, 1987); and Carol Witherell and Nel Noddings, *The Challenge to Care in Schools* (New York: Teachers College Press, Columbia University, 1992).

Multicultural education

Much recent educational concern has focused on values. For example, advocates of multicultural education stress not only knowledge of the diverse cultures and ethnic experiences of American society, but also appreciation and respect for cultures other than one's own. In this respect, multicultural education fits into a values-centered curriculum. Even more fundamentally, some educators, parents, and community members have come to the conclusion that too many students lack a strong sense of right and wrong. It is up to the schools, these people argue, to teach such basic values as honesty, responsibility, self-discipline, compassion, tolerance, and respect for the rights of others.

Basic moral values

Teaching valuing

But how should values be taught? Educators have developed various methods to teach valuing. For example, *value clarification* is a technique designed to overcome value confusion and to help people become positive and purposeful. According to Louis Raths and his associates, who have written one of the most popular books on the subject, the process of valuing follows seven steps: "choosing freely, choosing from alteratives, choosing after thoughtful consideration, prizing and cherishing, affirming, acting upon choices, and repeating [such choices] . . . as a pattern in life."[41]

In addition to value clarification, at least four other distinct teaching methods have appeared. The first is *inculcation*, in which accepted values are taught with the support of common law. Next is *moral development*, highlighting moral and ethical principles and their application. Third is *analysis* of issues and situations involving values. A fourth is *action learning*, by which values are tried and tested in real-life situations.[42] In addition, the humanistic approaches used by Abraham Maslow and Carl Rogers may be described as *evocation*, a calling forth from the individual of personal values and the ability to make choices and think creatively.

Lack of attention to cognitive learning

One drawback to humanistic and value-clarification theories is their lack of attention to cognitive learning. When asked to judge the effectiveness of their curricula, both humanists and value educators generally rely on testimonials and subjective assessments, rather than empirical evidence or student achievement scores. Even more important, value educators and community members often do not concur about the values to be taught or how to teach them. Parents may be enraged if a school attempts to teach values that differ from those of the home and family. Especially in such controversial areas as sex, religion, and social justice, values education may become a minefield.

Lack of agreement about values to be taught

Finding a consensus

Many educators contend, however, that it is possible — even with our multicultural, multireligious population — to establish a set of values that represent an American consensus.[43] The idea is not to prepackage a values curriculum that assumes there is only one right way of doing things, but to educate students to

---

[41]Louis E. Raths, Merrill Harmin, and Sidney B. Simon, *Values and Teaching,* 2nd ed. (Columbus, Ohio: Merrill, 1978), pp. 27–28. Also see Louis Raths et al., *Teaching for Thinking,* 2nd ed. (New York: Teachers College Press, Columbia University, 1986).

[42]Ronald C. Doll, *Curriculum Improvement: Decision Making and Process,* 8th ed. (Needham Heights, Mass.: Allyn and Bacon, 1992); James T. Sears and J. Dan Marshal, eds., *Teaching and Thinking About Curriculum* (New York: Teachers College Press, Columbia University, 1990).

[43]Merrill Harmin, "Value Clarity: Higher Morality: Let's Go for Both," *Educational Leadership* (May 1988), pp. 24–30; Richard W. Paul, "Ethics Without Doctrination," *Educational Leadership* (May 1988), pp. 10–19; and Edward A. Wynne, "Ethics vs. Morality: Should the Conflict Come to the Classroom?" *NASSP Bulletin* (October 1990), pp. 38–44.

be socially responsible adults. For example, a values curriculum can focus on readings that promote moral and ethical knowledge: for young readers, "Aesop's Fables" and "Jack and the Beanstalk"; for older children, *Sadako, Up from Slavery,* and *The Diary of Anne Frank;* for adolescents, *Of Mice and Men, A Man for All Seasons,* and *Death of a Salesman.* Students could also discuss political leaders such as Abraham Lincoln, Mohandas Gandhi, and Martin Luther King, Jr., and even religious leaders such as Moses, Jesus, and Confucius. A reasonable consensus on values education may be achievable if educators have the moral conviction to pursue it.

Curriculum Contrasts: An Overview

Subject matter and student needs

In summary, subject-centered and student-centered curricula each represent an extreme on a continuum that is rooted in the past and present practices of curriculum organization. Most schooling in the United States falls somewhere between the two — effecting a tenuous balance between subject matter and student needs, between cognitive outcomes and psychological factors.

Regardless of a teacher's personal bias or approach, decisions on what is taught and how curriculum is organized are usually influenced by the philosophical orientation of the school at which he or she is teaching. More traditional schools that subscribe to a perennialist or essentialist philosophy generally advocate a subject-centered curriculum. Schools that are oriented more toward progressive or reconstructionist education tend to use a student-centered curriculum. (Overview 14.1 summarizes the various subject-centered and student-centered curricula and their corresponding philosophies, content emphases, and instructional emphases.) Regardless of one's views or one's aims or goals, one need not take an extreme position on the subject matter–student interests continuum. We would expect some type of blend, although many educators would emphasize one curriculum approach (subject or student emphasis) over another.

Actually, the relative emphasis on subject matter or student interests is essentially a question of philosophical orientation and, to a lesser extent, learning theory. From these philosophical and theoretical concerns, we must eventually move to the area of curriculum development; this is a technical concern and involves systematic reflection and planning.

ISSUES IN CURRICULUM DEVELOPMENT

Curriculum at the national and state levels

Whether the curriculum is subject centered or student centered, the process of developing it involves (1) assessing the needs and capabilities of the learners and (2) selecting or creating the instructional materials and activities. At the national level, curriculum making is minimal and indirect, although the idea of national aims and standards has gained popularity. At the state level, curriculum development is often limited to the publication of curriculum guides and booklets. These are prepared by a professional staff in the state department of education, assisted by curriculum consultants and college professors. The state publications tend to focus on large-scale concerns, such as the need for stronger curricula in math and science. In many states, however, the guidelines are more

Overview 14.1

Curriculum Organization Approaches

Curriculum Approach	Corresponding Philosophy or Theory	Content Emphasis	Instructional Emphasis
Subject-Centered			
Subject-area curriculum	Perennialism, essentialism	Three Rs; academic, vocational, and elective subjects	Knowledge, concepts, and principles; specialized knowledge
Subject-structure curriculum	Essentialism	Science, math, and foreign language; academic disciplines; academic excellence	Concepts and principles; problem solving; intuitive thinking; learning how to learn
Perennialist curriculum	Perennialism	Three Rs; liberal arts; classics; timeless values; academic rigor	Rote memorization; specialized knowledge; mental discipline
Essentialist curriculum	Essentialism	Three Rs; liberal arts and science; academic disciplines; academic excellence	Concepts and principles; problem solving; essential skills
Back-to-basics curriculum	Essentialism	Three Rs; academic subjects	Specific knowledge and skills; drill; attainment of measurable ends or competencies
Higher standards curriculum	Perennialism, essentialism	Academic subjects; computer literacy; academic excellence and educational productivity	Knowledge; concepts and principles; learning how to learn; attainment of measurable ends or competencies

specific, including lists of instructional materials that are mandated or recommended for use in public schools.

Curriculum at the local level

The greatest responsibility for curriculum development generally falls on the local school district — or, as school-based management becomes more widespread, on the schools themselves. Large school districts often employ personnel who specialize in curriculum development, including subject-matter specialists and test consultants. In the smaller school districts, curriculum development is generally handled by a group of teachers organized by subject or grade level. In some cases the teachers work with parents, administrators, and student representatives.

College admission standards exert a strong influence on curriculum choices, for colleges establish minimum course requirements that applicants must have met. Increasingly, too, local curriculum developers must pay close attention to standards and academic requirements established by the state. For example, in

Curriculum Approach	Corresponding Philosophy or Theory	Content Emphasis	Instructional Emphasis
Core curriculum	Perennialism, essentialism	Common curriculum for all students; focus on academics	Common knowledge; intellectual skills and concepts; values and moral issues
Student-Centered Child-centered curriculum	Progressivism	Student needs and interests; student experiences	Play oriented; creative expression; free learning environment
Activity-centered curriculum	Progressivism	Student needs and interests; student activities; school-community activities	Active, experimental environment; project methods; effective living
Relevant curriculum	Progressivism, reconstructionism	Student experiences and activities; felt needs	Social and personal problems; reflective thinking
Humanistic curriculum	Progressivism, reconstructionism, existentialism	Introspection; choice; affective processes	Individual and group learning; flexible, artistic, psychological methods; self-realization
Values-centered curriculum	Reconstructionism, existentialism	Democratic values; ethical and moral values; crosscultural and universal values; choice and freedom	Feelings, attitudes, and emotions; existentialist thinking; decision making

a state where students take a statewide test to earn a high-school diploma, the curriculum must ensure that students acquire the knowledge and skills necessary to pass the test.

Influence of textbooks

A major influence on curriculum — one whose importance is often underrated — is the textbook. Traditionally, the textbook has been the most frequently used instructional medium at all levels beyond the primary grades. As such, textbooks can dominate the nature and sequence of a course and thus profoundly affect the learning experiences of students. In choosing a textbook, curriculum developers often shape the entire course. In effect, the course is based on the knowledge base and biases of the textbook's author. For this reason, it is important to understand some of the factors that govern textbook writing and publication.

Limitations of textbooks

In order to have wide application and a large potential market, textbooks tend to be general, noncontroversial, and bland. They are usually written for a

Getting to the Source ◄●►

Fundamental Questions on Curriculum

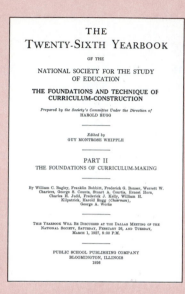

THE
TWENTY-SIXTH YEARBOOK
OF THE
NATIONAL SOCIETY FOR THE STUDY
OF EDUCATION

THE FOUNDATIONS AND TECHNIQUE OF
CURRICULUM-CONSTRUCTION

Prepared by the Society's Committee Under the Direction of
HAROLD RUGG

Edited by
GUY MONTROSE WHIPPLE

PART II
THE FOUNDATIONS OF CURRICULUM-MAKING

By William C. Bagley, Franklin Bobbitt, Frederick G. Bonser, Werrett W.
Charters, George S. Counts, Stuart A. Courtis, Ernest Horn,
Charles H. Judd, Frederick J. Kelly, William H.
Kilpatrick, Harold Rugg (*Chairman*),
George A. Works

THIS YEARBOOK WILL BE DISCUSSED AT THE DALLAS MEETING OF THE
NATIONAL SOCIETY, SATURDAY, FEBRUARY 26, AND TUESDAY,
MARCH 1, 1927, 8:00 P.M.

PUBLIC SCHOOL PUBLISHING COMPANY
BLOOMINGTON, ILLINOIS
1926

The twenty-sixth yearbook of the National Society for the Study of Education, published in 1930, is considered a landmark book on curriculum; it was the first attempt by a group of curriculum scholars to synthesize the meaning and practice of curriculum making. Volume II presented a list of "fundamental ques-

tions" on curriculum making, intended to stimulate discussion among teachers and curriculum leaders. The questions have stood the test of time; they are relevant today.

1. What period of life does schooling primarily contemplate as its end?
2. How can the curriculum prepare for effective participation in adult life?
3. Are the curriculum-makers of the schools obliged to formulate a point of view concerning the merits or deficiencies of American civilization?
4. Should the school be regarded as a conscious agency for social improvement?
    A. Should the school be planned on the assumption that it is to fit children to "live in" the current social order or to rise above and lift it after them? Are children merely to be "adjusted" to the institutions of current society or are they to be so educated that they will be impelled to modify it? Are they to accept it or to question it?
5. How shall the content of the curriculum be conceived and stated?

national audience, so they do not consider local issues or community problems. Because they are geared for the greatest number of "average" students, they may not meet the needs and interests of any particular group or individual.[44] In summarizing large quantities of data, they may become superficial and discourage conceptual thinking, critical analysis, and evaluation. Furthermore, with the possible exception of those on mathematics, most textbooks quickly become outdated; because they are expensive, however, they are often used long after they should have been replaced.

Advantages of textbooks   Considering these criticisms, why do teachers rely so heavily on textbooks? The answer is that textbooks do have many advantages. A textbook provides an outline that the teacher can use in planning lessons; summarizes a great deal of pertinent information; enables the student to take home most of the course ma-

---

[44]Allan C. Ornstein, "Textbook Instruction: Processes and Strategies," *NASSP Bulletin* (December 1989), pp. 105–111; Elliot W. Eisner, "Who Decides What Schools Will Teach?" *Phi Delta Kappan* (March 1990), pp. 523–525.

6. What is the place and function of subject matter in the educative process?

7. What portion of education should be classified as "general" and what portion as "specialized" or "vocational" or purely "optional?" To what extent is general education to run parallel with vocational education and to what extent is the latter to follow on the completion of the former? . . .

11. To what extent should traits be learned in their "natural" setting (i.e., in a "life-situation")?

12. To what degree should the curriculum provide for individual differences? . . .

14. What should be the form of organization of the curriculum? Shall it be one of the following or will you adopt others?
   a. A flexibly graded series of suggestive activities with reference to subject matter which may be used in connection with the activities? Or
   b. A rigidly graded series of activities with subject matter included with each respective activity? Or,
   c. A graded sequence of subject matter with suggestion for activities to which the subject matter is related? Or,
   d. A statement of achievements expected for each grade, a list of suggestive activities, and an outline of related subject matter, through the use of which the grade object may be achieved? Or,
   e. A statement of grade objectivities in terms of subject matter and textual and reference materials which will provide this subject matter without any specific reference to activities?

15. What, if any, use shall be made of the spontaneous interests of children?

Questions

1. What principles of psychology and school of philosophy do the questions reflect?

2. To what extent would you modify the questions set forth in the statement? Which questions do you find irrelevant?

3. What are the advantages and dangers in publishing a general statement or platform about curriculum making?

Source: "A Composite Statement by the Members of the Society's Committee on Curriculum Making," in G. M. Whipple, ed., *The Foundations of Curriculum Making*, Twenty-sixty Yearbook of the National Society for the Study of Education, Part II (Bloomington, Ill.: Public School Publishing Co., 1930), cover, pp. 9–10.

terial in a convenient package; provides a common resource for all students to follow; includes pictures, graphs, maps, and other illustrative material that facilitates understanding; and frequently includes other teaching aids, such as summaries and review questions. By relying on the textbook to provide the basic information, the teacher can spend more time preparing the lesson.[45] In short, the textbook is an acceptable tool if it is selected and used properly. However, it should not be the only source of knowledge for students, and it should not define the entire curriculum.

Censorship trends

Another issue in curriculum development is the question of censorship. In the states that prepare lists of instructional materials for their schools, the trend is growing to "limit what students shall read."[46] As Chapter 8 indicated, the list

---

[45]Ornstein, "Textbook Instruction."

[46]*Attack on the Freedom to Learn, 1989–90* (Washington, D.C.: People for the American Way, 1990).

of objectionable works has sometimes included such classics as *Little Red Riding Hood, Mary Poppins,* and *Huckleberry Finn.* Today, almost any book that contains political or economic messages, obscenity, sex, nudity, profanity, slang or questionable English, ethnic or racially sensitive material, or any material that could be interpreted as antifamily, antireligious, or anti-American is subject to possible censorship.

Subtle censorship

Although censorship is often overt, it can operate in subtle ways as well. Curriculum developers may quietly steer away from issues and materials that would cause controversy in the community. Moreover, textbooks often omit topics that might upset potential audiences or interest groups. Even pictures are important, for some organizations count the number of pictures of one ethnic group versus another group, of boys versus girls, of business versus labor. Professional associations can also exert a type of censorship when they recommend certain changes in subject content and implicitly discourage other approaches. Educators must be sensitive to censorship because it is always there in one form or another. In dealing with such issues, we often find that Herbert Spencer's fundamental question "What knowledge is of most worth?" becomes "Whose knowledge is of most worth?"

As teaching becomes more professionalized, teachers are increasingly expected to deal with curriculum choices and the complex issues they present. To avoid letting curriculum become "a political football," as Michael Apple terms it,[47] today's teachers need a full understanding of community concerns, statewide standards and goals, and student needs.

INSTRUCTIONAL APPROACHES

High hopes for reform

Although educators differ in the definition of curriculum, the majority recognize that curriculum and instruction are interrelated. To carry out the curriculum one must rely on instruction — programs, materials, and methods. The search for new programs and methods of instruction is continual. The last twenty-five years, in particular, have witnessed a major effort to improve learning outcomes, integrate technology into the lesson, and have students participate first hand with the new tools of instruction.

Although we cannot survey all the major instructional innovations of recent decades, the following sections describe several that have drawn considerable attention from educators. Chapter 16 will return to the subject of instructional approaches in the context of school reform and school effectiveness.

Individualized Instruction

In the past three decades, several models have been advanced for **individualized instruction.** Although these approaches vary somewhat, they all try to provide a one-to-one student-teacher or student-computer relationship. Stu-

---

[47]Michael Apple, "Is There a Curriculum Voice to Reclaim?" *Phi Delta Kappan* (March 1990), pp. 526–530.

dents are allowed to proceed at their own rate, and the instructional materials are carefully sequenced and structured, usually with an emphasis on practice and drill.

One of the early examples, the Project on Individually Prescribed Instruction (IPI), was developed at the University of Pittsburgh in the late 1950s and early 1960s.[48] For every student, an individual plan was prepared for each skill or subject based on a diagnosis of the student's needs. Objectives were stated in behavioral terms with specific proficiency levels. Learning tasks were individualized, and the student's progress was continually evaluated.

Individualized learning plan

The 1960s and 1970s saw the rise of two other well-known systems. The Program for Learning in Accordance with Needs (PLAN)[49] uses two-week modules arranged according to the student's level of achievement. Instructional materials are ungraded, and alternative sets of materials are available for each unit of instruction. In Individually Guided Education (IGE),[50] a total educational system introduced in several thousand schools, planned variations are made in what and how each student learns. In addition to individual objectives and one-to-one relationships with teachers or tutors, the program includes independent study, small-group instruction, and large-group instruction.

Use of modules

Adaptive instruction, a program that grew out of the IPI model, similarly emphasizes flexibility in teaching methods.[51] Different students pursue different objectives, spend different amounts of time learning each skill, and use different resources. Modular materials allow students to enter at different points, skip around, or go back to difficult items.

Adaptive instruction

A more behaviorist and teacher-directed approach is the Personalized System of Instruction (PSI), sometimes called the Keller Plan after its originator.[52] Developed initially for high-school and college students, PSI makes use of study guides (which break the course down into small units with specific objectives) and proctors (high-achieving students who assist others).

Study guides

Field testing of these individualized instruction programs has generally been positive. Some reports on IPI, PLAN, and IGE have shown significant gains in student achievement.[53] Adaptive instruction seems to benefit all kinds of students, especially low-achieving ones or students with mild disabilities,[54] and

Results positive

---

[48]Robert Glaser and Lauren B. Resnick, "Instructional Psychology," *Annual Review of Psychology* (no. 23, 1972), pp. 207–276.

[49]John C. Flanagan, "Program for Learning in Accordance with Needs" (Paper presented at the Annual Conference of the American Educational Research Association, Chicago, February 1968).

[50]Herbert J. Klausmeier and Richard E. Ripple, *Learning and Human Abilities*, 3rd ed. (New York: Harper & Row, 1971).

[51]Robert Glaser, *Adaptive Education: Individual Diversity and Learning* (New York: Holt, Rinehart and Winston, 1977); Lauren B. Resnick and Robert Glaser, *The Nature of Intelligence* (Hillside, N.J.: Erlbaum, 1976); and Margaret C. Wang, *The Rationale and Design of the Self Schedule System* (Pittsburgh: University of Pittsburgh, Learning Research and Development Center, 1974).

[52]Fred S. Keller, "Good-bye Teacher!" *Journal of Applied Behavioral Analysis* (April 1968), pp. 79–84.

[53]Herbert J. Klausmeier, *Learning and Teaching Concepts* (New York: Academic Press, 1980).

[54]Glaser, *Adaptive Education;* Margaret C. Wang and Herbert J. Walberg, eds., *Adapting Instruction to Individual Differences* (Berkeley, Calif.: McCutchan, 1985).

studies of PSI have reported a rise in student test scores.[55] Nevertheless, individualized plans are expensive to implement, and most schools today continue to employ group methods of instruction and group expectations.

Cooperative Learning

Reducing competition, increasing cooperation

Cooperative, rather than competitive, learning is becoming more and more accepted as an important way to instruct students. In the traditional classroom structure, students compete for teacher recognition and grades. The same students tend to be "winners" and "losers" over the years because of differences in ability and achievement. High-achieving students continually receive rewards and are motivated to learn, whereas low-achieving students continually experience failure (or near failure) and frustration. The idea of **cooperative learning** is to change the traditional structure by reducing competition and increasing cooperation among students — thus diminishing possible hostility and tension among students and continual failure among the same students.

Benefits of competition

This does not mean that competition has no place in the classroom or school. The chief advocates of cooperation tell us that competition can be utilized successfully and for increasing performance on simple drill activities, speed-related tasks (such as spelling, vocabulary, and simple math computations), in low anxiety games and psychomotor tasks (such as board games and puzzles), and on the athletic field.[56] Competition, under the right conditions with evenly matched individuals or groups, can be a source of fun, excitement, and motivation.

Benefits of cooperation

According to a review of the research, cooperation among participants helps build (1) positive and coherent personal identity, (2) self-actualization and mental health, (3) knowledge and trust of one another, (4) communication with one another, (5) acceptance and support of one another, and (6) wholesome relationships with a reduced amount of conflict. The data also suggest that cooperation and group learning are considerably more effective in fostering these social and interpersonal skills than are competitive or individualistic efforts.[57]

Of all the cooperative instructional arrangements, the two developed by Robert Slavin are most popular: Student-Teams Achievement Divisions (STAD) and Team-Assisted Individualization (TAI). Both methods have been found to increase student achievement, given the proper procedures.[58] In STAD, teams comprise four or five members, preferably four (an arrangement that contradicts

---

[55]Arthur L. Robin, "Behavioral Instruction in College Classrooms," *Review of Educational Research* (Summer 1976), pp. 313–354; James A. Kulik, Chen-Lin C. Kulik, and Peter A. Cohen, "Meta-Analysis of Outcome Studies of Keller's Personalized System of Instruction," *American Psychologist* (April 1979), pp. 307–318. Also see James A. Kulik, "Findings on Grouping Are Often Distorted," *Educational Leadership* (February 1990), p. 67.

[56]David Johnson and Roger T. Johnson, *Learning Together and Alone,* 3rd ed. (Needham Heights, Mass.: Allyn and Bacon, 1991); Robert E. Slavin, *School and Classroom Organization* (Hillsdale, N.J.: Erlbaum, 1988).

[57]David W. Johnson, *Reaching Out: Interpersonal Effectiveness and Self Actualization,* 4th ed. (Englewood Cliffs, N.J.: Prentice-Hall, 1990); Robert E. Slavin, *Cooperative Learning: Theory, Research, and Practice* (Englewood Cliffs, N.J.: Prentice-Hall, 1990).

[58]Robert E. Slavin, "When Does Cooperative Learning Increase Student Achievement?" *Psychological Bulletin* (November 1983), pp. 429–445; Slavin, "Synthesis of Research on Cooperative Learning," *Educational Leadership* (February 1991), pp. 71–82.

Balanced teams

other research indicating that groups of four tend to pair off). Teams are balanced by ability, gender, and ethnicity. Team members provide assistance and feedback to each other and receive a group performance score on quizzes. Teams receive recognition via bulletin boards, certificates, and letters to parents. The teams are changed every five or six weeks to give students an opportunity to work with others and to give members of low-scoring teams a new chance.[59]

The TAI approach puts more emphasis on mastery of particular skill sheets and on individual diagnosis through pre- and post-testing. Students first work on their own skill sheets and then have their partners or team members check their answers and provide assistance. Not until the student scores 80 percent or higher on a practice quiz is the student certified by the team to take the final test. Teams are scored and recognized in the same way as with STAD, although criteria are established for "super teams" (high performance), "great teams" (moderate performance), and "good teams" (minimum passing grade). Every day the teacher spends 5 to 15 minutes of the 45-minute lesson period with two or three groups that are at about the same point in the curriculum. The other teams work on their own during this time.[60]

Team recognition

Mastery Instruction

Mastery instruction is an instructional plan for all grade levels and subjects. The approach being used most widely in the public schools is the Learning for Mastery (LFM) model, often referred to as mastery learning and associated originally with John Carroll and later with James Block and Benjamin Bloom. Their ideas have gained supporters particularly in urban school districts, where there is an obvious need to improve academic performance among inner-city students.

Carroll pointed out that if students are normally distributed by ability or aptitude for some academic subject and are provided appropriate instruction tailored to their individual characteristics, the majority should achieve mastery of the subject.[61] He also maintained that if a student does not spend sufficient time to learn a task, he or she will not master it. However, students vary in the amount of time needed to successfully achieve or complete a task. Nearly all students (assuming no major learning disability) can achieve if given sufficient time. Carroll distinguished between *time needed* to learn (based on student characteristics) and *time available* for learning (under the teacher's control). High-achieving students need less time for learning the same material than low-achieving students do. The teacher can vary instructional time for different in-

Varying time needed to learn

---

[59]Robert E. Slavin, "Student Teams and Comparison Among Equals," *Journal of Educational Psychology* (August 1978), pp. 532–538; Slavin, "Student Teams and Achievement Division," *Journal of Research and Development in Education* (Fall 1978), pp. 38–49.

[60]Thomas L. Good and Jere E. Brophy, *Looking in Classrooms*, 5th ed. (New York: Harper Collins, 1991); Robert E. Slavin, "Team-Assisted Individualization: Combining Cooperative Learning and Individualized Instruction in Mathematics," in R. E. Slavin, ed., *Learning to Cooperate, Cooperating to Learn* (New York: Plenum, 1985), pp. 177–209.

[61]John B. Carroll, "A Model of School Learning," *Teachers College Record* (May 1963), pp. 723–733; Carroll, "The Carroll Model: A 25 Year Retrospective and Prospective View," *Educational Researcher* (January–February 1989), pp. 26–31.

dividuals (or groups of students), depending on the learners' needs and the teacher's own judgment.

Block and Bloom's approach is based on the central argument that 90 percent of public-school students can learn much of the curriculum at practically the same level of mastery. Although slower students require a longer period of time to learn the same materials, they can succeed if their initial level of knowledge is correctly diagnosed and if they are taught with appropriate methods and materials in a sequential manner, beginning with their initial competency level.[62]

To accomplish this goal, attention must be focused on small units of instruction, and criterion-referenced tests must be used to determine whether a student possesses skills required for success at each step in the learning sequence being taught. An entire course such as third-grade mathematics is too complex to be studied in large units. Instead, it should be broken into smaller modules, and the students should be maximally successful (scoring 80–90 percent correct) before moving to the next module.

A substantial body of data indicates that mastery learning can result in large learning gains for students. After reviewing hundreds of studies on mastery learning, three observers conclude that the results indicate that mastery strategies have moderate to strong effects on student learning when compared to conventional methods.[63] When entire school districts have been studied, the results show that mastery approaches are also successful in teaching basic skills, such as reading and mathematics, that form the basis for later learning; moreover, inner-city students profit more from this approach than from traditional groupings of instruction.[64]

Data favorable to mastery learning do not mean that all the important questions have been answered or that mastery strategies do not have critics. We do not know, for example, how well differing mastery approaches can work for "higher-order" learning, affective learning, or different types of students. Moreover, we are unsure to what extent teachers are teaching the test to their students in order to avoid blame for students' failure to master the material.[65] Other critics claim that reading, writing, and mathematics are being broken down into discrete skills that are mastered, but the students still cannot read, write, or compute any better. Students evidence gains on small skill-acquisition items, but this

---

[62]James H. Block, *Mastery Learning: Theory and Practice* (New York: Holt, Rinehart and Winston, 1971); Benjamin S. Bloom, *Human Characteristics and School Learning* (New York: McGraw-Hill, 1976). Also see James H. Block, Helen Efthim, and Robert Burns, *Creating Effective Mastery Learning Schools* (New York: Longman, 1989).

[63]Lorin W. Anderson, "Values, Evidence, and Mastery Learning," *Review of Educational Research* (Summer 1987), pp. 215–223; James H. Block and Robert B. Burns, "Mastery Learning," in L. S. Shulman, ed., *Review of Research in Education*, vol. 4 (Itasca, Ill.: Peacock, 1976), pp. 118–146.

[64]Daniel U. Levine and Eugene E. Eubanks, "A First Look at Effective School Projects in Milwaukee and New York," *Phi Delta Kappan* (June 1983), pp. 697–702; Daniel U. Levine, "Achievement Gains in Self-Contained Chapter I Classes in Kansas City," *Educational Leadership* (March 1987), pp. 22–23; and Daniel U. Levine and Allan C. Ornstein, "Research on Classroom and School Effectiveness," *Urban Review* (June 1989), pp. 81–94.

[65]Allan C. Ornstein, "Emphasis on Student Outcomes Focuses Attention on Quality of Instruction," *NASSP Bulletin* (January 1987), pp. 88–95; Robert E. Slavin, "Mastery Learning Reconsidered," *Review of Educational Research* (Summer 1990), pp. 300–302.

does not necessarily prove learning.[66] Traditionally, teachers have held time constant so that individual differences are reflected in achievement differences. A mastery learning situation that varies time among students will narrow achievement differences among students but will favor those who need extra time to complete tasks at the expense of other students.[67] Finally, like other individualized instructional systems, mastery learning is not easy to implement. Responsibility is placed on the teacher, who must adapt the instruction to each student. The teacher must continually monitor each student's work, determine what skills and tasks each student has mastered, and provide immediate feedback — not an easy instructional task in a class of twenty-five or more students. As more studies on mastery learning are conducted in various settings, educators will discover whether these problems and questions can be resolved.

Critical Thinking

Critical thinking and *thinking skills* are terms used today to denote problem-solving ability. Interest in this concept is evidenced by an outpouring of articles in the professional literature, by a host of conferences and reports on the subject, and by steps taken in a majority of states to bolster critical thinking for all students.

Critical thinking skills for elementary students

Most of the commentators argue that **critical thinking** is a form of intelligence that can be taught (it is not a fixed entity). The leading proponents of this school are Matthew Lipman and Robert Sternberg. Lipman seeks to foster thirty critical skills, generally designed for elementary school grades. Students are encouraged to develop, for example, (1) concepts; (2) generalizations; (3) cause-effect relationships; (4) allogistic inferences; (5) consistencies and contradictions; (6) analogies; (7) part-whole and whole-part connections; (8) formulations of problems; (9) reversibility of logical statements; and (10) applications of principles to real-life situations.[68]

In a text called *Philosophy for Children,* Lipman outlines a strategy for teaching critical thinking. In his approach, children spend a considerable portion of their time thinking about thinking and about ways in which effective thinking is distinguished from ineffective thinking. After reading stories in the text, children engage in classroom discussions and exercises that encourage them to adapt the thinking process depicted in the stories.[69] The assumption behind Lip-

---

[66]Linda Darling-Hammond, "Mad-Hatter Tests of Good Teaching," *The New York Times,* January 8, 1984, sect. 12, p. 57; Marilyn Cochran-Smith, "Word Processing and Writing in Elementary Classrooms," *Review of Educational Research* (Spring 1991), pp. 107–155.

[67]Marshal Arlin, "Time, Equality, and Mastery Learning," *Review of Educational Research* (Spring 1984), pp. 65–86; Arlin, "Time Variability in Mastery Learning," *American Educational Research Journal* (Spring 1984), pp. 103–120; and Martin Nystrand and Adam Gamoran, "Student Engagement: When Recitation Becomes Conversation," in H. C. Waxman and H. J. Walberg, eds., *Effective Teaching: Current Research* (Berkeley, Calif.: McCutchan, 1991), pp. 257–266.

[68]Matthew Lipman, "The Cultivation of Reasoning through Philosophy," *Educational Leadership* (September 1984), pp. 51–56; Lipman, "Critical Thinking — What Can It Be?" *Educational Leadership* (September 1988), pp. 38–43.

[69]Matthew Lipman et al., *Philosophy for Children,* 2nd ed. (Philadelphia: Temple University Press, 1980).

Philosophical issues of truth and fairness

man's program is that children are by nature interested in such philosophical issues as truth, fairness, and personal identity. Children can and should learn to think for themselves, to explore alternatives to their own viewpoints, to consider evidence, and to make distinctions and draw conclusions.

Sternberg seeks to foster many of the same intellectual skills. The behaviors that Sternberg emphasizes include (1) recognizing and defining a problem; (2) deciding upon processes needed to solve problems; (3) sequencing strategies for solving problems; (4) allocating mental and physical resources to problems; (5) monitoring and evaluating one's solution strategies; (6) responding adequately to external feedback; (7) responding effectively to novel tasks and situations; (8) effectively processing new information; (9) adapting effectively to one's immediate environment; and (10) shaping one's environment so as to best utilize one's abilities and interests.[70]

Adapting to one's environment

A holistic approach

Some critics of such approaches contend that teaching a person to think is like teaching someone to swing a golf club or tennis racket; it involves a holistic approach, not the piecemeal effort implied by Lipman and Sternberg. "Trying to break thinking skills into discrete units may be helpful for diagnostic proposals," according to two critics, "but it does not seem to be the right way to move in the teaching of such skills." Critical thinking is too complex a mental operation to divide into small processes; the result depends on "a student's total intellectual functioning, not on a set of narrowly defined skills."[71] Moreover, as Sternberg himself has cautioned, critical thinking programs that stress "right" answers and objectively scorable test items may be far removed from the problems students face in everyday life.[72] Thus, many educators believe that attempts to teach critical thinking as a separate program or as a particular group of defined skills are self-defeating. Ideally, one might argue, critical thinking should be integrated into all courses throughout the curriculum so that students are continually challenged to develop an inquiring attitude and a critical frame of mind.

Computerized Instruction

In the past decade, computers have played an increasing role in our schools, and their use continues to rise. In 1980 some 50,000 microcomputers were used by the nation's schools. By 1985 the number reached 500,000 in 92 percent of schools.[73] It is expected that in 1995 American schools will have more than 2 million computers in use in nearly 99 percent of the schools — that is, several per school. Many elementary schools already have students learning on computers once or twice a week, and educators project that most secondary schools

---

[70]Robert J. Sternberg, "How Can We Teach Intelligence?" *Educational Leadership* (September 1984), pp. 38–48; Sternberg "Intelligence, Wisdom, and Creativity," *Educational Psychologist* (Summer 1986), pp. 175–190; and Sternberg, "Technology and Testing," *Educational Psychologist* (Summer 1990), pp. 201–222.

[71]William A. Sadler and Arthur Whimbey, "A Holistic Approach to Improving Thinking Skills," *Phi Delta Kappan* (November 1985), p. 200.

[72]Robert J. Sternberg, "Thinking Styles: Key to Understanding Student Performance," *Phi Delta Kappan* (January 1990), pp. 366–371.

[73]*The Condition of Education 1987*, Tables 258–259, p. 314; Arthur S. Melmed, "Information Technology for U.S. Schools," *Phi Delta Kappan* (January 1982), pp. 308–311; and Denis Newman, "Organizational Impact of School Computers," *Educational Researcher* (April 1990), pp. 8–13.

will soon be offering students an average of 30 minutes a day at a computer terminal. Some 50,000 or more teachers are expected to be teaching computer technology as their main subject by 1995.[74]

Patrick Suppes, an early innovator of computer use in schools, coined the term **computer-assisted instruction (CAI).** Suppes defined three levels of CAI: practice and drill, tutoring, and dialogue.[75] At the simplest level, students work through computer drills in spelling, reading, foreign languages, simple computations, and so forth. At the second level, the computer acts as a tutor, taking over the function of presenting new concepts; as soon as the student manifests a clear understanding, he or she moves to the next exercise. The third and highest level, dialogue, involves a sophisticated interaction between the student and the computer. The student can communicate with the machine — not only give responses but ask new questions — and the computer will understand and react appropriately. Computers that can conduct a true dialogue with students are still in the developmental stage, but many educators expect them to reach the market before the end of the 1990s.

Recently the role of the computer has been envisioned in terms of three areas of application: (1) tool application, (2) computer-assisted instruction, and (3) computer-managed instruction.

1. *Tool application* is the use of microcomputers as a personal assistance device, say as an enrichment activity in school or at home to help with homework or a research project. Examples would include a student using word processing to analyze spelling or grammar or to write a report; another example would be a student using the computer to solve mathematical problems. The use of the computer is a personal decision on the part of the students and not one originated or requested by the teacher.

2. *Computer-assisted instruction* tends to emphasize tutoring and/or practice and drill programs and is appropriate when subject matter needs to be mastered or for practice of basic skills before advancing to higher levels of learning. This coincides with Suppes's first and second levels of computerized instruction.

3. *Computer-managed instruction* is the systematic control and organization of instruction, characterized by testing, diagnostic data, learning prescriptions, and thorough record keeping. If programmed properly, and if the computer has sufficient memory and storage capacity, the system can monitor, test, prescribe programs for, and keep the records of more than 100,000 students throughout the school district.[76]

Most teachers who use computers as an instructional aid operate at the first two levels of application. Increasingly, however, teachers of students with hand-

Practice, drill, tutoring, and dialogue

Word processing

Monitoring, testing, and record keeping

---

[74]Glen Bull et al. "The Electronic Academic Village," *Journal of Teacher Education* (July–August 1989) pp. 27–31; Allan C. Ornstein, "Effective Use of Computer Technology," *NASSP Bulletin* (March 1992), pp. 27–33.

[75]Patrick Suppes, "Computer Technology and the Future of Education," *Phi Delta Kappan* (April 1968), pp. 420–423.

[76]Alan M. Hofmeister, "The Special Educator in the Information Age," *Peabody Journal of Education* (Fall 1984), pp. 5–21; Rosemary Sutton, "Equity and Computers in the Schools: A Decade of Research," *Review of Educational Research* (Winter 1991), pp. 475–504.

Computer use for students with disabilities

icaps or learning disabilities are using computers at the third level for monitoring, testing, prescribing instruction, and storing information on each student they teach. In fact, the procedure is often part of the individualized education program (IEP) developed by the special educator. For slow students and students with disabilities, the computer can help the teacher to diagnose the student's difficulties, analyze instructional techniques, and replace ineffective techniques with alternative strategies. For average and rapid learners, the computer offers increased capacities for self-teaching, problem solving, and independent instruction.

Research on Computerized Instruction: Mixed Findings.   Summaries of the research on computer-assisted instruction suggest that it is effective as *supplement* to regular instruction. At higher grade levels, particularly college, it can be used as an effective *replacement* for regular instruction.[77] In other reviews of the re-

Short-term vs. long-term gains

search, CAI has been shown to be effective for short-term achievement gain (quizzes and examinations), but not for long-term gains (retention).[78] Some studies, in fact, show no significant differences in achievement between CAI and non-CAI students,[79] suggesting that CIA is not uniformly effective.

Given the computer craze, some words of caution are needed. Computerized instruction involves student interaction with machines and materials that have minimal emotional and affective components. Critics contend that substituting

Computers lack the human factor

a machine for a human teacher leaves the student with no true guidance and with too little personal interaction.

Still, the potential for computers is great, and they have already brought about changes in the day-to-day operation of the classroom and school. As Sey-

Building a sense of inquiry

mour Papert (the inventor of LOGO) argues, the computer can be used to build a sense of inquiry, to "mess about," to explore, and to improve thinking skills.[80] When students learn how to think with the computer, their potential for innovation and creativity is unlimited — their world has been expanded.

Video and Satellite Systems

The advent of video technology has made available another valuable tool for instruction. Videotapes, cassettes, and disks can be used for instruction in classrooms, libraries, resource centers, and the student's home. Since the video

---

[77]James A. Kulik, Chen-Lin C. Kulik, and Peter A. Cohen, "Effectiveness of Computer-Based College Teaching," *Review of Educational Research* (Winter 1980), pp. 525–544; Robert B. Kozma, "Learning with Media," *Review of Educational Research* (Summer 1991), pp. 179–212; and James A. Mecklenburger, "Educational Technology Is Not Enough," *Phi Delta Kappan* (October 1990), pp. 105–108.

[78]Gilbert R. Austin and Thomas Howie, "Leadership and Computers — A Winning Combination," *Principal* (September 1990), pp. 40–43; James A. Kulik, Robert L. Bangert, and George Williams, "Effects of Computer-Based Teaching on Secondary School Students," *Journal of Educational Psychology* (February 1983), pp. 19–26.

[79]Richard E. Clark, "Reconsidering Research on Learning from Media," *Review of Educational Research* (Winter 1983), pp. 445–459; Paul A. McDermott and Marley W. Watkins, "Computerized vs. Conventional Remedial Instruction for Learning Disabled Pupils," *Journal of Special Education* (Spring 1983), pp. 81–88; and Gavriel Salomon, "The Computer Lab: A Bad Idea Now Sanctified," *Educational Technology* (October 1990), pp. 50–52.

[80]Seymour Papert, "Computer Criticism vs. Technocentric Thinking," *Educational Researcher* (January–February 1987), pp. 22–30.

can be played at any convenient time, the student never has to miss a lesson. Hundreds of catalogs offer videos on a wide range of subjects; in addition, many school systems and teachers have begun to produce their own videos for specific instructional purposes. With the help of a videoprinter, individual images from the screen — photographs, tables, graphs, or any other useful picture — can be printed on paper for further study.

Simulations and interactive situations

Many videos interact with the viewer when used in conjunction with a computer. Realistic simulations and action-reaction situations can be presented as part of an instructional program. The program can tell the viewer if a response is right or wrong; or the viewer can be offered a choice of options, and the program will then display the outcome of the option chosen.[81] Interactive videos have an enormous teaching potential that educators are just beginning to explore. Such videos can be used either for individual lessons or for instruction in small groups.

Educators are also investigating ways to use the popularity of videogames for teaching purposes. Although videogames have been criticized for their escapism, they are by nature interactive — to each move by the player, the machine responds with a move of its own. Math, reading, and writing lessons can be written in a videogame format, and the student will find practice and drill more lively in a game atmosphere.

Integrating technology

According to one estimate, by the year 2000 more than 20 percent of instructional tools will include computers and videos. Teachers must not only keep abreast of this changing video technology but also plan ways to integrate it into the curriculum. In an era when the number of videos rented from video stores surpasses the total number of books checked out of libraries, teachers should help students become critical video consumers, aware of how visual images affect us as individuals and as a society.[82]

Distance Education. The idea of "distance education" originated in England in 1971 when the BBC began transmitting educational programs. Today, schools may select television programs specifically developed for educational purposes and have them beamed into the classroom by satellite. This is particularly useful for small, rural schools with limited local resources.[83] Some home cable systems also carry educational programming, but its quantity and quality will increase only if educators demand this resource and use it.

Widely used in business and industry, teleconferences have begun to appear in school systems, usually as an experiment on the secondary level. In a typical conference, a resource person, teacher, or group of students is viewed through the television screen, talking to or instructing other students or participants.

---

[81]Dennis M. Adams and Mary Hamm, "Changing Gateways to Knowledge: New Media Symbol Systems," *Tech Trends* (January 1988), pp. 2–23; Mary O'Sullivan et al., "Interactive Video Technology in Teacher Education," *Journal of Teacher Education* (July–August 1989), pp. 20–25.

[82]Allan C. Ornstein, "Video Technology and the Urban Curriculum," *Education and Urban Society* (May 1991), pp. 335–341; Harold Shane, *Teaching and Learning in a Microelectronic Age* (Bloomington, Ind.: Phi Delta Kappa, 1987).

[83]Jerry D. Pepple, Dale A. Law, and Sheri Kallembach, "A Vision of Rural Education for 2001," *Educational Horizons* (Fall 1990), pp. 50–58; Harold G. Shane, "Improving Education for the Twenty-first Century," *Educational Horizons* (Fall 1990), pp. 11–15.

Viewers can watch as if they were across the table, although they may be thousands of miles away. The viewing audience can ask questions and make decisions about what further information should be presented.[84] Again, the technique holds much promise for small, rural schools.

The fact is, instruction is going to come alive with interactive computers, videos, video discs, satellite and cable networks, and telecourses in all subject areas. Coupled with some 2 million computers already in classrooms, and increasing at a rate of 100,000 per year, we should see the demise of what some call "pencil technology": the point will no longer be made by the pencil. In the twenty-first century, the textbook will not be the norm; rather, it will be incidental and will probably take on different forms — talking to the student, monitoring his or her progress, and compensating accordingly. Acquiring new knowledge will not be the key because no one will be able to keep pace with it; instead, being able to access it and being networked into a call system will be critical.

EMERGING CURRICULUM TRENDS: AN AGENDA FOR THE FUTURE

In discussing video and communications technology, we have already begun to step from the present into the future. What other trends, we may ask, will the future bring to American classrooms? Opinions differ on the directions education will take, and library shelves are filled with volumes describing current and anticipated changes in society and education. Despite disagreements, however, it is likely that certain trends in particular will increasingly affect curriculum planning in the near future. Some of the most important of these trends are noted in the list that follows.

A more integrated and holistic curriculum

The emerging curriculum responds to the urge to break away from traditional disciplines, to develop more interdisciplinary approaches. In the curriculum of the future, subject matter most likely will be less compartmentalized and more integrated and holistic. Although traditional subject boundaries will remain, there will be increased cross-subject material; knowledge will no longer be considered fragmented or linear but multidisciplinary and multidimensional.

Growth of computer-related occupations

1. *Technical literacy.* Because of the revolution in technology, the schools must now educate citizens who are already familiar with computers, electronics, lasers, and robots. Computer literacy stands beside the three Rs as a fundamental skill. According to government projections to 1995, of the ten fastest-growing occupations, four require knowledge of computers (technician, systems analyst, programmer, and operator). Other trends suggest a heavy high-tech influence in such growth areas as biogenetics, computer/video software, robotics, telecommunications, microelectronics, toxic waste and pollution, space, and the oceans.[85] Soon there will exist technical occupations for which we do not yet even have names.

---

[84]Allan C. Ornstein, "Bringing Telecommunications and Videos into the Classroom," *High School Journal* (April–May 1990), pp. 252–257.

[85]*Occupational Projections and Training Data* (Washington, D.C.: U.S. Department of Labor, 1990). Also see Thomas Bailey, "Jobs of the Future and Skills They Will Require," *American Educator* (Spring 1990), pp. 10–15; Rosemary F. Klode, "Integrated Learning for a Competitive Workforce," *Phi Delta Kappan* (February 1991), pp. 453–455.

In cooperation with industry and government, schools must identify the emerging technologies and services and provide a curriculum that prepares students for viable careers. In part, this means educating future scientists who can design, develop, and apply the new technology. But not everyone needs to become a scientific expert. For many occupations, people simply need to understand the technological basics — what buttons to push under what conditions and how to make machines provide the service or information they were designed to offer. Only a small percentage of the workforce will require sophisticated technical or scientific knowledge, but many will need better cognitive and communications skills.

Pushing the right buttons

The National Science Teachers Association (NSTA) has endorsed a curricular approach called Science/Technology/Society, which emphasizes the social and technical aspects of science rather than pure science.[86] One of the purposes of such programs is to help students prepare for the impact of technology on daily life. Some traditional vocational/industrial programs are also being enriched with a focus on technology, especially on computers and robotic design. In still other cases, the entire vocational and industrial arts program is being revamped to meet new technological requirements; this demands updated equipment, the integration of computers into courses, and continual interaction among schools, government, and the workforce.

As the pace of technology accelerates, whole industries may be born, expand, and die in a matter of years. It will be nearly impossible to predict precise job skills needed for viable employment. Furthermore, there is still no nationwide plan — educational, industrial, or governmental — that assesses the future occupational needs of society and establishes corresponding guidelines for schools. Cooperative planning is needed — now.

No nationwide plan

2. *Lifelong learning.* The trend toward lifelong learning is occurring in all modern societies as a result of the knowledge explosion and rapid social, technological, and economic changes that force people to prepare for second or third careers and to keep themselves updated on new developments that affect their personal and social goals. Education will continue to become more of a "lifelong" enterprise and increasingly will take place outside the confines of the traditional school. Taking note of these trends, the Carnegie Commission has developed the concept of a "step-in, step-out" educational system for lifelong learning. This means that people could move in and out of educational programs throughout their lives.

Education outside the traditional school

Some observers believe that much of the learning that has been provided by elementary, secondary, and postsecondary schools may be provided by business and industry in the future, especially to meet the needs of a skilled workforce in high-tech and information-based industries.[87] By 1989, in fact, employers were spending $250 billion annually in training; in comparison, colleges and univer-

---

[86]John E. Penick and R. Meinhard Pellens, *Focus on Excellence: Science/Technology/Society* (Washington, D.C.: National Science Teachers Association, 1984); Robert E. Yager, *Centers of Excellence: Portrayals of Six Districts* (Washington, D.C.: National Science Teachers Association, 1983). Also see Robert E. Yager, "New Goals for Students," *Education and Urban Society* (November 1989), pp. 9–21.

[87]Michael W. Apple, "Curriculum in the Year 2000," *Phi Delta Kappan* (January 1983), pp. 321–326; Barbara L. McCombs, "Motivation and Lifelong Learning," *Educational Psychologist* (Spring 1991), pp. 117–128; and Roger J. Vaughan, "The New Limits to Growth," *Phi Delta Kappan* (February 1991), pp. 446–449.

sities spent only $120 billion.[88] Still other scenarios envision educating adolescents and adults through a network of community resources and small learning centers and libraries.

3. *International education.* Although historically the United States government has taken a relatively isolationist position, the increasing interdependence among nations demands that Americans become knowledgeable about developments in distant lands. Oil prices in Saudi Arabia and Iran affect job opportunities in Houston, Denver, and Tulsa. Auto and steel production in Japan and Korea influence the local economy in Detroit and Pittsburgh. We truly inhabit a "global village" in which our standard of living, our national economy, and even our air quality are vitally connected to events in other parts of the world. Satellite and aerospace communications, instant television reporting, supercomputer networks, laser technology, and jet travel have made this planet seem smaller, and other peoples' problems (or strengths) are harder to ignore. About 20 million children in Third World countries die of starvation each year, and another 800 million (about 15 percent of humanity) go to bed hungry or malnourished. Considering the rapid worldwide growth in population and the increasing scarcity of world resources, these figures indicate a planet in transition that may soon be unable to sustain even the industrialized nations.

One area of international education that U.S. schools may need to address in the future is foreign language instruction. The most common spoken language in the world is Mandarin, followed by English, Hindi, and Spanish, Japanese ranks tenth, and German and French rank even lower. Nearly all foreign language programs in American schools offer Spanish and French; in fact, 58 percent of secondary students enrolled in a foreign language study Spanish.[89] But fewer than .01 percent of U.S. high-school students study Japanese. Moreover, according to the best estimates, only two or three U.S. public high schools offer Mandarin, and none offer Hindi. Failure to train students in these languages may severely limit the future growth of U.S. trade.

Education in America must become more widely international in scope. Educators might expand travel exchange programs and perhaps make study in another culture a requirement for graduation. There should be emphasis on international geography, history, political science, and economics. As the world becomes more interconnected and interdependent, such needs will become more evident and more funds may be devoted to the area of global curriculum.

4. *Environmental education.* Mounting concern over such problems as pollution, overpopulation, and depletion of food and natural resources has created demands for more knowledge and new programs in ecology and environmental education. Much of the relevant content has long been included in traditional earth sciences, biology, and geography courses and in conservation programs. The new demand calls for a more meaningful and better coordinated program that raises the theme of crisis.

The list of environmental realities is a long one and is continually expanding. Scientists believe the depletion of the earth's ozone layer (already depleted

Interdependence of nations

Shrinking globe

Most common languages

Environmental problems

---

[88]*The Condition of Education 1991*, Vol. 1, Table 1.25–2, p. 225; *Digest of Education Statistics, 1990* (Washington, D.C.: U.S. Government Printing Office, 1990), Table 299, p. 302.

[89]Myriam Met, "Which Foreign Languages Should Students Learn?" *Educational Leadership* (September 1989), pp. 54–58.

some 5 percent), caused chiefly by manmade chemicals used in the manufacture of some plastics and in aerosol sprays and cleaning solvents, will increase the incidence of skin cancer, cataracts, and immune system disorders; it may also damage crops, trees, and marine organisms worldwide. If the ozone layer fades over populated regions (there is evidence that such a hole may already exist over northeast portions of the United States), the results could be devastating. The greenhouse effect, which may warm the atmosphere and increase sea level, may result in substantial harm to both farmlands and cities. Fish and wildlife, soil, water, and the air we breathe are often contaminated and affect our health. The deforestation of Third World countries, from Brazil to Malaysia, also affects our climate, wildlife, and entire ecological chain — and all are in jeopardy. Some even predict that the great wars of the twenty-first century will be fought for clean water and soil.[90]

Role of schools   Rather than terrifying students about ecological disaster, however, schools should prepare students for tomorrow's world by helping them understand how scientific, social, and political issues interact. Because mere possession of knowledge does not ensure proper action, the curriculum must also deal with the attitudes, values, and moral thinking that lead to responsible environmental behavior.

5. *Nuclear education.* The nuclear standoff between the United States and the Soviet Union has ended, and we are now less vulnerable to world nuclear confrontation than during the last fifty years. Indeed, the threat of computer malfunction and subsequent nuclear disaster has declined dramatically. But the nuclear bomb club, which now includes more than twelve nations, is expanding. Some countries, such as China, and private corporations in Germany and France continue to sell their nuclear knowledge to Third World countries. Considering the possibility that terrorists may use nuclear devices for their own purposes, the world may not be that safe from nuclear threat after all.

Nuclear problems   Even peaceful uses of nuclear energy — power plants, medical facilities, radiation therapy medicines — have come to seem more problematical, especially since the disasters at Three Mile Island and Chernobyl. The entire world would be affected by a serious meltdown — in terms of air, food, and water quality. Global weather patterns know no national boundaries; concentrated radiation can affect human populations thousands of miles away. The waste products of nuclear facilities also present a continuing problem: where in this world can we bury them? And try to convince the residents of Maine or Michigan that it is to their advantage, or that it is their patriotic duty, to have a nuclear (or toxic) dump site in their backyards.

Teaching peace strategies   Concern about nuclear energy has reached schools under such rubrics as "nuclear-sane programs," "peace education," and "peace-making strategies." In coming years these will continue to be important elements in a globally oriented

---

[90]See Paul Ehrlich and Anne Ehrlich, *Extinction: The Causes and Consequences of the Disappearance of Species* (New York: Random House, 1981); *The Limits of Growth: A Report to the Club of Rome's Projection of the Predicament of Mankind,* 2nd ed. (New York: New American Library, 1974); Rudy Abramson, "New Ozone Peril Seen," *Chicago Sun Times,* April 15, 1991, pp. 1, 18; Rudy Abramson, "Profile: Dr. Greenhouse," *Scientific American* (December 1990), pp. 33–34. Telephone conversations with Dan Blank, Public Information Coordinator, Environmental Protection Agency, Washington, D.C., June 24, 1991; and telephone conversation with Michael Korylo, Manager of Upper Atmospheric Research, NASA, Washington, D.C., June 25, 1991.

riculum. We must not reduce our concern about nuclear energy because of the demise of the Soviet Union; nuclear energy will play a great role in the future — and we will need a nuclear education program.

6. *Health education and physical fitness.* Trends in the health of the U.S. population are producing new pressures to expand or change the curriculum. For example, the epidemic of AIDS (acquired immunodeficiency syndrome), with its dire risk to sexually active adolescents, has forced educators to confront the issue of student health in a new way. Predictions are that by the year 2000 some 40 to 50 million people around the world will be affected by the disease; the majority will be from Africa, but some four to five million will be Americans.[91] Some educators see the AIDS epidemic as literally a life-or-death matter for their students. Schools have been slow, however, to include AIDS education in the curriculum.

AIDS education

One reason for the lack of AIDS education is the continued controversy over the disease and the recommended preventive measures. Many parents and educators have been particularly incensed by programs involving the distribution of condoms in big-city schools. A more basic reason for the lack of AIDS education, however, is that only twenty-seven states require any form of health or sex education, and American students average only 13.9 hours of such education annually. Moreover, nationwide there is only one certified health teacher for every 21,500 students.[92] Many educators believe this shortage must and will be addressed in the future.

Lack of health teachers

Dietary habits and exercise comprise another health concern. Citing medical evidence of high blood pressure and elevated blood fats among American youngsters, physicians have criticized the high-fat, burgers-and-fries diet common among school-age children. Many students appear to be eating their way toward heart disease and other maladies later in life. In addition, schoolchildren have been increasingly unable to pass basic physical fitness tests; they do poorly on measures of body development, strength, and flexibility.[93] Television and video viewing habits that include salt and sugar-coated snacks among American children and youth have contributed to this lack of fitness.

Poor diets

Physical fitness

Although the American adult population appears to have a love affair with physical fitness and sports, the schools ironically have cut back physical education and fitness programs because of budget considerations and renewed stress on academic excellence. Educators frequently assert that we will need to rebuild these programs in the curriculum of the future. Some schools are already recognizing the need to provide better guidance for diet and exercise. Sports, too, should be reoriented to increase the emphasis on aerobic and rhythmic activities (running, jumping, jogging, bicycling).[94] By the end of the 1990s, progressive

[91]Lawrence K. Altman, "W.H.O. Says 40 Million Will Be Infected with AIDS," *The New York Times*, June 18, 1991, p. B8.

[92]Anthony L. Manna and Cynthia W. Symons, "Promoting Student Health Through Children's Literature," *Educational Horizons* (Fall 1990), pp. 37–43.

[93]Nancy Benac, "Diet Guide for Kids Targets Cholesterol, Heart Disease," *Chicago Sun Times*, April 9, 1991, p. 22; Dick Thompson, "A How To Guide on Cholesterol," *Time*, October 19, 1987, p. 215; and "Time Out for Fitness," *Health Magazine* (April 1991), pp. 10, 11.

[94]Marian E. Kneer, "A New Emphasis on Physical Fitness," *Educational Leadership* (February 1987), pp. 93–94; Terri DeMarco and Ken Sidney, "Enhancing Children's Participation in Physical Activity," *Education Digest* (February 1990), pp. 58–61.

*Emphasis on
lifelong sports*
and far-sighted schools will be deemphasizing traditional competitive sports, which tend to cater to only a few students and involve activities that only the young can pursue. Instead, schools increasingly will emphasize lifelong sports such as tennis, golf, and swimming, as well as noncompetitive, intramural activities in which the average athlete and even the nonathlete can participate.

High rate of immigration

7. *Immigrant education.* Legal immigration now accounts for up to one-half of the annual growth in the U.S. population. It has already surpassed post–World War II rates and is approaching the peaks reached in the years prior to World War I. Despite its present economic ills, the United States still looks like the promised land to many people who are searching for a better life.

Sources of immigration

The new immigrant population differs in ethnic origins from that of the past. From 1930 to 1950, 80 percent of immigrants to the United States came from Western Europe and Canada. From 1970 through 1985, however, the leading source countries, with the highest first, were Mexico, the Philippines, South Korea, Taiwan, Vietnam, Jamaica, India, the Dominican Republic, and Guatemala. Today as many as 90 percent of immigrants come from non-Western or Third World countries. Moreover, estimates of *illegal* immigration, mainly from Mexico, Central America, and the Caribbean, total about one million people per year, with approximately 500,000 establishing permanent residence.[95] Partly as a result of these immigration trends, by the year 2000 nearly one-third of the U.S. population will be nonwhite and Hispanic, and in Arizona, California, Colorado, Texas, and New Mexico the proportion will approach 50 percent.[96]

*Difficulties faced by
immigrant families*

For some recent immigrants, life in America has been a remarkable success story. Many, however, face language barriers, ethnic prejudice, health problems, and a lack of good jobs. A significant number of immigrant families are "structurally poor," meaning that the family conditions are unstable or disorganized and the children have few chances to escape from poverty.[97] Because of cultural differences in learning styles or thinking patterns, the children may be labeled "learning disabled" or "slow." Even when this is not the case, value hierarchies vary widely across cultures, so that immigrant children have diverse attitudes about school, teacher authority, gender differences, social class, and behavior.

To assist these new immigrants, many educators are suggesting an increase in compensatory and bilingual programs in the schools. A multicultural curriculum can also help immigrant children achieve acceptance and respect in their new country. But in the future, if present immigration trends continue, schools will have to go even further in adapting their curricula for students who have been transplanted from another land and another culture.

8. *The return of geography.* Most adults over forty remember geography as a required unit in elementary school and as a separate subject in high school, usually taken for half a year along with civics or economics in the other half of

---

[95]John Fallows, "The New Immigrants," *Atlantic* (November 1983), pp. 45–68, 85–89; Jason Juffus, *The Impact of the Immigration Reform and Control Act on Immigration* (Washington, D.C.: Urban Institute, 1991).

[96]Allan C. Ornstein, "Urban Demographics with Educational Implications," *Education and Urban Society* (August 1984), pp. 477–496; Ornstein, "Enrollment Trends in Big City Schools," *Peabody Journal of Education* (Summer 1988), pp. 64–71.

[97]Frank D. Bean, George Vernez, and Charles B. Keely, *Opening and Closing the Doors* (Washington, D.C.: Urban Institute, 1989); Gary Imhoff, *Learning in Two Languages* (New Brunswick, N.J.: Transaction Press, 1990).

the year. During World War II and the Cold War period, geography was considered an essential subject, important for understanding military activities, international relations, and economic power.[98]

Disappearance of geography

However, geography gradually disappeared from the school curriculum; absorbed into social studies, it was often delegated to teachers who preferred to emphasize history. By 1960 only 14 percent of U.S. students in grades 7 to 12 were enrolled in geography courses, and in the mid-1970s the proportion dropped to 9 percent — a low point for the entire century.[99] Not only had geography been consolidated into social studies, but it also was no longer a requirement for college admission.

Geographic illiteracy

As a result of this neglect of the subject, American high-school and college students became geographically illiterate. A recent NAEP assessment of the nation's high-school students revealed that only 42 percent could locate Nigeria on a map of Africa, and only 37 percent could find Southeast Asia on a world map.[100] In another survey, 39 percent of young adults living in Boston could not name the six New England states; in Dallas 25 percent could not identify the country that borders the United States to the South.[101]

Renewed emphasis

The reform movement in education, starting with the publication of *A Nation at Risk* in 1983, has sounded the alarm. For the United States to remain a worldwide power, U.S. students must learn about the world around them, including its basic geography. Renewed emphasis on geography has become part of several different curriculum focuses, such as back-to-basics, cultural literacy, environmental education, and international education. As the drive toward restoring substantive content to the curriculum continues, geography will play an increasing role.

9. *Middle-grade education.* There is a growing recognition today that students between the ages of ten and fifteen are often distracted from their schoolwork because they are going through a time of rapid growth and development. Enormous variability exists among these students, even within the same age group and in the same classroom. The differences in physical, intellectual, and emotional development are so great that averages have little meaning. As one educator points out, these youth "experience the greatest change in their minds and bodies during this developmental period."[102]

The expanding use of middle schools is an attempt to make education more responsive to these students' social and psychological needs. Middle schools comprising grades 6 to 8 now enroll as many as 40 percent of U.S. students in

---

[98]Mary Crampton and David A. Lanegran, "Geography as an Independent Course," *NASSP Bulletin* (December 1989), pp. 24–30; Joseph P. Stoltman, "Geography in the Secondary Schools: 1945–1990," *NASSP Bulletin* (December 1990), pp. 9–13.

[99]Donald P. Gardner, "Geography in the School Curriculum," *Annals of the Association of American Geographers* (Washington, D.C.: The Association, 1986).

[100]*The Geography Learning of High School Seniors* (Washington, D.C.: U.S. Department of Education, 1990).

[101]David T. Kearns, "Helping to Restructure Public Education from the Bottom Up," *Harvard Business Review* (November–December 1988), pp. 70–75.

[102]Alan Knight, "The Magic Wand for Middle Level Educators," *NASSP Bulletin* (November 1988), p. 99.

this grade span. Schools concentrating on grades 7 and 8 — also called middle schools — account for another 25 percent. Today only 17 percent of U.S. students in this grade range attend a school comprising grades 7 through 9, the traditional junior high school.[103]

The differences between middle schools and junior highs are often confusing. Many middle schools were originally established for administrative reasons, such as the need to alleviate overcrowded elementary or high schools. Since the 1980s, however, middle schools have tended to represent a distinct way of thinking about the education of preadolescents and early adolescents. Compared to junior high schools, middle schools put more emphasis on socialization, less on academics; more emphasis on intramural sports, less on interscholastic or competitive sports. Their curricula are more interdisciplinary, and they offer more exploratory subjects, such as sex education, creative writing, and drama. Cooperative learning, heterogeneous grouping, flexible scheduling, and extended advisory periods are more common in middle schools than in junior high schools.[104]

Socialization and intramural sports

As middle schools become even more widespread, new curriculum approaches will continue to develop. Teacher-education programs will also reflect the change. Until now, only a tiny percentage of colleges have distinguished middle schools from elementary and secondary schools in their preservice programs.[105] In the near future, however, teacher-training institutions will focus increasingly on the skills and knowledge needed to teach in a middle school.

10. *Aging education.* Unless the U.S. birth and death rates both dramatically increase, we are heading for a society in which the young will play a diminished role. Our society is rapidly aging, and all of us are on the same conveyor belt — the only difference being that we got on at different times. By the year 2020, increased longevity and the aging of the post–World War II baby-boom group will increase the number of elderly Americans (age 65 or older) to an estimated 51.4 million, or 17.3 percent of the projected U.S. population. By comparison, this age group included only 25.5 million people, or 11.3 percent of the population, in 1980.[106]

Aging of U.S. society

The costs for medical and custodial care of elderly people will likely create an increasing burden on the younger working population. Moreover, the aging members of society constitute a growing political force, able to shift social spending dollars toward their own needs at the expense of school budgets. According to some projections, the increases in federal spending for Medicaid, Social Se-

Effects on social spending

---

[103]Joyce L. Epstein and Douglas J. MacIver, "The Middle Grades: Is Grade Span the Most Important Issue?" *Educational Horizons* (Winter 1988), pp. 88–94.

[104]William M. Alexander and C. Kenneth McEwin, *Schools in the Middle: Status and Progress* (Columbus, Ohio: National Middle School Association, 1989); Ornstein, *Middle School and Secondary Methods.*

[105]Paul George, "From Junior High to Middle School," *NASSP Bulletin* (February 1990), pp. 86–94; Gene I. Maeroff, "Getting to Know a Good Middle School," *Phi Delta Kappan* (March 1990), pp. 504–511.

[106]*U.S. Population: Where We Are: Where We're Going* (Washington, D.C.: Population Reference Bureau, 1992); William Van Wishard, "What in the World Is Going On?" *Vital Speeches of the Day* (March 1990), p. 314.

To help students overcome age stereotypes, schools can integrate retired people into the school workforce as volunteers, teacher aides, and resource people and thereby benefit from their collective wisdom. (© Carmen Chan/Amstock)

Education on aging

curity, and old-age benefits will reach 73 percent between 1990 and 1995, while spending on education dips 4 percent.[107]

Given this "graying of America" and the issues it raises, some educators believe that schools must teach students to understand the problems and prospects of aging: how to cope with aging personally (even though it may seem distant when we are young) and how to help loved ones (parents and grandparents) successfully confront this stage of life. On another level, schools should attempt to counter many of the existing stereotypes about the elderly. Retirement ages are changing as people stay in the workforce well past age sixty-five. We see more and more people in their seventies playing tennis and actively involved in business and community affairs. Soon the curriculum may treat age stereotypes and age discrimination as another "ism," like racism or sexism, that students should learn to overcome. Schools themselves should integrate semiretired and retired people into the school workforce, as volunteers, teacher aides, and resource people. The collective wisdom of these people is immense, and their political support for schools will become increasingly important.

11. *For-profit education.* A new form of separate and unequal schooling may increase in the years ahead. Privatization and profitization of education have

---

[107]Jack Hadley and Stephen Zuckerman, "Rising Hospital Costs," *Urban Institute: Policy and Research Report* (Winter–Spring 1990), pp. 9–10; George Kaplan, "Suppose They Gave an Intergenerational Conflict and Nobody Came," *Phi Delta Kappan* (May 1991), pp. K1–K12; and Wishard, "What in the World Is Going On?"

appeared in the form of nationwide nursery schools, day-care and after-school centers, private coaching and sports centers, franchised tutoring centers, private college counseling services (aimed at selected colleges), private coaching for SAT and professional tests, corporate training schools, and contracted out-of-school services. All of these trends have one thing in common: they turn education into business by marketing educational services for a fee.

Although we have always had private alternatives to public education, a growing number of affluent families are willing to pay for various types of educational services to enhance their children's education and opportunities. Tom Shannon, executive director of the National School Boards Association, put it this way: "Because of the profound emphasis on the importance of education in society and its importance to individual success, entrepreneurs have rightly judged there is a market [for supplementary services] — especially among well-to-do, high achieving parents."[108]

The largest private learning centers, as of 1991, were the Britannica Learning Centers, with 86 centers in eight states; Huntington Learning Centers, with 100 centers in twenty-six states; Kinder Learning Centers, with 1,250 centers in forty-one states and two Canadian provinces; and Stanley Kaplan Educational Centers, with 125 permanent centers and nearly 500 temporary centers.[109] About 3 to 5 percent of the U.S. school population participates in this type of proprietary school, twice the percentage that did so in 1987; the percentage is expected to increase further as the learning centers expand.

Some commentators have welcomed these private and profit-making schools as a means for radically changing American education. The present school structure, they contend, hinders school reform; educational services can be delivered more efficiently by the market system than by government. Myron Lieberman argues that public education discriminates against taxpayers who do not have children in school. Some proponents of profit-making schools see a worldwide movement in industrialized countries to privatize education.[110] In fact, it would not be surprising if large computer or publishing companies such as Apple, IBM, McGraw-Hill, and World Encyclopedia enter the market, or even begin franchising education for-profit centers.

On the other hand, many educators believe the rise of for-profit education will widen the gap between "have" and "have-not" children. Hourly fees for many learning centers and tutoring courses range from $15 to $40, a cost that prices out the great majority of parents. The price will probably increase as the demand for such services rises. To counter the trend, critics argue that public schools should offer more remedial education, supplementary help, and enrich-

[108]Sally B. Zakariya, "Is a New Era of Separate and Unequal Schooling About to Begin?" *American School Board Journal* (August 1987), p. 17. Also see Roger W. Hamm and Sandra Crosser, "What Happened to the Notion of a Free Public Education?" *American School Board Journal* (June 1991), pp. 29–31.

[109]Telephone conversations with David Hiatt, Vice President of Development, Kinder Learning Centers, July 11, 1991; Susan Meutchen, Manager of Franchise Services, Huntington Learning Centers, June 21, 1991; and Mary Verdon, Director of Public Relations, Britannica Learning Centers, June 24, 1991.

[110]Myron Lieberman, *Privatization and Educational Choice* (New York: St. Martin's Press, 1989).

ment programs — services that would benefit students and increase parents' confidence in local schools. In this way, the rise of private learning centers may soon stimulate changes in curriculum and instruction in the public schools.

12. *Futuristic education.* According to Alvin Toffler, many people are susceptible to "future shock"—that is, they are unable to cope with the rapid change of today's society. As he puts it, "To survive, [and] to avert . . . future shock, the individual must become infinitely more adaptable and capable than ever before." The principal aim of education "must be to increase the individual's 'cope-ability' — the speed and economy with which the person can adapt to continual change."[111]

One way of preparing students for the future is through studying the future itself. New courses or programs, called "futuristic studies," "futuristics," or "futurism," are now being offered at the college level, and they should soon filter down to secondary schools. This field of study considers technological developments and social events not as separate but rather as twin components that will determine our future. To generate accurate conceptions of the future is no small task, but presenting the future as a formal object of study helps students learn the implications of rapid change and how society can adjust to them.

Educators have identified several areas of competence that are important in a future-oriented curriculum. Understanding of technology is critical, of course, particularly communications technology. Other subjects of study include planning procedures, the organization of information, forecasting techniques, and decision making. Students would be taught to think in multidimensional as well as linear ways. Finally, the curriculum would enhance students' self-concepts and equip them to deal with the stress of international power shifts and rapid change.[112]

As Harold Shane asserts, the future is always evolving, and therefore the curriculum must also be evolving.[113] Whether in futuristic courses or in more standard ones, educators must begin to confront the twenty-first century.

Words of Caution

Although curriculum must evolve to serve a changing society, we caution the reader on several fronts. Change for the sake of change is not good; it must be tempered with wisdom, compassion, and justice. Schools throughout the ages have viewed their programs as being on the cutting edge of progress, and they have often been wrong. We may be misguided again as we view our schools and society; only the future will tell.

New knowledge, indeed, is not necessarily better than old knowledge. Are we to throw away most of Aristotle, Galileo, Kepler, Darwin, and Newton merely because they are not part of this century? If we stress only scientific and

---

[111]Alvin Toffler, *Future Shock* (New York: Bantam Books, 1970), pp. 35, 402.
[112]Allan C. Ornstein, "Planning the Curriculum in a World of Change," *Curriculum Review* (January–February 1987), pp. 22–24; Allan C. Ornstein and Francis P. Hunkins, "Curriculum Futures: Review and Outlook," *Kappa Delta Pi Record* (Summer 1989), pp. 107–111.
[113]Shane, "Improving Education for the Twenty-first Century."

Maintaining historical perspective

technological knowledge, we could languish physically, aesthetically, morally, and spiritually. As we try to maintain curriculum relevancy and plan for the future, there is no guarantee that we will not repeat the mistakes of the past; as educators, we should never lose historical perspective.

What knowledge we select and how we organize the curriculum requires continual attention; we must learn to prune away old and irrelevant knowledge and balance and integrate new knowledge into the curriculum. As we modify and update content, we must not throw away time-tested, enduring subjects, such as literature, history, even music or art (or the three Rs at the elementary level). Teachers, and especially curriculum specialists, must protect the schools and their students against fads and frills, and especially against extremism. They must keep in perspective the type of society we are, the values we cherish, and the educational aims we wish to achieve.

Fads and frills

Summing Up

1. In organizing the curriculum, most educators hold to the traditional concept of curriculum as the body of subjects, or subject matter. Nevertheless, a number of contemporary educators are more concerned with the experiences of the learner, and they regard the student as the focus of curriculum.

2. Examples of a subject-centered approach include the following types of curriculum: (1) subject-area, (2) subject-structure, (3) perennialist, (4) essentialist, (5) back-to-basics, (6) higher standards, and (7) core.

3. Examples of a student-centered approach include the following types of curriculum: (1) child-centered, (2) activity-centered, (3) relevant, (4) humanistic, and (5) values-centered.

4. The 1970s and 1980s produced a number of significant instructional innovations, including (1) individualized instruction, (2) cooperative learning, (3) mastery instruction, (4) critical thinking, (5) computerized instruction, and (6) the use of video and satellite systems.

5. As we near the end of the twentieth century, we must rely on new concepts and new courses to help us cope with change. Future curricular trends will likely focus on the following: (1) technical literacy, (2) lifelong learning, (3) international education, (4) environmental education, (5) nuclear education, (6) health education and physical fitness, (7) immigrant education, (8) geography, (9) middle-grade education, (10) aging education, (11) for-profit education, and (12) futuristic education.

Key Terms

curriculum *(521)*

subject-centered curricula *(522)*

subject-area curriculum *(523)*

subject-structure curriculum *(523)*

perennialist curriculum *(525)*

whole-language approach *(526)*

essentialist curriculum *(526)*

back-to-basics curriculum *(527)*

higher standards curriculum *(528)*

core curriculum *(530)*

student-centered curricula *(531)*

child-centered curriculum *(532)*

free schools *(533)*   individualized instruction *(544)*

alternative schools *(533)*   cooperative learning *(546)*

activity-centered curriculum *(534)*   mastery instruction *(547)*

relevant curriculum *(535)*   critical thinking *(549)*

humanistic curriculum *(536)*   computer-assisted instruction (CAI)
                                                  (551)

values-centered curriculum *(537)*

Discussion Questions

1. Define *curriculum* and support your definition with at least three examples.

2. Describe the differences in philosophy and instructional methods between a subject-centered and a student-centered curriculum.

3. Which of the instructional approaches discussed in this chapter best fits your teaching style? Why?

4. How should computers be used in the classroom? Should computers be provided for all students at once (thirty computers to a class) or for only a few students at a time (for example, in a lab setting)? At what grade should computers be introduced in the classroom, and for what purposes?

5. Discuss the problems and prospects of the curriculum trends described in this chapter. What other trends can you foresee?

Suggested Readings

Altbach, Philip G., ed. *Textbooks in American Society.* Albany, N.Y.: State University Press, 1991.
> *Focusing on how textbooks are produced and selected, this book explains the pressures placed on textbook authors and publishers.*

Connelly, Michael F., and D. Jean Claudinin. *Teachers as Curriculum Planners.* New York: Teachers College Press, Columbia University, 1988.
> *This gives a number of case studies on the role of teachers in planning and developing the curriculum.*

Doll, Ronald C. *Curriculum Improvement: Decision Making and Process,* 8th ed. Boston: Allyn and Bacon, 1992.
> *Doll provides an excellent overview of curriculum improvement, with emphasis on practical principles, problems, and solutions.*

Johnson, David H. *Reaching Out,* 4th ed. Englewood Cliffs, N.J.: Prentice-Hall, 1990.
> *The author describes the theory and practice of cooperative learning and how to enhance student self-actualization.*

Kozol, Jonathan. *Savage Inequalities: Children in America's Schools.* New York: Crown Publishers, 1991.
> *A description of rich and poor schools in America, this book suggests what needs to be done to improve inner-city schools.*

Schlechty, Phillip C. *Schools for the 21st Century.* San Francisco: Jossey-Bass, 1990.
> *The author tackles the question of how to make schools more responsive for the future and offers an overview of the possible future trends affecting education.*

Shane, Harold. *Teaching and Learning in a Microelectronic Age.* Bloomington, Ind.: Phi Delta Kappa, 1987.

> *Shane reviews the recent proposals for school reform and calls for a redesign of education that is integrated with the new high-tech society.*

Sizer, Theodore R. *Horace's Compromise: The Dilemma of the American School,* rev. ed. Boston: Houghton Mifflin, 1985.

> *Here is a timely book on school reform.*

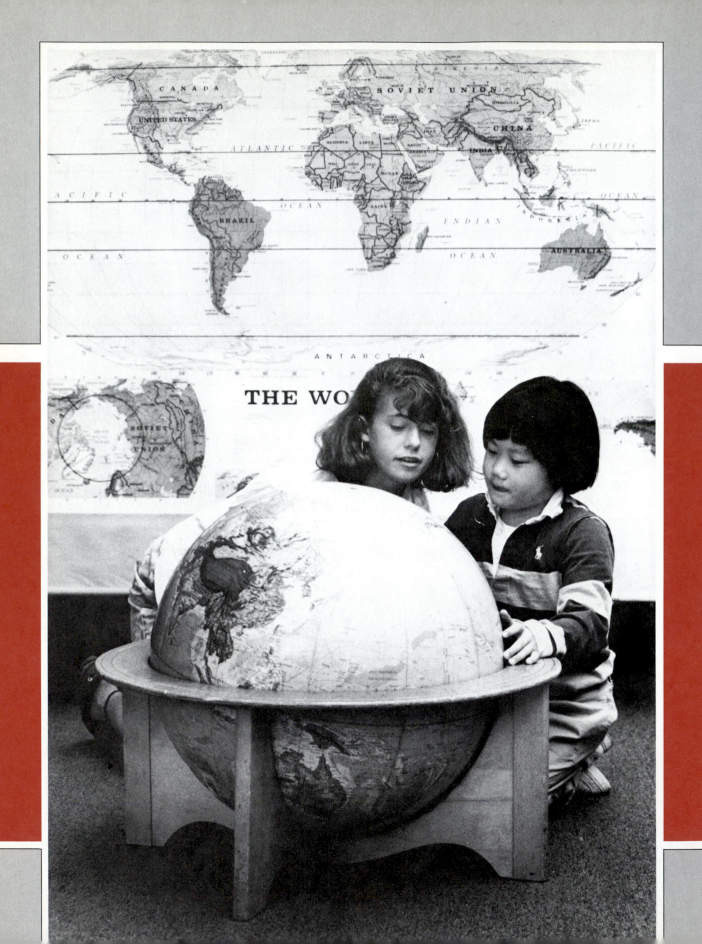

EFFECTIVE EDUCATION: INTERNATIONAL AND AMERICAN PERSPECTIVES

As education becomes more crucial to the success or failure of individuals and nations, increasing attention has been devoted worldwide to possibilities for improving the effectiveness of teachers and schools. Although educators everywhere face many difficulties in working to enhance their effectiveness, many plans are being introduced and comprehensive efforts are being undertaken to improve the opportunities available to children and youth.

Chapter 15 provides an overview of educational systems and developments in other countries. After describing major commonalities among and differences between national systems of education, the chapter briefly portrays exemplary educational services provided by some countries that may be worth emulating elsewhere. Particular stress is given to assessing U.S. education in an international context, and to inquiring about developments around the globe that may have important implications for the improvement of U.S. schools.

Chapter 16 discusses school effectiveness and reform in the United States. After highlighting the imperatives for reform, the chapter summarizes research on classroom and school effectiveness, recent efforts to make schools more effective, and the school improvement process. The chapter concludes with a discussion of several other major topics related to educational effectiveness, including cooperation between the schools and other institutions, improvement of rural education, performance of students in nonpublic schools, magnet and alternative schools, school choice proposals and developments, year-round schools, programs for the gifted and talented, and efforts to restructure U.S. schools.

15

International Education

FOCUSING QUESTIONS

What do educational systems in various countries have in common? In what respects do they differ?

How do educational systems differ with respect to the resources they devote to education and the percentage of students they enroll?

How does the achievement of U.S. students compare with that of students in other countries?

Which countries provide examples of outstanding educational activities that may be worth emulating elsewhere?

What should be done to improve education in developing countries?

How do the purposes and attainments of U.S. schools compare with those of other countries?

Many educational reformers have suggested that the United States could improve its educational system by emulating other countries. Japanese education has received particular attention because it appears to contribute in large measure to Japan's economic success. But can the United States simply adopt or imitate educational institutions and practices from other countries? Would they work in an American context? Do they mesh with American beliefs and values?

Before beginning to answer such questions, educators need to understand the varieties of educational systems that exist in other countries: how they resemble one another, how they differ, and which particular features are most effective in which contexts. This chapter offers an introduction to that kind of analysis. We begin with two examples that illustrate the wide range of educational opportunities and arrangements in other countries. Next, we examine worldwide similarities and differences in more detail before discussing particular educational features that seem especially effective. The chapter then considers education in developing countries and international studies of school improvement. Finally, the chapter offers a brief comment on the accomplishments of U.S. schools in an international context.

CONTRASTING EDUCATIONAL SETTINGS: TWO EXAMPLES

Because nations differ considerably in their history, customs, and stage of development, it is not surprising that educational systems vary dramatically. Contrasts are particularly apparent when Third World or "developing" countries, which can provide only limited educational opportunities, are compared with technologically advanced nations, in which most young people participate in comprehensive educational systems for twelve or thirteen years or more. As an illustration, we will consider two vastly different educational settings: a Sudanese village and contemporary Japan.

As in many other rural areas of low-income countries, educational opportunities for Sudanese village children are severely limited in comparison to those provided for young persons in highly industrialized countries. Until recently, most rural students in the Sudan attended school for only four or five years; few students proceeded to secondary and postsecondary schools. A typical Sudanese village school for boys has been described as follows:[1]

Sudanese rural village school

■ The building has no electricity. The walls are constructed of simple brick, and the earthen floor is uncovered. Each of the four rooms contains portable slateboards and long rows of benches with desks.

■ None of the four teachers has a high-school diploma, but three completed a two-year course at a teacher-training institute.

■ Instruction, delivered in accordance with the ministry of education's *Handbook for Elementary Education,* places great stress on memorization and reci-

---

[1]Harold B. Barclay, "A Sudanese Village: Buurri al Lamaab," in Robert J. Havighurst, ed., *Comparative Perspectives on Education* (Boston: Little, Brown, 1968), pp. 256–267.

tation. Nearly one-fifth of the curriculum focuses on the Koran and other aspects of Islamic religion and history. Science consists largely of basic information from biology and other natural sciences, math is simple computation, and language arts studies are intended to produce graduates who can read a daily newspaper. A "handwork" class provides instruction in manual arts, physical education classes usually consist of undirected play activities, and social studies classes impart fundamental information regarding geography as well as local and national history.

- Whenever a teacher or other adult enters the classroom, students are expected to rise and stand at attention until told to sit.

- Teachers may punish a student by beating him with a green switch, but can inflict no more than five lashes at a time. However, infractions of behavior codes are uncommon.

Although educational opportunities for rural students have been broadened in the Sudan and other developing countries in recent years, arrangements for schooling still tend to be rudimentary. In contrast, consider the educational arrangements and opportunities in Japan:[2]

Opportunities in Japan

- Nearly all students complete high school, and more than half of male graduates (but less than one-fifth of female graduates) proceed to postsecondary schools.

- Elementary and secondary students attend school for 240 days a year. Teachers generally have a college degree or equivalent preparation at a teacher-training institution, and most have considerable experience and pedagogical training. Although they are required to use methods and introduce materials specified by the ministry of education, Japanese teachers have latitude in devising activities and adapting materials that satisfy the national guidelines.

- Emphasis in curriculum and instruction is on developing *ningen* (i.e., human beings) in a manner that transcends basic skills and involves a holistic conception of social, moral, physical, and intellectual growth. The ideal thus is to educate the "whole person."

Instructional emphasis

- Particularly in elementary schools, many lessons are designed to develop students' thinking and problem-solving skills. Emphasis also is placed on active learning, on having students assist one another, and on helping low achievers improve their performance. In general, teachers have time to plan and to work collaboratively with colleagues in devising learning assignments aimed at ensuring that their students will attain a variety of academic and other goals.

- Parents and teachers work together to ensure that the school will function as the center of children's lives outside the home. Parents insist that their children meet the school's stringent homework and behavioral standards,

---

[2]Paul J. Buklarewicz, "The Me Generation," *Transpacific* (July/August 1990), pp. 30–35; Kunio Nishimura, "A Kinder, Gentler Generation," *Look Japan* (April 1991), pp. 4–8; Nancy Sato and Milbrey W. McLaughlin, "Context Matters: Teaching in Japan and the United States," *Phi Delta Kappan* (January 1992), pp. 359–366; and Harold W. Stevenson and James W. Stigler, *The Learning Gap* (New York: Summit, 1992).

In Japanese elementary schools, many lessons are designed to develop students' thinking and problem-solving skills. (© R. Bossu/Sygma)

and teachers advise students not to spend time at shopping malls, restaurants, or other places they might congregate. Given the fact that teachers usually assign large amounts of homework, it is clear that the typical Japanese student devotes much of his or her time to academic studies focused on development of basic skills. High-school students often are discouraged from participating in activities that might interfere with education, and only about one-fifth work part time.

COMMONALITIES IN EDUCATIONAL SYSTEMS

Some characteristics and problems are widespread

For reasons we will examine later in this chapter, educational arrangements in such countries as Japan and the Sudan differ significantly not only from each other but from arrangements in the United States. Before exploring these contrasts in more detail, however, we should stress that differences do not tell the whole story. Despite the great variety in educational systems worldwide, certain commonalities exist. The following sections describe some characteristics and problems that are virtually universal: the strong relationships between students' social-class origins and their success in school; the educational challenges posed by multicultural populations; the typical teaching approaches and the professional conditions that teachers face; and dilemmas arising from the relationship between education and economic development.

Social-Class Origins and School Outcomes

As we noted in Chapter 10, strong relationships between students' socio-economic background and their success in school and in the economic system have been reported in various national and international studies. For example, a report of the Organization for Economic Co-operation and Development (OECD) indicated that "glaring differences" in educational attainment between the "most and least privileged strata of society" are evident in all OECD countries, and a World Bank study reported that students' family socioeconomic background is a "salient" predictor of their achievement in both industrialized and developing countries. Studies in which Donald Treiman analyzed data for more than sixty countries found that individuals' social-class origins and background are related to their educational and occupational attainment regardless of whether their society is rich or poor or is politically liberal or conservative.[3] A multitude of studies such as these have demonstrated conclusively that the family and home environments of low-income students in other countries generate the same kinds of educational disadvantages as are found among students in the United States.[4]

International studies

Multicultural Populations and Problems

Except in a relatively few homogeneous countries, nationwide systems of education enroll diverse groups of students who differ significantly with respect to race, ethnicity, religion, native language, and cultural practices. (Because of its geographic isolation and cultural insularity, Japan is one of the exceptions to this generalization.) Most large nations historically have included numerous racial/ethnic and cultural subgroups, but the twentieth century seems to have greatly accelerated the mixture of diverse groups across and within national boundaries. World and regional wars, global depressions and recessions, migration and immigration to large urban centers that offer expanded economic opportunity — these and other destabilizing forces have led some historians to view recent decades as the era of the migrant and the refugee.[5]

Era of migrants and refugees

The diversity of student populations in other countries is associated with challenges in multicultural education similar to those the United States faces (see Chapter 11). This is because minority racial, ethnic, and religious groups in most nations frequently are low in socioeconomic status. Familiar problems arise: the ineffectiveness of traditional instruction, the provision of bilingual education, and the desegregation of minority students. England, France, the Netherlands, and other European countries have to cope with a large influx of students from Africa, Asia, the Caribbean, and other distant locations. Germany is struggling to provide effective education for the children of Romany (i.e., Gypsy), Slavic,

Multicultural challenges

---

[3]Donald J. Treiman, *Occupational Prestige in Comparative Perspective* (New York: Academic Press, 1977); *Educational Trends* (Paris: Organization for Economic Co-operation and Development, 1984); Marlaine E. Lockheed, Bruce Fuller, and Ronald Nyirongo, *Family Background and School Achievement* (New York: The World Bank, 1988); and Marlaine E. Lockheed, "Accounting for School Effects in Five Developing Countries" (Paper presented at the Annual Meeting of the American Educational Research Association, Chicago, April 1991.

[4]Alan C. Purves and Daniel U. Levine, eds., *Educational Policy and International Assessment* (Berkeley, Calif.: McCutchan, 1975); Annemette Sørensen, "Educational Systems Matter," *Educational Researcher* (March 1992), p. 36.

[5]Marcelo M. Suarez-Orozoco, "Migration, Minority Status, and Education," *Anthropology and Education Quarterly* (June 1991), pp. 99–118; George J. Church, "Surge to The Right," *Time*, January 13, 1992; and Alexander Stille, "Italy: No Blacks Need Apply," *The Atlantic Monthly* (February 1992), pp. 28–39.

Getting to the Source

Social Class and English Schools / Gene Maeroff

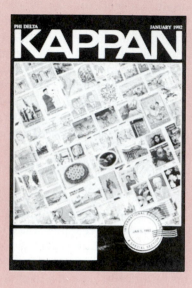

Gene Maeroff, a senior fellow at the Carnegie Foundation for the Advancement of Teaching, participated in a study group that visited English schools in 1990. Members of the study group were struck by the extent to which many working-class students in England were alienated from education. Comparing what he saw and heard with our situation in the United States, Maeroff found both similarities and differences.

An American visitor to one high school asked a small group of students who had stayed on after age 16 why they thought their fellow students had left school. This particular school served some 900 students in a working-class neighborhood, in which an estimated 20% of the fathers were unemployed because the economy had shifted and former employers had closed down production. The students said of the school leavers:

"Many of them lacked confidence that they could do the schoolwork."

"They wanted to make money."

"They were tired of school."

"Their parents may have needed them at home."

"They may have wanted more independence than there is in school."

There appeared to be a tendency among students in such schools to hide their interest in education and in achievement. Said one teacher, speaking of those who remained enrolled after age 16: "A potential achiever must be strong-willed. He could be subject to ridicule. We chaperone them and provide them with a haven from the others [those not yet eligible to leave school]. There are instances of the others destroying the folders of the achievers on the way to and from school."

What are we hearing here? Clearly, England and the U.S. share problems when it comes to the schools in which students are having the least success. Peer pressure against academic achievement, especially among disadvantaged students, is an obstacle to learning in both countries. Whether in England or in the U.S., the outlook for such young people once they leave school is grim. Legions of youths in both countries depart school utterly unequipped to make their way in a world that demands certain skills and attitudes on the job and that expects a kind of mainstream socialization to fit comfortably into society.

In England, there is the overlay of a historically intractable system of social class that has a devastating effect on the aspirations of young people in the lower class, who in England are overwhelmingly white. These students assume that social mobility is nearly impossible and appear not to aspire to higher education to the degree that poor Americans do. In turn, higher education in England does not play the role that it does in the U.S., where the educational hopes of the disadvantaged are reinforced by nonselective admissions policies and lots of available spaces.

Questions

1. In what ways do working-class students in England appear to exemplify the operation of "resistance theory" as described in Chapter 10?

2. Why do working-class students in England seem particularly likely to "assume that social mobility is nearly impossible" and to have little hope for advancement through higher education?

3. Why are educators and public officials in England and many other countries particularly concerned with improving opportunities for working-class students?

Source: Gene I. Maeroff, "Focusing on Urban Education in Britain, *Phi Delta Kappan* (January 1992), cover, p. 357. Reprinted by permission of the author.

Gypsy), Slavic, and Turkish migrants, and most central and West African nations include students from numerous disadvantaged tribal and minority language groups. Provision of educational and other opportunities for minority religious and ethnic groups also constitutes a serious problem throughout much of central and Southeast Asia.[6]

Teaching Approaches and Conditions

Cross-national similarities

Although instructional approaches vary considerably from one teacher to another and the conditions for teaching and learning change accordingly in different classrooms and schools, there also is much similarity in the practices typically emphasized across schools, districts, and entire regions and nations. In fact, research indicates that from some points of view there is relatively little variation internationally in the teaching practices most commonly used and the types of challenges and problems that teachers find rewarding or frustrating. Information on fifth- through ninth-grade classes in mathematics, social studies, and science in ten countries was collected as part of an international Classroom Environment Study. Two researchers who analyzed the data concluded that although there were some interesting differences between countries, overall there seems to be

Classroom Environment Study

> remarkable similarity with respect to the teaching and learning process across the ten countries. In general, classrooms in the ten participating countries can be characterized as follows:
>
> The primary activities include teacher presented lectures or demonstrations plus seatwork activity.
>
> Teachers are directly involved with the students for most of the time.
>
> The most frequently used resource materials are textbooks, workbooks and teacher prepared worksheets.[7]

Sources of professional discouragement and enthusiasm

Scholars in many countries report that teachers typically cite the following sources of "professional discouragement": lack of time to accomplish priority goals, a multiplicity of sometimes conflicting role demands, and lack of full support from administrators. Sources of "professional enthusiasm" generally center on relationships with students and satisfaction with students' accomplishments. Just as in the United States, these sources of teacher enthusiasm and discouragement in other countries inevitably reflect "the reality of schools."[8]

---

[6]John Eggleton, *European Multiethnic Education: A Comparative Perspective* (Coventry, United Kingdom, no date); Maurice Blanc, "The Multi-Ethnic European City and Educational Provision" (Paper presented at the Annual Meeting of the American Educational Research Association, New Orleans, April 1988); Franco Frabboni, "La Integracio Escola-territori," in *La Ciutat Educadora* (Barcelona: Ajuntament de Barcelona, 1990), pp. 147–156; and Margaret Shennan, *Teaching About Europe* (Rutherford, N.J.: Cassell, 1992).

[7]Angela Hilgard and Sid Bourke, "Teaching for Learning: Similarities and Differences Across Countries" (Paper presented at the Annual Meeting of the American Educational Research Association, Chicago, April 1985), p. 17.

[8]Herbert Eibler et al., "A Cross-Cultural Comparison of the Sources of Professional Enthusiasm and Discouragement" (Paper presented at the Annual Meeting of the American Educational Research Association, San Francisco, April 1986), p. 21.

Education and Economic Development

Resources limited

All countries, whether wealthy or poor, confront difficult decisions in determining how to provide educational programs and services that can improve the economic and social well-being of their populations. Expending financial, human, or other resources to provide one type of program or service usually requires deemphasizing or eliminating others that also may be beneficial and desirable. In addition, a particular program or service may prove ineffective or unsuccessful because prerequisite resources and programs have been neglected. The most central dilemmas include the following fundamental issues:[9]

Primary or postsecondary education?

1. Should special emphasis be placed on preschool and primary education to ensure a high degree of basic literacy so that secondary and postsecondary schools will have a developed pool of talent from which to draw? Alternately, should resources be allocated more to secondary or postsecondary schools to make sure that graduates can compete with the most skilled persons in other nations?

Vocational or general education?

2. Should priority be placed on vocational and technical education in order to encourage economic growth and prosperity that will provide resources later to support improvement in general education? Alternately, is it better to emphasize general education to ensure that the labor force will have strong reading and math skills that facilitate adaptation to changes in the future?

Centralized or decentralized?

3. Should decisions regarding curriculum, instructional methods, teacher selection, and other matters be made centrally to ensure that students receive equal opportunities and resources wherever they attend school? Alternatively, should decisions be decentralized so that teachers and administrators have opportunities to determine what works best in their own buildings or regions?

DIFFERENCES IN EDUCATIONAL SYSTEMS AND OUTCOMES

While the commonalities described above are present in educational systems throughout the world, each system also differs in important ways from other systems. Some of the most significant differences are discussed briefly in the following sections. (See endpapers.)

Resources Devoted to Education

Education vs. other priorities

One fundamental way in which nations differ is in the magnitude of their expenditures for education. Public expenditures on education as a percentage of gross domestic product (wealth produced annually) range from 4 to 4.5 percent in regions such as Asia and Latin America, where many countries are very low in average income and/or place relatively little priority on education, to nearly 7 percent in regions such as North America and Africa, where many countries

---

[9]Adriaan M. Verspoor, *Accelerated Educational Development* (Washington, D.C.: The World Bank, 1990); *Adult Illiteracy and Economic Performance* (Washington, D.C.: Center for Educational Research and Innovation, 1992).

have high average income and/or emphasize education compared with other possible priorities such as highways, health services, or military forces. Cross-national data on government expenditures also indicate that average per capita expenditures on military forces in the world's seventy-one poorest countries are nearly one-third greater than their per capita spending for education.[10]

Student-Teacher Ratios at the Primary Level. Nations that are relatively wealthy and/or that allocate many of their resources to education are able to provide a higher level of services than do poor nations that mobilize relatively few resources for their schools. One of the best indicators of availability (or lack of availability) of resources for education is the student-teacher ratio for the "first," or "primary," level of schooling attended. As one would expect, average student-teacher ratios at the primary level tend to be much higher in less-wealthy regions than in more-wealthy regions. Thus, 37 of 52 African nations and 16 of 41 Asian nations reported an average student-teacher ratio of more than 30 to 1 in 1988, whereas 24 of 33 European nations and 3 of 4 North American nations had average ratios of 20 to 1 or less.

Wealthier nations provide more services

Enrollment Ratios. Allocation and availability of resources for education also help determine whether most children and youth attend school and whether they obtain diplomas or degrees. As Table 15.1 shows, in some regions nearly all children between the ages of 6 and 11 attend school (Northern America, Oceania), but less than two-thirds of their counterparts in Africa do. Similarly, nearly all young people from age 12 through 17 and more than 60 percent between age 18 and 23 in the relatively wealthy nations of Northern America are enrolled in school, compared with much lower percentages for less-wealthy regions elsewhere. The table also shows, however, that the percentage of children and youth enrolled in school has increased substantially since 1960 in all regions.

Worldwide increase in enrollment

Male-Female Enrollment. Data provided in Table 15.1 show that expansion in the availability of education since 1960 generally has involved both male and female students. For example, enrollment of boys between 12 and 17 in Africa increased from 23 percent in 1960 to 55 percent in 1990, while enrollment of girls of comparable ages increased from 11 percent to 40 percent. However, enrollment ratios for females still are substantially lower than those for males in many countries, even though enrollment of females has increased much more rapidly than that of males in some regions. Scholars at the World Bank believe that the low enrollment ratio for females compared to males in many low-income countries in Africa and Asia is both a cause and an effect of economic development problems.[11]

Increase in female enrollment

The United States Among Industrial Nations. For some purposes it is more instructive to compare wealthy or highly industrialized nations with each other

---

[10]George Psacharopoulos, *Planning of Education: Where Do We Stand?* (Washington, D.C.: The World Bank, 1985); Antoine Schwartz and Gail Stevenson, *Public Expenditures Reviews for Education* (Washington, D.C.: The World Bank, 1990); and "Title XXI — Third World Development and Threat Reduction," *Congressional Record,* January 24, 1992, pp. 5359–5360.

[11]Wadi D. Haddad et al., *Education and Development* (Washington, D.C.: The World Bank, 1990).

Table 15.1 ━━━━━━━━

Estimated Enrollment Ratios by Region, Age Group, and Sex, 1960 and 1990, by Region

Region and Year	Ages 6–11		Ages 12–17		Ages 18–23	
	Male	*Female*	*Male*	*Female*	*Male*	*Female*
Africa						
1960	40	24	23	11	03	01
1990	68	58	55	40	17	08
Asia						
1960	62	42	49	32	11	06
1990	87	74	53	40	19	12
Europe						
1960	87	87	63	58	16	10
1990	89	89	84	84	33	32
Latin America						
1960	58	57	39	34	08	04
1990	88	87	72	71	28	27
Northern America						
1960	100	100	99	90	33	27
1990	100	100	98	97	61	66
Oceania						
1960	89	89	63	58	12	05
1990	99	97	75	76	24	24

Note: Enrollment ratios show the percentage of the appropriate population that is enrolled in school. Data for Europe include the former USSR. "Latin America" includes Central and South America, Mexico, and the Caribbean. "Northern America" includes Bermuda, Canada, Greenland, St. Pierre, and the United States. "Oceania" includes Australia, Guam, Polynesia, Samoa, Tonga, and other Pacific Islands.

Source: *UNESCO Statistical Yearbook, 1990* (Paris: UNESCO, 1990), pp. 2-32 and 2-33, Table 2.11. Copyright © UNESCO, 1990. Reproduced with the permission of UNESCO.

rather than with poor or economically underdeveloped nations. Other things remaining equal, nations that have less wealth and fewer resources have a much harder time supporting education or other government services than do those with a strong economic base. Thus, to analyze the adequacy with which the United States mobilizes resources to provide education, we will limit our discussion to comparisons with other highly industrialized and developed countries.[12]

Comparisons with other wealthy nations

Several recent controversies have focused on the extent to which the United States devotes resources to education. For example, officials of the Bush administration published data indicating that educational expenditures in the United States are "unsurpassed" by those in other industrialized nations (in the course of arguing that results have not been commensurate with expenditures), but a later study by staff of the Economic Policy Institute concluded that the United

─────────

[12]"Developed" nations as classified by the United Nations Educational, Scientific, and Cultural Organization (UNESCO) include Australia, Canada, Europe except for Yugoslavia, Israel, Japan, South Africa, the former USSR, the United States, and New Zealand. All others are classified as "developing" nations.

Differences in Educational Systems and Outcomes

Table 15.2

Estimated Gross Domestic Product per Capita, Educational Expenditures, and Student-Teacher Ratios, Excluding Higher Education, 15 Industrial Countries

	Gross Domestic Product per Capita		Education Expenditures per Capita		Expenditures per Pupil		Number of Students per Teacher	
	Dollars	Rank	Dollars	Rank	Dollars	Rank	Ratio	Rank
Australia	13,523	6	646	9	2,060	15	15.7	8
Austria	11,582	15	625	11	2,972	7	9.5	2
Belgium	11,755	14	613	12	2,492	9	10.5	4
Canada	17,355	2	1,153	1	4,054	2	16.2	10
Denmark	13,218	8	969	2	3,997	3	12.2	6
France	12,791	10	723	7	2,486	10	16.9	11
Italy	12,136	13	528	15	2,320	14	11.0	5
Japan	13,137	9	635	10	2,379	13	20.0	14
Netherlands	12,196	12	723	6	2,495	8	15.5	7
Norway	16,161	3	966	3	3,636	5	8.6	1
Sweden	14,052	5	911	4	4,279	1	10.3	3
Switzerland	15,570	4	715	8	3,733	4	NA	—
United Kingdom	12,529	11	604	13	2,474	11	15.7	8
United States	18,297	1	860	5	3,398	6	18.4	13
West Germany	13,296	7	536	14	2,450	12	18.3	12

Note: Expenditure data are for preschool through high school but exclude capital outlay and debt service. NA = not available. Original data are from OECD and UNESCO reports for 1986 and 1987. Student-teacher ratios are adjusted for part-time vocational enrollment. Various other adjustments were made to enhance comparability of the original data.

Source: F. Howard Nelson, *International Comparison of Public Spending on Education* (Washington, D.C.: American Federation of Teachers, 1991), pp. 32–34, Tables 4–6.

Data often not comparable

States does not rank high on expenditures when funding for higher education is subtracted and K–12 expenditures only are considered. Critics also identified problems with the comparability of data, inclusion or omission of private school students, definitions of schooling, assessment of cost-of-living factors, and other matters. Fortunately, F. Howard Nelson of the American Federation of Teachers and other researchers subsequently have been able to collect and analyze available data in a manner that takes better account of such problems and provides a basis for instructive comparisons.[13]

Ranking of United States

As indicated in Table 15.2, the data Nelson brought together indicate that except for Canada, the United States has had by far the highest gross domestic product per capita of any of the fifteen industrial countries for which he had adequate comparable information. At the same time, however, the United States ranks only fifth in expenditures per capita on education from preschool through grade twelve, and places only sixth among the fifteen countries in per-pupil

[13]John Hood, *Education: Is America Spending Too Much?* (Washington, D.C.: Cato Institute, 1990); Lawrence Mishel and Edith Rasell, *Shortchanging Education* (Washington, D.C.: Economic Policy Institute, 1990); Lawrence J. Perelman, *The "Acanemia" Deception* (Indianapolis, Ind.: Hudson Institute, 1990); F. Howard Nelson, *International Comparison of Public Spending on Education* (Washington, D.C.: American Federation of Teachers, 1991); and Gerald W. Bracey, "Of Elephants and Achievement," *Phi Delta Kappan* (April 1992), pp. 643–646.

expenditures when higher education is excluded. As the table shows, this level of expenditure translates into a much higher student-teacher ratio in the United States than is found in most of the other countries here compared. These kinds of data have led some observers to conclude that the United States is not placing as large an emphasis as it might on improving schools.[14]

Comparing teacher salaries

A strong debate also continues over whether teacher salaries in the United States are high or low in comparison with other industrial countries. Some observers have concluded that U.S. teacher salaries are relatively high, but others believe that the average pay is relatively low. Data on the average salaries of elementary and secondary teachers here and elsewhere indicate that for both beginning and experienced teachers, average salaries in some countries (e.g., Austria, Japan) are a good deal lower than in the United States, but in other countries (e.g., Canada, Switzerland) are substantially higher.[15]

Comparisons of educational expenditures in the United States and other industrial countries sometimes are expanded to examine other types of resources that support children's well-being and development. For example, Timothy Smeeding compared the United States with Australia, Canada, Germany, Sweden, and the United Kingdom, and found that U.S. governmental expenditures on children's education and health services as a percent of gross domestic product are about the same as the average for these five countries. However, he also found that U.S. government expenditures to help provide income security for

U.S. expenditures for low-income children

children's families is a little less than half of the average for these countries, perhaps in part because U.S. expenditures to help the poor have not been growing as fast as the percentage of low-income children in the youth population. Smeeding concluded that because high rates of divorce, out-of-wedlock births, and other social forces are creating a larger "urban and rural underclass," it is "becoming increasingly hard to argue that all U.S. children have equal life chances."[16]

Extent of Centralization

As we noted earlier, all governments must decide whether to emphasize decentralized decision making, which allows for planning and delivering instruction in accordance with local circumstances, or centralized decision making, which builds accountability up and down a national or regional chain of command. One can find examples that go very far in either direction. In the United States, for example, many or even most important decisions are decentralized across more than 15,000 diverse public school districts that have their own boards of education. At the other extreme, as in France, Greece, and Japan,

Examples of centralization

educational systems and decisions have been highly centralized, following na-

---

[14]F. Howard Nelson, *International Comparison of Public Spending on Education* (Washington, D.C.: American Federation of Teachers, 1991); Albert Shanker, "Core Knowledge," *The New York Times,* December 15, 1991, p. E7.

[15]F. Howard Nelson, "Shortchanged or Overindulged: Issues in Comparing Educational Spending in the U.S. to Other Countries" (Paper presented at the Annual Meeting of the American Educational Research Association, Chicago, April 1991).

[16]Timothy Smeeding, "Social Thought and Poor Children," *Focus* (Spring 1990), p. 14; Gene Koretz, ". . . And Other Nations Do Better Keeping Poverty at Bay," *Business Week,* February 24, 1992, p. 26.

tionwide policies concerning acceptable class size, teacher selection and assignment, and what will be taught in a given subject at a particular grade and time. Under such a centralized plan, for example, the same math lesson will be taught on the same day to about the same number of third-grade students in each school in the country, from distant villages to urban centers. One result of centralization, in some countries, is that long lines of citizens from all parts of the nation can be seen waiting outside the ministry of education for appointments with central school officials who determine what schools children will attend and how students will be treated.

Curriculum Content and Instructional Emphasis

Although, as we have seen, much instruction worldwide consists of teacher lectures and student seatwork, nations do differ with regard to curriculum content and instructional emphasis. Well-known practices that make some countries distinctive from most others include the following:[17]

Distinctive practices

■ New Zealand primary schools are known for their systematic emphasis on learning to read through "natural language learning." Using this approach, children learn to figure out words in context as they read, rather than through phonics and decoding instruction.

■ British "infant schools" historically have emphasized personal and social development and creative learning in preschools and in the primary grades.

■ Schools in some Islamic countries build much of the curriculum around religious content and emphasize didactic memorization of religious precepts.

■ Elementary schools in Japan place uncommon emphasis on in-depth study of instructional material and on learning of higher-order skills.

Vocational Versus Academic Education

Divergence after primary education

School systems around the world also differ greatly in the way they are organized to provide education through the postsecondary level. Although most nations now initially provide at least four years of first-level education during which all students attend "primary" or "elementary" schools, systems then diverge widely. Most students continue in "common" first-level schools for several more years, but in many countries students are divided between academic-track schools and vocational-type schools after anywhere from four to eight years of first-level education. This arrangement, which corresponds to the traditional European dual-track pattern described in Chapter 3, is often known as a **bipartite system.**

---

[17]Daniel A. Wagner and Abdelhamid Lotfi, "Traditional Islamic Education in Morocco: Sociohistorical and Psychological Perspectives," *Comparative Education Review* (June 1980), pp. 238–251; Brendon Burns, "In New Zealand, Good Reading and Writing Come 'Naturally,'" *Newsweek,* December 2, 1991, p. 53; James W. Stigler and Harold W. Stevenson, "How Asian Teachers Polish Each Lesson to Perfection," *American Educator* (Spring 1991), pp. 12–20, 43–48; and Elaine Jarchow, "Ten Ideas Worth Stealing from New Zealand," *Phi Delta Kappan* (January 1992), pp. 394–395.

Wide national variation

Academic and vocational tracks may each have more or less rigorous sub-tracks, and the proportions of students in various tracks may be high or low. For example, UNESCO reports indicate that the proportion of secondary students who are enrolled in primarily vocational programs varies from less than one-tenth in some industrial countries (e.g., Switzerland, United Kingdom) to more than one-third in others (e.g., Germany, Belgium). Nations in Africa and other developing regions also place varying degrees of stress on vocational and pre-vocational programs.[18] In contrast, beginning at the secondary level and extending into postsecondary education, large proportions of students in some countries are enrolled in academic schools that are established to produce an "elite" corps of high-school or college graduates. In other countries, such as Canada and the United States, most secondary students continue to attend "common" or "comprehensive" schools and many enroll in colleges that are relatively non-selective.

Enrollment in Higher Education

Nations that have different rates of participation in vocational education have subsequent differences in the percentages of students who attend and complete postsecondary education. In general, countries that channel students into vocational programs that prepare them for specific occupations have lower percentages of youth attending institutions of higher education; in countries that provide general academic studies for most high-school students, more youth go on to higher education. Other factors that help determine enrollment patterns in higher education include a nation's investment of resources in higher education, stress on postsecondary learning rather than entry into the job market, traditions regarding the use of higher education as a means to equalize educational opportunities, and the extent to which colleges and universities admit only high-achieving students.

Factors affecting enrollment

Developing countries that have relatively little funding available for higher education, and in any case are struggling to increase enrollments at the elementary and secondary levels, predictably have low proportions of youth participating in higher education. Thus Afghanistan, China, Ethiopia, Ghana, and many other developing nations enroll less than 5 percent of their 20- to 24-year-olds in higher education. Industrial countries provide postsecondary education for much higher proportions of youth and young adults (see Table 15.1). In most industrial nations, one-fourth to one-third of 20- to 24-year-olds are attending postsecondary schools, but in two countries — Canada and the United States — this proportion is nearly two-thirds.[19]

High enrollment in industrial nations

Once high-school graduates are enrolled in postsecondary institutions, numerous considerations determine whether they will stay enrolled and eventually gain their degrees: the rigor of the curriculum, the availability of financial support, the extent to which they are motivated, the accessibility of preferred insti-

[18]*Statistical Yearbook 1990* (Paris: UNESCO, 1990); Rosemary George, *Youth Policies and Programs in Selected Countries* (Washington, D.C.: The William T. Grant Commission on Work, Family, and Citizenship, 1987), p. 5; and Thomas Owen Eisemon and John Schwille, "Primary Schooling in Burundi and Kenya: Preparation for Secondary Education or for Self-Employment?" *The Elementary School Journal* (September 1991), pp. 23–40.

[19]*World Development Report 1991* (Washington, D.C.: The World Bank, 1991).

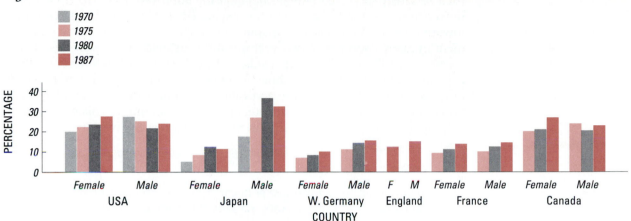

Figure 15.1

Higher Education Graduates As a Percent of All Persons 22 Years Old, by Country, academic years beginning 1970, 1975, 1980, and 1987 (all fields)

Source: *The Condition of Education 1991, Volume 2: Postsecondary Education* (Washington, D.C.: U.S. Government Printing Office, 1991), Chart 2:8, p. 37.

Numerous differences between nations

tutions and courses. Industrial nations differ greatly in the proportion of young persons who obtain postsecondary degrees, and in the educational opportunities available for females. As shown in Figure 15.1, for example, Canada, Japan, and the United States graduate a much higher percentage of 22-year-olds from post-secondary institutions than do England, France, and Germany. However, Japan's high percentage can be accounted for by the relatively high percentage of young men who obtain degrees; young women in Japan are significantly less likely to complete higher education than are their counterparts in Canada and the United States.

Higher education typology

National systems of higher education also differ substantially in their goals. One typology of higher education distinguishes between four fundamentally different approaches that specific groups of countries have historically followed. In the **research model,** best exemplified in Germany, teaching is closely linked with faculty members' research, and only a select group of students is admitted to study with research mentors. In the **personality development model,** best illustrated in England, emphasis is placed on "liberal education" to enhance students' academic and scientific preparation. In the **training model,** developed in France, colleges and universities prepare individuals in fields the government has identified as being worthy of public support. Finally, the **diversified model,** most clearly evident in the United States, attempts to satisfy all three of these goals (i.e., research, personal development, national training needs).[20]

---

[20]Claudius Gellert, "Higher Eduation: Changing Tasks and Definitions," *Higher Education in Europe* (no. 3, 1991), pp. 28–45. Also see Sheldon Rothblatt, "Education and Exclusion," *London Review of Books*, February 12, 1992, pp. 13–14.

Recently, governments nearly everywhere have been looking to higher education to meet national needs for a highly trained workforce. They have also tried to satisfy increased popular demand for improved access to colleges and universities. As higher education has expanded, many countries have moved toward diversified models. One manifestation of this movement is the establishment in many countries of two-year institutions similar to or even modeled on community colleges in the United States. The U.S. system of community colleges expanded rapidly during the middle of this century as part of our nation's efforts to make higher education more accessible and to provide postsecondary vocational preparation. Numerous adaptations of the community college model are helping to accomplish these purposes in many parts of the world.[21]

Community college movement

Nonpublic Schools

Depending on their histories, political structures, religious composition, legal frameworks, and other factors, nations differ greatly in the size and functioning of nonpublic sectors of education. In a few countries, such as the Netherlands, more than half of elementary and secondary students attend private schools. At the other extreme, governments in Cuba, North Korea, and some other nations have prohibited nonpublic schools in order to suppress ideologies different from those supported by the state. In general, private-school students constitute less than 10 percent of total enrollment in a large majority of countries.[22]

Suppression in some countries

Nations also vary widely in the extent to which they provide public support for nonpublic schools or students. They differ as to government regulation of nonpublic systems, people's perceptions of public and nonpublic schools, and the role that private schools should play in national development. In some countries, nonpublic schools enroll a relatively small, elite group of students who enter the most prestigious colleges; in others they serve a more representative sample of the nation's children and youth. Given this variety, it is not possible to say exactly what a "private school" is internationally, or to generalize about cross-national policies that encourage or discourage the growth and functioning of nonpublic schools. Clearly, productive national policies on nonpublic schools must reflect each country's unique mix of circumstances and challenges.

No standard definition of "private school"

Achievement Levels

Differences in school achievement among nations have received considerable attention since the **International Association for the Evaluation of Educational Achievement (IEA)** began conducting cross-national studies in the 1960s. One of the first major IEA projects collected and analyzed data on the achievement of 258,000 students from nineteen countries in civic education, foreign languages, literature, reading comprehension, and science. This study showed a wide range in average achievement levels across nations. In general,

First IEA study

---

[21]Joseph A. Greenberg, "Exporting the Community College Concept: Worldwide Variations," *New Directions For Community Colleges* (Fall 1991), pp. 69–77.
[22]*Statistical Yearbook, 1991* (Paris: UNESCO, 1991).

the United States ranked close to the middle among the nations included in the study.[23]

Mathematics comparisons

Assessment of mathematics achievement has been particularly emphasized in IEA activities, in part because math is widely viewed as a "gatekeeper" subject that helps determine later success in scientific and technical studies. Mathematics also lends itself to international comparisons because its content is relatively standard across cultures and does not much reflect historical and linguistic differences among countries. The first International Study of Achievement in Mathematics reported that high-ability students performed well in nearly all participating countries. A second International Study of Achievement in Mathematics assessed the performance of twelve- and thirteen-year-olds in educational systems in eighteen countries. Japanese students had the highest average scores in arithmetic, algebra, geometry, and measurement. Students in Hungary and the Netherlands also did unusually well in several of these categories, whereas students in Luxembourg, Nigeria, and Switzerland had low average scores. Eighth graders in the United States scored close to the overall average in arithmetic and algebra, and close to the bottom in geometry and measurement.[24]

U.S. scores not high

First IAEP study

Several years after the second study, the IEA and the U.S. National Assessment of Educational Progress (NAEP) worked together to help produce the first **International Assessment of Educational Progress (IAEP),** which compared math and science achievement among thirteen-year-olds in six countries. A follow-up study of math and science achievement in twenty countries was published in 1992. As shown in Table 15.3, mathematics scores of U.S. students were substantially below those for students in the other five countries in the first IAEP study (Canada, Ireland, Korea, Spain, and the United Kingdom), and their science scores were far below the averages for all the other nations except Ireland. Students in the U.S. sample also generally ranked low in the twenty-country study. Researchers at the Educational Testing Service who analyzed the first set of data offered the following comments:

> *Mathematics.* The position of the United States as last in overall achievement heightens concern for the future in an increasingly uncertain world. . . . [The data on advanced-levels performance] suggest that the pool of trained talent from which to draw our future scientists, engineers, and technicians is small indeed. . . .
>
> *Science.* The United States has traditionally thought of itself as technologically innovative and in the forefront in science. These results are sobering and pose a serious challenge to our position in the world community. . . . The findings of this study will present yet another opportunity to call the attention of policymakers, the business community, and America's parents to the potential problems the country will face if the mathematics and science curricula are not strengthened.[25]

Sobering results in the United States

---

[23]Purves and Levine, *Educational Policy and International Assessment*; Richard M. Wolf, *Achievement in America* (New York: Teachers College Press, 1977).

[24]Torsten Husen, *International Study of Achievement in Mathematics* (New York: Wiley, 1967); Curtis C. McKnight et al., *The Underachieving Curriculum* (Champaign, Ill.: Stipes, 1987); *National Education Goals Report* (Wasington, D.C.: National Education Goals Panel, 1991); and Elliott A. Medrich and Jeanne E. Griggith, *International Mathematics and Science Assessments: What Have We Learned?* (Washington, D.C.: U.S. Department of Education, 1992).

[25]Archie E. Lapointe, Nancy A. Mead, and Gary W. Phillips, *A World of Differences* (Princeton, N.J.: Educational Testing Service, 1989), p. 79. Also see Paul E. Barton and Richard J. Coley, *Performance at the Top* (Princeton, N.J.: Educational Testing Service, 1991), and *Learning Mathematics* and *Learning Science* (Princeton, N.J.: Educational Testing Service, 1992).

Table 15.3

Percentages of Thirteen-Year-Olds in Six Nations Scoring at or Above Designated Levels in Mathematics and Science

	Mathematics Levels			Science Levels		
	400	500	600	400	500	600
Korea	95	78	40	93	73	33
Canada	94	61	17	88	52	15
Spain	91	57	14	88	53	12
United Kingdom	87	55	18	78	59	21
Ireland	86	55	14	76	37	09
United States	78	40	09	78	35	12

Note: Mathematics levels as defined in the International Assessment of Educational Progress (IAEP) represent the following criteria for knowledge and skills:

   400   Can solve one-step problems and locate numbers on a number line, and understand the most basic concepts of logic, percent, and geometry.
   500   Can solve two-step problems; can use information from charts and graphs, convert fractions, decimals, and percents, and compute averages.
   600   Can multiply fractions and decimals, and demonstrate increased understanding of measurement and geometry concepts.

Science levels as defined in the IAEP represent the following criteria for knowledge and skills:

   400   Has basic knowledge of life sciences and physical sciences.
   500   Can design experiments and use scientific equipment.
   600   Can draw conclusions by applying scientific facts and principles.

Source: Adapted from Archie E. Lapointe, Nancy A. Mead, and Gary W. Phillips, *A World of Differences* (Princeton, N.J.: Educational Testing Service, 1989), pp. 17, 38, Tables 1.1, 4.1; *The National Education Goals Report* (Washington, D.C.: National Education Goals Panel, 1991), p. 18, Exhibits 12, 13.

Scholars who analyzed the IEA and IAEP mathematics and science data tried to determine whether aspects of instruction were associated with national performance levels. These analyses supported the following conclusions:[26]

1. Instructional characteristics generally were not correlated with average mathematics and science scores. These characteristics included class size, amount of time allocated to instruction, teachers' experience or training, and amount of homework.

2. As in other countries studied, mathematics instruction in the United States emphasized passive, rote, abstract learning that the analysts characterized as "tell and show" approaches. Since scores in some other countries were considerably higher, these approaches could not account for low U.S. performance levels except in interaction with other variables.

Passive "tell and show" instruction

3. In contrast to many other nations, the U.S. mathematics curriculum is "dramatically differentiated." That is, our eighth graders tend to be sorted into mathematics tracks that stress algebra and other advanced topics for high-

[26]McKnight et al., *The Underachieving Curriculum*; Lapointe, Mead, and Phillips, *A World of Differences*; David Robitaille and Robert Garden, *The IEA Study of Mathematics II: Contexts and Outcomes of School Mathematics* (Oxford: Pergamon, 1989); Ina V. S. Mullis, Eugene H. Owen, and Gary W. Phillips, *Accelerating Academic Achievement* (Princeton, N.J.: Educational Testing Service, 1991); and "U.S. Children Trail in Testing on Math and Science," *The New York Times*, February 6, 1992, p. A8.

achieving students and simple arithmetic for low achievers. Thus many students with low or medium achievement levels have little opportunity to proceed beyond basic skills. This is in marked contrast to Hong Kong, Japan, and some other locations where most students are challenged to perform at a higher level. Worse still, even high achievers in the United States frequently are in classes that introduce only low-level content. Most analysts who have reviewed these patterns believe that action must be taken to reduce or eliminate this kind of "curriculum differentiation," and to upgrade curriculum and instruction throughout our educational system.

Low-level content

Publication of the IEA and IAEP studies delineating low math and science performance in the United States compared with other countries has helped to ignite sustained and emotional controversies. On one side, some observers have expressed the belief that the functioning of our educational system is not as unsatisfactory as it frequently has been portrayed. While admitting that major improvements are needed, these observers point to issues and trends such as the following:[27]

Interpretation of U.S. scores controversial

■ International studies may underestimate U.S. performance in relation to other countries because they generally have questionable controls for social class and may be comparing our students with more elite groups of students elsewhere. In other words, samples of students tested in some of the comparison countries may consist disproportionately of high-achieving students or middle-class students.

Methodological issues

■ Much of the relatively low performance of our students may be due to cultural factors, not deficiencies in the schools. For example, the very high levels of mathematics achievement reported for Hungary, Japan, Korea, and several other countries may be attributable primarily to the great value their cultures attach to mathematics performance, strong family support for achievement, nationwide support for science and technology, and other sociocultural considerations.

Reasons for low scores

■ Contrary to the statements and assumptions of some critics, achievement in U.S. schools has improved during the past few decades, particularly considering the increased enrollment of minority students from low-income families. These improvements are attributable to the positive effects of compensatory education and school desegregation (see Chapter 11), to the introduction of minimum competency testing and other efforts to bring about educational reform, and even to enhanced verbal development associated with the spread of rap music.

Recent U.S. improvement

■ Analyses of relatively low performance among U.S. students typically fail to take account of the fact that, by some measures, expenditures for elementary

[27]Purves and Levine, *Educational Policy and International Assessment;* Michael Newman, "Software Soneteers," *The New York Times,* February 12, 1990, p. A11; Iris C. Rotberg, "I Never Promised You First Place," *Phi Delta Kappan* (December 1990), pp. 296–303; C. C. Carson, R. M. Huelskamp, and T. D. Woodall, *Perspectives on Education in America* (Albuquerque, N.M.: Sandia National Laboratory, 1991); Malcolm Gladwell, "2 Apples Plus 4 Oranges Equal 1 Uproar Over Math Skills," *The Washington Post National Weekly Edition,* December 2–8, 1991; Dale Whittington, "What Have 17-Year-Olds Known in the Past?" *American Educational Research Journal* (Winter 1991), pp. 759–780; and Charles Murray and R. J. Herrnstein, "What's Really Behind the SAT-Score Decline?" *The Public Interest* (Winter 1992), pp. 32–56.

and secondary education are low compared with those for some other industrial nations (see earlier sections in this chapter).

■   Assessments of the U.S. educational system should highlight the fact that
    our system produces higher percentages of high-school graduates and col-
    lege entrants than other countries, except for Canada and Japan.

"Bottom-line" findings

However, critics of U.S. performance have been unconvinced and unap-
peased by such arguments. Frequently pointing to the particularly low scores
that our students register on tests assessing higher-order skills such as math
problem solving, they reiterate the importance of improving students' skills in
comprehension, geography, math, science, and other subjects. They also stress
bottom-line findings such as the fact that only 6 percent of U.S. high-school
juniors could designate the amount of a loan to be repaid after calculating the
interest component. They conclude that low rankings obtained by U.S. students
in international achievement studies represent a deplorable performance level
that justifies radical efforts to reform or even replace our schools.[28]

Testing Policies and Practices

*Survey of
European practices*

Countries vary widely in the methods they use to measure student achievement, from the types of tests utilized and the grade levels tested to whether the
tests are administered nationally or locally. They also differ in the degree to
which tests are used to make final decisions about students' placement and careers, and the extent to which improved testing is seen as a means of reforming
schools. A team of analysts at the OECD recently surveyed student testing practices in seventeen industrialized countries to determine whether the data collected in these countries can be used for international comparisons. Team members concluded that assessment practices vary so greatly that the resulting data
are mostly incomparable.[29]

As we discuss elsewhere in this book, U.S. educators and political and civic
leaders have been debating whether to establish national tests that would determine certain skills and knowledge that teachers everywhere would be expected
to emphasize in classroom instruction. In effect, national tests would both reflect
and facilitate development of a **national curriculum,** which some policy makers strongly support and others oppose vociferously. Since many countries that
have centralized educational systems administer national tests to determine
whether students are mastering a standard curriculum, researchers can investigate how well this system works and whether it has discernible advantages and
disadvantages. Thomas Kellaghan and George Madaus have identified the fol-

---

[28]Chester E. Finn, Jr., *We Must Take Charge* (New York: Free Press, 1991); Norman Bradburn et
al., "A Rejoinder to 'I Never Promised You First Place,'" *Phi Delta Kappan* (June 1991), pp. 774–
780; Diane Ravitch, "U.S. Schools: The Bad News Is Right," *The Washington Post National Weekly
Edition*, November 25–December 1, 1991, p. 29; Robert Rothman, "Revisionists Take Aim at
Gloomy View of Schools," *Education Week*, November 13, 1991, pp. 1, 12–15; and Linda Darling-
Hammond and Ann Lieberman, "The Shortcomings of Standardized Tests," *The Chronicle of
Higher Education*, January 29, 1992, pp. B1–B2.

[29]Marilyn R. Binkley, James W. Guthrie, and Timothy J. Wyatt, *A Survey of National Assessment
and Examination Practices in OECD Countries* (Lugano, Switzerland: OECD, 1991).

Taking Issue ___•___

Establishment of a National Curriculum

In some countries in which public education is highly centralized, teachers generally are expected to follow a national curriculum that specifies the topics to be taught and the objectives and materials to be emphasized in each subject and grade level. In other countries that follow a decentralized pattern, decisions about subject matter and materials are made primarily at the level of a regional group of schools (such as a school district) or by individual faculties or teachers. Government officials in some highly centralized nations such as the United States are considering whether a national curriculum should be established to provide for a more standardized approach in planning and delivering instruction.

Question: For the United States, would a national curriculum be preferable to decentralized policies that allow individual school districts, schools, or teachers to select instructional objectives and materials?

Arguments PRO

1 Availability of a national curriculum is partly responsible for the high achievement levels attained in Japan, Korea, and some other countries.

2 A national curriculum based on the careful deliberation of subject-area specialists and experienced teachers makes it easier to achieve in-depth teaching of well-sequenced objectives and materials.

3 Uniformity in objectives and materials reduces the inefficiencies and learning problems that occur when students move from one classroom, school, or district to another.

4 A national curriculum will generate or, at least, facilitate improvements in teacher education because preparation programs can concentrate on objectives and materials that trainees will be required to teach when they subsequently obtain jobs.

5 Because it draws on a large base of resources, national curriculum planning can incorporate the best current thinking in each subject area and can be carried out in conjunction with the preparation of technically excellent tests.

Arguments CON

1 Establishment of a national curriculum runs counter to promising trends toward site-based management and professional autonomy for teachers.

2 A national curriculum is undesirable because it results in the use of objectives and materials that are too difficult for many students in some classrooms and too easy for many students in other classrooms.

3 Particularly in large and diverse countries such as the United States, the standardized materials that form the basis for a national curriculum will be uninteresting and demotivating for many students.

4 Despite possible efforts to allow for flexibility in selecting alternate objectives and materials when it may be appropriate to do so, teachers provided with a national curriculum will be pressured to use those specified nationally, and funds probably will not be available for alternate materials.

5 Since it is very difficult to prepare challenging materials that are appropriate for use across a wide range of classrooms, a national curriculum will reinforce tendencies to emphasize low-level skills and uncreative materials.

lowing potential problems associated with national tests or other "external examinations" administered across a diverse group of schools:[30]

1. External exams narrow the curriculum; objectives and materials that are not tested tend to be excluded from or neglected in instruction.

2. Costs of examining practical and oral skills are so high that they tend to be left untested.

3. It is extremely difficult if not impossible to prepare external exams that conclusively assess such aspects of student performance as perseverance and adaptability in executing projects.

4. External exams reinforce tendencies to emphasize low-order skills that are most easily taught and tested.

5. External exams generally are unsuitable for assessing the performance of low achievers.

6. Since external exams in effect determine much of the curriculum, they diminish the professional role of teachers.

7. If an external exam is implemented, systematic efforts should be made to identify and overcome predictable problems and disadvantages such as those identified above.

Kellaghan, Madaus, and other scholars who study testing practices have been particularly interested in developments in England and Wales, which have implemented a type of testing that resembles plans being considered for adoption in the United States. During the 1980s and early 1990s, the British government established a required national curriculum that is monitored and assessed partly through a new national testing system. In line with much current thinking concerning the disadvantages of standardized multiple-choice exams, the new tests are designed to assess a wide range of abilities and skills, such as students' ability to apply conceptual knowledge, to perform in both written and oral modes, and to understand complex subject matter. Methods of assessment require students to write essays, participate in group interviews, perform experiments, and compile portfolios or exhibits representing their capacity to carry out meaningful projects over a significant period of time.

Some analysts who have examined the initial implementation of England's national curriculum and testing system believe it may be having positive effects in terms of establishing and communicating nationwide standards for teaching and learning. However, they also report that large amounts of time, work, and money are required to select appropriate objectives and curricula, assess students' performance without dreadfully overloading teachers, plan and deliver large-scale staff development, and generally overcome the "dizzying" logistic challenges that teachers face when they must overhaul most of their lesson plans and testing practices.[31]

[30]Thomas Kellaghan and George F. Madaus, "National Testing: Lessons for America from Europe," *Educational Leadership* (November 1991), pp. 87–90; George F. Madaus and Thomas Kellaghan, *Student Examination Systems in the European Community: Lessons for the United States* (Washington, D.C.: United States Congress Office of Technology Assessment, 1991).
[31]Gene I. Maeroff, "Assessing Alternative Assessment," *Phi Delta Kappan* (December 1991), pp.

EXEMPLARY AND POTENTIALLY EXEMPLARY ACTIVITIES AND REFORMS

Many nations have introduced substantial reforms in their educational systems. Some countries have been respected for many decades for the quality and effectiveness with which they provide early childhood opportunities, mathematics instruction, vocational schooling, or other important educational experiences for their populations. In this section we will briefly review several such exemplary reforms. We have used the term "potentially exemplary" because some reforms either have been introduced only recently or may not have much applicability in other, very different countries.

Early Childhood Education in France

Variations in child-care arrangements

Recognizing that the preschool years critically determine a child's subsequent social, physical, and educational development, many countries have moved decisively to ensure that stimulating learning opportunities and positive day-care arrangements are available for most or all children. For example, more than 90 percent of three- to five-year-olds in Belgium and Hong Kong are enrolled in early childhood programs (compared with little more than half in the United States), and outstanding child-care arrangements for infants are easily accessible to families throughout Scandinavia. Although the mix of preschool and day-care programs varies considerably from one country to another, and the extent to which early childhood educators work with parents and families also varies greatly, early childhood education has become a topic of urgent interest throughout much of the world.[32]

"Vintage" French approach

The quality and comprehensiveness of early childhood programs in France have led many observers to view the arrangements in that country as a "vintage" approach to provision of preprimary services worthy of emulation elsewhere. Nearly all three- to five-year-olds are enrolled in preschool programs, and average salaries of preschool teachers are considerably higher than in the United States or most other countries. Stimulating activities are conducted for participating children before and after school, during vacation, and at other times when school is not in session. Equally important, parents are given financial incentives to enroll their children in high-quality programs that provide pediatric and other preventive health services. A team of U.S. child-care specialists and civic leaders who visited France and studied its early childhood programs concluded that the French system provides benchmarks against which to assess national arrangements elsewhere. In particular, team member Hillary Clinton

---

273–280; Susan Chira, "A National Curriculum: Fairness in Uniformity?" *The New York Times,* January 8, 1992, pp. A1, B9.

[32]James H. Tobin, David Y. H. Wu, and Dana H. Davidson, *Preschool in Three Cultures* (New Haven, Conn.: Yale University Press, 1989); Dra. Graby Fujnoto Gomez, "Seleccion Y. Capacitacion de Promotores," *International Journal of Early Childhood* (June 1990), pp. 10–13; Patricia Olmsted, ed., *How Nations Serve Young Children: Profiles of Child Care and Education in 14 Countries* (Ypsilanti, Mich.: High/Scope, 1990; and Robert Myers, *The Twelve Who Survive* (New York: Routledge, 1992).

Positive aspects of
French programs reported that the following aspects of early childhood programs in France are worth considering for implementation in the United States:[33]

■   A coordinated system linking early education, daycare, and health services is accessible to virtually all children.

■   Correlated arrangements for paid parental leave from jobs after childbirth or adoption help to nurture positive parent-child relationships.

■   Provision of good salaries and training for early childhood teachers helps to keep turnover low and program quality high.

■   Licensing of home-based providers, combined with regulations requiring provision of health services, social security, and other benefits for staff, function to protect and improve the quality of day care.

Choice and School-Based Management in England and Wales

As we discuss elsewhere in this book, plans for providing students with greater choice of schools to attend and for placing more decision-making responsibility at the level of the individual school have been receiving growing attention in the United States. Both these approaches to educational improvement are controversial because they involve relatively radical change and because it is not known how they might be introduced most productively or what their long-range effects are likely to be. Given these uncertainties, we may be

National movement
toward choice

able to derive useful lessons from developments in Great Britain, where recent national movement toward choice and school-based management probably has been faster and more comprehensive than in any other country.

Expansion of school choice has been an important national issue in the United Kingdom since 1982. (The United Kingdom consists of Great Britain and Northern Ireland; Great Britain consists of England, Scotland, and Wales.) De-

Education Reform
Act of 1988

bate on expanding choice and other reform proposals culminated in the Education Reform Act of 1988, which introduced in England and Wales a national curriculum and testing system, along with arrangements that allow students to attend any publicly financed school that will admit them. The provisions of the Act also stipulated that most decisions in such areas as allocation of budgets, scheduling of subjects and classes, and number and type of staff be made at the level of the individual school. Since the national government provides more than three-quarters of the funding for public schools and the amount provided depends on the number of students, schools thereby are not only encouraged but in effect are required to recruit and attract students. Those which do not succeed will have to close.[34]

As is true among many school choice advocates in the United States, proponents of the Education Reform Act believe it will benefit education by estab-

[33]*A Welcome for Every Child* (New York: French-American Foundation, 1990); Hillary Rodham Clinton, "In France, Day Care Is Every Child's Right," *The New York Times,* April 7, 1990, p. 15; and Susan Caminiti, "Preschool Around the Globe," *Forbes,* October 21, 1991, pp. 148–154.

[34]*Educational Developments in the United Kingdom 1982–87* (Strasbourg: Council of Europe Documentation Centre for Education in Europe, 1987); Gene I. Maeroff, "Focusing on Urban Education in Britain," *Phi Delta Kappan* (January 1992), pp. 352–358.

Free market of schools

lishing a free market of schools similar to a competitive business market that rewards effective organizations and requires unsuccessful ones to improve or perish. Combining school-based management with choice, the Act aims to bring about reform by giving decision makers at each school authority and incentives to improve the effectiveness and the attractiveness of their programs. While it is much too early to determine how well these systematic changes in English and Welsh education will succeed in the long run, observers have noted these initial developments:[35]

Neither catastrophic nor quickly rejuvenating

- After several years of implementation, school choice arrangements have had neither the catastrophic impact feared by many opponents, who thought they would lead to chaotic movement of students and rapid growth or decline in most schools' enrollments, nor the clearly rejuvenating effects many advocates predicted.

Urban schools still struggling

- Urban schools that enroll a large proportion of students from low-income backgrounds still struggle with the problems involved in educating a disadvantaged population. Giving school personnel more authority and incentive to decide how to improve instruction has not translated into rapid improvement in student performance.

Fears of critics

- Several hundred public schools among approximately 26,000 in England and Wales have "opted" out and obtained "grant-maintenance" status, which means they no longer function under Local Education Authorities (similar to our school districts); instead they obtain their funds directly from the national government. Reformers hope that allowing schools to function under grant-maintainance status will greatly reduce bureaucratic impediments and inefficiencies. Critics fear that allowing many schools to opt out will deplete the resources of the Local Authorities, thereby making it impossible for them to provide adequate curriculum development, staff training, evaluation, and other important services to the individual schools they supervise.

- Many faculties are recruiting students vigorously, even to the extent of employing full- or part-time marketing personnel.

- Some schools have waiting lists and others have declining enrollment but few have closed, although demoralized teachers at many schools may be participating in a "slow, lingering death."

Possible two-tiered arrangement

- Some schools may be trying to enhance their general attractiveness by screening out potentially troublesome students. To the extent that this may be happening, the system as a whole may be moving further toward a two-tiered arrangement consisting of "good" schools and "bad" schools, in accordance with the worst fears of English (and U.S.) critics of open-ended choice plans.

- Combined with national curriculum developments discussed earlier, the Act's school choice provisions appear to be generating worries about job security and overload among some teachers.

---

[35]Geoff Whitty, "The New Right and the National Curriculum: State Control or Market Forces?" *Journal of Educational Policy* (no. 4, 1989), pp. 329–341; Maeroff, "Focusing on Urban Education"; and Susan Chira, "'Choice' Can Be a Mirage as Schools Vie in Market," *The New York Times*, January 7, 1992, pp. A1, A9.

Vocational and Technical Education in Germany

Advantages and disadvantages

Most European countries and many developing countries channel a high percentage of high-school and postsecondary students into vocational or technical schools. There they receive high-quality training for specific occupations, which they enter immediately upon receiving their diplomas or certificates. The "up" side of this bipartite system — early separation into vocational and technical versus academic tracks — is that a high proportion of students who will not complete college can be successfully prepared for employment, provided the economy produces sufficient jobs. The transition from adolescence or young adulthood to work is smooth and easy. The "down" side is that these young people do not have numerous opportunities to enter or reenter academic studies and obtain a college degree, as they do in Canada, the United States, and a few other countries.

Movement to "de-track"

Responding to this dilemma, government officials in many countries with severe tracking are introducing general studies into vocational education, expanding opportunities to attend academic high schools and postsecondary institutions, and establishing "informal" mechanisms such as correspondence courses for obtaining college degrees. Conversely, officials in the United States are beginning to establish apprenticeship programs and other vocational or technical courses that may help prepare high-school students for employment without placing them in separate tracks that exclude them from higher education.[36]

German apprenticeship system

Many authorities on vocational and technical education view the traditional apprenticeship program in Germany as one of the most effective in the world. Only about a third of German students of high-school age attend college-preparatory institutions; the remainder are enrolled in vocational and technical schools that combine academics with job training as an apprentice. Students in apprenticeship positions sign contracts with a "training partner" in industry or business, agreeing to work for about three years while continuing academic classes. Their (paid) work is supervised by experienced personnel in their field, and each contract is monitored by an appropriate organization, such as state agencies for health workers and business or industrial associations for students with jobs in commerce or skilled crafts. The responsible organizations also administer qualifying exams that lead to completion certificates and often directly to employment. While experts in vocational education recognize that the German apprenticeship system evolved gradually over hundreds of years and

Not easy to copy

cannot be simply re-created in other countries, many believe that certain elements — such as close supervision of apprentices by skilled veterans and certification of a young person's employability — can be adapted and emulated successfully elsewhere.[37]

---

[36]*Annual Operational Review: Fiscal 1987 Education and Training* (Washington, D.C.: The World Bank, 1988); Lonnie Harp, "Demands of Information Age Renew Old Idea of Apprenticeships," *Education Week,* June 5, 1991, pp. 1, 18–21; Alison Wolf, "Assessment in European Vocational Education and Training: Current Concerns and Trends," *Journal of Curriculum Studies* (November–December, 1991), pp. 552–557; and Sam Nunn, "Amendment No. 1484," *Congressional Record,* January 24, 1992, S327–S332.

[37]Donna Harrington-Lueker, "Muscle Won't Make It," *The Executive Educator* (September 1991), pp. 34–38; Susan Tifft, "Ready, Willing and Able?" *Agenda* (Spring 1991), pp. 28–31; and Robert I. Lerman and Hillard Pouncy, "Why America Should Develop a Youth Apprenticeship System," *Congressional Record,* January 24, 1992, pp. S333–S334.

Many believe that certain elements of the German apprenticeship system — such as close supervision of apprentices by veterans and certification of employability — can be adapted and emulated successfully elsewhere. (© Robert Wallis/Sipa)

Adult Literacy in Cuba

Reducing illiteracy requires the resolution of many complex and controversial problems. Educators often disagree about how to define and measure literacy, about how to best mobilize literacy resources, and about whether literacy causes or reflects economic progress. Reduction of illiteracy has been a major goal of UNESCO, the World Bank, and other international organizations, which have provided substantial financial and technical assistance for this purpose during the second half of the twentieth century. Much success has been achieved: the percentage of Africans above the age of fifteen who cannot read at all declined from about 70 percent in 1970 to a little more than 50 percent in the late 1980s, and the comparable decline in Asia was from approximately 50 percent to about 33 percent.[38]

Decline in illiteracy in Africa and Asia

One country that has progressed rapidly and impressively in reducing adult illiteracy is Cuba. Many observers believe that Cuba has had a deplorable record with regard to economic production, civil liberties, and respect for human rights, but few disagree with the evidence that it has registered considerable progress in developing functional literacy. After a revolutionary dictatorship led by Fidel Castro took control of Cuba in 1959, a massive campaign was conducted to increase literacy nationwide. High schools were closed so that teachers could work as literacy instructors in rural areas, and several hundred thousand volunteers of all ages were mobilized as Brigadiers who taught illiterate persons in

Deplorable Cuban human rights record

Massive Cuban campaign

---

[38]Daniel A. Wagner, "Literacy Campaigns: Past, Present, and Future," *Comparative Education Review* (May 1989), pp. 356–360; Gabriel Carceles, "World Literacy Prospects at the Turn of the Century," *Comparative Education Review* (February 1990), pp. 4–20.

*Progress in
functional literacy*

both rural and urban areas. Within a year the proportion of the population that could not read at all fell from about one-fifth to less than one-tenth. Since then the government has conducted a variety of programs to raise literacy skills even higher. However, it should be kept in mind that general levels of education in Cuba before the revolution were high compared with most other low-income countries. Partly for this reason, the methods used to reduce illiteracy in Cuba are not necessarily workable or desirable in other countries.[39]

Comprehensive Schools in Sweden

As we pointed out earlier, there is a strong relationship worldwide between students' socioeconomic background and their educational performance and attainment. In many nations this pattern, combined with the systematic practice of dividing secondary (or upper-level) students into academic or vocational and technical tracks, has meant that students with high socioeconomic status have been much more likely than their peers to enter and graduate from academic high schools — and subsequently from colleges and universities.

Swedish changes in 1960s

Since the middle of this century, Sweden has provided exemplary leadership in modifying its educational system to provide more effective and equalized opportunities for students of all social backgrounds. In particular, elementary and middle-level schools were de-tracked in the 1960s; since that time high and low achievers for the most part have attended the same schools and studied the same curriculum in heterogeneous classes until the age of fourteen. As a result, lower secondary schools in Sweden have become the type of "comprehensive" high school that was historically considered an ideal in the United States, but that has become somewhat less prominent here as students are increasingly separated between big-city and suburban communities. The Swedish government took vigorous actions, including curriculum revision and staff development, as part of its overall plan for attaining an effective common system of education. Developments since the 1960s have included the following:[40]

*Subsequent developments
in Sweden*

■ Empirical as well as anecdotal data indicate that relatively high proportions of young people have been motivated to become "lifelong" learners.

■ Standards of performance for many low-achieving students increased substantially because they no longer study in low-level classes that communicate low expectations.

■ School completion rates increased and have been maintained at very high levels. Nearly all sixteen-year-olds and more than 80 percent of eighteen-year-olds are enrolled in public schools.

---

[39]Alfred Padula and Lois M. Smith, "The Revolutionary Transformation of Cuban Education," in Edgar B. Gumbert, ed., *Making the Future* (Atlanta: Georgia State University Press, 1988), pp. 117–139; Carlos Alberto Torres, "The State, Nonformal Education, and Socialism in Cuba, Nicaragua, and Grenada," *Comparative Education Review* (February 1991), pp. 110–118; and Vincente Echerri, "'Gains' of Cuban Revolution Built on Towers of Illusion," *The Wall Street Journal*, January 27, 1992, p. A13.

[40]"Swedish Schools," *The Economist*, November 12, 1988, pp. 15–18; Rolf Lander, "Quality, Equality, and Control in Education: Developments in Sweden" (Paper presented at the Annual Meeting of the American Educational Research Association, Chicago, April 1991); and Bennt Bengtson, "Computers in School: The Swedish Strategy," *T.H.E. Journal* (January 1992), pp. 68–71.

■ A national plan is being implemented to improve instruction through the use of computers and other technology.

Nevertheless, many parents are unhappy with national grading policies; teachers in Sweden give few low grades, and strong correlations still remain between students' social background and their academic achievement and entry into higher education. Dissatisfied with the performance of many low-income students and with other aspects of the educational system, Swedish government officials have been introducing changes aimed at decentralizing the system's highly bureaucratic organization and functioning. They are making efforts to improve national tests, revising curriculum to further enhance student motivation, training teachers to emphasize higher-order learning, and bringing about other contemporary reforms of the kinds we discuss elsewhere in this book.

Mathematics and Science Education in Japan

High performance

Studies conducted by the IEA and IAEP indicate that Japanese students consistently attain very high scores in mathematics, science, and some other subject areas. For example, the second International Study of Achievement in Mathematics reported that eighth graders in Japan on average answered 62 percent of the test items correctly, compared with 45 percent in the United States and 47 percent across the eighteen countries included in the study. With respect to science achievement among ten-year-olds, Japanese students attained an average score of 15.4, compared with an (unweighted) average score of 13.1 across the fifteen nations included in the IEA's most recent assessment.[41]

Numerous causes of high performance cited

Some aspects of Japanese education and society may help account for high achievement levels among Japanese youth. Most of the characteristics highlighted in the following list apply to Japanese education in general, not merely to math and science programs. The list of pertinent factors is long; researchers are not yet sure which of these characteristics are of crucial importance. Perhaps they all are.[42]

1. Intense parental involvement is expected and provided. In particular, mothers feel great responsibility for children's success in school. Families provide much continuing support and motivation, ranging from elaborate celebration of entry into first grade to widespread enrollment of children in supplementary private cram schools *(juku)*, which students attend after school and

---

[41] *Digest of Education Statistics 1991* (Washington, D.C.: U.S. Government Printing Office, 1991).

[42] Richard J. Deasy, "Education in Japan: Surprising Lessons," *Educational Leadership* (September 1986), pp. 38–43; Bonnie Gordon, "Cultural Comparisons of Schooling," *Educational Researcher* (August–September 1987), pp. 4–8; Robert Leetsma et al., *Japanese Education Today* (Washington, D.C.: U.S. Government Printing Office, 1987); Robert D. Hess and Hiroshi Azuma, "Cultural Support for Schooling," *Educational Researcher* (December 1991), pp. 2–12; Jon D. Miller and Masao Miyake, *Two Longitudinal Studies of Middle and High School Students in Japan and the United States* (DeKalb, Ill.: Northern Illinois University, 1991); Nancy E. Sato, "Japanese Education Where It Counts: In the Classroom" (Paper presented at the Annual Meeting of the American Educational Research Association, Chicago, April 1991); Harold W. Stevenson, "Japanese Elementary School Education," *The Elementary School Journal* (September 1991), pp. 109–120; and "Jet-setter," *Look Japan* (February 1992), pp. 20–21.

Getting to the Source

Snapshot of an Elementary Classroom in Japan / Merry White

After visiting Japan in the early 1980s, Merry White of the Harvard Graduate School of Education challenged the widely held myth that students in Japan spend most of their time in highly disciplined drill

and practice. Although there is some truth to this stereotype at academic secondary schools in Japan, White and other scholars have shown that Japanese educators place great emphasis on developing learning-to-learn skills and helping students acquire mastery of complex concepts and understandings. The following excerpt describes White's visit to a fifth-grade math class.

The day I visited, the class was presented with a general statement about cubing. Before any concrete facts, formulae, or even drawings were displayed, the teacher asked the class to take out their math diaries and spend a few minutes writing down their feelings and anticipations over this new concept. It is hard for me to imagine an American math teacher beginning a lesson with an exhortation to examine one's emotional predispositions about cubing (but that may be only because my own math training was antediluvian).

After that, the teacher asked for conjectures from the children about the surface and volume of a cube and asked for some ideas about formulae for calculation. The teacher asked the class to cluster into its component *han* (working groups) of four or five children

on weekends. Compared with U.S. parents, Japanese parents stress "effort" more and "ability" less when asked to identify causes of success or failure in school.

2. Students attend school 240 days a year (compared with about 180 in the United States), thus allowing for full, in-depth instruction in math, science, and other subjects.

3. Careful planning and delivery of a national curriculum contribute to students' acquisition of important concepts in a sequential and comprehensive framework.

4. Large amounts of homework correlated with classroom lessons contribute to high student performance in mastering and applying information and concepts.

5. Partly because much time and support are available to help slower students, there is less variability in achievement than is true in the United States and

each, and gave out materials for measurement and construction. One group left the room with large pieces of cardboard, to construct a model of a cubic meter. The groups worked internally on solutions to problems set by the teacher and competed with each other to finish first. After a while, the cubic meter group returned, groaning under the bulk of its model, and everyone gasped over its size. (There were many comments and guesses as to how many children could fit inside.) The teacher then set the whole class a very challenging problem, well over their heads, and gave them the rest of the class time to work on it. The class ended without a solution, but the teacher made no particular effort to get or give an answer, although she exhorted them to be energetic. (It was several days before the class got the answer — there was no deadline but the excitement did not flag.)

Several characteristics of this class deserve highlighting. First, there was attention to feelings and predispositions, provision of facts, and opportunities for discovery. The teacher preferred to focus on process, engagement, commitment, and performance rather than on discipline (in our sense) and production. Second, the *han:* Assignments are made to groups, not to individuals (this is also true at the workplace) although

individual progress and achievement are closely monitored. Children are supported, praised, and allowed to make mistakes through trial and error within the group. The group is also pitted against other groups, and the group's success is each person's triumph, and vice versa. Groups are made up by the teacher and are designed to include a mixture of skill levels — there is a *hancho* (leader) whose job it is to choreograph the group's work, to encourage the slower members, and to act as a reporter to the class at large.

Questions

1. Why has it been so difficult to dispel the myth that Japanese schools concentrate primarily on producing miniature soldiers who mostly repeat back material introduced by their teachers?

2. Teachers in Japan frequently refer to John Dewey in describing their methods and objectives. What Deweyesque ideas and practices are apparent in White's snapshot?

Source: Merry I. White, "Japanese Education: How Do They Do It" Reprinted with permission of the author from *The Public Interest*, No. 76 (Summer 1984) cover, pp. 87–101. Copyright © 1984 by National Affairs Inc. Reprinted by permission of the author.

Relatively few very low achievers

most other countries. There are relatively few very low achievers in Japanese schools.

6. The schools emphasize the development of students' character and sense of responsibility through such practices as assigning students chores and having them assist each other in learning.

7. Educators tend to take much responsibility for students' learning. For example, they may contact parents to recommend bedtime and homework schedules and curfews.

High status of educators

8. Japanese educators have relatively high social status, which enhances their authority in working with students and parents. Partly for this reason, there are numerous applicants for teaching positions, thus allowing administrators to select highly qualified candidates.

9. School schedules provide considerable amounts of time for counseling students, planning instruction, and engaging in other activities that enhance teacher effectiveness.

Little "bargaining" with students needed

10. Socialization practices in the family and in early childhood education help students learn to adapt successfully to classroom situations and demands. By way of contrast, U.S. schools tend to attain good discipline by making instruction attractive and by "bargaining" with students to obtain compliance (see Chapter 9), at great cost to academic standards and rigor.

11. Compared to classroom practices in the United States and in many other countries, lessons deemphasize rote learning; instead, they are explicitly planned and delivered to develop students' thinking skills and understanding of concepts.

Persons familiar with the Japanese educational system also point out, however, that it apparently exemplifies several negative characteristics and outcomes. Among the most frequently cited of these are the following:[43]

Too little divergent thinking

1. There appears to be relatively little emphasis on divergent thinking. Some observers believe that insufficient emphasis on creativity may severely hamper future social and economic development in Japan.

Postsecondary opportunity limited

2. To a greater extent than in the United States, opportunities for working-class students and women to attend postsecondary institutions and attain high occupational status appear to be severely limited. For example, one study found that only 11 percent of students in academic high schools that stress college preparation were from families in which the father had not completed high school, compared with 32 percent of students in less academic high schools. Postsecondary attendance is highly dependent on entering and succeeding at academic high schools.

3. Partly because of the restricted opportunities for higher education, secondary education is exam driven in the sense that instruction is geared to covering very large quantities of factual information likely to be tested on entrance examinations. In turn, examination pressures further stifle divergent thinking and frequently lead to mental distress and even suicide among some students, and alienation from schools and learning among others.

4. Relatively few demands are made of students once they are admitted to colleges and universities. Partly for this reason, performance standards and outcomes in higher education are relatively low.

5. Behavioral standards and expectations in many Japanese schools are so narrow and rigid that some educators believe they generate too much conformity. In accordance with the old Japanese proverb "The nail that sticks out gets hammered down," students are told what school uniform to wear at each grade beginning in kindergarten; in some cases, students have been required to dye their hair to conform to school regulations. However, rules governing student appearance and the details of their behavior have been significantly loosened in recent years.

---

[43]Leetsma, *Japanese Education Today;* Ken Schoolland, *Shogun's Ghost: The Dark Side of Japanese Education* (New York: Bergin and Garvey, 1990); Gerald K. LeTendre, "Educational Decisions, Family Background and Tracking in the Japanese Middle School" (Paper presented at the Annual Meeting of the American Educational Research Association, Chicago, April 1991); and Elizabeth Spalding, "A Critique of the Goals of Japan's National Council on Educational Reform," *National Forum of Applied Educational Research Journal* (no. 1, 1992), pp. 19–30.

*Behaviors and attitudes
of young people may
be changing*

6. More than ever before, young people in Japan seem to be rejecting the traditional customs and values on which the educational system is founded.

7. Many students with disabilities receive little help and have relatively poor opportunities to succeed.

In reviewing its various strengths and weaknesses, several thoughtful observers have concluded that we have much to learn from the Japanese educational system, but they add that we should make sure that promising practices from elsewhere are workable and appropriately adapted to our own situation. Likewise, governmental commissions in Japan have been considering reform proposals that incorporate the more positive aspects of education in the United States (for example, to reduce the emphasis on conformity). A professor of Japanese studies at Harvard University has summarized the situation this way: "As a mirror showing us our weakness and as a yardstick against which to measure our efforts," Japanese education has great value for us. But we should not "allow ourselves either to ignore or to imitate" its approach; instead we should "look periodically into the 'Japanese mirror' while we quite independently set out to straighten our schools and our system within our own cultural and social context."[44]

Neither ignore nor imitate

Multicultural Education in Europe and the United States

Satisfactory social and educational responses to the challenges posed by multicultural populations probably have not been attained anywhere. However, many nations have initiated significant efforts to deliver educational services suitable for diverse groups of students — particularly minority students who experience racial, ethnic, or religious discrimination or who do not learn the national language at home. Responses such as the following may prove to be exemplary means for improving equity and otherwise promoting educational goals through multicultural programs:[45]

*Possibly exemplary
educational responses*

■ As we discussed at length in Chapter 11, the United States is attempting to provide bilingual education for millions of limited-English-proficient and non-English-proficient students.

■ Canada has implemented sizable bilingual education programs, as well as numerous approaches for promoting multiethnic curriculum and instruction.

---

[44]Thomas P. Rohlen, "Japanese Education: If They Can Do It, Should We?" *The American Scholar* (Winter 1985–86), p. 43; Teruhisa Horio, "Problems of the Reform of Education in Japan" (Paper presented at the Annual Meeting of the American Educational Research Association, Boston, April 1990); and Alex Hendy, "Shining Morning Faces," *Look Japan* (March 1992), pp. 38–39.

[45]Maurice Blanc, "The Multi-Ethnic European City and Educational Provision" (Paper presented at the Annual Meeting of the American Educational Research Association, New Orleans, April 1988); E. Brian Titley, ed., *Canadian Education* (Calgary: Detslig, 1990); Maeroff, "Focusing on Urban Education in Britain"; Charles L. Glenn, "Educating the Children of Immigrants," *Phi Delta Kappan* (January 1992), pp. 404–408.

- France has provided in-service training nationwide to help teachers learn methods for teaching French as a second language.

- Belgium provides **reception classes** in which immigrant children receive six months to two years of instruction from both a Belgian teacher and a native-language assistant teacher (e.g., Moroccan), who use a carefully sequenced curriculum to develop skills in speaking Dutch.

- English schools that enroll many students whose families came from Asia or the Caribbean have been given "grant-maintenance" status (as described earlier in this chapter) that allows for unusual flexibility in adapting instruction to assist language-minority students.

PROBLEMS AND PROSPECTS IN DEVELOPING COUNTRIES

Education critical for economic development

Earlier in this chapter we saw that educational inadequacies in developing countries are both a cause and a result of poverty. For this reason, national governments and international organizations have placed great stress on working to enhance the economies of developing countries by expanding and improving their educational systems. Education usually is viewed as critically important for economic development because it can provide people with the skills and knowledge required to compete in international markets, and because it can help bring about a more equitable distribution of wealth and power that in turn contributes to political stability and long-term economic growth.[46]

Out-migration of educated persons

However, it has proven exceedingly difficult to achieve widespread, lasting, and balanced improvement of educational systems in many developing countries. For example, extreme poverty in countries such as Rwanda has been responsible in part for restricting the availability of funds to less than $100 per primary student per year. Numerous developing countries also confront a so-called **brain drain.** This phenomenon occurs when the number of high-school and university graduates increases but well-paid jobs commensurate with their level of education are not available; as a result these well-trained persons emigrate to wealthier countries with better employment opportunities. Some developing countries (e.g., India, Nigeria) also are struggling to overcome economic, social, and educational problems associated with the use of dozens or even hundreds of different languages among their diverse multiethnic populations.[47]

Researchers at the World Bank and elsewhere have identified areas that require particular attention if adequate progress is to be made in the future. To

[46]Haddad et al., *Education and Development;* Unna Huh, "Computers in Education in the Republic of Korea," *T.H.E. Journal* (January 1992), pp. 72–76.
[47]"Asia and Pacific Region," *Educational Innovation and Information* (March 1989), pp. 3–4; Kenneth B. Noble, "Nigeria's Plan: Adopt the (250) Mother Tongues," *The New York Times,* May 23, 1991, p. A4.

improve education in developing countries, these analysts suggest, the following steps should be taken:[48]

Guidelines for education

1. Invest more in primary education in order to broaden the base of young people who can later contribute to the economy and participate in secondary or higher education.

2. Since most students from largely illiterate populations must depend on the school rather than their families to support their educational development, invest in textbooks and other instructional materials, computer technology, and other means of disseminating knowledge.

3. Be careful about vocationalizing secondary schools, because curricula and skills emphasized in vocational education tend to be rapidly outdated.

4. Avoid great restrictions on enrollment in higher education, since students will tend to study abroad and may not return.

5. Find novel means to improve financing of education, possibly through recovering tuition costs from beneficiaries.

6. Make private schools an integral part of educational expansion plans.

7. Although many developing countries have substantially improved their educational infrastructure, equal effort must be devoted to improving students' cognitive functioning. Improvements in teacher training, instructional methods, and other aspects of the system are required to develop children's higher-order thinking skills.

8. Improving science and technology education is particularly imperative.

9. Providing at least a few years of education for all children in developing countries will require adding teachers and facilities for several hundred million students in the 1990s.

10. Many developing countries will need to make a special effort to overcome the social and economic obstacles that limit the education of girls and women.

SCHOOL IMPROVEMENT PROJECTS AND RESEARCH

Reforms widespread

As in the United States, educators in other parts of the world are introducing reforms to enhance school effectiveness and are examining research that may help guide their efforts to improve instruction in the future. In this context, educators and researchers increasingly are in contact with their counterparts in

---

[48]George Psacharopoulis, "Comparative Education: From Theory to Practice," *Comparative Education Review* (August 1990), pp. 369–380; Verspoor, *Accelerated Educational Development*; Fernando Reimers, "The Impact of Economic Stabilization Adjustment on Education in Latin America," *Comparative Education Review* (May 1991), pp. 319–353; and Tichatonga J. Nhundu, "A Decade of Educational Expansion in Zimbabwe," *The Journal of Negro Education* (Winter 1992), pp. 78–98.

*Sharing information
and research*

other nations, and are sharing knowledge about school reform possibilities and outcomes. Much of this cross-national information is transmitted through international conferences, implementation of joint research or development projects such as the International Assessment of Educational Progress and the International School Improvement Project, publication of journals such as the *International Review of Education,* and distribution of major reports by the World Bank, UNESCO, the OECD, and other organizations. For example, the American Educational Research Association (which has widespread and vigorous international participation) recently published a synthesis of research on improving science education in both industrial and developing countries, and a theme issue of the *International Journal of Educational Research* describes efforts in numerous countries to improve achievement through planning at the level of the individual school.[49]

Unusually effective schools

One topic that has received considerable attention is the functioning of unusually successful schools that produce higher achievement than most other schools with similar students. As we point out in the next chapter, research on these so-called effective schools has identified the characteristics that help account for their unusual success. Although the majority of school effectiveness studies have been conducted in the United States, important studies also have taken place in Australia, Canada, the Netherlands, the United Kingdom, and elsewhere. Educators have been disseminating information on the results of this research and discussing its implications for reform in their own unique settings.[50]

*Systematic and
comprehensive
reform needed*

In general, the conclusions of international research on improving school effectiveness have been similar to those of large-scale U.S. studies we summarize in the next chapter and other parts of this book. In particular, international research supports the conclusion that school reform is a difficult task requiring systematic change and substantial expenditure of human and fiscal resources. Thus an evaluation of projects sponsored by the World Bank concluded that curriculum development by itself is unlikely to produce lasting improvement; interventions also are required with respect to teacher training, organizational and instructional arrangements, and provision of technical assistance at the level of the individual school. Similarly, an assessment of school improvement efforts throughout the Netherlands concluded that innovations in curriculum made little difference in the absence of systematic reform of other aspects of schooling.[51]

[49]David Hopkins, ed., *Improving the Quality of Schooling* (New York: Falmer, 1987); Minda C. Sutaria, "Teaching for Maximum Learning: The Philippine Experience," *International Review of Education* (no. 3, 1990), pp. 243–250; Herbert J. Walberg, "Improving School Science in Advanced and Developing Countries," *Review of Educational Research* (Spring 1990), pp. 25–69; and David Hopkins and David Hargreaves, "Empowering Schools Through Development Planning," *International Journal of Educational Research* (1993, in press).

[50]Peter Mortimore et al., *School Matters* (Berkeley: University of California Press, 1988); Daniel U. Levine, "Creating Effective Schools," *International Journal of Educational Research* (1993, in press).

[51]Adriaan M. Verspoor, *Implementing Educational Change: The World Bank Experience* (Washington, D.C.: The World Bank, 1986); Bert Creemers, Tom Peters, and Dave Reynolds, eds., *School Effectiveness and School Improvement* (Amsterdam: Swets and Zeitlinger, 1990); and Greetje van der Werf, "School Based Curriculum Development and School Work," *International Journal of Educational Research* (1993, in press).

CONCLUSION: U.S. SCHOOLS IN AN INTERNATIONAL CONTEXT

This chapter has presented information illustrating the diversity that exists worldwide among educational systems and the ways in which educators are attempting to improve opportunities for children and youth. Despite their differences, educators and government officials everywhere confront the same general challenge: to provide effective schooling that will equip increasing proportions of young people with advanced skills and understandings required for successful participation in a modern economy. In this context, the United States can be viewed as an international leader in striving to educate all students regardless of their social background or previous achievement. Despite the many *Shortcomings* shortcomings and problems we describe at length in this book, the educational *and attainments* system in the United States probably has aimed higher and achieved more than any other in trying to provide equal educational opportunities for a diverse population. This view of U.S. schools has been partly summarized by Glen Latham of Utah State University:

> The American system of education, with all its faults, is still the most remarkable system on the face of the earth. It serves more children, with a broader range of ability, over a longer period of their lives, in the most enriched educational setting, for less money per pupil, than any educational system that has ever existed in the history of humankind.[52]

Summing Up

1. Although educational systems differ considerably internationally, they tend to confront the similar problem of providing effective instruction for large numbers of students whose opportunities and performance are related to their social and cultural background.

2. Teaching conditions throughout the world appear to be fundamentally similar. In most countries, teachers and curricula emphasize presentation of information, and teachers struggle to find time to accomplish difficult and sometimes conflicting goals.

3. Decision makers everywhere face difficult choices in the relative allocation of resources to early childhood education, elementary, secondary and post-secondary schools, and vocational education.

4. School systems around the world differ greatly with respect to the resources they devote to education, enrollments, student-teacher ratios, proportions of male and female students, the extent of centralization or decentralization, curriculum content and instructional emphasis, higher education and vocational education opportunities, the availability and role of nonpublic schools, student achievement, and national testing policies and practices.

5. Some countries have exemplary or potentially exemplary educational services and practices: early childhood education in France, choice and

---

[52]Glenn Latham, "Amerika Ni Dekimassen," *Principal* (February 1992), pp. 52–53.

school-based management in England and Wales, vocational and technical education in Germany, adult literacy in Cuba, comprehensive schools in Sweden, mathematics and science education in Japan, and multicultural education in Europe and the United States. Researchers can learn much from studying educational systems in other countries, but it is not always easy to identify the reasons for a system's success or failure or its implications for different societies. For example, it may be desirable for educators in the United States to adopt practices thought to be responsible for high mathematics and science performance in Japan, but some practices may not be easy to develop or may not function positively in our unique national setting.

6. Scholars studying education in developing countries believe that emphasis should be placed on improving primary education, academic curriculum in secondary schools, cognitive functioning of students, science and technology instruction, and education for girls and women.

7. Nations around the world have been initiating school-reform efforts similar to those being undertaken or advocated in the United States.

8. The United States is an international leader in the effort to provide equal and effective educational opportunities for all groups of students.

Key Terms

bipartite system (*583*)

research model (*585*)

personality development model (*585*)

training model (*585*)

diversified model (*585*)

International Association for the Evaluation of Educational Achievement (IEA) (*586*)

International Assessment of Educational Progress (IAEP) (*587*)

national curriculum (*590*)

reception classes (*604*)

brain drain (*604*)

Discussion Questions

1. Why is the distribution of curriculum subjects so similar from one nation to another? Who decides what subjects should be taught? Who should decide?

2. What are the most important educational problems in developing countries? What policies might be most appropriate in addressing these problems?

3. To what extent should education policies and practices in the United States emulate those in Japan? Which might be most "transportable," and which may be undesirable?

4. What are the advantages and disadvantages of offering higher education opportunities for a large proportion of young people? What might or should be done to counteract the disadvantages?

5. Should national tests or a national curriculum be introduced in the United States? What might be the dangers of moving in this direction?

Suggested Readings

Comparative Education Review.

> *Topics emphasized include development of national school systems, education and economic development, comparisons across nations, and international aspects of multicultural education.*

Coombes, Philip. *The World Crisis in Education.* Oxford: Oxford University Press, 1985.

> *This influential book summarizes the status of efforts to improve educational systems in both industrial and developing nations.*

Hargreaves, David H., and David Hopkins. *The Empowered School.* London: Cassell, 1991.

> *Drawing on research and analysis in many countries, this volume provides information and recommendations on how to improve instruction through development of individual school plans.*

Husen, Torsten, Albert Tuijnman, and William Halls. *Schooling in Modern European Society.* Oxford: Pergamon, 1992.

> *The authors describe emerging trends and discuss recent developments involving curriculum and testing, economics and education, schooling for minorities, and other contemporary issues.*

Verda, Gajendra K., ed. *Education for All.* London: Falmer, 1989.

> *This book provides background information and analysis regarding numerous aspects of education in the United Kingdom.*

Walford, Geoffrey, ed. *Private Schools in Ten Countries: Policy and Practice.* London: Routledge, 1989.

> *Essays deal with the history and status of private schools and their relationships with other social institutions.*

Wilson, Maggie. *Girls and Young Women in Education.* Oxford: Pergamon, 1990.

> *Educational systems in nine European countries are analyzed with reference to the performance and attainment of girls and young women, provision of equal opportunity for female students, impacts of national policy on career opportunities, and related issues.*

Yogev, Abraham, ed. *International Perspectives on Education and Society.* Greenwich, Conn.: JAI, 1992.

> *Scholars in various countries analyze the achievement effects of tracking, education of ethnic, racial, and religious minority groups, and economic aspects of education.*

16

School Effectiveness and Reform in the United States

FOCUSING QUESTIONS

Why is educational reform so important?

What are the characteristics of effective instruction and effective schools?

How can rural schools be made more effective?

What is the role of magnet and alternative schools?

Are nonpublic schools more effective than public schools?

Will expansion of school choice plans improve education?

What should be done for gifted and talented students?

Much of this book has been concerned with problems and trends in the reform of elementary and secondary schools. Chapter 1 described recent efforts to improve the teacher workforce in response to national dissatisfaction with the schools, and Chapter 2 considered merit pay and other methods of motivating teachers. Chapters 9, 10, and 11 examined reasons for the low performance of many disadvantaged students and explored the goal of educational equity. Chapter 13 provided a summary of major national reports on school reform.

The material in this chapter deals even more explicitly with selected issues in school effectiveness and reform. After highlighting several major challenges that confront the U.S. educational system, we will examine research into the characteristics of effective instruction and effective schools. We will also look at the process of school improvement and reform and a number of other important areas frequently discussed under the heading of school effectiveness.

IMPERATIVES TO IMPROVE THE SCHOOLS

Interrelated imperatives

Although there are many reasons for giving priority attention to the improvement of elementary and secondary schools in the United States, much of the concern focuses on the need to bolster the nation's international economic competitiveness and on the related imperative to improve the performance of disadvantaged students. Many observers believe that our response to these interrelated challenges will be of historic importance in determining whether the United States prospers or declines as we enter the twenty-first century.

International Competitiveness

A Nation Prepared

The importance of education in a world characterized by rapid technological change was stated forcefully in the report titled *A Nation Prepared: Teachers for the 21st Century,* prepared by the Carnegie Task Force on Teaching as a Profession. After noting the increasing importance of intentional economic competition, *A Nation Prepared* concluded that high wages and future prosperity will require an economic system based on highly skilled workers using sophisticated technology. To provide this workforce, the report said, "The educational system . . . must be rebuilt to match the drastic change needed in our economy." Too many U.S. students "lack the ability to reason and perform complex, nonroutine intellectual tasks."[1]

During the same year that the Carnegie Task Force issued its report, the National Assessment of Educational Progress (NAEP) reinforced concern about students' thinking skills when it released the results of a study of literacy among young adults between the ages of twenty-one and twenty-five. In line with ear-

---

[1]Carnegie Task Force on Teaching as a Profession, *A Nation Prepared: Teachers for the 21st Century* (New York: Carnegie Corporation, 1986), pp. 12, 14. Also see *The Bottom Line: Basic Skills in the Workplace* (Washington, D.C.: U.S. Department of Labor and U.S. Department of Education, 1988); Commission on Achieving Necessary Skills, *What Work Requires of Schools* (Washington, D.C.: U.S. Department of Labor, 1991); and Ira Magaziner and Hillary Rodham Clinton, "Will America Choose High Skills or Low Wages?" *Educational Leadership* (March 1992), pp. 10–14.

Getting to the Source ━━●━━●━━

A Day in the Life of an Eighth Grader /
John Lounsbury and Donald Clark

INSIDE GRADE EIGHT:
FROM APATHY TO
EXCITEMENT

JOHN H. LOUNSBURY
DONALD C. CLARK

NATIONAL ASSOCIATION OF SECONDARY SCHOOL PRINCIPALS
RESTON, VIRGINIA

Inside Grade Eight *summarizes the results of reports from observers who "shadowed" (i.e., accompanied) a national sample of 162 eighth graders throughout their day at school on March 8, 1989.*

Prepared by Donald Clark of the University of Arizona and John Lounsbury of the National Association of Secondary School Principals, Inside Grade Eight *concluded that students generally seemed "distanced from their own learning" and much of the time were "passive recipients, docile, and accepting of a routine that does not energize them very deeply" (p. 128). In the following excerpt, the authors criticize the focus on "prepackaged" information and the strong emphasis on testing.*

The predominant teaching methods appeared to be geared toward conveying a curriculum of prepackaged information. A lot of information passes from texts, blackboards, overhead screens, and teachers' mouths to students' papers (note papers and worksheets). Concern about covering material is carrying the day. Data manipulation, problem solving, and higher order decision making are getting short shrift in the very schools that are preparing students for the changing and uncertain world of the 21st century. We still seem to be teaching as though passing on the accumulated wisdom of the past is the best preparation for living in the future. While clearly there is a place for learning from the past, there doesn't seem to be a healthy balance

Not fully literate

lier NAEP data on reading scores, the study found that "sizable numbers" of young adults are unable to do well on tasks of moderate complexity and are "not fully 'literate' for a technologically advanced society." Related studies on mathematics achievement concluded that only about one-fifth of U.S. seventeen-year-olds are able to demonstrate competence in solving "challenging" mathematics problems. Similarly, data collected by the College Board indicate that less than one-third of high-school seniors can fully comprehend front-page and editorial material in newspapers.[2]

[2]Irwin S. Kirsch and Ann Jungeblut, *Literacy: Profiles of America's Young Adults* (Princeton, N.J.: Educational Testing Services, 1986); Lois E. Burrill, "How Well Should a High School Graduate Read?" *NASSP Bulletin* (March 1987), pp. 61–72; *The National Education Goals Report* (Washington, D.C.: National Education Goals Panel, 1991); and Bertram L. Koslin, Susan M. Zeno, and

between acquiring handed-down information from the past and learning how to manipulate information to prepare for the future. . . .

Testing has taken over classrooms to a very great extent. In the sample evaluated here, activities related to testing (taking them, reviewing for them, and going over returned tests) accounted for more teaching methods notations than any other activity including recitation, seatwork, and listening to explanations. The individual accountability binge that we are on in education seems to be taking up a lot of class time. . . . At a time when we need to be concerned about preparing students for the future, we seem to be becoming more locked into a focus on the past, on the easily testable. The impact of testing really stuck out in these shadow studies.

If I could sum up a day for these students it would be:

Come in school and sit down.

Take a quiz or test.

Go to study hall.

Take another quiz or test.

lunch

PE

Take another quiz or test.

band or art

Review for a test tomorrow.

Go home.

THINK NOTHING OF IT.

Questions

1. Why do we seem to have become "more locked into a focus on the past, on the easily testable"? What steps and proposals described in Chapter 1, in this chapter, and elsewhere in this text might help change our focus?

2. How can or should secondary schools be restructured to provide a very different schedule of activities from that described by Lounsbury and Clark?

3. Does this description generally agree with your memories of the eighth grade?

Source: John H. Lounsbury and Donald C. Clark, *Inside Grade Eight: From Apathy to Excitement* (Reston, Va.: National Association of Secondary School Principals, 1990), cover, pp. 126–127.

Equity and the Performance of Disadvantaged Students

Nearly all the recent reports and studies dealing with educational reform call for improving the performance of economically disadvantaged students in order to make educational opportunities and outcomes more equitable. For example, an analysis of NAEP data carried out for the Educational Testing Service concluded that the poor performance of disadvantaged students — particularly those who are African American or Hispanic — should be viewed as a "major national concern by educators and economic policymakers." Similarly, a state-

Major national concern

Steven H. Ivens, *Student Reading Ability, Reading Expectations and World Class Standards* (Brewster, N.Y.: Touchstone Applied Science Associates, 1992).

ment published by the Forum of Educational Organization Leaders concluded that "if we wish to maintain or improve our standard of living, we must work smarter . . . [but] it is not possible to succeed if only middle class people from stable families work smarter. . . . [This capacity] must — for the first time in human history — be characteristic of the mass of our population."[3]

CCSSO recommendations

Perhaps the most far-reaching proposal for helping disadvantaged or at-risk students is a policy statement of the Council of Chief State School Officers (CCSSO). Focusing particularly on students at risk of dropping out of school, the statement argues that state laws should "guarantee" educational programs and other services "reasonably calculated to enable all persons to graduate from high school." The statement recommends improving school instruction and staff development, using up-to-date learning technologies, and developing programs to engage families as partners in the learning process. Many CCSSO members view the statement as a mandate for radical school reform, and the CCSSO has indicated that implementation of its guarantee policy may include such strong measures as "state takeovers" of school districts that are educationally or financially distressed, support for students to transfer from low-achieving schools or districts to "successful" locations elsewhere, and reduction in the concentration of students at low-income schools.[4]

Decline in opportunity

Awareness of the plight of at-risk students has been spurred by data indicating that social and economic opportunities available to low-achieving students and those without good postsecondary credentials have declined rapidly. For example, researchers have found that young adults who have dropped out of high school have much lower earnings relative to other youth than was true before 1975. Numerous reports also have pointed out that even high-school graduates who acquire little or no further education have experienced increasing difficulty in the labor market and have substantially lower relative earnings than their counterparts in the early 1970s.[5]

Fewer workers

On the one hand, because the generation following the baby boom is relatively small, there should be less competition for good jobs in the next decade. Provided that disadvantaged youth acquire the skills necessary for rewarding employment, a "window of opportunity" will be open. On the other hand, the smaller size of this generation means that there will be relatively fewer workers to generate the economic production required to support a large population of retired baby boomers. From this point of view, the future welfare of much of the

---

[3]Richard Venezsky, Carl Kaestle, and Andrew Sum, *The Subtle Danger* (Princeton, N.J.: Educational Testing Service, 1987); "Meeting the Needs of Children and Youth At Risk of School Failure: A National Imperative" (Statement of the Forum of Educational Leaders, Washington, D.C., June 1987). Also see Ina V. S. Mullins, Eugene H. Owen, and Gary W. Phillips, *Accelerating Academic Achievement: A Summary of Findings from 20 Years of NAEP* (Princeton, N.J.: Educational Testing Service, 1990), and Lester C. Thurow, "The New Economics of High Technology," *Harper's* (March 1992), pp. 15–18.

[4]"Assuring Educational Success for Students at Risk" (Denver: Council of Chief State School Officers, 1987), pp. 1–6; Richard J. Coley and Margaret E. Goertz, *Children at Risk: The Work of the States* (Washington, D.C.: Council of Chief State School Officers, 1987); and *The Challenge and State Response* (Washington, D.C.: Council of Chief State School Officers, 1990).

[5]*The Forgotten Half: Non-College Youth in America* (Washington, D.C.: Youth and America's Future: William T. Grant Commission on Work, Family and Citizenship, 1988); Harold Howe II, "Thinking About the Forgotten Half," *Teachers College Record* (Winter 1990), pp. 293–305; and John O'Neil, "Preparing for the Changing Workplace," *Educational Leadership* (March 1992), pp. 6–9.

U.S. population depends directly on whether the schools and the society succeed in preparing disadvantaged students for productive employment.[6]

Inner-City Poverty. As we pointed out in Chapter 10 and elsewhere, educational problems are particularly severe in inner-city minority neighborhoods of concentrated poverty. Although less than 10 percent of the population of the United States living in poverty is located in such neighborhoods, they are home to millions of underclass families residing in an environment in which violence, teenage pregnancy, drug abuse, feelings of hopelessness and despair, and other manifestations of social disorganization have increased greatly during the past forty years.[7]

Increase in minority student population

Schools, like other social institutions, generally have not functioned effectively when overloaded with the problems associated with concentrated poverty; the result has been low educational achievement and attainment for the students who attend such schools. The situation in big-city districts has become more distressing as the percentage of disadvantaged minority students continues to increase (see Chapter 10). By the year 2010, minority children and youth under eighteen years of age may constitute 38 percent of this age group nationally, compared with 24 percent in 1976. At the same time, federal aid (adjusted for inflation) to big-city schools declined by more than 15 percent between 1980 and 1991, thereby exacerbating the problems of the very districts responsible for educating these students.[8]

Coordinated reform required

Although recognition of the importance of solving educational problems associated with disadvantaged populations in big cities appears to have increased in the 1980s, the difficulties also have increased. A comprehensive and workable response to the problems of inner-city neighborhoods will require coordinated efforts in employment, transportation, housing, social welfare policies, desegregation and deconcentration of poverty populations, crime and delinquency, affirmative action, and other components — and there is no doubt that elementary and secondary education must play a pivotal part in bringing about meaningful improvement.[9]

Appalachia and Concentrated Rural Poverty. Some rural areas have communities of concentrated poverty similar in many respects to those in big cities. Among these are the Appalachian region in the eastern United States and the Ozarks region in the South. Many other rural areas include smaller pockets of

---

[6]Diane Crispell, "Labor-Force Growth Expected to Ease," *The Wall Street Journal,* December 18, 1991, p. B1; Howard Banks, "Job Trends Across the Millenia," *Forbes,* January 6, 1992, p. 35.

[7]David T. Ellwood, *Divide and Conquer: Responsible Security for America's Poor* (New York: Ford Foundation, 1987), pp. 9–10; Karl Zinsmeister, "Growing Up Scared," *The Atlantic Monthly* (June 1990), pp. 49–66; and Jerome H. Skolnick, "Gangs in the Post-Industrial Ghetto," *The American Prospect* (Winter 1992), pp. 109–120.

[8]Michael Casserly and Nancy Kober, *Results 2000* (Washington, D.C.: Council of Great City Schools, 1990); Harold Hodgkinson, "Reform Versus Reality," *Phi Delta Kappan* (September 1991), pp. 9–16; and "Report Shows United States Per Pupil Spending Disparities," *Black Issues in Higher Education,* January 2, 1992, pp. 26–27.

[9]David T. Ellwood, *Poor Support* (New York: Basic Books, 1988); Nicholas Lemann, *The Promised Land* (New York: Knopf, 1991); and Carolyn Cody, "Teachers Need Help, Not Accusations," *Black Issues in Higher Education,* January 2, 1992, p. 22.

Social disorganization frequently serious

extreme poverty. Although many poor rural communities have mostly nonminority populations, indicators of social disorganization — high teenage pregnancy rates, widespread juvenile delinquency, very low school achievement, and pervasive feelings of hopelessness — are as high or nearly as high as those in poor minority neighborhoods in big cities.[10]

Rural populations in Appalachia and elsewhere frequently trace their roots to the eighteenth- and nineteenth-century migration of Anglo-Saxon and Scotch-Irish pioneer families who settled in mountainous locations and were isolated from social developments in towns and cities. In many cases, linguistic and dialect differences also contributed to isolation from the larger society and to students' lack of success in the schools. Scholars who have reviewed the limited data available on rural Appalachian students have concluded that cultural patterns stressing sex segregation, suspicion of contemporary society, and rejection of middle-class institutions and authorities have combined to hamper student progress in traditional educational settings.[11] For the U.S. economy as a whole to "work smarter," these rural students, like their inner-city counterparts, need effective education.

Student progress hampered

CHARACTERISTICS OF EFFECTIVE CLASSROOMS AND SCHOOLS

The push for greater educational effectiveness became a national growth industry in the 1980s, generating hundreds of research studies as well as thousands of discussion papers and school- and district-level improvement plans. The following sections describe some of the most important findings from this vast flood of materials.

Effective Teaching and Instruction

Much has been learned

One conclusion supported by recent research is that much has been learned concerning effective delivery of instruction in the classroom.[12] This section summarizes what this research into effective teaching and instruction has to say about classroom management, pedagogical methods, grouping of students, and related issues.

---

[10]John McCormick, "America's Third World," *Newsweek,* August 8, 1988, pp. 20–24; Alan J. DeYoung, "Economic Underdevelopment and Its Effects on Formal Schooling in Southern Appalachia," *American Educational Research Journal* (Summer 1991), pp. 297–315; Jonathan Weisman, "Rural America Is Quietly 'Hurting,' Educators Warn," *Education Week* (October 10, 1990), p. 10; and Deborah L. Cohen, "Conditions 'Bleak' for Rural Children, C.D.F. Finds," *Education Week,* January 8, 1992, p. 3.

[11]Susan Keefe, Una Mae Lange Reck, and Gregory G. Reck, "Ethnicity and Education in Southern Appalachia: A Review," *Ethnic Groups* (vol. 5, 1983), pp. 199–225; Maureen Sullivan and Danny Miller, "Cincinnati's Urban Appalachian Council and Appalachian Identity," *Harvard Educational Review* (February 1990), pp. 106–124.

[12]Andrew C. Porter and Jere Brophy, "Synthesis of Research on Good Teaching: Insights from the Work of the Institute for Research on Teaching," *Educational Leadership* (May 1988), pp. 74–85; Hersholt C. Waxman and Herbert J. Walberg, eds., *Effective Teaching: Current Research* (Berkeley, Calif.: McCutchan, 1990); and Barak Rosenshine, "Teaching Students to Create Questions: A Review of Research" (Paper presented at the Annual Meeting of the American Educational Research Association, San Francisco, April 1992).

Classroom Management. Research on classroom management indicates that effective teachers utilize a variety of techniques to develop productive discipline and to motivate students. Effective teachers emphasize such practices as the following:[13]

Effective practices

1. They make sure that students know what the teacher expects.
2. They let students know how to obtain help.
3. They follow through with reminders and rewards to enforce the rules.
4. They provide a smooth transition between activities.
5. They give students assignments of sufficient variety to maintain interest.
6. They monitor the class for signs of confusion or inattention.
7. They use variations in eye contact, voice, movement, and academic activities to maintain students' attention.
8. They do not respond to discipline problems emotionally.
9. They arrange the physical environment to complement instruction.
10. They do not embarrass students in front of their classmates.
11. They respond flexibly to unexpected developments.

Direct Instruction/Explicit Teaching. The terms **direct instruction** and **explicit teaching** (frequently used as synonyms) usually refer to teacher-directed instruction that proceeds in small steps and that research indicates is associated with high levels of student achievement. (Direct instruction also is sometimes referred to as "active teaching.") Barak Rosenshine identified these six teaching "steps" or "functions" as central to direct instruction:[14]

Active teaching

Lesson components

1. Begin lessons with review of relevant previous learning and a preview and goal statement regarding what is to be learned.
2. Present new material in small steps, with clear and detailed explanations and active student practice after each step.
3. Guide students in initial practice; ask questions and check for understanding.
4. Provide systematic feedback and corrections.
5. Supervise independent practice and monitor and assist seatwork.
6. Provide weekly and monthly review and testing.

---

[13]Edmund T. Emmer, Carolyn M. Evertson, and Linda M. Anderson, "Effective Classroom Management at the Beginning of the School Year," *The Elementary School Journal* (May 1980), pp. 219–231; Jere Brophy, "Classroom Management Techniques," *Education and Urban Society* (February 1986), pp. 182–195; Heather McCollum, "Instructional Strategies and Classroom Management," in Michael S. Knapp and Patrick M. Shields, eds., *Better Schooling for the Children of Poverty* (Berkeley, Calif.: McCutchan, 1991), pp. 273–310; and Anne Reynolds, "What Is Competent Beginning Teaching? A Review of the Literature," *Review of Educational Research* (Spring 1992), pp. 1–36.

[14]Barak Rosenshine, "Explicit Teaching and Teacher Training," *Journal of Teacher Education* (May–June 1987), pp. 34–36. Also see Jane A. Stallings and Jane McCarthy, "Teacher Effectiveness Research and Equity Issues," in H. Prentice Baptiste, Jr., et al., *Leadership, Equality, and School Effectiveness* (Newbury Park, Calif.: Sage, Corwin, 1990), pp. 186–208.

Several other prominent advocates of explicit teaching, such as Jere Brophy, Thomas Good, Madeline Hunter, and Jane Stallings, have outlined similar components of direct instruction.[15]

Active engagement

Time-on-Task.   Effective teaching as portrayed in a number of studies brings about relatively high student **time-on-task** — that is, time engaged in relevant learning activities. As one would expect, students who are actively engaged in relevant activities tend to learn more than students who are not so engaged. Studies of time-on-task have pointed out that classrooms can be managed in such a way as to increase the time students spend on actual learning activities.[16]

However, student learning is not simply a function of the time spent on academic work. Other variables, such as the suitability of the activities, the students' success or failure in the tasks attempted, and the motivating characteristics of methods and materials, are also important. These factors may themselves influence time-on-task; for example, a student who feels successful may spend more time on learning activities than one who feels less successful. But research

Challenging tasks

also indicates that academic tasks should be challenging, and student success should not be purchased at the cost of trivializing instruction.[17]

Questioning.   One way in which effective teachers stimulate student engagement in learning is to ask appropriate questions in a manner that ensures participation and facilitates mastery of academic content. Thus, several studies and analyses of classroom processes have identified questioning skills as an important aspect of effective teaching. In particular, research indicates that "wait

Wait time

time" (the interval between the posing of a question and selecting or encouraging a student to answer it) significantly influences student participation and learning. Some research also indicates that "higher-order" questioning that requires students to mentally manipulate ideas and information is more effective in improving achievement than is "lower cognitive" questioning that focuses on verbatim recall of facts.[18]

Explicit Comprehension Instruction and Strategic Teaching.   Explicit teaching frequently has been criticized for a tendency to neglect important

[15]Jere Brophy and Thomas I. Good, "Teacher Behavior and Student Achievement," in Merlin C. Wittrock, ed., *Handbook of Research on Teaching,* 3rd ed. (New York: Macmillan, 1986); Lorna Idol, Beau Fly Jones, and Richard E. Mayer, "Cognitive Instruction: The Teaching of Thinking," in Lorna Idol and Beau Fly Jones, eds., *Educational Values and Cognitive Instruction* (Hillsdale, N.J.: Erlbaum, 1991), pp. 65–119.

[16]Herbert J. Walberg, "Synthesis of Research on Time and Learning," *Educational Leadership* (March 1988), pp. 76–81; Herbert J. Walberg, "Productive Teaching and Instruction," *Phi Delta Kappan* (February 1990), pp. 470–478; and Jere Brophy, "Probing the Subtleties of Subject-Matter Teaching," *Educational Leadership* (April 1992), pp. 4–8.

[17]Mary Rohrkemper and Lyn Corno, "Success and Failure in Classroom Tasks: Adaptive Learning and Classroom Teaching," *The Elementary School Journal* (January 1988), pp. 297–311; Michael S. Knapp and Patrick M. Shields, eds., *Better Schooling for the Children of Poverty* (Berkeley, Calif.: McCutchan, 1991).

[18]Herbert J. Walberg, "Productive Teaching and Instruction," in Hersholt C. Waxman and Herbert J. Walberg, eds., *Effective Teaching: Current Research* (Berkeley, Calif.: McCutchan, 1991), pp. 33–62.

Questioning skills — such as ensuring long "wait times" and asking "higher-order" questions — are an important aspect of effective teaching. (© Frank Siteman/ Jeroboam)

Dangers in prescribed approaches

higher-order learning (reasoning, critical thinking, comprehension of concepts) in favor of small-step learning of factual material. Some critics believe that the format of explicit teaching or direct instruction — review, teacher presentation of material, guided practice, feedback, and independent practice — discourages higher-order thinking. Teachers in many schools have been told to follow a pre-scribed sequence of this kind, a practice that often has resulted in or reinforced emphasis on low-level learning and mindless regurgitation of facts.[19] In a classic description of this danger, Arthur Wise has portrayed such prescribed ap-proaches as leading to an educational world in which "passive learners" are "fed basic skills in bite-sized chunks to be regurgitated on command before the next scrap of spartan fare can be served" and in which there is a lack of concern for such themes as "individualism, individual freedom, creativity, [and] analytical thinking."[20]

[19]Linda M. McNeil, *Contradictions of Control* (New York: Routledge & Kegan Paul, 1986); Joseph O. Milner, "Suppositional Style and Teacher Evaluation," *Phi Delta Kappan* (February 1991), pp. 464–467; and Jane Hannaway, "Higher Order Skills, Job Design, and Incentives," *American Educational Research Journal* (Spring 1992), pp. 3–21.

[20]Arthur E. Wise, "Legislated Learning Revisited," *Phi Delta Kappan* (January 1988), pp. 328–329. Also see Arthur E. Wise, *Legislated Learning* (Berkeley: University of California Press, 1979), and Ann Lieberman, "The Shortcoming of Standardized Tests," *The Chronicle of Higher Education*, January 29, 1992, pp. B1–B2.

Nevertheless, the tendency to emphasize low-level learning is not necessarily inherent to direct instruction.[21] Higher-order questioning can and should be included as part of explicit teaching, and questions can be sequenced to develop students' thinking. Indeed, much has been accomplished during the last decade in refining classroom techniques for explicitly teaching comprehension in all subject areas. This has led one informed observer to characterize recent gains in teaching for comprehension as virtually a "revolution" in our pedagogy. David Pearson and his colleagues at the national Center for the Study of Reading refer to many of these techniques and approaches as **explicit comprehension instruction.**[22]

Revolution in teaching for comprehension

Like explicit teaching, explicit comprehension instruction emphasizes review and preview, feedback and correctives, and guided as well as independent practice. It also systematically stresses teacher modeling of conceptual learning, linking of new knowledge to prior learning, monitoring of students' comprehension, and systematic training for students in summarizing, inferencing, and other learning strategies. The techniques and strategies associated with explicit comprehension instruction include the following:[23]

Strategies to improve comprehension

"Prediction" activities in which students predict what will be found in the text based on their prior knowledge

"Reciprocal teaching," Student Team Learning, and other approaches to cooperative learning, through which students learn to take more responsibility for helping each other comprehend material

"Semantic maps" and "semantic networks" that organize information

Computer simulations specifically designed to develop concepts and thinking skills

"Metacognitive" learning strategies through which students monitor and assess their own learning processes

"Learning to learn" strategies

Problem-solving models that help students analyze learning situations

Teachers as strategists

Beau Jones and her colleagues have described the effective utilization of such techniques as **strategic teaching** — a "concept which calls attention to the role of the teacher as strategist . . . [who makes] decisions about the 'what,' 'how,' and 'when' of teaching and learning . . . the particular procedures needed

---

[21]Benjamin S. Bloom, "All Our Children Learning Well in Elementary School — And Beyond," *Principal* (March 1988), pp. 12–17; Joan D. Kozlovsky, "Integrating Thinking Skills and Mastery Learning," *Educational Leadership* (February 1990), p. 6; and Gerald G. Duffy, "Let's Free Teachers to Be Inspired," *Phi Delta Kappan* (February 1992), pp. 442–447.

[22]P. David Pearson, *The Comprehension Revolution* (Urbana: University of Illinois Center for the Study of Reading, 1985); P. David Pearson and Janice A. Dole, "Explicit Comprehension Instruction: A Review of Research and a New Conceptualization of Instruction," *The Elementary School Journal* (November 1987), pp. 151–165; and Georgia Garcia and P. David Pearson, "Modifying Reading Instruction to Maximize Its Effectiveness for 'All' Students," in Michael S. Knapp and Patrick M. Shields, eds., *Better Schooling for the Children of Poverty* (Berkeley, Calif.: McCutchan, 1991), pp. 31–60.

[23]Barbara Z. Presseisen, *Thinking Skills: Research and Practice* (Washington, D.C.: National Education Association, 1986); Lorna Idol and Beau Fly Jones, eds., *Educational Values and Cognitive Instruction* (Hillsdale, N.J.: Erlbaum, 1991); and "Comprehension Strategies," *Learning 92* (April/May 1992), pp. 31–46.

to implement a given strategy or skill . . . [and] the conditions under which it is appropriate." Emphasis in strategic teaching is on the student's construction of meaning and growth in independent learning, with the teacher serving as model and mediator of learning. As noted in Chapter 1, many analysts use the term *reflective teaching* in describing this kind of instructional approach.[24]

Cognitive Instruction for Low-Achieving Students.   Emphasis on passive learning of low-level skills seems to be particularly pervasive in schools with concentrations of working-class students and low achievers.[25] A change in this pattern will require new approaches for delivering cognitive instruction, as well as fundamental improvements in programming throughout the educational system.[26]

In addition to the comprehension-enhancement strategies described in the preceding sections, several other learning approaches offer particular promise for improving the thinking skills of low achievers. *Cognitive apprenticeships* immerse students in a motivating, real-world setting. *Cognitively guided instruction* builds on existing knowledge and intuitive reasoning to develop skill and understanding in problem solving. *Scaffolded instruction* provides step-by-step modeling and other forms of intellectual support that are gradually withdrawn as students acquire independent learning skills. *Situated cognition* involves multimedia simulations that are highly motivating and help students master learning-to-learn strategies.[27]

Cognitive scaffolds

Specific programs aimed at improving the thinking skills of low achievers include the Higher Order Thinking Skills Program (discussed later in this chapter), the Productive Thinking Program, and the Chicago Mastery Learning Reading (Insights) Program.[28] Research is beginning to support the conclusion that

---

[24]Beau Fly Jones et al., *Strategic Teaching and Learning* (Alexandria, Va.: Association for Supervision and Curriculum Development, 1987), p. x; Kenneth M. Zeichner and Daniel P. Liston, *Traditions of Reform in U.S. Teacher Education* (East Lansing, Mich.: National Center for Research on Teacher Education, 1990.

[25]Jean Anyon, "Social Class and the Hidden Curriculum of Work," in Henry Giroux and David Purpel, eds., *The Hidden Curriculum and Moral Education* (Berkeley, Calif.: McCutchan, 1983), pp. 143–167; Marshall S. Smith and Jennifer A. O'Day, "Educational Equality: 1966 and Now," in D. A. Verstegen and J. G. Wards, eds., *Spheres of Justice in Education* (New York: HarperCollins, 1991), pp. 53–100; and Cathy Collins and John M. Mangieri, eds., *Teaching Thinking* (Philadelphia: RBS, 1992).

[26]Daniel U. Levine, "Teaching Thinking to At-Risk Students: Generalizations and Speculation," in Barbara Z. Presseisen, ed., *At-Risk Students and Thinking: Perspectives from Research* (Washington, D.C.: National Education Association and Research for Better Schools, 1988); Daniel U. Levine and Eric J. Cooper, "The Change Process and Its Implications in Teaching Thinking," in Lorna Idol and Beau Fly Jones, eds., *Educational Values and Cognitive Instruction* (Hillsdale, N.J.: Erlbaum, 1991), pp. 387–410; and Daniel U. Levine and Robert J. Havighurst, *Society and Education*, 8th ed. (Needham Heights, Mass.: Allyn and Bacon, 1992).

[27]Lauren B. Resnick, "Literacy In School and Out," *Daedalus* (Spring 1990), pp. 169–186; Barbara Means and Michael S. Knapp, "Cognitive Approaches to Teaching Advanced Skills to Educationally Disadvantaged Students," *Phi Delta Kappan* (December 1991), pp. 282–289; and Barak V. Rosenshine and Carla Meister, "The Use of Scaffolds for Teaching Higher-Level Cognitive Strategies," *Educational Leadership* (April 1992), pp. 26–33.

[28]Stanley Pogrow, "Challenging At-Risk Students," *Phi Delta Kappan* (January 1990), pp. 389–397; Barbara Z. Presseisen, "Implementing Thinking in the School's Curriculum" (Paper presented at the Annual Meeting of the International Association for Cognitive Instruction, Riverside, Calif., February 1992).

such approaches have indeed improved performance. However, some specific obstacles need to be addressed, including the preference many students have developed for low-level learning, the low expectations many teachers have for low achievers, and the high financial cost of effective instruction that stresses cognitive development.[29]

Grouping and Tracking.   Although **homogeneous grouping** of students by ability or previous achievement frequently is utilized on the grounds that it facilitates teaching and learning, most research has concluded that it has little or no consistent positive effect. In fact, some studies have concluded that homogeneous grouping improves the performance of high achievers but depresses outcomes for low achievers. Detrimental effects reported for low achievers in some studies appear to occur in part because teachers have low expectations for low-achieving groups and pace instruction very slowly, and because students are demotivated and deprived of positive peer reinforcement and assistance when placed in such groups.[30]

Low expectations for low achievers

As we pointed out in Chapter 10, the implications of research on grouping are neither simple nor obvious. One can argue that individualized and small-group instruction in heterogeneous classes should have better results than homogeneous grouping, but such instruction is expensive and difficult to deliver effectively, and many schools have been unsuccessful at it. In addition, some research supports the conclusion that homogeneous grouping can be much more successful than it has been in the past.[31] The effects of grouping practices depend on a complex set of interacting considerations — the pacing and quality of instruction, adequacy of materials, class size, number of low achievers, instructional methods utilized (whole class or small group), and arrangements provided to differentiate instruction for high and low achievers. Much more needs to be learned concerning how such considerations intervene between grouping and achievement.[32]

Implications not obvious

The term **tracking** usually refers to the practice of separating high-school students into different curriculum paths, such as an academic track for college-

---

[29]Levine and Cooper, "The Change Process"; Jere E. Brophy, "Effective Schooling for Disadvantaged Students," in Michael S. Knapp and Patrick M. Shields, eds., *Better Schooling for the Children of Poverty* (Berkeley, Calif.: McCutchan, 1991), pp. 211–234; and Daniel U. Levine and Allan C. Ornstein, "Implications of International and NAEP Achievement Analyses," *NASSP Bulletin* (1993, in press).

[30]Jeannie Oakes, *Keeping Track: How Schools Structure Inequality* (New Haven, Conn.: Yale University Press, 1985); Robert E. Slavin, "Achievement Effects of Ability Grouping in Secondary Schools: A Best-Evidence Synthesis," *Review of Educational Research* (Fall 1990), pp. 471–499; and Jeannie Oakes and Martin Lipton, "Detracking Schools: Early Lessons from the Field," *Phi Delta Kappan* (February 1992), pp. 448–454.

[31]Gaea Leinhardt and Allan Pallay, "Restrictive Educational Settings: Exile or Haven?" *Review of Educational Research* (December 1982), pp. 199–210; Daniel U. Levine and Robert E. Leibert, "Improving School Improvement Plans," *The Elementary School Journal* (March 1987), pp. 397–412; and Christine Padilla and Thomas Parrish, *A Cost Analysis of Programs for Problem Learners* (Menlo Park, Calif.: SRI International, 1990).

[32]Rebecca Barr and Robert Dreeben, *How Schools Work* (Chicago: University of Chicago Press, 1983); Elfrieda H. Hiebert, "The Context of Instruction and Student Learning: An Examination of Slavin's Assumptions," *Review of Education Research* (Fall 1987), pp. 337–340; and Maureen T. Hallinan, "The Effects of Ability Grouping in Secondary Schools: A Response to Slavin's Best-Evidence Synthesis," *Review of Educational Research* (Fall 1990), pp. 501–504; and Mary McCarlin and Thomas L. Good, "Complaint Cognition," *Educational Researcher* (April 1992), pp. 4–17.

bound students, a general track for "business" students, and a vocational track for students who will enter a trade. Most of the research on tracking supports the conclusion that students in the general/business track have less opportunity to learn academic subject matter and make smaller academic gains than do college-track students with similar family and socioeconomic backgrounds.[33] For this reason, many recent proposals for educational reform strongly recommend that enrollment in general/business or vocational tracks should be reduced or eliminated and that academically oriented courses should constitute the basic curriculum for all or most students.[34]

Tracking limits opportunity

Effective Schools

The preceding sections addressed classroom-level implementation of effective teaching and instruction. However, much more than effective classroom instruction is required to bring about substantial, widespread, and enduring gains in student performance. Attention must be paid to the school as an institution and, in the final analysis, to the larger context of the school district and the environment in which schools operate. The effectiveness of the school and of the district as a whole helps to determine what happens in each classroom. In the words of one observer, "School performance is unlikely to be significantly improved by any measure or set of measures that fails to recognize that schools are institutions — complex organizations composed of interdependent parts, governed by well-established rules and norms of behavior, and adapted for stability."[35]

Schools are institutions

Elementary Schools. Most of the recent research on effective schools focuses on elementary education. Authors of various studies usually define effectiveness at least partly in terms of outstanding student achievement. One of the best-known studies is that of Ronald Edmonds and his colleagues, who defined an effective school as one in which working-class students score as high as middle-class students on basic skills tests. Based on analysis of such schools, Edmonds identified an effective school as one in which there is (1) strong leadership, (2) an orderly, humane climate, (3) frequent monitoring of student progress, (4) high expectations and requirements for all students, and (5) focus on teaching important skills to all students.[36]

Edmonds's research

---

[33]James E. Rosenbaum, *Making Inequality* (New York: Wiley, 1976); Barbara Benham Tye, *Multiple Realities* (Lanham, Md.: University Press of America, 1985); and Jeannie Oakes, "Can Tracking Research Inform Practice?" *Educational Researcher* (May 1992), pp. 12–21.

[34]William J. Bennett, *James Madison High School* (Washington, D.C.: U.S. Department of Education, 1988); John O'Neil, "Transforming the Curriculum for Students 'At Risk,'" *ASCD Curriculum Update* (June 1991), pp. 1–2.

[35]John E. Chubb, "Why the Current Wave of School Reform Will Fail," *The Public Interest* (Winter 1988), p. 29. Also see Pamela Bullard and Barbara A. Taylor, *Keepers of the Dream* (Needham Heights, Mass.: Allyn and Bacon, 1992).

[36]Ronald R. Edmonds, "Programs of School Improvement: An Overview," *Educational Leadership* (December 1982), pp. 4–11; *A Conversation Between James Comer and Ronald Edmonds* (Dubuque, Iowa: Kendall/Hunt, 1989); and "Is There Life After Correlates?" *Effective Schools News* (February 1992), p. 5.

Other observers and groups frequently extend this type of list. A good example is the analysis utilized by the Connecticut School Effectiveness Project, which describes an effective school as having the following characteristics:[37]

Characteristics of effective schools

1. A *safe and orderly environment* that is not oppressive and is conducive to teaching and learning.

2. A *clear school mission* through which the staff shares a commitment to instructional priorities, assessment procedures, and accountability.

3. *Instructional leadership* by a principal who understands and applies the characteristics of instructional effectiveness.

4. A climate of *high expectations* in which the staff demonstrates that all students can attain mastery of basic skills.

5. High *time-on-task* brought about when a large percentage of students' time is spent "engaged" in planned activities to master basic skills.

6. Frequent *monitoring of student progress,* using the results to improve both individual performance and the instructional program.

7. Positive *home-school relations* in which parents support the school's basic mission and play an important part in helping to achieve it.

Coordination of methods and materials

Another characteristic that contributes to school effectiveness is **curriculum alignment,** which refers to the coordination of instructional planning, methods, materials, and testing. When staff development focuses on such coordination, teachers are less likely to rely solely on textbooks and more likely to select or create materials that are most appropriate for teaching a specific skill to a particular group of students.[38]

Additional characteristics

According to several recent research reviews, other key features of unusually effective schools are (1) attention to goals involving cultural pluralism and multicultural education; (2) emphasis on responding to students' personal problems and developing their social skills; and (3) faculty that strive to improve students' sense of efficacy.[39] Researchers at the Northwest Regional Educational Laboratory have identified more than one hundred specific practices, grouped in seventeen categories, that contribute to school effectiveness.[40]

Secondary Schools.   Relatively few studies have concentrated solely on the characteristics of unusually effective secondary schools. (Our use of the term

---

[37]Joan Shoemaker, "Effective Schools: Putting the Research to the Ultimate Test," *Pre-Post Press* (1982), p. 241. Also see William J. Gauthier, Jr., Raymond I. Pecheone, and Joan Shoemaker, "Schools Can Become More Effective," *The Journal of Negro Education* (Summer 1985), pp. 388–408; Robert L. Crowson, *School-Community Relations, Under Reform* (Berkeley, Calif.: McCutchan, 1992).

[38]Daniel U. Levine and Joyce Stark, "Instructional and Organizational Arrangements That Improve Achievement in Inner-city Schools," *Educational Leadership* (December 1982), pp. 41–48. Also see Daniel U. Levine and Lawrence W. Lezotte, *Unusually Effective Schools* (Madison, Wis.: National Center for Effective Schools Research and Development, 1990).

[39]Lawrence Stedman, "The Effective Schools Formula Still Needs Changing," *Phi Delta Kappan* (February 1988), pp. 439–442; Daniel U. Levine, "Update on Effective Schools: Findings and Implications from Research and Practice," *The Journal of Negro Education* (Fall 1990), pp. 577–584.

[40]*Effective Schooling Practices: A Research Synthesis 1990 Update* (Portland, Ore.: Northwest Regional Educational Laboratory, 1990).

"secondary schools" refers to middle schools, which usually include a combination of grades six through eight; junior highs, which usually include grades seven through nine; and senior highs, which include grades nine or ten through twelve). Because the goals and programs of most secondary schools are so diverse and complex, it is difficult to conclude that one school generally is more effective than another, particularly when the social class of the student body is taken into account. In addition, hardly any secondary schools enrolling mostly working-class students stand out as being relatively high in achievement. However, there is strong support for the conclusion that effective secondary schools have made major modifications in the way students and teachers are assigned to classes, along with concomitant changes in school schedules, teacher selection, and related policies and practices.[41]

Basic changes

One of the few senior high schools for which concrete data indicate unusual effectiveness is South Boston High School. Reform of South Boston occurred over several years during a time of continuing turmoil in the Boston school system, but by 1980 impressive data were available on improvement in the performance of students. For example, average reading scores increased in one year from the 16th percentile to the 40th percentile in the ninth grade, and from the 18th to the 32nd percentile in the tenth grade. In addition, in four years the percentage of graduates attending postsecondary institutions increased from less than 8 percent to 40 percent. The changes that appear to account most for these improvements included the following:[42]

Developments at South Boston High School

Changes at South Boston

1. A new principal made major changes in organizational patterns and insisted that staff reexamine their methods.

2. More than two-thirds of the faculty were replaced by teachers willing to discard ineffective traditional methods.

3. Nearly all ninth and tenth graders were placed in reading and writing courses rather than in traditional English classes.

4. Students were placed in mathematics courses rather than in "business mathematics," which for the most part repeated beginning arithmetic.

5. A number of in-school and out-of-school alternatives were established. These alternatives included a school-within-a-school that emphasized academic learning and a mini-school that emphasized experiential learning and instruction.

6. Work-study programs based on learning opportunities in the community were made available to many students after the ninth grade.

7. Discipline, including strict attendance policies, was firm but fair.

---

[41]Daniel U. Levine and Eugene E. Eubanks, "Organizational Arrangements in Effective Secondary Schools," in John J. Lane and Herbert J. Walberg, eds., *Organizing for Learning* (Reston, Va.: National Association of Secondary School Principals, 1988); Loretta M. Shimniok and Mike Schmoker, "How We Made the Transition from Junior High School to Middle School," *Educational Leadership* (February 1992), pp. 27–29.

[42]This portrayal of South Boston is drawn from the authors' personal observations and from Geraldine Kozberg and Jerome Winegar, "The South Boston Story: Implications for Secondary Schools," *Phi Delta Kappan* (April 1981), pp. 565–569.

8. Guidance in personal development was made consistently available.

9. School pride and spirit were systematically emphasized.

Comparable changes have taken place at several other inner-city high schools, including George Washington Preparatory High School in Los Angeles and Ribault High School in Jacksonville, Florida.[43] Since no two schools share exactly the same problems and possibilities, one cannot say that other secondary schools should implement exactly the same set of changes as was introduced at South Boston, Washington, or Ribault. However, research on effective approaches at high schools with many low achievers has supported some particular changes, such as emphasis on firm but fair discipline, personalized guidance for students, insistence on more rigorous standards, increased stress on reading and math for students far below grade level, and activities to build school spirit.[44] In addition, according to several reviews of the literature, two of the most promising structural changes are a **school-within-a-school** and **achievement centers**.[45]

Support from research

1. *School-within-a-school for low achievers.* Students who can read but are more than two or three years below grade level are assigned to a school-within-a-school serving 80 to 120 students and staffed by four or five teachers (English, reading, math, science, and social studies) and a coordinator. If teachers in this type of program are specially selected for their ability and willingness to work with low achievers, participating students can make very large gains in reading and other basic skills.

School-within-a-school

2. *Achievement centers.* After specific learning objectives are identified for a given grade and subject area (for example, tenth-grade English), an achievement center is established for both remedial and developmental purposes. Students who do not have the skills prerequisite for a particular unit or who need special assistance in developing their full potential will attend the achievement center instead of or in addition to the regular class. Achievement center placement generally replaces the regular class for about two weeks, and close coordination is maintained between achievement center staff and the regular teacher.

Helping students improve

High-School Reform Proposals. In addition to recommendations for improvement contained in the national reports, several prominent educators have offered proposals for comprehensive reform of high schools. Two of the most

---

[43]U.S. Department of Education, *Schools That Work* (Washington, D.C.: U.S. Government Printing Office, 1987); Michael G. Fullan, "Change Processes in Secondary Schools: Toward a More Fundamental Agenda," in Milbrey W. McLaughlin, Joan E. Talbert, and Nina Bascia, eds., *The Contexts of Teaching in Secondary Schools* (New York: Teachers College Press, 1990), pp. 224–255.

[44]U.S. Department of Education, *Schools That Work;* Helen Featherstone, "Orderly Classrooms and Corridors: Why Some Schools Have Them and Others Don't," *The Harvard Education Letter* (September 1987), pp. 1–5; and Gary Wehlage, Gregory Smith, and Pauline Lipman, "Restructuring Urban Schools: The New Futures Experience," *American Educational Research Journal* (Spring 1992), pp. 51–96.

[45]Daniel U. Levine and John K. Sherk, Jr., "Organizational Arrangements to Increase Productive Time for Reading in High Schools" (Statement prepared for the International Reading Association response to *A Nation at Risk*, November 1983); Gary G. Wehlage et al., *Reducing the Risk* (New York: Falmer, 1989); and Daniel U. Levine, "Implications of an Urban School-Within-A-School Approach," in Hershholt C. Waxman et al., eds., *Students at Risk in At-Risk Schools* (Newbury Park, Calif.: Sage Corwin, 1992).

highly publicized proposals have been prepared by Ernest Boyer and by Theodore Sizer.

Boyer's *High School* was based on a three-year study in which twenty-five educators collected data at fifteen diverse senior high schools. Eighteen pages of proposals for improvement and reform stressed the following major themes:[46]

Boyer report goals

1. Goals must be more clearly focused on mastery of reading and writing, preparation for work and further education, and community service.

2. The core curriculum should expand from about half the units required for graduation to about two-thirds.

3. Working conditions of teachers must be improved.

4. Improvements must be made in instructional methods and materials.

5. Technology should be used to enrich curriculum.

6. More flexibility is needed in school size, schedules, and other arrangements.

Smaller teaching loads

Among Boyer's most important recommendations were those dealing with teachers' working conditions. He proposed that high-school teachers should have a daily load of only four regular classes and one small seminar, should have an hour a day for class preparation, and should be exempt from monitoring halls, lunchrooms, and recreation areas.

Theodore Sizer's major work, *Horace's Compromise: The Dilemma of the American High School,* was based on his visits to eighty high schools. In this book, a teacher named Horace must choose between "covering" a multitude of low-level skills in the prescribed curriculum and in-depth teaching of important concepts and understandings.[47] To enhance students' cognitive growth, Sizer recommends that the curriculum be divided into four major areas: inquiry and expression, mathematics and science, literature and the arts, and philosophy and history. He also advocates more active learning and reduced emphasis on minimal competency testing. Sizer particularly wants to eliminate the tacit understanding between students who say "I will be orderly . . . if you don't push me very hard" and teachers who respond "You play along with my minimal requirements and I will keep them minimal."[48]

Unproductive tacit understanding

Teams of teachers and students

Perhaps the greatest virtue of Sizer's proposals is that they explicitly recognize the difficulties of high-school teaching. After pointing out that teachers cannot provide appropriate coaching to 150 to 180 students a day, he suggests that teams of seven or eight teachers should work with groups of about 100 students. Sizer would make these teacher-student ratios possible by eliminating the separate functions of teachers now assigned to counseling, the arts, physical education, and other specialized areas. Sizer's recent book, *Horace's School: Redesigning the American High School,* provides information on developments at more

---

[46]Ernest I. Boyer, *High School* (New York: Harper & Row, 1983).

[47]Theodore R. Sizer, *Horace's Compromise: The Dilemma of the American High School* (Boston: Houghton Mifflin, 1984). Also see Reba N. Page, "Cultures and Curricula," *Educational Foundations* (Winter 1990), pp. 49–76.

[48]Theodore Sizer, "The Teacher as Coach: Fewer Facts, More Learning," *Education Week,* November 16, 1983, p. 23. Also see Annette Hemmings, "High-achieving Black High School Students and the Model Student Image" (Paper presented at the Annual Meeting of the American Educational Research Association, Chicago, April 1991).

than three hundred schools that have joined the Coalition of Essential Schools he organized to implement the ideas presented in *Horace's Compromise*.[49]

Evaluation of Effective Schools Research. In evaluating the research on effective schools, a number of points should be kept in mind. First, one should recognize that there is widespread confusion concerning the definition of an effective school; there are nearly as many definitions of effective schools as there are people discussing them. Some people have in mind a school with unusually high academic achievement (taking account of social class), but others are thinking about a "self-renewing" school that can identify and solve internal problems, a school that promotes students' personal growth, a school that has shown improvement in academic achievement, or a school that concentrates on developing independent study skills and love for learning. Still others apparently have in mind no specific definition at all when they write or talk about making schools more effective.[50]

Definitions differ

Second, most of the more rigorous studies have concentrated entirely or largely on inner-city schools. Those schools identified as unusually effective in such studies generally have been poverty schools in which academic achievement is higher than at most other schools with similarly disadvantaged students. It is more difficult to identify unusually effective schools outside the inner city, where high achievement is more common. In addition, the key components of effectiveness outside the inner city may differ somewhat from those at poverty schools.[51]

Research emphasizes poverty schools

Third, other methodological problems have left much of the research vulnerable to criticism. For example, schools identified as effective in a given subject (say, reading) during a given year may not be effective on other measures or the next year. In addition, controls for students' social class and family environment frequently are not adequate to attribute high achievement to school characteristics. This can happen, for instance, when magnet schools enrolling inner-city students are judged as unusually effective but further research would show that their students came from highly motivated poverty families dissatisfied with their neighborhood schools.[52]

Methodological problems

Fourth, the general level of most characteristics cited in the literature is such that they tend to beg the question of what teachers and principals should do in

More specificity needed

---

[49]Theodore Sizer, "High School Reform: The Need for Engineering," *Phi Delta Kappan* (June 1983), pp. 679–683; Theodore Sizer, "No Pain, No Gain," *Educational Leadership* (May 1991), pp. 32–34; and Theodore Sizer, *Horace's School: Redesigning the American High School* (Boston: Houghton Mifflin, 1992).

[50]Daniel U. Levine and Robert S. Stephenson, "Are Effective or Meritorious Schools Meretricious?" *The Urban Review* (no. 1, 1987), pp. 25–34; Allan C. Ornstein and Daniel U. Levine, "Urban School Effectiveness and Reform," *Illinois Schools Research and Development* (Spring 1991), pp. 111–117.

[51]Phillip Hallinger and Joseph F. Murphy, "The Social Context of Effective Schools," *American Journal of Education* (May 1986), pp. 328–355; Daniel U. Levine, "An Interpretive Review of Research and Practice Dealing With Unusually Effective Schools," *School Effectiveness and School Improvement* (1992, in press).

[52]John H. Ralph and James Fennessey, "Science or Reform: Some Questions About the Effective School Model," *Phi Delta Kappan* (June 1983), pp. 689–694; John F. Witte and Daniel J. Walsh, "A Systematic Test of the Effective Schools Model," *Educational Evaluation and Policy Analysis* (Summer 1990), pp. 188–212; and Billy Tashman, "Hobson's Choice," *The Village Voice*, January 21, 1992, pp. 9, 14.

the schools. For example, the claim that a school requires good leadership and a productive climate does not specify exactly what these are or provide much direct guidance on how to accomplish them.[53]

Despite these qualifications, the research on effective schools has identified a number of characteristics that deserve to be considered for implementation, and projects to improve schools in certain districts have met with notable successes. The next section will examine more of these success stories and the changes that lie behind them.

RECENT EFFORTS TO INCREASE SCHOOL EFFECTIVENESS

Many attempts to increase school effectiveness are under way. Educators in Chicago, Detroit, Milwaukee, Memphis, New York, and elsewhere are trying to create more successful schools by introducing practices identified in effective schools research. Departments of education in California, Connecticut, Florida, New Jersey, Ohio, and other states are providing services to help low-performing schools become more effective.

Successful School Effectiveness Projects

Encouraging data regarding achievement gains among disadvantaged students have been reported in a number of locations. For example, among eighteen Milwaukee elementary schools that have been participating in a project to raise achievement, the percentage of fifth-grade students reading in the lowest performance category decreased from 55 percent in 1979 to 30 percent in 1985, and the comparable decline in math was from 42 percent to 18 percent. Similarly impressive results have been reported for effective schools projects in several other big cities (see Table 16.1). In the past, successful inner-city elementary schools were considered "mavericks" whose success could be attributed mainly to the efforts of an atypical principal. It now appears to be possible to create such schools through careful planning and implementation of improved arrangements for curriculum and instruction.[54]

Milwaukee project

Probably the most impressive of the sizable projects undertaken to improve achievement throughout a group of schools or an entire school district has been the **Achievement Goals Program** (AGP) in San Diego. The AGP was devised in 1980 after a federal judge required the school district to improve achievement at twenty-three schools with 80 percent or more minority enrollment. The San Diego approach is twofold: (1) utilization of effective schools research on mastery learning, classroom management, time-on-task, direct instruction, provi-

San Diego project

---

[53]Aaron M. Pallas, "School Climate in American High Schools," *Teachers College Record* (Summer 1988), pp. 541–554; Kent D. Peterson, "Open Book," *Focus in Change* (July 1990), p. 3.

[54]Daniel U. Levine and Eugene E. Eubanks, "Achievement Improvement and Non-Improvement at Concentrated Poverty Schools in Big Cities," *Metropolitan Education* (Winter 1986–87), pp. 92–107; Barbara S. Taylor, ed., *Case Studies in Effective Schools Research* (Madison, Wis.: National Center for Effective Schools Research and Development, 1990); and "Project Canal: Creating a New Approach to Learning," *Reform Report* (February 1992), pp. 1–11.

Table 16.1

Improvements in Average Reading Comprehension Scores in Three Big-City School Districts

	Grade	Median Grade Equivalent Score			
		1978	1982	1990	National Norm
Kansas City, Missouri	3	3.1	3.3	3.4	3.8
	6	5.5	6.0	5.8	6.8
	8	6.7	7.6	8.3	8.7
Washington, D.C.	3	3.0	3.8	3.7	3.8
	6	5.1	6.2	6.4	6.8
	9	6.8	7.9	9.1	9.8

	Grade	Percent in Minority Isolated Schools Above National Median		
		1980	1990	National Average
San Diego	5	17	32	50
	9	22	35	50
	11	32	44	50

Source: Data provided by District of Columbia Public Schools; Kansas City Public Schools; San Diego Unified School District.

sion of staff development, and other topics and (2) expansion of magnet schools along with a radical curriculum alignment that makes it difficult for teachers to overemphasize low-level skills. As illustrated in Table 16.1, large gains in reading comprehension (along with language and math) have been registered since 1980 at every grade.[55]

Achievement generally still low

Unfortunately, however, school improvement projects do not seem to have been implemented successfully in many locations. Thus, the low achievement patterns and other indicators of educational problems that we cite elsewhere in this book do not appear to have changed significantly on a national basis. In order to attain national aims concerning cognitive growth of students, international competitiveness, and socioeconomic equity, more schools must make better use of the research on effective teaching and schooling.[56]

Exemplary Instructional Interventions

Promising interventions

Numerous recent intervention approaches appear to improve the cognitive functioning and performance of low achievers when educators implement them well. To illustrate what is being tried and accomplished in participating schools and districts throughout the United States, this section briefly describes several

[55]Levine and Eubanks, "Achievement Improvement and Non-Improvement"; Daniel U. Levine, "The Need to Assess Multiple Crucial Components in Evaluating Programs," in Josie G. Bain and Joan L. Herman, eds., *Making Schools Work for Underachieving Minority Students* (New York: Greenwood, 1990), pp. 195–200.

[56]Barbara O. Taylor and Daniel U. Levine, "Effective Schools Projects and School-Based Management," *Phi Delta Kappan* (January 1991), pp. 394–397; Nathan Glazer, "The Real World of Urban Education," *The Public Interest* (Winter 1992), pp. 57–75.

kinds of interventions for which positive achievement outcomes have been reported.

HOTS components

High Order Thinking Skills (HOTS) Program. Developed by Stanley Pogrow and his colleagues at the University of Arizona, the HOTS program is specifically designed to replace Chapter 1 remedial-reading laboratories in grades four through six. The HOTS approach has four major components: (1) use of computers for problem solving; (2) emphasis on dramatization techniques that require students to verbalize and that thereby stimulate language development; (3) Socratic questioning techniques; and (4) a thinking-skills curriculum that stresses metacognitive learning, learning-to-learn strategies, and other comprehension-enhancement techniques of the kind described earlier in this chapter. The developers of HOTS also are working to devise a thinking-based math curriculum and to identify materials and methods for improving low-achievers' comprehension in science, social studies, and other subjects. Achievement results of the HOTS program have been described as supporting the conclusion that "at-risk students . . . have tremendous levels of intellectual and academic potential . . . [but many do not] understand 'understanding.' . . . [This] fundamental learning problem can be eliminated if enough time and enough resources are made available."[57]

Accelerating the pace of instruction

Accelerated Schools. Originally initiated by faculty at Stanford University, the Accelerated Schools approach aims to bring about fundamental reform and improvement at elementary schools with a high proportion of disadvantaged students. After receiving training in group process and problem solving, participating faculties address major aspects of school operation such as grouping of students, delivery of instruction, improvement of expectations for students, and selection of materials. Particular stress is placed on accelerating the pace of instruction by reducing low-level learning experiences that are counterproductive for many students. By 1992, more than fifty elementary schools in several states were engaged in the Accelerated Schools approach, and plans were being developed to extend it to middle schools.[58]

Learning-to-learn stressed

Success for All. Probably the most comprehensive intervention that has been developed to improve the achievement of disadvantaged students, Success for All provides intensive instructional support along with family assistance for children in preschool classes and the primary grades. Curriculum and instruction stress language development and learning-to-learn skills for students who receive individualized help in small classes. Success for All also emphasizes cooperative learning and mastery instruction, with technical support and staff development provided by full-time coordinators and resource persons assigned to participating schools. The developers of Success for All have described its early results as supporting the conclusion that nearly all students can learn well be-

---

[57]Pogrow, "Challenging At-Risk Students," p. 392; Stanley Pogrow, "What to Do About Chapter 1," *Phi Delta Kappan* (April 1992), pp. 624–630.

[58]Jane McCarthy and Henry M. Levin, "Accelerated Schools for Students in At-Risk Situations," in Waxman et al., eds., *Students at Risk in At-Risk Schools;* H. M. Levin, "Accelerated Visions," *Accelerated Schools* (Winter 1992), pp. 2–3.

ginning in the earliest grades and thereby can avoid subsequent placement in remedial classes or special education.[59]

Reading Recovery.   Using linguistic theories originally elaborated in New Zealand, Reading Recovery is designed to provide systematic help for first graders who experience serious problems learning to read. Participating students receive individual tutoring every day for 12 to 20 weeks from a trained reading teacher. (A few students participate in additional tutoring after the first grade.) Emphasis in tutoring is on learning to read through oral and written expression, diagnosis and correction of individual learning problems, and use of short paperback books or other materials with only a few lines per page. In contrast to many compensatory-education programs, in which kindergarten and first-grade students have registered substantial reading gains but subsequently have declined in performance, Reading Recovery students have maintained relatively high reading scores in later grades.[60]

Sustained gains reported

Degrees of Reading Power Comprehension Development Approach.   Based in part on the Degrees of Reading Power (DRP) test originally developed by the College Board, the DRP approach is being implemented successfully at a number of secondary schools. The test is unlike other standardized reading measures in that it assesses how well a student actually can comprehend written prose he or she encounters in or out of school, not just whether the student is above or below some abstract grade level. After using the DRP to determine their students' comprehension levels, teachers in all subject areas align their instruction by selecting for homework or other independent assignments materials that are not so difficult that they frustrate students, and for classwork materials slightly beyond students' comprehension in order to help them improve. The largest component in this intervention approach is systematic in-service training to help teachers learn to use comprehension-enhancement strategies. Positive outcomes have been reported in both inner-city schools and suburban schools with socioeconomically diverse enrollment.[61]

Matching materials and students

Anchored Instruction and Other Technology-Based Approaches.   As we pointed out in the preceding chapter, numerous approaches are being developed and tested to improve student achievement through the use of computers, interactive video, multimedia, and other technological innovations. Many of these

---

[59]Nancy A. Madden et al., "Restructuring the Urban Elementary School," *Educational Leadership* (February 1989), pp. 14–18; Nancy A. Madden et al., "Success for All," *Phi Delta Kappan* (April 1991), pp. 593–599; and Nancy A. Madden, "Success for All: Fourth-Year Findings" (Paper presented at the Annual Meeting of the American Educational Research Association, San Francisco, April 1992).

[60]Gay Su Pinnell, "Success for Low Achievers Through Reading Recovery," *Educational Leadership* (September 1990), pp. 17–21; Gay Su Pinnell, *Restructuring Beginning Reading with the Reading Recovery Approach* (Bloomington, Ind.: Phi Delta Kappa, 1991); and Gay Su Pinnell, "Success for Low Achievers Through Reading Recovery," *Reform Report* (January 1992), pp. 1–5.

[61]Daniel U. Levine and John K. Sherk, "Implementation of Reforms to Improve Comprehension Skills at an Unusually Effective Inner City Intermediate School," *Peabody Journal of Education* (Summer 1989), pp. 87–106; Steven H. Ivens and Bertram L. Koslin, *Demands for Reading Literacy Require New Accountability Methods* (Brewster, N.Y.: Touchstone Applied Science Associates, 1991); and John E. George, Pauline Moley, and Donna S. Ogle, "CCD: A Model Comprehension Program for Changing Thinking and Instruction," *Journal of Reading* (April 1992, in press).

approaches either are specifically designed or have particular potential for improving the performance of low achievers. For example, the Anchored Instruction approach devised by the Cognition and Technology Group aims to improve the problem-formulating and problem-solving skills of low achievers by means of videodisc and computerized materials that provide a framework for substantial exploration of "authentic" tasks. Based on student and teacher reactions during pilot implementations, Group researchers concluded that students were participating actively and becoming more proficient at complex problem solving.[62]

Problem-solving stressed

Comer School Development Program. Developed by James Comer and his colleagues at Yale University, the School Development Program aims to improve achievement at inner-city elementary schools through enhanced social and psychological services for students, emphasis on parent involvement, and encouragement and support for active learning. Participating faculties involve parents in all aspects of school operation (including governance), and teachers, parents, psychologists, social workers, and other specialists form "Mental Health Teams" that design and supervise individualized learning arrangements for students experiencing or causing unusual problems. Curriculum and instruction are coordinated across subject areas in order to emphasize development of students' language learning and social skills. Several schools in New Haven, Connecticut, and Prince George's County, Maryland, have produced large achievement gains after implementing the School Development Program along with other innovations.[63]

Parent involvement and active learning

Algebridge. Jointly developed by the Educational Testing Service and the College Board, Algebridge was created to help students succeed in the transition from arithmetic to algebra. Participating students receive assistance in solving carefully sequenced problems as part of a year-long supplemental course prior to or in conjunction with prealgebra or algebra courses. Preliminary test scores support the conclusion that participating students frequently register large gains in mathematics performance.[64]

Transition to algebra

STL, CIRC, and TAI. For two decades, educators at Johns Hopkins University have been developing and refining techniques and materials for implementing cooperative learning arrangements in the classroom. As we pointed out earlier in the book, cooperative learning approaches can help teachers motivate students and respond to differences in learning styles. Student Team Learning (STL) provides specific techniques for implementing cooperative learning in any grade or subject. Drawing on STL, Cooperative Integrated Reading and

Cooperative learning approaches

---

[62]The Cognition and Technology Group at Vanderbilt, "Anchored Instruction and Its Relationship to Situated Cognition," *Educational Researcher* (August–September 1990), pp. 2–10; Ray Mabus, "A New Light in Education: Mississippi 2000," *T.H.E. Journal* (August 1991), pp. 53–56; and Marcia Linn, "The Art of Multimedia and the State of Education," *Educational Researcher* (February 1992), pp. 30–32.

[63]James P. Comer, "Educating Poor Minority Children," *Scientific American* (November 1988), pp. 42–48; James P. Comer and Norris M. Haynes, "Parent Involvement in Schools: An Ecological Approach," *The Elementary School Journal* (January 1991), pp. 271–278; and James P. Comer, "Opening the Door to Learning," *Agenda* (Winter 1992), pp. 26–28.

[64]Gary D. Keller, "Creating Candidates for Success," *The College Board Review* (Summer 1990), pp. 10–15, 28–29; "Algebridge," *Mathematics Education News* (Fall 1991), p. 41; and "Algebridge Users Report Success," *Mathematics Education News* (Spring 1992), pp. 1–2.

Composition (CIRC) uses specially prepared materials and comprehension-enhancement strategies at the elementary-school level, and Team Accelerated Instruction (TAI) combines STL with individualized mastery instruction in middle-grades mathematics. All three of these approaches have produced sizable gains among low achievers when they have been implemented well.[65]

Combinations of Approaches.   Exemplary interventions such as the ones described above are not mutually exclusive. Educators frequently combine promising approaches to school-based management, comprehensive staff development, changes in testing, and mastery instruction with other innovations and interventions described elsewhere in this book. For example, STL is combined with mastery instruction in implementing TAI, and HOTS incorporates computer technology. Teachers implementing the DRP approach frequently use comprehension-enhancement strategies such as semantic mapping as well as cooperative learning arrangements and computerized lessons. Accelerated Schools or School Development Program faculties can use STL, CIRC, mastery learning, and other substantive innovations in curriculum and instruction. School faculties throughout the United States currently are introducing and combining these kinds of exemplary interventions, frequently as part of districtwide or multischool projects.[66]

Logical combinations

AT-RISK STUDENTS AND DROPOUTS

As we pointed out earlier in this chapter, national concern for international competitiveness and for social equity has focused attention on education of disadvantaged students. Much of this concern has been expressed in terms of proposals to improve education for at-risk students — a term that is often not defined very specifically but seems to refer in most cases to students who generally are low achievers and/or are alienated from school and are at risk either of dropping out or of not acquiring sufficient secondary or postsecondary education to succeed in the economy. A high proportion of at-risk, low achievers consists of economically disadvantaged minority students.

Definitions seldom specific

In addition to the school reform projects already discussed, many other efforts have focused on alienated low achievers who are likely to drop out or already have withdrawn from high schools. Among the (not mutually exclusive) approaches most often advocated are the following:

Successful approaches

Alternative opportunities such as in-school suspension programs, magnet schools, and schools-within-a-school.[67]

[65]Robert E. Slavin, ed., *School and Classroom Organization* (Hillsdale, N.J.: Erlbaum, 1989); Robert E. Slavin, "Research on Cooperative Learning: Consensus and Controversy," *Educational Leadership* (January 1990), pp. 52–54.

[66]Thomas R. Guskey, Perry D. Passaro, and Wayne Wheeler, "The Thorpe Gordon School," *Principal* (September 1991), pp. 36–38; Brenda LeTendre, "Missouri's Accelerated Schools," *Accelerated Schools* (Winter 1991), pp. 8–9; and G. Alfred Hess, Jr., *School Restructuring, Chicago Style* (Chicago: Chicago Panel on Public School Policy and Finance, 1992).

[67]Mary A. Raywid, "Is There a Case for Choice?" *Educational Leadership* (January 1991), pp. 4–

THE ONE ON THE LEFT WILL FINISH HIGH SCHOOL BEFORE THE ONE ON THE RIGHT.

Most Latina teenage mothers never finish high school. To learn more about the challenges facing young Latinos today, request "Latino Youths At A Crossroads" by writing: *Children's Defense Fund, 122 C Street, N.W., Washington, D.C. 20001 ($7.45 postpaid).*

THE CHILDREN'S DEFENSE FUND

Employment linkages to provide part-time employment training and/or improvement in vocational education.[68]

12; Charles Dayton et al., "The California Partnership Academies," *Phi Delta Kappan* (March 1992), pp. 539–545.

[68]Victor Herbert, "Employment Strategies for Dropout Prevention," *Education Week*, January 27, 1988, p. 28; N. L. Gage, "Dealing with the Dropout Problem," *Phi Delta Kappan* (December 1990), pp. 280–285; and W. Norton Grubb, "Giving High Schools an Occupational Focus," *Educational Leadership* (March 1992), pp. 36–37, 40–43.

Special social services and counseling programs such as those for delinquents or pregnant girls.[69]

Modifications in curriculum and instruction to make education more motivating and relevant for disinterested students.[70]

Smaller classes and schools that provide for more personal contact between teachers and students and thereby create supportive communities.[71]

Selection of dedicated teachers who are willing and able to work with potential dropouts.[72]

Experiential learning that provides for active engagement in interesting activities.[73]

Mentoring and advocacy assistance from sympathetic adults.[74]

THE PROCESS OF SCHOOL IMPROVEMENT AND REFORM

Promulgating, legislating, and even packaging change are not the same as actually changing. Analysis of past efforts to improve schools has resulted in a much better understanding of the steps that must be taken to ensure that reform efforts have a significant and lasting impact. Some of the lessons that can be deduced from past efforts to innovate are described below.

Practical problems hamper good ideas

1. *Adaptive problem solving.* Implementation of an innovation frequently has little or no effect on students' performance because a host of problems arise to stifle practical application. For example, experts may devise a wonderful new science curriculum for fourth graders and school districts may purchase large quantities of the new curriculum materials, but teachers may choose not to use the materials or may not know how to use them. Innovations are not likely to be implemented successfully unless the organization introducing them is adaptive in the sense that it can identify and solve day-to-day implementation problems.[75]

---

[69]Dale Mann, "Can We Help Dropouts?" *Teachers College Record* (Spring 1986), pp. 307–323; Kathryn M. Henn-Reinke, "The Story Behind the 'Salsa' Study," *Equity and Excellence* (Fall 1991), pp. 47–54; and Lynn Liontos, *At-Risk Families and Schools: Becoming Partners* (Eugene, Ore.: ERIC Clearinghouse on Educational Management, 1992).

[70]Russell W. Rumberger, "High School Dropouts: A Review of Issues and Evidence," *Review of Educational Research* (Summer 1987), pp. 101–121; Jackson Toby and David J. Armor, "Carrots or Sticks for High School Dropouts?" *The Public Interest* (Winter 1992), pp. 76–90.

[71]Andrew Hahn, "Reaching Out to America's Dropouts: What to Do?" *Phi Delta Kappan* (December 1987), pp. 256–263; Gary Wehlage, "School Reform for At-Risk Students," *Equity and Excellence* (Fall 1991), pp. 15–24; and Mary Koepke, "All in the Family," *Teacher Magazine* (March 1992), pp. 21–22.

[72]Patricia S. Miller, "Increasing Teacher Efficacy with At-Risk Students," *Equity and Excellence* (Fall 1991), pp. 30–35.

[73]Gary Wehlage et al., *Reducing the Risk* (London: Falmer, 1989); Jeremy D. Finn, "How to Make the Dropout Problem Go Away," *Educational Researcher* (January–February 1991), pp. 28–30; and Stan Bernard, "A Day at the Box Factory," *Educational Leadership* (March 1992), pp. 50–51.

[74]James M. McPartland and Sandra M. Nettles, "Project RAISE," *CDS* (October 1991), pp. 9–10; Stephen F. Hamilton and Mary Agnes Hamilton, "Mentoring Programs: Promise and Paradox," *Phi Delta Kappan* (March 1992), pp. 546–550.

[75]Michael G. Fullan, *The New Meaning of Educational Change* (New York: Teachers College Press,

Each school must improve

2. *School-level focus.* Because the innovating organization must identify and solve day-to-day problems, the focus in bringing about change must be at the level of the individual school, where many of the problems occur.[76]

3. *Potential for implementation.* Successful school reform also depends on whether changes can be implemented, which means that teachers must perceive that they can adopt and utilize reforms effectively. Two characteristics that make successful implementation more likely are an innovation's *compatibility* with the social context of potential users and its *accessibility* to those who do not already understand or share the underlying ideas.[77]

Shared vision

4. *Leadership and shared agreements.* Meaningful innovation requires change in many institutional arrangements, including scheduling of staff and student time, selection and utilization of instructional methods and materials, and mechanisms for making decisions. The building principal usually is the key person in successfully implementing change, but the faculty also must have a shared vision of the kinds of changes that are possible and necessary. Otherwise, staff members are unlikely to seriously consider proposals that require them to significantly change their behaviors and classroom arrangements.[78]

Teacher's voice important

5. *Teacher involvement.* Because people who are expected to alter their working patterns will not cooperate fully unless they have a voice in designing and implementing change, teachers must have an opportunity to help select and evaluate innovations.[79]

Interactive staff development

6. *Training of staff.* Staff development is a core activity in the school improvement process. In the case of an elementary school, the entire staff should participate; in secondary schools, departments may be the appropriate unit for some activities. Staff development should be an interactive process in which teachers and administrators work together at every stage.[80]

1991); Michael G. Fullan, "Visions That Blind," *Educational Leadership* (February 1992), pp. 19–20.

[76]Linda Lambert, "Staff Development Redesigned," *Phi Delta Kappan* (May 1988), pp. 665–668; Marshall Sashkin and Herbert J. Walberg, eds., *School Leadership and Culture* (Berkeley, Calif.: McCutchan, 1993, in press).

[77]David P. Crandall, Jeffrey W. Eiseman, and Karen E. Louis, "Strategic Planning Issues That Bear on the Success of School Improvement Efforts," *Educational Administration Quarterly* (Summer 1986), pp. 21–53; Karen S. Louis and Matthew B. Miles, *Improving the Urban High School* (New York: Teachers College Press, 1990); and Ken Haycock, *Guiding Principles for Curriculum Implementation, Staff Development, and School-Based Management* (Vancouver, B.C.: Vancouver School Board, 1992).

[78]Joseph F. Rogus, "Developing a Vision Statement," *NASSP Bulletin* (February 1990), pp. 6–12; Kenneth A. Leithwood, "The Move Toward Transformational Leadership," *Educational Leadership* (February 1992), pp. 8–12.

[79]Gene I. Maeroff, *The Empowerment of Teachers: Overcoming the Crisis of Confidence* (New York: Teachers College Press, 1988); Susan Moore Johnson, *Teachers at Work* (New York: Basic Books, 1990); and Richard S. Sagor, "Three Principals Who Make a Difference," *Educational Leadership* (February 1992), pp. 13–18.

[80]Beverly Showers, Bruce Joyce, and Barrie Bennett, "Synthesis of Research on Staff Development," *Educational Leadership* (November 1987), pp. 77–87; Virginia Richardson, "Significant and Worthwhile Change in Teaching Practice," *Educational Researcher* (October 1990), pp. 10–18; Bruce B. Joyce and Marcia Weil, *Models of Teaching,* 2nd ed. (Englewood Cliffs, N.J.: Prentice-Hall, 1991); and Andrea Bartlett, "Teachers as Leaders of Staff Development" (Paper presented at the Annual Meeting of the American Educational Research Association, San Francisco, April 1992).

OTHER EFFORTS TO IMPROVE SCHOOL EFFECTIVENESS

Practically everyone who wants to change education says that the reason to reform schools is so that they will be more "effective."[81] We do not have space to describe all the projects that are under discussion nationally to achieve this end, but several of the more important efforts are discussed briefly in the following pages.

Cooperation with Other Institutions

Examples of cooperation

Many schools and school districts are attempting to improve the quality of education in elementary and secondary schools by cooperating with other institutions, particularly those in business and industry. Some of the most promising efforts along these lines include the following:

> "Partnership" or "adopt-a-school" programs in which a business, a church, a university, or some other community institution works closely with an individual school in providing assistance such as tutors or lecturers, funds or equipment for vocational studies, computer education, or help in curriculum development.[82]

> Cooperative implementation of activities such as health education or drug education.[83]

Joint conduct of projects

> Joint conduct of school improvement projects in which the emphasis is on helping faculty utilize research to improve curriculum and instruction.[84]

> Funding of student awards for reading books or other positive behaviors.[85]

Boston Compact

An even more far-reaching example of cooperation with public schools is the Boston Compact. In forming the compact in 1982, business leaders agreed to recruit at least two hundred companies that would hire graduates of the Boston public schools and also provide employment for students. In return, school officials agreed to establish competency requirements for graduation, increase placement rates of graduates into higher education as well as into full-time employment, and reduce dropout and absenteeism rates. The message sent to city

---

[81]For examples, see C. June Marker and Shirley W. Schiever, "Excellence for the Future," *Gifted Child Quarterly* (Winter 1984), pp. 6–8; Adrian Steinberg, "Guidance and Counseling: Too Little, Too Late?" *The Harvard Education Letter* (June 1988), pp. 1–5; and Harold M. Williams, "Why Ignore Art Education in Our Reforms?" *Education Week*, February 26, 1992, p. 32.

[82]Manuel J. Justiz and Marily C. Kameen, "Business Offers a Hand to Education," *Phi Delta Kappan* (January 1987), pp. 379–383; Joel Keehn, "How Business Helps the Schools," *Fortune*, October 21, 1991, p. 161; and Ann M. Farrell, "What Teachers Can Learn from Industry Internships," *Educational Leadership* (March 1992), pp. 38–39.

[83]Anne Tumbaugh Lockwood, "School-Community Collaboration," *Focus in Change* (Fall 1991), p. 1.

[84]James L. Johnson, "Creating Science Literacy," *The New York Times*, October 9, 1990, p. A15; Diana L. Pabst, "Human Retooling," *Agenda* (Winter 1992), pp. 52–53.

[85]Anne Lewis, "Business Gets Serious About Saving Our Schools," *Human Capital* (July 1990), pp. 28–31.

Many school districts are cooperating with business and industry to improve the quality of education in their schools. (© Charlie Archambault)

students is "If you stay in school, work hard, and master the basics, you will be helped to find a job."

By 1990 nearly four hundred companies were participating in the compact, activities had expanded to include more than twenty local colleges and universities, and tens of thousands of Boston students had been placed in summer jobs programs or had received help in obtaining full-time jobs after graduation. Data collected by compact officials indicate that very high proportions of high-school graduates in Boston either enter college or are employed full time, and most college entrants are persisting to graduation.[86] The apparent success of the Boston Compact has helped stimulate the initiation of similar projects elsewhere.[87]

Compact approach has spread

Among the other projects initiated by corporations in the late 1980s and early 1990s have been the following:[88]

---

[86]Robert Schwartz and Jeannette Hargroves, "The Boston Compact," *Metropolitan Education* (Winter 1986–87), pp. 14–25; Susan Diesenhouse, "Harvest of Diplomas for Boston Poor," *The New York Times,* May 24, 1989, p. 25; and Jonathan Weisman, "Uncertainties Over Funding Slow Start of New Assessment System in Boston," *Education Week,* December 12, 1990, p. 8.

[87]Robert Rothman, "Schools, Businesses Form Partnership in 7 Cities," *Education Week,* February 25, 1987, p. 4; Randy L. Dewar and Barbara Sprong, "No Diploma, No Job," *The American School Board Journal* (October 1991), pp. 38–39.

[88]Michael Timpane, "Business Has Rediscovered the Public Schools," *Phi Delta Kappan* (February 1984), pp. 389–392; Laurie Miller McNeill, "What America's Public Schools Really Need," *Human Capital* (July 1990), pp. 34–39; and Julia Angwin, "School Up for Adoption," *The New York Times Education Life,* January 5, 1992, p. 18.

Projects supported by corporations

- IBM set aside $25 million for school-reform projects.

- RJR Nabisco allocated $30 million to help implement educational improvements.

- Citibank announced it will spend more than $20 million to help improve the public schools.

- General Electric committed nearly $20 million to assist disadvantaged college-bound youth.

Foundations contribute

Philanthropic foundations also have become much more active (and generous) in providing funds to help improve education at all levels. For example, the MacArthur Foundation is providing $40 million to support reform efforts in the Chicago Public Schools, the Coca-Cola Foundation announced that it will donate $50 million to support education-improvement activities in the 1990s, and the Baltimore Foundation created a $25 million endowment to support that city's public schools.[89]

Privatization.   Recent efforts to involve business in public education have extended beyond the provision of financial support and staff assistance to the **privatization** of educational services. Privatization of public-school functions refers to arrangements wherein funds and responsibilities for operating a school or some of its programs are contracted out to private agencies. Several prominent analysts have argued that privatization can produce higher student performance at a lower cost than is likely at most public schools.

Contracting out

Dade County Project

The most publicized educational privatization experiment to date was initiated in the Dade County (Florida) Public Schools, where a corporation called Educational Alternatives, Inc., has contracted to operate an elementary school. Educational Alternatives promises to generate high achievement levels regardless of students' socioeconomic background. Numerous privatization experiments are being considered and, in some cases, initiated in other school districts, frequently in connection with the New American Schools (NAS) program proposed as part of the federal government's "America 2000" school-reform efforts.[90]

Guaranteed Postsecondary Access for High-School Graduates.   As noted above, a key component in the Boston Compact (and other similar projects elsewhere) is guaranteed support from business to help students attend postsecondary schools. In a growing number of communities, similar support is being provided by wealthy individuals, foundations, community agencies, colleges and

Support for college attendance

---

[89]"Baltimore Foundation Blazes New Trail," *Minority Funding Report* (May 1989), p. 2; Ann Bradley, "Chicago Reforms to Get $40 Million from MacArthur," *Education Week,* October 17, 1990, pp. 1, 22.

[90]Myron Lieberman, *Prioritization and Educational Choice* (New York: Saint Martin's Press, 1989); Kenneth J. Cooper, "Making It Better One School at a Time," *The Washington Post Weekly National Edition,* September 9–15, 1991, p. 34; Denis P. Doyle, "America 2000," *Phi Delta Kappan* (November 1991), pp. 185–191; and Alan November, "Breaking the Mold," *Electronic Learning* (January 1992), p. 50.

universities, and state or local governments. Well-known projects that help provide such support include[91]

- The *I Have a Dream Program* sponsored by Eugene Lang for students at P.S. 121 in New York City. In 1991, 38 of these students were attending postsecondary institutions.

- *Project Choice* in Kansas City, Kansas, and Kansas City, Missouri. A foundation organized by Ewing and Marian Kauffman provides funding and related services for 1,991 sophomores, juniors, and seniors at one high school and 150 students at five additional schools. Participating students must maintain acceptable academic and behavior standards and pass random drug tests.

- Indiana's *21st Century Scholars* project, which contributes the difference between tuition costs and financial aid for which a low-income applicant otherwise qualifies.

- Louisiana's *Taylor Plan*, which provides free tuition at state colleges and universities for students with low and moderate income.

Projects proliferate

Programs that guaranteed postsecondary access proliferated rapidly in the late 1980s and early 1990s. By 1991, 141 sponsors were helping to support programs similar to I Have a Dream in 41 cities. As the U.S. Government General Accounting Office reported, these programs generally combine "a financial aid guarantee, personal, often intense, mentoring, and a wide range of program elements aimed at increasing both motivation and academic skills."[92]

Rural Education

Diversity in rural communities

Much of the problem that educators face in trying to improve rural education derives from the extreme diversity of rural locations, which makes it difficult to generalize across many communities. One group of observers who attempted to address this problem agreed that rural school districts can be defined as those that have fewer than 150 residents per square mile and are located in counties in which at least 60 percent of the population resides in communities with populations under 5,000. However, within this definition rural communities exemplify hundreds of "subcultures," which differ from one location to another in racial/ethnic composition, extent of remoteness, economic structure, and other

[91]Michael Newman, "Rhode Island's 'Crusade' Offers College Aid, Mentoring Program," *Education Week*, September 9, 1989, p. 8; Don Wycliff, "Help Is Given in the Pursuit of Education Dream," *The New York Times*, June 20, 1990, p. B9; Jacqueline Conciatore, "The Louisiana Taylor Plan," *Black Issues in Higher Education*, July 4, 1991, pp. 3–4; Michael deCourcy Hinds, "Strangers' Generosity Steers Young to College," *The New York Times*, August 21, 1991, p. A17; and Millicent Lawton, "Lean on Me," *Teacher Magazine* (March 1992), p. 18.
[92]Eleanore Chelimsky, *Private Programs Guaranteeing Student Aid for Higher Education* (Washington, D.C.: General Accounting Office, 1990), p. 2. Also see Stephen F. Hamilton and Mary Agnes Hamilton, "Mentoring Programs: Promise and Paradox," *Phi Delta Kappan* (March 1992), pp. 546–550.

characteristics. Approximately one-fourth of U.S. elementary and secondary students attend rural schools.[93]

Delivering quality rural education

Partly because of this diversity, the particular problems of rural schools have received relatively little attention during the past fifty years. Recently, however, a small group of scholars has been trying to determine what should be done to provide high-quality education in a rural setting. Specialists in rural education have reached several major conclusions.[94]

1. The critical elements for rural school improvement are community dependent. For this reason, some innovations that are effective in urban areas tend not to work well in rural areas.

2. Because of the tremendous diversity in rural America, school improvement efforts also should be diverse.

3. The small scale of rural schools offers advantages. Teachers can know students personally, and schools can work closely with community agencies.

4. Economic recession has made public education an even more important force than it has been traditionally in providing skilled personnel and jobs in rural communities.

Other possible improvements

Other authors have concluded that teacher-training programs for rural areas should prepare teachers in a larger number of content areas for a broader age range of students than do conventional programs. As Chapter 6 points out, educators also are reassessing the desirability of school consolidation in light of the advantages that can be present for teachers and students in very small schools.[95]

Rural schools face increasing problems in the supply of qualified teachers. Because many states have increased certification requirements and reduced the flexibility that allowed teachers to be employed without proper certification, some rural districts have been unable either to find or to afford sufficient teaching personnel, particularly in science, math, and foreign languages.[96] This problem can be overcome, in part, by the use of television, interactive computers,

Distance education

and other forms of **distance education** that deliver instruction in a cost-effective manner. In addition to expanding access to high-quality teachers, distance education can accomplish several purposes, such as facilitating contact

---

[93]Michael Newman, "Too Many Districts?" *Teacher* (March 1990), pp. 12–13; Keith Geiger, "The Forgotten America," *Education Week,* January 15, 1992, p. 4.

[94]Paul W. Nachtigal, ed., *Rural Education* (Boulder, Colo.: Westview, 1982); Joyce D. Stern, ed., *Rural Education* (Washington, D.C.: U.S. Department of Education, 1989); Darryl J. Hobbs, *Education Reform and Rural Economic Health* (Charleston, W.Va.: Appalachian Educational Laboratory, 1990); and DeYoung, "Economic Underdevelopment and Its Effects."

[95]Sara Massey and Jeanie Crosby, "Special Problems, Special Opportunities: Preparing Teachers for Rural Schools," *Phi Delta Kappan* (December 1983), pp. 265–269; Alan J. DeYoung, "The Status of American Rural Education Research: An Integrated Review and Commentary," *Review of Educational Research* (Summer 1987), pp. 123–148; and "Multigrade Classroom Training Guide," *The Northwest Report* (May 1991), p. 5.

[96]E. Robert Stephens, "Rural Problems Jeopardize Reform," *Education Week,* October 7, 1987, pp. 25–26; William Celis 3d., North Dakota Districts Are Facing Rising Tide in Nation: Consolidation," *The New York Times,* April 3, 1991, p. B7; and Bruce O. Barker, *The Distance Education Handbook* (Washington, D.C.: ERIC, 1992).

between schools, delivering staff development programs, and providing special-ized courses.[97]

Cooperation among districts

Cooperation among school districts also appears to be expanding as a means to improve rural school effectiveness. Rural districts frequently share specialists in staff development, evaluation, and other areas, and many work together to provide vocational education, special education, and other services (see Chapter 6). Cooperation with business also may be helpful in developing more financial and community support.[98]

For low-income students in Appalachia and other areas of rural poverty, educators are trying to find ways to adapt curriculum and instruction to their students' social and cultural backgrounds. Examples of such adaptation can be found in the Foxfire approach, which utilizes oral history and local cultural ma-terials in order to help improve students' understanding and motivation inside and outside the school.[99]

Effectiveness of Nonpublic Schools

The question of whether nonpublic schools are more effective than public schools in bringing about high academic achievement and accomplishing other goals has emerged as an important issue in education. As we mention in Chapter 7, proposals have been made to provide families with vouchers and tax credits to support attendance at nonpublic schools, and some movement is occurring in these directions. To some extent, the desirability of such proposals hinges on the argument that nonpublic schools tend to be more effective than public schools.

Vouchers and tax credits proposed

Coleman study conclusions

Debate regarding the effectiveness of nonpublic schools has been spurred by studies in which James Coleman and his colleagues compared nonpublic and public schools.[100] Among the major conclusions of these studies were the follow-ing: (1) when family background variables are accounted for, students in non-public schools have higher achievement than students in public schools; (2) nonpublic schools provide a safer and more orderly environment; (3) except for

---

[97]Kenneth H. Hansen, *Distance Education and the Small School* (Portland, Ore.: Northwest Regional Educational Laboratory, 1987); Ruth E. Randall, "Trio of Telecommunications Projects Are Par-adigms for Rural Education," *T.H.E. Journal* (May 1991), pp. 71–72; and Lynne Schrum, "What Is Distance Education?" *Principal* (January 1992), pp. 56–57.

[98]Charles Dervarics, "Rural Educators Seek Answers to Funding Problems," *Education Daily*, Oc-tober 19, 1987, p. 3; Andy Sommer, *Rural School District Cooperatives* (Portland, Ore.: Northwest Regional Educational Laboratory, 1990); and "Schools Play Key Role in Distressed Rural Com-munities," *The Northwest Report* (January 1992), pp. 1, 5.

[99]Jane H. Arends, *Building on Excellence: Regional Priorities for the Improvement of Rural, Small Schools* (Washington, D.C.: Council for Educational Development and Research, 1987); Steve Nelson, "Small, Rural Schools Use Innovative Ideas to Renew Curricula," *The Northwest Report* (May 1991), pp. 1, 4–5; and Eliot Wigginton, "Culture Begins at Home," *Educational Leadership* (January 1992), pp. 60–64.

[100]James Coleman, Thomas Hoffer, and Sally Kilgore, *Public and Private Schools* (Washington, D.C.: National Center for Education Statistics, 1981); James Coleman, Thomas Hoffer, and Sally Kilgore, *High School Achievement: Public, Catholic, and Private Schools Compared* (New York: Basic Books, 1982); and James S. Coleman, *Equality and Achievement in Education* (Boulder, Colo.: Westwood, 1990).

Catholic schools, nonpublic schools are smaller, have smaller classes, and encourage more student participation than do public schools; (4) nonpublic schools require more homework and have better attendance; and (5) superiority in school climate and discipline accounts for the higher achievement of students in nonpublic schools.

Chubb and Moe conclusions

John Chubb and Terry Moe of the Brookings Institution also have conducted studies of achievement differentials between public and nonpublic schools. After analyzing their data Chubb and Moe concluded that nonpublic schools produce higher achievement than do public schools, and they further concluded that a major reason for this difference is that nonpublic schools tend to function more autonomously and with less bureaucracy. For example, principals of public schools are much more constrained than their counterparts in nonpublic schools with respect to hiring and firing teachers. In addition, public schools tend to be more complex and more susceptible to diverse pressures created by a variety of external constituencies (e.g., central offices, numerous groups representing taxpayers, state government officials) than are nonpublic schools; as a result, teachers and students in public schools are relatively more likely to receive mixed messages about the priority goals in their schools, and are relatively less inclined to work together to achieve these goals.[101]

Criticisms of research on nonpublic schools

Many analysts have published strong criticisms of the statistical methods and interpretations in studies reported by Coleman and his colleagues, Chubb and Moe, and other researchers who have concluded that nonpublic schools produce higher achievement than public schools. Critics give the following reasons for disagreeing with this conclusion: (1) obtaining better measures or otherwise taking better account of family background variables virtually eliminates the achievement superiority of nonpublic students; (2) taking account of achievement level upon entry to high school also eliminates the achievement difference between public and nonpublic students; (3) statistical methods the researchers employed were inappropriate and led to misleading and unjustified conclusions; and (4) whatever differences may exist between Catholic or other nonpublic schools on the one hand and public schools on the other are trivial and have few long-term effects.[102]

Coleman and his colleagues as well as Chubb and Moe have responded with data and arguments offering further support for their original conclusions. In particular, they have argued that nonpublic schools enhance achievement by placing a relatively high percentage of students in college-bound programs. But since it is difficult to isolate differences in student motivation even after one has

---

[101]John E. Chubb and Terry M. Moe, *Politics, Markets, and America's Schools* (Washington, D.C.: The Brookings Institution, 1990).

[102]Ellis B. Page and Timothy Z. Keith, "Effects of U.S. Private Schools: A Technical Analysis of Two Recent Claims," *Educational Researcher* (August–September 1981), pp. 7–22; Arthur Goldberger and Glen Cain, "The Causal Analysis of Cognitive Outcomes in the Coleman, Hoffer, and Kilgore Report," *Sociology of Education* (April 1982), pp. 103–122; Timothy Z. Keith and Ellis B. Page, "Do Catholic High Schools Improve Minority Student Achievement?" *American Educational Research Journal* (Fall 1985), pp. 337–349; Edward H. Haertel, Thomas James, and Henry M. Levin, eds., *Comparing Public and Private Schools* (Philadelphia: Taylor and Francis, 1987); John F. Witte, *Choice in American Education* (Madison: University of Wisconsin, 1990); and Bella Rosenberg, "Not a Case for Market Control," *Educational Leadership* (January 1991), pp. 64–65.

taken account of family background and social class, researchers probably will continue to argue over the relative effectiveness of public and nonpublic schools.[103]

Magnet and Alternative Schools

Many efforts to improve and reform the public schools have involved the establishment of magnet and alternative schools. **Magnet schools** are designed to attract voluntary enrollment by offering special programs or curricula that appeal to students from more than one neighborhood. Some magnet schools, such as the Bronx High School of Science in New York City, have existed for many years. Such schools usually were not referred to as magnets until the 1970s, when many big-city districts established magnet schools to increase voluntary desegregation.

Voluntary desegregation

Rather than serving only an academic elite, magnet schools today generally are designed to provide students of all ability levels with an opportunity to participate in a specialized or alternative instructional program not available in their local schools. This approach has been a major thrust of activity in many cities. Since 1977, for example, Milwaukee has established magnet schools in such areas as visual and performing arts, applied technology, marketing and business, college preparation, finance and commerce, communications and media, and health sciences. As we pointed out in Chapter 11, magnet schools have helped to increase desegregation significantly in many urban school districts.[104]

Milwaukee magnets

Alternative schools provide learning opportunities that are not available in the average public school. From this point of view magnet schools are a type of alternative school. So, too, are many parochial and other nonpublic schools; institutions such as street academies, storefront schools, and high-school "outposts" designed to make education more relevant for inner-city students; and "schools without walls," which draw heavily on community resources for learning.[105] Studies of alternative schools have indicated that they usually enroll students who have not succeeded in traditional schools or who want a different kind of education. Compared to traditional schools, alternative schools allow for greater individualization, more independent study, and more openness to the outside community; they tend to have small size, high staff morale, high atten-

Types of alternative schools

Characteristics of alternative schools

---

[103]James S. Coleman and Thomas Hoffer, "Response to Taeuber-James-Cain-Goldberger and Morgan," *Sociology of Education* (October 1983), pp. 218–234; James S. Coleman and Thomas Hoffer, *Public and Private High Schools* (New York: Basic Books, 1987); Robert Rothman, "Debate on Merits of Public, Private Schools Reignites," *Education Week,* September 18, 1991, pp. 1, 16; and John E. Chubb and Terry M. Moe, "Private Versus Public, Research Versus Rhetoric," *Education Week,* April 15, 1992, p. 19.

[104]Daniel U. Levine and Eugene E. Eubanks, "The Promise and Limits of Regional Desegregation Plans for Central City School Districts," *Metropolitan Education* (Spring 1986), pp. 36–51; Nolan Estes, Daniel U. Levine, and Donald R. Waldrip, eds., *Magnet Schools* (Austin, Tex.: Reho, 1990); and Robert A. Dentler, *The National Evidence on Magnet Schools* (Los Alamitos, Calif.: Southwest Regional Educational Laboratory, 1992).

[105]Daniel U. Levine, "Educating Alienated Inner City Youth: Lessons from the Street Academies," *Journal of Negro Education* (Spring 1975), pp. 139–148; Timothy W. Young, *Public Alternative Education* (New York: Teachers College Press, 1990).

dance, satisfied students, freedom from external control, and strong concern for noncognitive goals of education.[106]

Advocates of alternative schools point out that only one model of education typically is available to parents in any given public-school neighborhood. Some advocates argue for creating alternative schools within the system; others contend that the only true alternatives are outside the system. Either way, both types of advocates generally stress the value of providing students with opportunities to choose the type of school they wish to attend.[107] This consideration brings us to the hotly debated topic of school choice.

School Choice Proposals and Developments

In recent years, **school choice** plans have been advocated by a large collection of persons and groups who perceive them as a way to introduce greater flexibility and accountability into education. The basic idea is to enhance students' opportunities to choose where they will enroll and what they will study. Recent developments include the following:

Developments in school choice

■ After referring to school choice as "perhaps the single most promising idea" for advancing national efforts to improve education, President George Bush proposed that vouchers be made available so that students can attend whatever schools they choose, whether public or nonpublic. A component in part of the president's larger reform plan titled "America 2000," this voucher proposal encountered considerable opposition and was rejected by Congress.[108]

■ Legislators in Colorado, Minnesota, Washington, and other states have either introduced or approved laws expanding students' attendance options. Colorado's legislation requires that all districts allow students to transfer freely within their boundaries. Minnesota's comprehensive choice plan not only supports both intradistrict and interdistrict transfers but also provides for establishment and expansion of alternative schools and programs. Washington's legislation provides students who experience a "special hardship or detrimental condition" with an absolute right to enroll in another school district that has available space; it also requires districts to accept students

---

[106]Mary Anne Raywid, "Synthesis of Research on Schools of Choice," *Educational Leadership* (April 1984), pp. 70–78; Mary Anne Raywid, "Excellence and Choice: Friends or Foes?" *The Urban Review* (no. 1, 1987), pp. 35–47; and Mary Anne Raywid, "The Role of Alternative Schools in Urban Education," in John J. Lane and Edgar Epps, eds., *Restructuring Schools* (Berkeley, Calif.: McCutchan, 1992).

[107]Mario D. Fantini, *Public Schools of Choice* (New York: Simon & Schuster, 1973); Charles I. Glenn, "The New Common School," *Phi Delta Kappan* (December 1987), pp. 290–294; and William L. Boyd and Herbert J. Walberg, eds., *Choice in Education* (Berkeley, Calif.: McCutchan, 1990).

[108]Susan Chira, "A Sea of Doubt Swirls Around Bush's Plan to Change the Schools," *The New York Times,* July 22, 1991, p. A9; Edward B. Fiske, "Bush's Choice," *Agenda* (Fall 1991), pp. 9–13; and Edward Kennedy, "Strengthening Education for American Families Act," *Congressional Record,* January 24, 1992, pp. S385–S386.

who transfer in to locations close to their parents' place of work or child-care site.[109]

■ After stating that business involvement in education generally had accomplished little to bring about basic reform in the schools, the chairman of the Golden Rule Insurance Company announced that his company would provide $1.2 million to help low-income children transfer to nonpublic schools.[110]

Student transfer in Wisconsin

■ The Wisconsin legislature approved a plan that provides funds to support the transfer to nonsectarian private schools of a limited number of low-income students from the Milwaukee Public Schools. More than 500 students participated in 1992.[111]

As actions such as these have expanded school choice, vast numbers of recommendations for and against additional action have been put forward. Those who support complete choice recommend enrollment within and across school district boundaries, vouchers to attend nonpublic schools, magnetization of entire school districts and regions, creation of alternative-school networks, and other options to increase student opportunities for choosing among schools. Among supporters of choice the following arguments and assertions have been most prominent:[112]

Arguments favoring choice

■ Providing choice for disadvantaged students will enable them to escape from poorly functioning schools.

■ Because public schools generally are not very successful in working with low achievers, there is little to lose in facilitating their transfer to other schools.

■ Achievement, aspirations, and other outcomes will improve for many students because they will be more motivated to succeed at schools they select voluntarily.

■ Both existing public schools and alternative learning institutions (whether public or nonpublic) will provide improved education because their staffs will be competing to attract students.

■ Increased opportunities will be available to match school programs and services with students' needs.

---

[109]William Snider, "Wash. Lawmakers Adopt School-Choice Package," *Education Week,* April 11, 1990, p. 14; Ross Corson, "Choice Ironies: Open Enrollment in Minnesota," *The American Prospect* (Fall 1990), pp. 94–99; Lynn Olson, "Proposals for Private-School Choice Reviving at All Levels of Government," *Education Week,* February 20, 1991, pp. 1, 10–11; and "Save the Next Generation," *The Wall Street Journal,* May 7, 1992, p. A14.

[110]Chris Pipho, "The Vouchers Are Coming!" *Phi Delta Kappan* (October 1991), pp. 102–103; Hilary Stout, "Business Funds Program in Indianapolis Letting Poor Children Flee Public Schools," *The Wall Street Journal,* February 27, 1992, pp. B1, B5.

[111]Polly Williams, "Get the Hostages Out," *Agenda* (Fall 1991), pp. 59–60; Larry Hayes, "A Surprising Development," *Phi Delta Kappan* (February 1992), pp. 489–490.

[112]Chubb and Moe, *Politics, Markets, and America's Schools;* John E. Coons and Stephen D. Sugarman, "The Private School Option in Systems of Educational Choice," *Educational Leadership* (January 1991), pp. 54–56; John Hood, "Choice Challenges," *Reason* (October 1991), pp. 43–50; and Seymour Fliegel, "Choosing Your Public School," *The New York Times,* January 18, 1992, p. E19.

■ Parents will be empowered and encouraged to play a larger role in their children's education.

Critics of school choice plans question the assumptions and conclusions offered by the advocates, particularly in cases that involve public financing of non-public schools. Arguments advanced most frequently by opponents and skeptics include the following:[113]

Arguments questioning choice

■ Choice plans will reinforce stratification and segregation because highly motivated or high-achieving white and minority students will be disproportionately likely to transfer out of schools that have a substantial percentage of students with low achievement or low social status.

■ Much of the movement of students will constitute the transfer of middle-class students to nonpublic schools. This point of view was expressed by Wisconsin Commissioner of Education Herbert Grover: "You'll allow the informed and influential . . . the economic royalty of this country to get subsidies . . . [and in so doing] you'll absolutely nuke the public support for the institution that serves the predominant majority of young people."

■ Public financial support for nonpublic schools is unconstitutional.

Competition not the best reform

■ Competition among schools to attract transfer students will not by itself result in improved achievement; other emerging reforms described in this chapter are more important.

■ The opening and closing of numerous schools based on their competitive attractiveness will disrupt the fundamental operation of the entire educational system.

■ There is little or no reason to believe that most schools that presently enroll relatively few disadvantaged students will be more successful with such students than are their present schools.

■ Even if one assumes that schools capable of substantially improving the performance of low achievers are widely available in a choice plan, many students and parents lack the knowledge necessary to select them, and these outstanding schools may not accept many low achievers.

■ Complications arising from the massive movement of students will hinder implementation of other reform efforts that are beginning to report significant success.

■ Although accountability may increase in the sense that unattractive schools will lose students and may even be closed, overall accountability will be reduced because nonpublic schools receiving public funds will not be subject to government standards.

■ Public financing of nonpublic institutions will result in the establishment of "cult" schools based on divisive racist or religious ideologies.

---

[113]Herbert J. Grover, "Private School Choice Is Wrong," *Educational Leadership* (January 1991), p. 51; Paul E. Heckman, "Evidence, Values, and the Revitalization of Schools," *Educational Leadership* (January 1991), pp. 14–16; Elliott Negin, "Beyond the Rhetoric," *Agenda* (Fall 1991), pp. 50–53; Abigail Thernstrom, "Hobson's Choice," *The New Republic,* July 15 and 22, 1991, pp. 13–14; and Stan Karp, "Bush Plan Abandons Schools, *Substance* (January 1992), pp. 8–9.

*Worries shared by
advocates and opponents*

Many of the worries about school choice enumerated above are shared even by persons and organizations who have been mostly supportive of proposals to expand student options. For example, John Leo believes that school choice is "reform's best choice" but also is education's "new 600-pound gorilla" that may harm education by funding schools that encourage social, racial, and economic separatism. Given that both supporters and opponents recognize the dangers and benefits in expanding choice, it is not surprising that many analysts have been trying to identify policies that could make choice plans as constructive as possible. Policies frequently proposed to accomplish this goal include the following:[114]

Polices for choice plans

■ Ensure that students and parents receive adequate counseling and information.

■ Provide free transportation, scholarships, and other support to make sure that choices are fully available and do not depend on social status.

■ Include guidelines to avoid segregation and resegregation.

■ Ensure that enrollment and admissions procedures are equitable and do not exclude large proportions of students from the most desirable schools.

■ Include provisions to release government-operated schools from regulations not imposed on nonpublic schools.

■ Do not ignore other reform necessities and possibilities; instead, treat choice as part of a comprehensive reform agenda.

Year-Round Schools

Nearly 1.5 million students in more than 20 states now attend public elementary and secondary schools that function on a year-round schedule. Most commonly, each student in a **year-round school** attends classes for nine weeks and then is scheduled for three weeks of vacation. Although a substantial proportion of year-round calendars have been established primarily to relieve overcrowding and thereby avoid very large classes or double sessions (when students attend only in the morning or afternoon), some have been introduced to improve the efficiency and effectiveness of schooling. Many educators believe that students on a year-round calendar remember more of what they learn and require less review than do students who have a two- to three-month vacation. In addition, many advocates of year-round calendars believe they can be easily used to lengthen the academic year in accordance with recommendations in *A Nation At Risk* and other national reports.[115]

*Reasons for
year-round schools*

However, districts that have considered or implemented year-round calendars frequently have confronted serious obstacles. For example, many parents

---

[114]John Leo, "School Reform's Best Choice," *U.S. News and World Report,* January 14, 1991, p. 17; Diana T. Slaughter-Defoe, "Parental Educational Choice: Some African American Dilemmas," *The Journal of Negro Education* (Summer 1991), pp. 354–360; and Harry C. Weinberg, "For School Choice, Let's Follow the F.A.A.," *Education Week,* February 12, 1992, p. 40.

[115]Seth Mydans, "In an Assault on Tradition, More Schools Last All Year," *The New York Times,* August 18, 1991, pp. 1–12; Larry Hayes, "Support for a Longer School Year," *Phi Delta Kappan* (January 1992), p. 413.

Taking Issue ◂•▸

More Time in School

One suggestion for improving student achievement has been to increase the amount of time students spend in school by lengthening the school day or school year or both. This idea is based in part on observations of countries such as Japan, where students spend considerably more time in school than do American students. It also reflects research indicating that time-on-task is an important determinant of students' performance.

Question: Should the United States extend the amount of time students spend in school?

Arguments PRO

1   Extending the school year or school day will give teachers more contact time and an opportunity to teach students in depth. This is particularly vital for at-risk students, who need special services and remedial work.

2   Experience in countries such as Japan indicates that increased time spent in school can assist in raising achievement scores. Many national task-force reports have also recommended that time in school be extended.

3   The extension of school time will help to solve the problems of latchkey children, who must look after themselves while their parents work. In this way, schools can benefit the family as well as improve education.

4   Lengthening students' time in school will indicate to taxpayers that schools are serious about raising educational standards. Taxpayers will therefore be more willing to support the schools.

5   The present system of school attendance originated in an agrarian period when children were needed to assist in farm tasks. In an industrial society, the best use of students' time is to give them additional schooling that prepares them for the world of the twenty-first century.

Arguments CON

1   Extending time in school will not compensate for the poor teaching that takes place in too many schools. The problem is not quantity but quality of schooling, and longer hours could well mean *reduced* quality.

2   So many social and cultural differences exist between Japan and the United States that simple comparisons are not valid. There is little hard evidence that increasing students' time in school will raise achievement levels in the United States.

3   The growing institutional interference with basic family life will be increased by extending the time children spend in school. Such interference, however well intentioned, contributes to the fragmentation of the modern family.

4   Extending school time will require major new expenditures to increase salaries and refurbish buildings. Taxpayers will not willingly pay for these expenses.

5   We know too little about the effects of lengthening the school day or year. Do children in our culture *need* ample breaks from school? Do their originality and creativity suffer when they are kept too long in classes? Until we have answers, we should not make students spend more time in school.

object because their children do not have a common schedule to allow for extended family vacations. School buildings in some locations must undergo expensive rehabilitation to provide air conditioning, and teachers may find that year-round calendars interfere with rewarding opportunities for summer employment. In addition, year-round schedules that are advocated or introduced primarily to reduce student vacation time and thereby lengthen the academic year may require sizable increases in per-pupil expenditures.[116]

Gifted and Talented Students

Trends in gifted education

Research on the education of gifted and talented students has increased, as has the literature describing experimental efforts and demonstration programs to enhance their learning. Reviews of the research on these topics report that there are several widespread trends in developing programs for gifted students: "radical acceleration" of their learning opportunities; provision of special "mentoring" assistance; increased emphasis on independent study and investigative learning; utilization of individualized education programs (IEPs) as in the case of students with disabilities; delivery of instruction in accordance with students' learning styles; establishment of special schools, Saturday programs, and summer schools; and increased use of community resources.[117]

Approaches in gifted education

One of the major issues in providing education for gifted and talented students is selecting effective approaches to curriculum and instruction. Scholars and practitioners have tended to emphasize either acceleration through the regular curriculum or enrichment that provides for greater depth of learning, but some have argued for a "confluent" approach that combines both acceleration and enrichment. Specialists in gifted education have reviewed the literature on differing approaches and noted that the most popular practice seems to involve relatively ineffectual efforts to find some interesting current topics and ask students to conduct independent research on them. To improve instruction, these reviewers advocated the carefully planned use of combinations of approaches that involve: (1) the "content model," which emphasizes accelerated study; (2) the "process-product model," which emphasizes enrichment provided through independent study and investigative skills; and (3) the "epistemological model," which emphasizes understanding and appreciation of systems of knowledge.[118]

---

[116]Donald Singer, "Increasing 'Time on Task' Is No Free-Cost Panacea," *Education Week*, November 13, 1991, p. 23; Nancy Phillips, "As All-Year Schools Gain Headway, One Va. Town Looks Pretty Smart," *The Philadelphia Inquirer*, March 2, 1992, pp. A1, A4.

[117]E. Paul Torrance, "Teaching Creative and Gifted Learners," in Merlin C. Wittrock, ed., *Handbook of Research on Teaching*, 3rd ed. (New York: Macmillan, 1986); Beecham Robinson, "Blending Three Methods for Teaching Gifted Minority Children" (Paper presented at the Annual Meeting of the American Educational Research Association, Boston, April 1990); and Francis X. Archambault, Jr., et al., "Regular Classroom Practices with Gifted Students" (Paper presented at the Annual Meeting of the American Educational Research Association, San Francisco, April 1992).

[118]Joyce Van Tassel-Baska, "Effective Curriculum and Instructional Models for Talented Students," *Gifted Child Quarterly* (Fall 1980), pp. 162–168; Robert E. Slavin, "Are Cooperative Learning and 'Untracking' Harmful to the Gifted?" *Educational Leadership* (March 1991), pp. 72–82; and Debra Viadero, "Budget Cutters, School Reformers Taking Aim at Gifted Education," *Education Week*, March 18, 1992, pp. 1, 14–15.

Much concern has been expressed during the past two decades regarding the low participation of minority students and economically disadvantaged students in gifted education. Evidence indicates that commonly used selection criteria frequently fail to identify disadvantaged students who might benefit from participation.[119] As Paul Torrance has commented, the concern among educators has not produced much action:

> Despite strong arguments for developing programs to meet the needs of these groups and . . . imaginative proposals for accomplishing the task, very little seems to have actually been done. State departments of education and other authorities have been unwilling to modify identification criteria that would make possible the inclusion of many gifted disadvantaged and culturally different children who are now excluded.[120]

SYSTEMIC RESTRUCTURING AND REFORM

Throughout this chapter and the book as a whole, we have discussed many innovative proposals to reform the educational system. Efforts are being initiated to improve the preparation and professionalism of teachers, modify the organization and financing of school districts, empower faculties and parents as part of school-based management, and devise more successful policies on compensatory education, special education, and multicultural education. Reformers are also urging educators and state officials to alter testing and assessment of students to place greater emphasis on higher-order skills, establish magnet and alternative schools to enhance opportunities for at-risk students, upgrade the capabilities of teachers and entire faculties in accordance with research on effective instruction and effective schools, and implement numerous other changes intended to bring about widespread improvement of the system.

In recent years many of these reform efforts have been discussed in terms of **restructuring** all or part of the educational system. While this term has been interpreted in as many differing ways as the term *reform,* it increasingly is being used to indicate the need for systemic improvement (i.e., reform that simultaneously addresses all or most major components in the overall system). For example, officials of the Education Commission of the States have stated that all parts of the educational system from "schoolhouse to statehouse" must be restructured to bring about systematic improvement in teaching and learning.[121]

---

[119]Robert Rothman, "N.Y. Chief Bars the Use of Test Scores to Set Eligibility for Enrichment Classes," *Education Week,* January 9, 1991, p. 11.

[120]Torrance, "Teaching Gifted and Creative Learners," pp. 641–642. Also see Robert E. England, Joseph Stewart, Jr., and Kenneth J. Meier, "Second Generation School Discrimination as a Barrier," *Equity and Excellence* (Summer 1990), pp. 35–40.

[121]*Restructuring Schools* (Washington, D.C.: Council of Chief State School Officers, 1989), p. 1; Jane Armstrong, "A Road Map for Restructuring Schools," *Education Week,* March 28, 1990, p. 24; Jane L. David and Michael Cohen, *State Actions to Restructure Schools: The First Steps* (Washington, D.C.: National Governors' Association, 1990), p. 1; and Chris Pipho, "Reform Versus the Status Quo," *Phi Delta Kappan* (February 1992), pp. 430–431.

Systemic coherence

When many changes are being introduced simultaneously, restructuring and reform activities must be coherent; they must be compatible with and reinforce each other, rather than constituting isolated fragments that divert time and energy from priority goals. Recognizing this imperative, analysts concerned with bringing about systemic restructuring and reform have been trying to identify packages of changes that are sufficiently comprehensive and coherent to be successful in practice. Decision makers in many school districts and state governments are devising comprehensive improvement plans that coherently address each key aspect of restructuring and reform.[122]

Origins of Kentucky reform

A good example of a coherent systemic plan at the district level can be found in the Rochester Public Schools, which we reviewed in Chapter 1. Probably the best example of such a plan at the state level is in Kentucky, where in 1989 the state supreme court declared the state's "system of common schools" unconstitutional on the grounds that it was ineffective and inequitable. The court then instructed the legislative and executive branches to modify and improve the "entire sweep of the system — all its parts and parcels." Less than a year later, the state general assembly approved and the governor signed a massive education reform bill that consists of nearly 1,000 pages and weighs about 20 pounds. Among numerous other provisions, the following changes are to be phased in by 1996:[123]

Provisions of Kentucky reform

■ Curriculum, instruction, and student assessment will be performance-based, stressing mastery-oriented learning and criterion-referenced testing.

Governance and staff development emphasized

■ All schools will establish governance councils with substantial authority to make decisions on curriculum and instruction and on how budgets will be allocated to carry out improvement plans.

■ Staff development will be provided on an ongoing basis statewide.

■ Parents will be able to withdraw their children from schools they view as inadequate or unsatisfactory.

■ Monetary and other rewards will be given to successful schools and facilities, which also will receive waivers that exempt them from most state regulations.

■ Faculty at unsuccessful schools will be reviewed to determine if they should be replaced by state-appointed teachers and administrators.

■ Youth and family service centers will be established in communities where 20 percent or more of students are from low-income families.

[122]William H. Clune, *Systemic Educational Policy* (Madison: University of Wisconsin-Madison, 1991); Marshall S. Smith and Jennifer O'Day, "Putting the Pieces Together: Systemic School Reform," *CPRE Policy Briefs* (June 1991), pp. 2–9; and Consortium on Policy Research in Education, *Education Reform from 1983 to 1990* (New Brunswick, N.J.: Rutgers University, 1992).

[123]Chris Pipho, "Re-Forming Education in Kentucky," *Phi Delta Kappan* (May 1990), pp. 662–663; Lonnie Harp, "After First Year, KY. Reforms Called 'On the Move,'" *Education Week*, April 10, 1991, pp. 1, 20, 22; Michael Jennings, "Perestroika, Kentucky Style," *Agenda* (Fall 1991), pp. 32–35; and Allan Odden, "School Finance in the 1990s," *Phi Delta Kappan* (February 1992), pp. 455–461.

■ All districts will offer at least half-day preschool programs for all disadvantaged four-year-olds.

■ Preparation and certification programs for teachers and administrators will be redesigned, an alternative certification program will be introduced, and scholarships for prospective teachers will be expanded.

■ The state's new school finance formula will provide additional funds for low-wealth districts.

■ Taxes are to be increased by billions of dollars to pay for changes designed to accomplish systemic restructuring and reform.

CONCLUSION: THE CHALLENGE FOR EDUCATION

To help meet national challenges to compete internationally and to address the problems of disadvantaged citizens, education in the United States will have to become more effective than it is today. This is true with respect to the development of higher-order skills among all segments of the student population and specifically among disadvantaged students.

New teachers will be important

Recent national proposals for educational reform have reflected these emerging concerns. During the same time, much has been learned about improving educational effectiveness at the school and classroom levels — how innovations can be introduced successfully and what might be the potential value of choice in the educational system. However, using this knowledge to fundamentally improve the schools is a difficult and complex task. New educators entering the teaching force during the next ten to twenty years will play an important part in determining whether the U.S. educational system is successful in responding to overriding national imperatives.

Summing Up

1. The educational system is being challenged to improve achievement in order to keep the United States internationally competitive and to provide equity for disadvantaged and other at-risk students.

2. Research on effective teaching and instruction provides support for appropriate emphasis on efficient classroom management, direct instruction, high time-on-task, frequent questioning of students, explicit comprehension instruction, and other methods that promote achievement.

3. Research indicates that schools that are unusually effective in improving student achievement have outstanding leadership, high expectations for students, positive home-school relations, and an orderly, humane climate. Research also has identified somewhat more specific characteristics such as curriculum alignment and schoolwide emphasis on higher-order skills.

4. It now seems possible to create effective schools, provided educators recognize and utilize what has been learned about the school improvement and reform process.

5. Greater cooperation with other institutions and establishment of magnet and other alternative schools may help to improve the effectiveness of our educational system.

6. Some research indicates that nonpublic schools are more effective than public schools, but many researchers question this conclusion.

7. Many possibilities exist for improving education through expanding school choice, but there also are many potential dangers.

8. Much needs to be done to improve rural education and education for gifted and talented students.

9. Efforts now underway to bring about systemic, coherent restructuring and reform offer great promise for improving the quality and effectiveness of education.

Key Terms

direct instruction (*617*)

explicit teaching (*617*)

time-on-task (*618*)

explicit comprehension instruction (*620*)

strategic teaching (*620*)

homogeneous grouping (*622*)

tracking (*622*)

curriculum alignment (*624*)

school-within-a-school (*626*)

achievement centers (*626*)

Achievement Goals Program (*629*)

privatization (*640*)

distance education (*642*)

magnet schools (*645*)

alternative schools (*645*)

school choice (*646*)

year-round school (*649*)

restructuring (*652*)

Discussion Questions

1. How can schools and school districts become more effective than they are now? What kinds of resources are needed to make this possible?

2. What does the research say about the relative effectiveness of public and nonpublic schools?

3. Why should educators be somewhat cautious in reading and interpreting research on effective schools? What mistakes are most likely to be made in interpreting this research?

4. What are some of the major obstacles in working to improve students' higher-order skills? What can be done to attain this goal at the school and classroom levels?

5. Why is school effectiveness so dependent on what happens in the school as a whole, not just in individual classrooms?

Suggested Readings

Brookover, Wilbur, et al. *Creating Effective Schools*. Holmes Beach, Fla.: Learning Publications, 1982.

> *Chapters are devoted to improvement of school climate, high expectations for learning, and other aspects of effective schools.*

Fullan, Michael. *The New Meaning of Educational Change*. New York: Teachers College Press, 1991.

> *Fullan combines excellent analysis of both the theoretical basis and the practical implications of research on the school change process.*

Goodlad, John I. *A Place Called School*. New York: McGraw-Hill, 1984.

> *This is a thoughtful analysis of the problems and possibilities for reform in elementary and secondary schools, beginning with a chapter entitled "Can We Have Effective Schools?" and concluding with two excellent chapters, "Improving the Schools We Have" and "Beyond the Schools We Have."*

Jones, Beau Fly, and Lorna Idol, eds. *Dimensions of Thinking and Cognitive Instruction*. Hillsdale, N.J.: Erlbaum, 1990.

> *Here is much of what you always wanted to know about instruction to develop higher-order skills.*

Nachtigal, Paul M. *Rural Education*. Boulder, Colo.: Westview Press, 1982.

> *The author reviews the special problems of rural education and promising avenues for improvement.*

Strickland, Dorothy S., and Eric J. Cooper, eds. *Educating Black Children: America's Challenge*. Washington, D.C.: Howard University, 1987.

> *Selections address a diversity of topics on school reform and effectiveness.*

Insert and Endpaper Acknowledgments and Sources

Insert Page 1

Figure 1, Public School Enrollment, 1880–2000: *Historical Statistics of the United States* (Washington, D.C.: U.S. Bureau of the Census, 1960), p. 207; Valena D. Plisko and Joyce D. Stern, *The Condition of Education, 1985* (Washington, D.C.: U.S. Government Printing Office, 1985), p. 18; and *Projections of Education Statistics to 2002* (Washington, D.C.: National Center for Education Statistics, 1991), p. 9.

Figure 2, Private Elementary and Secondary School Enrollment, 1991: *Public and Private Elementary and Secondary Education Statistics: School Year 1991–92* (Washington, D.C.: National Center for Education Statistics, 1991), p. 4.

Insert Page 2

Figure 3, Racial/Ethnic Distribution of Students, 1976 and 1986: *1986 State Summaries of Elementary and Secondary School Civil Rights Survey* (Washington, D.C.: U.S. Department of Education, Office for Civil Rights, 1987); and *Common Core of Data Survey* (Washington, D.C.: National Center for Education Statistics).

Figure 4, Public School Enrollment by Race/Ethnicity, 1985–1992 (projected): Western Interstate Commission for Higher Education.

Figure 5, Children 5 Years and Older from Homes Where a Language Other Than English Is Spoken, 1980 and 1990: *1980 Census of Population, vol. 1, Characteristics of the Population* (Washington, D.C.: U.S. Department of Commerce, Bureau of the Census, 1984), chap. D, part 1, sec. A, table 1, table 256.

Insert Page 3

Figure 6, Public High School Graduates by Race/Ethnicity, 1985 and 1992 (projected): Western Interstate Commission for Higher Education.

Figure 7, Sources of U.S. Immigration, 1981–1990: *Household and Family Characteristics: March 1991* (Washington, D.C.: U.S. Department of Commerce, Bureau of the Census, Current Population Reports, 1991), p. 50, table 2.

Figure 8, Immigrants to the United States, 1820–1990: *Historical Statistics of the United States, Colonial Times to 1970* (Washington, D.C.: U.S. Department of Commerce, Bureau of the Census, 1975); *Statistical Abstract of the United States, 1991* (Washington, D.C.: U.S. Department of Commerce, Bureau of the Census, 1990).

Insert Page 4

Figure 9, Single-Parent Households, 1976–1991 (as Percentage of All Households with Children Under 18): *Statistical Abstract of the United States, 1985* (Washington, D.C.: U.S. Department of Commerce, Bureau of the Census, 1991), p. 46, table 64; *Statistical Abstract of the United States, 1987* (Washington, D.C.: U.S. Department of Commerce, Bureau of the Census, 1991), p. 48, table 66; *Statistical Abstract of the United States, 1988* (Washington, D.C.: U.S. Department of Commerce, Bureau of the Census, 1991), p. 49, table 68; *Household and Family Characteristics: March 1991* (Washington, D.C.: U.S. Department of Commerce, Bureau of the Census, Population Reports, 1991), p. 10, table G.

Figure 10, Changes in Make-Up of Single-Parent Families, from 1970 and 1991: "The Changes in One-Parent Families," *New York Times,* May 26, 1992, p. A12. Copyright © 1992 by The New York Times Company. Reprinted by permission.

Insert Page 5

Figure 11, Working Mothers, 1940–1990: U.S. Department of Commerce, Bureau of the Census, 1978; U.S. Department of Labor, Bureau of Labor Statistics, 1988; *Poverty in the United States: 1990* (Washington, D.C.: U.S. Department of Commerce, Bureau of the Census, 1991).

Figure 12, Percentage of Children Under 18 in Poverty, by Race/Ethnicity, 1960–1990: *Poverty in the United States* (various years) (Washington, D.C.: U.S. Department of Commerce, Bureau of the Census).

Insert Page 6

Figure 13, Teacher Characteristics, 1976 and 1991: *The Status of the American Public School Teacher* (Washington, D.C.: National Education Association, 1992).

Figure 14, Estimated Supply and Demand for New Teacher Graduates, 1970–1990: *Projections of Education Statistics to 1992–1993* (Washington, D.C.: U.S. Government Printing Office, 1985), p. 79, table B-23.

Back Endpapers

Figure 1, U.S. State Education Expenditures Per Student, 1990–91: *Estimates of School Statistics, 1990–91* (Washington, D.C.: National Education Association, 1991), p. 7.

Figure 2, Percentage of Total U.S. School Revenues from Federal, State, and Local Governments, 1929–30 to 1990–91: Joyce D. Stern and Marjorie O. Chandler, *The Condition of Education, 1987* (Washington, D.C.: U.S. Government Printing Office, 1987), p. 36, table 1.13; *Digest of Education Statistics, 1982* (Washington, D.C.: National Center for Education Statistics, 1982), p. 75, table 66; *Digest of Education Statistics, 1983–84* (Washington, D.C.: National Center for Education Statistics, 1984), p. 77, table 62; and *Estimates of School Statistics, 1990–91* (Washington, D.C.: National Education Association, 1991), pp. 6–7.

Figure 3, Education Expenditures Per Student in 15 Industrial Countries: F. Howard Nelson, *International Comparison of Public Spending on Education* (Washington, D.C.: American Federation of Teachers, 1991), pp. 32–34, tables 4–6.

Figure 4, Gross Domestic Product Per Capita in 15 Industrial Countries: F. Howard Nelson, *International Comparison of Public Spending on Education* (Washington, D.C.: American Federation of Teachers, 1991), pp. 32–34, tables 4–6.

Figure 5, Ratio of Pupils to Teachers in 15 Industrial Countries: F. Howard Nelson, *International Comparison of Public Spending on Education* (Washington, D.C.: American Federation of Teachers, 1991), pp. 32–34, tables 4–6.

Glossary

Academic freedom   A protection permitting teachers to teach subject matter and choose instructional materials relevant to the course without restriction from administrators or other persons outside the classroom.

Academy   A type of private or semipublic secondary school that was dominant in the United States from 1830 through 1870.

Accountability   Holding teachers, administrators, and/or school board members responsible for student performance, or relating education expenditures to outcomes.

Acculturation   The process beginning at infancy by which a human being acquires the culture of his or her society.

Activity-centered curriculum   A curriculum that emphasizes purposeful and real-life experiences and, more recently, student participation in school and community activities; a type of student-centered curriculum.

Aesthetics   The branch of axiology that examines questions of beauty and art.

Affirmative action   A method of redressing the wrongs of past discrimination against minorities and women in employment and education by giving preferential treatment to selected groups on the basis of sex, race, and ethnic background. Usually such plans require goals and timetables.

Aims   Broad statements that provide general guidelines for what schools should teach; these are value-laden statements frequently developed by national or state commissions or task forces.

Alternative certification   Teacher certification obtained without completing a traditional teacher-education program at a school or college of education.

Alternative school   A school, public or nonpublic, that provides learning opportunities different from those in local public schools.

At-risk students   Students who are low achievers and/or are alienated from school; students considered to be at risk of either dropping out of school or of not acquiring sufficient education to succeed in the economy.

Axiology   The area of philosophy that examines value issues, especially in ethics and aesthetics.

Back-to-basics curriculum   Emphasis on the three Rs at the elementary level and academic subjects at the secondary level; also includes a defined minimum level of academic standards; a type of subject-centered curriculum.

Bilingual education   Instruction in their native language provided for students whose first language is not English.

Block grants   General educational grants from the federal government to the states; each state is free to choose the specific programs for which the funds will be spent.

Board of education (local)   A group of people, elected or appointed, given authority by the state to operate the schools within a defined school district or location.

Career ladder   The arrangement of teaching positions in a series of steps, with inexperienced teachers at the bottom and the most highly qualified at the top; promotion from one step to the next usually brings additional responsibilities as well as a higher salary.

Categorical grants   Grants designated for specific groups and purposes; the method of federal education funding before the 1980s.

Certification   State government review and approval providing a teaching candidate with permission to teach.

Chapter 1   A portion of the federal Educational Consolidation and Improvement Act that provides funds to improve the education of economically disadvantaged students.

Chief state school officer A person serving as chief executive of the state board of education; sometimes called the state superintendent or commissioner of education.

Child-centered curriculum A curriculum rooted in the works of Rousseau, Pestalozzi, Froebel, and Montessori; combines academic work with play (at the primary grade levels) or with students' freedom to pursue their own interests (at higher levels); a type of student-centered curriculum.

Choice of schools *See* School choice.

Collective bargaining A procedure for resolving disagreements between employers and employees through negotiation; for teachers, such negotiation pertains to many aspects of their work and salary as well as their relationship with students, supervisors, and the community.

Common school A publicly supported and locally controlled elementary school.

Compensatory education An attempt to remedy the effects of environmental disadvantages through educational enrichment programs.

Competency-based teacher education An approach that requires prospective teachers to demonstrate minimum levels of performance on specified teaching tasks in actual or simulated situations.

Comprehensive high school A public high school that offers a variety of curricula, including a common core, to a diverse student population.

Consolidation The combining of small or rural school districts into larger ones.

Continuing teacher contract An employment contract that is automatically renewed from year to year without need for the teacher's signature.

Cooperative learning A form of instruction in which students are assigned to teams whose members work cooperatively on specific tasks or projects.

Core curriculum A curriculum of common courses that all students are required to take; emphasis is usually on academic achievement and traditional subject matter; a type of subject-centered curriculum.

Critical pedagogy An interpretation of schooling that views public school systems as functioning to limit opportunities for low-income students; proponents argue that teachers should be "transformative intellectuals" who work to change the system. Also known as "critical theory" or "critical discourse."

Critical thinking Solving problems by means of general concepts or higher-order relationships; instruction in critical thinking generally emphasizes basic analytical skills that can be applied to a wide variety of intellectual experiences.

Cultural pluralism Acceptance and encouragement of cultural, ethnic, and religious diversity within a larger society.

Curriculum Planned experiences provided through instruction that enable the school to meet its goals and objectives.

Curriculum alignment Coordination of instructional planning, methods, materials, and testing in order to accomplish important learning objectives.

Decentralization The division of large school districts into smaller units; although these local units have certain powers, the primary focus of authority generally remains in the central administration.

De facto segregation Segregation associated with and resulting from housing patterns.

De jure segregation Segregation resulting from laws or government action.

Department of Education *See* State department of education; U.S. Department of Education.

Desegregation Attendance by students of different racial backgrounds in the same school and classroom.

Direct instruction A systematic method of teaching that emphasizes teacher-directed instruction proceeding in small steps, usually in accordance with a six- to eight-part lesson sequence.

Distance education Instruction by people or materials that are distant from the learner in space or time; many distance education projects use television and other modern communication technologies.

Dual-track system The traditional European pattern of separate primary schools for the masses of population and preparatory and secondary schools for the upper socioeconomic classes.

Due process A formalized legal procedure with specific and detailed rules and principles designed to protect the rights of individuals.

Education The lifelong process of acquiring knowledge, skills, and values, whether by formal means such as schooling or by informal means such as discussion and personal experience.

Educational voucher A flat grant or payment representing a child's estimated school cost or portion of the cost; under a voucher system, the parent or child may choose any school, public or private, and payment is made to the school for accepting the child.

Effective schools Schools that are unusually successful in producing high student performance, compared with other schools that enroll students of similar background; sometimes defined as schools in which working-class students achieve as well as middle-class students.

Elementary school An educational institution for children in the earliest grades, generally grades one through six or one through eight; often includes kindergarten as well.

Epistemology The area of philosophy that examines knowing and theories of knowledge.

Essentialism The educational theory that emphasizes basic skills of reading, writing, and arithmetic and subject-matter disciplines such as mathematics, science, history, geography, and language.

Essentialist curriculum A curriculum based on essentialist theory and consisting of the three Rs at the elementary level and five major disciplines (English, math, science, history, and foreign language) at the secondary level; emphasis is on academic competition and excellence; a type of subject-centered curriculum.

Ethics The branch of axiology that examines questions of right and wrong and good and bad.

Ethnic group A group of people with a distinctive history, culture, and language.

Existentialism The philosophy that examines the way in which humans define their own selves by making personal choices.

Explicit teaching *See* Direct instruction.

Expulsion Dismissal of a student from school for a lengthy period, ranging from one semester to permanently.

Goals Statements of educational purpose at the school district or school level; intermediate between aims and objectives.

Head Start A federal government program that provides preschool education for economically disadvantaged students.

Hidden curriculum What students learn, other than academic content, from what they do or are expected to do in school.

High school A school for the upper grades of secondary students, commonly serving grades nine or ten through twelve.

Homogeneous grouping The practice of placing together students with similar achievement levels or ability.

Hornbook A single sheet of parchment, containing the Lord's Prayer, letters of the alphabet, and vowels, covered by the flattened horn of a cow and fastened to a flat wooden board; it was used during the colonial era in primary schools.

Humanistic curriculum A curriculum that stresses the personal and social aspects of the student's growth and development; emphasis is on self-actualizing processes and on moral, aesthetic, and higher domains of thinking; a type of student-centered curriculum.

Idealism The philosophy that construes reality to be spiritual or nonmaterial in essence.

Independent school A private school not sponsored by a church or religious group.

Individualized instruction Curriculum content and instructional materials and activities designed for individual learning; the pace, interests, and abilities of the learner are taken into consideration.

In loco parentis A Latin term meaning "in the place of a parent"; a concept whereby a teacher or school administrator assumes the rights, duties, and responsibilities of a parent during the hours the child attends school.

Instruction The methods and materials of the teacher designed to implement the curriculum.

Integration The step beyond simple desegregation whereby effective action is taken to develop positive interracial contacts and to improve the performance of low-achieving minority students.

Intermediate unit An educational unit or agency in the middle position between the state department of education and the local school district; usually created by the state to provide supplementary services and support staff to local school districts.

Junior high school A two- to three-year school intermediate between elementary and high school, commonly for grades seven through nine.

Kindergarten A school or division of a school for children below the first grade, usually for children between the ages of four and six; an educational environment first designed by Froebel in the mid-nineteenth century.

Land-grant college A state college or university, offering agricultural and mechanical curricula, funded originally by the Morrill Act of 1862.

Latin grammar school A college preparatory school of the colonial era that emphasized Latin and Greek studies.

Lead teacher *See* Master (or lead) teacher.

Least restrictive environment A term used in the education of students with disabilities to designate a setting that is as normal or regular as possible; federal law requires that children with disabilities be placed in special or separate classes only for the amount of time necessary to provide appropriate services.

Magnet school A type of alternative school that attracts voluntary enrollment from more than one neighborhood by offering special instructional programs or curricula; often established in part for purposes of desegregation.

Mainstreaming Placing students with disabilities in regular classes for much or all of the school day, while also providing additional services, programs, and classes as needed.

Master (or lead) teacher A teacher at the top rung of a career ladder who receives additional remuneration in return for increased responsibilities such as training beginning teachers or consulting on effective teaching methods.

Mastery instruction An approach in which students are tested after initial instruction, and those who did not master the objectives receive corrective instruction and retesting; emphasis is on short units of instruction and learning of defined skills.

Merit pay A plan that rewards teachers partially or primarily on the basis of performance or objective standards.

Metaphysics The area of philosophy that examines issues of a speculative nature dealing with ultimate reality.

Middle school A two- to four-year school intermediate between elementary and high school, commonly for grades six through eight.

Multicultural education Education that focuses on providing equal opportunity for students whose cultural and/or language patterns make it difficult for them to succeed in traditional school programs; many multicultural programs also emphasize positive intergroup and interracial attitudes and contacts.

National Assessment of Educational Progress (NAEP) A periodic assessment of educational achievement under the jurisdiction of the Educational Testing Service, using nationally representative samples of elementary and secondary students.

National curriculum A standard curriculum established by a national government and implemented in schools throughout the country; usually linked with a nationwide testing program to determine whether students are mastering the cirriculum.

Normal school A two-year teacher-education institution that was popular in the nineteenth century.

Objectives Statements of educational purpose for a subject, grade, unit, or lesson; commonly written in behavioral terms so that student experiences and performance can be observed and measured.

Parochial school A school governed and operated by a religious denomination.

Perennialism The educational theory that emphasizes rationality as the major purpose of education; it asserts that the essential truths are recurring and universally true.

Perennialist curriculum A curriculum based on perennialist theory and consisting generally of the three Rs at the elementary level and the classics at the secondary level; also carries a religious or moral overtone; a type of subject-centered curriculum.

Philosophical analysis A method of philosophy that uses linguistic analysis to clarify the language of both scientific and common discourse; widely used by contemporary philosophers of education.

Pragmatism The philosophy that judges the validity of ideas by their consequences in action.

Profession An occupation that is rated high in prestige and requires extensive formal education and mastery of a defined body of knowledge beyond the grasp of laypersons; members of many professions control licensing standards and have autonomy in their work environment.

Professional development school An elementary or secondary school operated jointly by a school district and a teacher-training institution, stressing thoughtful analysis of teaching and learning; the participants usually include future teachers as well as practicing teachers, administrators, and teacher educators.

Professional practice board A state or national commission that permits educators to set professional standards and minimal requirements of competency.

Progressivism An antitraditional theory in American education associated with child-centered learning through activities, problem solving, and projects; as an educational movement, progressivism was promoted by the Progressive Education Association.

Realism The philosophy that construes reality to be dualistic in nature; that is, it considers reality to have both a material and a formal or structural component.

Reflective teaching A style of teaching that emphasizes reflective inquiry and self-awareness; reflective teachers analyze their own teaching behavior and consider the factors that make their teaching effective or ineffective.

Relevant curriculum A curriculum that considers the interests and experiences of the student; consists of numerous course electives, extension courses, minicourses, and alternative courses; a type of student-centered curriculum.

Resistance theory The view that working-class students resist the school, in part because a hegemonic traditional curriculum marginalizes their everyday knowledge.

Scholasticism The intellectual and educational approach used by educators in medieval universities; it involved the study of theological and philosophical authorities.

School-based management A system of school governance in which many important decisions are made at the level of the individual school rather than by the superintendent or board of education; this system usually gives teachers substantial decision-making responsibility.

School board, local *See* Board of education (local).

School choice A system that allows students or their parents to choose the schools they attend.

School superintendent *See* Superintendent of schools.

Scientific method A systematic approach to inquiry in which hypotheses are tested by replicable empirical verification; although usually identified with the laboratory method in the natural sciences, the scientific method is also used in philosophy, where it is associated with pragmatism.

Secondary school A post-elementary school, such as a middle school or a junior or senior high school.

Sex roles Socially expected behavior patterns for girls and boys, men and women.

Social class A ranking of people according to their status in society; common divisions include upper class, middle class, and working class. *See also* Socioeconomic status (SES).

Socialization The process of preparing persons for a social environment.

Social reconstructionism The theory of education that advocates that schools and teachers act as agents of deliberate social change.

Socioeconomic status (SES) Relative ranking of individuals according to economic, social, and occupational prestige and power; usually measured in terms of occupation, education, and income and generally viewed in terms of social-class categories ranging from working class to upper class.

Socratic method An educational method attributed to the Greek philosopher Socrates by which the teacher encourages the student's discovery of truth by asking leading and stimulating questions.

Staff development Continued education or training of a school district's teaching staff; such programs often stress teacher input as well as collaboration between the school district and a college or university.

State board of education An influential and powerful state education agency that serves in an advisory function for the state legislature and establishes policies for implementing legislative acts related to education.

State department of education An agency that operates under the direction of the state board of education; its functions include accrediting schools, certifying teachers, apportioning state school funds, conducting research, and issuing reports.

State school code A collection of laws that establish ways and means of operating schools and conducting education in a state.

Student-centered curricula Curricula that focus on the needs and attitudes of the individual student; emphasis is on self-expression and the student's intrinsic motivation.

Subject-area curriculum A curriculum in which each subject is treated as a largely autonomous body of knowledge; emphasis is on the traditional subjects that have dominated U.S. education since the late nineteenth century, including English, history, science, and mathematics; a type of subject-centered curriculum.

Subject-centered curricula Curricula that are defined in terms of bodies of content or subject matter; achievement is judged according to defined outcomes such as test scores, correct answers, or responses deemed appropriate.

Subject-structure curriculum A curriculum that focuses on the concepts, rules, and principles of a subject; the structure of a subject delineates the appropriate body of knowledge and organizes it into a discipline; a type of subject-centered curriculum.

Superintendent of schools The executive officer of the local school district, whose function is to implement policies opposed by the school board.

Suspension Dismissal of a student from school on a temporary basis.

Taxonomy A classification system for organizing information; in education, it serves as a method for translating goals into more specific objectives.

Teacher empowerment The process of increasing the power of teachers and their role in determining school policies and practices.

Tenure Permanence of position granted to educators after a probationary period, which prevents their dismissal except for legally specified causes and through formalized due process procedures.

Town school The eighteenth- and early-nineteenth-century elementary school of New England that educated children living in a designated area.

Tracking Separation of students into different curriculum paths; the term usually refers to the high-school level, where students are often separated into an academic track, a general or business track, and a vocational track.

Transitional bilingual education (TBE) A form of bilingual education in which students are taught in their own language only until they can learn in English.

Tuition tax credits Tax reductions offered to parents or guardians of children to offset part of their school tuition payments.

Underclass Section of the lower working class that is subject to intergenerational transmission of poverty.

U.S. Department of Education One of twelve U.S. cabinet-level departments that operate in the executive branch of the federal government; now in charge of federal educational policy and the promotion of educational programs.

Values "Should" or "ought" imperatives that relate to ethical behavior or aesthetic appreciation.

Values-centered curriculum A curriculum that emphasizes affective learning and personal growth, focusing on morality, personal biases, personal choice, value clarification, and the social world in general; a type of student-centered curriculum.

Voucher *See* Educational voucher.

Whole-language approach An approach that integrates reading or language arts across the curriculum, emphasizing the ways language is used in real situations.

Author Index

Subject Index

Reader Response Form

We would like to find out what your reactions are to *Foundations of Education,* Fifth Edition. Your evaluation of the book will help us respond to the interests and needs of the readers of future editions. Please complete the form and mail it to College Marketing, Houghton Mifflin Company, One Beacon Street, Boston, MA 02108.

1. We would like to know how you rate our textbook in each of the following areas:

	Excellent	Good	Adequate	Poor
a. Selection of topics	_____	_____	_____	_____
b. Detail of coverage	_____	_____	_____	_____
c. Order of topics	_____	_____	_____	_____
d. Writing style/readability	_____	_____	_____	_____
e. Explanation of concepts	_____	_____	_____	_____
f. Study aids (e.g., marginal notes, focusing questions, Overview charts, Taking Sides charts, Getting to the Source boxes, glossary, summing up)	_____	_____	_____	_____
g. Attractiveness of design	_____	_____	_____	_____

2. Please cite specific examples that illustrate any of the above ratings. _____
_____
_____
_____

3. Describe the strongest feature(s) of the book. _____
_____
_____
_____

4. Describe the weakest feature(s) of the book. _____
_____
_____
_____

5. What other topics should be included in this text? _____
_____
_____
_____

6. What recommendations can you make for improving this book? _____
_____
_____
_____

Taking Issue Charts ◄●►

Overview Charts ◄●►